Construction Insolvency

Second Edition

Richard Davis
MA (Cantab)
Solicitor
Consultant with Masons

Foreword by
Gabriel Moss QC

Robert,
    With best wishes
            Richard.
            —

Palladian Law Publishing Ltd

© Masons
1999

Published by
Palladian Law Publishing Ltd
Beach Road
Bembridge
Isle of Wight PO35 5NQ

www.palladianlaw.com

ISBN 1 902558 17 0

The views expressed herein are for further consideration only and should not be acted upon
without independent consideration and professional advice. Neither Palladian Law
Publishing, Richard Davis nor Masons can accept any responsibility for any loss occasioned
to any person no matter however caused or arising as a result of or in consequence of action
taken or refrained from in reliance on the contents hereof.

Typeset by Heath Lodge Publishing Services
Printed in Great Britain by The Cromwell Press Limited

For my parents

· Contents ·

Foreword by Gabriel Moss QC		xi
Preface		xii
Introduction to the First Edition		xv
The Contributors		xix
Acknowledgements		xxi
Abbreviations		xxii
Table of Cases		xxiv
Table of Statutes		xliv
Table of Standard Forms		xlvii
1	**The Construction Industry** *(by Peter Fenn, UMIST)*	**1**
	Introduction	1
	Definition of the Industry	2
	Special Characteristics of the Industry	3
	Economic Criticisms of the Industry	7
	Industry Structure	8
	Operational and Organisational Features	11
	Forms of Construction Contract	15
	Dispute Resolution	17
	Conclusion	22
2	**Financial Protection**	**23**
	Introduction	23
	Pre-Contract Measures	23
	Contractual Terms	26
	Security	30
	Security for Payment	40
	Appropriate Use of Protection Measures	43
	Checklist of Weighting Criteria	46
	Conclusion	46

3	**Payment**	**48**
	Introduction	48
	Qualities of Payment	48
	Construction Receivables	49
	Retention	53
	Quantum Meruit	57
	Funding Cash Flow	58
	Housing Grants, Construction and Regeneration Act 1996	61
	Pay when Paid	63
	Book Debts	71
	Remedies for Non-Payment	73
	Security for Costs	78
	Conclusion	79
4	**Plant and Materials**	**81**
	Introduction	81
	Plant and Equipment Risk	81
	Rights against Plant	83
	Challenges to Vesting Clauses	96
	Plant not Owned by the Contractor	105
	Goods and Materials	108
	Fixed Materials	110
	Unfixed Materials	114
	Injunctions	119
	Insolvency Practitioners	123
	Conclusion	127
5	**Set-Off, Abatement and Deduction**	**128**
	Introduction	128
	Problem Solving	129
	Set-Off at Common Law	131
	Contractual Set-Off	137
	Statutory and Other Limitations	142
	Industry Cross-Claims	146
	Counterclaims and Summary Procedures	152
	Conclusion	154

6   Trust and Transferability   **156**
   Introduction   156
   General Principles of Trust Law   156
   Construction Trusts   159
   Assignment   163
   Benefit and Burden   164
   Assignability   166
   Non-Assignability   171
   "No Loss" Arguments   177
   Formalities   180
   Priorities   183
   Conclusion   185

7   Informal Insolvency   **186**
   Introduction   186
   Meaning of Insolvency   186
   Causes of Insolvency   190
   Informal Insolvency Procedures   199
   Restructuring   202
   Winding–up Petitions   206

8   Formal Insolvency   **210**
   Introduction   210
   Procedural Comparisons   210
   Company Voluntary Arrangement   224
   Individual Insolvency   224
   Application to the Industry   226
   Receivership   226
   Liquidation   230
   Administration   231
   Company Voluntary Arrangement   236
   Conclusion   238

9   Termination   **240**
   Introduction   240
   Termination at Common Law   240

Termination under the Contract   244
The Standard Forms   249
Sub-Contracts   255
Checklist of Steps for Sub-Contracts   257
Post-Termination Rights   258
Validity of Termination Clauses   272
Checklist of Steps before Termination   275
Conclusion   276

10 Novation and Completion Contracts   **278**
Introduction   278
Nature of Novation   278
Novation and Construction Contracts   283
Completion Contracts   288
Sub-Contractors   295
Mitigation of Loss   297
Conclusion   302
Case Study *(by Neil Burton, GVA Grimley)*   302

11 Trust Claims   **308**
Introduction   308
The Retention Trust   308
Rights of Recourse   311
Main Contract Retention Trusts   315
Management Contract Trusts   318
Mandatory Injunctions   323
Trust or Charge?   325
Sub-Contract Benefits   334
Breach of Trust   338
Termination of Trusts   340
Conclusion   343

12 Direct Payment   **344**
Introduction   344
Where the Contractor is Solvent   345
Construction of Direct Payment Clauses   347
Discretionary Direct Payment   351

Mandatory Direct Payment 363
Conclusion 369

13 Set-Off in Insolvency **371**
Introduction 371
Receivership Set-Off 371
Bankruptcy Set-Off 378
Voluntary Arrangements 378
Set-Off in Administration 383
Conclusion 383

14 Bonds and Guarantees **385**
Introduction 385
The Three Variables 385
Primary Obligations 388
Secondary Obligations 390
Hybrid Obligations 401
Retention Bonds 404
Tender Bonds 406
Advance Payment 408
Commercial Factors 408
Resolving Disputes 418
Relation to Other Securities 423
Conclusion 424

15 Insolvency Claims **426**
Introduction 426
Fraudulent Trading 427
Wrongful Trading 428
Preference 430
Avoidance of Transactions 435
Misfeasance 436
Other Claims 438
Conclusion 438

16 People **440**
Introduction 440

Directors	440
Employees	448
Insolvency Professionals	451
17 International Aspects	**453**
Introduction	453
Construction Liens	453
Stop Notices	458
Statutory Charges	460
Statutory Trusts	463
Holdback	465
Statutory Assignment	465
Restraining Bond Calls	466
Payment Bonds	468
Third Party Benefit	469
Restitution	470
Alternatives to Retention	471
Other Protective Devices	474
Far East	482
Scotland	486
Ireland	495
France	501
Conclusion	502
18 Images of Construction Insolvency	**503**
Introduction	503
The Legal Imagination	503
A Dialogue on Construction	510
The Love of Money	512
Images of Insolvency	513
The Myth of Construction Insolvency	521
Glossary	527
Bibliography	535
Index	555

· Foreword ·

The first edition of this work arrived in the midst of the great recession of the 20th century. It has proved an invaluable point of reference to everyone in the construction insolvency field. As we approach the start of the next millennium, the construction industry remains a high risk area for insolvency. A thorough knowledge of how to protect oneself as owner, employer, contractor, sub-contractor, bondsman etc from the effects of insolvency remain essential for survival.

The author's transition to consultant at Masons has given him the time not only to update this work but in many places to rewrite it and to add some very interesting material. This consists not only of the expected, such as the discussion of standard forms and case law. In terms of the unexpected, I can think of no other work which links construction and insolvency concepts with Greek myths! The degree of thought that has gone into exploring the underlying concepts shows how little most of us in the field step back and think what our work is really about.

There are in fact few places apart from this work where one can find such a detailed and clear discussion of the case law, old and new. Moreover, there is a feeling that the author has been able to step back and put the discussion in its proper context. This applies not only to cases in the construction insolvency area, but also to other significant developments in the law which any person in this area will need to be aware of.

One of the great attractions of insolvency law remains the fact that it constantly intersects with other interesting areas of law. This work brings together construction and insolvency law at their meeting point with the benefit of the author's expertise in both areas. That is why it remains in this new edition a fascinating work for anyone with an interest in the field.

Gabriel Moss QC
3-4 South Square
Gray's Inn
London WC1R 5HP

· Preface ·

It is a strange business revising a book after nearly ten years. Re-reading what I wrote then is a bit like coming across an old family photograph. I remember having taken it and recognise the people but neither I nor they are the same. Inevitably, therefore, although captioned as a second edition this is a different kind of book. Less than a third of the original text has survived.

The focus of this edition, as of the first, is on the phenomenon of insolvency as experienced by the construction industry and described in the language of the law. As before, I have drawn on the law reports and other sources from English speaking jurisdictions throughout the world as much for illustrations of facts as for propositions of law. In doing so, I do not advocate the homogenisation of law; one of the appealing aspects of this subject is learning about the remedies other jurisdictions have evolved to suit their own local conditions. What is new in this edition, and possibly unique for a book of this kind, is a consideration of the images underlying the subject. Law and imagination are often set against each other: the one viewed as a discipline which is structured, clear and logical, the other as a formless source of images which are ambiguous and unstable in their capacity to transform themselves. In fact this is not the case: the law is sometimes illogical and confused and images can be very precise. By taking our cue from the language of the law it is possible to see important connections between them.

It seems to me that legal textbooks tend to treat the law as if it were both separate from the factual context in which it is created and cut off from the images which really inform it. Hence, by becoming abstracted from the human dilemmas and conflicts brought to it and alienated from the images which give it life, law has tended to lose its value as a mediator of our inner and outer worlds. It has come to operate within its own world of definitions. In this book, I am attempting something different by beginning in Chapter 1 with a portrait of the industry and its fraught relations with money (the outer world) and ending in Chapter 18 with an exploration of the mythical background as it appears from the metaphors used by the law (the inner world). In between is a discussion of the relevant legal topics mainly by reference to case law. I see the reported cases as stories that interweave the factual with the imaginal, the conscious with the unconscious. Maybe that is the function of a law book: to act as a container holding abstract legal principles in balance between their practical application and imaginal derivation. As well as such *objective* functions, this time the writing has also had a *subjective* purpose. I have sometimes been aware of these three elements of insolvency, law and construction as if they held aspects of my own personality rather as Jung discovered that the alchemists, in their quest to change base metal into gold, were also engaged in a psychological process of soul-making by working with unconscious projections they were making onto their work. The work we do is often like the alchemist's crucible. It seems to have a symbolic function whose meaning lies beyond the grasp of our conscious minds.

With these ideas in mind, I have restructured the book loosely around three themes: building up (Chapters 1-6), falling apart (Chapters 7-9) and transformation (Chapters 10-18). I have omitted a few topics which were not of great commercial relevance, adding new sections on construction trusts, bonds and guarantees, restructuring, copyright, international aspects and related themes. This time round, I have slimmed down the amount of case references to the essentials, brought up footnotes into the main text and tried to avoid the tendency to write as if addressing the court. I have also included some further diagrams where it seemed appropriate and updated the Bibliography. The publishers have commissioned an extensive index. My overall aim is to produce a work which stimulates and surprises while also providing answers to specific problems, or at least an elucidation of the questions!

A work like this is a synthesis of others' views, insights and thoughts gathered from a large number of sources mixed up with a few original ideas of my own. I have set out the main sources in the Bibliography. I would particularly like to thank Gabriel Moss QC for his kind words in the Foreword and the specialist authors, Peter Fenn of UMIST, Neil Burton of GVA Grimley and Vincent Connor, Sharon Fitzgerald and Niav O'Higgins of Masons, for their contributions. I am grateful to Masons both for the consultancy without which the book would not have been written and specifically to Christopher Dering, Catriona Dodsworth, Alison Cull and Richard Williams for reading parts of the book in draft and making helpful suggestions, and to Alison Cull for researching and drafting the sections on personal insolvency and voluntary arrangements. Paul Newman very kindly sent me unreported aspects of the *Cosslett* litigation. I also thank James Hillman for his writings on archetypal psychology and personal encouragement and Benjamin Sells for sending me a copy of his book *The Soul of the Law*.

The actual process of writing was made immeasurably easier through Shirley Crabb's assistance with the typing and layout of the figures and help from Julie Kitchen and the librarians at Masons in finding references. I would also like to acknowledge the assistance of the librarians at the Institute for Advanced Legal Studies. Finally, it has been a particular pleasure to work once again with Andrew Prideaux and Jane Belford of Palladian Law Publishing who understand all about the needs (and foibles) of lawyers writing about the law. I have drawn on sources published as at 1 August 1999.

Richard Davis
30 Aylesbury Street
London EC1R OER
21 October 1999

Introduction to First Edition

There is something fascinating in the application of formal rules to the problems of everyday life. Where the rules consist of legal principles, the outcome of the exercise is of more than theoretical importance. The application of law to the construction industry arose out of the need for guidance on the interpretation of standard forms of building contract. Standard forms were first produced by bodies representing architects and builders in the last quarter of the 19th century. The earliest legal texts still in current use originated in 1882 (A E Emden) and 1891 (Alfred Hudson). These authorities have been supplemented in modern times by Donald Keating on building contracts (1955) and Max Abrahamson on engineering contracts (1965). The law applied by these works is largely contract and tort but construction law is also concerned with statutory duty and this trend is likely to increase with the influx of European directives.

Insolvency is the branch of law which concerns the ability to pay one's debts. Any kind of trading activity can give rise to insolvency and, as will be seen, the construction industry contributes more than its fair share to the annual toll of insolvencies. Just as law in general can be applied with benefit to an industrial sector so there is much to be gained by analysing a particular industry from the point of view of one area of law. This is the ultimate justification for this book.

What is construction insolvency? It is one aspect of applied insolvency and consists in the application of the law and practice of insolvency to the study of the construction industry, its members and activities. The industry has numerous special characteristics which make it especially vulnerable to insolvency. By studying this subject, it is hoped that more will become known about the causes of insolvency in the industry and, therefore, how best to avoid them. A study of construction insolvency should also assist in the identification of protective measures which can be taken to avoid the knock on effect which the insolvency of one member of the industry so often has on the financial stability of another. It may also be of use to insolvency practitioners in realising value in respect of the company over which they have been appointed and to lenders in giving them a better appreciation of the risk of lending to a construction company.

Apart from its intrinsic interest, it is hoped that this subject may also stimulate the reconsideration of some aspects of English law. It will be suggested that there are areas which seem to lag behind other jurisdictions and fail to provide a remedy where perhaps a remedy is needed. I have tried to assess how responsive English law is to the needs of its users in this field. For this reason, I have referred to overseas cases either to illustrate the course which English law might take should similar facts arise or a different and perhaps better approach taken to a problem by another jurisdiction. As far as I know, this is the first book to deal with construction insolvency at length. There is a short chapter in Totty & Crystal (1982) and longer contributions in Totty & Jordan (1986) and notably in Lightman and Moss (1986) (see the Bibliography). The discussion in these works was of necessity brief and does not pretend to explore this complex subject in detail. It may be wondered why the subject has not been tackled before. One reason may be that insolvency has only recently become acceptable as a subject worthy of academic study and inclusion in legal training courses. It may also reflect the different backgrounds of lawyers who specialise in construction and insolvency work: the former are expert in the common law of contract and tort; the latter in equity and property law, *e.g.* banking and finance work. The position is different in other jurisdictions. For example, in the United States there is a developed body of jurisprudence on construction insolvency. This has arisen largely because of the mechanics' lien legislation which protects the contractor by giving it a charge in certain circumstances on the land being developed as security for sums due to it. In addition, the United States has compulsory bonding on Federal and many State Government projects which means that work is completed by a surety where the contractor defaults. This situation unites common law concepts with the principles of equity through the doctrine of subrogation.

To appreciate the scope of the subject, it is necessary to have a basic understanding of the industry and also of insolvency law and practice. For this reason, the first group of chapters sets out the identifying characteristics of the construction industry and investigates why it is so prone to insolvency. The second and third chapters attempt to define insolvency in relation to the industry and to summarise the three main insolvency procedures of receivership, liquidation and administration.

The main body of the book consists in an exploration of the far reaching effects of the termination of a construction contract. The value of contracting companies lies in their work in progress which can only be realised in the event of insolvency by completing ongoing contracts. The right of the employer to terminate the contract before completion is therefore crucial (Chapter 4). Were the employer's powers to end at this point, an insolvency practitioner appointed over a contractor would still hope to salvage something. But the termination clause does not end there: it goes on to confer a series of rights which, when taken together, enable the employer to annihilate whatever value the contractor might have salvaged from the contract. Of these, the most far reaching is set off (Chapter 9). Other aspects covered are the means by which the works can be completed (Chapter 5) and sub-contractors and suppliers retained (Chapter 6); the rights of the parties to materials on and off site (Chapter 7) and to plant and equipment (Chapter 8); and the special position of sub-contractors (Chapter 10). The subjects of retention (Chapter 11) and bonds and guarantees (Chapter 12) are also examined at length.

Apart from the value of its contracts and work in progress, the most valuable resource of a contractor is its management. The last section considers the position of the company's employees and directors, in each case aiming to limit the discussion to industry specific issues. I end by drawing together the points which have emerged during the book which appear to me to merit further consideration. In an effort to keep the text down to manageable size, there have had to be omissions. Informal procedures and voluntary arrangements are not discussed but the issues raised in this book will be equally if not more relevant to those situations. Also omitted are issues relating to insurance and to nominated subcontractors which it is felt are fully dealt with elsewhere. The idea for this book grew from seminars given for Legal Studies and Services Limited, in-house talks for clients and trainee solicitors at Masons and lectures given at the Centre for Construction Law, King's College, University of London.

I would like to thank the many people who have contributed to this book. I am particularly grateful to Gabriel Moss QC for writing the Foreword and for the benefit of many discussions which I have had with him on construction insolvency over the years. Robert St J Buller and Stephen Hill of Grant Thornton read the whole book in draft and made many helpful suggestions. John Reid of E C Harris & Partners contributed the two worked examples which are found in Appendix 2. The following kindly sent me transcripts of unreported decisions:

Derek Firth and Anne Hinton of Simpson Grierson Butler White, Anita Patel of John Mowlem & Company Plc and Neil F Jones. Roy Radford of M J Gleeson Group Plc assisted with information relating to the industry.

Bill Heys and David Jones read individual chapters in draft and made helpful suggestions. I am also grateful to Richard Williams, James Elliott, Michael Battye, Jill Andrew, Nina Sandler, Peter Cassidy and Mark Harnett for their help in undertaking research and in checking specific points.

Shirley Crabb coped with the typing and retyping of the draft with her customary efficiency.

Tessa Hinton and Linda Rafter were indefatigable in tracking down source material. Lastly, I would like to record my thanks to Chancery Law Publishing for their encouragement throughout this project. Any errors which remain are my own. I have aimed to state the law from materials available as at 1 September 1991.

Richard Davis
30 Aylesbury Street
London EC1
October 1991

· The Contributors ·

Richard Davis was educated at Emmanuel College, Cambridge where he read law. He has practised for 20 years as a solicitor in the fields of construction and insolvency law. He joined Masons in 1984 and was a partner from 1988 until 1997, when he became a consultant with the firm. He published *Construction Insolvency* in 1991, which was the first study of insolvency in the construction industry. He co-edited *Security for Payment* in 1996. He is a contributor to Lightman and Moss, *The Law of Receivers of Companies* and Emden's *Construction Law* as well as other publications, and frequently chairs and speaks at conferences. He is a lecturer, tutor and examiner at the Centre of Construction Law and Management at King's College, University of London, is active in the training of lawyers within Masons, and has appeared regularly on Television Education Network, a system of legal education based on video. He served on numerous industry bodies and government committees in connection with the Latham Report and the Bill which led to the Housing Grants, Construction and Regeneration Act 1996.

Peter Fenn is a lecturer at the University of Manchester Institute of Science and Technology. He is a Chartered Surveyor, a Fellow of the Chartered Institute of Arbitrators and a Mediator on the President's Panel at the Royal Institution of Chartered Surveyors. During the academic year 1997/98 he was Visiting Professor at the University of Kentucky, USA. He is the joint co-ordinator of an International Working Commission investigating international construction conflict, and co-author of Dispute Resolution and Conflict Management: An International Review, published in 1998.

Neil Burton, is the senior quantity surveying partner with GVA Grimley. He has been advising insolvency practitioners, banks and companies on construction insolvency matters for many years. He is Past President of the Architects and Surveyors Institute and has lectured widely on construction insolvency matters.

Vincent Connor is a partner in Masons, based in their Glasgow office and works in the firm's Construction and Engineering practice area. He established Masons' Scottish base with Alastair Morrison in

May 1998. Vincent is experienced in advising on both standard form and bespoke building and engineering contracts and professional appointments and warranties, and specialises in contentious construction law, including tactical and strategic advice and the pursuit and defence of claims in a variety of forms of dispute resolution. In addition to having a strong reputation for advocacy on behalf of clients in both litigation and arbitration, he is a mediator and a member of the Mediation Accreditation Panel of the Law Society of Scotland. He is a member of the Society of Construction Law and the Technology and Construction Solicitors Association, and speaks regularly at construction conferences and seminars.

Dr Sharon Fitzgerald is an assistant solicitor in Masons, based in their Glasgow office and working in the firm's Construction and Engineering practice area. She specialises in non-contentious construction law and is experienced in advising on building and engineering contracts, professional appointments and warranties. She is experienced in Private Finance Initiative work and has been involved in the Masons team advising in a number of recent projects in the health and education sectors.

Niav O'Higgins is an assistant solicitor in Masons' Dublin office. She attended Sussex University where she studied Law and Italian and then went on to the European University Institute in Florence to do post-graduate research in comparative collective labour law. She trained at Masons in London and, on qualifying as a solicitor, she worked in the Construction and Engineering practice area in London for two years before transferring to the Dublin office.

· Acknowledgments ·

The following have kindly agreed to allow the reproduction of copyright material: RIBA Publications Limited in respect of JCT 63 and JCT 80; The Institution of Civil Engineers, The Association of Consulting Engineers and the Federation of Civil Engineering Contractors in respect of ICE form (5th edition); The Institution of Chemical Engineers in respect of the I Chem E Guide Federation Internationale des Ingenieurs-Conseils in respect of FIDIC (4th edition); Federation of Civil Engineering Contractors in respect of the ICE Blue Form; HMSO Publications in respect of Crown copyright for GC/Works/1; Building Employers Confederation, Federation of Associations of Specialists and Sub-Contractors and the Committee of Associations of Specialist Engineering Contractors in respect of the Green Form; David Morrell for permission to quote from Indictment: Power and Politics in the Construction Industry (Faber & Faber, 1987); The University of Reading (Department of Construction Management) for permission to reproduce Table 4.1 from The Modern Construction Firm, ed, Patricia M Hillbrandt and Jacqueline Cannon; Confederation of Construction Specialists in respect of its Model Form of Employer/Specialist Contractor Collateral Warranty Agreement; Lloyds Bowmaker Limited for the extract from Performance Comparisons (1990); County NatWest Securities Limited for the extract from Cash flow update 1990/1991. Extracts from GC/Works/1 are reproduced with the permission of the Controller of Her Majesty's Stationery Office.

· Abbreviations ·

Aust Const LR	Australian Construction Law Reports
ACILL	Australian Construction Industry Law Letter [Australian equivalent of CILL]
ACLB	Australian Construction Law Bulletin [formerly known as ACILL]
ACLR	Australian Company Law Reports
ACSR	Australian Corporations and Securities Report
ACTR	Australian Capital Territories Reports
ALJR	Australian Law Journal Reports
ALR	Australian Law Reports
Alta LR	Alberta Law Reports
BCC	British Company Cases
BCL	Building and Construction Law (Australian)
BCLC	Butterworths Company Law Cases
BLM	Building Law Monthly
BLR	Building Law Reports
BPIR	Bankruptcy & Personal Insolvency Reports
Bus LR	Business Law Reports (Canadian)
CBR	Canadian Bankruptcy Reports
CIB	Commercial Insolvency Bulletin (Canadian)
CILL	Construction Industry Law Letter
Con LR	Construction Law Reports
Con L Yb	Construction Law Yearbook
Const LJ	Construction Law Journal
CLD	Construction Law Digest
CLR	Construction Law Reports (Canadian)
CLY	Current Law Year Book
DLR	Dominion Law Reports (Canadian)
EG	Estates Gazette
EGD	Estates Gazette Digest
ER	English Reports
GLR	Gazette Law Reports (New Zealand)
HKLR	Hong Kong Law Reports
ICLR	International Construction Law Review
ICR	Industrial Cases Reports

IICRR	International Insolvency and Creditors' Rights Report [Journal of Committee J of the International Bar Association]
IL&P	Insolvency Law and Practice
IRLR	Industrial Relations Law Reports
JBL	Journal of Business Law
LMCLQ	Lloyd's Maritime and Commercial Law Quarterly
LQR	Law Quarterly Review
LT	Law Times
LJ	Law Journal
MLJ	Malayan Law Journal
NILR	Northern Ireland Law Reports
NLJ	New Law Journal
NSWLR	New South Wales Law Reports [replacing SR (NSW)]
NZLR	New Zealand Law Reports
OLR	Ontario Law Reports [replaced by OR]
OR	Ontario Reports
QdR	Queensland Reports
SA	South African Law Reports
SC	Courts of Session Cases (Scottish)
SCR	Supreme Court Reports (Canadian)
SJ	Solicitors Journal
SR (NSW)	State Reports (New South Wales)
STC	Simons Tax Cases
TLR	Times Law Reports
VR	Victorian Reports (Australian)
VLR	Victoria Law Reports (Australian, replacing VR)
WALR	West Australia Law Reports (1899 – 1959)
WAR	Western Australian Reports (1960 – current)
WN	Weekly Notes
WWR	Western Weekly Reports (Canadian)

· Table of Cases ·

Aboussafy v Abacus Cities [1981] 4 WWR 660   132
Acsim v Danish (1989) 47 BLR 55   134, 140, 141, 145, 151
Adams v Cape Industries [1990] Ch 433; [1990] BCLC 479   396, 442
Adelaide (Corporation of City of) v Jennings Industries [1984]
    156 CLR 274   270
ADI v State Electricity Commission of Victoria (1997) 13 BCL 337   467
Advanced Technology v Cray (1992) 63 BLR 59   79
Aectra v Exmar [1994] 1 WLR 1634   136
Afovos Shipping v Pagnan [1983] 1 WLR 195   245
Agip v Jackson [1992] 4 All ER 385   159
Agra Bank, *Re, ex parte* Tondeur (1867) LR 5 Eq 160   243
Aicken & Son v Bradley [1916] NZLR 659   183
Aktion Maritime v Kasmas [1987] 1 Lloyd's Rep 283   282
Alberta Mortgage & Housing Corporation v Strathmore Investments
    (1992) 6 Alta LR (3d) 159   282
Alexander v Administrator Transvaal [1974] 2 SA 248   293
Algons Engineering v Abigroup Contractors (1998) 14 BCL 215   139, 475
Allco Steel v Australian Capital Development Corporation
    (unreported, 14 Nov 1996) *noted* (1997) 14 BLM 1   121
Allied-Signal v Dome Petroleum (1991) 81 Alta LR (2d) 307   282
Alucraft v Costain Australia (1991) 7 BCL 179   119, 120
Alucraft v Growcon (1995) 11 BCL 20   74
Amantilla v Telefusion [1987] CILL 316   57
American Cyanamid v Ethicon [1975] 1 All ER 504   419
American Express v Hurley [1985] 3 All ER 564   216
Amman Aviation v Commonwealth of Australia [1988] 92 ALR 601   266
Analogy v Bell Basic Industries (1996) 12 BCL 291   432, 433
Anders v O/Y Louisa Stevedoring [1985] STC 301   261
Arbuthnot Leasing v Havalet Leasing [1990] BCC 627   436
Architectural Installation Services v James Gibbons Windows
    (1990) 16 Con LR 68   245, 246
Archivent v Strathclyde General Council (1984) 27 BLR 99   115, 116, 117, 494
Aries Tanker v Total Transport [1977] 1 WLR 185   132, 134
Armagh Shoes, *Re* [1984] BCLC 405   53
Armour v Thyssen [1990] 3 All ER 481   330
Arthur Sanders, *Re* (1981) 17 BLR 125   310, 312, 313, 314, 322, 332, 343
Ashby Warner v Simmonds [1936] 2 All ER 697   369

Asphaltic Limestone v City of Glasgow [1907] SC 463   382
Asphaltic Wood Pavement Co, *Re* (1885) 30 Ch D 216   243, 373, 381, 383
Astor Chemicals v Synthetic Technology [1990] BCC 97   219
Atlantic Computer Systems, *Re* [1990] BCC 859   124, 126, 216, 221
Atlas Cabinets v National Trust (1990) 68 DLR (4th) 161   470
Attock Cement v Romanian Bank [1989] 1 WLR 1147   418
Attorney General v Ko Hon Mau (1988) 44 BLR 144   97
Attorney General v McMillan & Lockwood [1991] 1 NZLR 53   51, 350,
    358, 359, 361
Attwood and Reid v Stephens [1932] NZLR 1332   174
Aurum Services v Greatearth Construction [1994] 3 SLR 330   478
Australian Conference v Mainline (1978) 141 CLR 335   406
Axel Johnson v M G Mineral [1992] 1 WLR 270   131
Ayerst v C & K (Construction) Ltd [1976] AC 167   215, 309

Babson v Village of Ulysses, 52 NW Rep (2d) 320   287
Bache v Banque Vernes [1973] 2 Lloyd's Rep 437   389
Bacon (MC) *Re* [1990] BCC 78   431
Ball v Scott Timber [1929] NZLR 57   124
Balfour Beatty v Britannia Life [1997] SLT 10   323, 493
Ballast Wiltshier v Thomas Barnes [1998] CILL 1417   53
Banbury v Daniel (1884) 54 LJ Ch 265   82
Banco de Portugal v Waterlow [1932] AC 452   297
Bank of Credit and Commerce International (No 8) [1997] 3 WLR 909   380
Bank of East Asia v Scottish Enterprise (unreported, 19 June 1992)   299
Bank of New South Wales v The King [1918] NZLR 945   184
Bankes v Jarvis [1903] 1 KB 549   376
Banque Paribas v Venaglass [1994] CILL 918   317
Barclays Bank v Quistclose [1970] AC 567   53, 162, 337, 433
Barlow Clowes v Vaughan [1992] 4 All ER 22   158
Barnett v Peter Cox (1995) 45 Con LR 131   134
Barrett v Livesey (unreported, 6 Nov 1980)   95
Barrett Steel v Amec (1997) 15 CLD 10-07   134
Barrow Borough Transport, *Re* [1990] Ch 227   101
Bateman v Eric Reed [1960] 4 SA 151   117
Baylis v Mayor of City of Wellington (1886) 4 NZLR 84   265
Beaufort Developments v Gilbert-Ash (1998) 88 BLR 1   246
Bedfordshire CC v Fitzpatrick Contractors (1998) 62 Con LR 64   242
Belgrave Nominees v Barlin-Scott [1984] VR 947   112
Bennett & White v Municipal District of Sugar City [1951] AC 786   85, 86,
    89, 95, 105
Biggerstaff v Rowatt's Wharf [1896] 2 Ch 93   170
Birse Construction v Co-Operative Wholesale Society (1997) 84 BLR 58   63,
    73, 334

Bishopgate v Homan [1994] BCC 868   158
Blake v Izard (1867) 16 WR 108   81, 103, 105
Blakey v Trustees of Property of Pendlebury [1931] 2 Ch 255   71
Blower v Alta (1983) 50 AR 66, *affirmed* 68 AR 156   113
Bocotra Construction v Attorney General of Singapore [1996] ADRLJ 312   417
Bocotra Construction v Attorney General of Singapore
   (No 2) [1995] 2 SLR 733   467
Bold v BGK Metals (unreported, 21 May 1997)   414
Bollore v Banque Nationale de Paris [1983] HKLR 78   416
Bond Worth, *Re* [1980] 1 Ch 228   123
Boscawan v Bajwa [1995] 4 All ER 769   157
Bouygues v Shanghai Links [1998] 2 HKLRD 479   483
Bovis v Whatlings Construction (1995) 75 BLR 1   248, 264
Bovis Construction v Ergon (unreported, 30 March 1994)   134
Bre-Aar v D'Angela Construction (1975) 21 CBR 260   464
Brice v Bannister (1878) 3 QBD 569   168, 172
Brightlife, *Re* [1987] Ch 200   329
Brightside v Hyundai (1988) 41 BLR 110   68
Brinks v Abu-Saleh [1995] *The Times*, 23 Oct   159
Bristol Meci v Ericsson (unreported, 25 Oct 1996)   421
British Columbia Hydro v Hallcraft Construction (1986) 6 BCLR (2d) 74   432
British Eagle v Air France [1975] 1 WLR 758; [1975] 2 All ER 390   143,
   275, 359, 360, 361, 362, 363, 366, 370
British Gas v Eastern Electricity [1996] *The Times*, 29 Nov   173
British Glanzstoff v General Accident [1913] AC 143   264
British Investment Trust v Foundation (unreported, 15 Dec 1930)   348, 349
Broken Hill v Xenakis [1992] Lloyd's Rep 304   418
Brooks Robinson v Rothfield [1951] VLR 405   115
Brown v Bateman (1867) LR 2 CP 272   86, 87, 103
Burch Construction, *Re* (1967) 10 CBR 307   464
Burns & Dutton v Yule (1969) 8 DLR (3d) 683   250
Business Properties, *Re* (1988) 4 BCC 684   212
Byblos Bank v Al-Khudairy (1986) 2 BCC 549   253
Byford v Russell [1907] 2 KB 522   94
Bysouth v Shire of Blackburn and Mitcham [1928] VLR 562   98, 266, 271

Callaghan v City of Glasgow (1988) SLT 227   98, 99
Calvert v London Dock Co (1838) 2 Keen's Rep 638   393
Canadian General Insurance v Dube (1982) 39 NBR (2d) 484   298
Canadian Imperial Bank of Commerce v Alberta Assessment
   Appeal Board (1990) 75 Alta LR (2d) 362   113
Canterbury Pipelines v Christchurch Drainage Board (1979) 16 BLR 76   74
Carecraft Construction, *Re* [1993] 4 All ER 499   446
Cargill v Bangladesh Sugar [1996] 4 All ER 563   421

Carpenter's Estates v Davies [1940] Ch 160   260, 261

Carreras Rothmans v Freeman Matthews Treasure [1985] 1 All ER 155   329

Carter v White (1883) 25 Ch D 666   392

Casson v Laing Construction (1974) 18 CBR 133, *upheld* (1975) 19 CBR 89   254

Castellain v Preston (1883) 11 QBD 380   279

Cavco Floors, *Re* [1990] BCC 589   234

Centre v Downie [1970] Qd R 414   466

Chandless v Whitton (unreported, 10 Dec 1986)   190

Channel Tunnel Group v Balfour Beatty (unreported, 27 Nov 1991)   74, 260

Chanthall Investments v F G Minter [1976] SC 73   264

Charge Card Services, *Re* [1986] 3 All ER 289   243

Charles Church v Cronin [1990] FSR 1   269

Charlotte Thirty v Croker (1990) 24 Con LR 46   166

Charterbridge v Lloyd's Bank [1969] 3 WLR 122   440

Chatbrown v Alfred McAlpine (1986) 11 Con LR 1   150

Chatsworth Investments v Cussins [1969] 1 All ER 143   171, 280

Cheffick v JDM Associates (1988) 22 Con LR 1   190

Chelsea Cloisters, *Re* (1981) 41 P & CR 98   434

Chip Hua Poly-Construction v Housing and Development Board [1998] 2 SLR 35   468

Church v Sage (1892) 67 LT 800   88, 89, 105, 176

Churchfield Construction v Waymans (unreported, 25 July 1996)   64

City Equitable, *Re* [1925] 2 Ch 407   441

Civil Service Co-Operative Society v Trustee of McGrigor [1923] 2 Ch 347   274

Clark v Bridgend Borough Council (unreported, 1998)   100

Clemence, *Re* (1992) 59 BLR 56   207

Climpson v Coles (1889) 23 QBD 465   104

Club Marconi v Rennat [1980] 4 ACLR 883   208

Clydebank v Fidelity & Deposit Company of Maryland [1916] SC 69   414

Coba Industries v Adams [1987] 15 BCLR (2d) 68   246

Coba Industries v Millie's Holdings [1975] 6 WLR 14   374

Coca-Cola v Finsat [1996] 3 WLR 849   141

Collins Trading v Maher [1969] VR 20   115

Colonial Bank v European Grain [1989] 1 Lloyd's Rep 431   133

Comco Constructions v Westminster Properties (1990) 2 WAR 335   251

Commercial Aluminium Windows Ltd v Cumbernauld Development Corporation (1987) SLT 91   490

Commercial Bank of Tasmania [1893] AC 313   287, 393

Community Development v Engwirda Construction [1969] 120 CLR 455   51

Company, *Re A* [1992] 2 All ER 797   207

Compaq Computer v Abercorn [1993] BCLC 602   328

Concorde Construction v Colgan (1984) 29 BLR 125   323, 324

Concrete Construction v Barnes [1938] 61 CLR 209   465, 466
Cone Textiles v Mather & Platt [1981] 3 SA 565   348
Connaught Restaurants v Indoor Leisure [1994] 1 WLR 501   141
Connolly v Superior Court of Merced County, Supp 132,
     Cal Rptr 477   458, 459, 460
Contemporary Cottages v Margin Traders [1981] 2 NZLR 114   72
Continental Assurance, *Re* [1996] BCC 888   440
Convent Hospital v Eberlin (1989) 14 Con LR 1   443
Cooper v Micklefield Coal (1912) 107 LT 457   181
Co-Operative Insurance v Argyll Stores [1997] 2 WLR 898   260
Cork, Corporation of v Rooney (1881) 7 LR Ir 191   98
Corrans v Transvaal Government (1909) TS 605   293
Cosslett (Contractors) Ltd, *Re* [1997] 4 All ER 115   45, 86, 90, 91,
     92, 94, 95
Costain v Scottish Rugby Union (1994) SLT 573   490
Costain Australia v Superior Pipe [1975] 1 ACLR 209   466
Costain International v Davy McKee (unreported, 25 Nov 1990)   405
Crabtree v GPT Communications Systems (1990) 59 BLR 43   79
Creasey v Breachwood Motors [1992] *The Times*, 29 July   282
Credit Valley Cable v Peel (1980) 27 OR (2d) 433   112
Creditel v Terrace Corporation (1983) 50 CBR 87   184, 292
Cretanor Maritime v Irish Marine [1978] 1 WLR 966   460
Crossley v Lee [1908] 1 KB 86   109
Crowfoot v London Dock Company (1834) 2 C&M 637   94
Crown House v Amec (1990) 6 Const LJ 141   154

D&H Distributing v United States, 102 F 3d 542   478
Dalinga v Antina [1979] 2 SA 56   108
Darlington BC v Wiltshier (1994) 69 BLR 1   179, 185
Davidson and Davidson v Claffey Constructions (1985) WALR 29   105
Davies v Mayor of Swansea (1853) 22 LJ Ex 297   100, 253, 271
Davies (A) & Company v William Old (1969) 113 SJ 262   65, 67
Dawber Williamson v Humberside County Council (1979) 14 BLR 70   117
Dawnays v Minter [1971] 1 WLR 1205   137, 138
Dearle v Hall (1828) 3 Russ 1   175
Decro-Wall International v Practitioners in Marketing [1971]
     2 All ER 216   74
D'Jan of London, *Re* [1993] BCC 646   444
De Mattos v Gibson (1858) 4 De G & J 276   333
Design Company v King (1992) 8 BLM 1   241
De Vere Hotels v Aegon Insurance [1998] CILL 1346   408
Diplock, *Re* [1948] 1 Ch 465   158, 332
DKG Contractors, *Re* [1990] BCC 903   198, 429, 431
Doe v Canadian Surety (1937) 1 SCR 1   363, 393

Doleman v Ossett Corporation [1912] 3 KB 257   373
Don King v Warren [1998] 2 All ER 608   34, 166, 175, 185
Doolaege v Solid Resources (1990) 74 Alta LR (2d) 406   282
Douglas (RM) v Bass Leisure (1990) 53 BLR 119   148
Drew v Josolyne (1887) 18 QBD 590   51, 183, 311, 368
Dunlop & Renken v Hendall Steel [1957] 3 All ER 344   51, 368
Duquemin v Slater (1993) 35 Con LR 147   133
Durham Brothers v Robertson [1898] 1 QB 765   176
Dyer (ER) v Simon Build, Peter Lind Partnership (1982) 23 BLR 23   255

Earle (G & T) v Hemsworth RDC (1929) 140 LT 69   51, 183, 270, 332, 368
Edward Owen v Barclays Bank [1978] 1 QB 159   388, 419
Egan v State Transport (1982) 31 SASR 481   94, 101, 102, 116, 245
El Ajou v Dollar Land Holdings [1993] 3 All ER 717   505
Elian v Matsas [1966] 2 Lloyd's Rep 495   420
Elitestone v Morris [1997] 2 All ER 513   112
Eller v Grovecrest Investments [1995] 2 WLR 278   132
Elliott v Wheeldon [1992] BCC 489   443
Ellis v Dixon-Johnson [1924] 1 Ch 342   380
Ellis v Wates (1976) 2 BLR 57   147
Ellis Tylin v Co-operative Retail Services [1999] BLR 205   134, 253
Elwes v Maw (1802) 3 East 38   110
Emson Eastern v EME Developments (1992) 55 BLR 114   266
Endowments Society, *Re* (1870) 5 CL App 118   282
Engineering Construction v Attorney General [1994] 1 SLR 687   485
Equitable Life v Kenchington Ford [1996] CILL 1163   299
Erimis v Banque Indosuez (unreported, 26 Feb 1997)   421
Esal Commodities v Oriental Credit [1985] 2 Lloyd's Rep 546   401, 402
Esso v Kago Petroleum [1995] 1 MLJ 149   467
Esso v Milton [1997] 2 All ER 593   131, 132, 141, 142, 146
Europa Holdings v Circle Industries (1992) 33 Con LR 34   78
Exchange Mutual v Haskell, 742 F 2d 274   480

Fairclough v Cigna Insurance (unreported, 11 Sept 1991)   396
Far East Consortium v Airedale (unreported, 27 Dec 1991)   281
Farley v Housing and Commercial Developments (1984) 26 BLR 66   380
Farnsworth v Garrard (1807) 1 Camp 38   382
Farrier-Waimak v Bank of New Zealand [1965] NZLR 426   362
Fearman (WF) (1988) 4 BCC 139   234
Felt and Textiles v Hubrich [1968] NZLR 716   377
Ferguson v Sohl [1992] *The Times,* 24 Dec; (1993) 62 BLR 95   271, 297
Filross Securities v Midgeley [1998] 3 EGLR 43   134
Financings v Baldock [1963] 2 QB 104   247
Finbo Engineering, *Re* [1998] 2 HKLRD 695   482

Finnegan v Ford Sellar Morris (No 1) (1991) 53 BLR 38　　　　324, 438
Finnegan v Ford Sellar Morris (No 2) (1991) 27 Con LR 41　　　164, 317,
　　　　　　　　　　　　　　　　　　　　　　　　　　　324, 369
Fischer v Multi Construction (1995) BCC 310　　　　　　　　　　396
Fletcher Development v New Plymouth Hotels [1986] 2 NZLR 302　　207
Flint, *Re* [1993] Ch 319　　　　　　　　　　　　　　　　　　438
Flood v Shand Construction (1996) 81 BLR 31　　　　　　　　　173
Fonthill v Bank of Montreal [1959] OR 451　　　　　　　　　　339
Forestry Commission v Stefanetto [1975] 133 CLR 507　　　　　98, 99
Fortescue v Lostwithiel and Fowey Railway [1894] 3 Ch 621　　　282
Forth Shipbuilding v Tonnevold (1923) 12 Ll L Rep 554　　　　290, 291
Foster Wheeler v Chevron (unreported, 29 Feb 1996)　　　　　134
Fulton v Dornwell (1885) 4 SC 207; (1885) 4 NZLR 207　　　185, 299

Gallemos v Barratt (1990) SLT 98　　　　　　　　　　　　　137
Galway Concrete, *Re* [1983] IRLM 402　　　　　　　　　　　122
Gardner and Yeoman v Watson (1937) GLR 141　　　　　　　　184
Garrett v Banstead and Epsom Downs Railway (1864)
　　4 De GJ & Sm 462; (1865) 12 LT 654　　　　　　　　　96, 272
Garrud, *Re, ex parte* Newitt (1881) 16 Ch D 522　　　　　　　103
General Steam Navigation v Rolt (1859) 6 CB (NS) 550　　　　393
General Surety v Francis Parker (1977) 16 BLR 16　　　　　　386
Gerald Cooper, *Re* [1978] Ch 262　　　　　　　　　　　　　427
Geraldton Building v Christmas Island (1995) 11 BCL 23　　　　74
Geraldton Building v Woodmore (1993) 8 ACSR 585　　　　　　57
Gericevich Contracting v Sabemo [1984] 9 ACLR 452　　　　356, 432
Gibbs v Tomlinson (1992) 35 Con LR 86　　　　　　　　　　248
Gibraltar Homes v Agroman (unreported, Gibraltar CA 15/96)　　421
Gilbert-Ash v Modern Engineering [1973] 3 All ER 195; [1974] AC 689　64,
　　　　　　　131, 138, 139, 147, 148, 149, 246, 347, 476, 477
Gillis-Mason Construction v Overvaal Crushers [1971] 1 SA 524　209
GKN Contractors v Lloyds (1985) 30 BLR 48　　　　　　　　419
Gleeson (MJ) v Taylor Woodrow (1989) 49 BLR 95　　　　　　147
Glen Music v City of Glasgow DC (1983) SLT 26　　　　　　489
Gloucestershire CC v Richardson [1968] 3 WLR 645　　　　　　114
Glow Heating v Eastern Health Board (1992) 8 Const LJ 56　356, 364, 499
Goldcorp Exchange, *Re* [1994] 2 All ER 806　　　　　　　　157
Golden Sand v Easy Success Enterprises (unreported, 31 March 1999)　181,
　　　　　　　　　　　　　　　　　　　　　　　　　　　360, 369
Goodman v Napier Harbour Board [1939] NZLR 97　　85, 266, 271, 297
Gordon Durham v Haden Young (1990) 52 BLR 61　　　　　　335
Goscott (Groundworks) Ltd, *Re* (1988) 4 BCC 372　　　　　　234
Gough v Timbalok [1997] 1 NZLR 303　　　　　　　　　　　477
Gough v Wood [1894] 1 QB 713　　　　　　　　　　　　　109

GPT Realisations v Panatown (1992) 61 BLR 88 312, 323
Grant Plant Hire v Trickey (1961) 105 SJ 255 51, 53, 368
Grayan Building Services, *Re* [1995] BCC 554 446
Gray's Inn Construction, *Re* [1980] 1 All ER 814 438
Grayson-Robinson v Iris Construction (1960) 168 NE 2(d) 377 261
Great Eastern Railway v Lord's Trustee [1909] AC 109 94
Griffiths v Hodge (1979) 2 BPR 9474 474
Grills v Dellios [1988] VR 136 117
Groutco v Prince Constructions (1987) BCL 372 97
Grys Building Services (le) v Sealand Associates
    (unreported, 29 March 1990) 280
GSAR Realisations, *Re* [1993] BCLC 409 447
Guinness v CMD Property Developments (1995) 76 BLR 40 392
Gulf Bank v Mitsubishi [1994] 2 Lloyd's Rep 145 415
Guyana and Trinidad Mutual Fire Insurance v Plummer (1992)
    8 Const LJ 171

Halesown Presswork v National Westminster Bank [1972] AC 785 380
Hallett's Estate, *Re* (1880) 13 Ch D 696 158
Halls v O'Dell [1992] 2 WLR 308 437
Hamlet International, *Re* (unreported, 19 Feb 1998) *noted* (1998) 2 BLM 1 94
Hanak v Green [1958] 2 QB 9 131, 150, 376, 383, 384
Hanson v Rapid Civil Engineering (1987) 38 BLR 106 116, 117, 119, 124
Harbottle v National Westminster Bank [1978] QB 147 409
Hargreaves v Action 2000 (1992) 36 Con LR 74; [1993] BCLC 1111 135,
    367, 373
Harrington v Co Partnership (1998) 88 BLR 44 42, 314, 319, 320,
    322, 325, 343
Harris Simons, *Re* [1989] 1 WLR 368; (1989) 5 BCC 11 195, 214, 233
Harrison, *Re, ex parte* Jay (1880) 14 Ch D 19 99, 100
Harry Bibby v Neill Construction [1973] EGD 52 309, 323
Hart v Porthgain [1903] 1 Ch 690 87, 88, 89
Hawker Siddeley Power v Peterborough Power (unreported, 9 May 1994) 421
Hawthorn v Newcastle upon Tyne Railway (1840) 3 QB 734 94
HEB Contractors v Verrissimo [1990] 3 NZLR 754 282
Hegarty v Royal Liver Friendly Society (unreported, 11 Oct 1985) 500
Helstan Securities v Hertfordshire CC [1978] 3 All ER 262 172
Hempseed v Durham Developments [1998] 3 NZLR 265 477
Henderson Investment Corp v International Fidelity Ins Co,
    575 So 2d 770 480
Hendry v Chartsearch [1998] *The Time*s, 16 Sept 173
Henry Boot v The Croydon Hotel (1985) 36 BLR 41 324
Herbert Construction v Atlantic Estates (1993) 70 BLR 46 316, 319
Herkules Piling v Tilbury Construction [1992] CILL 770 174

Hertz v Itzig (1865) 3 M 813   490
Hewitt v Official Assignee of Barnes and Keble [1930] NZLR 416   184
Heyman v Darwins [1942] AC 356   241, 242
High Mark v Patco Malaysia (1984) 28 BLR 129   269
Hill v London Borough of Camden (1980) 18 BLR 31   244
Hobson v Gorringe [1897] 1 Ch 181   111
Hobbs v Turner (1900) 17 TLR 83   348
Hodgson v Miller Construction (unreported, 1995)   133
Holidair, *Re* (7 March 1994, Supreme Ct of Ireland)   501
Holland v Hodgson (1872) LR 7 CP 328   111, 112
Holme v Brunskill (1878) 3 QBD 495   392
Holt, *Re, ex parte* Gray (1888) 15 LJQB 5   346, 354, 355
Hong Kong Teakwood v Shui On [1984] HKLR 235   68
Hounslow (London Borough of) v Twickenham Garden [1971]
    1 Ch 233   260, 274
Housing Guarantee Fund v Yusef [1991] VR 17   287, 393
Hsin Chong Construction v Yaton Reality (1986) 40 BLR 119   314, 322
Hughes v Trustees of the Roman Catholic Church (1994) 10 BCL 335   252
Hughes (CW & AL) *Re* [1966] 1 WLR 1369   449
Hulme v Brigham [1943] 1 KB 204   112
Hunter v Fitzroy Robinson (1977) 10 BLR 84   268, 269
Hutchens v Deaville Investments (1986) 68 ALR 367   177, 412
Hutchinson v Harris (1978) 10 BLR 19   133
Hydrodam (Corby) Ltd, *Re* [1994] 2 BCLC 180   440, 442

IE Contractors v Lloyd's Bank (1990) 51 BLR 1   389
ILG Travel, *Re* [1995] 2 BCLC 129   175, 330
IM Properties v Cape & Dalgleish [1998] 3 All ER 203   76
Iezzi Constructions v Currumbin (1994) BCL 408   256
Imodco v Wimpey (1987) 40 BLR 1   154
Independent Automatic Sales v Knowles & Foster [1962] 1 WLR 974;
    [1962] 3 All ER 27   71, 101
Intepro Engineering v Sin Heng Construction [1998] 1 SLR 694   485
International Factors v Rodriguez [1979] QB 351   174, 338

Jack Frost v Minister of Public Works [1980] 3 SA 20   118
Jackson v Horizon Holidays [1975] 1 WLR 1468   337
Jaks (UK) Ltd v Cera Investment Bank [1998] 2 Lloyd's Rep 89   386
James Graham v Southgate Sands [1986] QB 80   412
Jartay Developments, *Re* (1983) 22 BLR 134   40, 316, 317
Jason Construction, *Re* (1972) 16 CBR 297   184, 381
Jersey (Earl of) v Great Western Railway (1893)   282
John Dee v WMH (21) Ltd [1997] BCC 518, *affirmed* [1998] BCC 972   142,
    267, 374, 377

John Holland Construction v Majorca Projects (1996) 12 BCL 135   435
John Lee v Railway Executive [1949] 2 All ER 581   67
John Sisk & Son v Lawter Products (unreported, 15 Nov 1976)   500
Johnson (B) & Co (Builders) Ltd, *Re* [1955] 1 Ch 634   436
Johnson v Davies [1998] BPIR 607   393
Johnstone v Milling (1886) 16 QBD 460   247
Jones, *Re, ex parte* Nichols (1883) 2 Ch D 782   184
Jones v Farrell (1857) 1 De G & J 208   164
Joo Yee Construction v Diethelm [1990] MLJ 66   360

Kamlee Construction v Town of Oakville (1960) 26 DLR (2d) 166   297, 298
Kay's Leasing Corporation v CSR Provident [1962] VR 429   113
Kayford, *Re* [1975] 1 WLR 279   156, 434
KBH Construction v Lidco (1991) 7 BCL 183   315
Keen and Keen, *Re, ex parte* Collins [1902] 1 KB 555   86, 89
Kennedy v Collings Construction (1991) 7 BCL 25   248, 271
Kerr v Dundee Gas Light Company (1861) Ct of Sess 343   95
Kinsela v Russell (1986) 4 NSWLR 722   435, 442
Kirames v Federal Land [1991] 2 MLJ 198   469
Kon Struct v Storage Developments (1990) 6 BCL 171   369
Kraft Construction v Guardian Insurance (1984) 57 AR 118   298
Kratzmann v University of Queensland [1982] Qd R 682   266
Kum Leng v Hytech Builders [1996] 1 SLR 751   478
Kuwait Asia Bank v National Mutual Life Nominees [1991] AC 187   441
Kvaerner v Midland Bank (1998) CLC 446   389, 413, 419
Kvaerner Singapore v UDL Shipbuilding [1993] 3 SLR 350   467

L/M International v The Circle Limited Partnership (1992) 37 Con LR 72   153
L/M International v The Circle Limited Partnership (1995) 49 Con LR 12   33, 165, 176, 179
Lagos v Grunwaldt [1910] 1 KB 41   58
Laidlaw v Smith (1836) 16 F 267   489
Laing and Morrison-Knudson v Aegon Insurance (1997) 86 BLR 70   29, 180, 243, 244, 247, 248, 250, 275, 411, 501
Lane v Shire Roofing (1995) IRLR 493   451
Lawson Constructions, *Re* [1942] SASR 201   71
Leigh v Taylor [1902] AC 157   112
Lemina v Phillips Construction (1988) BCL 56   172
Lett v Morris (1831) 4 Sim 607   135, 163
Levy v Gardner (1964) SLT (Notes) 68   489
Lewis's of Leicester, *Re* [1995] 1 BCLC 428   312, 435
Leyland Motors v Napier Harbour Board [1930] NZLR 113   251
Linden Gardens v Lenesta Sludge (1992) 30 Con LR 1; (1992) 57 BLR 57;
    [1994] 1 AC 85   165, 166, 171, 173, 174, 178, 245, 280

Lintest Builders v Roberts (1978) 10 BLR 120, *affirmed* (1980)
   13 BLR 38   271, 373
Lipe v Leyland DAF [1993] BCC 385   120, 126
Lloyd's v Harper (1880) 16 Ch D 290   336, 337
Lo-Line Electric Motors, *Re* [1988] Ch 477   445
Lockland Builders v Rickwood (1995) 77 BLR 38   246
Lombard North Central v Butterworth [1987] QB 527   249
London Wine Shippers, *Re* [1986] PCC 121   157
Lord Advocate v Royal Bank of Scotland (1977) SC 155   490
Lorne Steward v William Sindall (1986) 35 BLR 109   336
Lovell Construction v Independent Estates [1994] 1 BCLC 31   33, 42,
                                                            325-329, 330
Lowe v Holme (1883) 10 QBD 286   150
Lucas' Trustees v Campbell and Scott (1984) 21 R 1096   489

McAlpine, Alfred v BAI [1998] 2 Lloyd's Rep 694   415
McAlpine, Alfred v Panatown (1998) 88 BLR 67   180
McAlpine, Alfred v Unex (1994) 38 Con LR 63   421
McAlpine, Sir Robert v Semisquare (1994) ORB 19   120
McCosker v Lovett (1996) 12 BCL 146   474
McIlwee v Foley Brothers (1916) WWR 5   301
MacJordan Construction v Brookmount Erostin (1992) 56 BLR 1   309, 317,
                                                      324, 331-333, 435
McKeown, *Re* [1974] NILR 226   162
Macleod v Alexander Sutherland (1977) SLT 44   261
McNeill v Ja Ron Construction (1979) 35 NSR (2d) 150   123
McPhail v Cunninghame District Council (1985) SLT 149   250, 282
Maidenhead Electrical Services v Johnson (1997) 15 CLD 10-03   65
Mancetter Developments v Garmanson (1986) 2 BCC 98924   444
Marathon v Mashreqbank [1997] 2 BCLC 460   169, 175
Marsden v Sambell (1880) 43 LT 120   123, 252
Mayflower Foods v Barnard (unreported, 9 Aug 1996) *noted* (1997)
   14 BLM 1   121
Melbourne Glass v Corby Constructions (1998) 14 BCL 409   149
Mellowes Archital v Bell Projects (1997) 87 BLR 26   133
Melluish v B & I [1996] AC 454   112
Melville Dundas v Team Management (unreported, 1 Dec 1994)   492
Mercantile Bank of Canada v Leon's Furniture (1989) 42
   Business Law Rep 1   375
Mercantile Bank of India v Chartered Bank of India [1937]
   1 All ER 231   101
Mercers Company v New Hampshire [1992] 2 Lloyd's Rep 365   392,
                                                            393, 398
Merchants' Trading v Banner (1871) LR 12 Eq 18   261

Merco v McMichael, 372 F Supp 967 469
Meridian Global Funds v Securities Commission [1995]
   3 All ER 918 440, 505
Mertens v Home Freeholds [1921] 2 KB 526 270, 289
Midland Engineeering v John Hall, 398 F Supp 981 (1975) 68
Midland Land v Warren Energy [1997] CILL 1222 173, 249
Milburn Services v United Trading Group (1995) 2 Con LR 130 256
Milestone v Yates Brewery [1938] 2 All ER 439 347, 348, 349
Miller Gibb & Co, *Re* [1957] 2 All ER 266 338
Min Thai v Sunlabel [1999] 2 SLR 368 467
Mine v Henderson Drilling [1989] 1 ACSR 118 208
Minneapolis-Honeywell v Empire Brass [1955] SCR 694 463
Minion v Graystone (1990) 2 ACLB 7 253
Minshall v Lloyd (1837) 2 M & W 450 112
Minter v WHTSO (1980) 13 BLR 1 75
Modern Brokerage v Massachusetts Bonding & Ins Co, 54 F Supp 939 480
Modern Structural (Scotland) Plastics v Tayloroof (unreported,
   3 Dec 1990) 494
Modern Weighbridge v ANR (1996) 12 BCL 224 172
Mohan and Holmes v Dundalk Railway (1880) LR Ir 477 98, 102
Moncton (City of) v Aprile Contracting (1977) 17 NBR (2d) 678 298
Mondel v Steel (1841) 8 M & W 858 132, 133, 140, 147
Monkhouse (CG) Properties, *Re* [1968] SR (NSW) 429 356, 363, 432
Moody v Amoco Oil, 734 F 2d 1200 481
Mooney v Henry Boot (1996) 80 BLR 66 337
Morgan v Allen [1971] Tas SR 285 55
Morgan v Martin Johnson [1949] 1 KB 107 376
Morris v Harris [1927] AC 252 279
Morrison, Jones & Taylor, *Re* [1914] 1 Ch 50 113
Moschi v Lep Air [1973] AC 331 391
Mottram v Bernard Sunley [1975] 2 Lloyd's Rep 197 140
Mowlem v Carlton Gate (1990) 21 Con LR 113 148, 196
Mowlem v Eagle Star (1992) 33 Con LR 131 139, 427
MPS Constructions v Rural Bank of New South Wales (1980)
   4 ACLR 835 380
Mullan v Ross (1996) 86 BLR 1 360
Multi Guarantee, *Re* [1987] BCLC 257 156
Munroe v Wivenhoe and Brightlingsea Railway Company (1865)
   12 LT 656 249, 263
Murphy Brothers v Morris (unreported, 6 Oct 1975) 489

Nam Fang Electrical v City Developments [1997] 1 SLR 585 484
Napier and Ettrick v Hunter [1993] 1 All ER 385 93, 335
Natal Administrator v Magill Grant & Nell [1969] 1 SA 660 357, 358, 361

National House-Building Council v Fraser [1983] 1 All ER 1090   401,
                                                                  408, 411
National Trust v Mead [1990] 2 SCR 410   282
National Westminster Bank v Halesowen [1972] 1 All ER 641   143
National Westminster Bank v Hardman [1988] FLR 302   401
National Westminster Bank v Riley [1986] BCLC 268   393
National Westminster Finance, *Re* [1991] 1 Qd R 130   72
Nelson Carlton v Hatrick [1965] NZLR 144   245
Nene Housing Society v National Westminster Bank (1980) 16 BLR 22   399
New, *Re* [1901] 2 Ch 534   343
New Zealand Shipping v Société des Ateliers [1919] AC 1   250
Newfoundland (Government of) v Newfoundland Railway Co
   (1888) 13 App Cas 199   374
Ng v Clyde Securities [1976] 1 NSWLR 443   268, 269
Nicholas Acoustics v H & M Construction, 695 F 2d 839 (1983)   68
Nokes v Doncaster Amalgamated Collieries [1940] AC 1014   172, 214
Norman Kennedy v Norman Kennedy Ltd [1947] 1 SA 790   357
North v Bassett [1892] 1 QB 333   278
Northwood v Aegon Insurance (1994) 10 Const LJ 157   399
Nova (Jersey) Knit v Kammgarn [1977] 2 All ER 463   146

O'Driscoll v Manchester Insurance Committee [1915] 3 KB 499   51
Oasis Merchandising, *Re* [1997] 1 All ER 1009; [1997] BCC 282   167, 426
Oatway, *Re* [1903] 2 Ch 356   158
OCWS Logistics v Soon Men Construction [1999] 2 SLR 376   478
Odebrecht v North Sea Production Co [1992] 2 All ER
   (Comm) 405   404, 423
Official Assignee v Mayor of City of Wellington [1885] 3 NZLR 159   266
Ogdens v Weinberg (1896) 95 LT 567   57
Olsson v Dyson [1970] 120 CLR 365   283
Olympia & York, *Re* [1993] BCLC 453   383
Orion Finance v Crown Financial Management [1994] 2 BCLC 607   173
Otis v Girvan (1990) 2 ACLB 70   115
Oval (717) Ltd v Aegon Insurance (1997) 85 BLR 97   392, 399, 414, 415
Ovington Investments, *Re* (1975) 5 OR 320   375

Paddington Churches v Tower & General Guarantee [1999] BLR 244   400
Pan Ocean v Creditcorp [1994] 1 All ER 470   169
Paramount Airways, *Re* [1990] BCC 130   126
Partridge v Morris [1995] CILL 1095   30
Patrick Carr v Marosszeky [1982] 7 ACLR 59   208
Paul & Frank v Discount Bank [1967] Ch 348   71
Pauling v Mayor of Dover (1855) 10 Ex 753   249
Pavex Constructions, *ex parte* [1979] Qd R 318   461

Payzu v Saunders [1919] 2 KB 281   298

Pearson Bridge v State Rail Authority of New South Wales (1982)
    1 Aust Const LR 81   466, 467

Perar v General Surety (1994) 66 BLR 72   244, 246, 250, 398, 399

Perbadanan v Teo Kai Huat [1982] MLJ 165   107

Perrins v State Bank of Victoria [1991] 1 VR 749   72

Perry v National Provincial Bank [1910] 1 Ch 464   287

Pettkus v Becker (1980) 117 DLR (3rd) 257   470, 471

Philip Head v Showfronts [1970] 1 Lloyd's Rep 140   115

Phontos v New South Wales Land & Housing Corporation (1988) BCL 45   97

Photo Production v Securicor [1980] AC 827   242

Pillar v Croudace (unreported, 19 Dec 1984)   140

Pillar v DJ Higgins (1986) 10 Con LR 46   149

Pioneer Concrete v Ellston [1985] 10 ACLR 289   430

Polly Peck (No 2) *Re* [1998] 3 All ER 812   333

Popular Homes v Circuit Development [1979] 2 NZLR 642   297

Pratt v George Hill (1987) 38 BLR 25   30

Premier Products, *Re* [1965] NZLR 50   243

President of India v La Pintada [1985] AC 104   76

Press Construction v Penspen (unreported, 16 April 1996)   421

Primrose Builders, *Re* [1950] Ch 561   449

Pritchett & Gold v Currie [1916] 2 Ch 515   114

Produce Marketing, *Re* [1989] 5 BCC 569   428, 429

Public Bank v Perbadanan [1980] 1 MLJ 214   266

Pullan v Koe [1913] 1 Ch 9   316

Pysogea v Rightfairs Development [1991] 1 HKC 341   483

R v Webb [1960] Qd R 443   466

Rafidain Bank v Saipem (unreported, 2 March 1994)   160, 322, 340, 343

Rafsanjan v Reiss (1990) 7 CLD 7.30   444

Rajaram v Ganesh [1995] 1 SLR 159   467

Ramsden v Dyson (1866) LR 1 HL 129   110, 470

Ranger v Great Western Railway (1854) HLC 72   99

Rasbora v JCL Marine [1977] 1 Lloyd's Rep 645   286

Rawson v Samuel (1841) Cr & Ph 161   131

Rayack Construction v Lampeter Meat (1979) 12 BLR 30   312, 315

Raymond Construction v Low Yang Tong (unreported,
    Suit No 1715 of 1995)   467

Read Construction v Kheng Seng (1999) 15 BCL 158   467

Reeves v Barlow (1884) 12 QBD 436   89, 101, 104, 105

Remm Construction v Allco (1990) 53 SASR 471   122, 257

Rendell v Doors & Doors [1975] 2 NZLR 191   377

Reynolds v Ashby [1904] AC 466   111

Richborough Furniture, *Re* [1996] 1 BCLC 507   440

Right Time Construction, *Re* (1990) 52 BLR 117   369, 438
Roach v Great Western Railway Company [1841] 1 QB 51   100, 258, 271
Road Surfaces v Brown [1987] 2 Qd R 792   461
Robbie v Witney Warehouse [1963] 1 WLR 1324   377
Robert Salzer Constructions v Elmbee (1991) 10 ACLR 64   245
Roberts v Maurbeth Investments [1974] 1 NSWLR 93   98
Roberts Petroleum v Kenny [1983] 2 AC 192   333
Robertson v Grigg (1932) 47 CLR 257   72
Rogersons Development v The Housing Corporation (unreported,
    14 Oct 1994) *noted* (1995) 12 BLM 4   110
Rohan Construction v Antigen [1989] IRLM 783   500
Rolfe v Amey Construction (unreported, 13 Nov 1992)   449
Roscoe v Winder [1915] 1 Ch 62   158
Rosehaugh v Redpath Dorman Long (1990) 50 BLR 69   139
Rother Iron v Canterbury Precision Engineers [1974] QB 1   377
Rouse v Bradford Banking [1894] 2 Ch 32   278, 280
Royal Bank of Canada v Wilson (1963) 4 CBR 300   293
Royal Bank of Scotland v Slinn (unreported, 10 March 1989)   401
Royal Brunei Airlines v Tan [1995] 3 All ER 97   159
Royal Design Studio v Chang [1991] 2 MLJ 229   467
Rumput v Islamic Republic of Iran [1984] 2 Lloyd's Rep 259   373
Rushpass v G Percy Trentham (unreported, 10 May 1991)   64

Sabema v De Groot (1991) 8 BCL 132   476
Sable Contractors v Bluett Shipping [1979] 2 Lloyd's Rep 33   149
Samuel Allen, *Re* [1907] 1 Ch 575   113
Samuel Properties v London Borough of Richmond (unreported,
    22 July 1983)   250, 298
Sandy v Yukon Construction [1961] 33 WWR 490   52
Sauter Automation v Goodman (1986) 34 BLR 81   118, 119, 123
Savory Holdings v Royalo Oak Mall [1992] 1 NZLR 12   476
Scarf v Jardine (1882) 7 App Cas 345   279
Scheibler, *Re, ex parte* Holthausen (1874) LR 9 Ch App 722   270
Schenkers v Overland Shoes [1998] 1 Lloyd's Rep 498   142
Schindler Lifts v Shui On (1984) 29 BLR 95   68
Schott-Kem v Bentley [1990] 3 All ER 850   437
Schott-Kem v G Percy Trentham (unreported, 15 May 1985)   336, 345
SCL Building Services, *Re* (1989) 5 BCC 746   234
Scobie & McIntosh v Clayton Bowmore (1990) 49 BLR 119   256
Scottish Discount v Blin [1985] SLT 123   111
SEA Housing v Lee Poh Choo [1982] 2 MLJ 33   132
Seath v Moore (1886) 11 App Cas 350   117
Seawind Tankers v Bayoil [1999] 1 Lloyd's Rep 211   207
Sevenoaks Stationers, *Re* [1990] BCC 765   446

Seventeenth Canute v Bradley Air-Conditioning [1987] 1 Qd R 111 461
Shamia v Joory [1958] 1 All ER 111 177
Shanning v Wimpey [1985] 3 All ER 475 154
Sheffield v Conrad (1987) 22 Con LR 108 249
Shipley v Marshall (1863) 14 CB (NS) 566 71
Shipton v Micks, Lambert & Co [1936] 2 All ER 1032 272
Siebe Gorman v Barclays Bank [1979] 2 Lloyd's Rep 142 53
Simon (LU) Builders v Fowles [1992] 2 VR 189 476
Skipskredittforeningen v Emperor Navigation [1998] 1 Lloyd's Rep 66 142
Slater v Duquemin (1992) 29 Con LR 24 271
Smallman Construction v Redpath Dorman Long (1988)
    47 BLR 15 154, 232
Smith (HL) Construction v Albany Estates (noted in Dean 1996) 319
Smith and Smith Glass v Winstone [1992] 2 NZLR 473 66
Sneezum, Re, ex parte Davis (1876) 3 Ch D 463 272
Sotiros Shipping v Sameiet Solholt [1983] 1 Lloyd's Rep 605 297
South East Thames RHA v YJ Lovell (1985) 32 BLR 127 164
Spencer Constructions v Aldridge (unreported, 29 July 1997) 209
Sperry v Government of Israel, 689 F 2d 301 418
Sport International v Inter-Footwear [1984] 2 All ER 321 261
St Martin's Corporation v Sir Robert McAlpine [1994] 1 AC 85 178
Standard Electric v Royal Bank of Canada (1960) 1 CBR 64 464
Stanford Services, Re (1987) 3 BCC 326 446
Stanley Brown v Maryland Casualty, 442 SW 2d 187 (1969) 67, 289
Star Rider v Inntrepreneur (unreported, 8 Dec 1997) 132
Star-Trans v Norske-Tech [1996] ADRLJ 62 282
Starline Furniture, Re [1982] 6 ACLR 111
State Trading Corporation of India v Man [1981] Com LR 235 420
Stein v Blake [1995] 2 All ER 961; [1996] AC 243 373, 378, 380
Stenning, Re [1895] 2 Ch 433 158
Stephens v Venables (1862) 30 Beav 625 372
Stewart Gill v Horatio Meyer [1992] 2 All ER 257 142
Stimpson v Smith [1999] 2 WLR 1292 393
Stocznia v Latvian Shipping [1998] 1 All ER 883 245
Stonegate Securities v Gregory [1980] Ch 576 206
Stonehenge Constructions, Re [1986] 2 NZLR 302 208
Stooke v Taylor (1880) 5 QBD 569 136, 152, 169
Stovin-Bradford v Volpoint [1971] Ch 1007 269
Straume (A) (UK) Ltd v Bradlor Developments [1999]
    *The Time*s, 29 June 232
Stroud Architectural Systems v John Laing (1993) 35 Con LR 135 123
Swartz v Wolmaransstad [1960] 2 SA 1 407
Swiss Bank v Lloyd's Bank [1980] 2 All ER 419 330

T & D Services, *Re* [1990] BCC 592   447
Tailby v Official Receiver (1888) 13 App Cas 523   52
Tancred v Delagoa Bay Railway (1889) 23 QBD 239   176, 181
Tapp v Jones (1875) LR 10 QB 591   52
Tapper v Bodley (1884) 3 NZLR 4   105
Tatung v Galex (1989) 5 BCC 325   330
Taylor v Pace Developments [1991] BCC 406   430
Taylor (George E) v G Percy Trentham (1980) 16 BLR 15   335
Taylor Woodrow v Sears Investment Trust (1991) SLT 421   490
Taylor's Industrial Flooring, *Re* [1990] BCC 44   187
Taymech v Rush & Tompkins (1990) SLT 681   122, 490
Taymech v Trafalgar House Construction (1995) SLT 202   490
TBV Power v Elm Energy (unreported, 21 Nov 1995)   402, 403, 421
Team Services v Kier (1993) 63 BLR 76   137
Tern Construction v RBS Garages (1992) 34 Con LR 137   247, 266
Tersons v Stevenage Development Corporation [1963] 2 Lloyd's Rep 333   67
Thiess Watkins White v Commonwealth of Australia (1998)
   14 BCL 61   271, 272
Thames Ironworks, *Re* (1912) WN 66   291
Themehelp v West [1995] 4 All ER 215   389, 419
Thomas Construction v Grafton Furniture [1986] 4 SA 510,
   affirmed [1988] 2 SA 546   251, 265, 270
Thomas Feather v Bradford [1953] 52 LGR 30   248
Thomas Graham v Glenrothes [1967] SC 284   116
Thomas Saunders v Harvey (1989) 30 Con LR 103   443
Thompson (NEI) v Wimpey (1987) 39 BLR 65   147, 152
Three Rivers v Bank of England [1996] QB 292   181
Tilley's Will Trusts, *Re* [1967] 1 Ch 1179   158
Timbro Developments v Grimsby Diesel (1988) 32 CLR 32   66
Tins Industrial v Kono Insurance (1987) 42 BLR 110   397
Tito v Waddell (No 2) [1977] Ch 106   170, 280
Tolent Construction v Kustow (unreported, 28 June 1994)   325
Tolhurst v Associated Portland Cement [1902] 2 KB 660   167
Tony Cox v Jim 5 (1996) 14 BLM 6   53
Tooth v Hallett (1869) LR 4 Ch App 242   184
Total Gas v Arco [1998] 2 Lloyd's Rep 209   244
Tout & Finch, *Re* [1954] 1 WLR 178; [1954] 1 All ER 127   181, 185,
   308, 309, 310, 311, 318, 355, 364
Toward, *Re, ex parte* Moss (1884) 14 QBD 310   183
Tower Housing v Technical & General Guarantee (1997) 87 BLR 82   264,
   266, 301, 399
Townsend v Stone Toms (1984) 27 BLR 26   30
T R Nominees v Multiplex (1996) 12 BCL 219   107
Trade Indemnity v Parkinson (1995) BCL 39   41

Trade Indemnity v Workington Harbour and Dock Board [1937] AC 1   397
Trafalgar House v General Surety (1994) 66 BLR 42; *overruled*
   [1996] AC 199   393, 399
Trendtex v Crédit Suisse [1982] AC 679   167
Triangle v John Burroughs [1958] 3 SA 810   106
Triden Contractors v Belvista (1987) 3 BCL 203   476
Trident v Manchester Ship Canal [1990] BCC 694   189
Tripp v Armitage (1839) 4 M & W 687   123
Trollope and Colls v Gresham (1984) 2 CLD 7.16   190
Turkiye v Bank of China [1993] 1 Lloyd's Rep 132   418
Twin City v Penwood Construction (1980) 44 NSR (2d) 418   243

UDL Holdings, *Re* [1999] 2 HKLRD 817   483
Ultra Refurbishing v John Goubran (1997) 13 BCL 330   35
Underground (Civil Engineering) Ltd v London Borough of Croydon
   (1990) BLM 7   261, 262
United City Merchants v Royal Bank of Canada [1983] 1 AC 168   419
United Railways, *Re* [1960] 1 Ch 52   284
United Trading v Allied Arab Bank [1985] 2 Lloyd's Rep 554   402, 419
Universal Cargo Carriers v Citati [1957] 2 QB 401   241
University of Reading v Miller Construction (1994) 75 BLR 91   421

Vaswani v Italian Motors [1996] 1 WLR 270   241
Venios v Macon (1986) 3 BCL 171   474
Ventura v Svirac [1961] WAR 63   270
Victorian Railway Commissioners v Williams (1969) 44 ALJR 32   356
Vigers Sons & Co v Swindell [1939] 3 All ER 590   289, 347
Vitol v Norelf [1996] AC 800   242, 243

Wadsworth v Lydall [1981] 2 All ER 401   76
Wahda Bank v Arab Bank [1996] 1 Lloyd's Rep 470   418
Wahda Bank v Arab Bank (unreported, 16 June 1999)   389, 416
Wakefield & Barnsley Banking Co v Normanton Local Board
   (1881) LT 697   372
Walker, *Re, ex parte* Barter (1884) 25 Ch D 510   272, 273, 274, 275, 277
Warren, *Re* [1938] Ch 725   163
Wates Construction v Franthom (1991) 53 BLR 23   312, 316, 471
Watkins v Cairns Meat [1963] Qd R 21   54
Watpack v K-Crete Industries (1996) 12 BCL 103   461
Watson v Mid Wales Railway (1867) LR 2 CP 593   373
Waugh, *Re, ex parte* Dickin (1876) 4 Ch D 524   94
Welfab Engineers, *Re* [1990] BCC 600   442
Welsh Development Agency v Export Finance [1990] BCC 393   105
Welsh Irish Ferries Ltd, *Re* [1985] WLR 610   329

West Cumberland Farmers v Ellon Hinengro (1988) SLT 294   489
West Mercia Safetywear v Dodd [1988] BCC 250   436, 441
West Street Properties v Jamison [1974] 2 NSWLR 435   377
Westdeutsche v Islington BC [1996] 2 WLR 802   77
Western Credit v Alberry [1964] 2 All ER 938   394
Western Webb Offset Printers v Independent Media [1995/6]
    CILL 1122   271
Westminster (City of) Properties v Mudd [1959] Ch 129   67
Westminster City Council v Reema Construction (No 1) (1990)
    24 Con LR 16   282
Westminster City Council v Reema Construction (No 2) (1990)
    24 Con LR 26   281
Westralian Farmers v Commonwealth Agricultural Service Engineers
    [1935] 54 CLR 361   257
Whenuapai Joinery v Trust Bank [1994] 1 NZLR 406   113
White v Ensor (1882) 11 NZLR 207   185
Whitmore v Mason (1861) 2 J & H 204   274
Wilkinson, *Re, ex parte* Fowler [1905] 1 KB 713   349, 350, 352,
    354, 355, 360, 361, 362
William Brandt v Dunlop Rubber Company [1905] AC 454   180
William Hockley, *Re* [1962] 2 All ER 111   209
William Thorpe, *Re* (1989) 5 BCC 156   213
Williams, *ex parte* Official Assignee, *Re* (1899) 17 NZLR 712   462
Williams v Natural Life Health Foods [1998] 2 All ER 577   444
Williamson v Murdoch [1912] WAR 54   265
Willment Brothers v North West Thames RHA (1984)
    26 BLR 51   266, 381
Wilson v Lloyd (1873) LR 16 Eq 60   283
Wilson v Metropolitan Property [1975] 2 All ER 814   367
Winter, *Re, ex parte* Bolland (1878) 8 Ch D 228   98
Wire Industries v Certes [1953] 2 SA 531   357
Wolverhampton Corporation v Emmons [1901] 1 KB 515   259
Wong v Ratesharp [1994/5] CILL 1001   443
Wood v Rural Sanitary Authority of Tendring (1886) 3 TLR 272   98, 99
Wood Hall v Pipeline Authority (1978) 141 CLR 443   406
Woodar v Wimpey [1980] 1 WLR 277   241, 242
Worcester v Cooden [1972] 1 QB 210   116
Workington Harbour v Trade Indemnity (No 2) [1938] 2 All ER 101   414
Wright (S & D) *Re* [1992] BCC 503   438
Wyett v Smith and Smith [1908] 28 NZLR 79   114

Yagerphone, *Re* [1935] Ch 392   426
Yeadon Waterworks, *Re* (1895) 72 LT 538   98, 185, 265, 293
Yeandle v Wynn Realisations (1995) 47 Con LR 1   163

Yeoman Credit v Latter [1961] 1 WLR 828   415
Young v Kitchen (1878) 3 Ex D 127   147, 150, 374
Young v Matthew Hall Mechanical & Electrical Engineers Pty Ltd
    [1988] 13 ACLR 399   89, 90, 93
Young & Marten v McManus Childs [1969] 1 AC 454   114
Yorkshire Joinery, *Re* (1967) 111 SJ 71   109
Yukong Line v Rendsberg [1996] 2 Lloyd's Rep 604   243

· Table of Statutes ·

Acton Burnell (Statute of) 1283 507
Arbitration Act 1975 136

Bankruptcy Act 1914 254
Bankruptcy (Scotland) Act 1985 487
  s 7 253
  s 37(4) 489
Bankruptcy (Scotland) Act 1993 487
Bills of Sale Act 1854 103
Bills of Sale Act 1878 102, 103, 104
Bills of Sale Act (1878)
  Amendment Act 1882 104

Companies Act 1948
  s 165(b) 251
Companies Act 1985 202, 214, 222, 282
  s 319(4) 449
  s 320(3) 445
  ss 330, 334 441
  s 395 32, 103, 216, 327
  s 396 32, 102, 329
  s 458 427
  ss 651, 653 279, 520
  s 726 78, 189, 221
  s 727 444
Company Directors
  Disqualification Act 1986 445
  s 15 446
Contracts (Applicable Law)
  Act 1990 418
Copyright Designs and Patents
  Act 1988 267

Debtors Act 1869 507

Employment Rights
  Act 1996 369, 448

Finance Act 1971 450
Finance Act 1995
  Sched 27 450
Frauds (Statute of) 1677 391

Housing Act 1980 387
Housing Grants, Construction
  and Regeneration Act 1996 21, 51, 61 et seq, 143, 155, 214, 502
  s 109 62, 145
  s 110 70, 145
    (1) 62
    (2) 63, 143, 144, 145
  s 111 74, 144, 145, 146
    (1) 143, 145
    (4) 69
  s 112 74
    (4) 75
  s 113 65, 68, 69, 70
    (1) 64, 68
    (2) 69

Income and Corporation Taxes
  Act 1988
  s 560 450
  Sched D 449, 450
  Sched E 450
Insolvency Act 1986 70, 143, 202, 210 et seq, 487
  s 9(4) 239
  s 10 125, 212
    (2) 239
  s 11 212, 383
  s 15 124, 217, 498
    (5) 125
  s 17(2) 239
  s 19(5) 125
  s 27 125

Insolvency Act 1986, *cont.*

s 34	212
s 40	216, 350, 370
s 44	215
s 61	490
s 86	213
s 98	327
s 107	99, 211
s 123	73, 254
(1)	186
(a)	187
(2)	186, 249
s 127	438
s 143	211
s 175	211, 448
s 178	219, 274
(5)	274
s 183	367
s 186	273, 383
s 212	436
s 213	427
s 214	427, 430
(6)	430
ss 217, 219	213
s 234	91, 217
s 238	435
s 239	251, 430, 434
(4)	433
s 245	217, 438
s 249	431
s 251	124, 125, 217, 442
s 281	378
s 285	225
s 306	225
s 323	378
s 345	225
s 378	156
s 382(3)	379
s 386	448
s 388	452
s 389	451
s 390	215
s 423	436
s 436	263, 272

Insolvency Act 1986, *cont.*

Sched 1	212
Sched 4	212, 231
Sched 6	448
Insolvency (Scotland) Act 1986	487
s 185(1)	489
s 242	488
s 243	488
Insurance Companies Act 1982	
Sched 2C	282
Judgments Act 1838	77
Late Payment of Commercial Debts (Interest) Act 1998	76, 194
s 5	76
Law of Property Act 1925	31
s 136	79, 180
Limited Liability Act 1855	504
Sale of Goods Act 1893	
s 25	117
Sale of Goods Act 1979	
s 25	115, 116, 117, 118, 122, 126, 127, 494
s 53	133
Supply of Goods and Services Act 1992	115
Supreme Court Act 1981	
s 35A	76
Third Parties (Rights against Insurers) Act 1930	368, 415
Torts (Interference with Goods) Act 1977	123
s 3	102
Trustee Act 1925	
s 57	340
Unfair Contract Terms Act 1977	68, 142

Australian Statutes

Building Contracts (Deposits) Act 1962	466

Building Services Authority
  Act 1991 475
Contractors' Debts Act 1897
  (New South Wales) 465
Subcontractors Charges Act
  1974 (Queensland) 460
Trust Accounts Acts 1923-59
  s 3E 466
Workmen's Liens Act 1893 461

Canadian Statutes
Ontario Construction Lien
  Act 1983 454
  s 21 465
  s 70 ..... 456, 479

French Law
Law of 16 July 1971 501
Law of 31 Dec 1975 501

Irish Statutes
Bankruptcy Act 1988 496
  First Sched 500
Companies Acts 1963-90 486
Companies Act 1963
  s 284 500
Companies (Amendment)
  Act 1990 496

New Zealand Statutes
Contractors' and Workmen's
  Lien Act 1892 ..... 461, 462

United States Law
Bankruptcy Code
  Chap 11 480-481
  Prompt Payment Act 1982 479

· Table of Standard Forms ·

UK main contracts

ACA 82 (3rd ed)	251
ACE 98 (2nd ed)	268
CCC/WKS/1	309
FIDIC (4th ed)	83, 251, 401
cl 1.1(f)	82
cl 3.1	171
cl 54.7	106
cl 59.5	349
cl 63.1	253-254
GC/Works/1	249, 251, 353, 356
cl 3(1)	118-119
cl 30(2)	119
cl 57(2)	270
ICE (4th ed)	
cl 13	172
ICE (5th ed)	75, 163, 251, 399, 401
cl 1	82
cl 53	82, 91-95, 108
cl 59C	349
cl 63	91, 92-94
(1)	255
ICE (6th ed)	63, 76, 254, 401
cl 3	171
cl 63(1)	253
IFC 84	161
IFC 98	161
JCT 63	115, 161, 312, 364, 432
cl 2(1)	136, 314
cl 13	314
cl 14	116
cl 17	172
cl 19(1)	314
cl 22	314
cl 25(3)(b)	353

JCT 63, *cont.*	
cl 27(c)	181, 314, 352, 353
cl 30(4)	314, 315
JCT 67	120, 161
JCT 80	63, 161, 164, 235, 251, 290, 319, 325, 326, 329
cl 4.1.2	312
cl 19	171
cl 19.1.2	174
cl 19.4	119
cl 21.1.3	312
cl 26	265
cl 27	266
cl 27.4.2.1	263
cl 27.4.4	270, 271
cl. 27.6.6.1	265
cl 30.3	119
cl 35	231, 288, 352, 365
JCT 81	64, 161, 179, 207, 251, 331, 398, 408
cl 27	400
cl 27.4	360
JCT 87	149, 161, 314, 319, 325
cl 4	494
cl 4.3.2	320
cl 4.6.2	320
cl 4.8	493
cl 4.8.1	320
cl 4.8.3	494
cl 4.11	320, 321
cl 4.23	320
cl 7	494
cl 7.4.4	320
JCT 98	63, 75, 161
cl 27.5.3	290, 377
cl 27.7	266
cl 27.8	246

JCT 98, *cont.*
  cl 30   134
  cl 30.1.1.2   311
  cl 30.4   316
  cl 30.5   315
  cl 30.5.1   311
  cl 30.5.3   316
MF/1   249
  cl 1.1   82
  cl 37-38   82
  cl 49   82
NEC 95   161
RIBA 1909   347
RIBA 1931
  cl 25(d)   318
RIBA 1978   109
  cl 21(c)   355
  cl 30   317
SEACC 93   161
SFA/92   267
SFA/99   267

UK sub-contracts
ASI
  cl 6.41   310
DOM/1   62, 70, 146, 161, 256
  cl 21.4   125
DOM/2   161
FASS   313
  cl 11(h)   310
FCEC   65, 66, 70, 173, 255
  cl 10(2)   337
NAM/SC   257
  cl 22   162
NSC/2   364
  cl 7.2   366
  cl 35   366
NSC/2A   364
NSC/4   256, 310
  cl 12   148
  cl 23   311

NSC/4A
  cl 23   149
  cl 31.2.1   256
NSC/C   161, 336
  cl 1.11   337
  cl 1.13   334-335, 337
  cl 2.7   334
  cl 3.11   334
  cl 4.20   334
  cl 4.22.1   309
WC/2   161, 319
  cl 4.29   309
Blue Form   106
  cl 15(2)   150
Green Form   65, 120, 310

Australia
AS 2124-1992   318
AS 4000-1997   56
JCC-1994   263
JCC-D (1994)
  cl 5.06   467
NWPC3-1981   271
SC JCC A (1985)   314

Ireland
CIF   499
  lc 11(d)   499
GDLA   496, 499
IEI   496
RIAI   496, 499

Singapore
SIA
  cl 32(8)(c)   353

United Sates
AIA Doc A201/CM-1980
  cl 9.6.1   352

Chapter 1 *

· The Construction Industry ·

Introduction

This chapter sets the scene by examining the construction industry from an economic standpoint. The first question is: what is the construction industry? This is not as facile as it might seem since there are problems in fitting all the activities which account for construction into one industry. Most economic discussion of the construction industry concentrates on certain features which it is claimed make construction a special case, summarised by the anecdote which says that contractors bidding for work are "attempting to forecast the cost (to turn into a price) of something never designed or constructed before and which may never be done again, the design for which is incomplete, the site as yet unknown, for which planning permission may not be granted, and the labour force and the materials not yet identified". All that is certain is that the building is required (or is it?): the employer is not bound to accept the lowest or indeed any tender.

The author does not agree with the line of economic debate that seeks to excuse the construction industry from its failings by pointing to the special features of construction. This fails to separate the excellent, successful, dynamic and competitive parts of the industry from those that give the industry its image as producer of projects which are expensive, slow and of poor quality. Economists, who can almost never agree on anything, have mostly avoided any analysis of the construction industry. This is surprising when the size of the industry is considered. There are, of course, notable exceptions to this. The work of Raftery, Hillebrandt and Cannon in particular is seminal (see the Bibliography). Many other works offer alternative analyses, Michael Ball's *Rebuilding Construction* being a fine example. The classical definitions of economics concentrate on the allocation of scarce resources which have alternative uses. Construction economics, which is a relatively new discipline, is a branch of economics and concerns the allocation of scarce construction resources. At a simple level these are labour, materials, equipment, money and land. They are

* by and © Peter Fenn, UMIST

all restricted by a further scarce resource: time. In order to accommodate the many activities involved in construction it is necessary to sub-divide the labour resource into the specialist areas of design, production and management. A shortfall in any of these resources can lead to insolvency, the subject of this book.

Definition of the industry

The construction industry is a large and diverse industry in many nations. In the United Kingdom the Standard Industrial Classification is used by the government to define industrial categories for the purposes of official statistics. It includes the following activities within construction: erecting and repairing buildings; constructing and repairing roads and bridges; erecting steel and reinforced concrete structures; other civil engineering works such as laying sewers and gas mains, erecting overhead line supports and aerial masts, open cast mining; the building and civil engineering establishment of defence and other government departments and of local authorities; establishments specialising in demolition work or in sections of construction work such as asphalting, electrical wiring, flooring, glazing, installing heating and ventilating apparatus, painting, plumbing, plastering, roofing; hiring of contractor's plant and scaffolding; other activities where the major elements of the work are building, civil engineering, other installation of products and systems either in buildings or in association with civil engineering works.

Construction is a very large industry. In 1998 its output on a value added basis was over £60 billion (DETR). This is almost 8% of the UK's gross domestic product. It also employed a large portion of the work force in employment. The industry is highly fragmented and consists of a large number of small firms. Construction data has to be treated with caution, not least because of the difficulties in defining the industry. The fragmentation of the industry creates problems in measuring employment. Are persons engaged in fabrication of building products classified under manufacturing or under construction? Most professionals in the construction industry are included as part of the services sector and are not counted as part of the construction industry. There is also a problem with under-reporting due to fraud. The industry is often sub-divided into sectors, *e.g.* the civil engineering, building and process plant industries. The Standard Industrial Classification definition recognises that building and civil engineering projects, unlike most other industries, are split into separate operations of design and production. Further, design and production operations are separated from the eventual use of the building. The manufacture of some components and materials, *e.g.* bricks, cement, timber, doors and windows comes under manufacturing and quarrying gravel and sand under mining and quarrying.

Construction is a crucial part of a nation's economy. Its importance stems from three characteristics: size, the production of investment goods, and the nature of its client (Hillebrandt 1985). Many comparisons have been drawn with other industries. For example, construction output is greater than the transport industries and it employs three times more people than agriculture and the gas, water and electricity industries combined. The product of the construction industry is, for the most part, an investment good. That means that construction's new products are not wanted for their own sake, but for the goods or services which the new buildings and structures can create or help to create. In addition the price of the building and structures is high in relation to the income of the purchaser. The purchaser normally borrows capital to pay for this investment good and this makes the purchasing of construction sensitive to fluctuations in the cost of capital. The public sector is a major client of the industry. This has reduced as successive governments have sought to reduce public sector expenditure but as construction produces the major infrastructure sector projects, which must necessarily be driven by the public sector, it will remain a major construction client. Public expenditure on construction output still approaches 40% as shown in Figure 1.1.

Special characteristics of the industry

The construction industry has certain characteristics which are common to other industries but appear nowhere else in the same combination. These fall into four headings:

- the physical nature of the product
- the structure of the industry and the organisation of the construction process
- the determinants of demand
- the method of price determination.

The product produced by construction is large and heavy. Buildings and structures are produced in the open air with all the associated uncertainties. Substantial portions are constructed in and below the

Type of Work	£ 000's	£ 000's	£ 000's	%
New Work				
Public Housing	1185			
Public Non-housing	3854			
Infrastructure	6330			
Total Public New Work		11369		19
Private Housing	7215			
Private Industrial	3692			
Private Commercial	8716			
Total Private New Work		19623		33
TOTAL NEW WORK			30992	
Repair and Maintenance				
Public Housing	6461			
Public Non-housing	5091			
Total Public R&M		11552		19
Private Housing	9649			
Private Non-housing	8105			
Total Private R&M		17754		29
TOTAL R&M			29306	
TOTAL ALL WORK			60298	100

Source: DETR Construction Market Intelligence Division

Fig 1.1

ground. Even in densely populated countries the nature of sub-soil conditions is unknown. For the main part structures are unique and bespoke. The operation of design is separated from the operation of production. These are often quoted as reasons why construction cannot share the advantages enjoyed by other industries in which factory production can be employed with the concomitant benefits of scientific management.

The characteristics of the product are used to explain the structure of the industry and the organisation of the process, *i.e.* the industry structure is determined by the product. Large, heavy and expensive products require many different actors and the separation of design and build. The result is a fragmented industry where projects require the bringing together of many parties with differing objectives for each project. The structure of project teams is described as "temporary multiple (management) organisations" and the necessary repetition of learning curves is seen as wasteful. The organisation of the process is discussed at length later.

The demand placed on the construction industry for its products is for investment goods with a variety of uses:

- as the means of further wealth creation (factories)
- as infrastructure for social, commercial, industrial and joint use (roads)
- as direct social investment (schools and hospitals)
- as an investment for direct enjoyment (housing).

The determinants of demand for each of these categories are different and need to be considered separately. It is often stated that it is impossible to talk of one construction industry when the demands are so varied. The status of government as a construction client means that it can directly or indirectly affect construction and use the industry to regulate the economy. The state of the construction industry is often used as a barometer of the state of the general economy.

Construction has a long history of discrete price production for each and every project. Clients arrange for their demands to be split into unique projects that are priced individually. Competitive tendering became the usual practice: either open where all were free to tender or selective where some pre-qualification process was introduced. Each project is similarly split into pieces of work. Main contractors do not have the ability to carry out all of the work and a system of competitive sub-contracting developed.

The special economic features of construction are often used to explain the poor performance of the industry when compared with other industries, and indeed construction in other countries. The poor performance is summarised under three headings: cost, time and quality (Figure 1.2). Simply put, the construction industry produces products which are over-priced, over-budget and not to the quality expected. A requirement in one of the factors will have an effect on the others, *e.g.* a demand for a building of exceptional quality will inevitably result in extra cost and a longer production period.

Recent economic conditions in the industry have highlighted the supply and demand factors which are active. Figure 1.3 shows the relationship between the cost of resources (labour and materials etc) and the price charged by contractors measured as the tenders received for work. Between 1985 and 1990, commonly referred to as the

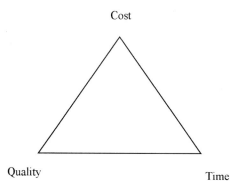

Cost

Quality   Time

Fig 1.2

"Thatcher-Lawson boom", prices rose in excess of input costs. Costs rose by 30% while prices rose by 39%. The explanation was that contractors increased their margins as demand exceeded available supply. During the deep recession that ensued between 1990 and 1994, building costs rose by 19% while the prices charged for projects fell by 16%. Here supply exceeded demand and contractors slashed overheads and margins to retain work and maintain cash flow. The over supply which exists in the construction market has been identified as a significant problem and many, including contractors themselves, maintain that the market correction can only be complete when supply has been further reduced, *i.e.* the number of contractors falls.

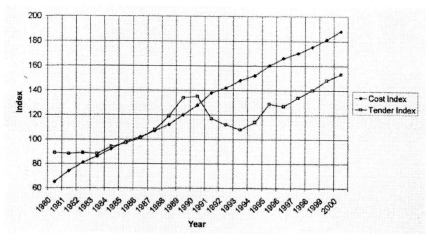

Fig 1.3

Economic criticisms of the industry

Many commentators point to the special features of construction. Before examining the organisation and production methods used by the industry it is useful to draw attention to the special features of the demand for and the supply of the product. The particular features of demand for construction can be summarised as follows:

1. Most buildings are "one-off", bespoke or tailor-made to the client's individual specification. Further factors such as site surroundings and the user's requirements mean there is very little standardisation. This reduces opportunities for mass production and to a large extent determines the method of pricing.

2. Buildings and structures are durable. Because of this one half of the value of the output of the construction industry is in repairing and maintaining these durable products: see Figure 1.1.

3. Durable goods are mainly capital goods. Borrowed funds are used to purchase buildings and structures which are expensive relative to income. The demand for buildings and structures is therefore dependent upon the cost and availability of credit to fund these capital purchases.

4. Demand is subject to fluctuations, seasonal and cyclical. In many countries activity is confined to spring and summer months. Cyclical fluctuations are often claimed to be more serious. As an investment goods industry, construction is vulnerable to fluctuations in demand resulting from changes in expectations.

5. Since the construction industry is a major percentage of a country's economic output it is vulnerable to government intervention. Changes in taxes and subsidies can affect the rate of redevelopment. Since demand is dependent on the cost and availability of credit, the government is tempted to use the industry as a major "regulator" of the economy.

The distinctive features of the supply of construction products are:

1. Unlike most manufacturing industries which can carry out all their operations concurrently, construction is an assembly industry where the operations are consecutive.

2. Production takes place in the open air on site giving rise to problems of weather protection, storage of materials, moving labour and equipment and supervision of the work.

3. In economic terms, for most projects the minimum technical unit is small: a traditional house can be built by two bricklayers, two labourers and a carpenter with other tasks being sub-contracted. This is the same for many large projects which can be carried out by a relatively small labour force by putting the work out to specialist firms by vertical disintegration.

4. Construction is labour intensive. Labour costs form a high proportion, between one third and one half of total costs. Skilled labour accounts for some two thirds of total labour costs. The casual and cyclical nature of the work results in the high rate of unemployment. Unemployment in the industry is a higher percentage than unemployment of workers in general.

Industry structure

The origin of all construction industries lies in man's primary need for shelter. Initially, as society develops, families build shelters for themselves and groups of neighbours co-operate to build churches, bridges and other infrastructure for communal needs. This spirit of co-operation remains in many developing and developed countries. However, this informal sector of construction often escapes legal regulation and statistical numeration. This introduces a shadow economy consisting of an innocent informal sector and an illegal sector, the so called "black economy". Black economies in western countries have been estimated as 3-5% of gross domestic product in the United Kingdom and less than 5% in West Germany (Smith and Wiede-Nebbeling 1986). Many commentators have described the importance of black economies in poorer and developing countries. Raftery (1991) says this is a reason why the World Bank plays a role in helping the development of informal sector construction activities in many countries.

The presence and size of an informal sector in the construction industry is a further indication of the imprecision of the quantitative descriptions of construction industries. It is evidence of further fragmentation and possibly a source of many disputes. The World Bank (1984) has described the structure of the construction industries in various countries and points to variations in structure being dependent on three factors:

- type of work to be done, which may depend on the size of a country, its climatic and geographical features, the dispersion and density of its population

- the choice of technology, which may again depend on physical and climatic conditions, the state of technological development, the availability of resources, labour and materials and plant, and governmental intervention in the overall development of the economy
- social and economic factors which are often a function of cultural and historical conditions, the political and economic organisation of the country and the state of its economy.

The structure of construction organisations, that is the production unit in the industry, will be consequent on these three factors. Construction units normally fall into four types: state owned, private sector enterprises, informal sector individual enterprises and self help or communal organisations.

The economic factors outlined above have produced an industry in the United Kingdom dominated by a few large firms while most construction activity is carried out by small firms on a sub-contract basis. This trend towards small firms has increased recently, fuelled by a government committed to free market strategies and the encouragement of self-employment, and a move by firms to reduce overhead cost. The structure of the industry shown in Figure 1.4 demonstrates a dramatic growth in the number of very small firms between 1973 and 1997.

The result of these economic factors is that many major firms have grown from family businesses. Some have remained private concerns and have never gone to the markets. Sir Robert McAlpine and Shepherd Construction remain private, family-owned businesses. Again it might

Size of firm in no. of employees	1973	1978	1989	1993	1997
1200+	80	35	48	33	38
600-1119	125	71	66	53	60
300-599	246	143	153	96	107
115-299	872	507	530	330	381
60-114	1440	849	871	577	692
25-59	4662	3027	2936	2164	2332
8-24	15626	11559	10811	7759	6888
1-7	73525	158904	86391	184095	149607

Fig 1.4

be proposed that for an industry which is responsible for such a major part of the nation's gross domestic product, the constituent firms are unsophisticated, some would say naïve. The stock market's perception of the industry reinforces this view. The paucity of construction industry firms in the market indicator indices speaks for itself. Standard company analyses are misleading when applied to construction. Hillebrandt *et al* (1995) describe how company directors are frustrated at the perceptions of market analysts and complain that the analysts do not understand construction. The main problem in analyses is that construction is a cash positive process and while profit on turnover may be very low, profit on investment is very high. Construction companies employ quantity surveyors and commercial managers to optimise cash flow and careful management can result in projects becoming self-financing through interim payments very quickly, indeed some are self-financing from the outset. It might be thought that the structure described above is unique to the United Kingdom, the outcome of its history and development. However an examination of EU statistics demonstrates that other countries have the same characteristic fragmentation. Figure 1.5 shows the dominance of the small enterprises in construction.

Country	No. of building firms	No. of firms with up to 20 employees	% of totals
Belgium	26000	24000	92
Denmark	27600	25000	90
France	340000	32700	96
Greece	75000	71000	95
Ireland	N/A	N/A	85
Italy	410000	398000	97
Luxembourg	1494	1264	85
Netherlands	18680	16208	94
Portugal	28400	26800	94
Spain	182000	178000	98
Switzerland	35822	31530	88
United Kingdom	209000	203700	97
West Germany	280000	260000	93

Source: European Commission

Fig 1.5

Operational and organisational features

Operational and organisational features have evolved different solutions in different countries but they share a common theme. Organisational features may be split into:

- initiating and funding
- design
- construction and supervision management
- construction activities.

In the United Kingdom the traditional arrangement for buying buildings and structures was via an architect or master builder controlling craftsmen, journeymen and labourers. The architect and the work force made their name by repute. The risk of the cost and duration of the construction remained with the client, normally the Crown, the aristocracy or the church. Nevertheless, disputes arose. Ferry and Brandon (1983) have described how building Blenheim Palace almost bankrupted the Duke of Marlborough. The industrial revolution changed this. Building projects became business led and the need arose for risks to be apportioned between the parties to the contract, the client and the builder.

A system of main contracting developed. Building organisations used their skills to manage labour and materials, at first directly employed but more recently sub-contracted, in a highly competitive tendering market. The result was a fragmented market of poorly qualified firms and the scope for disputes vastly increased. The traditional form of procurement became one where a separate designer employed by the client produced a complete design which was priced by a contractor responsible for the construction. The tendering contractors at first joined forces to pay for a measurement surveyor to produce a survey of quantities of materials and labour to avoid the need for repetition. Later a system developed where the client employed the surveyor to produce a complete set of tender documents for use by all the tenderers. The profession of quantity surveying grew from this technical background. Civil engineering developed along similar lines with an engineer designing the works for a contractor to build.

The separation of design from production has been roundly criticised for many years.

> "In no other industry is the responsibility for design so far removed from the responsibility for production. The most urgent problem which

confronts the construction industry is the necessity of thinking and acting as a whole ... it has come to think of itself ... as a series of different parts. These attitudes must change" (Banwell 1964).

The arrangements whereby the client who initiates and funds the proposed building or structure deals with the construction industry have been described as "procurement". Procurement arrangements may be classified into three types: the so called traditional system, the design and build and the management type. The organisational and contractual arrangements for these three systems are shown in figures 1.6, 1.7 and 1.8. The traditional system, which is mainly a UK approach, involves the client or building owner in separate contractual relationships.

The owner might consult the following: architect, quantity surveyor, structural engineer, services engineer, interior designer and building contractor. Traditionally, the architect took the lead and it was his job to liaise with the client to ensure that the building met with his expectations. A claimed advantage of this system is the client having on

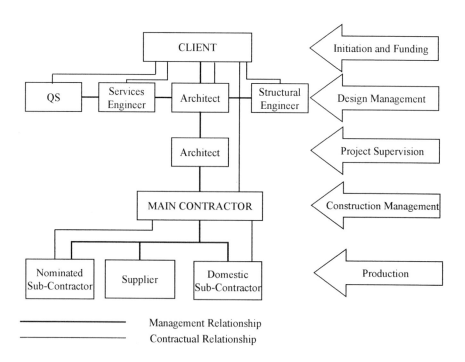

Fig 1.6

hand an array of specialist advisers. These specialists were and are all members of separate professional institutions. The vested interests of those institutions meant that little collaboration took place. For this reason the traditional system fell into disrepute and lines of responsibility and authority became notoriously unclear. Higgins and Jessop (1965) describe the immense difficulties in communication. By the 1970s the traditional system had developed a reputation for delivering buildings which were over budget, over-programme and not to the desired quality.

Many alternative forms of procurement are now offered to clients and much literature exists. The major systems might be classified as: traditional (lump sum, measure and value, cost plus), design and build, and management types (construction management, management contracting). Within the classification many specialist systems are also offered. Serious quantitative studies of the usage of the differing systems are rare and it is often claimed that one particular system is more prevalent. Received wisdom is that design and build has steadily taken a larger market share since the 1980s and that, although the management types were popular in the boom of the late eighties, notably for very large projects, they have declined since. Some data is available from the Royal Institution of Chartered Surveyors. A survey carried out on behalf of the junior organisations captures data on new building projects (civil engineering and repair and maintenance are not covered). The researchers claim to cover 15% by value of new orders and that the survey can be taken as broadly representative of the industry as a whole. The data on procurement methods used between 1984 and 1995 is shown in Figure 1.9.

Procurement method	1984 %	1985 %	1987 %	1989 %	1991 %	1993 %	1995 %
Lump sum	72	70	70	62	55	50	56
Measure and value	7	5	3	4	3	4	2
Cost plus	4	3	5	1	0	0	1
Design and build	5	8	12	11	15	36	30
Management type	12	14	10	22	27	10	11
Totals	100	100	100	100	100	100	100

Source: Davis, Langdon and Everest (1996)

Fig 1.9

The increasing internationalisation of construction has brought pressure to bear on the UK construction industry by international clients and marketing from international contractors. These pressures resulted in the so-called alternative arrangements of design and build and management systems. Figure 1.7 shows the arrangements for design and build procurement. The salient feature is the replacement of many contractual arrangements with one link between client and contractor. This system is closer to a traditional system in other countries *e.g.* the United States where the professional demarcations developed in the United Kingdom have not arisen. The advantages claimed for this system include single point responsibility, producer input into design and speed when compared to sequential approaches.

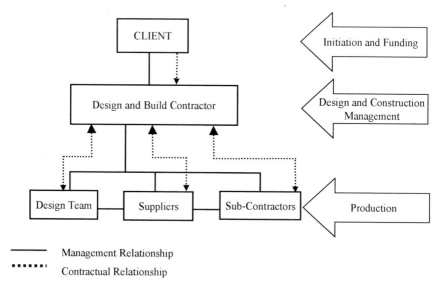

Fig 1.7

There are many variants of management procurement methods but essentially the contractor offers the client a consultancy service based on a fee for co-ordinating, planning the construction and managing and executing the process. The benefits claimed for these systems are centred on the early involvement of management expertise ensuring maximum construction experience being fed into the design and production. Figure 1.8 shows management contracting where the contracts are held by the management contractor. The other major system is construction management where the contracts are held by the client.

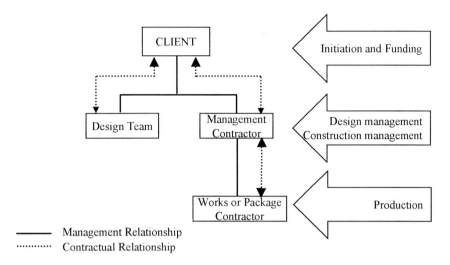

Fig 1.8

Forms of construction contract

Construction contracts are unique in the sense that negotiations continue throughout the project. It might be argued that construction contracts are in fact one long negotiation from beginning to end. The contract requires the parties to agree a whole host of matters including valuation of variations, extension of time and quality of workmanship. This has led to the evolution of a complex set of standard forms.

As the concept of a price in advance developed following the industrial revolution there were calls for standard forms of contract in building work. From about 1870 the bodies representing contractors discussed with the Royal Institution of British Architects (RIBA) the issue of a standard contract. The main areas of contention were the scope of the arbitration clause in reviewing decisions of the architect and the question of quantities forming part of the contract. As a consequence the RIBA and the contracting bodies issued their own contracts. However, in 1903 a settlement was finally reached following the intervention of the then Institute of Builders. This intervention has been described as a mediation! An agreed form of contract was issued, further amendments were discussed and a revised form was issued in 1909.

Problems arose in connection with the operation of the 1909 form. The contracting bodies gave notice to the RIBA rescinding their agreement to the 1909 form and issued their own building standard code. Following this, in 1922 a conference was held between representatives of architects, surveyors and contractors and a joint drafting committee was established under independent chairmanship, any points of difficulty being referred for final decision to Sir William McKenzie. The main area of disagreement was whether the architect should be sole judge between the contractor and the client on financial aspects of the contract. In 1928 the conference approved a draft form of contract which provided for arbitration on all matters. Relationships having been restored and confidence and goodwill re-established, discussions continued and from these the 1931 form emerged. A special mechanism was introduced in the form of the Joint Contracts Tribunal (JCT) in recognition by sponsoring parties of the fact that the most experienced committee of practitioners working with the most skilled legal draftsmen could never anticipate every difficulty which might arise during a project. The JCT was established to discuss difficulties and agree amendments. In 1937 an adaptation of the 1931 form was issued for use in the public sector. A further revised edition was published in 1939 whose terms were further revised during the Second World War to meet all the conditions likely to be experienced after the war had ended. In 1955 the JCT announced a general revision of its forms of contract and invited comments and proposals from all those interested. It was reported that some 1400 points were raised indicating the degree of interest within the industry. These revisions resulted in the 1963 edition of the JCT Standard Form of Building Contract.

Following the 1963 Form, the JCT went on to produce a wide range of standard forms to meet the needs of clients. The current versions of the Standard Form of Building Contract (1998) are: local authority with quantities, local authority without quantities, local authority with approximate quantities, private with quantities, private without quantities, and private with approximate quantities. Amendments are issued to deal with inflation and sectional completion. A supplement is printed where the contractor undertakes part of the design work. Other JCT forms are: agreement for minor building works, fixed fee form of prime cost contract (1967), standard form of building contract with contractor's design (1981), intermediate form of building contract (1984), standard form of management contract (1987), standard form of measured term contact (1989). The JCT is a widely representative body. In 1990 some 217,000 copies of JCT documents were purchased. Civil engineering forms developed along similar lines and are published by the Institution of Civil Engineers (ICE). A reflection of the different risks in civil works meant that the initial form was a measure and value type contract, and lump sum and cost plus contracts followed later. Debate about the plethora of standard forms has reappeared periodically as the industry aspires to a single standard form. Most recently this was addressed by Sir Michael Latham in the joint government and industry review of procurement (Latham 1994). A single model form of construction contract has been introduced by the ICE as The New Engineering and Construction Contract.

Dispute resolution

The development of the construction industry brought about a need for binding methods of settling disputes. Initially the methods were limited to litigation or arbitration. As the industry became more sophisticated, less formal procedures became available. Standard forms of contract introduced an employer's agent, either an architect or an engineer, who became responsible for the administration of the contract and was given varying powers to adjudicate on contentious matters under the contract. The industrial revolution and the advent of limited liability brought about the formation of corporate bodies. It became apparent that the civil courts were hardly the ideal place for the resolution of corporate disputes. Business complained of the vagaries of the system and took their disputes elsewhere, notably the arbitrator's room. The construction industry in particular was quick to take on board the developing process of arbitration. Baden Hellard (1988) describes the formation of the Chartered Institute of Arbitrators which included several construction professionals on the founding committee. Arbitration became the preferred method of resolving disputes in the industry and in other areas, notably shipping. Litigation and arbitration continued in an atmosphere of mutual distrust.

All the widely adopted standard forms of contract for construction works include an arbitration agreement and arbitration is still generally seen as the common method for resolving disputes. The major traditional advantages proposed for arbitration are the speed and cost of proceedings, privacy and the technical expertise of arbitrator. Some industries now propose arbitration as an alternative dispute resolution technique (ADR) demonstrating how an established technique in one area can be seen as new in another. Construction professionals would hardly consider arbitration to be ADR. Recently arbitration has been accused of suffering from the same problems which afflicted the civil courts after the industrial revolution, the very deficiencies which allowed arbitration to flourish (Acland 1990, Tillotson 1985). The perceived advantages of cost, speed and expertise have all but disappeared as arbitrators have increasingly mimicked High Court procedures. Parties are frequently represented by counsel, the rules of evidence follow court procedures and proceedings have become protracted. The parties have turned to the courts in appeals against arbitrators' awards. The Arbitration Act 1996 moved to correct this and arbitrators have been given stronger powers and the grounds for appeal limited. The principles behind the Act are:

1. The object of arbitration is to obtain the fair resolution of disputes by an impartial tribunal without unnecessary delay or expense.

2. The parties should be free to agree how their disputes are resolved, subject only to safeguards necessary in the public interest.

3. The court should not intervene.

An important dividing point in the dispute resolution process in construction disputes is the stage at which the dispute passes from the site (out of the hands of those involved with the success of the project) and into the hands of third parties who may be head office-based or external consultants. The importance of this distinction was confirmed by some American research by the Construction Industry Institute. Once this point has been reached, the site-based personnel lose control of the resolution of the dispute, leaving the issues of entitlement and quantification to be dealt with by those least familiar with the project. The head office staff or external consultants will not be sensitive to the on-site relationships; they tend to live in an environment where adversarial techniques are the norm and so the dispute is likely to escalate, adding to the cost and time it will take to resolve. In many countries it is normal for large construction disputes to be resolved off-site by a costly after the fact determination. It has long been recognised that once the dispute resolution process passes from the site, matters can soon get out of hand. For this reason construction contracts now make conscious attempts to resolve disputes on site. A variety of techniques and procedures have been introduced for this purpose. These are described in more detail below. For a review of dispute resolution and conflict management processes in 20 jurisdictions see Fenn, O'Shea and Davies (1998).

Mediation

Mediation is the leading ADR technique in construction contracts and consists of a neutral person, the mediator, assisting the parties to reach a negotiated settlement. Mediation is quick, cheap and usually effective. Its advantages have been described in terms of "the five Cs":

- Commercialism: at the heart of mediation lies the concept of helping commercial people make commercial decisions.
- Consensus: a joint objective to find the commercial and business solution.
- Continuity: a desire to find a solution in the context of an ongoing business relationship.
- Control: the ability to tailor a solution geared towards a commercial result rather that one governed by a rule of law which may be restrictive or inappropriate.
- Confidentiality: maintaining confidentiality in commercial matters, no washing of dirty linen in public.

Parties to a mediation are free to talk in confidence to the mediator in private sessions (caucuses) where they can focus on what they would really like to achieve. The true interests of the parties are often different from the positions presented to each other in the negotiation. It is usual for the mediation process to be treated as privileged and this means that nothing said or done in a mediation may subsequently be referred to in arbitration or litigation should the mediation fail.

Dispute review board

In America dispute review boards have been an outstanding success. This is an expedited non-binding ADR procedure whereby an independent board, usually of three persons, is established to evaluate disputes in the form of settlement recommendations to the parties. The board members become knowledgable about the project by periodically visiting the site. The board meets at regular intervals and hears presentations on any disputes which have arisen since they last met. The goal of the process is not only to resolve disputes but also to prevent them. The same board will sit on all disputes occurring during the project and the parties will soon become familiar with how the members look at particular types of issue. They will then be able to predict how the board will react and will take that into account when negotiating between themselves. As a consequence many disputes settle before reaching board level. A form of review board (the panel) was used on the Channel Tunnel project between England and France and review boards are being used successfully on several major projects in the United States. The World Bank now insists on them on infrastructure projects where it provides finance.

The dispute resolution adviser

This is a flexible pre-contract and post-contract dispute avoidance and resolution system. At the pre-contact stage it is used for identifying commonly occurring problem areas and unrealistic risk allocation in the project documentation or proposed project structure. Suggestions are made by a neutral person following a confidential information gathering exercise on how contract documentation or contract arrangements might generally be modified so as to reduce the potential for conflict.

At the post-contract stage, the employer and the contractor choose a mutually acceptable construction industry professional who is well versed in dispute resolution techniques to serve as the adviser. In a similar manner to a dispute resolution board member, the adviser visits the site on a regular basis to keep abreast of construction activities and to advise the parties how best to deal with disputes or disagreements as and when they occur. The adviser also has a proactive role and will focus the parties' attention on potential problem areas. In this way matters can be addressed in a constructive manner and mitigating measures taken as soon as possible. The adviser will also act as a facilitative mediator and attempt to persuade the parties to resolve their disputes by non-binding means if at all possible. As an incentive for the parties to solve their own disputes, a short form arbitration is built into the system as a swift and cheap method for resolving those disputes which the parties are unable to settle by themselves or with the assistance of a neutral person. The system also uses partnering and "step negotiating" techniques.

The mini-trial

The mini-trial or executive tribunal is not a trial at all but a highly structured form of mediation and like the adviser system it is a hybrid of several alternative resolution techniques. It combines evaluative and facilitative mediation with negotiation. The mini-trial typically involves two chief executives and a neutral person listening to an exposition of a particular dispute from both sides. The procedure is carried out in the manner of an arbitration hearing or trial in that arguments are presented and witnesses called and cross-examined on both sides. The presentation normally takes place within a relatively short time frame, perhaps half a day, and this enables the executives and the neutral person to get a good overview of the dispute. The executives then attempt to resolve the matter by negotiation using the neutral person as an evaluative mediator if they reach an impasse.

Partnering

Partnering is a technique pioneered by the US Army Corps of Engineers and is essentially a consensus building process that re-orientates the parties from an "us and them" mentality to a "we" mentality. Partnering has also been used successfully in Hong Kong and in the United Kingdom where major retail clients have for a long time entered into arrangements with preferred contractors which are not project based. Partnering arrangements often combine a useful technique known as "step negotiation". This is a process whereby the representatives of the parties to whom the dispute is referred are required, if they cannot resolve the problem, to refer the matter to their respective superiors. This provides an additional incentive to the representatives to resolve problems without having to involve their superiors.

Adjudication

This is a procedure in which a neutral person acting as an expert and not an arbitrator investigates a dispute and gives a decision which is binding on the parties, normally for the duration of the contract. An adjudicator's decision is permanent unless a notice of arbitration is given within a set time frame. If notice of arbitration is given, the arbitration does not normally take place until after project completion, whereas adjudication can take place immediately or very shortly after a dispute has arisen. Adjudication has been championed in the United Kingdom by a joint government and industry review of procurement (Latham 1994). The Housing Grants, Construction and Regeneration Act 1996 now imports statutory adjudication into all construction contracts, with specific exceptions, unless the parties have included their own procedure which complies with the Act.

Conclusion

This chapter has set the scene for a book on construction insolvency by considering the industry from an economic standpoint. The construction industry forms a major part of a nation's economy. It is highly labour intensive. It also plays a crucial role in government's social objectives and tends to be subject to government intervention. As a result the industry has several special features. It is highly fragmented so that many small companies serve a few powerful major players. Access to the market place is easy for small firms in that there are few restrictions to entry.

The industry is based on a system of payment as the work proceeds and firms have little or no investment in projects. With careful commercial management and the use of quantity surveyors, companies can ensure that contracts are almost entirely self-financing. Clients pay for the work on a monthly cycle and suppliers allow lines of credit for materials. The result is that income flows before expenditure. Cash flow has been described as the life blood of the industry and construction companies are highly sensitive to delays in the flow.

The construction industry is often discussed in very critical terms. It is not unusual to hear it described as a "backward industry" where productivity is low and innovation unusual. The counter argument is that criticism of the industry, while in some cases justifiable, fails to acknowledge and appreciate its great diversity. This argument goes on to say that a study of the conditions of supply and demand relating to the industry reveals that its organisation is largely a result of, and a response to, economic factors. The critics of the construction industry confuse technical efficiency with economic efficiency; they concentrate on the supply side and ignore the special aspects of construction demand.

Chapter 2

· **Financial Protection** ·

Introduction

To procure construction work is to wade into a sea of risk. Will it be fit for its purpose? Will it cost more than you can afford? Will delays to completion cause loss to your business? These risks are real enough but they can be managed. Ultimately, they come down to the contractor's ability to remedy the problem, either physically or by paying damages. But what if the contractor becomes insolvent? The employer stands on the edge of an abyss.

Employers have evolved a wide range of procedures and legal devices to give them the maximum possible financial protection against the contractor's insolvency. The aim of this chapter is to summarise these devices and examine how they relate to each other and assess their relative importance in the overall scheme of things. It will be seen that they often cover the same risk, which raises questions about their real function and their impact on the cost of construction.

Attitudes towards financial protection depend on who you are: funder, employer, contractor, sub-contractor, supplier. The law sees protection in terms of rights and obligations: rights as contractual or proprietary and obligations as primary or secondary. Commercially, protection consists in the cost effective management of risk, which may well vary among the specialist industry sectors, *e.g.* because of different ways of structuring interim payments. Each approach casts a different light on the subject. To provide some structure to the discussion, this chapter focuses on the project as a whole and examines protection under three main headings: pre-contract measures, contractual terms and security. These headings include a mixture of processes, concepts and documents, each of which may have its own commercial, financial and legal aspects (Figure 2.1).

Pre-contract measures

Successful companies understand the value of planning. Projects often fail or experience difficulties because not enough care is taken at the

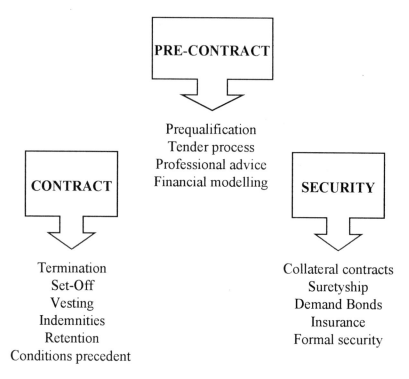

Fig 2.1

early stages. Each project has its own unique needs but most will require the following elements to some degree. The modern construction project has become so complex that it needs input from a number of specialist professional advisers including merchant bankers, accountants, lawyers, designers and surveyors. It is vital that the advisers act as a team and are properly co-ordinated.

The basic question is whether the project makes financial sense. This is likely to involve detailed projections involving many different assumptions. For major projects, accountants and merchant bankers prepare a financial model which is the key to the "bankability" of the project. Once the model has been agreed, it will form the basis on which lending is structured and be the source of the principles governing the allocation of risk among the various parties. It follows that the financial model dictates the way in which financial protection measures are selected and the degree of overlap between them.

The procurement method is critical. "Procurement" can refer to a number of different aspects:

- the choice of contract structure: design and build, management contracting etc
- the statutory procurement rules that must be followed
- the joint venture vehicle: contractual, partnership, special purpose company
- the division of responsibilities between the co-venturers
- the creation of a new company to act as concessionaire and the grant of the concession
- the allocation of ownership of the land (or of the works if they are not fixed to land) among companies investing in the project and the timing of its transfer to others.

Getting procurement right ensures the best possible start to a project.

Pre-qualification is probably the key area for pre-contract financial protection. It is difficult to overstate the importance of good pre-qualification procedures. Pre-qualification comprises at least five elements. The first is the identity of the contractor. "Identity" in this context is a combination of the prospective tenderer's group structure, its legal domicile, its owners, whether any group companies are involved in capital intensive businesses, whether there are any cross guarantees within the group and, most important for parent company guarantees, the ownership and location of the group's principal assets. The second factor is reputation. What do people say about the company? Ask its bankers, credit agencies, competitors, suppliers, clients, industry professionals, stockbrokers and analysts. Does it have appropriate external accreditations such as IIP or ISO 9000? The third element of pre-qualification protection lies in the company's expertise. The employer needs to know details of recent work undertaken, make visits to the contractor's premises and current projects, ascertain its involvement in professional bodies, licences held, industry awards, and check for any prosecutions under health and safety and other legislation. The fourth and critical factor is its people. What is the quality of the management? Who is likely to be important to your project? Are they committed to it? Is there evidence of a commitment to on-going training? What is the level of staff turnover? Is the firm's culture open or closed? Finally, the contractor's own financial resources need to be checked. The employer will need to be satisfied on the firm's balance sheet and cash flow positions, current trends, profitability, strength of core areas to withstand downturns in demand, business plans, management accounts and projections, any recent (or planned) major changes with financial consequences, acquisitions, exceptionally large projects, off balance sheet liabilities.

After pre-qualification, the next area of pre-contractual protection is the tender process. This enables prospective bidders to be compared against each other to allow the employer to obtain the best value for money (not necessarily the lowest price). As additional protection against wasted costs incurred in the tender process, tenderers may be required to provide a bid bond or a cash deposit as a condition of their bid. Prospective tenderers are sometimes asked to agree the text of certain documents, *e.g.* parent company guarantees, before invitations to tender are sent out. This is intended to limit the scope for negotiation after the tender has been accepted.

Finally, there are several legal devices which are useful:

1. Mark all pre-contract correspondence and draft documents with the words "subject to contract".

2. Ensure that any letters of intent contain clear financial limits or appropriate safeguards so that the client only becomes liable to pay for work it has asked the contractor to do and at rates which are reasonable.

3. Agree adequate procedures so that everyone knows when a contract has been formed, for example, making execution of formal contract documents a condition precedent to contract.

Contractual terms

When preparing the construction contract, the procurer of the project has to decide how the terms should relate to those implied at common law. In particular, employers usually have two aims: to exclude or heavily qualify the common law rights of the contractor and to enlarge as far as possible their own common law rights. Whether this is in the overall interests of the project is debatable.

Cutting down the common law

It is common for contracts to exclude the common law in its entirety, limiting the parties' rights and obligations to the terms of the contract. The contractor will resist such an attempt since there are still some areas where the law is unclear and relies on the implication of a term, *e.g.* the duty to account for the proceeds of an on demand bond insofar as they exceed the beneficiary's loss: *Cargill* v *Bangladesh Sugar* [1996] 4 All ER 563. Ambiguities may remain in the contract drafting as the consequence of the parties' failure to come to terms. Modern projects can be so complex and involve so many variables that matters can arise which have not been foreseen and dealt with in the express terms. The common law is often qualified or excluded in connection with the contractor's rights of assignment, set-off, title to materials and equitable remedies, such as subrogation, indemnity and contribution. These and other areas are considered in later chapters.

Expanding the common law

As well as cutting down the contractor's common law rights, the employer usually wants to enhance its own. Areas to consider are:

- set-off, abatement and deduction
- accrual of the right to payment
- specific kinds of indemnity
- conditions precedent
- sub-contractors and suppliers
- solvency warranties
- title to product,
- termination of the contract.

There are gaps in the common law of set-off which can be filled by appropriate drafting. The major lacuna is where the employer's cross-claim is independent and unliquidated. GC Works/1 is an example of a contract which deals with this problem by allowing each party to set off against the other all cross-claims for damages whether arising under that contract or others between them. Where there is extensive trading between groups of companies, it may be appropriate to include a group set-off clause, allowing set-off in circumstances where the common law would deny it for want of mutuality between the parties. A particularly contentious issue is the term by which a project procurer is entitled to set off cross-claims which have not yet accrued due, *e.g.* where the project manager considers in good faith that the contractor's actions are likely to lead to a breach in the future. Abatement can be extended by agreement to cover contracts for professional services. In addition to set-off and abatement, construction contracts often confer specific rights of deduction, although at times they may be interpreted simply as contractual set-offs. Common examples are liquidated damages and retention.

One of the major protections of the project procurer is the certification process whereby its nominee in the form of an architect, engineer or project manager decides the level of interim payments. This is intended to ensure the contractor gets a fair payment on account, but the closeness of the certifier to the employer sometimes leads to under-certification. Even so, as the certifier has a duty to act independently of the project procurer, there is a perception among funders and their lawyers that a further buffer is necessary. There may be a requirement for the approval of a monitoring agent to certificates before they can be issued or become due for payment. This additional level of checking occurs in some completion contracts following a contractor's insolvency or where the capital cost of a construction contract is being funded by the Arts Council with lottery money. On lottery contracts the approval of the monitoring contractor is not, however, made a condition precedent to payment of the contractor carrying out the work.

In addition to normal indemnities found in commercial agreements, construction contracts often require the contractor to indemnify the employer against damage to the existing structure caused by the negligence of the contractor or its sub-contractors. It is very important to be clear about the interface between such an indemnity and any insurance obligations. There have been a number of cases on the JCT forms where the contractor has been excused from liability under its indemnity, even where a fire was caused by its negligence, because the employer had agreed to insure the risk indemnified against.

Conditions precedent are useful control mechanisms and fall under two headings: conditions precedent to contract and to payment. Conditions precedent to contract include the execution of bonds and guarantees, the provision of opinion letters from foreign lawyers and the execution of formal contract documents. Conditions precedent to payment include certificates, monitoring agents' approvals, compliance with accounts procedures and "pay to be paid" clauses. A pay to be paid clause could make payment contingent on proof of payment of sub-contractors from the previous certificate or it might oblige the contractor to pay sub-contractors in advance.

The protection given to the employer under the main contract needs to be reinforced by the inclusion of parallel terms in sub-contracts and agreements with suppliers. Unless these terms are back to back with those of the main contract, the employer may lose significant protection on the contractor's insolvency. Some main contracts go further and impose express duties on the contractor to act in a particular way with sub-contractors, *e.g.* to pay them promptly, even making it a condition of the contract that they do so. This can be useful in the event of an insolvency termination where the termination clause has not been properly drafted or operated. The employer may be able to treat the contractor's non-payment of sub-contractors as a repudiatory breach, as was assumed in *Laing and Morrison-Knudson* v *Aegon Insurance* (1997) 86 BLR 70.

A covenant to observe a solvency ratio is normally only contained in bank security documents. With the increasing reliance on public-private financing, solvency warranties are becoming more common in construction contracts and are also found in parent company guarantees. There are three approaches to a warranty of solvency:

- a covenant to maintain the current net worth of the company as at the date of contract or to satisfy a solvency formula
- a duty to satisfy the employer on request of the ability to finance the completion of the contract
- a duty to provide cash flows and updates on other pre-qualification information on request.

This ensures that the basic protection given by pre-qualification procedures is continued throughout the contract period.

In order to "feed" its security, the project funder is interested in the employer converting its contractual rights into proprietary rights as quickly as possible. This can result in contract terms which attempt to pass title to materials as early as possible.

The effect of an insolvency termination clause is to empower the employer to exclude the contractor from site to allow the employer to build out in its own way and to maximise its claim for compensation against the insolvent contractor. In practice, this is achieved through the legitimised suspension of the contractor's rights to payment to allow the employer time to establish its cross-claim for loss caused by the termination. It is as if the employer is allowed to take as hostage any receivables owed to the contractor and any tangible property on site pending the building out. As well as vertical agreements between parties to the contract chain, termination clauses are highly relevant in horizontal agreements between joint venturers. These follow a similar pattern, in that they exclude the insolvent venturer from further participation in the project and suspend any entitlement to payment of cost or profit share until the project has been completed.

Some of the risk associated with the contractor's insolvency is allocated to the certifier. For example, if the builder is overpaid through deliberate over-certification, the architect will be liable to compensate the employer for the excess if it cannot be recovered from the insolvent contractor: *Townsend* v *Stone Toms* (1984) 27 BLR 26 at 46. Equally, an architect who recommended an incompetent contractor as reliable, whose work proved to be defective and resulted in a claim in arbitration was held liable for the costs of the arbitration left unpaid as a result of the contractor's insolvency. The incurring of the costs flowed from the architect's breach of duty and the intervention of insolvency was immaterial to his liability: *Pratt* v *George Hill* (1987) 38 BLR 25. An architect can also be liable in negligence for failing to check the financial standing of a contractor during the tender process: *Partridge* v *Morris* [1995] CILL 1095.

Security

Under the contract, the contractor has either to perform its obligations or pay damages. The employer has the right to performance or to compensation. On the contractor's liquidation, these rights are commuted to the right to a dividend, *i.e.* a fixed percentage of the employer's claim which is arrived at by dividing the amount of cash in hand after disposing of the contractor's property by the total amount owed to all the unsecured creditors. The purpose of security is to give the employer a right, in priority to other creditors, to satisfy its claim out of a particular asset of the contractor. If there is a shortfall after having sold the asset, the employer proves for the difference as a dividend. Any surplus must be paid to the liquidator for the benefit of the other creditors.

Contractors offer the following kinds of asset as security for debt finance: freehold or leasehold land, plant, machinery and equipment, motor vehicles, the benefit of contracts (*e.g.* for building, hire-purchase or options), building materials, shares in group companies, receivables (certified sums, retention, claims), loans made to others and intellectual property rights. Similarly, the employer offers the following as security for project finance: the benefit of the construction contract and any direct agreements with sub-contractors and suppliers, any bonds and guarantees, copyright in design documents etc (Jones 1992). In addition, under the facility agreement, the employer is likely to covenant not to vary or terminate the construction contract without the funder's consent. This can become a cause of friction with the contractor.

The contractor always has the right to recover the asset by performing the secured obligation. This is known as the "equity of redemption". If the arrangement between the parties does not give rise to an equity of redemption, it will not be a security in the strict legal sense. Some contractual rights can have an effect similar to security and these are considered later under the heading "informal security". The common law in this area has largely concerned security for payment of a debt rather than performance of complex obligations such as those undertaken by contractors. It can be difficult to apply the law of security to construction contracts for this reason.

Formal security

English law recognises four types of security: the charge, the mortgage, the contractual lien and the pledge (Goode l988, compare Oditah 1991). A charge describes an obligation to be secured and identifies a particular asset (*e.g.* a specific contract) or type of asset (*e.g.* "all current contracts") as security for that obligation. The person offering the asset is known as the "chargor", and the person who receives it as the "chargee". The chargor remains the owner of the asset but the chargee obtains a security interest in it. A charge may be fixed or floating.

Under a fixed charge the chargor loses control over the asset. Fixed charges are often granted over interests in land, fixed plant and machinery and book debts. In the case of a charge on book debts, the charge attaches as soon as the debt is created and the proceeds of collection must be paid to an appropriate account. Where the chargor defaults on the secured obligation, the chargee can appoint a receiver whose powers over the asset derive from the terms of the charge and from the Law of Property Act l925. Receivers appointed under a fixed charge are known as "LPA receivers" or "fixed charge receivers". Where land is given as security, the charge normally confers wide powers to sell the site, build out, lease it or exercise other options, but LPA receivers may have to apply to the court for further powers if those in the charge are insufficient.

By contrast, under a floating charge the chargor retains ownership and control, and can use assets falling within the description in the charge in the ordinary course of business. A floating charge is often given over stock and cash at bank and other types of property which the contractor needs to recycle for the purposes of its business. It could, however, be given over land or any type of property. The charge states the events which entitle the chargee to enforce the security by the appointment of an "administrative receiver" who has wide powers of managing the company and its business. The moment the receiver is appointed (or the company ceases to trade if earlier), the charge converts from floating to fixed. This process is known as "crystallisation". Until crystallisation, the chargee's security interest in the charged assets is actual but incomplete (Lightman and Moss 1994).

A mortgage is a species of charge (a charge by way of mortgage), with the difference that ownership in the asset is transferred to the employer ("the mortgagee") as security on terms that the contractor ("the mortgagor") is entitled to have the property transferred back after having performed the secured obligation (Halsbury 32/404). The most common example is a house mortgage from a building society. A mortgage or a charge can be granted over any kind of property and does not involve the transfer of possession.

Liens and pledges apply only to personal property. A lien can arise in many different contexts but consists in the right to retain an asset for a purpose other than that for which it was originally received (Halsbury 28/501-600). For example, property originally received for repair can be retained as security for the repairer's charges. The lien is unlike the charge and the mortgage in that it does not give the lien-holder the right to sell the asset, only to detain it until performance of the secured obligation. If the lien arises under a contract which allows the person in possession of the asset to sell it, it is really a pledge (Goode 1988 at 14). Contractors sometimes claim a "lien on the site" as security for unpaid sums but this is conceptually impossible under English law. In other jurisdictions with special legislation, the lien takes effect as a charge on the land or the employer's interest in it (Odams 1996). A pledge arises on the delivery of an asset to a creditor by way of security (Halsbury 36/101-200). The creditor ("the pledgee") becomes entitled to sell the asset in the event of non-payment by the debtor. As with a charge, but unlike a mortgage, ownership remains with the person giving the security ("the pledgor").

A charge granted by a limited company falling within the following categories must be registered with the Registrar of Companies within 21 days of its creation otherwise it will be void against a liquidator, administrator or creditors of the company under ss 395-396 Companies Act 1985:

- a charge on land or any interest in land

- a charge on book debts
- a floating charge
- a charge created or evidenced by an instrument which, if executed by an individual, would require registration as a bill of sale.

Security can arise without any special formalities, provided there is an obligation to be secured, an asset dedicated to that obligation, and an equity of redemption. If other legal devices are used, such as assignment and trust, it can be difficult to tell whether a security has been created. For example, in *L/M International* v *The Circle* (1995) 49 Con LR 12 the court had to consider an assignment by way of legal mortgage of a management contract, and in *Lovell Construction* v *Independent Estates* [1994] 1 BCLC 31 a liquidator appointed over an employer argued unsuccessfully that a trust of the contract sum was a trust by way of floating charge and not binding on him for want of registration. Both cases are discussed later.

Informal security

"Security" is also used when speaking of informal protective devices. Informal security takes various forms.

It is sometimes possible to achieve protection without obtaining a security interest. This can be done through contractual provisions or by obtaining a proprietary right. Classic examples are set-off, non-assignability, vesting clauses, insurance, bonds and guarantees, warranties and escrow agreements. These are considered in detail in later chapters. For the moment, it is useful to look at the roles they play as security.

One of the most powerful contractual rights is the right of set-off. Construction contracts allow the employer to satisfy a cross-claim against the contractor by applying against it any claim the contractor may have against the employer. The employer is thus "secured" up to the value of the contractor's claim. The right of set-off is not a security interest in the contractor's claim in the legal sense but has a similar effect (Neate 1990). Set-off is most valuable after the employer has exercised its right of termination. Termination clauses contain a bundle of rights, many of which enlarge the employer's rights of set-off under the general law. For example, the employer can pay sub-contractors and suppliers direct and set off the direct payments against sums otherwise due to the contractor.

Another useful contractual right is the non-assignability clause which prevents the contractor from disposing of the benefit of the contract. The employer is protected in the sense that its own benefit and burden are not split and the contractor retains a personal interest in the payments accruing due under the contract. When a clause prevents the contractor assigning the benefit of the contract as security it is known as a "negative pledge" clause (Goode 1988, 17-23). This can be overcome by using another device such as the trust: *Don King* v *Warren* [1998] 2 All ER 608.

Where plant and equipment is critical to the project, the funder may require the employer's contractual rights to be buttressed by obtaining rights against the plant and equipment. Vesting clauses used in engineering contracts are intended to prevent the contractor removing plant and equipment from site for use on another project until the work has been completed. It is a question of construction in each case whether the vesting clause gives the employer a proprietary right, a security interest or just a personal right against the contractor. These clauses are sometimes referred to as if they were uniform and have the same legal effect. In fact there is a wide variety of clause types, of which it is worth noting three:

- The plant vests in the employer on delivery to site with no provision for re-vesting.
- The plant vests in the employer on delivery to site and re-vests in the contractor on final completion.
- There is no vesting but the contract prevents the contractor removing the plant from site without the engineer's approval until the works have been completed.

The first type of clause could operate as an absolute transfer or the grant of an equitable interest. The second could be a mortgage or an outright transfer coupled with an undertaking to re-transfer in certain events (Halsbury 32/409). It is sometimes hard to tell these two apart (Oditah 1991). The third example could be a contractual lien or, if there is a power of sale on the contractor's default, a fixed or floating charge or a pledge. It could simply be a contractual restriction. The contract might even contain an express charge. Everything depends on the precise words used.

Insurance can cover a risk which is not specifically allocated to any of the parties to the project. Typical examples of insurance used in the industry are employer's liability, professional indemnity (which may exclude cover for other protection devices such as warranties and indemnities), public liability (for existing structures) and all risks cover (for damage to the works).

One particular kind of collateral agreement which deserves special mention is the escrow agreement. Escrows can be used for various purposes: to protect source codes in information technology, an increasingly important element of construction procurement; to protect the proceeds of sale of units in a commercial property development until the time comes for them to be distributed among the venturers; as trust accounts for construction contracts protecting the contract sum; and for other project finance uses. There are other miscellaneous agreements which may or may not provide informal security, *e.g.* letters of comfort and opinion letters obtained from foreign lawyers.

Next and perhaps most controversially come bonds, guarantees and warranties. There is a complex overlap between the risks they are each intended to cover. Bonds and guarantees perform a number of functions, some general, some specific:

1. Financial long-stop

A guarantee stands as a certain source of compensation, once liability and quantum of the beneficiary's claim have been established. The beneficiary wants certainty not speed, and takes into account the risk of having to incur costs in enforcing the guarantee. Insurance has a similar function.

2. Cash flow

The aim here is to provide the beneficiary with certainty of payment and cash on demand. As between the employer and the issuing bank there is an absolute obligation to pay on presentation of a document. Although there is an implication that the employer will use the proceeds of the bond as cash flow for the project, it has complete discretion over the application of the money. The philosophy underlying this function is that the bank should "pay now, argue later". Escrow accounts can have a similar function. The Australian JCC-D (1994) form provides that payments to a completion contractor as well as direct payments can be deducted from or paid out of the proceeds of any security provided by the contractor, including an on demand bond: see *Ultra Refurbishing* v *John Goubran* (1997) 13 BCL 330.

3. Group cover

If the contractor is part of a group, it may not be possible for the employer to check its financial standing. Even if they are significant at the start of the contract, the contractor's assets may be switched to another group company later. Obtaining a parent company guarantee gives some comfort but the parent may have no assets except shares in its subsidiaries. Only a composite guarantee jointly and severally from all group companies will overcome the group problem, but this is usually only given to banks.

4. Allocation of risk

A project risk may be met by only one device, *e.g.* insurance. Similarly, if there is no overlapping of remedies, a bond may be the only container for a particular risk. An example would be an advance payment bond, where the employer has not required a performance or retention bond.

5. Proof of solvency

It is sometimes said that if a contractor can afford to procure a bond, then it must be strong enough financially to perform the contract.

6. Overcome privity of contract

This is usually the function of a collateral warranty or a direct agreement (*e.g.* employer/sub-contractor or contractor/funder), but bonds are also used for this purpose, for example, when a funder requires sub-contract bonds to be assigned to the employer.

7. Project management

Some bonds allow the bondsman to carry out the works after default by the contractor. Such involvement is usually limited to putting forward a recommendation for the completion contractor. This may help employers who lack the experience or the resources to manage this process themselves, *e.g.* housing associations or local authorities.

8. "Sword of Damocles"

Where the employer and the contractor are in dispute, the employer may make oblique references to the bond or even expressly threaten to call it unless the contractor accepts the employer's terms. Usually a covert purpose, this has been accepted as an actual function of a performance bond by an Australian court: *Olex Focas* v *Skodaexport* (1997) 13 BCL 318.

9. Object of security

On a project financing, there is a tendency in banks to require the creation of obligations solely in order to take security over them. This may simply be a question of habit or it may be that the bank intends to include a value for the obligation in its financial modelling for the project. This is especially the case with on demand bonds.

10. Unique source of recovery

Contracts frequently exclude or place a limit on certain kinds of liability, *e.g.* a cap on damages. As on demand bonds take effect independently of the contract, some employers have used them in an attempt to deprive the contractor of the benefit of limitations of liability.

11. "Belt and braces" approach

Project lenders sometimes adopt a "belt and braces" approach to financial protection. The idea behind this seems to be that the integrity of the project is paramount. This results in the indiscriminate use of all possible financial protection measures, regardless of the adequacy of pre-contract procedures or the terms of the contract.

12. Increase the contractor's liability

A contractor who agrees to provide a parent company guarantee or a collateral warranty does so on the basis that it assumes no wider liability than already exists under the construction contract. In practice, drafts put forward by intended beneficiaries extend the scope of the contractor's liability, *e.g.* "primary obligor" clauses in guarantees and fitness for purpose obligations in warranties.

13. Compensate for pre-contract errors

Risks are created by the employer's failing to ascertain its needs and requirements, rushing the preparation of the tender documents and inviting tenders based on incomplete designs. These risks filter through sooner or later to the contractor. The employer may unconsciously project risks of this kind on to a bond.

14. Personal liability

Where the contractor is a small company, clients sometimes seek personal guarantees from the directors.

Bonds required for specific purposes include:

15. Tender

A tender or bid bond is sometimes required as security for the employer's wasted costs should the successful tenderer fail to enter into the contract.

16. Advance payment

An advance payment bond is required as security for the earning of any advance payment by performance.

17. Performance

A performance bond is required as security for performance generally. Lenders use this term to mean an "on demand", primary obligation. The construction industry uses it to mean a "default", secondary obligation. Each document has to be separately construed to ascertain which it is.

18. Retention

A retention bond is required as security for re-payment of retention released early or never withheld.

19. Efficiency

This bond is used as security for certain obligations after completion, *e.g.* to satisfy performance and output tests. It may extend further than this, going some way into the limitation period, in which case it performs a similar function to latent defects insurance.

20. Liquidated damages

A separate bond is sometimes required as additional security for payment of liquidated and ascertained damages.

21. Customs and freight

Customs and Excise will agree to defer liability to pay VAT and duty if the importer provides a bond as security. Freight bonds are security for payment of duty where equipment originally intended for re-export after completion of a project (and therefore exempt from duty) is left in the country where the works were carried out.

22. Payment

Payment bonds deal with the situation where a contractor has failed to pay others. Advance and down payment bonds cover the risk that the contractor will not earn a pre-payment. Stage or repayment bonds are used where the contractor is paid by reference to milestones or dates and cover the risk of over-payment, *i.e.* if the payment does not reflect the value of the work carried out at that time.

23. Maintenance

The aim of this bond is to secure the contractor's performance during the maintenance period, which might be 12 months after substantial completion. A retention bond is usually available for enforcement from the inception of the contract, whereas a maintenance bond is intended to come into force only at the start of the maintenance period. It ought to come into force only on the expiry of any performance bond. A separate bond is sometimes required where the performance bond expires on substantial completion, the contract concerns a specialist installation which demands a high level of attention after substantial completion or the contract has an unusually long maintenance period.

The main function of a warranty for a tenant is protection against liability to repair. For a purchaser, a warranty protects its investment, giving a right to sue for latent defects and use plans and drawings. Warranties often say that, on the insolvency of the employer, the contractor will not terminate its employment without having given the beneficiary a period of notice in advance. This is to enable the beneficiary to negotiate a novation of the contract if appropriate. Such terms are also found in step-in or direct agreements with project funders.

Security for payment

The measures discussed so far provide funders and employers with security for performance, *i.e.* having the works constructed to the required quality, time and cost. Contractors seek the same protection, so far as they can, from their sub-contractors and so on down the contract chain. Looking upwards, the main protection is security for payment. There are comparatively few devices available for this purpose. They fall under the same broad headings of pre-contract, contractual terms and security.

The contractor also needs to ask whether the project makes commercial sense. If it were the employer, would it be entering into a transaction of this kind? If the project is speculative, is there a committed end user in terms of a prospective tenant or purchaser? Payment problems tend to occur towards the end of the project, which can be the first time the contractor realises the inadequacy of the project financing. Perhaps it was always the employer's intention to fund the final stages itself but it has not been able to raise the money. There may be unexpected liability for VAT, extras or loss and expense which were not budgeted for. These risks can be managed to an extent by "pre-qualifying" the employer. A key question to ask is the extent to which the project will be financed by the employer. How does it propose to do it? Are there realistic contingency funds? What are the external sources of funding? If at all possible, the contractor needs access to the financial model, the development appraisal or the finance agreement. The relationship between the finance agreement and the construction contract can become highly material later on, *e.g. Re Jartay Developments* (1983) 22 BLR 134.

The contractor is given some financial protection by the contract terms. For example, it is comparatively common for limitations to be placed on the nature and amount of the damages recoverable by the employer. Sub-contracts enhance the contractor's rights under the common law by allowing specific rights of deduction, *e.g.* trade and cash discounts. Contingent payment clauses protect the contractor against sub-contractor's claims to the extent that they are mirrored in its own claims against the employer. Such "pay when paid" clauses afford a kind of security to the contractor against insolvent employers by passing risk on to sub-contractors. The security could be described as the right to treat non-payment to the contractor as payment by it.

It is theoretically possible to insure against non-payment (Wright 1997) but credit insurance is little used because of exceptions to the cover, such as retention, and because premiums are assessed on the contractor's turnover rather than the value of the vulnerable contract in question (Hughes *et al* 1998, at 52). Even if it is available, the policy wording may not reflect industry practice and be unenforceable against the insurer. In *Trade Indemnity* v *Parkinson* (1995) BCL 39, a sub-contractor took out credit insurance. One of the terms of the policy was that sub-contracts had to provide a maximum of 45 days for payment after the delivery of goods or provision of services. The insurer was not liable in respect of a bad debt arising through a contractor's insolvency where the sub-contract included an entitlement to payment within 14 days after the contractor had been paid subject to actual receipt by the contractor, *i.e.* a pay when paid clause. Similarly, bonds in support of payment of the contract sum are rarely used, whether given by employers or contractors. Where the employer takes out latent defects insurance under which the insurer waives its rights of subrogation, however, contractors and those working lower down the contract chain can be protected from future claims. Parent company guarantees are useful but depend on the parent holding the assets of the group, which is not necessarily so. Likewise letters of comfort are useful but are based on trust. Perhaps the weakest security is the personal covenant by the employer that it will have access to funds to meet its commitments. It was reported, for example, that bidding documents for the Channel Tunnel Rail Link included the following term: "The employer shall not accept the tender referred to unless it is satisfied on reasonable grounds and obtains information from [its parent] to this effect that it has and shall continue to have sufficient financial and other resources in order to meet its obligations" (*Building*, 30 January 1998).

Formal security for payment is rare. It tends to arise on unusual projects or when the contractor has the upper hand, *e.g.* where it is threatening to issue a winding–up petition against the employer for non-payment. The employer may offer security as quid pro quo for the contractor's forbearance, *e.g.* over land, even if only a second or third charge. In practice, apart from letters of credit or bank guarantees, the only legal device which is used to protect payment is the trust. Trusts are used to protect the whole contract sum or, in the case of JCT forms, retention. In both cases, the trust is integrated with the terms of the contract. The most common trust of the contract sum is along the lines considered in *Lovell Construction* v *Independent Estates* [1994] 1 BCLC 31. At the inception of the project, the employer and contractor divide up the contract sum into equal monthly amounts or varying sums reflecting the anticipated work flow. They then agree a schedule of dates by which the employer agrees to make the payments into a trust account. These are intended to be one month before the work represented by the payment is carried out. The contractor is paid from the trust account by presenting certificates to the trustees, often the solicitors for the parties. The contractor is given rights of suspension and termination in the event of the employer failing to make payments into the account on time. Although the trust is for the sole benefit of the contractor, the fact that the contractor will have some protection in the event of the employer's insolvency reduces the risk of non-payment to sub-contractors. Sir Michael Latham proposed a different scheme under which the employer sets aside money into a trust fund along the lines of the *Lovell* trust, but if the contractor becomes insolvent before completing the work, a secondary trust arises in respect of any balance in the account in favour of the first line of sub-contractors, who share rateably in the fund (Latham 1994). There are some conceptual difficulties with this idea, but they are not insuperable. These and other trusts of the contract sum are considered later.

Retention trusts are now firmly established as a feature of the JCT forms. Retention is a fixed percentage withheld from certified sums until practical completion when half is released to the contractor, with the balance being paid after making good of defects. In view of the time lag between the contractor's earning the retention and acquiring an unconditional right to it, the employer agrees on request to set aside an equivalent amount in a separate account to be held on trust on the terms of the contract. The contractor can only become absolutely entitled to the fund if the employer has no cross-claim which it is entitled to set off. Where the trust account is set up under JCT 87 for the benefit of the management contractor and the works contractors, the employer's right of set-off is limited to the portion withheld from the contractor's fee: *Harrington* v *Co Partnership* (1998) 88 BLR 44. The effect of this decision is to give a genuine security for payment to works contractors in the event of the contractor's insolvency. Whether this is the true construction of JCT 87 is discussed later. It has been suggested that the retention trust takes effect as a charge (Oditah 1991). If so, and the charge is registrable under the Companies Act 1985, the beneficiaries will be unsecured creditors in the employer's liquidation. This issue is also discussed later.

Appropriate use of protection measures

In 1998, the Reading Construction Forum carried out extensive research on the use of financial protection devices in the industry (Hughes *et al* 1998). Figure 2.2 indicates the frequency with which some of the more common devices are used and the approximate percentages by which the contract sum increases annually to pay for them.

Protection device	Frequency (% of contracts on which the device is used)	Cost (% annual addition to the contract sum)
Retention	77 (91 on contracts over £10m)	0.30
Retention bond (default-based)	4	0.03
Performance bond (default-based)	45	0.10
Performance bond (demand)	10	0.33
Parent company guarantee	43	Nil
Collateral warranty	55	Uncertain
P.I. insurance	62	0.40

Source: Hughes *et al* (1998)

Fig 2.2

The table assumes retention of 3% which could have earned interest at 10%, half being withheld over a contract period of two years. The performance bonds were assumed to be for 10% of the contract sum. The research found that if all of the devices were used, they could cost an average of 0.34% of the contract sum per annum. The report concluded:

> "In general, the money cost of these various measures is marginal and it is important for industry policy makers to focus more on the costs of loss of liquidity caused by payment problems, whether legitimate or spurious. This is an aspect of protection for payment obligations. Perhaps the industry should be less defensive about performance protection and more proactive about security for payment" (at 59).

Security for payment was given by the employer in only 6% of the contracts analysed. The selection of protection device appeared to be governed more by a desire to wield bargaining power than an informed assessment of risk. It is tempting to regard the use of contractual security measures as a compensation for inadequate pre-contract measures, rather than filling a genuine gap in the matrix of risk. The starting position ought to be to take adequate pre-contract measures, to draft a fair contract sticking to the common law position as far as possible and to seek the absolute minimum by way of additional security.

Apart from tender and maintenance bonds, all other bonds and guarantees in common use are concurrent rather than consecutive (Figure 2.3).

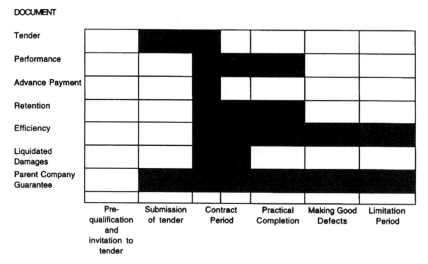

Fig 2.3

It can be seen that the tender bond expires on the entry into the contract by the successful tenderer and the provision of a performance bond. On a major protect, where retention is not being withheld, it would not be unusual for there to be concurrent bonds covering performance in general, retention and advance payment. Although contractors regard retention, and by extension retention bonds, as security for rectification of defects, the employer is often entitled to set off any cross-claim against retention. It follows that, despite its name, retention is simply additional performance security. Similarly, although an advance payment bond is security for the advance payment, it also stands as performance security. Vesting clauses in engineering contracts are a form of performance security although their principal function is operational, to prevent the contractor removing plant from site before completion: see the discussion on the *Cosslett* case later.

It is for the contractor to negotiate specific provisions in the contract and in the bonds that restrict the employer's use of these devices to specific purposes which do not overlap. For example, each bond could say that a claim under one automatically reduces the bonded amounts under the others but this rarely happens in practice. Unless the boundaries between these devices are respected, the position can easily get out of hand. If the contract provides for a 10% performance bond, 5% cash retention and an advance payment bond for 15% of the contract price, then 30% of the contract sum will be subject to security. It is critical to include appropriate accrual and reduction provisions in bonds dealing with retention and advance payment. It should be noted that, assuming the contractor is paid monthly in arrears and the contract period is, say, two years, the employer has further security of 4% in terms of the contractor's uncertified work in progress and even more if the employer abuses its position by delaying payment and conniving at under-certification. If the contractor has undertaken design obligations, the employer should also take the contractor's PI insurance policy into account.

A performance bond should only be required for good reason. A parent company guarantee might be enough. If a bond is thought necessary, the first two of the 23 functions referred to earlier would be appropriate uses, although a bond protecting cash flow ought to be used only in exceptional circumstances, perhaps where the project is of unusual complexity or very high risk. The transferability of assets within groups makes it reasonable in principle to seek parent company guarantees. If the bond answers a project risk not covered by anything else, then again it would be an appropriate function. Using a bond as evidence of solvency is a mistake, based on a misunderstanding of the way bonds are in fact issued. This is an issue for the pre-qualification and tender stages. Many of the general functions are abuses, as may in context be some of the specific purposes. Perhaps an employer who uses bonds for abusive purposes thinks it is getting an advantage, but its relationship with the contractor will be soured and this cannot be in the interests of the project.

Given that almost all risks are managed by the contract itself, it would appear that the real reason for requiring all this security is the risk of the contractor's insolvency. Can this be justified? One of the clients interviewed for the Reading report thought it could make money out of a contractor's insolvency. Uncertified work in progress and non-payment could give a six-week buffer. The client may be legally entitled to set off a cross-claim for management time expended in dealing with the problems caused by the insolvency. The focus groups suggested that many clients do so. Last, contractors keen to impress new clients may take on a completion contract at cheaper rates (at 18).

Checklist of weighting criteria

The following questions are relevant when weighting the full range of protective devices available to employers:

- What percentage of the total project risk can the device bear?
- Does the device consist of cash or is it equivalent to cash?
- How much does it cost to put the device in place? Is the cost passed on to the project procurer?
- Does the device wholly or partly overlap with another device? Is the overlap one of time or obligation?
- Is there security over security, *e.g.* a charge over a performance bond or a parent company guarantee of a collateral warranty?
- Does the overlap confer any additional benefit on the employer which answers a project risk not otherwise allocated?
- How frequently is the device enforced in practice by the industry (isolating those which are never, or rarely, called upon in practice)?
- Is the function of the protection device recognised as part of the project risk management or is it covert or unofficial, perhaps conferring a benefit over and above that contracted for by the contractor?
- Is the function of the device general and/or specific? If both, can its scope be reduced without disadvantaging the employer?

Conclusion

The question remains whether the risk of the contractor's insolvency is so great as to make all this protection necessary. It is hard to identify the consequences of "over-management" of risk. It is not just a question of increasing the cost of construction. The boundaries between the available devices are not being respected. This blurring is mirrored in the relationships between employers, contractors and sub-contractors. An inevitable consequence is conflict and mistrust. The lack of discrimination in the approach to financial protection by employers, perhaps at the insistence of funders, is a contributory factor to the lack of trust in the industry (Latham 1993).

The power imbalance between employers and contractors means that attention is usually focused on financial protection of the paying party rather than security for payment for contractors and sub-contractors. Sir Michael Latham tried to redress the balance a little by recommending that employers set up trust accounts and make a payment monthly in advance into the account as security for the contractor, to "prime the pump" as he put it (Latham 1994). The proposal was universally condemned by clients. Maybe his idea will come back onto the political agenda one day. In the meantime, there should be a shift away from the emphasis on security and unbalanced contract terms to greater sophistication in pre-contract measures.

There is a case for developing financial models that accurately assess insolvency as one of many project risks, allocate the risks among all the project participants, match appropriate protection devices against relevant risks and take proper account of overlaps of time and obligation.

Chapter 3

· **Payment** ·

Introduction

In the manufacturing industry, an order is completed on delivery of the goods and payment becomes due on receipt of the supplier's invoice. In construction, concepts like completion and entitlement to payment are much more complex. Completion is progressive and has to be defined: phased, practical, making good defects, final. The right to payment depends on a certificate of the employer's representative and on other conditions being met. Interim payments are provisional until final completion and subject to retrospective abatement. Construction contracts are shot through with conditionality. The fact that construction work is carried out using chains of contracts gives rise to the idea that payment is linear. In the industry people speak about payment as if it were a thing, but in law a right to payment is an intangible, enforceable only by bringing proceedings. There is nothing for the contractor to "pass on".

Qualities of payment

Payment has temporal, relational and structural qualities. As a function of money it also has archetypal, imaginal qualities (see Chapter 18). These qualities are apparent from the words used in connection with payment.

The language of payment is time. The industry talks of payment as slow, delayed, in arrears or deferred on the one hand and advanced, accelerated or prompt on the other. In relational terms, payment is defined by the identities of payer and payee (not necessarily debtor and creditor). In a simple situation, A agrees to pay B £x. In construction, since the vast majority of work is sub-contracted, A agrees to pay B £x of which £y is to be paid to C, £z to D and so on. The industry therefore speaks of payment being made "direct" by A to C or D. Payment is also indirect (by set-off), retained and withheld by A or B.

Payment's temporal and relational features are very important, but in construction insolvency its structural qualities are more important still.

The industry speaks of "payment structures" when distinguishing between, say, payment by value over time (interim certificates) and payment of a percentage of the contract sum by work stage (milestones). The "structure" of a payment is also apt to describe inherent limitations in the chose in action. For example, retention is a conditional debt defeasible by set-off. The failure to bring the works to completion means the condition will never be satisfied, providing the employer with a complete defence to proceedings. The debt is defeasible if the employer has a right of recourse under the contract.

As Peter Fenn emphasised in Chapter 1, a construction contract is very unusual in that the consideration is continually being negotiated. A agrees to pay B £x to be valued by C and certified by D, where C is the employer's quantity surveyor and D is the architect. Inherent in any construction receivable is the exercise of judgment by A (in respect of its rights of abatement, deduction and set-off), C (in exercise of its duties of valuation) and D (in exercise of its duties of checking C's valuation and certification). A further structural consideration is whether the payment is secured, guaranteed, or contingent (in the sense of a pay when paid clause). The consequences of non-payment by the employer are not as immediate as the consequences of the contractor's ceasing work. Non-payment of one or even two certified sums is unlikely to be a repudiation by the employer, whereas the contractor's ceasing work could well be an abandonment of the contract. For all these reasons construction receivables are regarded as "flawed" and "vulnerable" compared with those of other industries. This chapter examines various of the structural qualities of payment. Set-off is dealt with in Chapters 5 and 13 while direct payment is considered in Chapter 12.

Construction receivables

It is hard to say exactly what a receivable is. Its elusiveness reflects the mysterious nature of money which, unless in the form of coins or notes or a document like a cheque, is purely intangible. At its broadest, a receivable embraces any actual or potential right to payment. It can include a present debt which may never confer the right to sue the creditor to judgment and an inchoate entitlement which may never become a debt at all. It is not much easier to tell when a receivable is a debt because, instead of enunciating clear principles in this area, the court has tended to resolve the issue before it by applying a subtly different definition of a debt. A debt is therefore like a chameleon which adapts itself to its environment. For example, set-off, assignability, statutory demands, winding-up petitions, attachment of debts, retention, and charges over book debts all adopt slightly different criteria. Debts are described as actual, future, contingent, conditional, defeasible, present, maturing, accruing due, due, owing and payable. For the purposes of obtaining a judgment against a debtor, the receivable must be payable. Hence the standard definition of a debt as a liquidated sum of money which is due and payable and enforceable by action. However, this does not mean that a receivable falling in the other categories listed above would not be regarded as a debt for other purposes.

This section attempts to set out some general principles and then to apply them to receivables arising under a construction contract. First, it is worth noting that any definition of a debt will not apply in all situations, partly in view of the differing contexts referred to above and partly because a debt comes into being under a contract by which the parties can choose whatever criteria they like of when and how a debt will arise. Secondly, the accrual of a right to payment, and its correlative duty to pay, may entitle the creditor to issue proceedings but not to obtain judgment. Judgment can only be obtained where all the contractual conditions for recovery of the debt have been satisfied. The most common is the expiry of a grace period. Where a contract allows time for payment, it is usual to refer to a debt becoming "due" at the beginning of the period and "payable" at the end. If there is no grace period, a debt will become due and payable at the same time. Although it sounds paradoxical, it depends on the construction of the contract whether a receivable can become a debt before it becomes due for payment. For example, under a sale of goods payable by instalments, the contract may be construed as creating a debt for the whole price on delivery of the goods which accrues due as each instalment date is reached. It is uncertain exactly how far this concept of a debt "accruing due" goes. Some would extend it to situations where a seller has provided the consideration but a condition of a purely administrative nature has not been satisfied or even where the condition is structural so that the debt itself is conditional.

The position under a construction contract is much more complicated because the contractor's right to payment is usually dependent on the issue of a certificate by a third party. However, it is possible for a receivable to become a debt due for immediate payment without a certificate. This can arise where the contract provides for payment monthly in advance on receipt of the contractor's invoice.

Alternatively, the contract may provide for stage payments entitling the contractor to specific amounts at defined stages of the works, *e.g.* second stage brickwork or the building being watertight, or for specific sums to be paid on agreed dates under a cash flow schedule regardless of the amount of work actually done. In either case, the debt will become payable as each stage or date is reached.

In any event, the Housing Grants, Construction and Regeneration Act 1996 now provides that every construction contract must have an adequate mechanism for ascertaining when a sum becomes due and the date of the "final date for payment", which simply seems to mean the date it becomes payable. The Act does not define a debt for the purposes of a construction contract and says nothing about the structural issues which can arise. The case law has not really addressed the issue. In *Community Development* v *Engwirda Construction* [1969] 120 CLR 455 at 459, it was said that, on entering into a lump sum contract for building work, the employer becomes liable to pay the lump sum as a debt. However, the debt is conditional on the contractor providing the consideration: *Attorney General* v *McMillan & Lockwood* [1991] NZLR 53. The debt will not become enforceable until all contract terms for payment have been satisfied. It is not clear, however, whether, after having provided the consideration by doing the work, but before the work has been certified for payment, the contractor has a debt accruing due or simply an inchoate right to have the contract terms of certification operated. The only context in which the court has considered the issue is in the attachment of debts following judgment, also known as the garnishee procedure.

A garnishee order may be obtained in respect of debts "due or accruing due" to the contractor under RSC Order 49. Under English law, the creditor can only attach a certified sum although it is immaterial whether the sum is payable at the date of attachment: *Dunlop & Renken* v *Hendall Steel* [1957] 3 All ER 344. It appears that retention cannot be attached until certified for payment: *Grant Plant Hire* v *Trickey* (1961) 105 SJ 255, *Drew* v *Josolyne* (1887) l8 QBD 590, *Earle* v *Hemsworth* RDC (1928) 140 LT 69. This view limits "accruing due" to the situation where the debt is in existence and will become payable by effluxion of time. Such a construction is apt for the garnishee procedure, otherwise the court could become involved in very difficult questions of interpretation of the standard forms which are unsuited for consideration at the enforcement stage, but is inconsistent with the law's general approach to debts: *O'Driscoll* v *Manchester Insurance Committee* [1915] 3 KB 499,

Tapp v *Jones* (1875) LR 10 QB 591, Prentice 1983. It appears to confuse the distinction between a condition precedent to a debt coming into existence and its recoverability by action.

Compare this approach with the Canadian case of *Sandy* v *Yukon Construction* [1961] 33 WWR 490 in which a judgment creditor of a sub-contractor obtained a garnishee order against the contractor. The sub-contract provided that amounts should not become payable to the sub-contractor until 14 days after the contractor received the appropriate architect's certificate and payment from the employer. No sums were payable when the order was served but money was later paid into court. It was held that the order attached money accruing due to the sub-contractor even though it did not become payable until a later date. It was unnecessary for the contractor's debt to be enforceable by the sub-contractor at the date of the garnishee order.

A contractor's receivables naturally fall within six categories: debts (certified sums, retention), loss and expense, finance charges, claims for damages, quantum meruit and claims for interest.

Retention is a special case. Although it is not recoverable by action until certified for release, it is quantified by each interim certificate and is thus regarded as a conditional debt (see below). Retention is therefore more analogous to a future instalment under a sale of goods contract than uncertified work in progress under a contract for work and materials.

A receivable needs to be a debt in the strict sense, *i.e.* recoverable by action, before it can be the subject of a statutory demand. In practice, the same applies to the issue of a winding-up petition. This is understandable since the court does not want to place a company in liquidation without a high degree of certainty that the money is owed. It is possible that the criteria for a book debt are wider and embrace not only certified sums but also retention and claims made under the contract which are normally recorded in the contractor's books (see below). Any receivable can be assigned, however inchoate, even those which accrue due under a future contract: *Tailby* v *Official Receiver* (1888) 13 App Cas 523. To be eligible for legal set-off a cross-claim must be for a debt in the strict sense, whereas contractual set-off and set-off in bankruptcy and liquidation apply even to inchoate uncertified amounts, ascertainment being a matter either for the contract or the insolvency procedure. A cross-claim for equitable set-off need not be ascertained and would probably fall in the same category. For *quantum meruit*, see later.

Fixed charges are taken over "book debts and other debts now and from time to time due or owing to the company": *Siebe Gorman* v

Barclays Bank [1979] 2 Lloyd's Rep 142. If a receivable falls within this description, the charge-holder will gain priority over preferential creditors. The description of charged assets may be wider than this, *e.g.* "all receivables, debts … now or at any time hereafter belonging to the mortgagor": *Re Armagh Shoes* [1984] BCLC 405. If a company has granted more than one charge, the precise status of a receivable might determine who takes priority. Similar wording is used in agreements for the sale of businesses.

It is sometimes argued that, where retention or the whole contract sum is subject to a trust, the obligation of the payer is not in debt but in equity and that such receivables should not be regarded as debts. However, the law accepts that an obligation can be owed in trust and contract at the same time (*Barclays Bank* v *Quistclose* [1970] AC 567), so a trust receivable can be a "book or other debt" for the purposes of a fixed charge. Where the benefit of such a contract is sold and the purchaser undertakes to account to the receiver for receivables representing work done before the transfer, they would be book debts. This is because a receivable under the sale of business agreement or a novation would ordinarily be a debt.

Retention

The right of retention is a longstanding feature of building contracts. Retention is part of a certified sum which has been earned by the contractor but which is not payable until the final stages of the contract. Retention is regarded as a debt even where a condition for its release has not been satisfied. An action can be brought on it, although it can be defended by reliance on the condition. If the condition is satisfied before trial, the contractor is entitled to judgment even though the condition was a good defence when the proceedings were issued: *Ballast Wiltshier* v *Thomas Barnes* [1998] CILL 1417, a case on the DOM/1 sub-contract. Until retention falls for release, however, it is not regarded as a "debt due or accruing due" which can be attached by garnishee proceedings: *Grant Plant Hire* v *Trickey* (1961) 105 SJ 255. In order to avoid bringing retention into account on a repudiation by the contractor, very clear words would be necessary: *e.g. Tony Cox* v *Jim 5* (1996) 14 BLM 6.

The term "retention" is used in the United Kingdom, Australia and New Zealand. Confusingly, "retention fund" and "retention moneys" are also used, whether or not the employer has segregated retention from its own property by paying an amount equivalent to it into an account. Such imprecise language has caused confusion in the context of the retention trust which is considered in more detail in Chapter 11. American contracts use "retainage" but this appears to have the same function as retention (Sweet 1994). Canadian statutes and standard forms use "holdback". Although this is a percentage of the contract sum retained by the employer, it fulfils a different function from retention and is not directly comparable (Goldsmith and Heintzman 1988). The Canadian statutes are interesting and instructive and are briefly considered in Chapter 17.

Commercial function

Retention is usually a fixed percentage of the contract sum, which varies from contract to contract. In the 19th century, as much as 25% was withheld. Nowadays, the norm is 3% or 5% but higher percentages are still encountered, particularly on local authority contracts. In some jurisdictions, the maximum percentage is fixed by statute. The timing of its release depends on the terms of the contract. Usually, half is paid to the contractor on practical completion (or substantial completion or taking over) and the balance is paid after the end of the defects liability period (also known as the maintenance period), but this is not necessarily so. In an Australian case, the taking over provisions in a standard form were deleted and the following words substituted: "the retention amount shall be payable in six months after the Certificate of Acceptance is granted, which shall not be withheld unduly, providing all works are wind and weathertight": *Watkins v Cairns Meat* [1963] Qd R 21. The court referred to deleted words from which it was inferred that the parties had intended something different from a taking over certificate. The clause meant that retention was to be released only six months after defects had been completed, even though the employer had gone into occupation of the building.

The timing of payment of retention is the clue to its principal function, which is said to be "to encourage the contractor to fulfil his obligations during and after the completion of the works and to provide some form of insurance to the client should he fail to do so" (Banwell 1964 at 9.1). According to this definition, retention has a dual purpose: an incentive to the contractor and protection of the employer. Retention has been described as a forced loan providing free financing to the employer (McGuinness 1983). It is also seen as a safeguard against over valuation; it does have a quality of provisional abatement about it. It is a claim against which the employer can make a set-off in the event of the contractor's default. Retention is protection against failure to rectify defects since a certificate of making good is a condition of its recoverability. The JCT forms also anticipate deductions from retention in respect of liquidated damages for delay, insurance premiums, the cost of completion of part of the work by an alternative contractor, or direct payment made to sub-contractors or suppliers. Retention is defeasible in respect of these other risks. These two aspects, conditionality and defeasiblity, make retention a flawed asset in the contractor's balance sheet: see Hayton CLY 1994.

As retention accumulates gradually during the contract period, it is only towards the end of a contract that it can give worthwhile protection. It is at this time that the employer may need it most as, apart from any final account balance due to the contractor, there will be no further sums against which the employer could set off a cross-claim: *Morgan* v *Allen* [1971] Tas SR 285.

Significance of retention

At first sight it seems unjustifiable to devote much time to a detailed consideration of retention in view of the fact that it accounts for so small a proportion of the contract sum. On closer examination, it can be seen that retention is of considerable significance, not least when the contractor becomes insolvent. It is useful to summarise the reasons why retention is important. Margins in the construction industry are low when compared to other sectors. Even if the retention is only 3%, its loss may deprive the contractor of its profit on the contract. Non-recovery of retention could mean a loss on the contract. It is also important to appreciate the figure to which the retention percentage is applied. It is not uncommon for a modest project to have a contract sum in excess of £1 million. On larger projects that sum may be payable under a monthly certificate alone.

In theory the cost of retention to a contractor is loss of interest but, if it could not have borrowed the amount of the retention, its cost may be better expressed as the loss of opportunity.

> "This might be a profit on a development or it might be the ability to pay off an existing loan or to finance the business and avoid insolvency. The focus group interviews revealed that the true cost of retention was … the problem of the final payment never being released at all" (Hughes *et al* 1998 at 22).

Provided the employer remains solvent, however, retention is relatively neutral to contractors as they obtain back-to-back retentions from sub-contractors, nor does it increase the contract sum as the employer can earn interest on it or put it to other uses.

The retention percentage can be increased by agreement in substitution for other security, *e.g.* a performance bond. This may arise because the contractor has exhausted its bonding capacity at its bank or for other reasons. Retention falls within a fixed charge on book debts and can be collected by a receiver and paid in full to the charge-holder in priority to other creditors. Although retention counts as an asset in the contractor's balance sheet, it is vulnerable. Apart from the additional credit which it represents to the employer during the execution of the work on site, the employer has free use of half of the retention during the maintenance period which could be 12 months or more. As the retention is usually unsecured, and the contractor may have little contact with the employer during the maintenance period, it becomes less recoverable as time goes by. The Cork Committee received extensive representations on retention when reviewing the law and practice relating to insolvency between 1977 and 1982 (Cork 1982 at 1057-1075), but it was outside their terms of reference to report on the subject.

On the contractor's insolvency, the employer, the contractor's general creditors and its lender all look towards the retention to satisfy their claims. Priority disputes over retention involving guarantors are discussed in Chapter 10. In the United Kingdom, the major difficulty concerns the nature and effect of the security given over the retention to the contractor by the standard forms (see Chapter 11).

Alternatives to retention

Some standard forms provide for other forms of security in lieu of retention. For example the Australian form AS 4000-1997 defines security as:

> "cash, retention moneys, bonds or inscribed stock or their equivalent issued by a national, state or territory government, interest bearing deposit in a bank carrying on business at the place stated in Item 9(c), an approved unconditional undertaking ... or an approved performance undertaking given by an approved financial institution or insurance company or other form approved by the party having the benefit of the security."

In the United Kingdom, it is more common for retention to be replaced (or released early) by the provision of a retention bond or a maintenance bond. Philip Wood has considered other alternatives, such as charge back or trust back arrangements whereby the contractor charges or declares itself trustee of amounts representing a given percentage of the contract value (Wood 1989 at 227). The Banwell Committee suggested an experiment under which contractors would tender on the alternative bases that retention was and was not withheld. It considered that retention in excess of 3% was unjustified where the contractor had both pre-qualified and been chosen through selective tendering (Banwell 1964 at 9-11). Further options are discussed in Chapter 17.

Quantum meruit

A receivable frequently encountered in the construction industry is the claim in quasi contract for a *quantum meruit*. This is a right to be paid a reasonable sum for work done at the employer's request without a contract, or pursuant to a letter of intent, or where variations are ordered outside the scope of the contract. A *quantum meruit* is also available as an alternative to damages to a person accepting the other's conduct as a repudiation of the contract (see Chapter 9). In these circumstances, it has been held in Australia that a *quantum meruit* for work in progress remaining uncertified at the date of termination could not be a debt because it was not ascertained or readily ascertainable by the court: *Geraldton Building* v *Woodmore* (1993) 8 ACSR 585. The court applied *Ogdens* v *Weinberg* (1896) 95 LT 567 which defined a debt as a sum recoverable by an action for debt which had to be ascertained or capable of being ascertained by the court.

In *Amantilla* v *Telefusion* [1987] CILL 316, an Official Referee reached the opposite conclusion.

> "A *quantum meruit* claim for a reasonable sum lay in debt because it was for money due under a contract; it was a liquidated pecuniary claim because a 'reasonable sum' was a sufficiently certain contractual description for its amount to be ascertainable. Such a claim was for a specific sum and was no less specific for being described in words rather than in figures. The nature of a claim for unliquidated damages was wholly different; the function of the court was not one of interpreting the contract, but of deciding, in accordance with legal principles, what compensation, if any, should be paid to redress any harm done by its breach. A claim for unliquidated damages could not be a liquidated pecuniary claim, even if claimed at a definite figure."

In that case, the *quantum meruit* was for variations included in a final account claim brought by a receiver and manager appointed over a contractor. A claim for *quantum meruit* would probably be regarded as a debt for the purposes of legal set-off: *Lagos* v *Grunwaldt* [1910] 1 KB 41 at 48, *Aectra* v *Exmar* [1994] 1 WLR 1634 at 1647. It is hard to understand why the test should be different for other purposes.

Funding cash flow

Contractors are usually paid monthly in arrears. At the outset, dates are agreed for monthly valuations of the contractor's work. Under standard forms of building contract, the contractor provides the quantity surveyor appointed by the employer with sufficient information for him to value the work seven days before each of the agreed dates. The quantity surveyor then submits his valuation to the architect appointed under the contract who issues an interim certificate by which the employer has to pay the net sum due to the contractor within 14 days or such other period as is stated in the contract. The contractor will, as far as possible, so arrange its affairs that it does not have to meet outgoings until payment has been received under an interim certificate (Upson 1987). This is achieved in the case of sub-contractors by appropriate contract terms. In many cases, a significant amount of labour on site is engaged by labour-only sub-contractors who will not be paid until the contractor is paid. Builders' merchants give extended credit to contractors in respect of direct supplies which ought to make it unnecessary to settle invoices before receipt of certified sums. Nevertheless it is necessary for a contractor to meet some site outgoings and it has to meet its head office overheads in the meantime. The delay between payments and receipts gives rise to the requirement for working capital (Pilcher 1985).

Working capital consists of current assets including cash, debtors and stock. Stock in the case of a construction company largely consists of materials and work in progress. Unless an advance payment has been made, there is at least a month's delay before a project starts to generate cash and so the contractor must look to other sources of finance to fund its working capital. These sources consist of debt and equity.

Debt is basically borrowing. With most small to medium contractors, debt is provided by means of a bank overdraft, trade credit or unsecured loans from the directors. Motor vehicles, plant and equipment are commonly financed by hire purchase or leasing.

Factoring is not often encountered since construction contracts tend to be long-term and there is a serious risk that the factor's claim would be defeated by set-off (Salinger 1991). Funding debt by means of an overdraft and trade credit is a cause of instability because both sources of finance are short-term. Once these have been exhausted, the contractor may have no other source from which to pay its creditors. Historically, there has been a tradition of generalism among banks and insolvency practitioners. The logistics of their businesses did not fit with industry specialisation. This is changing. A recent example is the "Safeguard" facility introduced by the Bank of Ireland, who have also recruited industry professionals for their newly formed construction division. Safeguard is a two-year rolling facility, renewed every 12 months, under which the bank agrees not to make a demand for the repayment of the overdraft unless there has been a default. The cost is 0.5% over their normal facility rate.

Medium to large contractors are better placed since they can fund debt by means of term loans, bond issues and other methods. Equity means shareholders' funds. These consist of the capital contributed by the company's shareholders, retained profits from previous years' trading, reserves established by revaluation of properties held and the share premium account representing the premiums received from the issue of shares at a price above their nominal value. An equity investment depends on the financial success of the company. Its reward consists in dividends declared by the company but the investor takes a high risk which is not secured against the company's assets. A debt investment is not so dependent on the company's financial success. Its reward is interest payable at agreed rates and the investor's risk is lower as the debt is normally secured against the company's assets. Types of security were considered in Chapter 2. The relationship which debt bears to equity ("gearing") is one of the major financial ratios by which a contractor's financial health can be assessed. Gearing indicates a company's ability to borrow in order to meet short term commitments.

It is also important to know the extent to which a company can pay interest on its borrowing out of its operating profits ("profit before interest and tax"). The proportion which interest bears to profit ("interest strain") is the other major solvency ratio. In 1990, average gearing among publicly quoted contractors was 50% and interest strain 40%, but there can be considerable fluctuation from year to year. The level of gearing is important but the ultimate cause of insolvency is lack of liquidity. Creditor pressure may be such that the contractor has no time to dispose of assets or organise a rights issue to raise cash. There are two guides to liquidity: the current ratio which is the proportion which current assets bear to current liabilities and the acid test ratio which is the proportion which current assets less stock bear to current liabilities. Figure 3.1 shows how these ratios varied between 1984 and 1990 (County Natwest 1991).

Ratio %	1984	1985	1986	1987	1988	1989	1990
Gearing	43.4	40.3	40.1	33.1	37.6	50.3	48.9
Interest strain	22.1	25.8	21.5	17.3	15.2	23.8	39.9
Current	1.58	1.58	1.67	1.80	1.71	1.81	2.07
Acid test	0.47	0.45	0.44	0.46	0.44	0.45	0.51

Fig 3.1

A company must also show a return on investment to its shareholders. What profit margins do contractors achieve? And how profitable are they by comparison with companies undertaking construction-related activities? A contractor's margin is the proportion which profit (before interest and tax) bears to sales. Profitability can be assessed by return on capital employed ("ROCE"). ROCE is the proportion which profit, before interest and tax, bears to the capital employed in the business. Capital employed is the total of fixed assets and working capital. An analysis was carried out in 1990 of key financial ratios for 60 companies involved in contracting, housebuilding and plant hire with turnover ranging from £0.7 million to £35 million (Lloyd's Bowmaker 1990). The results are set out in Figure 3.2.

	Construction	Housebuilding	Plant-hire
ROCE (%)	16.5	15.4	22.7
Margin (%)	3.0	24.2	16.8
Asset Turnover	5.5	0.6	1.4
Stockholding Period (days)	35	298	19
Collection Period (days)	47	34	69
Payment Period (days)	56	42	48
Current Ratio	1.3	1.9	0.8
Acid Test	0.9	0.6	0.7
Debt/Equity (%)	19	89	70
Interest Cover	7.1	3.5	5.6
Turnover per Employer (£)	13704	13897	11621
Profit per Employee (£)	1897	51195	8963

Fig 3.2

Figure 3.3 compares the finance required by seven company types in the construction industry (Hillebrandt and Cannon 1989). Once a contract has been under way for some months, it should start to generate positive cash flow. This is enhanced by the practice adopted by many contractors of weighting items occurring early in the contract known as "front-end loading".

Purpose of Finance	Type of Business						
	Con-tracting	House-Building	Plant Hire	Materials Production	Mining	Property develop-ment	Property Invest-ment
Working capital	1	2	2	2	2	2	2
Speculative stock & WIP	-	3	-	2	1	3	3
Stocks ordered & WIP	1	1	1	1	1	1	-
Unexpected liabilities	3	1	2	1	3	-	2
Operating assets other than land	-	1	3	3	3	-	3
New ventures	-	1	-	2	1	2	2
Land	-	3	-	-	2	3	-

Notes

WIP – Work in progress

The numbers from 1 to 3 indicate the relative importance of requirements of finance for each type of business:

1 – low

2 – medium

3 – high

Fig 3.3

Housing Grants, Construction and Regeneration Act 1996

Payment under a construction contract entered into after 1 May 1998 is governed by the Housing Grants, Construction and Regeneration Act 1996. The Act applies to all construction contracts except those with residential occupiers and in certain specialist sectors, such as oil and gas, mining, nuclear and manufacturing of building components. The Act is intended to provide "a framework for fairer contracts and better working relationships within the construction industry" (DOE 1995). The Act requires the parties to agree a procedure for payment which complies with the Act. Failure to do so will result in the implication of the Scheme for Construction Contracts into the contract in order to supplement or replace the non-compliant contractual term.

By s 109 a contractor is entitled to be paid by instalments, stage payments or other periodic payments unless either the contract period is less than 45 days or the parties estimate that the work will take less than 45 days. The parties are "free to agree" both the amounts and the intervals of payments or the circumstances in which they become due. If not set out in the contract, the Scheme for Construction Contracts provides that payment intervals will be monthly in arrears. The Act does not require an instalment to represent the value of the work done since the previous instalment. Under a deferred payment contract, for example, there might be 10 instalments, nine for nominal amounts and the tenth for £10 million.

Before the Act, the domestic sub-contract, DOM/1, provided for monthly payments to the sub-contractor, the first being one month after the sub-contractor started work on site. Payment was within 17 days of the date it became due. So if the sub-contractor started on site on 1 July, its first payment would be due on 1 August, and payable on 18 August. The next payment would be due on 1 September and so on. In practice, this contractual mechanism was often not operated (Price 1994). Instead, sub-contractors were paid within a certain period after the date of a main contract certificate or after the contractor had been paid. This left the sub-contractor in a difficult position. DOM/1 did not reflect what actually happened. There was no requirement for domestic sub-contractors to submit applications for payment, although they usually did. Their works were valued by the employer's quantity surveyor when he valued the whole of the main contract works for certification. Then it was for the main contractor to allocate an amount in respect of the domestic sub-contractor's work and make the payment.

Section 110(1) is intended to provide greater clarity in this area. It requires that every construction contract should provide an "adequate mechanism" for deciding what is due, when it becomes due and when it becomes payable. The parties are "free to agree" all these things but, in the absence of agreement, the Scheme provides that the amount due will be the amount applied for by the sub-contractor. An amount will become due when the sub-contractor serves its application on the contractor, and payable within 21 days after it becomes due (or 45 days in the case of a final payment). Obviously, there is scope for discussion as to what an "adequate mechanism" would be. Section 110(2) requires the contractor, no later than five days after a payment has become due, to serve a payment notice stating the amount if any of the payment made or proposed to be made and the basis on which that amount was calculated. If the Scheme applies, the payment notice must be served within five days after receipt of the sub-contractor's application for payment. Contractors have to decide how to incorporate the payment notice requirement into their existing procedures (see Chapter 5).

Both the JCT and ICE forms have been amended following the Act. Amendment 18 to JCT 80 is now incorporated in JCT 98. Arguably, the JCT form fails to say with sufficient clarity when payments become due, but by inference this is on the issue of an architect's certificate. The employer issues a payment notice no later than five days after the certificate. In theory this means the employer could insert a lower figure in the payment notice than that in the certificate. The final date for payment as defined in the Act is 14 days from the certificate. A withholding notice must be served not later than five days before that. ICE (6th edition) takes a slightly difference approach. The engineer's certificate takes effect as the payment notice. Payment is due on the certificate which must be issued within 25 days of delivery of the contractor's monthly statement. The final date for payment is 28 days after delivery of the monthly statement, *i.e.* three days after the certificate. The withholding notice must be given at least one day before the final date for payment. Both JCT and ICE have excluded the enforcement of an adjudicator's decision from the jurisdiction of an arbitrator, enabling the decision to be enforced by the court. Each party bears its own costs of an adjudication under either form.

Pay when paid

On a construction project, the contractor bears the risk of the employer's insolvency, unless the sub-contract clearly provides otherwise:

> "Where one has a chain of contractual rights and liabilities, the party in the middle is normally exposed to the risk of insolvency on the part of the other parties. If the [JCT] scheme set out to avoid that consequence one would expect it to do so by clear and express provision": *Birse Construction* v *Co-Operative Wholesale Society* (1997) 84 BLR 58 at 75.

Pay when paid clauses in construction contracts are now regulated by s 113(1) Housing Grants, Construction and Regeneration Act 1996. Before looking at the Act it is useful to bear in mind the background to pay when paid clauses. Problems arise in four situations: the employer's insolvency, the termination of the main contract, the completion of the main contract and disputes between the employer and the contractor.

The general background

Outside insolvency, although not directly in issue, the efficacy of pay when paid clauses was impliedly accepted in *Gilbert-Ash* v *Modern Engineering* [1974] AC 689 where the sub-contract stated:

> "14. Payments (both interim and final) as stated overleaf will be made to the sub-contractor as and when the value of such works under the terms of the principal contract is included in a certificate to the contractor and the contractor receives the moneys due thereunder."

Viscount Dilhorne commented: "Under the sub-contract [the contractor] became only liable to pay when he received the money from the employer." The English cases in this area have focused on the effectiveness on a pay when paid clause after the completion or termination of the main contract.

In *Rushpass* v *G Percy Trentham* (unreported, 10 May 1991), a main contract under JCT 81 was determined. The termination was disputed and referred to arbitration. The sub-contractor was entitled to payment "within 7 days of receipt by [the main contractor] of payment of the said work pursuant to the said main contract". The sub-contract provided that where the main contract was determined, the sub-contract would automatically determine, and the sub-contractor's rights would be the same as those of the main contractor in that situation under JCT 81. The sub-contractor obtained summary judgment on the ground that JCT 81 did not provide for contingent payment.

> "If a pay when paid clause is to survive the determination of a contract, then it must be clearly drafted in order to achieve that effect. In the present case not only is it not so clearly drafted but for the reasons set out above, the drafting of [the termination clause] clearly precludes such a construction".

In *Churchfield Construction* v *Waymans* (unreported, 25 July 1996), a contractor was in dispute with an employer over a claim for loss and expense. Practical completion of the main contract had been achieved. The contractor had agreed a final account with a domestic sub-contractor and there was no dispute as to defects or otherwise between them. The sub-contract provided for payment within 28 days after any interim certificate which included the value of work done by that sub-contractor provided that the contractor had received payment in respect of it. It appears that the amount claimed by the sub-contractor had not been certified or paid to the contractor. Garland J awarded summary judgment to the sub-contractor:

> "I read these provisions as being abundantly clear that the pay when paid provision bites only on interim certificates and not once the works have reached the stage of practical completion, still less of course, final certificate ... [The sub-contractors] were only dependent on pay when paid so far as interim certificates were concerned ... I averred in passing that these pay when paid clauses can cause great difficulties, and are not to be encouraged at every stage".

These cases imply that a pay when paid clause would have been effective before practical completion or termination, and even on those events if the sub-contract had been clear enough. The validity of a clause making payment contingent on the employer's solvency is impliedly recognised by s 113 Housing Grants, Construction and Regeneration Act 1996. Before the Act, there was some doubt over the effectiveness of a pay when paid clause on the employer's insolvency, mainly because clauses in regular use referred to payment but not the cause of non-payment. For example, under the FCEC form of sub-contract, a contractor had to pay the sub-contractor "within 7 days of his receiving from the employer on account of the main work any payment which includes a sum in respect of the sub-contract works". The Green Form had a similar provision. The use of pay when paid clauses is associated with the introduction of management contracting as a means of procurement in the 1960s. Until 1987, when the JCT issued a standard form, contractors used their own forms of sub-contract or had special conditions for use with the standard forms of sub-contract: *A Davies & Company* v *William Old* (1969) 113 SJ 262. In *Maidenhead Electrical Services* v *Johnson* (1997) 15 CLD 10-03, a sub-sub-contract consisted partly of the sub-contract conditions and the sub-contractor's own purchase order. The order stated that the sub-sub-contractor was entitled to payment: "within 14 days of the receipt by the Company of any payment pursuant to such applications the Company [Johnsons] shall account to the Contractor [Maidenhead] for all monies properly due hereunder to the Contractor in respect of the Works less any sums which may be deducted from such payments ...". It was held that this term did not take effect as a pay when pay clause, although the report does not set out the judge's reasons.

There is a significant body of case law in America, Canada and New Zealand on the ability of a pay when paid clause to withstand the employer's insolvency. Broadly speaking, in America there are two opposing lines of authority for and against the validity of pay when paid clauses (Hill and Evans, 1998). The courts of Canada have tended to validate them as conditions precedent to payment, unless non-payment has been caused by a default of the contractor: *Timbro Developments* v *Grimsby Diesel* (1988) 32 CLR 32. The courts of New Zealand have tended to invalidate pay when paid clauses. The main issue is whether the restriction imposed by the clause is intended to be temporal (pay when paid) or structural (pay if paid): *e.g. Smith and Smith Glass* v *Winstone* [1992] 2 NZLR 473, which concerned a claim by a sub-sub-contractor after the contractor had gone into receivership. The sub-sub-contract was in similar terms to the FCEC sub-contract. It was held that to be effective against the contractor's insolvency, the pay when paid clause would have to be a condition precedent, rather than an ordinary term of payment, but the words used were not strong enough to support such a construction.

Condition precedent

A condition precedent is a term which suspends an obligation pending fulfilment of a condition. If a term is a condition precedent, the court will examine it carefully as to its intended effect. One of the main functions of construction contracts is to allocate risks between the parties and there is no reason in principle why the risk of employer insolvency should be allocated to the contractor alone. Even with a pay when paid clause the contractor will suffer loss in that its own proportion of the monthly certificate will be lost. Such a term spreads the risk between contractor and sub-contractor. The court will normally presume that it was not the intention of the parties that either should be entitled to rely on its own breach in order to avoid the contract or obtain a benefit under it. Thus, if the pay when paid clause contains a condition precedent, the term may be construed so as to render the contractor liable to pay if fulfilment of the condition precedent has been made impossible by its conduct. Default of this kind could be mis-management under a management contract, failure to enforce payment by the employer where the employer could pay but chooses not to or perhaps a failure by the contractor to prove in the liquidation of an employer. It is a well established legal principle that a person cannot rely on his own wrong.

It is not uncommon for a sub-contractor to discuss a contractor's pay when paid clause when negotiating the sub-contract. If the sub-contractor protests and asks for it to be deleted but the contractor asks that it should remain and assures the sub-contractor that it will not be used against it, the contractor's promise may give rise to a collateral contract from which the contractor may not be allowed to withdraw: *City of Westminster Properties* v *Mudd* [1959] Ch 129. This principle highlights the importance to sub-contractors of registering a protest at tender stage in case the contractor induces it to enter into the sub-contract by means of such a promise. In the case of ambiguity, the court has much wider scope for investigating the background to the contract and can take into account other factors, such as the nature of the contract, the normal allocation of risk in the industry and the state of the market in which the contracting parties are involved. Where the contract containing the pay when paid clause is a standard form, there will be no presumption either for or against the construction contended for by either party: *Tersons* v *Stevenage Development Corporation* [1963] 2 Lloyd's Rep 333 at 368. Where it is the contractor's own form, however, it will be construed more strongly against the contractor: *John Lee* v *Railway Executive* [1949] 2 All ER 581 at 583.

Where it can be established that the sub-contractor made enquiries of the employer's financial position but still entered into the sub-contract, the court may be more readily satisfied that the sub-contractor assumed the risk of employer insolvency. The same may be the case where the sub-contractor obtained credit risk insurance or was aware of the owner's financial state from previous dealings or the financial or construction press. The position is stronger still where the employer entered into the main contract after having entered one of the recognised insolvency procedures: *Stanley Brown* v *Maryland Casualty*, 442 SW 2d 187 (1969). Consider the position where the contractor is in administration and the administrator is seeking new contracts or where a receiver is continuing to trade while seeking purchasers for the business. In *Davies* v *William Old* (1969) 113 SJ 262, the court considered that sub-contractors would be bound if they entered into a sub-contract knowingly, voluntarily and on more or less equal terms.

This case preceded the Unfair Contract Terms Act 1977 but the Act is unlikely to have affected the position (Keating 1983). The terms of s 113 Housing Grants, Construction and Regeneration Act 1996 now make it strongly arguable that a pay when paid clause operating on the employer's insolvency cannot be an unfair contract term. This section is considered below.

Where the evidence is that the sub-contractor is in default, an American court has allowed a contractor to rely on a pay when paid clause, at least to prevent summary judgment: *Nicholas Acoustics v H & M Construction*, 695 F 2d 839 (1983). Where the only issue was a dispute between contractor and employer, which does not concern the sub-contractor's work, the court awarded summary judgment to the sub-contractor: *Midland Engineering v John Hall*, 398 F Supp 981 (1975). If the contractor has not been paid because the employer has set off liquidated damages against a sum due under an interim certificate, can the contractor still defend itself by relying on the pay when paid clause? There is very limited authority on this point. In two Hong Kong decisions, the court held in favour of the contractor although both were summary judgment applications and the issues were not fully argued: *Hong Kong Teakwood v Shui On* [1984] HKLR 235, *Schindler Lifts v Shui On* (1984) 29 BLR 95. In a Singapore case, the judge considered the point was "highly arguable" but again stayed the action to arbitration: *Brightside v Hyundai* (1988) 41 BLR 110. There appear to be two main issues raised by these cases which might be resolved as follows:

1. If the contractor is innocent, payment can be made by means of contractual set-off under the main contract, although not by legal or equitable set-off (see Wood 1989, 725-727, Goode 1988, 147-148, Halsbury 42/410, Goode 1983);

2. If the liquidated damages were deducted through a default by the contractor, the sub-contractor ought to succeed, otherwise the contractor would be relying on its own wrong. Receipt of a dividend in the liquidation of the employer would not constitute payment to the contractor for the purposes of a pay when paid clause.

The effect of section 113

Section 113(1) provides that pay when paid clauses will now be effective only on insolvency. It states:

"A provision making payment under a construction contract conditional on the payer receiving payment from a third person is ineffective, unless that third person, or any other person payment by whom is under the contract (directly or indirectly) a condition of payment by that third person, is insolvent."

The definition of insolvency for companies in s 113(2) is limited to formal insolvency events, *e.g.* an administration order, the appointment of a receiver and a resolution or an order for winding-up. It does not include informal insolvency or voluntary arrangements or compositions with creditors. This omission can lead to an anomaly. If the employer enters administration, the contractor can rely on a pay when paid clause as a complete defence to proceedings brought by sub-contractors. One of the purposes of the administration might be to facilitate a voluntary arrangement. If that purpose is successful, and the employer proposes an arrangement, could the contractor lose the protection of the pay when paid clause? If so, the contractor may well vote against the arrangement. Perhaps this situation could arise where only the contractor's employment has been terminated and the sub-contracts remain in being. Even if the operation of s 113 is "once and for all", it may encourage a contractor to seek the employer's formal insolvency when previously it may not have done so.

Contractors will have to take a policy decision whether or not to include a pay when paid clause in their sub-contracts. If they wish to do so, it is essential that they draft their own clause and make sure it is properly incorporated. This is because there is no pay when paid clause in the Scheme. One potential difficulty with the Act is that it appears to require that the formal insolvency event occurs before the payment date. If it occurs after the payment date, then the contractor is liable to make the payment without set-off or abatement even though the contractor's cheque would simply be cashed by the contractor's insolvency practitioner. One solution to this problem, at least when a contractor is aware of an employer's impending insolvency, is to defer the payment date by serving a withholding notice, inviting the sub-contractor to refer the dispute to adjudication. Under s 111(4) where a dispute has been referred to adjudication and the adjudicator decides in favour of the sub-contractor, the payment becomes due seven days after the decision or after the date which, apart from the withholding notice, would have been the payment date, whichever is the later. In most cases, it is likely that the payment will be due seven days after the adjudicator's decision.

This is not necessarily the end of the story for contractors. The Act does not resolve other difficulties with pay when paid clauses created by ambiguous or confusing drafting. Reference will still have to be made to the principles to be derived from the cases (McCosker 1995). It is not the intention of the Act that s 113 should strike down legitimate agreements for deferred payment. Payment may depend in practice on contingencies other than receipt of payment from a party up the line. Consider the following examples:

- a PFI contract in which no payment is to be made without specific consents from funders
- a contract funded by lottery money where the procedures require a number of compliances before funding can be released
- a secured payment contract where payment is deferred until a particular stage or until completion
- asub-contract under which payment to sub-contractors is conditional on the issue of a completion certificate under the main contract
- a sub-contract with conditions of payment to sub-contractors such as a certificate from the main contractor or a certificate from the employer under the main contract which the contractor could make a condition precedent under the sub-contract
- a sub-contract with strict contractual deadlines for submission of applications for payment, in default of which payment will be deferred until the following period
- a sub-contract with a requirement for a certain level of detail for a valid payment application.

Whether or not devices like these would comply with the payment provisions of s 110 or 113 of the Act will have to be decided by an adjudicator. In common with their approach to other legislation whose provisions have been more in the nature of a framework than a detailed statement of the law, such as the Insolvency Act 1986, tribunals can be expected to give the Act a purposive interpretation. In other words, tribunals will regard it as their duty to observe the spirit of the legislation and not be distracted by obstructive, technical or pedantic arguments.

The FCEC sub-contract now contains a pay when paid clause which conforms with s 113. DOM/1 was amended to include an insolvency pay when paid clause (Amendment 10), but a subsequent re-issue of the form published in 1998 omitted this clause. The intention is therefore that the contractor bears the risk of the employer's insolvency, although the loss claimable by the sub-contractor from the contractor in that event still excludes loss of profit.

Book debts

"The question of what is a book debt has regrettably remained one of those mysteries of company law" (Oditah 1991 at 23). Whether a debt is a book debt is a mixed question of law and accounting practice. A book debt is a debt arising in the course of a business which is normally entered in the books of a business of that description whether actually entered or not: *Shipley* v *Marshall* (1863) 14 CB (NS) 566. Classification depends on the accounting treatment given to the industry concerned and the activity undertaken in that industry. The definition of a book debt is capable of changing from time to time. In the case of contingency contracts such as insurance policies or surety bonds, receivables will not be book debts in view of uncertainty whether they will arise or not: *Paul & Frank* v *Discount Bank* [1967] Ch 348. If the contract is not contingent, such as a building contract, a debt could be a book debt even though the right to payment could not arise until sometime in the future: *Independent Automatic Sales* v *Knowles & Foster* [1962] 3 All ER 27. In that case, the court defined a book debt as "a debt arising in the course of the business and due or growing due to the proprietor of that business". It was seen earlier that "growing due" has been construed in several different ways, *e.g.* in a different context, the Court of Appeal construed the phrase as "something that in the course of the trade or business will ripen into a debt, although not a debt, and only in an inchoate state at the commencement of the bankruptcy": *Blakey* v *Trustees of Property of Pendlebury* [1931] 2 Ch 255 at 264.

Cases in the construction industry have not yielded a clear or comprehensive test. Even if the receivable is a book debt, it may have been the subject of an outright assignment rather than a charge. In one case, a contractor resolved that one of its shareholders should complete outstanding contracts and receive 50% of any resulting profits. It was held that the arrangement was an equitable assignment of the profits: *Re Lawson Constructions* [1942] SASR 201. In another case, it was held that debts arising under road construction contracts undertaken by a person whose normal business was that of a storekeeper were not book debts because they did not arise out of that person's normal business: *Robertson v Grigg* (1932) 47 CLR 257. The authorities were reviewed in *Contemporary Cottages v Margin Traders* [1981] 2 NZLR 114. A contractor carried on the business of selling and erecting prefabricated cottages. Having obtained a contract to build a cottage, it manufactured units for assembly and sub-contracted the construction of the units on site. The benefit of each contract was assigned to a finance company as security for loans and notice of assignment was given to each employer. Assignments were generally made before commencement of construction and in all cases before completion. Under some of the contracts the price was payable by way of:

- a small deposit
- the balance of the purchase price save a small retention within 14 days of notice that the package was ready for delivery
- the balance within seven days after completion.

It was held that all categories were book debts.

What of contractors' claims? In *Re National Westminster Finance* [1991] 1 Qd R 130, the court considered a construction company whose main business "was the construction of home units and commercial buildings for sale". The case concerned the status of money held in the company's solicitor's account in respect of damages recovered from defaulting purchasers who had agreed to buy building units. It was held that:

> "When received by the present solicitors, the relevant amounts of damages took on the character of debts due to the company, because, subject to clause 3 of the agreement they were the company's money and held by the present solicitors on the company's behalf ... The evidence shows that these amounts were due to the company on account of or in connection with its construction business, so that they should be regarded as 'book debts' of the company falling within the scope of the above statutory definition."

It has also been held that money received where a claim is compromised constitutes a book debt since the original obligation did not disappear but was transformed by the compromise into an obligation to pay a lesser sum: *Perrins v State Bank of Victoria* [1991] 1 VR 749 at 756. It is also possible that a book debt will arise under a nominated sub-contract as soon as an award is issued under a main contract arbitration which identifies sums in respect of measured work and loss and expense claimed by the sub-contractor: *Birse Construction* v *Co-Operative Wholesale Society* (1997) 84 BLR 58.

Before a claim has been settled or converted into a judgment or an award, its status is less clear. An argument could be constructed that "loss and expense" and "finance charges" under a JCT form or "costs" under an ICE form are debts in the sense that they are earned by performance under the express terms of the contract. The contractor might routinely enter amounts for such items in a "claims ledger" before they have been ascertained. It is possible that they are all debts "growing due" to the contractor and, in view of their accounting treatment in the contractor's records, are properly regarded as book debts, but this would depend on the court taking a relaxed view on the question of ascertainability.

In summary, it seems likely that construction book debts will not be limited to sums certified for payment. Sums invoiced by the contractor under contracts with different payment structures could be book debts provided the payment event giving rise to the invoice had occurred. Its conditionality and defeasibility gives retention a different quality but it is strongly arguable that it is a book debt even before being certified for release. Conditionality is not the same as contingency: retention is sufficiently certain to be a debt: only its recoverability is uncertain until after completion. An agreed final account could be a book debt even though the contract makes a certificate a condition of payment. It appears the same will apply to loss and expense and finance charges under the JCT forms and costs under the ICE forms.

Remedies for non-payment

Adjudication

If the employer fails to pay, and does not serve a withholding notice in the time limit, the contractor can refer the dispute to adjudication. An adjudicator's decision can give rise to a debt. This can be enforced by an application to the court (provided there is no arbitration clause in the contract or the enforcement of the adjudicator's decision has been excluded from his jurisdiction), or by an arbitrator, although in that event the arbitrator's award has to be enforced by the court. The beneficiary of the decision may also serve a statutory demand under s 123 Insolvency Act 1986 on the payer or issue a winding-up petition. Once the adjudicator's decision has been converted into a judgment, the creditor will have access to all the usual remedies: execution against the debtor's property, charging orders over land and shares, garnishee orders against money due or to become due to the debtor, and the right to have the debtor orally examined before the court.

Suspension

A failure to pay a debt which is due and payable is not likely to be a repudiation of the contract: *Decro-Wall International* v *Practitioners in Marketing* [1971] 2 All ER 216 at 227. The law appears to discriminate in favour of the payer in this situation. Unlike civil law jurisdictions, the common law does not recognise any right in the payee to take equivalent action by suspending work: *Canterbury Pipelines* v *Christchurch Drainage Board* (1979) 16 BLR 76. The contractor unsuccessfully attempted to rely on the civil law concept of exceptio at first instance in *Channel Tunnel Group* v *Balfour Beatty* (unreported, 27 November 1991) on the ground that, unusually, the proper law of the contract was stated to be the common principles of English and French law.

Non-payment was held to be a repudiation by the employer in the Australian case of *Alucraft* v *Growcon* (1995) 11 BCL 20. Where a contractor terminated the contract for non-payment, an employer was still entitled to make a call under an on demand bond in respect of unliquidated damages arising from breaches by the contractor before the termination: *Geraldton Building* v *Christmas Island* (1995) 11 BCL 23.

Section 112 Housing Grants, Construction and Regeneration Act 1996 introduced a right of suspension for non-payment to construction contracts. The right to serve a suspension notice only arises where there has been no effective withholding notice served by the paying party. "Effectiveness" means formal compliance with s 111, so the notice will be effective provided it states the amount and the grounds for withholding payment even if it is later found by the adjudicator that the withholding was wrongful. This could be a significant drawback to suspension. The JCT main contract forms now have a contractual right to suspend work. This is in addition to the statutory right under s 112 of the Act. The ICE form does not provide for contractual suspension, leaving it to the Act to provide this right.

At least seven days' notice of intention to suspend has to be given. The Scheme does not (and cannot) alter this period. Despite extensive lobbying by industry bodies, neither the Department of the

Environment nor the draftsman of the Bill was able to grasp the concept that delay caused by a suspension could be much greater (or even less than) the period of suspension itself. Section 112(4) may well give rise to problems in practice and cannot be relied on as giving sufficient protection for a contractor or sub-contractor operating the suspension procedure.

It has been argued that the new statutory right of suspension "might provide the raw framework which could lead to a conclusion of a contractor's acceptance of an anticipatory repudiation by the employer in non-payment circumstances" (Lyndon 1996). Statutory suspension is a novel idea for an English contract. It is possible that non-payment of one instalment could, as well as being an actual breach, also be an anticipatory breach of the duty to pay future instalments, but it is hard to see how the exercise of a right of suspension of work under a contract could ever amount to an acceptance of repudiation.

Interest

Interest is often a large part of a contractor's claim. It is one way of describing the cost of financing additional working capital to resource additional work required by, for example, variations or delay caused by the employer. Depending on the method adopted, this cost could be claimed as interest, finance charges or damages. There are five variables of a claim for interest: the rate, the period, the subject of the claim, whether the interest represents an actual or notional loss and whether simple or compound interest can be claimed.

Interest is recoverable under a contract, by statute or in equity. The level of recovery varies depending on the nature of the claim. Interest can be recovered contractually by means of an express term or as special damages for breach. The express term may entitle the contractor to simple interest for late payment at a specified rate. For example, JCT 98 now provides for interest at 5% above base on unpaid certificates. The contractor may also be able to claim interest under an express term allowing it to recover additional amounts in respect of "direct loss and/or expense" under the JCT forms: *Minter* v *WHTSO* (1980) 13 BLR 1. In this context, interest is referred to as "finance charges". Interest may also be recovered as "costs" under ICE (5th edition). It is not clear whether this word limits a contractor's claim to interest actually paid as a cost of borrowing additional capital or whether it would also extend to interest lost on capital which could not be invested. Under the ICE (6th edition), the definition of costs has been widened to include finance provided it is "expenditure properly incurred".

English law does not recognise a claim for interest as general damages for breach of contract. Interest can be recovered as special damages if they represent a loss reasonably in the contemplation of the parties as a probable result of the breach at the time they made the contract: *Wadsworth* v *Lydall* [1981] 2 All ER 401. The contractor would have to show that the employer had knowledge of circumstances from which it was reasonable to infer that delay in payment would lead to the loss being claimed. Only simple interest is recoverable: *President of India* v *La Pintada* [1985] AC 104 at 120.

Interest can be claimed under three statutes: during the contract, as part of litigation or after judgment. Under the Late Payment of Commercial Debts (Interest) Act 1998, a contractor or sub-contractor with fewer than 50 employees trading with another business or a local authority can claim simple interest at 8% above the official dealing rate of the Bank of England from the date a payment becomes due. By s.5, the rate and period can be reduced in the interests of justice as a result of the conduct of the payee. This might apply where the payee caused the delay by failing to provide appropriate information or by failing to provide goods or services in accordance with the contract entitling the creditor to abatement. The Act is intended to be extended to all businesses in due course.

The court has power to award simple interest under s 35A Supreme Court Act 1981. In practice, the court normally exercises its discretion in favour of a successful litigant wherever the breach has deprived it of an opportunity to put the subject-matter of the claim to work to earn profits or income, and awards interest from an appropriate time depending on the facts of the case. Where the claim is for an unpaid debt, interest will be payable from the day on which the debt became due and payable. Where the claim is for damages, interest will be payable from the date of the cause of action, which usually means the date of the breach. The court has a discretion to order interest to run from a later date where it is satisfied that the plaintiff has unreasonably delayed in bringing his claim. In both cases interest is payable until the day on which judgment is entered. Where a claim for debt or damages is paid before proceedings are issued, the court has no jurisdiction to make an award of interest: *IM Properties* v *Cape & Dalgleish* [1998] 3 All ER 203. This is one reason why it is in the contractor's interests to issue proceedings without undue delay. The court will not make an award of interest where it has accepted a claim for interest or financing charges brought under the contract. There is no requirement to prove the loss actually suffered. The rate of interest to be awarded under the Act is within the court's discretion. The court will adopt the rate of interest which would have been payable by a person in the commercial position of the plaintiff, rather than the interest actually paid. There are three possible rates:

- the Judgments Act rate of 8%
- the commercial rate of 1% above LIBOR
- a higher rate than 1% above LIBOR if justified in all the circumstances. Under the Judgments Act 1838, interest at 8% per annum is added to judgment debts until payment.

The court also has an equitable power to award interest, *e.g.* in cases of fraud or where the plaintiff is claiming an equitable remedy or has a fiduciary relationship with the defendant. Examples of a fiduciary relationship are trust, agency and partnership. In this kind of case, the court is sometimes prepared to award compound interest: compare *Westdeutsche* v *Islington BC* [1996] 2 WLR 802.

Defences to interest claims

A debtor may defend a claim to interest on a number of grounds.

1. It has a substantive defence to the claim in respect of which the claim for interest is ancillary, *e.g.* that the contractor incurred additional working capital through its own default, inefficient methods of working, underbidding etc.

2. The creditor failed to comply with procedural requirements: whether notices are a pre-condition to the recovery of interest depends on the type of claim chosen. If a claim for financing charges is part of a variations claim then whatever contract procedure has to be followed for the variation would also have to be followed for the interest element. A right to special damages depends on proof of loss rather than contemporary notification of it. The court will usually exercise its discretion to award statutory interest from the date of the cause of action but could adopt a later date if it considered that notice of the claim should have been given.

3. The interest was included in the contract sum or the parties excluded rights to interest or finance charges.

4. The claim for interest fails through the exercise of set-off or deduction rights.

5. The creditor has failed to satisfy a condition precedent to payment in the contract, *e.g.* prior approval before engaging reimbursable personnel, the agreement of measurement and pricing of milestones, the contractor's obligations to issue invoices with supporting documents, make applications for payment, make submissions in respect of claims for new/changes in legislation, give notices and proper records in respect of variation claims.

6. It is also possible that the employer will argue that, where its liability is limited by a financial cap, the cap will include any potential liability for interest.

7. The employer may alternatively have an express right of withholding or it may argue that the contractor has failed to mitigate its loss.

Security for costs

Under s 726 Companies Act 1985, the court has jurisdiction to order a plaintiff to provide security for a defendant's costs if there is reason to believe that the plaintiff will be unable to pay them if the defendant is successful. The court then has a discretion whether or not to order security. In *Europa Holdings* v *Circle Industries* (1992) 33 Con LR 34, the claim represented work done at Canary Wharf. There was no system of certification. Instead, the contractor valued the sub-contractor's work, passed the valuation to the contract administrator for approval, and then paid it after deducting retention. The claim was for a valuation previously approved and for extra work done since then which had been valued by the sub-contractor. The claim was disputed on the ground that it represented work actually carried out by the contractor and that the sub-contractor had already been overpaid. The court predicted "an extremely expensive action" and considered that if the plaintiff were asked to pay the defendant's costs immediately, it would not be able to do so. On the facts, retention could not be included as an asset in the defendant's accounts and there was no evidence of on-going work. The court therefore had jurisdiction but declined to exercise it as to order security would be oppressive and stifle a genuine claim.

The relevant factors were:

1. The company was solvent before bringing into account a prospective order for costs against it.

2. It was apparently well and prudently managed.

3. It had a genuine claim which was founded in part on the contractor's own valuation.

4. "There are few small but well-managed companies in the construction industry which would have resources to meet the costs of both sides in unsuccessful litigation before an official referee" (at 40).

5. The abandonment of the claim would mean that that the company would have to close down and begin the business again.

6. If security were ordered, it would not be sufficiently high to give the defendant much protection.

If security is ordered but cannot be paid, the plaintiff may assign the claim to allow it to be pursued by someone else. In a spate of cases in the 1990s, the assignment was made to one of the directors who tried to avoid the security problem by obtaining legal aid.

In *Advanced Technology* v *Cray* (1992) 63 BLR 59, a company was able to put up security but unable to fund the action further. It assigned the claim on the basis that it would take two-thirds of the proceeds and the assignee one-third. The assignee obtained legal aid subject to the outcome of an application to the court to join him as an additional plaintiff. The application failed as the court regarded the assignment as a sham, a device to overcome the company's inability to fund the action. The assignment provided for deemed re-assignment if the claim were not pursued. The court held that the assignment was absolute for the purposes of s 136 Law of Property Act 1925.

One relevant factor is whether the issues the court would have to consider on the counterclaim are the same as those raised by the claim. In one case the court refused security for costs of the claim for this reason: *Crabtree* v *GPT Communication Systems* (1990) 59 BLR 43.

Conclusion

As might be expected in an industry in which cash flow is of paramount importance, payment issues have become extraordinarily subtle and complex. So much so that one of the main roles of a construction lawyer is to help clients recover money or resist claims for money made against them. Perhaps this also reflects the mercurial nature of money itself and its ability to reflect the attitudes of contract parties towards each other and to the project itself. This aspect is taken further in Chapter 18.

Perhaps in no other context has the court shown greater respect for the facts. While adopting a basic definition of a debt as a claim for money which is ascertained or easily ascertainable and recoverable by action, the law seems content with apparently contradictory applications of the definition so as to deal fairly in any given situation. In this the law shows its imagination, to the frustration of all in search of a "yes" or "no" answer.

Chapter 4

· **Plant and Materials** ·

Introduction

Plant and materials are tangible property and attract different legal principles from receivables. The fundamental issue concerning plant and equipment is how far a contract can ensure its availability until final completion by contractual, proprietary or security rights. Any consideration of goods and materials raises two fundamental differences between construction and other contracts: the rule that anything attached to the land becomes part of it and the sophisticated standard forms which attempt to regulate passing of title up the contract chain.

The approach taken today is derived from 19th century building leases and contracts for construction of the railways and other major projects. These contained clauses vesting plant and materials brought to site in the employer but, as will be seen, their commercial function has since changed. On the contractor's insolvency, its tangible property becomes a magnet for unpaid suppliers, the employer and execution creditors.

Plant and equipment risk

The standard forms allow the employer to seize, use and sometimes sell the contractor's plant and equipment after termination. Some engineering contracts vest the contractor's plant and equipment in the employer on its delivery to site. The purpose of these provisions can best be understood by looking at the historical background. Under building lease agreements, employers in the 19th century bought the materials themselves or made advance payments to builders to pay their suppliers. In *Blake* v *Izard* (1867) 16 WR 108 Counsel for the employer submitted that:

> "the lessors now very often sell the materials to the builders, and advance so largely on the works as they progress that builders without any capital accept large contracts, and become virtually merely the foremen of the

lessors. In this case, the materials were originally nearly all the property of the lessors, and the lessors would, without such an agreement as this, have no security for the value of their materials until they were used on the land, and so became part and parcel of the freehold. The builder having no capital to purchase them with, is, by giving this security to the landlord, enabled to get everything that he wants, either directly from the landlord, or by the otherwise unsecured pecuniary advances of the landlord from tradesmen who are paid with the landlord's money."

Having provided or paid for materials, it was only reasonable that ownership should vest in the employer on their delivery to site. This protected the employer against claims by the builder's creditors or his trustee in bankruptcy, unless the trustee could prove that the materials had remained in the reputed ownership of the builder, a concept abolished by s 235 Insolvency Act 1985.

From quite early on, contracts included plant and equipment on site within the scope of these clauses. Perhaps the employer also provided the plant (*e.g. Banbury* v *Daniel* (1884) 54 LJ Ch 265, a railway contract under which the contractor was paid 75% of the value of the plant in advance) or simply sought more security by "belt and braces" drafting. Whatever their original function, vesting clauses have gradually disappeared from building contracts. Instead contractors agree not to remove materials from site without the architect's consent. This change may have occurred through the emergence and increasing financial strength of main contractors, the growing use of sub-contractors or the replacement of building lease agreements by other forms of contract. At any rate, Alfred Hudson did not include vesting clauses in the precedents in his book published in 1891. Although they have been dropped from building contracts, they have remained in contracts for engineering work. Their commercial function has obviously changed, but what is it now?

There are specific risks associated with plant and equipment. These will vary depending on whether the items in question are intended to become part of the works or are just the means of constructing them. The standard forms now make a distinction between plant and equipment: see clauses 1 and 53 of ICE (5th edition), clause 1.1(f) of FIDIC (4th edition), clauses 1.1, 37, 38 and 49 of MF/1. They use "plant" when referring to a structure fixed to the land as part of the permanent works *e.g.* a chemical plant or a mechanical handling plant. "Equipment" is used in two senses: items intended to be fixed to the land but only as temporary works, *e.g.* sheet piling or a tower crane; and a range of items from hand tools at one end of the spectrum to a tunnel boring machine at the other. Part 2 of FIDIC (4th edition) gives the example of a dredger for reclamation work whose capital value might exceed the contract sum. The distinction between plant and equipment is comparatively new, however, and this chapter concerns anything in the nature of plant and equipment which is not intended for the permanent works.

Plant and equipment is more diverse in engineering than in building work. It is more likely to be specifically designed for the works. The main risk attaching to it is lack of availability to meet the contractor's programme. This might be caused by periods of high activity in the industry when suppliers cannot meet the demand for specific plant, problems in the design or manufacture of the plant leading to delays in replacement, the contractor diverting the plant to other contracts, the contractor defaulting in payment to leasing companies leading to repossession and claims by the contractor's creditors. It may well be that vesting clauses have survived in engineering contracts owing to the employer's belief, perhaps mistaken, that they could help manage these "availability risks". Removal of materials from site can be an early warning sign of a contractor's impending insolvency. Vesting clauses also have a general function as indirect financial protection against the contractor's insolvency.

Rights against plant

Contractual rights

It is useful to consider the employer's rights against the contractor's plant under three headings: contract, property and security.

Before a termination, the employer's rights under the standard forms are personal against the contractor but afterwards they are also possessory and proprietary against the contractor's plant. Several issues arise.

1. Does the employer have an adequate remedy should the contractor remove plant from site before termination? Removal would be a breach of contract but not a termination event allowing the employer access to post-termination rights. The employer may not want to terminate. Even if the breach were repudiatory, the employer may not want to accept the repudiation. It may just want the contractor to return the plant.

2. Specific performance would not be available if the court thought damages would be an adequate remedy or if the obligation to return the plant was one requiring the court's supervision.

3. Will the rights reserved after termination be enforceable if the termination is for insolvency? Some might be invalidated by the *pari passu* rule if liquidation or bankruptcy were the termination events. The employer has therefore tried to improve its position by obtaining property interests in the contractor's plant at the inception of the contract.

Proprietary rights

The employer has various options. Does it want to own the contractor's plant outright or to obtain some lesser right in it? Is the proprietary interest intended to be permanent or for a specific period? Unfortunately, the language used in contracts has been highly ambiguous. The courts have also had to construe subtly different wording and for different purposes, for example, questions whether building lease agreements were registrable as bills of sale, whether plant fell within with the "reputed ownership" of a bankrupt or whether the employer had a property interest sufficient to defeat claims by the contractor's creditors or his trustee in bankruptcy. These issues have generated a substantial body of case law some of which is inconsistent and unsatisfactory (summarised in Wallace 1995). Nevertheless, out of these conflicts between landowners, chattel mortgagees, execution creditors and bankruptcy trustees, it is possible to see a pattern emerging.

The employer has three options when drawing up the contract: (1) include a vesting clause but do not refer to plant in the termination clause, (2) omit a vesting clause but reserve wide powers to seize, use and sell the plant on termination, and (3) include both a vesting clause and wide powers on termination.

If the employer chooses (1), the issue for the court will be whether the employer has acquired a property right in the plant and if so of what kind. With (2), the issue is whether the express powers are both adequate to enable the employer to do what it wishes and enforceable against the contractor and strangers to the contract. If the employer selects (3), the court will have to construe the two clauses and, if they are ambiguous, decide which should take precedence. If one is ineffective, will the other give the employer sufficient protection?

If the contract says that title passes to the employer on delivery to the site, the employer will acquire unlimited ownership rights to the contractor's plant. For example, in *Goodman* v *Napier Harbour Board* [1939] NZLR 97 the employer determined the contract on grounds not associated with insolvency and seized and sold the contractor's plant. The contract contained a vesting clause which said that:

> "All plant and material delivered or brought on to the works for the purpose of being used or employed in or about the same shall be the absolute property of the board in like manner as though they had been legally vested in the board by absolute assignment ...".

The clause also restricted the removal of plant during the contract and prevented any assignment or other dealing with the plant without the engineer's consent. The termination clause provided that the plant should become the absolute property of the board without making any payment for it. The court was impressed by the clarity of the vesting clause. The effect of the termination clause was merely that the board was allowed to keep its own property.

Bennett and White v *Municipal District of Sugar City* [1951] AC 786, on appeal from the Supreme Court of Canada, is a similar case. The contractor had been assessed for tax on plant and equipment used on a government contract. Tax was payable on items owned by or in the legal possession of the contractor. The contract provided:

> "15. All machinery, tools, plant, materials, equipment, articles and things whatsoever, provided by the Contractor shall from the time of there being so provided become, and, until the final completion of the said work, shall be the property of His Majesty ...".

Lord Reid construed these words literally so as to pass ownership to the employer on delivery to site. There was then "a notional or actual bailment or redelivery of possession to the builders for the purpose of carrying out the building contract" (at 815), so the contractor remained in legal possession. Both employer and contractor had legal interests in the plant, the former derived from an absolute title, the latter from possession (Goode 1995, at 39).

It was put to the court that, as the contractor did not have exclusive control over the plant, in view of the engineer's powers, it could not have legal possession. This argument was rejected as it "would seem to confuse control of operations with control of the physical instruments by which the operations are to be carried out. These may well be in different persons" (at 815). The inference is that the contractor did not lose control over the plant: it was simply subject to operational decisions by the engineer. Alternatively, it could perhaps have been held that the plant was in the joint possession of contractor and employer (Goode 1995 at 48). In the end, the contractor escaped liability for tax on other grounds.

If the contract is allusive and "deems" the employer to be the owner or says the employer is to "be considered" as the owner for the purposes of the contract, the court will regard the contract as ambiguous and enquire further: *Re Cosslett (Contractors) Ltd* [1997] 4 All ER 115.

1. If the court concludes that the contractor intended to transfer an equitable interest, it will so hold: *Brown* v *Bateman* (1867) LR 2 CP 272, which concerned materials which were deemed by the terms of a building lease to be attached to the land on delivery. Lord Reid's reference to bailment in *Bennett and White* suggests the employer had the general property in the plant and the contractor the special property. Jonathan Parker J, reasoning on similar lines at first instance in *Cosslett* where the wording was different, thought the employer had the special property.

2. Otherwise, the court will not give effect to the provision, leaving it to the employer to rely on any protection given by a termination clause: *Re Keen and Keen, ex parte Collins* [1902] 1 KB 555. Similarly, if there is no vesting clause, there can be no transfer of ownership or any lesser right before termination.

Security interests

Instead of obtaining a property interest, an employer has tried to reinforce its contract rights by obtaining a security interest in the contractor's plant. The employer: (1) identifies the liability of the contractor to be secured, (2) chooses a recognised form of security, and (3) decides whether the security requires registration.

Security is the dedication of an asset owned by A to support a personal liability owed by A to B, so that if A fails to discharge the liability B can do so by realising the asset. The law relating to security, like assignment, was developed in the 19th century in cases on the liability for debt.

Vesting clauses originally reflected the fact that the employer had advanced money to the builder to pay for materials. The court has on occasion described vesting clauses as security for re-payment of the advances but this is not strictly accurate as the contractor discharges that liability by using the advances to buy the materials. After the replacement of the building lease by standard forms in which the builder received interim payments as the works progressed, the original purpose of vesting clauses was lost. Advance payments are now more likely to be secured by a bond. The only payment obligations owed by the contractor before termination are for general or liquidated damages or sums recoverable as a debt in respect of specific breaches. Vesting clauses are not expressly dedicated to these payment obligations; it seems more likely they are intended as security for the performance obligation not to remove the plant without authority. English law recognises four forms of security: mortgage, charge, lien and pledge (see Chapter 2). There is authority on each of these in the context of construction contracts, some of which is considered below in relation to vesting clauses.

Fixed charges

The court has construed vesting clauses as a fixed charge in only two cases: *Brown* v *Bateman* (1867) LR 2 CP 272 and *Hart* v *Porthgain* [1903] 1 Ch 690. Where the vesting clause is intended to operate as a security but the words used are not sufficiently clear to transfer ownership to the employer, it could take effect as an equitable charge or an equitable assignment by way of security. This appears to be the basis of the decision in *Hart* v *Porthgain* where a contract for the construction of a tidal harbour required the erection of a temporary dam to keep out the sea during the excavations. Before his bankruptcy, the contractor had completed the temporary works and mortgaged them to the employer together with plant and materials on site. In the event of the contractor's bankruptcy, the contract gave the employer the right to possession of the contractor's plant and materials and to complete the works using an alternative contractor. It also provided that:

"All such plant and materials shall be considered the property of the Company until the engineers shall have certified the completion of the contract, and no plant or materials shall be removed or taken away without the consent or order in writing of the engineers."

The judge decided that:

"In my opinion the true construction of the clause ... is that it vests the property in the materials in the Company at law subject to a condition that, when the engineer shall have certified the completion of the contract, the contractor shall be at liberty to remove them. ... Further if a man makes a contract under which he hands over his property to the person with whom he is contracting in such a way that it is to be treated as security for the due performance of the contract, and then he himself makes default in performing the contract, in my opinion it is not possible for him to say that he is entitled to recover such property when he is not able to show that he has performed his part of the contract ... In my opinion these clauses are put in for the purpose, not merely of enabling the contract to be performed, but also as a due security for its performance" (at 696).

In other words, the right to re-vesting on completion was an equity of redemption.

Contrast this decision with *Church* v *Sage* (1892) 67 LT 800 where a builder assigned the benefit of a building contract together with all plant and materials on site, or which were to be brought on site during the contract, as security for a loan from a third person. A creditor obtained judgment against the builder and levied execution on the plant and materials. The court accepted the execution creditor's argument that the assignment was invalid as an unregistered bill of sale. It was held that the assignment:

"is not an agreement between landowner and builder, but is a mere mortgage by a builder of his interest in a building agreement to a stranger to secure money advanced by the stranger to enable the builder to carry out the building agreement, and is subject to all the ordinary incidents of a mortgage. It purports to assign the plant and materials now or hereafter to be brought on the ground or adjoining thereto to the lender absolutely, subject to redemption, and authorises him in case the builder impairs the security by delay in building etc. to enter on the land and complete the buildings, and for that purpose to take possession of the land, and of all plant and materials thereon. In the absence of authority I should have thought that this was a legal assignment of the existing plant and materials, with a power to take possession, and as regards the future plant and materials, either an equitable assignment ... or an agreement whereby a right in equity to the chattels, or a charge or security upon them was created" (at 801).

Because of earlier decisions, the court distinguished between cases where lenders and employers took the benefit of the security. The basis of the distinction was that the employer was the landowner or landlord under a building lease agreement. Where the employer is not the landowner, *e.g.* a subsidiary of the landowner or a joint venture company, it seems that *Church* v *Sage* ought to apply where a construction contract uses a vesting clause. This is, however, not the case in view of *Reeves* v *Barlow* (1884) 12 QBD 436 considered later.

In *Re Keen & Keen, ex parte Collins* [1902] 1 KB 555, (a reputed ownership case), the contract was in essentially the same terms as in *Hart* v *Porthgain* but the court reached the opposite conclusion that the words were not sufficient to pass ownership to the employer. The court did not consider the security function of the vesting clause in the context of the contract as a whole. The court placed reliance on the restriction on removal of the plant from site during the contract as evidence that the parties did not intend to transfer ownership. The case was criticised in *Bennett & White* v *Municipal District of Sugar City* [1951] AC 786. Perhaps the decision can be explained on the basis that the clause took effect as a charge on the plant in favour of the employer.

By contrast to these decisions, *Young* v *Matthew Hall Mechanical & Electrical Engineers Pty Ltd* [1988] 13 ACLR 399 concerned an express charge contained in a termination clause in an engineering sub-sub-contract which had been terminated by the sub-contractor. A few weeks later a liquidator was appointed to the sub-sub-contractor (Nordtech) who claimed delivery up of certain plant and equipment in the possession of the sub-contractor (Matthew Hall) on the ground that the sub-sub-contract constituted an unregistered charge which was not binding on him pursuant to the Western Australian equivalent of s 395 Companies Act 1985. There was no clause vesting plant and equipment in Matthew Hall before termination but there was an extended termination clause entitling Matthew Hall to take possession of and use Nordtech's plant without any duty to pay rent for it.

> "19.5 … On the completion of such work all tools and equipment and the surplus of the materials so taken possession of shall be handed over to Nordtech but without payment or allowance for the fair wear and tear they may have sustained in the meantime, provided that, if there be a deficiency as referred to in this article, and if Nordtech fails to make

good such deficiency [they] may be sold and a sufficient part of the moneys received retained by Matthew Hall and applied in payment of such deficiency.

19.6 (a) If default is made by Nordtech and not remedied and Matthew Hall exercises all or any of the powers provided by art 19.3 then (to the full extent permitted by law and by Nordtech's existing contractual obligations to others): (i) Matthew Hall shall have and Nordtech hereby grants to Matthew Hall a charge over all construction equipment owned by Nordtech and the right to register bills of sale over such construction equipment; and (ii) Matthew Hall shall have the right to retain possession of all construction equipment owned by Nordtech and then situated on the work site for the purposes of ensuring the completion of the works pursuant to the powers granted to Matthew Hall in this art 19; (b) Nordtech acknowledges and agrees that construction equipment brought onto the work site for the purpose of the works is deemed to be in the possession of Matthew Hall for so long as it remains on the work site; and (c) Matthew Hall's rights pursuant to para (a) of this art 19.6 shall be extinguished with respect to any item of construction equipment if Matthew Hall gives written approval to Nordtech pursuant to art 6.6 of the sub-contract for any such item to be removed from the work site and in that event Matthew Hall will at the request and expense of Nordtech supply to Nordtech a Memorandum of Satisfaction of any bill of sale which Matthew Hall has registered over such item of construction equipment".

Matthew Hall conceded that the charge and the power of sale were void against the liquidator for lack of registration, but their argument that their rights of possession and use remained contractually enforceable was accepted by the court. These rights were not enough to confer a security interest in the plant. If anything, they amounted to a lien which would be lost if the employer lost possession of the plant. Since the charge could only come into effect on a termination, it was not registrable until that event happened. The terms of the sub-sub-contract in this case are radically different from the English cases. By the time the charge came into effect, the only liability it could secure was for any net deficiency. *Young's* case and the earlier law were reviewed by the Court of Appeal in *Re Cosslett (Contractors) Ltd*, considered below.

Floating charges

In *Cosslett* the contractor agreed with a local authority to provide among other things two coal washing plants designed to separate coal from shale to enable the local authority to sell off the coal and use the shale for purposes of land reclamation. It was estimated that the two plants would have to operate for at least four years before this process would be completed. The contract was the ICE (5th edition), amended so as to define the coal washing plants as "plant", *i.e.* they were to be treated as construction plant rather than temporary works. The plants in question were large and valuable. A year later, the contractor went into administration and left site following disputes with the employer. Administration was not a termination event under the contract. The engineer certified that the contractor had abandoned the site and it was then expelled under clause 63. The employer took possession of the two plants and sold them to the completion contractor.

In 1997, before the works had been finally completed, the administrator claimed delivery up or compensation under s 234 Insolvency Act 1986, The administrator failed at first instance and in the Court of Appeal, but on different grounds. Jonathan Parker J construed the contract as a whole and found the employer had obtained a fixed charge over the plant: [1996] 3 WLR 299. The Court of Appeal held the employer's pre-termination rights and post-termination rights of possession and use to be merely contractual but construed the power of sale exercisable after termination as a floating charge: [1997] 4 All ER 115. The employer's rights before termination are set out in clause 53:

> "53(2) All plant, goods and materials owned by the Contractor or by any company in which the contractor has a controlling interest shall when on site be deemed to be the property of the Employer. The washing plant must be owned by the Contractor or by a company in which the Contractor has a controlling interest ... (6) No Plant (except hired Plant) goods or materials or any part thereof shall be removed from the Site without the written consent of the Engineer which consent shall not be unreasonably withheld where the same are no longer immediately required for the purposes of the completion of the Works but the Employer will permit the Contractor the exclusive use of all such Plant goods and materials in and for the completion of the Works until the occurrence of any event which gives the Employer the right to exclude the Contractor from the Site and proceed with the completion of the Works".

On termination, the employer becomes entitled to:

> "63(1) ... complete the Works and the Employer or such other contractor may use for such completion so much of the Constructional Plant Temporary Works goods and materials which have been deemed to become the property of the Employer ... [and] may at any time sell any of the said Constructional Plant Temporary Works and unused goods and

materials and apply the proceeds of sale in or towards the satisfaction of any sums due or which may become due to him from the Contractor under the contract ...".

Both the trial judge and the Court of Appeal agreed that clause 53 was not clear enough to give the employer a property right in the plant. The issue was whether the employer had obtained a contractual right or a security interest, and, if the latter, whether the security was enforceable against the contractor in administration. Viewing the contract as a whole, the trial judge concluded that Cosslett had given the employer a fixed equitable charge over the plant: fixed, in the light of the restrictions against removal in clause 53; equitable, in that the vesting provisions in clause 53 showed an intention to confer an interest in the plant short of legal ownership; and a charge, in view of the power of sale in clause 63 and the right to set off the proceeds against sums due or to become due to the contractor.

Construing the clauses separately, the Court of Appeal concluded that clause 53 was purely contractual whereas clause 63 conferred a floating charge over the plant securing the contractor's contingent duty to pay any final account deficiency. Before termination there was no liability a charge could secure since the court had found no debt owing by the contractor at that time. After termination, the charge could only secure a payment obligation as the contractor's duty to perform had been commuted to a potential liability to account. Although the floating charge had not been registered and was therefore unenforceable against the administrator, it did not taint the employer's other rights under clause 63 to take possession and use the plant for the purposes of a completion contract. As the works had not been completed by the time the proceedings were issued, the employer was still relying on the contractual rights which had not been affected by the administration order.

Commentary on the Cosslett case

Although at first sight an attractive analysis, the decision throws up a number of issues. Millett LJ relied on clause 53 when considering whether clause 63 created a fixed or a floating charge. Clause 53 defines "plant" for the purposes of the contract and is therefore the source for identifying the assets subject to the floating charge. The plant became subject to the charge only when brought on to site pursuant to clause 53. An essential aspect of the floating charge was that the contractor had the right to withdraw assets from the security before it crystallised. That right, albeit qualified by the engineer's powers, is only contained in clause 53. Clause 53 was integral to the court's decision. It seems odd to construe clause 53 on its own and hold it to be ineffective in law to create a property or security right while construing clause 63 in conjunction with clause 53 and holding clause 63 to contain a floating charge.

The finding that the security was a floating charge seems artificial on the facts of this case. The whole point of the contract was the provision of two coal washing plants and it was not the parties' intention that the contractor should be entitled, subject to the engineer's consent, to substitute other items for them. At the end of his judgment, Millett LJ said that he was in full agreement with the court in *Young* v *Matthew Hall*. This is strange given that:

1. The judge in that case found that rights to possession and use after termination amounted to a possessory lien, whereas Millett LJ expressly rejected any lien.

2. It appears the judge in *Young's* case thought the charge was fixed not floating, attaching to all plant in the contractor's ownership on the employer entering into possession following a default.

3. *Young's* case concerned a contract with no equivalent to clause 53 of the ICE form and some highly individual terms, including an express charge, in the termination clause.

The court could have given effect to clause 53 by construing it together with clause 63 as a fixed equitable charge securing performance of all obligations under the contract, whether arising before or after termination. If the contractor broke its specific obligation not to part with possession of plant before completion, the employer could not exercise its power of sale as that was postponed until after termination, but it could have applied to the court for specific performance of clause 53(6): compare *Napier and Ettrick* v *Hunter* [1993] 1 All ER 385 at 409. It would also have justified the engineer in witholding his consent to removal if there were, at the time the contractor made its request, circumstances making it likely that a termination event would occur. This view is consistent with the risk analysis referred to earlier. The court focused on the traditional purpose of the charge as a security for a debt. In this context, security for payment is a secondary purpose, the primary purpose being to ensure that plant is not removed from site.

Lien

In the *Cosslett* case Counsel for the employer argued that clauses 53
and 63 when taken together were a possessory lien with a power of
sale, relying on *Great Eastern Railway* v *Lord's Trustee* [1909]
AC 109. This was rejected on the ground that the employer's rights
against the plant were exclusively contractual and not derived from
any voluntary delivery of possession. It only obtained possession by
exercising an express right arising on the contractor's default which
was more in keeping with an equitable charge than a lien. This view
was followed in *Re Hamlet International* (unreported, 19 February
1998, noted in (1998) 2 BLM 1). It can be compared with *Crowfoot* v
London Dock Company (1834) 2 C&M 637 in which a contractor
went bankrupt before completing the contract. Retention was 25% of
the contract sum payable within one month after full completion. He
was to be paid under engineer's certificates issued every two months.
This was not enough to finance the work and the employer agreed to
make advances to the contractor in consideration of his agreement
that all the plant, equipment and materials on site and to be brought
to site should be a security for the advances. On the contractor's
bankruptcy, the employer marked the plant with its initials and used
it to complete the works. It emerged that the contractor had been
overpaid by £13,000. The plant was worth £5,000 and the
contractor's assignee sued the employer for its value. The assignee's
claim failed since the effect of the contractor's agreement was to give
the company a lien over the plant as security for its outstanding debt.
See also *Hawthorn* v *Newcastle upon Tyne Railway* (1840) 3 QB 734,
Re Waugh, ex parte Dickin (1876) 4 Ch D 524, *Byford* v *Russell*
[1907] 2 KB 522, *Egan* v *State Transport* (1982) 31 SASR 481.

Pledge

Professor Norman Palmer has argued that if the ICE form confers a
security it is as likely to be a pledge as anything else (Palmer 1996,
1997). The argument against this is that the contractor has possession
of the plant until the event arises which activates the employer's power
of sale. Professor Palmer suggests that the possessory element of the
pledge could be supplied by construing the employer's position before
termination as that of a bailee with special property in the plant (and
see earlier under "Proprietary rights"). Against this is the fact that
under clause 63 the employer's right to possession is expressly made

contingent on a termination. Further, the only clear delivery of possession was involuntary through the operation of the termination clause. Professor Palmer counters this by arguing that a pledge can arise where possession of a chattel has been given for some other purpose: *Barrett* v *Livesey* (unreported, 6 November 1980, Court of Appeal).

It is a pity that the Court of Appeal did not hear reasoned argument on these points. In the only other relevant case in this area, *Kerr* v *Dundee Gas Light Company* (1861) Ct of Sess 343, the contract conferred an express pledge on the employer in respect of plant and materials brought to site "for the due performance of the contract". After the original contractor went bankrupt, the works were completed and the employer had to return the plant. It could not sell it and set off the proceeds of sale against sums due from the bankrupt because on its true construction the liability secured by the pledge was completion of the works rather than payment of any deficiency.

Conclusion

It may well be that the intent behind vesting clauses in modern engineering contracts is to enable the employer to treat removal of plant from site as if it were an event of default under a charge. The contractor's breach of clause 53 would then be remediable by the employer taking possession of the plant by enforcing the charge. Unfortunately for employers using the ICE form, the drafting falls short of articulating this intent. The chargee's remedies of possession and sale are contained in the termination clause: the vesting and termination clauses are not integrated.

The *Cosslett* decision is the first reported English case on vesting clauses since *Bennett & White* in 1951 and it may be a long time before the court revisits the issues. The case has a number of practical implications. If the ICE (5th edition) is used, the contract needs to be registered as creating a floating charge. The charge may be in breach of negative pledge covenants given by the contractor to its lenders. Should negative pledges make an exception in favour of the ICE floating charge? Will lenders require amendments to contracts of this kind by stipulating for the employer to take a fixed equitable charge? The close involvement of lawyers advising banks on the drafting of PFI contracts might precipitate this. The ICE may choose to amend the standard form (Newman 1998). In view of the plethora of security, formal and informal, now demanded of contractors, there is something to be said for scrapping vesting clauses altogether. Standard forms other than the

ICE contracts have subtly different provisions vesting plant and materials in the employer (Barber 1998).

Challenges to vesting clauses

Vesting clauses have been challenged in the following situations:

- where a termination is disputed and the contractor has lost possession of the site but wants to safeguard its plant
- the contractor argues that the clause is void as a penalty
- a contractor's liquidator or trustee in bankruptcy argues that the terms of the contract are in breach of the *pari passu* rule
- a claim is made against the employer in conversion or the tort of interference with goods
- a liquidator argues that the clause is invalid as an unregistered bill of sale.

Disputed termination

Where termination is disputed and the contractor has left site, the court has to consider whether, on a balance of convenience, the employer should be allowed to use the contractor's plant and equipment for the purpose of completing the works pending determination by litigation of the validity of its actions.

In deciding on the balance of convenience, the court takes all the circumstances into account. In *Garrett v Banstead & Epsom Downs Railway* (1864) 4 De GJ & Sm 462 the contractor was in such delay that, after 14 days' notice, the employer removed the works from his hands and had them completed by another contractor. The contract did not vest plant and equipment in the employer at the outset but provided that on the contractor's default it:

> "shall thereupon become the absolute property of the company, and the whole thereof shall be valued or sold, and the amount of such valuation or sale shall be credited to the contractor in reduction of the moneys recoverable from him ... and the contractor shall not in any manner ... hinder [the employer] or any person engaged by or for them, in the execution of the works, or in using for that purpose any materials, plant, or implements theretofore belonging to the contractor, but [the employer] shall not be bound to use the materials, plant, or implements."

The contractor was refused an injunction entitling him to return to site but was successful in obtaining an injunction restraining the employer from removing any of the plant or selling it until the outcome of an arbitration between them. It was not doubted that the employer was entitled to use the plant but it could only sell it on proof that damages were recoverable and this had yet to be established.

Attorney-General v *Ko Hon Mau* (1988) 44 BLR 144 concerned the Hong Kong Public Works Highways Maintenance Contract (1972 edition) which had a vesting clause with re-vesting on completion or termination for non-payment or if the employer obstructed the issue of a certificate. The contractor terminated but the employer cross-claimed for an entitlement to terminate for failure to proceed with due diligence. The court was asked to rule on the fate of the plant pending an arbitration.

> "The contractor puts its value at $1.8 million. This he says he wishes to realise to satisfy the pressing demands of his creditors. Government wishes to retain the apparent 'security' the plant affords (in addition to that provided by the $0.45 million performance bond provided under the contract); to use the plant on site; and if necessary to sell it to its advantage. Underneath the rival claims to possession lie the competing claims of creditors between whom hereafter different considerations may apply ..." (at 150).

On balance, the court allowed the contractor to repossess its plant. The employer therefore lost its security but the court may have been influenced by the fact that the contractor had also provided a bond. Contrast *Groutco* v *Prince Constructions* (1987) BCL 372 where a contractor was allowed to retain a sub-contractor's plant until their dispute on the validity of the termination of the sub-contract had been concluded, otherwise the court felt the contractor would have irrevocably lost any proprietary rights it may have had.

If the contract gives the employer the right on the contractor's default either to cancel the contract or take over the works and use the contractor's plant and equipment, the employer cannot use the plant if it decides to cancel the contract: *Phontos* v *New South Wales Land & Housing Corporation* (1988) BCL 45. That case concerned a disputed termination but the court assumed for the purpose of the contractor's application for the return of its plant that the employer had validly cancelled the contract. The contract gave the employer a lien over the plant until the contractor had paid the net deficiency arising after the contract had been completed. Since the lien only arose where the works had been taken over, however, it was held that the contractor was entitled to the immediate return of its plant. The contract also contained a restriction on removal of the plant but this was only effective while the contractor was carrying out the work. Once the contract was cancelled, the restriction was removed.

Generally, where the contractor is ordered to leave site, it will be protected either by being allowed to go on to the site and remove its materials or by the employer's undertaking in damages: *Mohan and Holmes* v *Dundalk Railway* (1880) LR Ir 477; *Callaghan* v *City of Glasgow* (1988) SLT 227 (obligation to return plant or pay its value), *Wood* v *Rural Sanitary Authority of Tendring* (1886) 3 TLR 272 (plant returned), *Corporation of Cork* v *Rooney* (1881) 7 LR Ir 191 (undertaking in damages); *Roberts* v *Maurbeth Investments* [1974] 1 NSWLR 93 (contractor allowed on site to collect plant); *Re Winter, ex parte Bolland* (1878) 8 Ch D 228. Compare *Re Yeadon Waterworks* (1895) 72 LT 538 (CA) (sell or use or cause to be used gratuitously, the plant tools and materials of the contractor), and *Forestry Commission* v *Stefanetto* [1975] 133 CLR 507 (considered below).

Penalty arguments

Whether a clause is a penalty is a question of the construction of the contract. In a case concerning a road-making contract, it was held that forfeiture of plant on termination of the contract was a penalty. There was a vesting clause but it only concerned materials. Plant was referred to only in the termination clause: *Bysouth* v *Shire of Blackburn and Mitcham* [1928] VLR 562. The court may have been influenced by the fact that the employer was entitled to terminate for trivial breaches, *e.g.* execution of work on a Sunday. The court also found that the notice given under the contract was invalid. In *Forestry Commission* v *Stefanetto* [1975] 133 CLR 507 the employer was entitled to seize and use the contractor's plant and equipment on a termination.

> "The Contractor shall have no right to any compensation or allowance for any action taken by the Principal pursuant to this sub-clause, other than a right to require the Principal to maintain in good working order the Constructional Plant referred to in the preceding paragraph. On completion of the work all Constructional Plant and the surplus of the materials and other things so taken possession of will be handed over to the Contractor but without payment or allowance for the fair wear and tear they may have sustained in the meantime provided however, that if there is

a deficiency as referred to in sub-clause 43.4 and if the Contractor fails to make good that deficiency, the Principal may retain in his possession the said Constructional Plant, materials and other things until the deficiency is made good pursuant to the provisions of sub-clause 43.4."

It was held that the employer was not entitled to possession of plant in which the contractor had only a limited interest under hire purchase and lease agreements. It was also held that this provision was not a penalty and the level of liquidated damages and the amount of any security deposit were irrelevant.

"It must be observed that the appellant is not primarily interested in obtaining damages for breach of contract. It is primarily concerned with the completion of the work within a stipulated time. Both the provisions as to liquidated damages and as to the provision of security are means to that end, coupled with an ease of recovery of damages in the event of breach. But the possession and use of the machinery and plant are, to my mind, a direct means of achieving the purpose of the contract, namely, the completion of the work. They are not a means of providing the appellant with any form of compensation in respect of the breach of the agreement. ... It seems that the provision allowing the appellant to complete the work with the aid of the respondent's plant is both reasonable and in the interest of both the parties, *i.e.* the interest of both parties to effect early completion. True it is that the respondent is denied the immediate use of the machinery and plant: but he is in default" (at 515-516).

Had there been provision for compensation or allowance for use of the plant in the completion contract, there could have been no objection: *Ranger* v *Great Western Railway* (1854) HLC 72, *Wood* v *Rural Sanitary Authority of Tendring* (1886) 3 TLR 272, *Callaghan* v *City of Glasgow* (1988) SLT 227.

The pari passu rule

Where the contract has no vesting clause but allows the employer to seize and sell the contractor's plant should the contractor become bankrupt or go into liquidation, it will be struck down as infringing the *pari passu* rule now contained in s 107 Insolvency Act 1986. In *Re Harrison, ex parte Jay* (1880) 14 Ch D 19 the contract provided that on the contractor's bankruptcy:

"all improvements, materials, implements, plant, chattels, and effects [on site] shall be and become absolutely forfeited" to the employer who would have the right to:

> "re-enter and take possession of [the site], chattels, and effects, without any formal proceeding, and to re-let or sell the same to any person, or otherwise use and enjoy the same as fully as if this agreement had never been entered into."

The contractor went bankrupt and the Court of Appeal had to decide claims to wood, bricks, tiles, scaffolding and other building materials made by the employer and the contractor's trustee in bankruptcy. The court had no hesitation in deciding that they belonged to the trustee and stated the principle as follows:

> "A simple stipulation that, upon a man becoming bankrupt, that which was his property up to the date of the bankruptcy should go over to someone else and be taken away from his creditors, is void as being a violation of the policy of the bankrupt law ... everything that [the contractor] was bound to do under the agreement had been performed by him up to the date of the bankruptcy, and therefore no right was vested in the lessor except by virtue of the bankruptcy" (at 25).

A power to forfeit plant would, however, be upheld where the right is exercised on another ground in the absence of insolvency: *Davies* v *Mayor of Swansea* (1853) 22 LJ Ex 297. A right to forfeit must have arisen before the start of the bankruptcy. For example, in *Roach* v *Great Western Railway Company* [1841] 1 QB 51, two partners acted together as contractor. The contract provided that on their default, their tools and materials on site should "be in all respects considered as the absolute property" of the employer. They did not vest in the employer on delivery to site. The contractors were in delay and the engineer served a seven-day notice prior to termination. Before the period expired, both partners went bankrupt. It was held that the contractors would only have been in default after the notice had expired. As bankruptcy had intervened, title had passed to the contractors' trustees placing the plant and materials beyond the employer's reach.

Conversion

A substantial interim payment on account of damages for conversion was ordered in *Clark* v *Bridgend Borough Council* (unreported, 1998). This was an application by the administrator of Cosslett (Contractors) Ltd following the decision of the Court of Appeal discussed earlier in this chapter. The Court of Appeal had refused the administrator's application for delivery up of the coal washing plants on the ground that the contract conferred a right to possession and use on the council until the completion of the works by an alternative contractor. At that point, however, the council would have to return the plant. It emerged in evidence that the council had agreed that the plant should become the completion contractor's property. The council refused to pay for the plants' use or value on the ground that, although the power of sale in the termination clause was void as an unregistered floating charge as against the administrator, it was not void against the company: *Independent Automatic Sales* v *Knowles & Foster* [1962] 1 WLR 974 at 981. This was important because it enabled the employer to set off a cross-claim for the cost to complete of £2.2 million against the administrator's estimated value of the plant. As between the employer and the administrator the floating charge had the effect of allowing the administrator to deal with the sale proceeds of the plant free of the charge: *Re Barrow Borough Transport* [1990] Ch 227 at 233. As between the employer and the contractor, however, the employer sold the plant as mortgagee and the contractor's entitlement was limited to the proceeds of sale subject to the employer's right of set-off. As the employer had taken possession of the plant before the administrator was appointed, the floating charge had crystallised into a fixed charge which was valid as against the administrator: *Mercantile Bank of India* v *Chartered Bank of India* [1937] 1 All ER 231. A fixed charge over a chattel is not regarded as a registrable bill of sale: *Reeves* v *Barlow* (1884) 12 QBD 436. The employer argued that the administrator had no personal right to bring the claim which was vested in the company. The court rejected the employer's submissions but without giving reasons. The case is under appeal.

In *Egan* v *State Transport Authority* (1982) 31 SASR 481, the contract provided that on termination the employer could seize the contractor's plant and materials which would then become the employer's property. The employer wrongfully terminated but relied on the express rights against the plant and materials. Fifteen years later, after extensive litigation, the court declared the termination to have been wrongful and awarded damages in conversion or detinue at the contractor's election. Exemplary damages in detinue were also awarded against the employer.

> "The immediate effects of the termination were traumatic. Men were stranded in remote areas without pay. Recent large deliveries and materials were not paid for. Creditors contacted the police and Egan was

threatened with arrest and possible imprisonment. In the longer term he was a man left without an occupation; his credit worthiness and general business reputation were in ruins; he was foreclosed by clause 35 from claiming damages for breach of contract; he was harried by hostile creditors, the number and extent of whose claims had just been revealed to the railways. These disastrous consequences arose out of the initial unlawful detention of plant and further detention in the early stages more than out of the subsequent conversions of plant in later months and years" (at 532).

The court had declared that clause to be a penalty at an earlier trial: (1979) 24 SASR 5. Detinue was abolished as a separate tort in English law by the Torts (Interference with Goods) Act 1977, but the remedy of delivery up was retained under s 3 of the Act.

Where a contract allowed the employer to use the contractor's plant and materials:

> "without making any payment for the same, or being answerable for any loss, damages or deterioration which might happen thereto (save from unlawful neglect or default of [the employer])"

it was held that the employer was entitled to use the plant and materials without being liable in conversion to the contractor: *Mohan and Holmes* v *Dundalk* (1880) LR Ir 477.

Bills of sale

Under the Bills of Sale Act 1878 a bill of sale is a document executed by an individual which is:

1. An assignment, a transfer or other assurance of goods or chattels, or

2. A licence to possession of chattels as security for a debt, or

3. An agreement by which an equitable right to or a charge or a security on personal chattels is conferred.

If the bill is given as security for payment of money, it is known as a "security bill", otherwise it is called an "absolute bill": Halsbury 4(1)/602 (by R M Goode). Both types of bill must be properly witnessed, show consideration and be registered in the Central Office of the Royal Courts of Justice within seven days in order to be valid against a trustee in bankruptcy or an execution creditor (Halsbury 4(1)/735, 832). Under s 396 Companies Act 1985 "a charge created or evidenced by an instrument which, if executed by an individual, would require registration as a bill of sale" is void against a liquidator, administrator or creditor of the company under s 395 unless details are delivered to the Registrar of Companies within 21 days of its creation. Looking at this matter without the benefit of case law an insolvency lawyer might well conclude that many of the clauses referred to earlier would fall within categories (1) or (3) or even (2), but the court has exempted vesting clauses in construction contracts from registration altogether. Why? The answer is a mixture of the common law, statutory interpretation and public policy.

In *Brown* v *Bateman* (1867) LR 2 CP 272, the contract provided that all materials brought onto the site by the contractor for the purposes of the works "should be considered as immediately attaching to and belonging to the premises." The court rejected an execution creditor's claim that the clause was a bill of sale. It expressed no view whether the words used were clear enough to transfer the materials to the employer outright but considered they were sufficient to create "a clear equitable right" or "an equitable charge". However, at the time the case was decided, an agreement creating an equitable interest was not a bill of sale. In *Blake* v *Izard* (1867) 16 WR 108, the contract provided that all materials brought on to site "should become the property of" the employer. The court again rejected a claim by an execution creditor:

> "The court has in the case of *Brown* v *Bateman* decided to respect the evident intention of the parties under these agreements. It was intended to preserve the rights of landlords [under building leases], and I consider it was a most wholesome decision. It has been contended that it is a bill of sale, or that it comes within the scope of the Bills of Sale Act, but I apprehend that that question is set at rest by *Brown* v *Bateman*, which shows that stipulations of the nature of building agreements are not within the scope of the Bills of Sale Act."

Here the court reveals a policy basis for the earlier decision, to protect the interests of landowners. This may explain why *Brown* v *Bateman* was not distinguished since there the equitable interest arose as the materials were considered part of the land. In *Blake* v *Izard*, they became the property of the employer and there was no deemed incorporation. These cases were decided under the Bills of Sale Act 1854 which only concerned the first and second categories of bill.

In *Re Garrud, ex parte Newitt* (1881) 16 Ch D 522, the contract had no vesting clause but gave the employer a right of re-entry on default by the contractor and the right to forfeit any materials on site "as and for liquidated and settled damages". On the contractor's bankruptcy, the trustee argued that the clause was void as an unregistered bill of sale. The court held that, in the absence of a vesting clause, the first and third categories of bill could not apply. The second category was also rejected on the ground that the clause was given as security for damages not as debt. (This is doubtful as liquidated damages are regarded as a debt for the purpose of legal set-off: see Chapter 5). If that was incorrect, the trustee's claim still failed because the materials had not been taken as security for the debt but in discharge of it. Could the trustee have succeeded on the alternative ground that the seizure clause contravened the *pari passu* rule in confiscating the bankrupt's property? Contrast *Climpson* v *Coles* (1889) 23 QBD 465.

The Bills of Sale Act 1878 added the third category of bill, namely agreements transferring an equitable interest or conferring a charge or security over chattels. This statute was amended to require security bills to be in a specific form by the Bills of Sale Act (1878) Amendment Act 1882. The next case to come before the court was *Reeves* v *Barlow* (1884) 12 QBD 436. There, the contract provided that:

> "all building and other materials brought by the intended lessee upon the land shall, whether affixed to the freehold or not, become the property of the intended lessor."

The report does not give any further details of the contract. Once again the court rejected the claim of an execution creditor that the clause was an unregistered bill of sale. The Court of Appeal considered that the two earlier decisions were "unshaken decisions of a court of great weight" which "we are not prepared to review." Unless new legislation had been passed after those decisions which altered the position, the claim had to fail. The only significant change was the third category of bill introduced by the 1878 Act which the court held inapplicable on the ground that, as soon as the materials were delivered to site:

> "property in them passed in law, and nothing was left upon which any equity as distinct from law could attach ... The builder's agreement accordingly was at no time an equitable assignment of anything, but a mere legal contract that, upon the happening of a particular event, the property in law should pass in certain chattels which that event itself would identify without the necessity of any further act on the part of anybody, and which could not be identified before" (at 442).

The same reasoning could be applied to the first category (although it was not a ground for the earlier decisions) since a bill of sale will become spent and the legislation cease to apply:

"if after the execution of the bill and before the occurrence of the avoiding event the grantee either perfects his title in some other manner, as by exercising a right to take possession of the chattels or by taking a new and valid bill, or exercises a right to dispose of the chattels." (Halsbury 4(1)/615, 624, 630).

In the construction context, even if the vesting clause were a bill of sale, the court seems to be saying that the bringing of materials to site or their fixing to the structure, depending on the terms of the contract, would render the bill spent. See also *Welsh Development Agency* v *Export Finance* [1990] BCC 393 at 411.

Reeves v *Barlow* is firmly established and has been followed many times (*e.g. Tapper* v *Bodley* (1884) 3 NZLR 4, *Bennett and White* v *Municipal District of Sugar City* [1951] AC 786), but it would put it too highly to say the case is authority for the proposition that a vesting clause in a construction contract can never be registrable as a bill of sale. Each contract has to be construed separately. If the plant is designed specifically for the contract, it will be identified before being brought to site. Delivery to site is not necessarily a transfer of possession to the employer. Some financial obligations owed by contractors are debts. *Church* v *Sage* (1892) 67 LT 800 is authority for the view that an assignment by a builder to a mortgagee of plant to be brought on to land requires registration. The court in that case appeared to indicate towards the end of the judgment that a distinction could be drawn between a clause which said that plant should be deemed attached to the land and other types of clause. It may remain arguable that a vesting clause requires registration as a bill of sale where the employer is not the owner of the land. The policy basis of *Blake* v *Izard* could be reviewed in the light of changes in social conditions. It is clear, however, that in the absence of a vesting, user or seizure clause, a simple provision for payment to a builder under interim certificates cannot be a bill of sale: *Davidson and Davidson* v *Claffey Constructions* (1985) WALR 29.

Plant not owned by the contractor

The discussion so far has assumed that the contractor owns the plant and equipment. This is now unlikely as the majority of the work is normally carried out by sub-contractors. The sub-contractor may be a subsidiary of the contractor but whether the plant is owned by the contractor or a sub-contractor, it may be fully charged. There is also the possibility that the plant was hired or subject to a finance lease. The employer may try to anticipate as many of these possibilities as it can so as to enhance the security given by the vesting clause. One form obliges the contractor to mark all plant delivered to site as the employer's property (Pike 1992 at 445).

Sub-contractors

Where a vesting clause in the main contract is not mirrored in the sub-contract, the court will not infer it merely because the sub-contractor agrees to carry out work in accordance with the terms of the main contract. In *Triangle* v *John Burroughs* [1958] 3 SA 810, the main contract contained a clause vesting plant and machinery in the employer together with rights of enforcement similar to the ICE form. Some of the work was to be done by a nominated sub-contractor but the sub-contract did not contain a clause vesting the sub-contractor's plant and equipment in the contractor or the employer. The court considered that the vesting clause, having been inserted for the benefit of the building owner, should be construed against it. As it only referred to plant and equipment brought on to site by the contractor, it could not include plant and equipment brought on to site by sub-contractors. The court felt it would be unjust to construe the clause in any other way as it could lead to the sub-contractor's plant being forfeited if the main contract were terminated through no fault of the sub-contractor. In any event, there was no privity of contract permitting the employer to enforce direct against the sub-contractor.

To overcome this difficulty, clause 11 of the Blue Form designed for use in conjunction with the ICE form provides for ownership in the sub-contractor's plant to pass to the contractor immediately before it is due to vest in the employer and then revert to the sub-contractor immediately after it has re-vested in the contractor. The standard forms also require contractors to ensure that sub-contracts include back to back terms regarding the vesting of plant and equipment, *e.g.* clause 54.7 of FIDIC (4th edition). Where there is no incorporation of terms and the sub-contract does not contain a vesting clause neither the employer nor the contractor is entitled to retain the sub-contractor's plant. In a Malaysian case, a sub-contract was terminated following the termination of the main contract. The employer retained and used a hoist, a dumper and three concrete mixers owned by the sub-contractor. There was no dispute that the retention was wrongful: the issue was whether the sub-contractor's claim lay in the tort of conversion or detinue. Damages were awarded in detinue representing the value of the plant at the time of the judgment and an amount in respect of its fall in value between the wrongful detention and the judgment together with loss of hire at the market rate over the same period: *Perbadanan* v *Teo Kai Huat* [1982] MLJ 165.

Where the plant is hired

Both ICE and FIDIC have elaborate provisions enabling the engineer to identify plant not in the ownership of the contractor so that arrangements can be made for the employer to take over the hire after forfeiture. The possibility of the employer taking over the hire of contractor's plant is recognised in conditions published by the Construction Plant Hire Association. These conditions and FIDIC both restrict the employer's obligation to payment of hire charges incurred after termination. As the contractor may have defaulted in payment under its hire agreement before termination, this appears to envisage that the owner will not claim pre-termination arrears from the employer, but this is unlikely. It may refuse to allow the employer to take over the hire contract at all. To meet this risk, clause 16(4) of SIA (2nd edition) gives the architect power to refuse to allow plant not owned by the contractor to be brought on to site unless its owner gives the employer a written undertaking that, in consideration of the plant being admitted to the site, the owner would assign the benefit of its hiring contract with the contractor on the contractor's default. Notwithstanding the collateral contract effected by the undertaking to assign the contract, the owner could still insist on payment of all arrears otherwise the contract would sooner or later be repudiated by the contractor and its benefit would become worthless (Wallace 1986).

If the hirer cannot satisfy the criteria required for a mandatory injunction for delivery up of the plant, the court may allow the plant to remain in the possession of the employer until the project has been finished. In *T R Nominees* v *Multiplex* (1996) 12 BCL 219, the hirer failed in a claim for delivery up of two tower cranes and a hoist which had been hired to a sub-contractor which had repudiated its sub-contract. The evidence was that the equipment would be needed for a further nine months. The application failed for two reasons:

1. There was a common director between the hirer and the sub-contractor and it was not at all clear whether the hirer had an immediate right to possession for non-payment under the hire agreement.

2. In any case, the balance of convenience lay with the contractor as the hirer had no present use for the plant, its true claim was for damages in conversion, the inconvenience to the contractor of dismantling the cranes and the hoist would be considerable, the hirer's financial position meant that an undertaking in damages would be of little value, and the order sought was in the nature of final relief.

No condition was imposed that the contractor should pay a reasonable hiring charge as it would represent payment of damages before trial (inappropriate in the absence of facts which could support a Mareva injunction), the payments would be irrecoverable if the contractor ultimately succeeded and, if the sub-contractor went into liquidation (as was possible as a petition had been issued) the contractor would be exposed to the risk of double payment.

Subsidiaries

Clause 53 of ICE (5th edition) attempts to vest in the employer all plant brought to site owned by the contractor "or by any company in which the contractor has a controlling interest". It is questionable whether this is enforceable against a subsidiary of the contractor as there is no privity of contract and the contractor may not be authorised to act as agent for its subsidiary for this purpose. The plant may also be subject to a prior charge. The only safe method is by a direct agreement between the employer and the relevant subsidiary. Clause 53 is like a group set-off clause or a cross-guarantee in attempting to bind the whole group.

Goods and materials

On the insolvency of a construction company, there is often a contest between the employer and the receiver, suppliers, sub-contractors and execution creditors of the contractor over the ownership of goods and materials. Disputes of this kind arouse strong feelings and some of the cases portray difficult situations in which suppliers have attempted repossession, *e.g. Dalinga v Antina* [1979] 2 SA 56 where a lift installation sub-contractor disabled a lift by removing a vital mechanism to force payment. The situation usually calls for quick advice and this section aims to set out the basic principles.

There is one respect in which a construction contract differs from any other: it concerns fixing things to land. This has a drastic effect on the ownership of those things because of the principle that anything fixed to land becomes part of it: *quicquid plantatur solo, solo cedit* (Holdsworth 1956). This rule is in conflict with another rule of English law that you cannot give what you do not have: *nemo dat quod non habet*. This is the reason why suppliers include clauses in their terms and conditions that ownership will not pass to the purchaser until the goods have been paid for. A clause of this kind is known as a retention of title clause (McCormack 1995, Goode 1989). A retention of title clause is defeated where the goods are fixed to the land: *Re Yorkshire Joinery* (1967) 111 SJ 71. Where the employer is not the owner of the land, the supplier has no cause of action against the landowner for the price: *Gough* v *Wood* [1894] 1 QB 713, *Crossley* v *Lee* [1908] 1 KB 86. The tension between employers who do not want to pay for goods until they have title and suppliers who do not want to pass title until they have been paid is at the heart of the problem discussed in this section.

The greater the number of intermediate parties between the supplier and the landowner, the more complex the position becomes. The *quicquid plantatur* rule transfers risk to the contractor just as a pay when paid clause transfers risk to sub-contractors and suppliers. A retention of title clause might be seen as the supplier's answer to the pay when paid clause: money going down the chain is held up by a pay when paid clause; title going up the chain is held back by a retention of title clause. Standard forms of main and sub-contract attempt to resolve this tension. The intention behind the JCT scheme, for example, is that title to unfixed materials should pass to the employer as soon as the employer pays the contractor for them (RIBA 1978), but it is worth noting that the employer is not always the owner of the site. As the construction process involves payment monthly in arrears, the landowner obtains at least a month's credit in respect of the work, takes the value of fixed materials by operation of law rather than payment and can only be sued by a direct contracting party. Credit opens up the risk of non-payment and the owner of the land benefits at the expense of those carrying out the work. The injustice of this situation has long been recognised and recommendations have been made to change the law, but so far without success (Crowther 1971, Latham 1994).

There are three important distinctions to bear in mind:

- between fixed and unfixed materials
- between materials on and off site
- between a sale of goods and a supply of goods and services.

It seems appropriate to start with the first of these distinctions.

Fixed materials

The *quicquid plantatur* rule derives from Roman law, as far back as the Twelve Tables of the fifth century BC (Buckland 1963). The policy behind it was to prevent the needless demolition of buildings. The Roman concept of *accessio* applied where ownership of a thing was acquired by incorporation into another thing. This could be a movable to another movable (a jewel set in a ring), immovable to immovable (silt attaching to a river bank) and a movable to an immovable (building on land). The last situation was known as *inaedificatio*. The principles of Roman law were adopted by medieval lawyers and the *quicquid plantatur* rule gradually emerged as part of the common law. As it evolved, it concerned three legal categories: heirs and executors, tenants for life and remaindermen, and landlords and tenants. The strict rule was relaxed in the case of the last category because it was recognised that a tenant would need to fix things to the land for business purposes and it was accepted that these could be removed before the end of the term. The law was restated in *Elwes* v *Maw* (1802) 3 East 38 which concerned a tenant farmer who had erected buildings for the better running of the farm. Before the end of the term, he demolished the buildings and removed the materials but was held liable in conversion to the freeholder. The exception given to trading tenants did not apply as farming was not regarded as a trade and it was held that after the end of the term, the buildings "became a gift in law to him in reversion and were not removable" (at 52).

There appears to be only one exception: where a builder works on another's land by mistake and the owner stands back and accepts the benefit without telling the builder of his mistake, the owner can be liable to compensate the builder: *Ramsden* v *Dyson* (1866) LR 1 HL 129. So it is that a contractor or sub-contractor working on a modern construction project confers a gratuitous benefit on the landowner as title to its materials vanishes as they are transformed into land. In *Rogersons Development* v *The Housing Corporation* (unreported, 14 October 1994, noted in (1995) 12 BLM 4) the employer, a housing association, went into liquidation after practical completion but before paying the last stage payment and retention. The builder sued The Housing Corporation who had been funding the development against a mortgage over the site. The Corporation had failed to inform the builder of its decision taken before practical completion to discontinue funding the employer, but this could not give rise to any claim based on estoppel nor could the builder argue an entitlement on an implied assignment by the employer of its rights against the Corporation since, on the employer's liquidation, it became liable to repay to the Corporation all the sums it had received.

Meaning of fixture

In view of the drastic effect of the *quicquid plantatur* rule, it becomes very important to identify when materials are fixed to the land. What are the criteria? In the leading case of *Holland* v *Hodgson* (1872) LR 7 CP 328 Blackburn J said:

> "There is no doubt that the general maxim of law is that what is annexed to the land becomes part of the land, but it is very difficult, if not impossible, to say with precision what constitutes an annexation sufficient for this purpose. It is a question which must depend on the circumstances of each case, and mainly on two circumstances as indicating the intention, viz, the degree of annexation and the object of the annexation .... Perhaps the true rule is that articles not otherwise attached to the land than by their own weight are not to be considered as part of the land unless the circumstances are such as to show that they were intended to be part of the land, the onus of showing that they are so intended lying on those who assert that they have ceased to be chattels; and that, on the contrary, an article which is affixed to the land, even slightly, is to be considered as part of the land, unless the circumstances are such as to show that it was intended all along to continue a chattel, the onus lying on those who contend that it is a chattel" (at 334-335).

A minimal degree of annexation shifts the burden of proof that a chattel is a fixture away from the landowner: *Reynolds* v *Ashby* [1904] AC 466, *Scottish Discount* v *Blin* [1985] SLT 123, and the Australian case of *Re Starline Furniture* [1982] 6 ACLR 312 in which a liquidator who had detached and sold fixtures was made to account for the proceeds to the mortgagor of the land. Each case depends on its own facts and the intention of the parties is relevant only insofar as it can be derived from the degree and purpose of annexation: *Hobson* v *Gorringe* [1897] 1 Ch 181 at 193. The court will not admit extraneous evidence of the subjective intentions of the parties, but the amount of damage which would be caused to the building or the chattel by its removal is a relevant factor: *Holland* v *Hodgson* (1872) LR 7 CP 328. The court takes account of changing times:

"... you must have regard to all the circumstances of the particular case to the taste and fashion of the day as well as to the position in regard to the freehold of the person who is supposed to have made that which was once a mere chattel part of the realty. The mode of annexation is only one of the circumstances of the case, and not always the most important: its relative importance is probably not what it was in ruder or simpler times": *Leigh* v *Taylor* [1902] AC 157 at 162.

An agreement between the owner of the land and the person fixing the chattel only affects the right to sever the chattel acquired by the contractor or others with an equitable right: *Melluish* v *B & I* [1996] AC 454 at 473. In *Elitestone* v *Morris* [1997] 2 All ER 513, the House of Lords distinguished between a chattel, a fixture and a part of the land. The House of Lords held that a chalet resting on a concrete base had become part of the land since it could not be taken down and re-erected elsewhere like a portakabin: it could only be enjoyed *in situ*, giving rise to a strong inference that its purpose was to become part of the land. The House approved the approach taken in *Holland* v *Hodgson*. Building components normally fall within the third category. Equipment or other items which are fixed to a built structure are a fixture. A fixture may or may not be part of the land depending on the degree and purpose of annexation.

It has been held that:

"something as basic as doors, windows and shutters, in the construction of a building are so much part of the structure that it would bring an air of unreality ... to suggest that the joinery did not become a fixture": *Minshall* v *Lloyd* (1837) 2 M&W 450.

The same would apply to panels in a suspended ceiling: individually, they are easily removable but they rest on a frame which is fixed. Modern building techniques and new technology, especially computers, are likely to challenge the criteria of a fixture as time goes by. In the Canadian case of *Credit Valley Cable* v *Peel* (1980) 27 OR (2d) 433, for example, it was held that television cable installed in conduits within an apartment building was not a fixture because it was not for the permanent enjoyment of the building but installed as a service to the residents. Contrast this with the Australian case of *Belgrave Nominees* v *Barlin-Scott* [1984] VR 947 where the court issued a mandatory injunction against a sub-contractor ordering it to return air-conditioning plant removed after it had been installed on the roof of a building on the basis that it had become a fixture. See also *Hulme* v *Brigham* [1943] 1 KB 204 (printing machines remained chattels), *Blower* v *Alta* (1983)

50 AR 66, affirmed 68 AR 156 (two-ton crane sitting on track bolted to floor remained a chattel), *Canadian Imperial Bank of Commerce* v *Alberta Assessment Appeal Board* (1990) 75 Alta LR (2d) 362 (bank cash dispensing machines remained chattels).

The retention of title supplier

Where the supplier is in contract with the owner of the land and reserves a right of re-entry in the event of non-payment for the purpose of detaching its goods the supplier obtains an equitable interest in the land: *Re Samuel Allen* [1907] 1 Ch 575, *Re Morrison, Jones & Taylor* [1914] 1 Ch 50. If the right of re-entry is exercised and the materials are detached, they regain their former identity as chattels. The supplier's equitable interest takes priority over a later equitable interest in the land, *e.g.* where a receiver is appointed under a floating charge over land, but will be defeated by anyone taking a later legal interest in good faith for value without notice of the supplier's interest: *Kay's Leasing Corporation* v *CSR Provident* [1962] VR 429.

The problems which arise in practice can be illustrated by *Whenuapai Joinery* v *Trust Bank* [1994] 1 NZLR 406 which concerned a contract to build "what was intended to be one of the finest residences in New Zealand." Substantial sums were lent by the bank against a mortgage on the property. When construction was at an advanced stage, a joinery supplier who had made substantial deliveries to site was owed nearly $180,000. The supplier's terms included a retention of title clause with a right of re-entry and the right to re-take possession of joinery which had been fixed to the building. Following the collapse of the property market in New Zealand, the developer was unable to finance the completion of the project. The supplier re-entered and removed its joinery and the bank entered into possession and sold the property. The joinery was in fact used to complete the works without prejudice to all parties' claims. The bank succeeded in its claim against the supplier on the ground that the joinery had become a fixture. It was possible that the bank could have consented by implication to an agreement made by the developer with third party suppliers allowing the latter rights of entry and repossession in case of default. However, in this case, the mortgage prohibited the removal, dismantling or structural alteration of buildings or improvements by the developer without the written consent of the mortgagee which had not been given. The supplier had an equitable interest in the joinery despite the fact that it had become a fixture. Under New Zealand legislation the bank's mortgage took effect as a fixed equitable charge. At first instance the bank took priority as it had gone into possession before the supplier had re-entered and without notice of the supplier's rights. On appeal, the court held the bank's priority did not stem from the act of possession but from the prohibition against removal in the mortgage. The moral for suppliers to construction companies is that it is not sufficient to rely on a retention of title clause in the supply contract. The supplier must ascertain the identity of the employer (and the landowner if different) and at the least give notice of the retention of title clause. A right of re-entry or repossession can only be effective, however, where a supplier is in contract with the landowner, and then subject to registration if applicable.

Unfixed materials

A supplier's rights to repossess unfixed materials will depend on the terms of the contract, in particular whether it is for the sale of goods or the supply of goods and services. Only if it is a contract for the sale of goods can the purchaser pass title without paying for them to a sub-purchaser receiving the goods in good faith and without notice of the original seller's rights. This is considered later. The House of Lords has acknowledged that the expression "contract for work and materials" is one of considerable imprecision and that many work and materials contracts closely resemble contracts of sale: *Young & Marten* v *McManus Childs* [1969] 1 AC 454 at 476, *Gloucestershire CC* v *Richardson* [1968] 3 WLR 645. For example, in *Pritchett & Gold* v *Currie* [1916] 2 Ch 515 a sub-contractor agreed to supply and erect a battery. The contractor went into liquidation before the battery was installed and the sub-contractor sued the contractor and the employer who paid the balance of the contract sum into court. It was held that there were two contracts: one for the sale of the battery and another for its installation. The consequence was that title to the battery passed on delivery so that the money in court had to be paid to the liquidator. The position would have been different had the contract been for work and materials as title would have passed to the employer on installation.

The precise dividing line is not easy to draw. A contract to supply and hang wallpaper has been held to be two contracts: one for the sale of the wallpaper and the other for the provision of services: *Wyett* v *Smith and Smith* [1908] 28 NZLR 79). A contract to supply and lay a carpet was held to be a contract for the sale of goods: *Philip Head* v *Showfronts* [1970] 1 Lloyd's Rep 140. The proportion which the work content bears to the overall contract price is the key factor. The higher the work content, the more likely the contract will be for work and materials: *Brooks Robinson* v *Rothfield* [1951] VLR 405, *Collins Trading* v *Maher* [1969] VR 20, *Otis* v *Girvan* (1990) 2 ACLB 70. If the agreement provides for progress payments on account of the contract price, it is more likely to be a contract for work and materials and governed by the Supply of Goods and Services Act 1992.

Sale of goods contract

If the contract is found to be for the sale of goods it is governed by the Sale of Goods Act 1979. Under s 25 of the Act:

> "where a person having bought or agreed to buy goods obtains, with the consent of the seller, possession of the goods ... the delivery or transfer by that person [the purchaser] ... of the goods ... under any sale, pledge or other disposition thereof, to any person [the sub-purchaser] receiving the same in good faith and without notice of any ... right of the original seller in respect of the goods ... "

transfers title to the sub-purchaser. *Archivent* v *Strathclyde General Council* (1984) 27 BLR 111 is a good illustration of the application of s 25 to construction contracts. Archivent was a direct supplier to the contractor. The main contract was in the JCT 63 form. Archivent had not supplied to the contractor before and its normal policy was to ask for cash before delivery but by an oversight they supplied goods to site without obtaining payment in advance. Some of the goods had been fixed by the time the contractor went into receivership. At that time the contractor had been paid for them, but Archivent had not. It was held that s 25 applied and title to the unfixed goods had passed to the employer when it paid the contractor without notice of the retention of title clause.

The crucial aspects were that the goods were delivered to site under a contract of sale and the employer could prove it had paid the contractor in good faith and without notice of the retention of title clause. The decision is of interest because of the implicit finding that the transfer to the employer under JCT 63 satisfied the requirement of a "sale, pledge or other disposition". As JCT 63 is a contract for work and materials, the transfer could not have been a sale. Even if there had been a constructive delivery to the employer, it was not by way of pledge. The only basis for the decision was that the transfer was a "disposition". In *Worcester* v *Cooden* [1972] 1 QB 210 at 220 the Court of Appeal considered that "disposition" meant "some transfer of an interest in property" (see also Goode 1995 at 51, ch 16). This test is satisfied by clause 14 of JCT 63 which provides that unfixed or off-site materials should become the employer's property where their value is included in an interim certificate that has been paid. It was this kind of term that was missing in *Egan* v *State Transport* (1982) 31 SASR 481 considered earlier.

The facts in *Archivent* can be contrasted with those in *Hanson* v *Rapid Civil Engineering* (1987) 38 BLR 106 where the supplier had traded with the contractor for some years. The supplier's terms included a retention of title clause which could be waived at its discretion "where goods or any part of them have been incorporated in building or constructional works." The contractor went into receivership without paying the supplier for the unfixed materials. It was held that s 25 could not apply.

Goods had been supplied to three sites and it appears from the report that no standard form had been used. On two of the contracts, there was provision for monthly progress payments of 97% of the value of work done including the value of unfixed materials. Property in the materials would not pass to the employer until payment of the valuation which included them. There was no provision for certificates. The absence of payment meant that there could be no "disposition". The third contract was silent on progress payments and the passing of property but the parties seem to have adopted informally the arrangements which applied on the other two. Unless the contract otherwise provides, an interim payment is on account of the contract sum and does not pass ownership of materials whose value may have been included in a certificate: *Egan* v *State Transport* (1982) 31 SASR 481 at 542. In the absence of any express term, the section had no application to the third contract either.

Under s 25, title to goods passes from supplier to employer by statute. This position can be compared with fixed goods where title passes from supplier to landowner by operation of the common law. *Hanson* v *Rapid* can be contrasted with the Scottish decision in *Thomas Graham* v *Glenrothes* [1967] SC 284 in which the Court of Session held it was arguable that s 25 was satisfied where goods were supplied direct to a contractor and their value included in a certificate of which 80% had been paid to the contractor before it went into liquidation. The employer then sold the goods on to the completion contractor. Presumably it was possible to appropriate the payment to specific goods.

Work and materials contract

In both *Archivent* and *Hanson*, the materials were supplied under a sale of goods contract. Section 25 cannot apply where the claimant is a sub-contractor supplying the goods under a contract for work and materials. In *Dawber Williamson* v *Humberside County Council* (1979) 14 BLR 70, a domestic sub-contractor supplied slates to a contractor which went into liquidation before paying for them. None of the slates had been fixed. It seems from the report that the contractor had been paid for them before it went into liquidation. The employer relied on s 25 Sale of Goods Act 1893 (essentially the same as the 1979 Act) as a defence but its counsel did not pursue the argument, rightly in the judge's view. As a result it was unnecessary for the court to explain why the concession was rightly made by looking at the Act.

The sub-contractor submitted that the slates had been brought to site under a supply and fix contract not a contract of sale and it seems that the s 25 defence would have failed on that ground. The court was influenced by *Seath* v *Moore* (1886) 11 App Cas 350 where it was held at 381 that materials could not be regarded as "appropriated to the contract or as sold unless they have been affixed to or in a reasonable sense made part of the corpus" but this statement could not apply to the sub-contract which appears to have been in the Blue Form as it expressly provided for passing of property in the materials after payment of interim certificates which included their value. The parties to a construction contract are free to agree that property in materials shall pass other than on incorporation: on "appropriation" off site, on delivery to site, when their value is included in a valuation or a certificate, when the contractor is paid or when the sub-contractor is paid or on some other event: *Bateman* v *Eric Reed* [1960] 4 SA 151, *Grills* v *Dellios* [1988] VR 136.

The employer failed on a further argument that as the sub-contractor was deemed to have notice of the main contract it had agreed that title to its goods should pass to the employer on payment to the contractor. It was held that deemed notice was insufficient to create privity of contract between employer and sub-contractor and as a result the employer could only have obtained title if it had been the contractor's to transfer. It follows that, in the absence of privity, the only way to pass title to the employer is by express provision in the sub-contract.

The question of incorporation of terms arose in *Sauter Automation* v *Goodman* (1986) 34 BLR 81. Sauter agreed to supply and commission a boiler which was to be installed by others. The equipment had been delivered but the contractor had not been paid for it at the time it went into liquidation. The employer wanted to use the equipment and Sauter attempted to hold the employer to ransom by seeking a declaration of ownership. The main contract was GC/Works/1 which would have allowed the employer to pay Sauter direct but the employer was not prepared to do so. Sauter included a retention of title clause in its tender but it was not incorporated in the contract, having been killed by a counter-offer made by the contractor which was accepted by Sauter's conduct in delivering the equipment. It was held that, in the absence of a retention of title clause, Souter could not recover. There are numerous points of interest in this decision. Although described as a sub-contractor, it seems that Sauter really had a contract for the sale of goods. They were not to instal the equipment: the only element of site work involved was commissioning which made up a small proportion of the contract sum. Section 25 could therefore have applied but did not because the employer had not paid the contractor. The contractor's order to the supplier incorporated GC/Works/1 which has two relevant provisions: clause 3(1) by which anything brought on to the site in connection with the contract and owned by the contractor (or which vests in it under any contract) vests in the employer; and clause 30(2) which obliged the contractor to include in any sub-contract a provision that anything brought on to site by a sub-contractor should vest immediately in the contractor. Clause 3(1) was applicable because for "contractor" it was permissible to read "sub-contractor". Two points arise here:

1. It appears that automatic vesting on delivery to site is equivalent to passing of property on delivery for the purpose of ascertaining when property is to pass under the Sale of Goods Act.

2. There are problems in the wholesale incorporation of main contract conditions into a sub-contract. For example, in *Jack Frost* v *Minister of Public Works* [1980] 3 SA 20, the main contract was not incorporated and an unpaid sub-contractor repossessed its materials on the contractor's liquidation even though the employer had paid the contractor for them.

The court in *Sauter* speculated on the position had the retention of title clause and GC/Works/1 both been incorporated in the sub-contract and held that the two were inconsistent. Clause 3(1) of GC/Works/1 reads:

"From the commencement to the completion of the Works any things (whether or not for incorporation) brought on to the Site in connection with the Contract and which are owned by the Contractor or vest in him under any Contract shall become the property of and vest in the Authority ...".

Read alone, there is no necessary conflict because, by reason of the retention of title clause, the goods will not be owned by the contractor on delivery to site. In view of the direct conflict between the retention of title clause and clause 30(2), the retention of title clause would probably take priority, as special conditions are given precedence over a standard form. This view is supported by the judgment in *Hanson* v *Rapid*.

In response to the decision in *Sauter Automation*, clause 19.4 of JCT 80 was amended to oblige contractors to include in sub-contracts a term that title to materials should pass to the employer as soon as the contractor was paid. This may also reflect the industry's experiences during the recession of the early 1980s (Williams 1987). Contractors often provide a "certificate of indemnity" to the architect as an inducement to certify payment for off site goods and materials under clause 30.3 of JCT 80. However, they may be of no effect if as a matter of law property has not passed to the contractor or where the contractor becomes insolvent. Architects are nervous about certifying for off-site materials in view of the potential risk of a claim for negligence by the employer in this situation.

Injunctions

An unpaid supplier or sub-contractor claiming the benefit of a retention of title clause has various remedies: to apply to the court for an order for delivery up, to apply for an injunction restraining the buyer or contractor from dealing with its goods, to repossess its goods by taking "self help" action, or to sue the buyer for damages in conversion. Assuming the supplier can show it still owns the goods and that damages would not be an adequate remedy, the prospect of an injunction depends on showing that the balance of convenience is in the supplier's favour.

An injunction for delivery up was refused in *Alucraft* v *Costain Australia* (1991) 7 BCL 179. Costain as main contractor delivered materials to Alucraft as sub-contractor for processing and fabrication into cladding. Alucraft issued proceedings alleging that Costain had repudiated the sub-contract claiming damages. Costain counterclaimed that it had properly terminated the sub-contract and claimed a mandatory injunction for the return of materials previously supplied. The injunction was refused on the ground that damages were an adequate remedy and that the balance of convenience lay with Alucraft. The particular facts were important. Alucraft accepted that Costain could collect fabricated panels which had been paid for. There were sufficient quantities of completed panels on site already to ensure that the progress of the works would not be impeded by refusing an injunction. Alucraft undertook to return glass and aluminium which had not yet been used in the fabrication process some which had been only partially used. Alucraft had a lien on partially or fully fabricated panels which had not been paid for which extended to the added value of the materials accrued from the fabrication process. Alucraft was entitled to retain raw steel, reinforcement, fixings, rubber sections, silicone and insulation which had not been used but for which it had not been paid.

One of the best known disputes over steelwork arose out of the last recession in connection with the development of Battersea Power Station. The main contract was under the JCT 67 form as amended which provided that materials and goods brought on to site would become the property of the employer when their prime cost was included in a certificate for which the contractor had been paid. The contractor engaged a sub-contractor under the Green Form to fabricate and erect temporary support steelwork for over £1 million. The contractor paid the sub-contractor but was not paid by the employer. Nearly five years went by before a writ was issued claiming a declaration that property in the steelwork remained with the contractor: *Sir Robert McAlpine* v *Semisquare* (1994) ORB 19. Presumably one of the issues in the case would have been whether the steelwork had become part of the land.

The objective of the unpaid supplier or sub-contractor is not usually the return of its materials but payment. Where payment can be adequately protected, the court is unlikely to grant an injunction for delivery up, even if the paying party is insolvent. In *Lipe* v *Leyland DAF* [1993] BCC 385 a supplier claimed about £100,000 in respect of vehicle parts. A major part of Leyland's business consisted in the sale of spare parts. If the supplier's claim succeeded, it would be followed by hundreds of others which would could wreck the receivers' chances of selling Leyland's business as a going concern. The receivers offered the supplier a personal undertaking in their own names that should its claim be accepted, the receivers would either return the goods or if they had been sold would pay the suppliers their invoice values. The supplier rejected the undertaking since it would have had to take on trust the receivers' personal ability to pay. This was not accepted by the court on the ground that those dealing with receivers rely on the fact that as an agent of the company a receiver is entitled to an indemnity from the company's assets and that as a professional a receiver would not risk bankruptcy by incurring personal liability unless satisfied that there were sufficient assets of the company to enable the liabilities to be paid. In the circumstances, to grant an injunction would be to yield to unfair commercial pressure from the supplier. Although undoubtedly a fair result, the reasoning will come as a surprise to people in the industry whose enquiries as to the level of receivers' PI insurance and indemnity from their firms suggests that they do in fact rely on the receivers' personal assets.

In *Mayflower Foods* v *Barnard* (unreported, 9 August 1996, noted in (1997) 14 BLM 1) the court discharged an injunction obtained *ex parte* preventing receivers disposing of fixtures attached to business premises in circumstances where the receivers had given an undertaking along the lines of the *Lipe* case. The undertaking extended to consequential losses that might be suffered by the claimant, who was an equipment lessor, and any liability the receivers may have for inducing or procuring a breach of the lease, damages being limited to the value of the goods.

If both main and sub-contracts provide that title to unfixed materials identified in an application will pass on payment, the employer will become the owner of the materials when the sub-contractor is paid even if that occurs after the employer pays the contractor for them: *Allco Steel* v *Australian Capital Development Corporation* (unreported, 14 November 1996, noted in (1997) 14 BLM 1). In that case structural steelwork remained on the sub-contractor's premises. The main contract was terminated and the contractor negotiated a settlement of the sub-contract under which the sub-contractor was allowed to keep all materials in its possession. On the sub-contractor selling the materials, the employer successfully claimed damages from it in conversion. The Court of Appeal of New South Wales held that it did not matter in what order payment for the steel had been made. Property in it would pass to the employer as and when the contractor obtained title. If both contracts had been for the sale of goods under retention of title, title would have passed to the employer on its paying the sub-contractor, regardless of whether the supplier had been paid (Goode, 1995, at 475).

In the Australian case of *Remm Construction* v *Allco* (1990) 53 SASR 471 a sub-contract for the supply and erection of structural steel was forfeited by the contractor on the ground of delay. The contractor had paid the sub-contractor for raw steel and steel in course of fabrication off site at sub-sub-contractors' premises. Other payments in respect of the steel had not been made because the contractor claimed a set-off and relied on a right to suspend payment conferred by the forfeiture clause. The sub-contractor warned the sub-sub-contractors not to co-operate with the contractor who obtained an injunction against the sub-contractor preventing it from interfering. The balance of convenience lay in favour of minimising delay to the project rather than conferring a security for payment on the sub-contractor for claims it was pursuing in arbitration. The sub-contractor argued that, although it had been paid, property in the steel had not passed to the contractor because it had not been appropriated to the contract. This was rejected as "appropriation" was a sale of goods concept which could not apply to the sub-contract in this case. The court seems to have assumed that the contractor owned the steel: as between contractor and sub-contractor, the court would stop the sub-contractor interfering in the contractor's attempts to negotiate with the sub-sub-contractors; but as between the contractor and the sub-sub-contractors, the latter may have retained ownership under the terms of their sub-sub-contracts. Had the case been brought in England, s 25 Sale of Goods Act 1979 may well not have applied. Interestingly, the court held that the right to pay sub-sub-contractors direct conferred by the contract operated independently of the forfeiture clause. The fact that the forfeiture clause conferred an express right to use "on site" materials but was silent about "off-site" material was not relevant.

Where the materials are fixed to the land but are "tenant's fixtures" so that as between landlord and tenant they could legally be removed before the end of the term, it has been held in an Irish case that a retention of title supplier could require the tenant (with whom he was in contract) to detach the materials or to exercise the tenant's right of removal: *Re Galway Concrete* [1983] ILRM 402. The court also considered that the supplier would have had a right of re-entry to detach its materials even without an express term to that effect but this aspect is questionable. See also *Taymech* v *Rush & Tompkins* (1990) SLT 681 (removal of an inhibition after receivers appointed).

"Self-help" by sub-contractors by removing goods from site is not uncommon. After the contract has been terminated, the court will grant an injunction restraining removal of goods and materials and in appropriate cases award damages to the employer in conversion: *Marsden* v *Sambell* (1880) 43 LT 120. In the Canadian case of *McNeill* v *Ja Ron Construction* (1979) 35 NSR (2d) 150, a sub-contractor who suspected he might not be paid laid a sceptic tank in the ground but took care not to connect it to the house. On the contractor absconding, the sub-contractor simply turned up with a lorry and removed the tank and other items. It was held that the sub-contractor had not committed any trespass as the employer had never revoked the contractor's licence to the site which the sub-contractor also enjoyed. The employer was liable in conversion to the sub-contractor for refusing to hand over other items taken before the sub-contractor could come back and collect them. Applying *Tripp* v *Armitage* (1839) 4 M&W 687, in the absence of any express provisions regarding passing of title, a sub-contractor's materials would only pass to the landowner on incorporation which had not occurred. The sub-contractor caused no damage to the owner's property in removing the septic tank which had been since installed on another site. This situation could happen in England where the contractor is informally insolvent but no termination event has yet occurred allowing the employer to terminate its employment.

In *Stroud Architectural Systems* v *John Laing* (1993) 35 Con LR 135 a supplier to a sub-contractor claimed damages in conversion against a contractor in respect of glazing units which the sub-contractor had not paid for before its insolvency. The claim relied on a retention of title clause which reserved "equitable and beneficial ownership" to the goods. The court rejected the claim on the ground that the clause created an unregistered floating charge by the sub-contractor in favour of the supplier, following *Re Bond Worth* [1980] 1 Ch 228. Since title had passed to the sub-contractor, the supplier had no interest in the goods and therefore no right to conversion damages.

Insolvency practitioners

Goods and materials belonging to a third person are not property of the company and are beyond a liquidator's reach. If a third party claims unfixed materials on site, a liquidator must investigate the claim, taking legal advice where appropriate, or risk personal liability in conversion or under the Torts (Interference with Goods) Act 1977. The liquidator of the contractor was joined as a party in *Sauter Automation* but avoided liability as property in the supplier's goods had passed to the contractor before liquidation.

Receivers are in greater danger of personal liability as they are more likely to continue trading. The receiver's notice to creditors usually states that deliveries will not be accepted unless they have been signed for by an authorised representative. If a supplier makes a delivery under an existing contract, the receiver will not be personally liable for it; his liability arises only out of contracts entered into by him: *Re Atlantic Computer Systems* [1990] BCC 859 at 866. However, it could be difficult for a receiver to be certain whether the delivery is made under a pre-existing contract: it could in all the circumstances create a new one: *Ball* v *Scott Timber* [1929] NZLR 57.

The facts in *Hanson* v *Rapid* (1987) 38 BLR 106 are instructive. The contractor went into receivership on 15 August. The supplier made a delivery to site the following day. It is not clear from the report what the driver was told but when the supplier demanded payment or return of the goods, both were refused by the receivers. On 17 August, the supplier was allowed access to the site to compile an inventory of the goods but the employer refused to undertake not to use them and proceedings were issued. Assuming that the fresh delivery was not a new contract, the receiver was not personally liable and it seems he played no further part in the proceedings. If, however, he had decided to continue trading and, with knowledge of the supplier's claim, allowed the materials to become fixed, he could have been personally liable in conversion. The same applies where, after a receiver has been appointed, materials are included in an interim certificate and paid for by the employer without notice of a retention of title clause. If property passes to the employer under s 25, again a receiver on notice of the claim could be liable in conversion.

What is the position where the contractor goes into administration? An administrator has power to dispose of property in which another person has a security interest under s 15 Insolvency Act 1986. This includes property subject to a "retention of title agreement" which is defined in s 251 of the Act as:

> "an agreement for the sale of goods to a company, being an agreement (a) which does not constitute a charge on the goods, but (b) under which, if the seller is not paid and the company is wound up, the seller will have priority over all other creditors of the company as respects the goods or any property representing the goods."

A supplier under a retention of title agreement cannot repossess its goods or take proceedings in relation to them without permission from the administrator or leave of the court: s 10 Insolvency Act 1986.

The definition in s 251 is oddly expressed (Goode 1997, 305) and appears to extend beyond a simple sale of goods. Some sub-contract forms provide that title to materials passes when the value of the materials has been included in a certificate which has been paid to the contractor, *e.g.* clause 21.4 of DOM/1. Title is lost under the *quicquid plantatur* rule where the materials are incorporated into the building if this occurs before the contractor has been paid. Where neither of those events has occurred, title will remain in the sub-contractor who would be entitled to repossess the materials. The section refers to "the seller" which is not an appropriate description of a sub-contractor. But this could be overridden by giving the Act a purposive construction. It is as important to the administrator to be able to deal with materials owned by sub-contractors as those owned by suppliers. A sub-contractor should therefore contact the administrator as soon as possible and give notice of its claim to the materials.

Where materials have been brought to site under a retention of title agreement, the administrator has power, with leave of the court, to dispose of the materials as if they were not subject to retention of title. The court will make it a condition of granting leave that the net proceeds of disposal are applied "towards discharging the sums secured by the security": s 15(5) Insolvency Act 1986. On a construction contract, the administrator can destroy the supplier's title by incorporating its materials into the building. This may be treated as a disposal under the Act. The net proceeds would be paid to the administrator under the next certificate.

The retention of title creditor could be prejudiced by the administrator's use of its materials in this way. As title is lost before the administrator is paid for the materials, the availability of the proceeds depends on the solvency of the employer. But a creditor may feel with some justification that it should decide who receives its credit. If the goods were supplied before the administration order and the supply contract was not entered into by the administrator, the creditor's debt would not be a charge on the company's property recoverable in priority to the administrator's remuneration under s 19(5) Insolvency Act 1986. This would leave the creditor with the right to petition the court under s 27 Insolvency Act 1986 on the ground that the company's affairs were being managed by the administrator in a manner unfairly prejudicial to that creditor. This remedy can be expensive and slow and has not so far shown itself of great value to creditors. Retention of title creditors could also be prejudiced where the land is not owned by the employer. Under the *quicquid plantatur* rule, their materials would have passed to a third person with no obligation to pay the administrator for them. Creditors should therefore seek confirmation of the ownership of the land under development and notify the landowner of their retention of title clauses, since this would at least deprive the landowner of a defence under s 25 Sale of Goods Act 1979 in respect of unfixed materials.

It cannot have been the intention of the Act to treat the disposal of materials belonging to a supplier or a sub-contractor differently from an ordinary sale. As the Court of Appeal has stated: "It cannot be right that the appointment of an administrator has the effect of turning a secured into an unsecured creditor": *Re Paramount Airways* [1990] BCC 130 at 151.

> "An intention to take away the property of a subject without the right to compensation is not to be imputed to Parliament unless that intention is expressed in unequivocal terms ... to the extent that the prohibition of s 11 precludes an owner of land or goods from exercising his proprietary rights, s 11 does not have an expropriatory effect. But that is provided for in unequivocal terms. The safety valve which Parliament has built into the system is the owner's ability to make an application to the court. Built into s 11 itself is provision for an application to the court for leave, in the absence of agreement by the administrator" *Re Atlantic Computers* [1990] BCC 859 at 870.

Guidelines have been laid down to assist administrators in exercising their discretion whether to allow creditors to repossess their property: *Re Atlantic Computers*. This requires a delicate balancing exercise. Perhaps retention of title creditors whose property consists of materials intended for incorporation in a building are a special category where permission should be given to repossess unless the administrator can earmark a sum equivalent to their value from another source to pay the creditor in the event their value is not recovered from the employer. Alternatively if the administrator were to give a personal undertaking the court might regard that as sufficient protection by analogy with administrative receivers: *Lipe* v *Leyland DAF* [1993] BCC 385.

Possible relevant factors when considering leave are the importance of the materials in relation to the works as a whole, whether they are readily available or can only be obtained from a specialist supplier with a long lead time, and the terms of payment between employer and administrator. Also relevant are the terms of the sub-contract or supply contract. If it contains a pay when paid clause it could be unjust on the creditor to dispose of its materials without securing their value in advance or, perhaps, deleting the clause. Where the materials are important, the sub-contractor should be involved at the inception of the administration so that its concerns can be taken into account in negotiations with the employer. Continued availability of labour, plant and materials is a significant factor to an employer in deciding whether to allow the administrator to complete current contracts.

Conclusion

The considerable body of case law on construction plant and materials is partly a reflection of their importance on an insolvency but it also stems from the ambiguous words of the standard forms. The treatment of plant shows the limitations of formal security as a way of protecting contractual rights to performance as opposed to payment of a debt. Perhaps because contractors have limited assets, security for an obligation is taken over the very asset needed to perform that obligation. It is highly arguable that vesting clauses are an inappropriate way of managing the commercial risk of unavailability of plant and equipment when needed on site. The discussion on the registrability of vesting clauses also shows the court's reluctance to import questions of security such as bills of sale into the context of a construction contract. There is an intricate relationship between construction receivables and plant and materials. All are susceptible to being "taken hostage" by the employer whether before or after a termination. They are subtly linked in that pay when paid clauses are answered by retention of title clauses and vice versa. They come together in the operation of s 25 Sale of Goods Act 1979 where a payment to a contractor causes title to materials to leapfrog from a supplier to an employer. The overall impression is one of congestion brought about by the employer's quest for total security.

Chapter 5

Set-Off, Abatement and Deduction

Introduction

Assume that A is claiming money from B and that B has a money claim against A. Set-off is the process by which the two claims are set against each other producing a balance. For convenience, let us say that A has a claim and B has a cross-claim. Set-off is a progressive defence to payment, to the extent that the cross-claim approaches the amount of the claim. Once the cross-claim exceeds the claim, it amounts to a complete defence. Set-off can be contrasted with abatement, counterclaim and valuation: see Figure 5.1. Abatement is a defence that a claim should be reduced by the value of goods or services which are not in accordance with the contract. Counterclaim is not a defence but a separate cause of action which the rules of the court allow a defendant to assert in proceedings brought by a plaintiff. Valuation is

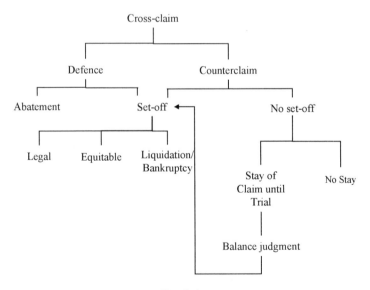

Fig 5.1

neither a defence nor a claim but a procedure to determine the amount of a claim, although it might also involve set-off if it involved a genuine balancing of claims. All three aspects will be considered later.

Set-off cannot arise if the claim or the cross-claim is for property other than money. A cross-claim for delivery up of a chattel, for a declaration or for possession of land cannot be set off against a claim for money. Nor can set-off exist unless both claims are owed between the same persons in the same capacity. A cannot set off against B a cross-claim against B which it is asserting as trustee for C. Nor can A set off against B a cross-claim it may have against C. This is because B's claim is against A whereas the cross-claim against B is really made by or against C.

Set-off performs several different functions. Where both parties are solvent, set-off exists for commercial convenience: why insist on two payments, when one will do? In this sense set-off is a means of payment. If a dispute arises, set-off avoids unnecessary proceedings: why have two actions, when a writ for the balance will do? Set-off is also a way of simplifying disputes. Where one of the parties goes into liquidation or becomes bankrupt, set-off is intended to do justice between them, otherwise the liquidator or the trustee would be able to recover the claim in full, leaving it to the other person to prove for a dividend in respect of its cross-claim. This is a question of public policy, and does not apply to receivership, administration or any other insolvency procedure.

Problem solving

Unlike the law of assignment, set-off is well served by textbooks which give a very comprehensive account of the subject (Wood 1989, Derham 1996). This chapter explains the law of set-off by adopting a problem-solving approach. It is suggested that there are six questions which need to be considered:

1. What is the nature of the claim and the cross-claim?

2. Would the common law allow them to be set off?

3. Is there an arrangement between the parties which alters the common law position?

4. Would the insolvency of either party make any difference?

5. Are there any limitations on the enforceability of set-off?

6. Are there any procedural alternatives to set-off?

It may not be necessary to look at all six stages. Outside insolvency, disputes in the industry tend to revolve around the third question. Set-off in insolvency is considered in Chapter 13. The particular nature of industry cross-claims based on breaches of obligations as to time, quality and cost are dealt with later.

Types of money claims

One of the most important criteria for the availability of set-off is whether the two claims are quantified or quantifiable without the intervention of a third party. In this context, the law regards a claim as quantified if it is easily ascertainable by a simple calculation. It may help to consider examples of both kinds of claim: see Figure 5.2.

QUANTIFIED/QUANTIFIABLE	UNQUANTIFIABLE
Sums due	Work in progress
Invoiced amounts	Quantum meruit
Book debts	Future debts
Rent and mesne profits	General damages
Hire charges and freight	Interest as special damages
Taxed costs	Untaxed costs
Judgment debts	Order for damages to be assessed
Liquidated damages	Restitutionary claims
Contractual interest	Damages in tort
Money lent	

Fig 5.2

Distinctions like this are important in other contexts too: assignability, accounting treatment, litigation, fixed and floating charges and so on. With set-off, the issue is not so much the correct legal classification of a claim as its quantifiability without recourse to a third party. A claim for liquidated damages is regarded as quantified even though it is a claim for damages. A claim for an indemnity would be quantified if it were an indemnity against liability for a judgment debt but not for damages.

Set-off at common law

Owing to its historical origins, the common law of set-off is clear but illogical. There are two kinds of set-off to consider: equitable and legal. Equitable set-off arises where the two claims are so closely connected that it would be unjust to allow the claim to proceed without setting off the cross-claim. It does not matter whether the claim or cross-claim is quantified or unquantifiable. Legal set-off arises where the two claims are unrelated and is restricted to claims and cross-claims which are both quantified or easily quantifiable. There is therefore a gap in the common law which does not allow the set-off of a cross-claim which is unrelated to the claim and is unquantifiable without reference to a third party: *Axel Johnson* v *M G Mineral* [1992] 1 WLR 270. As might be expected, the two kinds of common law set-off have different origins. Equity intervened to provide relief where a debtor had a cross-claim which "impeached the title" to the claim: *Rawson* v *Samuel* (1841) Cr & Ph 161. In other words it was a question of conscience. Legal set-off arose to avoid the practical problem of a debtor being sent to prison for non-payment of a claim when he had a cross-claim exceeding the claim which could not be taken into account in equity because it was not connected with it.

Equitable set-off

The test is whether the cross-claim is so closely connected to the claim as to make it unjust not to allow it to be set off. Two general points arise from this. The first is that set-off will not necessarily be available just because both claims arise out of the same transaction: *Esso* v *Milton* [1997] 2 All ER 593. In view of *Hanak* v *Green* [1958] 2 QB 9, it seems that the court is more generous in upholding claims for set-off with construction contracts than other commercial arrangements. The endorsement of this decision by the House of Lords in *Gilbert-Ash* v *Modern Engineering* [1974] AC 689 means it cannot be regarded as an aberration. The second point is that equitable set-off is not simply a matter of discretion for the judge. It involves a careful and thorough examination of the facts and the application of equitable principles. It is as if the cross-claim were woven into the fabric of the claim. In recent cases, the court has asked the following questions: has the act or omission giving rise to the cross-claim prevented the cross-claimant from deriving a significant benefit from the transaction? apart from any transactional link, does the cross-claim have any relevance to the claim? does it ethically undermine it? was the cross-claim in existence when the claim arose? has either party acted manipulatively? See *Eller* v *Grovecrest Investments* [1995] 2 WLR 278, *Esso* v *Milton* [1997] 2 All ER 593, *Star Rider* v *Inntrepreneur* (unreported, 8 December 1997).

It may be useful at this stage to illustrate the distinction between equitable and legal set-off by reference to a Canadian case, *Aboussafy* v *Abacus Cities* [1981] 4 WWR 660. There were three separate contracts between employer and contractor. In 1974 the contractor sold the site to the employer, in 1975 the contractor agreed to build on the site for the employer, and in 1977 the contractor agreed to manage the building for the employer. The contractor went into receivership and the receiver sued for recovery of sums due under the management agreement. The employer claimed set-off in relation to claims it had under the sale and construction contracts but set-off was refused. The cross-claims were unliquidated so legal set-off was not available. The three contracts were not sufficiently connected to qualify for equitable set-off: it was just a coincidence that the employer happened to have cross-claims under the other agreements.

In a Malaysian case a purchaser agreed to buy land from a builder who in turn agreed to construct a "shophouse" on the land within 18 months. It was completed five months late, by which time the purchaser still owed the final instalment of the purchase price. The purchaser successfully claimed the amount by which liquidated damages for the builder's delay exceeded the unpaid balance of the purchase price. She was not in breach of contract in withholding the final instalment since she was entitled to an equitable set-off which gave her a complete defence: *SEA Housing* v *Lee Poh Choo* [1982] 2 MLJ 33.

Abatement

Abatement is a defence that a claim should be reduced by the value of goods or services which are not in accordance with the contract: *Mondel* v *Steel* (1841) 8 M & W 858. In that case the claim was for the balance of the contract price and an amount for extra work due under a shipbuilding contract. The ship had needed the repairs after a voyage from London to Australia because of breaches of specification and the owner was held entitled to abate the claim by the cost of the repairs. Abatement has been recognised and confirmed in many subsequent decisions: *Aries Tanker* v *Total Transport* [1977] 1 WLR 185, *Colonial*

Bank v European Grain [1989] 1 Lloyd's Rep 431. A valuation of the goods or services actually delivered has to be made which is then deducted from the value they would have had if they had conformed with the contract. It may be possible to make this valuation simply by referring to the contractor's tender or invoice, but if he has simply charged a lump sum a fair assessment has to be made by the customer, supported if necessary by an expert's report. It is incorrect to reduce the claim by the cost of having the goods or services made to conform with the contract requirements: *Duquemin* v *Slater* (1993) 35 Con LR 147. The defence goes to the quality of the product or service rather than the performance of some other contractual obligation. A contractor's claim for payment cannot therefore be reduced by the loss suffered by the employer through delayed performance: *Mellowes Archital* v *Bell Projects* (1997) 87 BLR 26. Abatement is by reference to the value of the service as a whole rather than specific elements of it. If a contractor agrees to construct a reinforced concrete beam but omits the steel, the employer is likely to be able to abate the whole price rather than just the value of the missing reinforcement: *Hodgson* v *Miller Construction* (unreported, 1995, noted in Neil F Jones 1999).

Abatement is a common law doctrine but it is now contained in s 53 Sale of Goods Act 1979, as far as contracts for the sale of goods are concerned. Abatement applies to the supply of work and labour but not to contracts for professional services. The defence was refined by the Court of Appeal in a case where the court refused to abate an architect's claim for unpaid fees: *Hutchinson* v *Harris* (1978) 10 BLR 19. There were four grounds:

1. Abatement was contended in respect of damages for negligent supervision and over-certification but there was evidence that these had already been set off.

2. It had not been established that the principle could apply to a claim for professional services at all.

3. It was not disputed that the architect had performed the work represented by the fees claimed.

4. The claim was essentially different from *Mondel* v *Steel* because that case concerned a reduction in the value of the subject matter of the action by a breach of contract. Here the claim arose from the architect's contract for services, rather than the building work which was the subject of a separate contract.

The distinction between contracts for work and labour and for professional services is not always clear. Relevant factors are the nature of the personnel involved, the scope of work and the question whether the obligations assumed are those ordinarily undertaken by professionals: *Foster Wheeler* v *Chevron* (unreported, 29 February 1996).

The same facts can give rise to abatement and equitable set-off as alternatives: *Barnett* v *Peter Cox* (1995) 45 Con LR 131. It is possible that the cost of rectifying defective work could be the same as the difference between the value of the work done and the value it would have had if it been carried out in accordance with the contract: consider *Barrett Steel* v *Amec* (1997) 15 CLD 10-07. This could arise where the replacement builder is not called on to take down defective work and make good or perhaps where the cost of labour or materials falls after the original work is done. In most cases, however, the amount of an equitable set-off will be higher than an abatement in order to take account of preparatory work, increased costs and the fact that the original builder may have under-estimated for the work in its tender.

The distinction between abatement and equitable set-off is most relevant in the context of exclusion clauses. It will be a question of construction whether the contract excludes abatement or equitable set-off or both: *Acsim* v *Danish* (1989) 47 BLR 55. Abatement is not subject to the law of limitation in view of its character as a defence rather than a claim. Neither is an equitable set-off provided the facts giving rise to the cross-claim also amount to a defence on the merits: *Filross Securities* v *Midgeley* [1998] 3 EGLR 43. If the cross-claim is merely a counterclaim for damages, it cannot be set off in equity if it has a shorter limitation period than the claim, and the claimant waits until after the cross-claim has expired before issuing proceedings: *Aries Tanker* v *Total Transport* [1971] 1 WLR 185. The right to abate is implicit in the words "work properly executed" in clause 30 of JCT 1998: consider *Barrett Steel* v *Amec*. In *Ellis Tylin* v *Co-operative Retail Services* [1999] BLR 205 at 221, the employer reserved an express right of abatement under a maintenance contract, with an additional right to deduct a 10% retention from future payments if the work represented by the abatement was not done.

Accounting process

An accounting process determines the amount of a claim or when the claim will become due. It does not usually involve set-off but can act as a defence: *Bovis Construction* v *Ergon* (unreported, 30 March 1994,

Court of Appeal). This case arose out of the insolvency of the Olympia & York Group, the employer on the Canary Wharf project. Ergon achieved practical completion of its work and signed an agreement in full and final settlement of its final account before the employer went into administration. The issue was who was to bear the loss: Bovis as management contractor or Ergon as works contractor. Ergon obtained summary judgment but lost on appeal. On its true construction, the works contract entitled Ergon to payment within 21 days after Bovis submitted an application to the employer. Bovis had not done this when the employer went into administration and there was no allegation of breach in having failed to do so. The termination clauses commonly found in construction contracts are examples of accounting processes involving an element of set-off.

Legal set-off

Legal set-off is also known as "common law" "independent" or "statutory" set-off. Disputes usually arise over the nature of the claim and the cross-claim rather than the question whether they are related to each other or not: the issue is the quantifiability of the two claims rather than their recoverability after taking into account available defences. In the early case of *Lett* v *Morris* (1831) 4 Sim 607, a contractor carried out repairs and alterations for a bank. The contractor went bankrupt before receiving payment and his trustees sued the bank to recover the value of the building work. The bank had a cross-claim against the builder as assignee of sums owing by the builder on a bank account at a different bank. The builder had given security to its banker which had also been assigned. After the security had been realised, the proceeds were found to be insufficient to discharge the debt which exceeded the builder's claim. Legal set-off was allowed as claim and cross-claim were independent mutual debts which preceded the bankruptcy.

Legal set-off is not particularly common in the industry since at least one of the claims tends to be unliquidated. A cross-claim for an over-payment for example which relies for quantification on a surveyor's report prepared on behalf of only one of the parties will be treated as unliquidated: *Hargreaves* v *Action 2000* (1992) 36 Con LR 74. The case concerned nine sub-contracts between Action 2000 as contractor and Hargreaves as sub-contractor. They were all signed on the same day and related to nine petrol stations which Action 2000 was building to the same design for the same employer. The sub-contractor went into receivership and there was a sum due from the contractor on one of the sub-contracts. Action 2000 attempted to set off cross-claims for overpayment arising under two of the other sub-contracts. The cross-claims could not be set off in equity as they were unconnected or at law because the cross-claim was unquantifiable.

Legal set-off can apply, where a claim for a certified sum is met by a cross-claim for liquidated damages (Wood 1989 at 2-84). This may be subject, however, to the satisfaction of conditions such as a certificate. If liquidated damages are the subject of a claim, the question of the certificate will be dealt with as an ordinary defence at a summary judgment hearing before the court goes on to examine the proposed defence of set-off. Where liquidated damages are asserted as a cross-claim, the position is less clear. Legal set-off is perhaps least likely between contractor and sub-contractor as liquidated damages clauses are less common in sub-contracts. Legal set-off is more likely between suppliers where mutual trading is on the basis of invoices, as in the manufacturing and retailing industries. Another possible application is where a contractor is carrying out more than one contract for an employer. The employer may have a liquidated cross-claim if the contractor has refused to remove defective work and the employer has engaged an alternative sub-contractor for that purpose. Clause 2(1) of JCT 63 provides that the cost is recoverable from the defaulting contractor as a debt.

Legal set-off is a purely defensive right: it can only be used as a shield, not as a sword. It can only arise as a defence in proceedings brought by the creditor. The court encourages the claimant to give credit for the debtor's cross-claim where legal set-off is available. So much so that if credit is not given, the claimant may be penalised in costs: *Stooke* v *Taylor* (1880) 5 QBD 569. As a consequence of its historical origins, legal set-off is not available where either claim is subject to arbitration: *Aectra* v *Exmar* [1994] 1 WLR 1634. This restricts the use of legal set-off in the industry still further. In *Aectra*, there was a claim for a sum due pursuant to a settlement agreement which was met by a cross-claim for a liquidated sum arising under a separate dispute which had been stayed to arbitration under the Arbitration Act 1975. The cross-claim could not be set off since it was not being pursued by action. Only a contractual set-off clause can cure this problem. The choice of forum is not relevant where the cross-claimant seeks equitable set-off. In summary, a cross-claim can be set off in arbitration where it amounts to an abatement or equitable set-off but not where the respondent claims legal set-off or makes a counterclaim which is not also an equitable set-off (Aeberli 1992).

Contractual set-off

In its purest form, contractual set-off creates a set-off where none would otherwise be available, but it is also a useful way of describing terms which expand, re-state, exclude or cut down common law remedies. A contract can expand on the common law in several ways: (1) by allowing set-off of unliquidated claims arising from unrelated contracts, (2) by removing the restrictions on equitable set-off by allowing any cross-claim relating to the contract to be set off whether or not it is connected to the claim, and (3) by allowing either or both parties to exercise group set-off, rather as the Crown does on government contracts. There is little case law dealing with group set-off clauses: *Gallemos* v *Barratt* (1990) SLT 98 is a Scottish example.

As well as expanding common law set-off, contracts also confer rights of deduction which are not available under the common law. In the industry, these include retention of a percentage of the value of work done until completion and cash discounts of a percentage of the difference between the value of the work done and the retention. Perhaps surprisingly, the expression "cash discount" may not be construed as a discount depending on prompt payment unless the context is clear: *Team Services* v *Kier* (1993) 63 BLR 76.

Dawnays' case

It is common for construction contracts to restate the common law without intending to affect either party's rights. The only problem with this approach is that, where the clause only sets out some of the rights available under common law, it opens up the possibility that the parties may be taken to have intended to have excluded the common law except for those rights. Lord Denning MR treated a clause of this type as the peg on which to hang the proposition that claims for payment under a certificate were exempt from set-off unless and until they were enshrined in a court order or arbitrator's award: *Dawnays* v *Minter* [1971] 1 WLR 1205. This became known as the "rule" in *Dawnays'* case. The court had before it a claim by a sub-contractor for payment under a certificate which was met by a contractor's cross-claim for damages for delay. The contract provided that:

> "The contractor shall notwithstanding anything in this sub-contract be entitled to deduct from or set off against any money due from him to the sub-contractor (including any retention money) any sum or sums which the sub-contractor is liable to pay to the contractor under this sub-contract."

Set-off was refused as the court construed this clause (in particular the word "liable") as restricting the contractor's right of set-off to liquidated and ascertained sums established by a judgment or an arbitration award or otherwise admitted due. It is not stated in the judgment whether submissions were made on the question whether the general law had been excluded. Damages were estimated initially at £47,000 and later revised to £61,000 and exceeded the sub-contractor's claim. The court seems to have considered that the revision to the calculation indicated a lack of credibility in the cross-claim as a whole and may have rejected it as shadowy. It does, however, appear from the report that the delays were on the critical path of the works. It also seems that the architect had not issued a certificate of delay which may have been a condition precedent to the set-off of any cross-claim for delay related costs. The decision could perhaps be justified on either of these grounds but the court went on to elaborate a more general principle that interim certificates created a special class of debt against which set-off was not possible apart from fraud. Lord Denning MR stated:

> "Every businessman knows the reason why interim certificates are issued and why they have to be honoured. It is so that the sub-contractor can have the money in hand to get on with his work and the further work he has to do ... an interim certificate is to be regarded virtually as cash, like a bill of exchange. It must be honoured. Payment must not be withheld on account of cross-claims, whether good or bad except so far as the contract specifically provides. Otherwise any main contractor could always get out of payment by making all sorts of unfounded cross-claims. All the more so in a case like the present where the main contractors have actually received the money" (at 1209).

Lord Denning thus departed from the mainstream of existing law by attempting to restrict equitable set-off to judgment debts or sums admitted as due. *Dawnays* was followed in a series of later decisions in the Court of Appeal before they were all overruled by the House of Lords in *Gilbert-Ash* v *Modern Engineering* [1974] AC 689. The law is therefore that a certified sum is not insulated from set-off like freight or a bill of exchange unless the contract clearly provides otherwise.

Modifying the general law

The majority of industry disputes over set-off concern the contractual exclusion or restriction of common law rights. It is a question of construction of the contract in each case whether the parties have excluded or modified the general law. The House of Lords decided that the contract in *Gilbert-Ash* had not excluded the general law. Lord Reid thought that the contract term dealing with set-off was "intended to supersede and be substituted for the common right of set-off" (at 698) but the majority were of the view that although the contract gave a right of deduction, it did not go far enough to exclude the contractor's rights under the general law:

> "… when one is concerned with a building contract one starts with the presumption that each party is to be entitled to all those remedies for its breach as would arise by operation of law, including the remedy of setting up a breach of warranty in diminution or extinction of the price of materials supplied or work executed under the contract. To rebut that presumption one must be able to find in the contract clear unequivocal words in which the parties have expressed their agreement that this remedy shall not be available in respect of breaches of that particular contract" (at 718).

The absence of "clear unequivocal words" excluding the general law meant that the set-off clause merely re-stated the general law.

It sometimes forgotten that *Gilbert-Ash* v *Modern Engineering* [1974] AC 689 also decided that the common law of abatement and set-off could be excluded by implication as well as by clear words. In the United Kingdom, the court has focused on the adequacy of words attempting to exclude set-off, and has not considered how set-off can be excluded by implication. In a series of decisions, the Australian courts have gone down this road by looking at the contract as a whole. In *Algons Engineering* v *Abigroup Contractors* (1998) 14 BCL 215, a contractor claimed to set off liquidated damages for delay and damages for defects against a sub-contractor's progress payment claim but failed because the common law of set-off had been excluded (see Chapter 17).

The court also requires very clear words to show the parties' intention that a bona fide estimate of future loss should be sufficient to ground a set-off. The introduction of construction management as a new form of procurement has led to many one-off contract forms. In *Rosehaugh* v *Redpath Dorman Long* (1990) 50 BLR 69 two claims were made by the employer for £5.2 million and £3.1 million respectively, representing bona fide estimates made by the construction manager. Summary judgment was refused by the Court of Appeal on two grounds: the trade contractor's set-off rights had not been excluded by the contract and it had arguable cross-claims for variations, loss and expense or damages. The text of a similar prospective set-off clause is given in *Mowlem* v *Eagle Star* (1992) 33 Con LR 131 at 135.

The House of Lords has decided that the parties are perfectly free to exclude the principle of abatement as well as the general law of set-off: *Mottram* v *Bernard Sunley* [1975] 2 Lloyd's Rep 197. The decision arose from the deletion from a printed form of contract of the following words:

> "Any amount which the employer or the co-ordinator on his behalf shall be entitled to deduct from or set off against any money due from him to the contractor (including any retention money) in virtue of any provisions of the contract or any breach thereof by the contractor."

It was held that there were no "clear unequivocal words" excluding abatement and set-off. There had however been clear words conferring such rights which had been deleted by the parties. The court was entitled to take the deleted words into account when construing the contract. It appears that abatement was excluded by the parties' deletion of the word "deduct" as "deduction" had been specifically referred to in *Mondel* v *Steel*.

A contract can exclude the general law and confer strictly defined set-off rights which can only be exercised in certain circumstances. The court requires clear drafting to exclude the general law and the parties may inadvertently fail to exclude every category of set-off or abatement. This can be illustrated by *Acsim* v *Danish* (1989) 47 BLR 55. The facts were rather unusual because, as well as owning the site, Dancon was main contractor and architect. Its contract with Acsim was in the Blue Form of non-nominated sub-contract, substantially amended by the parties, but there was no main contract. The Blue Form provided for payment within 14 days of Acsim's invoice and contained the following term in respect of set-off: "The rights of the parties to this sub-contract in respect of set-off are fully set out in these conditions and no other rights whatsoever shall be implied as terms of this sub-contract relating to set-off." The court construed this clause as excluding rights of set-off under the general law but not the principle of abatement and Dancon was allowed to abate Acsim's claim.

One of the peculiarities of the industry is that the parties sometimes fail to form a contract at all, even where substantial works are involved. In this situation, a cross-claim for set-off may be answered by the argument that no contract had been formed and that the plaintiff's claim could only be for a reasonable sum under a *quantum meruit*. In *Pillar* v *Croudace* (unreported, 19 December 1984) a sub-contractor's claim for an interim payment under the Green Form was met by a counterclaim for charges and services rendered, defective work and damages for delay and disruption. The sub-contract provided that:

"Notwithstanding anything contained in this sub-contract, Croudace Limited or any associated companies will be entitled to deduct from this sub-contract, any monies due, whether under this sub-contract or otherwise."

On the evidence, the Official Referee concluded that no contract had been formed and dismissed the application but granted leave to the sub-contractor to amend its pleading to claim payment on a *quantum meruit.*

Outside construction, loan agreements, guarantees and leases are examples of contracts which frequently exclude the common law, *e.g.* in one case a combined loan agreement and guarantee stated:

> "All payments under this agreement ... shall be made in United States dollars, in immediately available funds, free and clear of any right of set-off or counter-claim or any withholding or deduction whatsoever ...".

The clause was effective to give the claimant summary judgment. An application to stay execution of the judgment pending the hearing of the borrower's cross-claims in New York was refused: *Coca-Cola* v *Finsat* [1996] 3 WLR 849.

Each clause will be carefully examined by the court, with particular reference to the facts. Several points are worth drawing out. First, if the clause prohibits deduction rather than set-off, it may in context not be clear enough to exclude common law set-off rights. The term "deduction" is not a legal term of art: *Connaught Restaurants* v *Indoor Leisure* [1994] 1 WLR 501. Secondly, if an agreement excludes the withholding of payment of "sums properly due", it may not be sufficient to exclude set-off. The court may distinguish withholding payment from discharging a claim by way of set-off. Agreeing not to withhold payment of sums "properly due" begs the question of the claim's validity: *Esso* v *Milton* [1997] 2 All ER 593. Thirdly, abatement and set-off are separate processes. A contract excluding the one will not automatically be taken to exclude the other. In the leading case on this point, a sub-contractor claimed for sums due, relying on the following term adapted from the Blue Form of non-nominated sub-contract: "The rights of the parties to this sub-contract in respect of set-off are fully set out in these conditions and no other rights whatsoever shall be implied as terms of this sub-contract relating to set-off". The Court of Appeal concluded that the clause was effective to exclude set-off but not abatement: *Acsim* v *Danish* (1989) 47 BLR 55.

Statutory and other limitations

Legal set-off and liquidation and bankruptcy set-off are derived from statute. As well as creating rights of set-off, however, statute also restricts such rights in certain situations. The most significant are set-off clauses which are deemed to be unfair, or to contravene the policy of insolvency law or fail to comply with construction industry legislation.

Unfair Contract Terms Act 1977

Where a set-off exclusion clause is contained in standard terms of business, it may fall within the ambit of the Unfair Contract Terms Act 1977. The issue for the court is whether a relevant term, when construed as a whole, is reasonable, rather than the particular part relied upon as excluding set-off rights: *Esso v Milton* [1997] 2 All ER 593 at 602. It is hard to generalise as the court will carefully scrutinise the wording of the contract and the factual background. A clause in a contract for the provision of mechanical plant was held unreasonable on the ground that it prevented the withholding of payment by reason of any "payment, credit, set-off, counterclaim, allegation of incorrect or defective goods or for any other reason whatsoever which the customer may allege excludes him for performing his obligations hereunder": *Stewart Gill* v *Horatio Meyer* [1992] 2 All ER 257. In contrast, a term was held to be reasonable where it excluded set-off against payment "in cash or as otherwise agreed [of] all sums immediately when due". The term was contained in standard conditions adopted by the freight forwarding industry after extensive negotiations between representative bodies and was in widespread use: *Schenkers* v *Overland Shoes* [1998] 1 Lloyd's Rep 498. The Act also applies to attempts to exclude set-off for cross claims for misrepresentation: *Skipskredittforeningen* v *Emperor Navigation* [1998] 1 Lloyd's Rep 66. However, the aim is to strike down clauses limiting liability rather than setting out a procedure for dealing with claims. There is no policy bar against a clause excluding set-off of cross-claims for fraud. It is clauses excluding liability for fraud which are at risk. The court has accepted that one of the reasons for excluding set-off is to protect the creditor in case it gets into financial difficulty or the debenture holder where receivers are appointed: *John Dee* v *WMH (21) Ltd* [1997] BCC 518 at 522, affirmed [1998] BCC 972 at 976.

Insolvency Act 1986

Contracts attempting to exclude liquidation or bankruptcy set-off will not be upheld by the courts. This is on the ground of public policy: *National Westminster Bank* v *Halesowen* [1972] 1 All ER 641, *British Eagle* v *Air France* [1975] 2 All ER 390.

Housing Grants, Construction and Regeneration Act 1996

Set-off in connection with construction contracts is now regulated by the Housing Grants, Construction and Regeneration Act 1996 (see Chapter 3). The Act does not exclude the common law of set-off or abatement but imposes certain procedural conditions to the valid exercise of such rights. Non-compliance would mean the loss of such rights against the payment concerned but the payer would still have another opportunity to make the set-off or abatement at the following payment interval. The relevant sections of the Act read:

> "110(2). Every construction contract shall provide for the giving of notice by a party not later than five days after the date on which a payment becomes due from him under the contract, or would have become due if (a) the other party had carried out his obligations under the contract, and (b) no set-off or abatement was permitted by reference to any sum claimed to be due under one or more other contracts, specifying the amount (if any) of the payment made or proposed to be made, and the basis on which that amount was calculated.
>
> 111(1). A party to a construction contract may not withhold payment after the final date for payment of a sum due under the contract unless he has given an effective notice of intention to withhold payment. The notice mentioned in section 110(2) may suffice as a notice of intention to withhold payment if it complies with the requirements of the section. (2) To be effective such a notice must specify (a) the amount proposed to be withheld and the ground for withholding payment, or (b) if there is more than one ground, each ground and the amount attributable to it, and must be given not later than the prescribed period before the final date for payment."

Assume a sub-contractor values its work at £100. The contractor disagrees and considers the value of the work to be £80. The contractor also wishes to set off £30 for defective work previously carried out. Assume the Scheme for Construction Contracts applies. The effect of the Act on abatement is not entirely clear, but it seems that the position would be as follows:

1. The amount due to the sub-contractor would be £100. Under the Scheme the date of submission of the application is also the due date for payment.

2. The contractor must serve a payment notice within five days saying what it intends to pay. If the contractor has all the available information, it may be able to make the deductions of £20 and £30 at this stage. If so, then the payment notice would have to contain the same information required of a withholding notice. The payment notice would then state that £50 would be paid that month.

3. If the contractor could only substantiate a deduction of £20 on valuation grounds by payment notice stage, the notice would state that £80 was due. The contractor could then serve a withholding notice witholding a further £30 for defects, which would be effective provided it was served at least seven days before the final date for payment. If the sub-contractor wished to challenge the deductions, it could refer the dispute to adjudication.

The contractor may prefer to draft its own payment procedure rather than rely on the Scheme. There are various possibilities. The contractor could adopt a system based on certification to the sub-contractor. Under this procedure, a sub-contractor could apply for £100, but the contractor would issue a certificate for £80, and only that amount would become due. In this way, the contractor has exercised a right of abatement and had an influence on what becomes due and when. The sub-contract certificate could count as the payment notice if it complied with s 110(2). The contractor could reserve the right to serve a payment notice to cater for situations where it wished to make a further deduction after issuing its payment certificate, enabling it to make a further abatement or a set-off. If the contractor wished to make a set-off (*e.g.* for defects under this contract or for another cross-claim under a different contract), its payment notice would have to comply with the requirements of a withholding notice set out in s 111. However, to achieve this result, it would require very careful drafting. There may be complications with set-off across two contracts where the Act applies to both of them. Would a withholding notice be required under both contracts? The contractor could then make a further set-off after serving a withholding notice within the required period before the payment date. If this is right, a contractor could have up to three opportunities to make an abatement of the monthly sum payable to the sub-contractor and two opportunities to operate a set-off. The sub-contractor may protest that this is against the spirit of the Act. If the Act were intended to invalidate spurious set-offs, that might be so. However, it seems more directed to ensuring certainty as to what becomes payable to the sub-contractor and when. It does not address the question whether a cross-claim could be set off at common law.

Section 110(2) and the second sentence of s 111(1) were introduced into the Bill at a very late stage, only a few weeks before it gained Royal Assent at the end of July 1996. The wording beginning "… or would have become due …" is a little hard to understand. It seems to be relevant only for the purposes of timing when considering whether the payer has provided its payment notice within five days after the date an amount became due. This is a rather complicated way of preventing the payer arguing that it need not serve a payment notice because the sub-contractor is in breach of another contract and, by reason of the set-off arising from that breach, nothing will become due for payment.

It has been argued that s 110(2) refers not to abatement but to deductions such as discount and retention and that s 111 may not require any notice where an abatement as opposed to a set-off is intended (Barrett 1998). The rationale is that the section only requires a notice where the payer wants to withhold payment against a "sum due", but abatement would normally reduce the sum due against which withholding can be made rather than constitute a withholding in itself (see the discussion earlier on *Acsim* v *Danish*). The contrary argument is that the Act uses the term "witholding" which, if given a purposive construction, is wide enough to include abatement as well as set-off. It also goes against the intention of the Act which is to prevent any reduction of payment for whatever reason which has not been fully notified in advance. In the industry, abatement can cause as much damage to cash flow as set-off.

It is useful to bear in mind the key concepts for ss 109 to 111. The statutory language of "final date for payment" is unusual: it may simply reflect the distinction between a sum being due and becoming payable. The grace period means that the contractor will not be in breach if it makes a payment on or before the payment date. Secondly, there is a distinction between rights at common law and rights under the contract. The Act operates as a statutory gloss on common law rights of set-off and (arguably) abatement. Although it might be thought that the requirement of a payment notice and a withholding notice would be an improvement in the sub-contractor's position in that it imposes more hurdles to set-off for the contractor to overcome, this need not be the case. Carefully drafted payment procedures and their reflection in contractual terms could mean that the contractor has rights of set-off similar to those it had before the Act. After the Act, if a construction contract fails to provide for advance notice of any set-off, such a term is automatically included by operation of the Scheme for Construction Contracts. Will this deprive the payee of an argument that the common law of set-off has been excluded by implication, having reference to all of the contract terms? After all, if a contract provides for notice before set-off, even if only by statutory implication, it affirms the common law rather than excludes it.

The Act introduces a set-off procedure into all "construction contracts" as defined in the Act. It is important to note, however, that the statutory procedure is different from set-off clauses found in sub-contract forms in use before the Act. For example, there is no express requirement to set out the ground for withholding payment "in detail and with reasonable accuracy" as was the case under DOM/1. It remains to be seen whether the courts will apply the same test as they did in that context. Although helpful, the numerous cases reported in the 1980s on the operation of these clauses by contractors may not be regarded as precedents when hearing disputes under s 111, especially if the court takes a purposive approach to the legislation.

Common law restrictions

Apart from statute, there are some common law restrictions on set-off. The first is that a claim brought on a dishonoured cheque is immune from set-off unless the cross-claim be based in fraud, duress, invalidity or a total failure of consideration: *Nova (Jersey) Knit* v *Kammgarn* [1977] 2 All ER 463. The second is that set-off is not available where the claim is brought in respect of a cancelled direct debit arrangement, subject to the same exceptions: *Esso* v *Milton* [1997] 2 All ER 593.

Industry cross-claims

In practice there are two scenarios:

1. A contractor has a claim for payment for work done and materials supplied which is resisted by a cross-claim for delay and disruption, bad workmanship or over-valuation, and

2. An employer has a claim for damages against the contractor under the above headings which is met by a cross-claim for monies due under a contract or damages for its breach.

It is immaterial whether the cross-claim is made by the employer or the contractor. For the purposes of the following discussion, it is assumed that the employer is defending the contractor's claim.

Delay

A contractor's claim for payment for work done and materials supplied may be defeated by equitable set-off of a cross-claim for delay. In *Young v Kitchen* (1878) 3 Ex D 127 a contractor agreed to construct two buildings for an employer. On completion, over £6,000 became due and payable which the contractor assigned to Young. Young gave notice of assignment to the employer. On the employer's failure to pay, the assignee sued for the balance of the contract sum but was met by a cross-claim of £2,400 for delay and £800 for defects. The two buildings were due for completion by August and September 1876 but were not completed until November 1876 and August 1877 respectively. The employer had been unable to let them for commercial purposes. It was held that the employer was entitled to set off its cross-claim for damages in reduction of the assignee's claim. Although it was unliquidated, the cross-claim flowed out of the same transaction and the criteria for equitable set-off were satisfied.

In *Ellis v Wates* (1976) 2 BLR 57 a sub-contractor claimed release of retention after the main contract had been terminated. The contractor's cross-claim included an element of delay related costs incurred on a different contract between the parties. Although both contracts concerned the same development, the employers were different and set-off was refused for lack of mutuality. The Court of Appeal later considered a claim by a sub-contractor for an interim payment which was met by a cross-claim from the contractor for damages based on a nine week delay which over-topped the claim: *NEI Thompson v Wimpey* (1987) 39 BLR 65. Applying *Gilbert-Ash*, it was decided that the contractor could "rely on their cross-claim by way of set-off under the rule in *Mondel v Steel*." This is not strictly correct because that case concerned abatement which gives a defence not a right of set-off and delay costs could not abate the claim. The real basis of this decision appears to have been equitable set-off along the lines of *Young v Kitchen*.

In *M J Gleeson v Taylor Woodrow* (1989) 49 BLR 95, a management contractor's cross-claim to set off damages for delay against a sub-contractor's claim was refused on the ground that liquidated damages had already been deducted: to allow set-off would permit double recovery. The management contractor was responsible for certifying interim payments and had deducted liquidated damages and general damages for delay before ascertaining the sum stated as due in the certificate. As the Official Referee said:

> "The only thing which was wrong about [the management contractor's] statement of account was that it treated the deduction which I have mentioned as a certifiable matter capable of reducing the sum certified ... that would be tantamount to saying that a cross-claim unrelated to the value of work done and materials supplied diminishes their value which would, of course, be nonsense."

Such deductions could only give rise to a set-off but that had already been made by deducting liquidated damages. Even if the contractor complied with the set-off procedure, it might still be refused set-off in the absence of the necessary certificate of delay, *e.g.* if the architect's certificate under clause 12 of NSC/4 had not been issued before the date on which the monies became due.

The court is constrained by the criteria for summary judgment and interim payment applications. In one case, the court refused summary judgment and stayed the contractor's claim to arbitration on the ground that the employer's cross-claim gave rise to arguable points of law:

> "I do also have in mind that where a construction contract provides for interim payments it is usually for the very good reason that people doing the work need the money to continue with the project. The sums involved are so large that even the large construction companies feel the pinch when payment is withheld" *John Mowlem* v *Carlton Gate* (1990) 21 Con LR 113 at 118.

The cross-claim was for delay and the amount set off exceeded £1.1 million. Nevertheless, the contractor's arguments that set-off notices had not followed the machinery, were not issued in good faith and relied on counterclaims arising after the date when certificates should have been paid were adjudged too complex for summary judgment.

Care needs to be exercised when referring to case law on particular forms of contract. The court has frequently emphasised that decisions on one form of contract are of limited value when considering a contract whose terms are different: *Gilbert-Ash* v *Modern Engineering* [1974] AC 689 at 699. In *R M Douglas* v *Bass Leisure* (1990) 53 BLR 119 the court allowed set-off of a cross-claim for delay and other breaches of contract by an employer against a management contractor where JCT 87 had been used. That contract does not exclude the general law and provides that:

> "the employer is entitled to exercise any right under this contract of deduction from monies due or to become due to the management contractor against any amounts due under an interim certificate whether or not retention is included in that interim certificate."

There is no compliance procedure to be followed as a condition precedent to the right to set-off.

> "As a matter of law, it seems to me that if the defendants have a counterclaim arising out of any breach of this contract, the defendants are entitled to set off that counterclaim against any claim made under the contract, even though there is machinery provided by the contract for dealing with that counterclaim in a different way. The point against the plaintiffs is that the contract does not expressly and clearly provide that the contractual machinery is to be the only way of dealing with such a counterclaim, although such a result could be achieved by contract and it may have been the intention of some of the members of the committee which drafted this contract that that should be the effect of the contract" (at 133).

In *Gilbert-Ash*, part of the contractor's cross-claim against the sub-contractor related to delay. The House of Lords allowed equitable set-off of the delay costs although the decision may also be justified on the basis that delay costs could be set off under an express term of the contract. In practice, set-off for delay requires substantiation otherwise a cross-claim is at risk of being rejected, as in *Sable Contractors* v *Bluett Shipping* [1979] 2 Lloyd's Rep 33 in which a cross-claim for rent under a prospective lease failed as being too speculative, and the Australian case of *Melbourne Glass* v *Coby Constructions* (1998) 14 BCL 409.

Disruption

If the issue turns on a short point of law or on the construction of the contract, the court will decide it on an application of summary judgment. The Court of Appeal has refused a contractor's claim for set-off based on disruption on the ground that, properly construed, clause 23 of NSC/4a required compliance with the set-off machinery in respect of disruption as well as delay: see *Pillar* v *D J Higgins* (1986) 10 Con LR 46.

The cases do not often deal with set-off for disruption costs. Some guidance can be obtained from *Chatbrown* v *Alfred McAlpine* (1986) 11 Con LR 1 in which Kerr LJ said:

> "I certainly do not suggest that clause 15(2) can never be used in a situation such as the present, and that it is always necessary, in cases of delay or disruption, to wait until the end of the main contract period before any loss or expense can be said to have been actually incurred. On the other hand, there may be great difficulties in using the sub-clause in such situations, whatever the draftsman may have intended. While one can of course easily think of cases where a contractor would be able to claim that he has already incurred additional expense by reason of disruption, delay is likely to present greater problems, because the site would often have been fully operational in any event" (at 9).

Clause 15(2) of the Blue Form (1971 edition, July 1978 Revision) permitted set-off of "any claim for loss and/or expense which has actually been incurred by the contractor." If the contractor's cross-claim is prospective under this form it will not qualify for set-off.

Defective work

Cross-claims in respect of defective work are treated either as giving rise to equitable set-off of the cost of rectification or an abatement of the claim by the value of the defective work: *Lowe* v *Holme* (1883) 10 QBD 286. Part of the successful cross-claim brought by the employer in *Young* v *Kitchen* represented defective work.

In *Hanak* v *Green* [1958] 2 QB 9, an employer sued for the cost of rectifying defects. The contractor had unliquidated cross-claims for the value of variations on a *quantum meruit*, expenses incurred through a denial of access to the site and damages for trespass to goods. It was decided that the contractor had the right of set-off for all of the cross-claims. Those for *quantum meruit* and damages in tort did not arise out of the contract but were held to be so incidental to or closely associated with it as to satisfy the criteria for equitable set-off. This shows the liberal attitude adopted by the English courts to equitable set-off where claim and cross-claim arise out of the same project. It is difficult to understand how a claim for damages for trespass to goods could impeach a defects claim. This aspect was not necessary for the decision and only Sellers LJ actually dealt with it. The allowance of set-off of the claim for a quantum meruit has also been criticised (Spry 1969, Derham 1996, Meagher, Gummow and Lehane 1992).

Over-valuation

The principle of abatement is extremely important where a paying party wishes to challenge the value of work carried out. In *Acsim* v *Danish* (1989) 47 BLR 55 a contractor succeeded in abating a sub-contractor's claim for payment where the sub-contract set-off procedure had not been followed and where the general law of set-off had been excluded. The contractor failed in its cross-claim in respect of damages for delay but succeeded in reducing the claim on the basis that it did not represent "the total value of the sub-contract works properly executed and of the materials and goods properly on site." The contractor had not lost the right

> "either to show that the sub-contractor had not in fact earned all of the sum claimed, or his right to defend the action by showing that by reason of breach of contract the work was worth less than the sum claimed" (at 70).

The contractor argued that part of the sub-contractor's claim had not been earned because some of the work had not been done or the amount claimed in respect of it had not been included in the contract sum. The court concluded that the contractor had a defence in respect of:

- work omitted from the contract
- unauthorised variations or work deemed to have been included in the contract sum
- over-valuation of authorised variations
- over-valuation of incomplete work
- work not properly executed.

There can also be room for argument about the correctness of a method of measurement, the true interpretation of a bill item, the effect of an instruction etc. However, as Lord Denning has said:

> "That is all very well; but, as all of us with experience of building and construction cases are aware, there is inevitably something due. In most cases it can be said with certainty that x is due. In such a case the court gives judgment for the x and gives leave to defend as to the balance. Otherwise it would mean that the builders and contractors could be kept out of a great portion of their money indefinitely by the employer simply saying 'I want to investigate the account'": *Ellis* v *Wates* (1976) 2 BLR 57 at 62.

In that case there was no expert valuation evidence from the contractor but its Counsel, the late Donald Keating QC, challenged the accuracy of the certificate by relying on the sub-contractor's own evidence, *e.g.* that materials off site had been wrongly certified and the value of materials on site was wrong because the valuation had not been restricted to materials where ownership had passed to the contractor. He also argued that fluctuations were erroneous and excessive. Set-off was refused on the basis that:

> "The ordinary practice is that there must be some real basis, not a shadowy basis, for showing that there is an issue worthy of investigation by the courts. The defendants' answer amounts to no more than 'we dispute the claim'. That is not enough" (at 64).

In deciding against the contractor, the court was influenced by the fact that a valuation had been prepared between the employer and its quantity surveyor supporting the sub-contractor's claim after the decision at first instance. This was accepted in evidence even though it had no binding effect on the contractor as the main contract had been terminated. In *NEI Thompson* v *Wimpey* (1987) 39 BLR 65 the Court of Appeal considered a claim by a contractor for payment which was met by a cross-claim from the employer alleging that the figure in the certificate relied on was incorrect. There appeared to be no firm evidence other than:

1. The sub-contractor's account had considerably increased although there had been few architect's instructions in relation to the work.

2. The final account was double the original contract sum.

3. The contractor had not submitted a claim for loss and expense despite an overrun.

The Court of Appeal considered that this evidence was "just enough" but ordered that a bank guarantee for two thirds of the claim be provided as a condition of the action being stayed to arbitration. If the employer has an arguable case that a certificate is open to challenge in good faith and on reasonable material, the court is prepared to accept a defence of abatement.

Counterclaims and summary procedures

A counterclaim is a cross-claim which could be brought by separate proceedings, but which the rules of the court allow to be made in the proceedings brought by the creditor: *Stooke* v *Taylor* (1880) 5 QBD 569. A counterclaim differs from set-off and abatement in three ways. It can be used to claim any form of relief and is not restricted to a claim for money. Set-off admits a claim and then asserts a cross-claim up to the value of the claim whereas a counterclaim does not use a claim but is asserted independently of it. A counterclaim is offensive in character and puts forward an autonomous cause of action, whereas set-off and abatement are essentially defensive (Figure 5.1). There are some cross-claims which can only take effect as a counterclaim:

1. An independent, unliquidated claim cannot be the subject of legal or equitable set-off unless the contract so allows.

2. Where set-off is excluded by the contract or where contract machinery made a condition precedent to set-off has not been complied with.

3. Where the cross-claim exceeds the claim, the excess can only be advanced as a counterclaim.

However, if a counterclaim falls within any of the recognised categories of set-off discussed earlier, it will be allowed as a set-off in the proceedings.

It has been seen how set-off performs a security function by allowing the debtor to use the creditor's claim to pay the cross-claim. A counterclaim which cannot be set off can still function procedurally as a security. For example, if the court stays execution of the creditor's judgment pending the hearing of the counterclaim, the result is the same as if set-off had been ordered. This is because, assuming the counterclaim succeeds, the court will either give a balance judgment (having deducted the judgment from the counterclaim or vice versa) or give judgment on both claim and counterclaim and then set off one against the other. It follows that even if there is no right of set-off, a defendant may be able to persuade the court to exercise its discretion so as to achieve the same result. A defendant has two opportunities to convert a counterclaim into a set-off: before the trial, if the plaintiff applies for summary judgment or an interim payment, and at the trial itself. The outcome of either type of pre-trial application is often decisive of the future of the action, never more so than where the plaintiff is insolvent: a receiver often decides not to proceed further if a summary judgment application is unsuccessful.

Whether a counterclaim can be set off is highly material when considering an application for security for costs against a defendant. In *L/M International* v *The Circle Limited Partnership* (1992) 37 Con LR 72, the court ordered an employer to provide security for a counterclaim of £15 million against a construction manager suing for an unpaid balance of prime cost. The report includes a discussion on the nature of equitable set-off under a construction management agreement.

Where a contractor or sub-contractor believes there is no defence to its claim, it can apply for summary judgment under CPR Part 24 (formerly RSC Order 14). This procedure is restricted to cases where there is no real dispute on the facts and, if there is a point of law involved, that it can be easily and crisply dealt with by the court. In view of the size of a monthly progress payment on a modern construction project, this is the usual procedure to take where an employer has failed to pay on a certificate. If it is possible but improbable that a defence to the claim will succeed, the court has discretion to make a conditional order requiring a payment into court to be made or particular steps taken. This procedure replaces the former practice of granting leave to defend whether conditionally or unconditionally. The court also has power under CPR Part 25 (formerly RSC Order 29) to order a defendant to make an interim payment of such amount as it thinks just where liability is admitted or the court is satisfied that if the action proceeded to trial, the plaintiff would obtain judgment for a substantial sum. This application will only get past the first stage where the court has taken into account any set-off or counterclaim on which the defendant might be entitled to rely. This suggests that the court will anticipate the trial and estimate the likelihood of success on the counterclaim and only consider an interim payment as a proportion of a balance judgment after having deducted the counterclaim from the claim: *Shanning* v *Wimpey* [1985] 3 All ER 475, *Crown House* v *Amec* (1990) 6 Const LJ 141, *Imodco* v *Wimpey* (1987) 40 BLR 1. The security function of the counterclaim is therefore preserved in its entirety. In a case where an administrator of a steel erection sub-contractor applied for an interim payment, it was held that, taking cross-claims into account, the court could not make the order (*Smallman Construction* v *Redpath Dorman Long* (1988) 47 BLR 15), but when the case was remitted to the Official Referee, he was prepared to order summary judgment of part of the claim.

Conclusion

Set-off is best seen as a series of layers (common law, contract, statute, insolvency) which require an archaeological approach. This reflects the hoarding instincts of the law, *e.g.* the right to legal set-off was not lost when the original need for it disappeared. Set-off has become an integral part of the law of payment. The effect of insolvency on the position is considered in Chapter 13. It remains to be seen how the Housing Grants, Construction and Regeneration Act 1996 will work in practice. The Act leaves some issues unresolved, in particular its effect on the defence of abatement.

Chapter 6

· Trust and Transferability ·

Introduction

The law of trusts is a special area of law developed by the courts of equity. If property is held on trust, it falls outside the estate of a bankrupt and is not available for distribution to creditors: s 378 Insolvency Act 1986. The same applies to trust property held by insolvent companies, although the Act does not expressly say so. Similarly, property assigned before formal insolvency is beyond the reach of an insolvency practitioner. In cases of trust and assignment, issues often arise as to the adequacy of the evidence of transfer. If it is incomplete in some essential respect, the transfer will not be sufficient to divest the person or company of the property.

General principles of trust law

Creation of a trust

There are three essential requirements for a trust: A as settlor must intend to create a trust; the property held by B as trustee must be ascertained and identified; and B must know the identity of C as the beneficiary of the trust to whom he is accountable (Underhill and Hayton 1995). Most trusts are constituted by a formal instrument recording the transfer of property to trustees to hold on trust for named beneficiaries, but it is not essential for the word "trust" to be used provided the settlor's intention is clear: *Re Kayford* [1975] 1 WLR 279. Setting money aside into a separate account is helpful but not conclusive evidence of a trust. In *Re Multi Guarantee* [1987] BCLC 257, money was paid into a joint account in the names of the parties' solicitors pending resolution of a dispute. One of the parties intended the account to be held on trust for its customers, but the other envisaged its being used for general purposes after the dispute had been resolved. There were no agreed terms on how money could be withdrawn from the account. It was held that the money had been paid to the solicitors for a purpose which had never been finalised and reverted by resulting trust to the person who had paid it in.

It must be possible to ascertain the subject matter of the trust. If the property is unique ("my Picasso"), there can be no doubt but where the property is generic equity requires specific property to be segregated from the mass before it can be held in trust. For example, if A declares a trust in favour of B of "£5,000 of the £10,000 standing in my account" there is no trust unless and until A transfers £5,000 into a new account. Similarly, if A declares a trust in favour of B of "20 bottles of Chateau Lafite 1961 now in my cellar" and there are more than 20 bottles answering that description, there can be no trust until they have been set aside: *Re London Wine Shippers* [1986] PCC 121, *Re Goldcorp Exchange* [1994] 2 All ER 806. A trust can exist over any property. For example, a trust of the benefit of a contract will apply to all present and future choses in action in respect of it. Thus, the trust would extend to any debt arising out of the contract, any cheque representing that debt, and any cash or credit to a bank account representing that cheque.

There must be a beneficiary to whom the trustee can be accountable, but a trustee can hold property on trust for itself and another as beneficiaries. The terms of the trust may entitle the trustee to specific rights against the trust property without naming the trustee as co-beneficiary. A as trustee would hold the property subject to its express rights on trust for B as beneficiary. A would be an active self-interested trustee. Self-interested trusteeship is a defining characteristic of construction trusts (Hayton CLY 1994). As well as obtaining protection against insolvency, a beneficiary under a trust obtains a proprietary right to trace any trust property which is misapplied and a personal right against anyone who knowingly receives trust property or actively assists in a breach of trust.

Equitable tracing claims

Tracing is a process of following property as it changes from one form to another. Strictly speaking, it

> "is neither a claim nor a remedy but a process ... by which the plaintiff traces what has happened to his property, identifies the persons who have handled or received it, and justifies his claim that the money which had been handled or received (and if necessary which they still retain) can properly be regarded as representing his property": *Boscawan* v *Bajwa* [1995] 4 All ER 769 at 776.

The question is whether the court can "see" the original property or its value in its substituted form. As a process of following transformations, tracing has an affinity with construction and insolvency, both of which are transformative by nature. Trust assets can be traced into all kinds of property. There are detailed rules dealing with bank accounts. An account is a debt owed by the bank to its customer. There will normally be many payments in and out of the account. When making a withdrawal, the customer is deemed to be taking out the earliest payment in. If a customer pays trust money into his personal account, he is deemed to make withdrawals of his own money first, as the law assumes he would not intend to commit a breach of trust.

Where trust money, or the proceeds of sale of trust property, are mixed with the trustee's own money, the beneficiary is entitled to a charge over the account as security for the trust property. If trust money is used to buy an asset, the beneficiary can either claim the asset or a lien over it: *Re Hallett's Estate* (1880) 13 Ch D 696. Where an asset is purchased from a mixed fund containing trust money and the trustee's own funds, it is subject to a charge securing payment of the misappropriated assets: *Re Oatway* [1903] 2 Ch 356. If the asset increases in value, the beneficiary becomes entitled to a proportionate share of the increase: *Re Tilley's Will Trusts* [1967] 1 Ch 1179. If at any time a mixed account goes into overdraft, the beneficiary loses all tracing rights. If the trustee then makes a payment into the account with his own money, the beneficiary acquires no right of tracing unless it can be shown that the trustee intended to replenish the trust assets: *Roscoe v Winder* [1915] 1 Ch 62. If two or more trust funds are mixed together and withdrawals are made from the account, the trustee is deemed to withdraw first from the earliest payment in: *Re Stenning* [1895] 2 Ch 433. If the beneficiaries always intended their funds to be mixed, however, the withdrawal will be deemed to be of the same percentage of each fund: *Barlow Clowes v Vaughan* [1992] 4 All ER 22. Where an asset is purchased using an overdraft, with the intention of repaying the overdraft by misappropriating trust property, it may be possible to trace "backwards" into the asset: *Bishopgate v Homan* [1994] BCC 868. If trust property is transferred to a bona fide purchaser for value without notice of the trust, it cannot be traced: *Re Diplock* [1948] 1 Ch 465.

Personal claims

If A receives trust property obtained in breach of trust and parts with it without accounting to the beneficiary, he can be personally liable as constructive trustee: *Agip* v *Jackson* [1992] 4 All ER 385. A will be liable where his knowledge is actual, by turning a blind eye to the obvious or deliberately failing to make enquiries which an honest person would make ("knowing receipt"). A person can be accountable as an accessory to a breach of trust, even if he has not personally handled trust property ("knowing assistance"). There are four elements to this claim:

- the existence of trust property
- a breach of trust by the trustee
- assistance by the person in that conduct
- the person's own dishonest state of knowledge in assisting the breach.

A person can be liable for knowing assistance if he is dishonest even if the original breach of trust was committed honestly and in good faith: *Royal Brunei Airlines* v *Tan* [1995] 3 All ER 97. It is however essential to prove the dishonesty of the person assisting the breach of trust. In *Brinks* v *Abu-Saleh* [1995] *The Times*, 23 October which arose out of the Brinks Matt bullion robbery in 1983, a man was caught carrying £3 million in cash by car which had been traced to the robbery. All that could be proved against him was that he thought the money was being moved in order to evade tax. A claim against the man's wife failed since there was no evidence that she knew it was either trust money or had been obtained through a breach of trust in that a security guard had given the robbers a key and photographs of the warehouse. Knowing receipt depends on receiving trust property for your own benefit and is restitutionary. Knowing assistance means acting as an accessory to a fraudulent breach of trust and is compensatory (McCormack 1997).

Construction trusts

When a trust is used in connection with a construction contract, it is almost always intended as the means of payment. The trust may be the source of payment for the whole contract sum, or a part of it such as retention, or a part which is in dispute. The trust can arise from a clause in the contract or a separate agreement. Whichever method is used, the trust will consist of a mixture of contractual and trust obligations. In essence, the terms of the trust will be the terms of the contract: the contractor is not intended to have a better right of payment as beneficiary of the trust than as an ordinary contract party. There are, however, exceptions to this: see the discussion on *Rafidain Bank* v *Saipem* (unreported, 2 March 1994) in Chapter 11.

Trusts of the contract sum

There are many ways in which a trust can be used to protect the contract sum. The most useful device from the contractor's point of view is the "Lovell trust" described in detail in Chapter 11, since the employer has to make a payment into the account one month in advance of the work being carried out. The difficulty is that sub-contractors benefit only indirectly in that improved security of payment for the contractor reduces the knock-on effect of employer insolvency. A similar arrangement is used on international contracts where the employer's lack of access to foreign currency to pay the contractor can be overcome by barter. An example is *Rafidain Bank* v *Saipem* in which Italian contractors agreed to build a pipeline in return for oil. The oil was supplied by an associated company of the employer (both Iraqi state-owned entities) to Saipem (a company associated with the contractor) who paid for it by transferring US dollars into a trust account with its own bankers in London from which the contractor was paid on presentation of invoices to Rafidain, an Iraqi bank named as trustee of the account.

Some sub-contracting organisations advocate the "cascade" system whereby sums received on account of the contract sum are held on trust by the contractor to pay itself, its sub-contractors and suppliers. The sub-contractors will receive payment for themselves and their sub-sub-contractors and so on down the chain until either the last supplier to the project has been paid or a person is reached whose contract sum is less than a given amount. Under this system, which is operated in some American states and most Canadian provinces, the trust is not expressly written into the contract but arises by statutory implication. As such, the trust is not the means of payment in contrast to the Lovell trust but a source of proprietary and personal remedies. Some aspects of the cascade system are considered in Chapter 17. One of the main problems with it is its complexity. It also restricts the availability of capital since banks mainly lend against receivables: if all construction debts were held on trust the level of debtors available as security would dramatically fall.

A third kind of trust is that proposed in *Constructing the Team* (Latham 1994). This provides a composite scheme protecting the contractor and the first line of sub-contractors and suppliers. The employer sets aside money into a trust fund along the lines of the Lovell trust and the benefit of the account is held by the employer on trust for itself and the contractor to pay the contractor in accordance with the building contract. The difference is that if the contractor becomes insolvent before completion, the primary trust fails and a secondary trust arises in respect of any balance in the account in favour of the first line of sub-contractors, who share rateably in the fund. This ingenious solution resolves the problem created by the *British Eagle* case since a statutory trust would fall outside the *pari passu* rule. It was accepted as a viable solution by the contractors in their response to *Constructing the Team*. This idea is only given in outline and there are various issues which would have to be resolved before it could be taken further (Davis 1996). Unfortunately, it was roundly rejected by employers.

There are currently two standard forms incorporating a trust of the contract sum. Under the SEACC form published in 1993, the employer opens a special account from which the contractor and specialist sub-contractors are paid. The principal feature of the trust is that the employer loses all rights of set-off against the fund, even in respect of liquidated damages. The second standard form trust is that contained in optional clause V of the second edition of the New Engineering Contract published by the ICE in 1995 (now re-named The Engineering and Construction Contract). This is contrary to Latham's recommendation that the trust should be included as a core clause. For a detailed comparison of the Lovell trust with the SEACC and NEC forms see Davis (1996).

Retention trusts

Trusts of retention are only found in the JCT standard forms, *i.e.* the Standard Form of Building Contract (JCT 63, 80, 98), the Standard Form With Contractor's Design (JCT 81, 98), the Intermediate Form (IFC 84, 98), the Fixed Fee Form (JCT 67), and the Management Contract (JCT 87, 98). The trust is stepped down into the conditions of nominated sub-contract (NSC/C) and works contract (WC/2) but not to named sub-contracts (NAM/C) or domestic sub-contracts (DOM/1 and DOM/2).

The status of beneficiary has led to some confusion over the rights of recourse given by the contract to employers and contractors in their roles as trustee. The other major difficulty consists in the ascertainment of trust property, whether in the form of money set aside in a separate account or other choses in action, such as the employer's rights under a development or finance agreement. Issues of this kind and others arising on formal insolvency are discussed in Chapter 11.

Stakeholder accounts

JCT forms of sub-contract provide for payment to a trustee-stakeholder to hold on trust for the contractor and the sub-contractor until otherwise directed by the arbitrator or the parties, *e.g.* clause 22 of NAM/SC. Interest is added to the fund and the stakeholder is entitled to deduct its expenses from the fund.

Trust accounts

Occasionally an employer will agree to place money in a trust account as security for its own payment obligation rather than as the means of payment, the intention being that the money will remain in the account until the contract sum has been paid in full. In the rare cases where employers are prepared to give security, it is more usual for them to provide a bond or guarantee than a trust account of this kind. Escrow accounts are also advocated in lieu of on demand bonds from contractors (Stebbings 1997/98). Apart from tying up cash, this option also raises questions over its accounting treatment.

"Quistclose" trusts

Money advanced to enable a debtor to pay his creditors, but which has not been paid to them by the time the debtor goes into liquidation, is held on a resulting trust in favour of the person who advanced the money: *Barclays Bank* v *Quistclose Investments* [1970] AC 567. The concept was applied to the industry by *Re McKeown* [1974] NILR 226. A contractor borrowed money to pay an arbitrator's fees before taking up the award. The loan was on condition that it be used to pay the arbitrator's fees only and that it was to be repaid out of the proceeds of the award. The contractor went bankrupt after taking up the award but before receiving payment. It was held that the loan had been advanced for a specific purpose and did not form part of the bankrupt's estate, which could only receive the proceeds of the arbitration award subject to the obligation to repay the loan from it first.

Assignment

Assignment is a very versatile device and is widely used in the industry. As security for a loan to acquire the site and pay the construction cost, an employer will often assign agreements relating to the development to the lender. In *Re Warren* [1938] Ch 725 a builder financed the development of four houses on a bank overdraft guaranteed by the vendor of the land who also made a small cash advance in consideration of the builder's agreement that the sale proceeds would be paid to the vendor's solicitors to be applied first in repayment of the builder's overdraft. The last payment was made to the vendor on the very day that the builder went bankrupt. It was held that the contract was an equitable assignment of the anticipated proceeds of sale from the development and the trustee in bankruptcy was not entitled to the balance which had been paid to the vendor.

Trade credit is sometimes given to contractors and sub-contractors by assignment of receivables. In the early case of *Lett* v *Morris* (1831) 4 Sim 607 a builder agreed to demolish and rebuild a tavern for £2,360 payable by instalments. A timber merchant agreed to give credit of up to £700 on security of payment of £80 from each of the first three instalments and £460 from the balance. The arrangement was held to be a valid assignment to the timber merchant. Such arrangements are no longer common because contractors have to undertake to lending banks not to offer their receivables as security to another creditor. These are known as "negative pledge" clauses. Even where assignments of debts are permitted, they may not be accepted by factoring companies in view of the comparative ease with which debtors in the industry can make a set-off. In *Yeandle* v *Wynn Realisations* (1995) 47 Con LR 1, a contractor in administration had a contract with a local authority under ICE (5th edition). A sub-contractor under the FCEC Blue Form claimed extra remuneration for unforeseen ground conditions but the engineer rejected the claim. The sub-contractor then assigned its debts, including receivables under the sub-contract, to a factor at a discount. The factoring agreement was guaranteed by the managing director. The sub-contractor went into liquidation and the factor enforced the director's guarantee. The factor's claim was settled and the debts re-assigned to the sub-contractor who then assigned to the director all monies payable by the contractor pursuant to the sub-contract. The director failed in his claim as assignee against the contractor as the assignment did not pass the right to challenge the engineer's decision.

Assignment is also used as a means of facilitating the disposal of a business or settlement of disputes: *South East Thames RHA* v *Y J Lovell* (1985) 32 BLR 127. It is used in leasing agreements in respect of plant and equipment and is often used in the transfer of assets between companies in a group. Lastly, a debtor may assign property in part payment in response to pressure from its creditors. In *Jones* v *Farrell* (1857) 1 De G & J 208 a timber merchant had already given substantial credit to two partners trading as a contractor in relation to a factory under construction. Partly as payment and partly as security for a further advance, the contractor assigned £1,000 which was to become due from the employer. One of the partners became insolvent and the other absconded before the supplier had been paid and the employer refused to pay him without an indemnity. It was held that the employer was obliged to pay the supplier as the arrangement was a valid equitable assignment.

Benefit and burden

If the property concerned is a chattel or land, an assignee acquires the right to possession, but an assignment of a chose in action such as a debt, goodwill, intellectual property or the benefit of a contract can only be enforced by taking proceedings. A contract is a chose made up of four distinct elements: the benefit and burden respectively of the seller and the buyer. Only the benefit is assignable, so the buyer can assign the right to the goods but not the duty to pay for them, and the seller can assign the right to payment but not the duty to deliver them.

With a construction contract, things are rather more complicated. From an employer's point of view, the benefit and burden of a construction contract extend much further than the right to the building on completion and the duty to pay the contract price. The most important elements are set out in Figure 6.1.

So where an employer assigned the benefit of a contract in JCT 80 form to a funder after practical completion, it was held not to have passed the burden of having to fund retention on request from the contractor: *Finnegan* v *Ford Sellar Morris* (No 2) 27 Con LR 41. It is often assumed by project funders that an assignee from an employer can exercise all of the rights making up the benefit of a contract, but there are dicta to the contrary:

BENEFIT	BURDEN
to issue variation orders	to pay
to terminate in certain events	to appoint the professional team
to levy liquidated damages	to give possession of the site
to claim general damages	to co-operate, or not to hinder or prevent
to possession of the building on completion or in sections	to procure the performance of the professional team: the proper issue of instructions, certificates and valuation of the work
to be jointly named in an insurance policy taken out by the contractor	not to interfere with the independent functions of the certifier
	to insure against certain risks

Fig 6.1

"A contract that A will build a house for B, and follow his instructions on such variations as the contract may allow, cannot be converted by assignment into an obligation to follow the instructions of C": *Linden Gardens* v *Lenesta Sludge* (1992) 30 Con LR 1 at 13, per Staughton LJ.

Although the judgment of the Court of Appeal from which this quotation is taken was overturned on appeal, this particular point was not expressly dealt with in the House of Lords. Staughton LJ repeated it later in *L/M International Construction* v *The Circle Limited Partnership* (1995) 49 Con LR 12 at 22:

"When the benefit of a contract is assigned, the character of the obligation is not changed. Before the assignment the [construction] managers were, in some respects, obliged to act on the instructions or directions of [employer]. The assignment could not change that and render them subject to the orders of [the assignee banks]. A new agreement would be needed to achieve that."

This view has attracted support:

" ... the better view appears to be that the employer who has wide powers of variations and of expending prime cost sums cannot assign the contract benefit while the building is uncompleted. The contractor expects that employer to be the one exercising the benefits as well as remaining subject to the burdens" (Megens and Ang 1994 at 324).

The court appears to be limiting the assignment to money obligations such as liquidated damages or general damages awarded as a surrogate for performance. If correct this is a limitation on the general law whereby assignees are entitled to specific performance or injunctions in respect of non-money obligations if such relief would have been available to the assignor (Jones & Goodhart 1996). In *Linden Gardens* v *Lenesta Sludge* [1994] 1 AC 85 it was decided that a prohibition against assignment of a contract invalidated the assignment of the whole benefit of the contract. From the employer's point of view, the benefit includes the right to call for further performance from the contractor as well as a right to damages. Prima facie the converse is also true: in the absence of clear words to the contrary, an assignment of the benefit of the contract transfers both kinds of right. The House of Lords spoke of the right to performance mainly as the right to possession of the building on completion free from defects. In other words, there was no discussion of other rights which form part of the benefit but which are exercised through the architect, such as the right to issue instructions or variation orders. It is the unique position of the certifier that makes it hard to fit construction contracts into the law of assignment, which has historically been based in the transfer of debts. Perhaps this is the crucial point: it is not so much that certain aspects of the employer's benefit are by nature personal, but rather that the benefit of the power to vary the works is subject to the burden of doing so through a third party who owes independent obligations to the contractor. Could this be an example of the so called "pure principle of benefit and burden"? Perhaps Lightman J had this kind of situation in mind in when he said that

> "if the contract requires any judgment to be exercised whether by the obligor or the obligee, an assignment cannot alter who is to exercise it or how that judgment is to be exercised or vest the right to make that judgment in the court": *Don King* v *Warren* [1998] 2 All ER 608 at 634, affirmed [1999] 2 All ER 218.

In assessing whether an assignment of the benefit of a construction contract was to the prejudice of the contractor, the court has taken into account in one case that the employer could not "extend the job at will by calling for extras": *Charlotte Thirty* v *Croker* (1990) 24 Con LR 46, 55.

Assignability

Unless the contract otherwise provides, a creditor can assign a debt without the debtor's consent because it is in the interests of society as a whole that property should be freely transferable. It has long been accepted that it is immaterial to a debtor who it pays provided it gets a good discharge.

> "The special right of ignoring altogether the consent of the person upon whom the obligation lies to the substitution of one person for another as the recipient of the benefit would seem in principle and in common justice to be confined to those cases where it can make no difference to the person on whom the obligation lies to which of two persons he is to discharge it ... ": *Tolhurst* v *Associated Portland Cement* [1902] 2 KB 660, 668.

This is subject to a few exceptions: the burden of the contract, a contract which is personal to the parties (to paint a portrait), a bare cause of action unless the assignment concerns the transfer of a property right or the assignee has a genuine commercial interest in the action: *Trendtex* v *Credit Suisse* [1982] AC 679, and in some insolvency situations, *e.g.* a liquidator cannot assign a claim for wrongful trading: *Re Oasis Merchandising* [1997] BCC 282.

The court is prepared to assume that it is of no importance to the contractor who is to take the benefit of its work or to the employer as to whom it pays. On the other hand it is of concern:

- to the contractor that the employer in whom it placed confidence by entering into contract retains the liability to pay
- to the employer that the contractor entrusted with the works actually carries them out.

The assumption that there is no detriment to either party in allowing the benefit and burden of a contract to be split is not well founded in practice. For example, the lender financing a project may require the employer to assign to it the benefit of the contract, *i.e.* the right to call for performance. If this occurs, the contractor owes a duty to the lender to continue working on site but can only look to the employer for payment (see Figure 6.2). As the works proceed, their value may be under-certified or the employer may make wrongful set-offs against certified sums. Either matter can seriously damage the contractor's cash flow but not alone be sufficient to justify the contractor in suspending work or leaving site.

In such circumstances, the contractor cannot protest that continued under-certification will delay completion as the duty to complete will be owed to the lender. Indeed, the lender will probably be pressing the contractor to maintain programme. If the employer becomes insolvent

	Benefit	*Burden*
Employer	None	Duty to pay
Contractor	Right to payment	Duty to carry out and complete building
Lender (assignee of benefit)	Right to the building on completion	None

Fig 6.2

but no event occurs entitling the contractor to terminate its employment, the contractor could be obliged to continue even in the knowledge of an increasing risk that it will never be paid. Had the benefit and burden not been split, it would have been easier for the contractor to "go slow" and await a repudiation by the employer as only then could the contractor safely suspend the works or leave site. Unfortunately for the contractor, this process could take several months. If it decided to abandon the site during that period, the contractor could find itself in repudiation and the lender would be entitled to claim as damages the increased cost of having the works completed by a new contractor together with consequential losses. Commercially, if the contractor dealt only with the employer, it might be able to leave site much earlier.

This point is well illustrated by *Brice v Bannister* (1878) 3 QBD 569 which concerned a shipbuilding contract under which the builder was to receive £1,375 by stage payments. The builder experienced financial difficulty and persuaded the owner to make advance payments ahead of the agreed stages. The builder owed a solicitor a substantial amount and assigned £100 "out of money due or to become due" to him under the contract. Notice of the assignment was immediately given to the owner. At the date of the assignment, the builder had received £1,015 leaving a balance of only £360 of the contract price unpaid. The amount the builder had received was more than the value of the work done and it would require considerably more than £360 to finish the ship. The builder became unable to continue without further payments from the owner who was concerned at the extra cost of terminating the contract and engaging another builder. The report is unclear but this appears to be the reason why the owner continued to pay the builder rather than the assignee.

Although the court sympathised with the owner, he was found liable to pay the £100 to the solicitor. As the cost to complete exceeded the balance of the contract price, the owner had no choice but to fund the builder to completion. Having allowed the builder to split the benefit and the burden, the owner had to pay twice. In fact, the owner may have been fortunate that only £100 of the balance of £360 had been assigned. It might still have been cheaper for the owner to have risked additional liability to the assignee than the greater cost of the completion contractor, although this was presumably outweighed by the legal costs involved. The report is silent on the value of the work at the date of receipt of the notice of assignment.

Assignment can have other adverse consequences to a debtor. First, there is the inconvenience of having to pay someone other than its creditor. In the 19th century, it was recognised it would be most tiresome for a gentleman to have to pay the assignees of his tailor, butcher or baker. To avoid problems his only recourse was to pay the assignee without delay and produce the receipt to his creditor or to interplead and allow the various claimants to the debt to fight it out amongst themselves: *Jones* v *Farrell*. It would certainly be very inconvenient if all the sub-contractors employed on a project were to assign sums due to them from the contractor. This is of course unlikely for the reasons outlined above. Apart from the inconvenience involved, assignment adds to a contractor's risk because there is always a possibility that it would be overlooked and the assignor paid by mistake. If a builder is paid monthly in advance, and assigns its right to payment, the employer cannot claim against the assignee for repayment of sums not earned by performance: *Pan Ocean* v *Creditcorp* [1994] 1 All ER 470. The duty to earn the advance is part of the burden which remains with the builder.

These concerns are insignificant when compared with the fact that after receipt of notice of assignment, the debtor can build up no new rights of set-off. In the absence of assignment, a debtor could (unless the contract forbade it) set off a cross-claim under an entirely different contract provided it was for a debt which was payable when the claim was brought by the creditor: *Stooke* v *Taylor* (1880) 5 QBD 569. If the creditor assigned its claim, the debtor will be denied this right of set-off unless its debt had already accrued due: *e.g. Marathon* v *Mashreqbank* [1997] 2 BCLC 460.

Thus, by allowing a creditor to assign its claim, a debtor can lose a right of set-off it would otherwise have had. The injustice of this is obvious when one considers that assignment is supposed to be a special right exerciseable only where identity of the payee is not important to the debtor. The same situation arises when an administrative receiver is appointed because the appointment crystallises a floating charge and operates as an equitable assignment of all the charged assets to the floating charge holder: *Biggerstaff* v *Rowatt's Wharf* [1896] 2 Ch 93. The right of a receiver to resist cross-claims arising after the debtor receives notice of assignment is loosely known as "receivership set off". Although strictly the subject belongs to the law of assignment, it will for convenience be dealt with in Chapter 13. A debtor may be asked to confirm receipt of the notice of assignment. In some cases, the notice will set out a new term not contained in the contract, *e.g.* a duty to pay without set-off or counterclaim. Care is needed lest, by counter-signing the notice of assignment, the debtor undertakes a wider obligation to the assignee than it had to its creditor.

There are two possible exceptions to the rule that only the benefit can be assigned: the "conditional benefit" rule and "the pure principle of benefit and burden". Where a contract confers only conditional or qualified rights, an assignee takes them subject to the condition or qualification. "Such restrictions or qualifications are an intrinsic part of the right: you take the right as it stands, and you cannot pick out the good and reject the bad": *Tito* v *Waddell* (No 2) [1977] Ch 106, 190. A conditional right under a construction contract would include a right subject to a condition precedent. For example, the contract may make the execution of a collateral warranty or the provision of a bond a condition precedent to the right to payment. An assignee of the right to payment would have to satisfy the condition before being able to enforce the right. In this sense, the benefit is inextricably bound to the burden and cannot be separated. The pure principle of benefit and burden is a more elusive concept. The principle is that a person who takes the benefit must bear the burden. How can this principle be reconciled with the rule that only the benefit can be assigned? In his analysis of this principle in *Tito* v *Waddell*, Megarry V-C stated as follows:

> "As it has developed, I do not think that the pure benefit and burden principle is a technical doctrine, to be satisfied by what is technical and minimal. I regard it as being a broad principle of justice, to be satisfied by what is real and substantial ... It seems to me that the principle ought to embrace anybody whose connection with the transaction creating the benefit and burden is sufficient to show that he has some claim to the

benefit, whether or not he has a valid title to it. ... It may be founded on acceptance, so that he who accepts the benefit is taken also to have accepted the burden, or it may be a rule of law, so that he who accepts the benefit is bound by the burden, irrespective of any acceptance of it. In the conditional benefit type of case it may perhaps be easier to rest the doctrine on acceptance than in cases of the pure principle of benefit and burden: if you accept the benefit you cannot escape the consequence that you have accepted what forms part of the benefit, or is annexed to it, whereas under the pure principle, the burden may be the price the law compels you to pay for taking the benefit" (at 302, 305, 308).

It was held that the pure principle of benefit and burden applied. There, the benefit was a right to mine phosphate and the burden was an obligation to restore the land to its former owners and replant it with trees when the phosphate had been extracted. The replanting was not a condition of the right to mine. The assignment was the culmination of a complex series of changes of control from a company to special commissioners who were replaced from time to time. It is difficult to see how the pure principle can apply to a construction contract. Some guidance may be found in the judge's view that the principle would apply where a person takes an assignment of the whole contract from a company on the point of going into liquidation and undertakes to discharge the burden and to indemnify the company (at 287). This is close to the facts in *Chatsworth Investments* v *Cussins* [1969] 1 All ER 143 and might be a better explanation for the decision in that case than implied novation.

Non-assignability

Standard clauses

Construction contracts often contain a clause preventing either party from assigning the benefit without the consent of the other (*e.g.* JCT 80 clause 19, FIDIC (4th edition) clause 3.1, ICE (6th edition) clause 3). Assignment in breach of such a clause will be invalid as between the assignee and the other contract parties: *Linden Gardens* v *Lenesta Sludge* [1994] 1 AC 85. Lord Browne-Wilkinson confirmed in that case that

> "a party to a building contract ... can have a genuine commercial interest in seeking to ensure that he is in contractual relations only with a person whom he has selected as the other party to the contract".

There are many reasons for this. He gave as examples the fact that some employers are more reasonable than others in dealing with disputes and a contractor suing the employer for payment might be met by the defence of abatement even though a cross-claim in respect of defects had been assigned. The contractor might have to join the assignee in the proceedings to avoid being penalised twice for the same breach (at 105). In *Modern Weighbridge v ANR* (1996) 12 BCL 224 an assignee failed to recover the balance of the contract price from the employer due to a non-assignability clause in the contract. The assignee could not establish an estoppel against the employer because although the assignee acted to its detriment in completing the contract for the assignor, to the knowledge of the employer, the employer had made it clear that it did not consent to the assignment.

Linden Gardens concerned clause 17 of JCT 63 which provides that "the employer shall not without written consent of the contractor assign this contract". A contract comprises a benefit and a burden and it is established law that a burden cannot be assigned: *Nokes v Doncaster Amalgamated Collieries* [1940] AC 1014. The court construed "assign this contract" as "assign the benefit of this contract". The standard forms vary in their treatment of non-assignability. Clause 13 of ICE (4th edition) provides that "the contractor shall not assign the contract or any part thereof or any benefit or interest therein or thereunder without the written consent of the employer". This was an effective restriction on the assignment of the whole benefit: *Helstan Securities v Hertfordshire County Council* [1978] 3 All ER 262. A contract can restrict the assignment of part of the benefit leaving the remainder freely assignable, but it would have to be very clearly drafted.

The reasons why parties opt for non-assignability range from case to case: it removes the risk of double payment by overlooking assignment; it rids the debtor of the inconvenience of having to deal with a potentially large number of assignees; it avoids the problem which arose in *Brice v Bannister* where the employer was exposed because of advance payments it had made; some creditors are faster than others in enforcing their rights; and it might prejudice the debtor's rights to legal and liquidation set-off. A non-assignment clause means that one party has to ask the other's consent to an assignment. This can work both ways: such a clause can be used by a contractor as a lever to extract payment from an employer: *Lemina v Phillips Construction* (1988) BCL 56. On the other hand, a contractor in financial difficulties whose lender asks for an assignment of the benefit of contracts as security, might be forced to reveal its financial position to the employer as a condition of obtaining its consent. As a result, the employer might start delaying payment or preparing claims against the contractor. A non-assignability clause can survive the repudiation of the contract: *Hendry* v *Chartsearch* [1998] *The Times*, 16 September (noted in (1998) 15 BLM 1). It was reasonable to withhold consent to assignment in that case as the relationship between the parties had broken down and was likely to result in litigation.

Qualified assignability

A contract may also qualify the right to assign. It may be unassignable without the consent of the other party (as in *Linden Gardens*) or it may be assignable with the consent of the other party, which is not to be unreasonably withheld. In *Orion Finance* v *Crown Financial Management* [1994] 2 BCLC 607, a computer lease contained a clause preventing assignment without the consent of the end user. The dealer assigned the right to rental under the agreement without consent to Orion as security for payment under a hire purchase agreement. Orion gave notice of the assignment to the end user who counter-signed the notice. The court held that the end user was estopped from relying on the non-assignability clause. Objectively, the assignment was one to which no reasonable objection could have been made. Subjectively, the end user always knew the dealer intended to assign the lease and was aware that Orion did not know about the non-assignability clause. By countersigning the notice, the end user had represented to Orion that there was no assignability point to be taken. Similarly, in *British Gas* v *Eastern Electricity* [1996] *The Times*, 29 November the court held that the withholding of consent for a collateral purpose was not reasonable. Nor would it be reasonable to withhold consent at trial, having been informed of the assignment before it was made and made no objection: *Midland Land* v *Warren Energy* [1997] CILL 1222.

Assignability may not be reciprocal. This sometimes occurs in construction contracts where assignability is restricted to the employer. The contract may provide that only some rights are assignable. This occurs in assignments of sale of business agreements where the original purchaser excludes from the assignment the benefit of warranties and indemnities given by the original vendor. A construction example is the FCEC form of sub-contract which only allows the assignment of "sums which are or may become due and payable". The assignment of other rights is therefore excluded: *e.g.* to claim general damages (*Flood* v *Shand*

Construction (1996) 81 BLR 31), to arbitrate (*Herkules Piling* v *Tilbury Construction* [1992] CILL 770), or to apply to set aside an engineer's rejection of a claim for additional remuneration due to adverse ground conditions (*Yeandle* v *Wynn Realisations* (1995) 47 Con LR 1). It is also possible to limit the number of assignments that can be made. This occurs in collateral warranties where one or two assignments may be allowed. The benefit may become assignable at a particular stage of the contract, *e.g.* clause 19.1.2 of JCT 80 which allows assignment only after practical completion where the employer has also transferred its interest in or granted a lease of the whole of the property concerned. The contract gives the parties the option of incorporating this qualification on assignability or making assignability dependent on consent. Last, the contract may be assignable only to a named person or class, *e.g.* to a named banker or to"any lender to the project" or "any group company". In such a case, it will be a question of construction of the clause whether the assignee will be subject to the same restriction.

It was held in *Linden Gardens* (at 108) that:

> "a prohibition on assignment normally only invalidates the assignment as against the other party to the contract so as to prevent the transfer of the chose in action: in the absence of the clearest words it cannot operate to invalidate the contract as between the assignor and the assignee and even then it may be ineffective on the grounds of public policy".

This is illustrated by *Attwood and Reid* v *Stephens* [1932] NZLR 1332 which concerned road contracts for a public works department which denied the contractor the right to

> "assign all or any of the monies payable or to become payable under the contract or all or any part of any other benefit whatsoever arising or which may arise under the contract, without the previous consent in writing of the engineer-in-chief"

and provided that any money assigned in breach of the contract was to be forfeited to the employer. The case did not concern the employer but was a priority dispute between the contractor's assignee and one of its creditors who had obtained a garnishee order. It was held that assignments which had been made were valid and took priority over the garnishee.

Where the contract has a non-assignment clause and the debtor pays the assignor, it will not be obliged to pay again to the assignee, but the assignor will hold the money on trust for the assignee or its successor in title: see *e.g. International Factors* v *Rodriguez* [1979] QB 351. If a creditor in financial difficulty assigns the same debt to more than one person, the first to give notice of assignment to the debtor will take priority provided the assignee was unaware of any prior assignment: *Dearle* v *Hall* (1828) 3 Russ 1.

Assignment by way of trust

A declaration of trust can avoid the effect of a non-assignment clause (Allcock 1983 at 343). In *Don King* v *Warren* [1998] 2 All ER 608, affirmed [1999] 2 All ER 218 management and promotion agreements between Frank Warren and professional boxers were unassignable by nature as personal contracts or through non-assignability clauses. Warren entered into partnership with King and agreed to hold the agreements "for the benefit of the partnership absolutely". This was held to be a valid declaration of trust of the benefit of the agreement. The trust extended to all rights under the agreement and was not limited to the fruits, *i.e.* money derived from the agreement received by Warren. The court held that "the purpose of the non-assignment clause is a genuine commercial interest of a party of ensuring the contractual relations are only with the person he has selected as the other party to the contract and no one else". The judge stated that non-assignability was "still undeveloped" as a field of law.

A declaration of trust might prejudice the debtor's rights of set-off in two ways. First, as with equitable assignment, once the debtor receives notice of the trust it can no longer build up rights of set-off in respect of an unrelated liquidated cross-claim which accrues due after notice has been received: *e.g. Marathon* v *Mashreqbank* [1997] 2 BCLC 460. Secondly, the debtor may lose the right to liquidation set-off in respect of its cross-claim for lack of mutuality, title to the claim having passed to the creditor in a different capacity as trustee. It is possible that the court would protect the debtor against such consequences by restricting the effect of the trust: *Re ILG Travel* [1995] 2 BCLC 129, 161.

Assignment by way of charge

Perhaps the most common assignment in the industry is of the benefit of a building contract by way of security. To overcome a non-assignment clause in a standard form, tender documents frequently make it a condition of the building contract that the contractor will consent to the assignment of the benefit by the employer to the lender. The Court of Appeal has held the following to be an equitable assignment by way of charge:

> "In consideration of money advanced from time to time we hereby charge the sum of £1,080 which will become due to us from [the employer] on the completion of the above buildings, as security for the advances, and we hereby assign our interest in the above-mentioned sum until the money with added interest to be repaid to you": *Durham Brothers v Robertson* [1898] 1 QB 765.

The lender gave notice of the assignment to the employer but failed in an action against the employer on the ground that the document created an equitable assignment which did not entitle the lender to sue in its own name. If the assignment had transferred plant or materials to a lender as security it would only give the lender priority over an execution creditor of the contractor on registration as a bill of sale: *Church v Sage* (1892) 67 LT 800.

If an assignment is by way of charge, the assignor retains the right to sue for any loss suffered through breach by the debtor. If there is an outright assignment coupled with an entitlement to re-assignment once the secured obligation has been performed, it takes effect as an assignment by way of legal mortgage: *Tancred v Delagoa Bay Railway* (1889) 23 QBD 239. By this arrangement, the mortgagor remains the beneficial owner of the property subject to the mortgagee's security interest. It follows that, despite the assignment, the assignor-mortgagor retains the right to sue for its own losses during the period of the assignment. If the assignee issued proceedings, it could only recover the loss actually suffered by the assignor and would then hold the proceeds on trust for the assignor as mortgagee. After reassignment, the original assignor would sue on its own account and not as successor in title to the assignee: *L/M International v The Circle Limited Partnership* (1995) 49 Con LR 12.

Attornment

An attornment (or acknowledgement) arises where (1) A holds a fund on behalf of B, (2) B directs A to pay C from the fund, (3) A accepts the direction, and (4) A promises to pay C direct. C can seek restitution from A by an action for money had and received (Chitty, 2132). It has been suggested that this principle might apply where a contractor asks an employer to make a direct payment to a sub-contractor and, in response to the contractor's request, the employer promises the sub-contractor to pay it direct (Prentice 1983). If this situation falls within the principle of attornment, the sub-contractor may have an action for money had and received against the employer enforceable on the contractor's liquidation.

The problem with this argument is that the employer does not normally hold a fund for the contractor. The nearest equivalent would be some kind of construction trust. The difficulty is that the employer could not accept the direction because it could lead to personal liability for breach of trust. There is authority that the employer need not hold a fund and that attornment can be effective where the employer merely owes a debt to the contractor: *Shamia* v *Joory* [1958] 1 All ER 111. In the absence of more recent case law, the position is uncertain (Goode 1976).

Flawed assignments

It was seen earlier how the assignment of the benefit of a construction contract may only pass the right to payment rather than the right to order a variation. By the same reasoning, it is possible that the assignment of an on demand bond may transfer the right to the proceeds of a call but not the power to sign the demand. If a default guarantee is assigned, but there is no assignment of the underlying contract or obligation, the assignee cannot enforce the guarantee: see the Australian case of *Hutchens* v *Deaville Investments* (1986) 68 ALR 367. The rationale is that a creditor cannot convert one obligation into two: the original contract duties owed to itself and the guarantor's duties owed to the assignee. This reflects the secondary nature of a guarantor's obligation (Chapter 14).

Conclusion

To avoid problems of non-assignability a contract must be explicit and prohibit all means of transfer: assignment, trust, mortgage, attornment or any disposition or dealing whether absolutely or by way of security without consent.

"No loss" arguments

Under common law a plaintiff cannot normally recover damages for loss sustained by someone else. What happens if the assignor has a cause of action but suffers no loss while the assignee has suffered a loss but has no cause of action? This conundrum arises in the context of non-assignability clauses, and is resolved by reference to the context of the transaction as a whole.

1. Ordinary property assignment

If a builder is asked to refurbish a building for an owner, assignment of the benefit of the contract is prohibited and the builder is unaware of any intention of the owner to transfer the property, the assignee from the employer cannot recover damages against the builder: *Linden Gardens* v *Lenesta Sludge* [1994] 1 AC 85.

2. Inter-group agreement

The position is different if all parties are aware before work begins that the employer intends to transfer the building on completion. Assume that A assigns to B a property and the benefit of a building contract with C. After completion of the works, leaks appear which were caused by breaches by C after the assignment. C's consent to the assignment, a requirement of the contract, had not been obtained. C defended proceedings brought by A and B on the grounds that A had suffered no loss as it had received full value for the property and B had no cause of action as the assignment had been made without C's consent. It was held that C was liable on two grounds:

1. It was foreseeable that defective work could cause loss to an assignee since C knew it was likely that A would sell the property on completion.

2. The non-assignability clause could not be taken to exclude C's liability to a subsequent purchaser and the parties must have intended that A would be able to enforce the contract to recover losses suffered by B: *St Martin's Corporation* v *Sir Robert McAlpine* [1994] 1 AC 85.

3. Development agreement

Where the employer intends to assign the property on completion to the landowner who is intimately involved in the construction process, the court will allow the owner the benefit of the employer's rights. A wanted to have a new leisure centre built on its land. It asked B to enter into a building contract on its own account with C. A would pay B all sums due under the building contract to C and A would act as B's agent for most purposes under the contract. B would not be liable to A for defects in the work and A agreed to indemnify B against any liabilities incurred to C. After practical completion, B assigned the benefit of the contract to A. On defects appearing in the work, A sued C. C defended on the ground that A was a stranger to the contract and B had suffered no loss having assigned the benefit, having no interest in the property and no obligation to A for the quality of C's work. C was held liable on the ground that it knew that the contract was being performed for the ultimate benefit of A and that the agreement between A and B entitled A to call for an assignment of the benefit of the building contract on completion. In the circumstances, the arrangement constituted B as constructive trustee of any causes of action against C: *Darlington Borough Council* v *Wiltshier* (1994) 69 BLR 1.

4. Construction management

A commissioned B to redevelop a site in consideration of the development costs plus 10%. B entered into a construction management agreement with C. On C suing for unpaid fees, B cross-claimed for damages for delay. C argued that B had suffered no loss, as any loss could only be sustained by A. The Court of Appeal held that B could assert the cross-claim in its own right. As a matter of contract, B suffered the loss in the first instance. B had a duty to keep the development costs down, and not to increase them in order to increase its own reward. It was as if A were an undisclosed principal whose intervention was excluded or B were claiming for a loss covered by insurance: *L/M International* v *The Circle Limited Partnership* (1995) 49 Con LR 12.

5. Duty of care deed

A had two subsidiaries, B and C. B owned a development site and C entered into a JCT 81 contract with D, a contractor, for work on the site. D entered into a duty of care deed with B warranting it would exercise reasonable skill and care under the main contract and that it also owed a duty of care to B. There were substantial differences in scope and strictness of obligation between the two documents. The

Court of Appeal held D liable to C on the ground that, properly construed, the main contract showed an intention that D would be liable to C for all losses suffered by B flowing from a breach of the main contract subject to a duty in C to account for them to B. The court inferred an intention not only that B's losses should be recoverable despite the absence of privity and the existence of the separate duty of care deed but also that D could be liable to B for more than C could suffer itself: *Alfred McAlpine* v *Panatown* (1998) 88 BLR 67.

6. Management contracting

The unique relationship between an employer and a management contractor sometimes gives rise to a "no loss" argument. In *Laing Management and Morrison-Knudson* v *Aegon Insurance* (1997) 86 BLR 70 a claim by a management contractor under a surety bond provided by a works contractor which had gone into receivership was met by a defence from the surety that the contractor had suffered no loss since it was entitled to recover the additional cost to complete and its own losses from the employer as part of the prime cost. The argument was rejected since the management contractor was responsible for bringing the whole works to completion and the protection conferred by the contract against loss caused by works contractors was limited in scope.

Formalities

Assignment is an informal process. "All that is necessary is that the debtor should be given to understand that the debt has been made over by the creditor to some third person": *William Brandt* v *Dunlop Rubber Company* [1905] AC 454. In practice, there are only two issues to consider on formalities: when can the assignee sue the debtor? who does the debtor have to pay in order to get a good discharge? An assignee can only take proceedings in its own name to enforce the chose without having to join the assignor where the assignment is legal. A legal assignment is one that complies with s 136 Law of Property Act 1925:

> "(1) Any absolute assignment by writing under the hand of the assignor (not purporting to be by way of charge only) of any debt or other legal thing in action, of which express notice in writing has been given to the debtor, trustee or other person from whom the assignor would have been

entitled to claim such debt or thing in action is effectual in law (subject to equities having priority over the right of the assignee) to pass and transfer from the date of such notice (a) the legal right to such debt or thing in action; (b) all legal and other remedies for the same; (c) the power to give a good discharge for the same without the concurrence of the assignor".

It follows that the following can only take effect as an equitable assignment: oral assignments, assignments by way of charge, assignments of part of a chose, where notice of assignment is not given to the debtor and agreements to assign. An equitable assignee can sue in its own name but has to join the assignor. After an assignment, the assignor cannot sue in its own name without joining the assignee: *Three Rivers* v *Bank of England* [1996] QB 292. The section only excludes assignments by way of charge; an assignment by way of mortgage will fall within the section if the other conditions are met: *Tancred* v *Delagoa Bay Railway Co* (1889) 23 QBD 239. Giving notice of assignment has at least four advantages: until it receives notice, the debtor can obtain a good discharge by paying the assignor; giving notice ensures priority to the assignee over successive dealings with the chose; the notice may bring the assignment within s 136 and allow the assignee to sue in its own name; after receipt of the notice, the debtor cannot raise any fresh and independent equities in defence to an action brought by the assignee. In practice, "the assignee cannot insist on the continued performance of the contract unless either his assignor is able and willing to satisfy the obligation to pay or the assignee himself is willing to do it for him": *Cooper* v *Micklefield Coal* (1912) 107 LT 457.

An equitable assignment can arise informally. A term in a nominated sub-contract that the contractor holds the sub-contractor's proportion of retention in trust has been held to be an equitable assignment to the sub-contractor of the appropriate proportion of the contractor's interest in the retention: *Re Tout and Finch* [1954] 1 WLR 178. In an insolvency situation, time is often of the essence. Whether acting for a creditor pressing for payment or an insolvency practitioner wishing to conclude an agreement, equitable assignment may be the preferred means of transfer. For example, in *Golden Sand* v *Easy Success Enterprises* (unreported, 31 March 1999) a contractor in financial difficulty was unable to prove payment of nominated sub-contractors who approached the employer for direct payment under the equivalent of clause 27(c) of JCT 63. Instead, it was agreed between the employer, the contractor and nominated sub-contractors that all future payments to nominated sub-contractors would be made direct by the employer. The works were completed, the defects liability period expired and the final account was agreed. Approximately $380,000 was due to one of the nominated sub-contractors which included retention of $175,000. Before this was paid by the employer, the contractor went into liquidation. It was held by the High Court of Hong Kong that the direct payment agreement divested the contractor of its rights in respect of money due to nominated sub-contractors, the element representing retention being held in trust in any case. The court ordered payment to the nominated sub-contractor of money the employer had paid into court. The basis of the decision seems to have been that the agreement amounted to an equitable assignment to the sub-contractors of the proportions of certified sums ascertainable from the architect's certificates. Equally, assignment can be a means of holding a reluctant party to its bargain, for example, where an agreement is made informally which can later be enforced as an effective equitable assignment. Figure 6.3 summarises the essential differences between legal and equitable assignment.

LEGAL	*EQUITABLE*
Formalities required – must be in writing signed by the assignor	No formalities required – could be oral provided there is adequate evidence
Written notice must be given to the debtor	No requirement for notice (although notice would preserve priority over later assignees and ensure that debtor can only obtain a good discharge by paying assignee)
Debtor can only obtain a good discharge by paying assignee	Debtor can obtain good discharge by paying assignor (unless notice of assignment has been served)
Assignee can sue in its own name	Assignee needs to add assignor as co-plaintiff or, if it refuses, as co-defendant
No consideration required	Probably no consideration required
Must be absolute – *i.e.* whole debt or interest must be transferred.	Need not be absolute, assignor could retain some interest
Must not be by way of charge only	Can be by way of charge only

Fig 6.3

Priorities

Apart from its use as a mechanism for procuring a completion contract, assignment is often encountered in the twilight period before formal insolvency. A contractor may pacify its most aggressive creditors, particularly those threatening to issue a winding-up petition, by assigning sums due or to become due from employers. Such assignments could give rise to competing claims between the assignee, a liquidator or receiver appointed over the contractor, a mortgagee, an execution creditor, a guarantor, or (in jurisdictions with lien legislation) employees, and any sub-contractors or suppliers whose work was connected with the improvement to the land. The question of priorities will be looked at first where money assigned has already been earned and then where it has not been earned by the date of notice of assignment.

Money already earned

An assignment for value of a sum already earned before liquidation will be valid against a liquidator, even if payment does not become due until after the start of the liquidation. So where six-sevenths of the work had been performed and two-sevenths remained to be paid for, an assignment of less than one-seventh of the contract sum before the contractor's bankruptcy was valid against the trustee even though it did not become due for payment until after the trustee had completed the work: In *Re Toward, ex parte Moss* (1884) 14 QBD 310, *G & T Earle* v *Hemsworth RDC* (1929) 140 LT 69. There is no distinction between an assignment of the value of work payable on completion of an agreed stage and an assignment of retention: *Drew* v *Josolyne* (1887) 18 QBD 590. Where money is lent to a builder on the security of freehold land on which the builder is engaged and the lender/employer retained a proportion of the loan pending completion of the building, and the contractor assigned part of the loan to a judgment creditor before its bankruptcy, it was held that the assignee took priority as the sum assigned was already the contractor's property at the date of the assignment: *Aicken & Son* v *Bradley* [1916] NZLR 659.

If the value of work on a stage payment contract, retention and money already borrowed are all regarded as "earned", what is the position where a contractor has a claim for a *quantum meruit*? As the test is whether the sum assigned has been earned by the date of assignment not whether it is due and/or payable, it appears that an assignment of sums due or to become due from an employer in respect of defined works ought to be valid against a contractor's liquidator, although there appears to be no authority. The same appears to be the case where the contract provides for payment against interim certificates. An assignment of sums due or to become due would probably attach the value of uncertified work in progress executed before liquidation as the value had been earned before liquidation and merely required ascertainment. Thus, it is important for a liquidator or receiver to value work completed before deciding whether to complete a contract.

An employer does not want to risk paying twice for the same work. An assignee will be anxious to obtain payment of the whole amount assigned. And a receiver wants to ensure that the company recovers the amount budgeted against the cost to complete in order to recover the projected profit. A bank or other holder of a fixed charge over book debts will take priority against an assignee of sums due or to become due insofar as they are represented by certified sums or retention at the date of liquidation: *Re Jason Construction* (1972) 16 CBR 297. It is thought that this principle would apply also to an assignment of an entitlement under an arbitration award: *Bank of New South Wales* v *The King* [1918] NZLR 945.

Money not yet earned

In the example referred to above, if the fractions had been reversed and two-sevenths of the work was still to be done but only one-seventh of its value remained to be paid for, an assignee would not take priority against the contractor's trustee in bankruptcy or liquidator if the latter completed the contract because there was nothing due at the date of the assignment: *Tooth* v *Hallett* (1869) LR 4 Ch App 242. Compare the Canadian case of *Creditel* v *Terrace Corporation* (1983) 50 CBR 87 where no money became payable to the assignee as the trustee elected not to continue the contract. The same applies to an assignment of profits where it can be shown that they would only be earned at the end of a contract: *Hewitt* v *Official Assignee of Barnes and Keble* [1930] NZLR 416, *Re Jones, ex parte Nichols* (1883) 22 Ch D 782. It is always important to examine the terms of the assignment carefully. If the assignee is entitled to be paid out of specific progress payments (*e.g.* the first and second certified sums), it will not take priority over a liquidator if those particular payments are insufficient to pay the assignee in full: *Gardner and Yeoman* v *Watson* (1937) GLR 141. The assignee may also lose priority if, after deduction of liquidated damages payable prior to receipt of the notice of assignment, there is no net sum payable to the assignor: *White* v *Ensor* (1882) 11 NZLR 207. Compare *Fulton* v *Dornwell* (1885) 4 NZLR 207 where an assigned debt was extinguished by the cost to complete and the employer was held to have acted reasonably and mitigated its loss, and *Re Yeadon Waterworks* v *Wright* (1895) 72 LT 538 at 832. Assignment is also important in the context of the transfer of collateral warranties where there is some uncertainty over the assignee's right to recover damages (Cartwright 1990, 1993).

Conclusion

In the eyes of the law, trust and transferability are intimately connected. A trust is constituted by the transfer of property from settlor to trustee, but the connection is deeper than this. A trust can arise by way of assignment (*Darlington* v *Wiltshier*) and an assignment can be effected by way of trust (*Re Tout & Finch*). Trust, transferability, direct agreements and automatic novation were all important elements in the restructuring of the Channel Tunnel Rail-Link (Bowles & Reingold 1999). If a contract says it cannot be assigned by either party, the law still allows them to transfer it in any other way. So a non-assignability clause in a contract can be overcome by a declaration of trust (*Don King* v *Warren*).

This approach is based on the presumed intention of the parties. But is such *laissez-faire* consistent with a construction contract, which depends on mutual co-operation? The philosophy behind assignability is that it should not prejudice the obligor. Prejudice can be caused in two ways: (1) by splitting the benefit and the burden of a contract, and (2) unless the law implies some restriction on the concept, assignment also increases the benefit by reducing the obligor's rights to legal and liquidation set-off. Contrary to the underlying philosophy, therefore, an assignee can be in a better position against the obligor than the assignor. Confusion also occurs in splitting the benefit in that it seems to be the law that only financial rights (*e.g.* liquidated damages) and the benefit of full performance (e.g. the right to the building on completion) can be transferred, rather than other performance rights (*e.g.* to order variations).

Chapter 7

· **Informal Insolvency** ·

Introduction

This chapter looks at the two statutory definitions of insolvency and how they apply to the industry. It then considers the causes and indicators of insolvency as manifested by contractors, with specific reference to the major construction insolvencies of English contracting firms in recent years. The procedures available outside formal insolvency to a contractor in financial difficulty are then reviewed, concluding with the criteria adopted by the court when hearing winding-up petitions, again by reference to construction companies.

Meaning of insolvency

"Insolvency" covers the financial failure of individuals and companies and their position before and after the start of a formal insolvency procedure. Insolvency may be experienced in the short or long term. Short term insolvency usually means a cash flow crisis where not enough money is coming in to meet a company's outgoings. Long term insolvency applies where the company is able to pay its debts as they fall due but its balance sheet shows a deficiency of assets over liabilities. The situation is recognised by the Insolvency Act 1986 which provides two alternative tests of insolvency: the "going concern" test under s 123(1) which assesses the company's current cash flow and the "balance sheet" test under s 123(2) which compares the company's assets with its current and long term liabilities. The purpose of both tests is to determine whether or not the company is able to pay its debts: if the company fails either test, it will be insolvent.

The going concern test

Under the going concern test, also known as the "cash flow" or "commercial insolvency" test, a company is insolvent if it is unable to pay its debts as they fall due. A contractor is insolvent if it is unable to pay a sub-contractor within the period allowed by the sub-contract or a supplier within the supplier's credit terms. It is important at the outset to distinguish between inability to pay, deferment of payment and refusal to pay. Inability to pay is the consequence of inadequate cash flow and shortage of working capital which can have many different causes. Alternatively, non-payment may be the result of a deliberate policy of postponing payment to creditors until the last possible moment, *e.g.* service of a writ or a winding-up petition. This is a dangerous line to take because of the serious effect of a winding-up petition on a company's credit rating and on the confidence of its lender. Refusal to pay may result from defective performance by the sub-contractor or failure to comply with a condition precedent.

Even where the contractor is unable to pay, it will not be insolvent under the going concern test if it has a defence to the sub-contractor's claim. Proof of inability to pay is sometimes difficult. The best evidence is a written admission, which may be forthcoming if the contractor is seriously insolvent and driven to relying on the creditors' goodwill in a last ditch attempt to avoid formal insolvency. In the absence of other evidence, insolvency can be proved by the service of a statutory demand under s 123(1)(a) Insolvency Act 1986. This is a simple form which is served at the registered office of the company requiring it to pay a due debt exceeding £750 within 21 days. If payment is not made within that period, and the company has no justifiable reason for non-payment, it is deemed to be insolvent and no further proof of insolvency will be required at the hearing of a winding-up petition.

There is no requirement that the creditor must serve a statutory demand. In *Re Taylor's Industrial Flooring* [1990] BCC 44 the Court of Appeal stated that the vast majority of creditors seeking a winding-up order do not serve statutory demands as the 21-day period merely gives the company time in which to dissipate its assets. Where "a debt is due and an invoice sent and the debt is not disputed then failure of the debtor company to pay the debt is itself evidence of inability to pay" (at 49). In that case, a plant hire company invoiced a contractor for its charges. The contractor raised an argument that its credit period had not expired but this was rejected by the court on a finding of fact.

The balance sheet test

As its name suggests, this test assesses a company's solvency by reference to its assets and liabilities rather than its cash flow. It is more difficult to apply than the going concern test. The Insolvency Act 1986 does not define assets and liabilities. Although the Act contemplates that a snapshot will be taken as at a particular date, rather like a balance sheet, the criteria for inclusion and valuation of an asset are not the same as for a statutory audit. The main problem arises out of the long term contracts carried out by contractors. On the asset side, there may be disagreement on whether profit or a claim should be included as an asset and, if so, at what point. Where the contractor is involved in property development, problems arise on the treatment of interest on land acquisition and construction costs and on the valuation of the land and buildings in course of construction. In addition, liabilities financed off balance sheet not required to be shown in audited accounts may have to be taken into account in the balance sheet test. It is the treatment of contingent and prospective liabilities which gives rise to most difficulty (see generally Ernst & Young 1999).

Valuation of liabilities

Risk in contracting relates to overruns of cost or time and to disputes over the quality of work. Cost is relevant when considering claims for variations from sub-contractors which the contractor may have ordered without authorisation from the architect. Cost may also be relevant where there has been an overpayment and there is insufficient value in future work for its recovery by deduction. Time is relevant in the context of employers' claims for liquidated and ascertained damages or in sub-contractors' claims for loss and expense or unliquidated damages following delay to completion. Quality is the most difficult area. The ascertainment of liability for defective work may require a lengthy trial and be the subject of considerable disagreement between the parties' experts. The court may conclude that the contractor is not liable for the defects because they arose exclusively from the architect's design. Even if the contractor is found liable, the court may conclude that damages should be restricted to the cost of repair rather than replacement. Thus, depending upon the circumstances, it is possible to say that a defects claim could be worth everything or nothing.

In these circumstances, how should the court apply the balance sheet test? One approach is to take the whole value of the claim into account, but this could be unfair to the contractor. The creditor may be using its claim oppressively in order to stifle the contractor's genuine cross-claim. Both parties' views may be tenable at the date of the test but the employer's claim may be sufficient to convert a fully solvent contractor into a grossly insolvent one. The balance sheet test is applied in various contexts and at different dates (Goode 1997 at 68). In the event of difficulty, the court could adjourn the application to allow the contingent claim to be valued. This may be done by litigation or arbitration or by the procedure for appealing against rejection of proof as appropriate. These methods would promote certainty but be a slow and expensive means of valuation.

Totty & Moss propose taking a range of potential liability (at A1.08). They suggest that the lowest figure in the range should be deducted from the highest figure in order to ascertain the area of uncertainty. The figure representing the area of uncertainty is then multiplied by the percentage probability that the claim will succeed, and the result is then added to the lowest figure in the range to arrive at a valuation. The authors of UK GAAP disapprove of a method of valuation which relies upon the multiplication of a claim by a probability factor. The addition of the minimum value of the claim in the calculation proposed by Totty & Moss adds credibility to their approach but it presupposes that it is possible to arrive at realistic figures to establish the range in the first place. Where the claim depends upon the existence of a contract, and this is in dispute, the range may be between 0% and 100%. What are the alternatives? Valuation of contingent claims is necessary in the following contexts: the statutory audit of companies, security for costs applications, breach of warranty claims and valuation of proofs by liquidators.

Auditors are concerned with questions of accrual and disclosure in accounts, so as to show a true and fair view. Where a contingency is reasonably certain to occur (95% to 100% likelihood) it will be included. Where it is probable (50% to 95% likelihood) an amount is accrued if it can be estimated with reasonable accuracy, otherwise it is disclosed in a note to the accounts. Where an outcome is possible (5% to 50% likelihood) no amount is accrued but the potential liability is disclosed. Where liability is unlikely (less than 5%) disclosure is not required although good practice may recommend it. As with Totty & Moss's approach, the application of auditing techniques presupposes that liability and a range of quantum can be established. The auditors' approach is therefore of limited value to the balance sheet test.

Where there is evidence that a plaintiff will be unable to pay a defendant's costs if the defendant succeeds in its defence, the court may order the plaintiff to provide security for costs under s 726 Companies Act 1985. One of the criteria is the plaintiff's prospects of success but the court will not become involved in a lengthy examination of the merits of the case: *Trident v Manchester Ship Canal* [1990] BCC 694.

The claim must have a reasonable prospect of success or, at least, be brought in good faith and on competent advice in order to give rise to the jurisdiction to award security: *Cheffick* v *JDM Associates* (1988) 22 Con LR 1. The judges of the Technology and Construction Court have found it difficult to assess the probability of success in defects claims. If they experience difficulty given their experience of the industry and familiarity with the issues, courts with insolvency jurisdiction may find themselves in an even more difficult position. Attempts to value contingent liabilities in the context of agreements for the sale of shares or assets in the company have not enjoyed greater success: *Trollope and Colls* v *Gresham* (1984) 2 CLD 7.16. Claims in the construction industry, whether made by employer, contractor or sub-contractor, are often inflated. They suffer from "exaggerations which in all good faith everybody is inclined to make in estimating the expenses which they can recoup from someone else": *Chandless* v *Whitton* (unreported, 10 December 1986, Browne-Wilkinson VC). The acceptance of the full value of the contingent claim for the purpose of the balance sheet test fails to take this important factor into account. Insolvency practitioners and those advising them would benefit from the court's guidance on these issues.

The pari passu rule

A creditor with a security interest or proprietary right in the debtor's property is much more likely to be paid in the event of the debtor's insolvency. An ordinary unsecured creditor often receives nothing. Hence the scramble for assets which precedes many insolvencies. The position changes with the start of a liquidation or a bankruptcy when a creditor's debt is converted into the right to claim in the proceeds of sale of the assets after they have been realised by the insolvency practitioner. The claim is known as a "proof of debt" which, if admitted, entitles the creditor to a dividend, each creditor receiving the same percentage of its debt. This principle of fair treatment is known as the *pari passu* rule (meaning literally "with the same step").

This rule underpins much of insolvency law (Goode 1997). It is the basis of the liquidator's power to claw back property transferred by the company before the start of the procedure by avoiding transactions which have unjustly enriched one person at the expense of the general body of creditors. This applies to directors, shadow directors, connected persons, associates, creditors, sureties, participators in fraud and others. The idea is that the transactions have, by diminishing the company's assets, conferred an unfair or improper advantage on the other party. It is the fact that the company participated in these transactions which justifies their avoidance. The liability of directors and others in connection with the avoidance of transactions is considered in Chapter 15.

Causes of insolvency

Contractors are renowned for having low profit margins, low fixed assets and low capital but high cash flow and high return on capital employed. Financing is generated internally from positive cash flow and retained profits and externally from short term finance, usually an overdraft repayable on demand. Short term finance can support working capital, stock and work in progress; but for growth, long term external finance is needed in the form of equity investment and long term loans.

Structural consequences

As a consequence of positive cash flow and the lack of an asset base:

1. Contractors diversify in order to use the cash earned from contracting to generate higher profits, create assets as security for loans and seek financial stability by venturing into businesses counter-cyclical to construction.

2. There are no financial barriers to entry into the industry.

3. Given the absence of need to raise equity funds from shareholders, there are many family firms of contractors.

4. Conglomerates seeking positive cash flow are attracted to contractors.

5. Management buy-outs are more feasible than in other industries (Hillebrandt and Cannon 1989).

Here are the seeds of insolvency.

1. Diversification

Diversification was a major cause of insolvency between 1989 and 1995. Whether the move was into property as with Rush & Tompkins and Lilley or into sub-contracting and materials supply as with Conder, failed acquisitions poisoning the financial health of the group have been a feature.

2. Absence of barriers to entry

The ease of entry into the industry has a number of consequences: a proliferation of small firms with little management expertise, a tendency to over-capacity even at the height of a market and the lack of financial barriers to entry has created an industry where market forces are at their most ruthless (BCIS 1994). This is why analysts press for mergers and the increased use of on demand bonds, contractors protest at banks supporting "lame ducks" and insolvency practitioners argue that proposed reforms to insolvency law may prop up companies which should be forced out by the market for the good of the industry: there are just too many contractors. Yet calls for a licensing system as practised in Australia, for example, have not found favour with the legislature.

3. Family firms

The predominance of family firms also contributes to the level of financial failure. This is because ingrained attitudes lead to financial complacency and an inability to adapt to a changing market.

4. Conglomerates

With conglomerates, one thinks of Lonrho which bought Sunley. Sunley in turn purchased Turriff on its insolvency, only for Sunley Turriff to purchase part of Lilley on its receivership.

5. Management buy-outs

Management buy-outs have been a common exit from receivership: examples are Graham Wood, Conder Structures and Henry Barrett. However, there have been cases where a management buy-out has been followed by receivership due in part to the level of debt required to finance it. An example is Elliott Northern, where the business was acquired through a buy-out from the receiver of J A Elliott, which went into receivership in March 1993 and was then dispersed through novations. It may be possible to plan the receivership by appointing receivers to the parent company, allowing the target company to continue trading while a buy-out is negotiated. This occurred with the Dew Group in 1992.

From time to time, contractors experience a sharp decline in demand leading to reduced turnover and lost cash flow. In the 1990s recession, excessive competition forced many to tender at below cost. Tenders for long term contracts have been based on prices for sub-contractors and materials which are now rising. These features cannot be sustained by the unstable sources of finance used by contractors. Cash reserves built up in previous years have been lost and contractors have to turn to their bankers and shareholders for support.

Business sector ratios

As Peter Fenn explained in Chapter 1, demand for the industry's products is cyclical and fluctuates in accordance with Government policy and the general economic climate. Insolvency is more likely to occur in the construction industry than most others.

It has been suggested that the way the figures are compiled and presented gives a misleading picture of the relation between construction and other industries (Hillebrandt 1984). The industry appears so prominent because it is the largest industrial category which is not subdivided in the statistics and is bound to have a larger number of failures because of its unusual fragmentation. As Patricia Hillebrandt points out, "there is a greater chance of a construction firm failing than other firms but it is less than twice as much, not five times as much as some statements imply" (Hillebrandt 1977).

Poor financial control

Successful contractors are expert at cash control and management. They have evolved highly sophisticated techniques of cash flow forecasting and monitoring. A well managed contractor maintains detailed financial, cost and management accounts which allocate cost in as much detail as possible to specific contracts and to individual elements within them but, unfortunately, many fall short of this standard. Insolvency practitioners have long ceased to be surprised at the lack of proper accounts in construction companies. Many contractors fail to collect debts, particularly retentions, allowing them to accumulate until their age makes them difficult to collect. The adage of cash flow is to "collect early and pay late". Late payment is, however, a two-edged sword. It is a serious problem in the industry and a contributory factor to the large number of insolvencies. The Banwell report concluded:

> "Prompt payment for work done is of such importance and all concerned are so sensitive to delay that the industry generally must be willing to make use of procedures which will ensure that contractual obligations are met promptly and that there is no impediment to the proper flow of money." (Banwell 1964, at 9.6).

Delay in payment affects all parties involved in the contractual chain. It is hard to say at this stage what difference the Late Payment of Commercial Debts (Interest) Act 1998 will make. Last in line is the builders' merchant, colloquially known as the "industry's banker".

The "knock-on effect"

The vast majority of contractors are small firms with few employees. Small firms often fail because of the financial failure of another company higher in the contractual chain. A significant number of insolvencies occur as a direct result of the insolvency of another party. This phenomenon is sometimes described as the "domino" or "knock-on" effect. It has three aspects. First, the knock-on effect is felt up or down the chain. The insolvency of a contractor may bring down a series of sub-contractors and suppliers; but it may also cause the failure of an employer set up for a project which becomes unviable after the contractor's failure. Secondly, the effect can be felt across different companies in the same group. Thirdly, the knock-on effect is experienced across industrial sectors. The property industry is cyclical and experiences boom and bust periods. A sharp decline in the property market reduces the demand for construction work which causes insolvency among contractors. The fall in orders is felt by sub-contractors, suppliers and manufacturers of plant, equipment and transport. A slump in house-building inevitably leads to a contraction in demand for home furnishings, household appliances and DIY services.

The failure of a parent company may lead to the collapse of the entire group. This may arise where each company has guaranteed the liabilities of the others. Similarly, the failure of one partner may cause the insolvency of the joint venture company if the other partner is unable or unwilling to assume responsibility for its debts. The failure of one partner may also lead to the insolvency of the other. A common reaction to a substantial bad debt is the purchase of work at low or negative margins in order to maintain turnover. Suicidal bidding of this kind only makes the problem worse, increasing the risk of further insolvencies.

How can the knock-on effect be avoided? Protection against insolvency can be obtained by a combination of measures and especially by avoiding excessive concentration on a particular client, industrial sector, region or even country. A pattern of growth commonly seen is where a small contractor forms a relationship with one particular client. If that client becomes insolvent or decides to place its work elsewhere, the contractor cannot support its overheads and debt and is forced into insolvency. In *Re Harris Simons* [1989] 1 WLR 368 a contractor went into administration after increasing its turnover from £830,000 in 1985 to £17 million in 1987 and £27 million in 1988. Almost all of the increase was attributable to one client. The contractor became unable to pay its debts after substantial sums were withheld as a result of a dispute. This is a potential risk in "partnering". The same point applies to companies concentrating in one sector. During the 1980s, many contractors expanded into house-building and commercial property and were badly affected when both markets collapsed in 1989. Diversification during a recession is extremely difficult because the influx of competition drives down margins forcing newcomers to buy in work with the attendant risks referred to earlier. Geographical spread ought to give some protection against insolvency since demand fluctuates across the country. Finding work overseas is not necessarily the answer: the property ventures in the United States undertaken by Rush & Tompkins were a significant cause of its receivership and liquidation in 1990.

Overwhelming contract claims

If a construction contract goes wrong, it can go badly wrong. An exceptional claim against the contractor under one contract can be enough to cause insolvency. One example is liability for liquidated damages following a failure to complete the works on time. The greatest danger is that management is forced to concentrate on one problem contract and the effort to extricate the company draws in resources from the rest of the company or group. There have been some striking examples in recent years, notably the contract for the construction of the Kariba Dam in Zambia undertaken by Mitchell Construction in the early 1970s. In his account of the contract and the subsequent receivership of the company, David Morrell, Mitchell's former chairman, argues that problems on the Kariba contract arose out of chronic under-certification and the refusal by the employer to allow compensation for unforeseen ground conditions:

> "The most crucial fact we faced was that between October 1971 and April 1972 we had suffered an adverse cash flow at Kariba of £1 million and, at a time when we should really have been in our stride, work was almost at a standstill. In the previous October we had raised £1 million through the issue of debenture stock, because it was considered prudent to augment the company's working capital; but in those few months the whole of that sum had disappeared down a large hole in Central Africa. Not only that, but the drain was continuing and would go on unless and until the engineer acknowledged that the rock was treacherous and gave us some financial relief. Our reaction in April 1972, when the storm clouds had unmistakably gathered, was twofold. We stopped tendering for new projects. At the same time we turned our attention to trying to collect some of the huge sums which were owing to us. We also made some internal reorganisation in order to limit the disruption to the rest of our business. In cutting back on tendering we were, of course, taking the opposite action to a contractor who is seriously unstable. He is likely to seek his solution in a vastly inflated order book, with a great deal of 'front-end loading', in the hope of gaining liquidity relief while putting his house in order. Our position was different. We had many assets to protect, and our biggest fear was that they would all be absorbed by this one disastrous contract" (Morrell 1987, at 165).

By January 1973, when the receiver was appointed, Mr Morrell estimates that Mitchell had been under certified by £4.1 million. Under-certification is an area of risk in contracting which the contractor is not well placed to resist. In *Mowlem* v *Carlton Gate* (1990) 21 Con LR 113 a contractor alleged bad faith on a part of a certifier but the court could not decide such a serious allegation on an application for summary judgment and stayed the claim to arbitration.

Another example of an overwhelming contract claim bringing down a substantial contractor is that of Davy Corporation. Davy was founded in 1830 but was forced to dispose of its main businesses in 1991 following a disastrous contract for the conversion of an oil rig in the North Sea. The contract sum was in excess of £120 million and agreed as a fixed price, no allowance being made for progress payments. Davy's problems started with the withdrawal of a joint venture partner and were compounded by increased safety requirements, industrial relations problems and difficulties experienced in the course of construction. Liquidated damages eventually exceeded the contract sum.

Imprudent diversification

Contractors look to other sectors in search of higher profits than are to be made from contracting. Successful contractors need outlets to invest positive cash flow. During the 1980s, many contractors were tempted into property development for these reasons, but have since withdrawn from the sector or have become insolvent. The largest insolvency was the Rush & Tompkins Group which went into receivership in April 1990 with liabilities thought to exceed £300 million. The company was formed in 1930 and was floated on the Stock Exchange in 1971. Its core business of contracting and minor civil engineering was reasonably successful. The company experienced a liquidity problem in 1986 but was able to reduce borrowing by a rights issue. New management was introduced which decided to close the civil engineering side and diversify into property development. The company would enter into a joint venture with a partner who would provide the land and obtain planning permission. Projects would be financed through a jointly owned company whose assets would be charged to the lender. Rush & Tompkins assumed all the risk, however, because it both guaranteed the liabilities of the joint venture company and acted as contractor to it. A further rights issue was planned in 1989 but was not proceeded with. Cash flow problems emerged towards the end of 1989 and a programme of property disposals was launched, but by February 1990 additional financing was sought from the company's bank which was refused. After additional security was provided in March 1990, the bank lent a small amount of new money, but, after negotiations for further equity from existing shareholders failed, the company's shares were suspended in early April 1990 and, two weeks later, the company ceased trading. Receivers were appointed by the bank on 48 hours' notice. Unusually, for such a large company, there had been no prior investigating accountant's report.

Diversification can also be achieved by moving from one method of procurement to another. An example in the early 1990s is Harry Neal, a long established contractor, which decided to move from lump sum to management contracting but could not adjust to the different culture. Insolvency could also result from an acquisition which turns out to be a financial liability. Substantial sums can be incurred in supporting a new subsidiary, even by means of an orderly wind down of its activities, and in litigation to recover losses from the vendor. For some, the urge to build an empire is just too strong: many insolvencies have resulted from corporate aggrandisement.

Indicators of insolvency

Most indicators of insolvency are matters of common sense but sometimes the same action can be interpreted either as prudent management or a distress signal. An early indicator of insolvency could be a missed payment deadline or a request for an extended payment period. A request for accelerated payment or reduced retention is frequently a sign of a cash flow problem: *Re DKG Contractors* [1990] BCC 903 at 911. In the medium term, increasing creditor pressure results in the service of writs and notices of arbitration. Damaging rumours may start to circulate on site. A contractor in difficulty tries to reschedule payments by raising disputes, making unjustified contra charges or set-offs and by refusing to make payments on account when only a small element is in dispute. A cash crisis causes rapid management turnover on and off site. Reduction in site supervisory staff leads to defective workmanship which aggravates the company's existing difficulties in getting paid. A company may become known for under-bidding to win work and take on excessive numbers of surveyors to launch claims against employers.

An auditor's report qualified on a going concern basis is an indicator that the company is on the road to formal insolvency in the short to medium term. Accounts are, however, an unreliable basis for decision-making as they may be out of date or prepared on misleading assumptions, *e.g.* a contractor may have included profit and claims before they should properly have been taken into account. If the contractor is concerned in property development, it may have capitalised interest or have substantial liabilities off balance sheet. Access to internal accounts is difficult to obtain for all but secured lenders and these may also be unreliable. If a company is quoted on the Stock Exchange, its share price is one indication of its financial worth but this can be illusory if information available to analysts fails to disclose the true picture. The financial press publishes details of transactions by directors in shares of their own companies, but this is not necessarily a distress signal: it may simply record a particular director's need for cash rather than any problem with the company. Many lack the capacity or the time to analyse financial data or are unable to give each item of information or financial ratio its appropriate weighting. One indicator is a system known as the Z-score based on research by Syspas which analyses the published results of failed companies and identifies and quantifies the characteristics which distinguish them from financially sound companies. The system has developed a score which discloses whether a company is above or below a solvency threshold.

By the time a creditor becomes aware of a problem, it may be too late. A company may be forced to admit to its client that it cannot continue trading without an *ex gratia* payment. The client may feel that it is in its own best interest to make a payment rather than suffer the consequential costs of engaging a completion contractor. At the terminal stage, the contractor may be refused trade credit other than on a pro-forma basis. Before a company goes into receivership or liquidation, there is a twilight period when it is known to be financially vulnerable. During this period, creditors stalk the company's assets hungry for payment or security to improve their position in the impending insolvency. The law of the jungle prevails and the most powerful (or the best advised) succeed in getting paid in preference to others.

Informal insolvency procedures

When asked for money, investors turn to a company's balance sheet. What assets does it have? Unlike property companies, contracting firms have few tangible assets which can be carved up and redistributed among the creditors or offered as security to lenders. A company which has never diversified out of contracting will have debtors, retention, claims and work in progress: assets derived from construction contracts which are regarded by banks as a flawed form of security. Contractors may also own a lease, stock and vehicles but these are unlikely to be of much value to a lender.

In reviewing its options a contractor has to consider the interests of lenders (including banks, building societies, venture capitalists and holders of debt instruments), trade creditors such as sub-contractors and suppliers, bondsmen, employers, preferential creditors, shareholders, landlords, asset lessors, public utilities and employees. If a contractor approaches a bank with a request to increase the overdraft facility, the bank may require the contractor to commission a viability report from an accountant (ICAEW 1992). This may be either the result of a full investigation which may take weeks or a quick review lasting a day or two, known as a "quick and dirty".

A "quick and dirty" may conclude that the business cannot be saved and that the bank should take immediate action. The overdraft limit is likely to be cut causing an immediate cash flow crisis resulting in the voluntary liquidation of the company unless the directors can find another source of short term finance. The reduction may be followed by a requirement that the overdraft limit is further reduced by the amounts of additional sums paid into it. Timing is important and the bank may act immediately after a large payment is received from an employer before the contractor can pay trade creditors. This is more likely where a contractor has failed to keep the bank fully informed or where there is no market for its services. The annual survey of the Society of Practitioners of Insolvency is significant in recording loss of market in the top three causes of insolvency (SPI 1999).

If a more detailed investigation is commissioned, what factors will influence the lending decision? The key question is whether the business is viable. Viability is in the eye of the beholder (Adamson 1991). An objective assessment can only be made by an outsider. This is usually an insolvency accountant. Some firms publish special briefings on the industry for the benefit of lenders (Grant Thornton 1999). An initial review is taken of the company's cash flow since uninterrupted cash flow enables a company to continue trading while the options are sorted out. The best approach is to look for positive aspects of the business while recognising the negative ones. The accountant will also appraise the quality of the management. There is no standard form of report but it is likely to deal with the history of the company, its future profitability, projected cash flows and balance sheet. The report is then presented to the bank and a lending decision made. This can result in the company entering "intensive care" and conditions of further lending being imposed. There is a wide range of possibilities.

Operational measures

These include cutting overheads and "non-productive" staff, managing working capital by improving collections and obtaining more generous credit, alternative finance such as factoring, asset refinancing or venture capital.

Reorganisation

This involves an alteration to the group's structure by winding down loss-making businesses, merging separate businesses to reduce cost and create "synergy" or separating businesses to take advantage of new markets. Where businesses are discontinued, careful timing is required to take advantage of tax losses and allowances. Tax is a major concern in the swaps of businesses and shares between group members, sale and lease backs, hive down and sale arrangements, the creation of new subsidiaries and asset refinancing.

Merger or takeover

For some years, analysts have been pressing for mergers and takeovers in the industry, recommending privatised water or power companies as potential bidders. Arrangements such as swaps of divisions between contractors are advocated.

Secondment

Secondment of managers from one part of the group to another may be sufficient. Alternatively, the appointment to the board of a company doctor, an insolvency practitioner or even a retired bank manager is worth considering.

Rescheduling

Rescheduling is the postponement of payment of the principal or interest of a debt. For example, a trustee of an 8% loan note maturing in 2001 might agree to reschedule repayment of the principal to 2005 provided that interest is paid at 10% after 2001. Rescheduling can include the reduction of interest rates, waiver of debt and other possibilities.

Moratorium

A moratorium is a consensual freeze on the enforcement of rights contingent on an agreed date or event. For example, where a company has comparatively few creditors, they might be prepared to suspend their rights pending the sale of a major asset. In practice, a moratorium is implemented in conjunction with one or more of the other options.

Composition

A composition is a contract between the company and its creditors to pay less than the face value of its debts. For example, the creditors might agree to accept 60 pence in the pound in full and final satisfaction of their debts to enable the company to continue trading.

Arrangement

The word "arrangement" is wide enough to embrace most informal processes, as well as voluntary arrangements under the Insolvency Act 1986 considered in Chapter 8, and schemes of arrangement under the Companies Act 1985 (Goode 1997, at 20).

Rationalisation

Similar to reorganisation but involving the disposal of assets or businesses. The decision to sell depends on whether the proceeds of sale will exceed the loss of cash flow generated by those assets or businesses.

Restructuring

Restructuring is the alteration of a company's balance sheet by agreement between the company and its lenders. It may include elements of all of the above together with an alteration to the company's share capital. This is now considered in more detail.

Restructuring

A restructuring is an expensive process involving heavy professional fees of merchant banks, accountants and lawyers in addition to the costs of redundancies and asset disposals. Even the high cost of restructuring may, however, be less than the cost of a full blown receivership. Restructuring may preserve the financial viability of other businesses in the region to whom the bank may have lent, preserve a significant customer for future lending, enable the customer to continue to pay interest and leave open the possibility of the bank's recovering the principal after the business has recovered sufficiently to be sold or floated. Restructuring is more likely to take place where the contractor has acquired tangible assets in the form of property and subsidiary companies with viable businesses. The aim is to persuade the company's lenders that they have more to gain by co-operating with each other than by enforcing their securities. The company will involve subsidiaries and shareholders where it is contemplated that a rights issue, a debt-equity conversion or a guarantee will be required. Trade creditors will not usually be involved but continue to be paid in the ordinary course of business in order to prevent a winding-up petition being issued.

Under the London Approach developed by the Bank of England, lenders act in unison and agree to allow the company to continue to draw on facilities which have not been exhausted (Kent 1997). Lenders also agree to postpone enforcement of their securities and in appropriate cases to provide further working capital in proportion to their existing commitments on the basis that further advances will be given priority. There are three stages: standstill, refinancing and workout.

Standstill

The aim of a standstill is to arrive at a short term interim agreement between the banks in order to stabilise the position. The lawyers acting for the banks will need the following information: a group structure chart, full details of joint ventures and other off balance sheet activities, existing facilities and security, an inventory of the company's property, copies of all negative pledges etc (White 1998). The standstill agreement will deal with waiver of default, a moratorium and the basis on which new money is to be provided. It may also lay down further conditions precedent to drawdown. A standstill enables the banks to work out what their respective positions would be on a notional liquidation of the borrower. This will influence their respective negotiating positions when dealing with the refinancing agreement. A steering committee is chaired by a co-ordinating bank which is often the clearing bank with the largest debt. The committee represents a number of diverse interests including banks, leasing companies, bondholders etc. Their loans may be secured or unsecured, long or short term, from a parent or subsidiary, guaranteed, subordinated etc. The company should take advice from its lawyers, auditors and merchant bank who may be appointed especially to advise on the restructuring.

Refinancing

The refinancing agreement will determine the basis on which the company's existing and future borrowing is to be dealt with. This will vary in each case. The agreement should authorise the steering committee to approve the terms of all asset disposals and lay down the priority in which the proceeds of sale are to be paid to the banks. It will also provide the machinery for the conversion of debt into equity (as occurred for example with Costain and Y J Lovell), the subordination of existing borrowing to enable lenders of new money to take prior security and a moratorium on the enforcement of existing securities. The agreement will provide a termination date for completion of the rescue or the wind down as the case may be and the refinancing period will end by expiry, default or repayment. Detailed monitoring arrangements are needed. Default under the refinancing agreement will include the presentation of a winding-up petition which is not withdrawn within, say, 10 business days. Changes in the termination date or interest rates would probably require the unanimous approval of the banks, whereas other matters might require the approval only of the steering committee or of a group of banks.

Workout

After the refinancing agreement has been executed, the workout has to be closely monitored. Banks do not want a permanent stake in construction companies and will take an active interest in the means whereby their shareholding can be realised. If problems emerge during the workout which were not previously known, the company may be forced into receivership. The restructuring of Lilley failed through the discovery of large "black holes" in the balance sheet of joint venture companies which had environmental problems which might have cost £14 million to put right.

Lending criteria

What are the factors influencing lenders when deciding whether to accept one of these options rather than appointing receivers? The bank's perspective is governed by a number of factors. The first is stability. If the borrower's position is unstable, lenders may prefer to enforce their security by appointing receivers than risk its erosion by creditors enforcing judgments against the company's assets. One of the factors preventing the restructuring of Lilley was the extent of creditor pressure: there were over 300 writs issued against the company by the time receivers were appointed. The second factor is security. If lenders are fully secured, or nearly so, they are more likely to appoint receivers than agree a restructuring. Conder was not supported because the banks were nearly fully secured. Costain was supported because a receivership would not have resulted in a good recovery for the banks who were forced to take risks to get their money back. With Lilley, a restructuring would still have left the banks 50% secured and a receivership was thought to be the better option. Where possible, the bank will improve its security before appointing a receiver, as happened with Rush & Tompkins. The third factor is the prospect of recovery. Banks will appraise the quality of the management and the underlying viability of the business. Banks place comparatively little weight on the value of contractors' claims and discount the chances of contractors squeezing margins from sub-contractors and suppliers especially as a market begins to rise. Evidence of previous tendering on negative margins is also likely to deter lenders. Another relevant factor is the question of new money. Banks regard the conversion of debt into equity and the provision of new money as options of last resort. If new money is required, they are happier for shareholders to raise it through a rights issue or a new placing of shares or for a venture capitalist to provide it on the basis of new security taking priority over existing security. If debts are so great that interest would not be recovered for many years, banks might prefer to convert the interest rather than the principal into secured loan stock or preference shares. Retention of debt with the option of conversion into shares later is a more attractive proposition than conversion into equity at the start of a restructuring. If a contractor has a weak balance sheet, it will be excluded from tender lists, be unattractive as a joint venture partner and fall prey to aggressive creditors who might not otherwise have woken up to the existence of a financial problem until after a rights issue had been underwritten.

Impediments to informal procedures

Inevitably the process of trading through insolvency involves many areas of law. A major restructuring, for example, requires expertise in company law, security law, tax, insolvency, pensions, employment, finance and commercial law and other areas. As the intention would be to continue paying trade creditors, the restructuring may pay little attention to the terms of the company's ongoing contracts.

The use of on demand bonds causes considerable problems. It was reported that the restructuring of Costain involved a special facility of £65 million for these bonds. On demand bonds are being increasingly used on UK projects and result in bank facilities being needlessly committed to the detriment of the contractor's working capital position. A bondsman can also exert considerable pressure over banks involved in a rescue.

> "Once the bond provider has paid it becomes an actual, rather than a contingent, creditor and is in a position to pull the group down unless it is bound by the terms of the rescue not to do so. Accordingly the lead bank has to make the difficult decision, at the outset, whether to bring the bond providers within the rescue party knowing that many of them will not be familiar with the rescue culture, or whether to take the gamble that the company will perform all its contracts properly so that a bond will never be called. However, if the lead bank's judgment is wrong, and the bond is called then the bond provider who has paid is in a singularly strong position to force the rest of the creditor group to put the company in funds to reimburse the bond provider lest it destroy the whole rescue" (White 1998).

Another area of concern is the power of an unsecured creditor to present a winding-up petition based on a contingent or prospective debt, *e.g.* where a contract has been completed but a final account not yet agreed. If the creditor can show an entitlement to a minimum sum and that the company is insolvent, it will be able to present a petition which the company's lenders may be forced to settle. This is because the restructuring may have involved the creation of new security and the giving of composite cross guarantees by all companies in the group which could be vulnerable as preferences or transactions at an undervalue on an investigation by a liquidator.

There is always a concern by directors (and lenders) that they could become liable to contribute to the assets of the company for wrongful trading. Although this risk is probably small in many cases, it is always present in any restructuring.

Winding-up petitions

Where a statutory demand or a winding-up petition is served, and the debt on which it is based can be disputed in good faith and substantial grounds, the court will grant an injunction restraining further proceedings: *Stonegate Securities v Gregory* [1980] Ch 576. In the case of the demand, the injunction is against the issue of a petition; where the petition has been issued, the injunction restrains its advertisement (Oditah 1995).

It is sometimes said that any dispute arising out of a building contract must be referred to the Technology and Construction Court and cannot be dealt with on the hearing of a petition, but this is not the case. The Companies Court will grant a winding-up order where it is satisfied that the debt on which it is brought cannot properly be disputed. However, where the company has a "genuine and serious" counterclaim for an amount greater than the creditor's claim, which it has been unable to litigate, the petition should be dismissed in the absence of special circumstances: *Seawind Tankers* v *Bayoil* [1999] 1 Lloyd's Rep 211.

Petitions against employers

The only recent construction cases in England have concerned petitions against employers. The petition was dismissed in *Re A Company* [1992] 2 All ER 797 as the contractor's debt was disputed on bona fide and substantial grounds. It was based on an unpaid application under JCT 81 which is normally payable within 14 days. In this case, the employer claimed an oral agreement varying the dates for submitting applications and had terminated the contractor's employment. Both aspects were contested by the contractor. There was also evidence that the employer had net assets exceeding £100 million and that the contractor had cash flow problems. The petition was granted in *Re Clemence* (1992) 59 BLR 56. It was based on unpaid certified sums. The employer raised a counterclaim for defects which could have abated the contractor's claim and thus disputed the petition debt, but it was not properly quantified and in any event was for less than the claim.

Overseas cases involving petitions against the employer are instructive. In another case, a contract to build a hotel accommodation block and a tavern for $5.3 million provided for release of retention of $20,000 13 weeks after practical completion and $30,000 39 weeks after that date: *Fletcher Development* v *New Plymouth Hotels* [1986] 2 NZLR 302. The first tranche was certified due for release but no certificate was issued for the balance. Statutory demands were served for both tranches and the employer applied to restrain the issue of a petition. The judge at first instance was initially minded to allow the petition to proceed in relation to the first tranche of retention but concluded that the injunction should be granted because the dispute arose out of a building contract, the amounts at stake were very small compared with the overall contract sum (which had been paid on time during the contract) and that, by threatening to petition, the contractor was using improper pressure to recover a debt. This decision was reversed on appeal on the ground that the employer's evidence of defective work was inadequate and that it had failed to disclose in its evidence that it was in receivership.

An Australian case concerned a claim by a contractor for drilling work in respect of which a statutory demand had been served: *Mine v Henderson Drilling* [1989] 1 ACSR 118. The employer resisted payment on the ground that the drilling had been carried out at depths greater than specified and the contractor was not entitled to payment for the over-drilling; that some work had not been authorised by the employer and that other work had had to be redone at the employer's expense. In refusing the injunction, the court was influenced by payments which had been made by the employer, the absence of criticism of workmanship in contemporary correspondence and the fact that the employer had never threatened or issued proceedings. It also appeared that the employer was insolvent on its own evidence.

By contrast, an injunction was granted in *Club Marconi v Rennat* [1980] 4 ACLR 883 where a management contractor had agreed a guaranteed maximum cost. Any variations were to be charged at cost plus a 4.5% fee. The contractor's claim exceeded the maximum cost and the employer relied on an apparent absence of authorisation signed by the architect in respect of variations. Other claims for extras were not properly documented. The employer argued that until the contractor put forward a particularised claim it was impossible to ascertain the true position. Although there was evidence that the employer had suffered a liquidity crisis, it was not possible to conclude that that was the cause of non-payment. In another Australian case, an injunction was granted where there was clear evidence of a dispute over the quality of workmanship and valuation. Unusually, the contractor was also named as architect under the standard form. Although the court found it likely that a considerable sum would be found payable to the contractor at the conclusion of an arbitration, the winding up was not the proper forum for the dispute: *Patrick Carr v Marosszeky* [1982] 7 ACLR 59.

Petitions against contractors

Petitions against contractors tend to be factually messy. In *Re Stonehenge Constructions* [1986] 2 NZLR 302 a sub-contractor agreed orally to construct an entrance road and car park. The contractor disputed payment contending that the sub-contract was on a schedule of rates rather than a lump sum basis and that the sub-contractor had already been paid what was due to it. Relying on an oral pay when paid term, the contractor argued that no further sum was then payable. The evidence showed that the contractor had in fact been paid more on a rates basis than the amount of the sub-contractor's petition and the court refused to grant an injunction restraining the issue of the petition. The Federal Court of Australia refused to set aside a statutory demand against a contractor in *Spencer Constructions* v *Aldridge* (unreported, 29 July 1997). An underpinning sub-contractor claimed release of retention. The contractor disputed the debt on several grounds:

1. That the employer had terminated the main contract and agreed to assume direct responsibility for sums due to sub-contractors;

2. In any event there was a pay when paid clause in the sub-contract and the contractor had not received any sums in respect of the sub-contractor's retention.

Neither contention was supported by the evidence. Even if they could be established there was no evidence that the sub-contractor had released the contractor by an implied novation of the sub-contract, and the employer claimed to have paid the contractor in respect of the retentions.

The criteria to be applied where the contractor petitions on a contingent or prospective debt are not entirely clear (Lee Beng Tat 1993). A contingent liability arises under an existing obligation under which "the company may or will become subject to a present liability on the happening of a future event or at some future date": *Re William Hockley* [1962] 2 All ER 111 at 113. One of the problem areas is where the petition is based on a claim for damages for breach of contract. In a South African case, *Gillis-Mason Construction* v *Overvaal Crushers* [1971] 1 SA 524, a sub-contractor was unable to comply with its contract to supply crusher stone and the contractor was unable to obtain an alternative supply. Such supplies as were available were at rates exceeding those in the sub-contract. The contractor was also at risk of failing to complete the main contract on time. The sub-contract had made time of the essence. The sub-contractor accepted it had repudiated the sub-contract but relied on the contractor's duty to mitigate its loss. There was evidence that the sub-contractor was insolvent. In all the circumstances, the court exercised its discretion and made a winding-up order on the basis of the sub-contractor's contingent liability.

Chapter 8

· **Formal Insolvency** ·

Introduction

There are different procedures for individuals and companies. For an individual, the main alternatives are voluntary arrangement and bankruptcy. For a company, they are administrative receivership, liquidation, administration and voluntary arrangement. In the year 1997-1998 there were 7960 voluntary liquidations, 4873 compulsory liquidations, 1307 administrative receiverships, 487 company voluntary arrangements and 225 administrations (SPI 1999). The first part of this chapter is intended for those who are unfamiliar with the law and practice of insolvency, and various aspects have been simplified. It deals with the three major corporate procedures, company voluntary arrangements and the two types of individual insolvency. The second part describes how the various procedures have been used in the industry. Unless otherwise stated, all references are to the Insolvency Act 1986.

Procedural comparisons

A formal insolvency procedure affects every aspect of a company. This section compares the three major procedures by asking twelve key questions which are relevant in any insolvency.

1. What is the purpose of the procedure?

Each of the procedures has a specific objective. If statutory, its purpose is the implementation of public policy. Where it is purely consensual, its objective is the enforcement of a contract. Whether a procedure is statutory or contractual will determine its scope and effect. The purpose of the procedure can be gathered from how it affects the company's assets and its creditors (Figure 8.1).

Although receivership is primarily a security enforcement procedure, it can also have a rescue function. If the receiver sells a business as a

Receivership	Liquidation	Administration
Security enforcement by selling charged assets and paying net proceeds to lender until loan repaid, any surplus being paid to the directors or the liquidator, if appointed.	Preservation and collection of the company's assets, conversion into cash and distribution to creditors in accordance with the statutory order of priority.	Rescue of the company and the whole or part of its business; or the promotion of a voluntary arrangement or scheme of arrangement; or getting a better value for the assets than liquidation would achieve.

Fig 8.1

going concern, so that the purchaser engages the company's employees and completes current contracts, the receiver may enhance the recovery for the lender and save the business at the same time. Unfortunately, unsecured creditors often receive no return at all, a factor which led the Cork Committee to recommend that 10% of the net floating charge recoveries should be dedicated as a fund for unsecured creditors, but the recommendation was rejected by Parliament (Cork 1982, at 1538). A case has also been made for the abolition of receivership as part of a more truly rescue-oriented insolvency regime (Phillips 1996).

A liquidator has power to continue trading but this is rarely exercised and the assets are normally sold on a break-up rather than a going concern basis. A liquidator's main function is the realisation and distribution of the assets. This includes clawing back assets misapplied by directors within certain time limits before the start of the liquidation (see Chapter 15). Litigation, or at least the threat of proceedings, is often required. Property held on trust by the company is not an asset of the company. Once the assets have been collected in, they must be sold in order that the proceeds of sale can be distributed to creditors. The pay-out is in accordance with the statutory scheme which lays down the following order of priority: (1) petitioning creditor's costs (in a compulsory liquidation), expenses of the liquidation, liquidator's remuneration (2) preferential creditors (3) floating charge-holders (4) unsecured creditors (5) shareholders: ss 107, 143, 175, r 4.218 Insolvency Rules 1986. In many cases, the assets are insufficient to make any distribution to unsecured creditors or shareholders.

Administration was introduced by the Insolvency Act 1986 which provides a broad framework but Parliament left it to the courts to work out the procedure in detail. The object of an administration can range from the survival of the company to a quasi-liquidation, but whatever the object, the administrator has no power to make distributions to creditors: *Re Business Properties* (1988) 4 BCC 684. This can only be done by a subsequent procedure, *e.g.* voluntary arrangement or liquidation. There is a moratorium on all claims and enforcement of security both prior to and during the administration, unless in the first case leave is obtained from the court or once the order is made, leave of the court or the consent of the administrator is obtained: ss 10 and 11. Administration provides a "breathing space" to allow the company to consider its options before letting the creditors decide what should be done.

Administrative receivers and administrators have similar powers which cover all aspects of running a business. Liquidators also have wide powers but the emphasis is on investigation of the company's affairs, claims against directors and others to recover misappropriated property and agreeing creditors' claims: Schedules 1 and 4.

2. How is the procedure started?

The transition from informal to formal insolvency is of critical importance because of its effect on the ownership of the company's property and the rights and duties of its employees, directors, creditors, shareholders, guarantors, insurers and others. Commencement of the procedure is an event provided for in most construction contracts entitling the other person to terminate. Almost all receiverships are initiated by secured creditors without reference to the court. Many liquidators are court appointees but administrators can only be appointed by the court. Both liquidation and administration derive from statute; a receiver can be appointed under statute but the vast majority are appointed under a contract, usually a fixed and/or floating charge (Figure 8.2).

Receivership commences when the receiver is appointed by the charge-holder. Receivers normally seek legal advice on the validity of their appointment and ideally will obtain an indemnity from the charge-holder in respect of personal liability arising out of actions properly taken during the receivership. If it later appears that their appointment was invalid, receivers can apply to the court for a statutory indemnity against the charge-holder: s 34. A voluntary liquidation starts when

Receivership	Liquidation	Administration
Out of court (but the court has power to appoint in appropriate cases).	The court can appoint if a creditor successfully petitions for a winding-up order.	Only the court can appoint and the petition is in most cases issued by the directors who also choose the administrator.
If the lender has advanced money on overdraft, a receiver could be appointed once a borrower fails to meet a demand for repayment.	Alternatively shareholders can appoint out of court at a meeting convened by the directors.	
Otherwise, the lender has to establish a default before becoming entitled to appoint.	In both cases the creditors have the opportunity to replace the liquidator with their own choice.	

Fig 8.2

the shareholders pass a resolution that the company should cease trading and be wound up: s 86. A compulsory liquidation starts on the date of presentation of the petition: s 129. A hearing is fixed when the petition is presented and, once a winding-up order is made, it is retrospective to the date of the petition. In the interim, all dealings by the company with its assets are void unless validated by the court before or after they are made: s 127.

Both types of liquidation considered so far are creditors' procedures. Where the directors conclude, after making a full enquiry into the company's affairs, that the company will be able to pay its debts in full with interest within 12 months after the start of liquidation, and the directors swear a statutory declaration to that effect, the shareholders can pass a resolution for the liquidation of the company. Creditors are not involved in this procedure which is known as a members' voluntary liquidation. The danger for the directors is that, if they did not have reasonable grounds for their opinion that the company would be able to pay its debts in full with interest within 12 months, they can be liable to imprisonment or a fine. In *Re William Thorpe* (1989) 5 BCC 156 a contractor whose assets consisted of a freehold property, debts and work in progress, went into members' voluntary liquidation. The directors estimated in their declaration that the company would have a surplus of assets over liabilities of £100,000. As a result of trading losses during the liquidation, the company incurred net liabilities of £600,000 and the court ordered that the company be placed in compulsory liquidation. The assessment of contingent and prospective liabilities poses special difficulties in this context (Simmons 1996).

An administration order is only granted where the company is unable to pay its debts or is likely to be unable to do so. The procedure is available in cases of imminent as well as actual insolvency. It must be shown that the order is likely to achieve one or more of the four purposes: the survival of the company, the approval of a CVA, the sanctioning of a compromise under the Companies Act 1985 or the more advantageous realisation of the company's assets than would be effected by a winding up. This means the company must show a "real prospect" that one of the purposes will be achieved, although this can be less than a 50:50 chance: *Re Harris Simons* (1989) 5 BCC 11. In another context, the House of Lords has held that:

> "we should avoid a construction which would reduce the legislation to futility and should rather accept the bolder construction based on the view that Parliament would legislate only for the purpose of bringing about an effective result": *Nokes* v *Doncaster Amalgamated Collieries* [1940] AC 1014 at 1022.

The same point applies to the Housing Grants, Construction and Regeneration Act 1996.

Accepting that "likely to achieve" can mean less than a 50% chance of success requires vigilance in the exercise of the court's discretion to avoid oppressive use of the procedure. The time scale is much shorter than compulsory liquidation and the petition is usually supported by a report from an insolvency practitioner which explains the likelihood of the specified purpose being achieved.

3. What effect does the procedure have on the ownership of the company's assets?

The assets of a company are owned by the company. The company is owned by its shareholders. An insolvency procedure may alter this position by transferring the assets owned by the company to a third party. This depends on the purpose of the procedure (Figure 8.3).

Receivership	Liquidation	Administration
Assets falling within the charge under which the receiver is appointed are assigned to the holder of the charge on the receiver's appointment.	A trust is created over all the company's free assets in favour of the unsecured creditors.	No change.

Fig 8.3

In an administration, there is no change of ownership. This reflects the temporary nature of the procedure, its function as a breathing space and the administrator's inability to distribute the proceeds of sale of assets. The position is different in both receivership and liquidation. Receivership is primarily for the benefit of the charge-holder. The effect of the receiver's appointment is to complete an equitable assignment of the charged assets to the holder of the charge. This emphasises the basic function of receivership as a security enforcement procedure.

Liquidation on the other hand divests the company of ownership of its assets and imposes a trust over them in favour of the creditors: *Ayerst* v *C & K (Construction) Ltd* [1976] AC 167. The trust extends to all assets owned by the company wherever they are situated. This means that a liquidator appointed in England can, in theory, realise assets located abroad. Just as a liquidator collects and realises assets all over the world, so foreign creditors are allowed to participate in the distribution of the proceeds of sale of those assets. This is known as the principle of universality. English law differs from other jurisdictions in this respect.

4. What is the status of the office holder?

Only a licensed insolvency practitioner can act as an administrative receiver, liquidator or administrator: s 390. The basic position is that each office holder acts as agent of the company (Figure 8.4).

Receivers and administrators are personally liable on contracts entered into by them after their appointment unless their personal liability is expressly excluded. A receiver loses the right to act as agent of the company if the company goes into liquidation and cannot act as agent if appointed after the start of a liquidation: s 44. If the charge-holder interferes with the conduct of the receivership, the receiver may

Receivership	Liquidation	Administration
Agent of the company (unless winding-up order is made in which case the receiver acts as principal or as agent for the charge-holder who appointed him).	Agent of the company and a trustee of its assets. Officer of the court (in compulsory liquidation).	Agent of the company (which cannot be in liquidation or receivership while an administration order is in force). Officer of the court.

Fig 8.4

become the agent of the charge-holder rather than the company, which could make the charge-holder liable as principal on contracts entered into by the receiver: *American Express* v *Hurley* [1985] 3 All ER 564. The office-holder does not become personally liable on contracts entered into by the company before formal insolvency which are continued afterwards: *Re Atlantic Computers* [1990] BCC 859 at 865.

5. What effect does the procedure have on secured creditors?

The purpose of security is to give the secured creditor an interest in the company's property enforceable in the event of the company's insolvency. A secured creditor wants immediate access to the secured property in that case and is concerned to ensure that its rights are not prejudiced by the actions of an office-holder. The three procedures differ in the rights given to office-holders over property subject to a security interest (Figure 8.5).

It is not always easy to decide whether an asset falls within the scope of a charge. One of the most frequent issues to arise is whether a receivable is a book or other debt falling within a fixed charge. The question is important because if the receivable falls within a floating charge, it will be available to meet the claims of preferential creditors in priority to the floating charge-holder: s 40.

Liquidation does not alter the rights of secured creditors. Creditors with security are only prejudiced if the validity of the security can be challenged. Where a registrable charge has not been registered before the start of the liquidation it is invalid against the liquidator, administrator or other creditors: s 395 Companies Act 1985. Where a floating charge is granted within 12 months before the start of the

Receivership	Liquidation	Administration
Full rights of sale over the property comprised in the charge under which the receiver was appointed, but can dispose of other charged property with the court's authorisation.	None, unless secured creditors renounce their security and prove in the liquidation or a security is invalidated for want of registration or some other cause.	Full rights of sale, coupled with a duty to account to the charge-holder for the proceeds of sale. Leave of the court is required before sale of secured property unless it is subject only to a floating charge.

Fig 8.5

liquidation but no new value is provided in return, a liquidator may apply to have the charge declared invalid, in which case the creditor becomes unsecured: s 245. Administration does alter the rights of secured creditors. The administrator has power to sell charged property but only on condition that the proceeds of sale are paid to the charge-holder. To protect the charge-holder against a sale at an undervalue, the administrator is liable to pay the difference between the proceeds of sale and the market value of the property: s 15.

When an administration order is made, fixed charge receivers vacate office, floating charge-holders lose the right to appoint an administrative receiver and any winding-up petition is dismissed. If an administrative receiver is appointed before the hearing of the petition, no order can be made. Apart from losing the right to appoint receivers, secured creditors can take no other steps to enforce their security without the administrator's consent or leave of the court. Security is given an extended meaning and covers hire purchase agreements and "retention of title agreements" as defined in s 251. This is an unusual expression which could conceivably include contracts for work and materials. This possibility is discussed in Chapter 4.

6. How does the procedure affect unsecured property?

Property which the company has not offered as security before formal insolvency intervened is available to preferential and unsecured creditors (Figure 8.6).

In a liquidation or administration, the office-holder has full rights of disposal. In a liquidation, the disposal will normally be to convert the assets into cash for distribution to creditors. In an administration, the purpose is the achievement of the object of the administration within the framework of the administrator's proposals.

Receivership	Liquidation	Administration
None	Full	Full

Fig 8.6

A receiver's main function is to dispose of the charged assets. In so doing, he may deal with property which appears to be owned by the company but in fact is owned by someone else. The most common example is property supplied under a contract containing a retention of title clause. An administrative receiver is entitled to dispose of such property without becoming liable in conversion provided that the existence of the clause could not have been revealed through reasonable enquiry: s 234. If the receiver was on notice of the clause when the property was sold, he will have to account to the owner of the property for the proceeds of sale and any shortfall between them and the property's market value.

7. What effect does the procedure have on current contracts?

Receivership	Liquidation	Administration
No change but receiver not bound to cause company to perform.	No change (unless nature of the contract meant it was automatically repudiated, *e.g.* a contract of employment). Right to disclaim onerous property or contracts.	No change.

Fig 8.7

Neither receivership nor administration has the effect of terminating current contracts. Receivers have the power to allow the company to break its contract where completion is not beneficial to the charge-holder. Administrators are in a different position and can be restrained from breaking contracts: *Astor Chemicals* v *Synthetic Technology* [1990] BCC 97. Liquidation is different in two respects. First, the liquidator has the right to decide whether to perform the contract or not. If he decides that the contract is unprofitable, it can be disclaimed, leaving the other party with the right to prove for damages: s 178. Secondly, the nature of the contract may be such that liquidation would be an anticipatory breach entitling the other party to accept the repudiation and claim damages. In practice, many contracts include receivership, liquidation and administration as events of default entitling the other party to terminate. Questions arise on the validity of such clauses. These are discussed in Chapter 9.

8. What effect does the procedure have on the parties' rights of set-off?

Set-off applies where a debtor uses a creditor's claim to satisfy its own claim. It is an important subject in insolvency because of its security function. Set-off does not give the debtor a security interest in the creditor's claim but it has a similar effect. Set-off in insolvency can only be understood after ascertaining the parties' rights before insolvency. This is a good example of how insolvency law is an overlay over the normal position. The three procedures are completely different in this respect (Figure 8.8).

Receivership	*Liquidation*	*Administration*
Company's claims are assigned to debenture holder but liabilities remain with the company. Cross claims denied unless they arise before receipt of notice of appointment, unless they also qualify for contractual or equitable set-off.	Mandatory set-off of all mutual dealings.	No change.

Fig 8.8

As receivership alters the ownership of the charged assets, a claim which arises against the company after the receiver has been appointed cannot normally be set off against a claim owed by the company before the receiver's appointment (see Chapter 13). The explanation is that receivership destroys the mutuality between the claims. Before receivership, there was a claim owed to the company. On the receiver's appointment, that claim (as a charged asset) was transferred to the charge-holder. If after the receiver's appointment a claim arose against the company, nothing would remain against which it could be set off as the claim had been transferred to the charge-holder.

Whatever the rights of set-off may have been before insolvency, they are replaced on liquidation by a form of statutory set-off which applies in all cases. The parties cannot contract out of it. It is much wider than the general law and applies to claims arising under separate contracts, whether for debt or damages, whether present or future etc. Under the general law, the purpose of set-off is to prevent multiplicity of proceedings by allowing claim and cross-claim to be dealt with in the same action. The purpose of liquidation set-off is to do justice between the parties (see Chapter 13). An administration order has no effect on the beneficial ownership of the company's property: there is no reference in the Insolvency Act 1986 to any alteration in the parties' rights of set-off in the event of administration.

9. What effect does the procedure have on existing litigation?

By the time a company enters formal insolvency, it is often involved in litigation with its creditors. Where the company is plaintiff, the claim is part of the company's property. Recovery of the asset depends on the successful conclusion of the proceedings (Figure 8.9).

Receivership	Liquidation	Administration
No change.	No change, unless compulsory winding-up in which case proceedings cannot be commenced or continued without the leave of the court.	No proceedings can be continued or commenced without the consent of the administrator or leave of the court.

Fig 8.9

None of the procedures affects the company's ability to commence or continue proceedings where it is plaintiff. The defendant may however be entitled to security for its costs. Where the company is in liquidation, security may be ordered where the defendant can show that the company would be unlikely to meet an order for costs if made against it: s 726 Companies Act 1985. Where the company is in receivership, the defendant can rely on the alternative ground that the company is nominal plaintiff, suing on behalf of the charge-holder as the true owner of the claim.

Where the company is defendant, receivership has no effect on the position. Where the defendant is in liquidation, the plaintiff can continue without leave where the liquidation is voluntary but needs leave of the court on a compulsory winding-up. The court will consider whether the dispute should be continued in court or whether it should be dealt with in the liquidation by way of an appeal against rejection of proof. Where the company is in administration, the administrator is required to give careful consideration whether to consent to the proceedings continuing. The Court of Appeal has laid down a series of guidelines which the administrator has to take into account: *Re Atlantic Computer* [1990] BCC 859. If the administrator refuses to consent, the plaintiff can apply to the court.

10. What rights do creditors have to participate in the procedure?

Creditors' rights vary considerably from passive receipt of information in a receivership to the approval of proposals in an administration (Figure 8.10).

Before the Insolvency Act 1986, creditors had few rights to information from receivers and felt shut out of the procedure. A receiver must now convene a creditors' meeting within three months of his appointment and provide copies of his receipts and payments account. In practice, receivership creditors' committees have no real function but they can provide an opportunity for creditors to meet the receiver to discuss specific points.

Creditors have always had a more active role in liquidations through their right to elect the liquidator and form a creditors' committee. The main function of the committee is to approve the liquidator's remuneration and to act as representatives of the general body of creditors to approve proposed courses of action, *e.g.* the issue of

Receivership	Liquidation	Administration
Very limited. Receiver owes duty of care to the company and to guarantors of its secured debt but not generally to its creditors.

The receiver is under a limited duty to convene creditors' committee meetings. | Fairly wide. Creditors have the right to elect the liquidator and to appoint a committee to oversee the conduct of the liquidation. | Wide. Creditors have the right to approve, vary or reject the administrator's proposals. Some creditors' rights to repossess goods are curtailed. Creditors are given the right to petition for unfair prejudice. Creditors form a committee to oversee the conduct of the administration. |

Fig 8.10

proceedings. Administration is primarily a creditors' procedure and is unique in allowing the creditors to shape the course of the procedure by voting on the administrator's proposals. This right is ineffective, however, where the administrator disposes of the assets before convening the meeting of creditors. A meeting must be called within three months of the administration order or such extended period as the court may allow.

11. What is the directors' role in the procedure?

Receivership	Liquidation	Administration
Directors' powers are suspended and exercised by the receiver but the directors remain liable under the Companies Act 1985 to file accounts and annual returns and retain the power to act in the name of the company in limited circumstances.	Directors lose all powers.	Administrator has the right to retain, appoint or dismiss directors.

Once dismissed, directors lose all residual powers. If retained, their powers are subordinated to the administrator's instructions. |

Fig 8.11

English insolvency law takes a harsh line with the directors. They are usually regarded as the cause of the problem and lose all rights of management (Figure 8.11).

Directors often feel that the insolvency procedure would have been more successful had they been allowed a more active role. The degree of participation during the procedure is a matter for the insolvency practitioner's discretion. A judgment has to be made on the director's personal and managerial qualities and whether his involvement is necessary or desirable to fulfil the procedure's purpose. Directors owe a statutory duty to co-operate with the office-holder.

12. What effect does the procedure have on contracts of employment?

Employees will be concerned to know their position. One of the first things an insolvency practitioner does is to talk to the company's employees and briefly explain what has happened and tell them his immediate intentions as far as continued trading is concerned. Each procedure has a different effect on the company's contracts of employment (Figure 8.12).

The effect of insolvency on the rights of employees is an important aspect of any insolvency procedure. Apart from those features highlighted in Chapter 16 there are few industry specific matters which call for consideration under this heading.

Receivership	Liquidation	Administration
Contracts of employment continue but receiver has 14 days to review the position before adopting contracts of employment.	On compulsory liquidation, contracts of employment automatically terminated. Voluntary liquidation has no effect.	No effect on contracts of employment.

Fig 8.12

Company voluntary arrangment (CVA)

A CVA is a court procedure enabling a company to propose a compromise with its creditors. All creditors receiving notice of the proposal and entitled to vote on it will be bound by the composition, provided at least 75% in value of creditors attending the meeting vote in favour. A CVA does not prejudice the rights of secured creditors, preferential creditors or suppliers who have retained title. The directors make a proposal to an insolvency practitioner who files a report with the court stating whether in his view a creditors' meeting should be called to consider it. There is no standard form of CVA (see Lingard 1988), but the Insolvency Rules 1986 set out the minimum it needs to contain.

It is fundamental that the creditors are realistic when considering the company's proposal (especially in relation to the percentage of their debt which is to be written off), and that the company is realistic when proposing the dates by which sums will become payable. The CVA will set out the means by which payments will be funded, *e.g.* the disposal or refinancing of assets, a management buy out, other external finance or from future profits. Without a good core business and competent management, a company would have difficulty in persuading its creditors to accept a CVA. The insolvency practitioner's role will probably be limited to supervising the disposal or refinancing of assets earmarked for payment of the dividend to creditors, organising the payment of the dividend and ensuring that the directors comply with undertakings given in the CVA.

Individual insolvency

There are two formal insolvency procedures for an individual, bankruptcy and individual voluntary arrangement. They are distinct procedures and can result in a dramatically different outcome.

The purpose of bankruptcy is the same as liquidation, *i.e.* the collection, realisation and distribution of the debtor's estate in accordance with the Act. A trustee in bankruptcy has powers similar to those of a liquidator to claw back assets misapplied by the debtor within certain time limits before the start of the bankruptcy. Once the assets have been collected in, they must be sold, usually on a break-up basis, in order that the proceeds can be distributed to creditors. The pay-out is in accordance with the statutory scheme.

Bankruptcy proceedings are commenced by petition, either by the debtor or, more commonly, by a creditor and the bankruptcy commences on the date the petition is issued by the court. The bankrupt's estate automatically vests in the trustee in bankruptcy on his appointment without the need for any formal transfer documents: s 306. A bankruptcy order does not affect the debtor's secured creditors, who will only be prejudiced if the validity of their security can be challenged. There are no issues whether assets fall within a floating charge as only a company can grant such a charge.

A trustee in bankruptcy has powers of disclaimer similar to those of a liquidator, in that he can disclaim onerous property, leaving the creditor to prove for damages. Contracts often make bankruptcy a termination event but this approach is questionable (see Chapter 9). Bankruptcy entitles the other parties to a contract to apply to the court for an order discharging their obligations on such terms as to payment of damages as appears to the court to be equitable: s 345. Such damages are provable as a debt in the bankruptcy. As with liquidation, any rights of set-off prior to bankruptcy are replaced by a form of statutory set-off which applies in all cases. This is much wider than the general law and arises in respect of all mutual credits, mutual debts and other mutual dealings between the bankrupt and the other party (see Chapter 13).

Any cause of action owned by the bankrupt vests in his trustee by virtue of s 306 unless it is personal to him. When a petition has been issued or an order made, the court has a discretion to stay any action, execution or other legal process against the property or person of the bankrupt under s 285. After a bankruptcy order has been made, creditors have no remedy in respect of a pre-bankruptcy debt against the property or person of the bankrupt and cannot commence or continue any action or other legal proceedings without the leave of the court.

An individual voluntary arrangement (IVA) is, like a company voluntary arrangement, a court procedure enabling an individual to make a compromise with his creditors. The purpose of an IVA is to provide the machinery whereby a debtor can make a proposal to and enter into an arrangement which is binding on all his creditors and thereby avoid bankruptcy. The one key difference between an individual and a company voluntary arrangement is that an individual can apply to court for an interim order before sending out proposals to creditors. The interim order has the effect of staying all proceedings against the debtor and is designed to allow the debtor a breathing space: no creditor can take action against the debtor or execute a judgment without leave of the court. It is fundamental that the creditors are realistic when considering the debtor's proposal, especially in relation to the percentage of their debt which has to be written off and that the debtor is realistic when proposing the terms and the dates by which sums will become payable. The proposals should be carefully drafted as their viability will be considered by the court.

Application to the industry

One of the peculiarities of the construction industry is that, on the insolvency of a contractor, there is almost a presumption against payment of genuine debts to the insolvency practioner. This even applies where the contractor has fully performed so that the second half of retention is due and payable. The employer sometimes argues that it has suffered a loss in such a case because, if a defect were to arise during the limitation period, it would not be remedied. This has been described as loss of "expectancy" or "the chance of a remedy" (Bingham 1993). The employer therefore withholds the retention until the limitation period has expired. The issue was addressed in SPI Technical Bulletin 13 which advised insolvency practioners to "take a robust line" with employers in this situation. In law, an employer would not have any right to withhold payment unless perhaps the contractor had covenanted not to become insolvent before the expiry of the limitation period or the contract contained a right of set-off in respect of a prospective breach on a certificate from the architect or project manager. Both would be novel and it is not clear to what extent they would be enforced by the court.

This section looks at how formal insolvency procedures work in the construction industry. There is little empirical research but construction insolvencies do pose special challenges to insolvency practitioners. A significant amount of time is spent in packaging and negotiating a disposal of the company's contracts. With a medium sized contractor with subsidiaries in construction related activities, it may be easier to sell the subsidiaries in separate packages. With a large player, like Rush & Tompkins, the procedure requires a detailed strategy.

An analysis in 1994 found that the combined turnover of the 10 largest contractors to become formally insolvent in the previous three years was £2.1 billion whereas the loss of capacity suffered by the industry in the same period was only half that amount. Even formal insolvency procedures are not sufficient to balance supply and demand (*Contract Journal*, 5 May 1994). It is arguable that the return on scarce managers who are difficult to replace should be considered as the criterion of financial performance rather than return on capital employed, management expertise being the principal scarce resource limiting the expansion of a construction business (Hillebrandt and Cannon 1989, at 71).

Receivership

Receivership is primarily a security enforcement procedure but is also a means of business rescue since the receiver is keen to realise the whole value of the company and this is best done by selling the business as a going concern. Receivership does save businesses and jobs but the perception of receivers in the industry is very negative.

Receivers are usually appointed after informal options have been explored and rejected. Receivers were appointed to Conder, for example, in 1992 after an attempt to raise working capital failed and the proposed sale of a subsidiary company fell through. Receivership does not necessarily mean the loss of the name of the company. Bovis novated numerous contracts from Lelliott and formed a new Lelliott division retaining the services of John Lelliott as head of the division. When Sunley Turriff acquired Lilley Construction (Scotland) they preserved the Lilley name and livery and retained 300 of the 500 employees. Even where the company is broken up and its assets and contracts dispersed among a number of different purchasers, there is a chance that jobs will be saved. Where a significant package of contracts is novated to the same purchaser, the prospects are good. In a sense, receivership is a natural process of the industry:

> "Because of the nature of the building industry, if a company fails it is usually only money that is lost. The basic resources of a skilled labour force, plant and administrative expertise are dissipated to other companies with little or no disruption to the industry as a whole" (Upson 1987).

The ideal scenario for a receiver is to sell the business or novate all the contracts to the same purchaser within a few days of the appointment. This occurred in the receivership of Farr Group in December 1990. The group had 40 current contracts, 34 of which were novated to Amey Construction within a couple of days. "Amey diverted dozens of senior staff to phone all 40 clients and accompany Farr contract staff to site to negotiate terms with the clients' representatives" (*Building*, 17 January 1992). 200 of the 400 staff were kept on as a result.

Other companies entering receivership in the last 10 years have included Dunning (1989), Farr, Brims, Harry Neal, Rush & Tompkins (1990), Conder, Isis, Turriff, J A Elliott, Shepherd Hill, Locker & Riley, Allied Partnership, Graham Wood (1992), Lilley, Budge, McLaughlin & Harvey, Dove Brothers, Thompson Mechanical and Electrical, Lelliott, Tubeworkers, Rees Hough, Clayton Bowmore, Elliott Northern (1993), VAT Watkins, M F Kent, Kentz, Johnson & Bailey (1994), Donelon Tyson (1995), Rawlings (1997), Ruddy, Wolfe (1998).

Unless he has already investigated the company and prepared a report on its financial position, a receiver's first action is to identify the company's property and have it valued. This exercise requires specialist advice because it involves issues of asset valuation, quantity surveying and insolvency and construction law. The receiver will therefore assemble a team including a surveyor, a valuer and a lawyer while at the same time mobilising his own staff to visit the company's offices and sites. Having taken possession of such books and records as the company may have kept, the receiver establishes a system for logging correspondence, invoices, tender enquiries etc and attempts to reconcile the company's accounts. The receiver ascertains the whereabouts of the company's motor vehicles, plant, equipment and other assets and arranges to schedule them and have them professionally valued. The surveyor will carry out an appraisal of the company's completed and current contracts to enable the receiver to decide which should be completed, sold or abandoned. The lawyer will advise on the validity of the receiver's appointment and any other legal problem areas. The receiver may also consider entering into new contracts.

The surveyor's contract appraisal is the key exercise (see Chapter 9). Priority is given to current contracts which are scheduled as short, medium and long term. A complete financial profile of each contract is then prepared showing the net amount, if anything, payable by the employer on completion compared with the cost to complete. The difference between the two represents the receiver's profit or loss as the case may be. Loss-making contracts are likely to be abandoned. The receiver is aiming to sell the contracts (as a whole if possible) rather than to complete them himself but may be prepared to continue trading in order to preserve their value pending disposal. The preservation of the company's asset value while a sale is negotiated is not at all easy and requires good judgment and commercial skill from the receiver and sound and robust advice from the professionals. The surveyor's contract appraisal will ascertain the time and cost required to complete each contract. Marginal contracts may be completed in order to preserve value on other completed contracts with the same employer. The receiver will analyse claims and cross-claims in cost benefit terms and may conclude that it is cheaper to incur a small loss on one contract than to risk the uncertainty, delay and cost of litigation.

Once a decision has been made to dispose of particular contracts, the receiver decides the value he wants for them. Experienced receivers know which major contractors and sub-contractors are interested in making acquisitions and may be assisted in this aspect by their professional advisers. It may be necessary to advertise the sale. Previous tenderers on contracts on which the company is involved should also be contacted. The directors and estimating staff will be able to assist in this connection. Once a list has been compiled, information needs to be assembled and disclosed to potential purchasers on a confidential basis. After basic heads of terms have been negotiated, they need to be formalised into a binding agreement. The standard procedure is a novation. There are a large number of permutations to novation agreements, some of which are considered in Chapter 10. The consideration is sometimes deferred or payable out of profits earned from the contract or the business, whichever has been sold. The possibility of purchaser default makes it particularly important for the receiver to be satisfied with the purchaser's solvency and reputation before formalising terms, or a guarantor may be required.

Heads of agreement may not be fully comprehensive and there is scope for the lawyers for both parties to improve their clients' positions. There is a tension between the need for expedition and the desire for the best possible deal. The receiver may decide that the anticipated receiver's profit in a contract makes it worthwhile building out. The uncertainties in the contracting process mean that this is only done where there is a high probability that the profit will be recovered. The receiver will wish to avoid asking the charge-holder to finance building out and will instead attempt to obtain advance payments from the employer in respect of labour and materials. In addition, the employer may be amenable to purchasing materials and entering into sub-contracts direct. The receiver may also re-negotiate the contract terms to remove or restrict the employer's right of set-off, liquidated damages, retention, maintenance obligations, the payment period and any other term affecting cash flow, end profit and liability. All these factors are matters for negotiation depending on the circumstances of the case. Receivers are wary of completing current contracts because of the risk of previous over-certification. In such cases, the architect reduces the gross value of the works shown in future certificates. As a consequence, receivers carefully analyse the accuracy of pre-receivership certificates and discuss the situation in detail with the employer. Difficulties are experienced with trade creditors regarding future supplies. These may only be available by paying cash on delivery or on receipt of orders, hence the need to negotiate advance payments from the employer. Problems are also experienced with office and site staff. Motivation is difficult as staff realise that they are working themselves out of employment. The promise of a completion bonus if targets are met alleviates the position.

If the company cannot be sold as a going concern, the receiver turns to the realisation of the value of completed contracts. This involves three assets: the collection of retention, the recovery of final account balances, and claims for loss and expense or damages for breach of contract. Many contractors are poor at collecting retentions and final account sums because they lack in-house skills necessary to pursue employers. A large number of uncollected retentions is often a sign of poor financial management. A cost benefit analysis has to be made comparing the investment required in terms of receiver's time costs and professional fees against the amount of the likely judgment and the prospects of enforcement. This requires specialist legal advice. Receivers often rely on the quantity surveyor for legal advice on contractor's claims. This can lead to under recovery, particularly where no contract was signed. This may indicate that no contract was formed at all which would entitle the receiver to recover a reasonable sum for the work done by the company prior to receivership without the risk of set-off by the employer. In view of the widespread use of letters of intent by employers and contractors, this is a significant aspect for receivers to consider. The question whether a contract has been formed is in many cases one of considerable legal sophistication.

Liquidation

A liquidator has no power to deal with charged assets unless the charge-holder prefers not to appoint a receiver or take possession of the assets but to leave it to the liquidator to realise them. This occurs where the amount owed to the charge-holder is comparatively small and would not justify the expense of appointing a receiver. The liquidator is allowed his costs of enforcing the security for the charge-holder. Where receivers have sold the charged assets, there may be nothing left for the liquidator to realise and distribute. Where there are current or completed contracts which are not charged, the liquidator undertakes a review similar to that of the receiver. A quantity surveyor will be appointed to appraise the contracts and employers approached to ascertain whether they would be prepared to agree to a novation. Unless a provisional liquidator is appointed, this is done by voluntary liquidators because of the time lag between the issue of a petition and the making of an order in a compulsory liquidation. During that period, the employer will have terminated and decided on its own method of procuring completion. A liquidator has no power to trade unless it is necessary for the beneficial winding-up, and only with the sanction of the court on a compulsory liquidation: Schedule 4.

Liquidators have the following functions:

- location, valuation and disposal of unsecured assets
- acceptance and rejection of proofs of debt
- investigation of claims against the directors and others
- reviewing the conduct of receivers and the validity of the security and their appointment, and ensuring they comply with their duties in disposing of assets
- investigation of the directors' conduct with reference to their fitness to act
- distributions to creditors.

Whereas the emphasis in a receivership is on speed in order to preserve the company's goodwill, liquidation requires the patient and detailed investigation of the company's affairs.

It is conceivable that a receiver might petition to wind up the company in order to prevent a direct payment being made under clause 35 of JCT 80 (see Chapter 12). This will be rare as receivers prefer to maintain their agency of the company which is lost if the company goes into liquidation. A petition is possible where the receiver is unable to realise any value from current contracts and confines himself to completed contracts where there is no need to trade. Insolvency claims are discussed in Chapter 15.

Companies working in the industry which went into liquidation rather than receivership or administration have included Declan Kelly (1990), Zimmcor, Clifford Barnett (1991), Nugent (1994).

Administration

The administration of a construction company has many similarities to a receivership. An administrator has the same problem of preserving the value of the company's assets and goodwill while searching for purchasers. Administration does, however, have some advantages.

1. Proceedings against the company can only be continued with the consent of the administrator or leave of the court. Hostile claims divert resources away from productive work on other contracts which may themselves become subject to claims as a result. Administration breaks this vicious circle. This also applies to adjudication under s 108 Housing Grants, Construction and Regeneration Act 1996: *A Straume (UK) Ltd* v *Bradlor Development* [1999] *The Times*, 29 June, in which leave to seek adjudication against an insolvent employer was refused. The court held that for this purpose adjudication was closer to arbitration than an expert procedure.

2. Retention of title creditors are prevented from repossessing their materials. This can be a useful bargaining point with an employer.

3. Where the administrator is ready, willing and able to continue the contract, the employer may be refused leave to re-enter the site. This aspect is considered further in Chapter 9.

4. Where the contractor's cash flow has been damaged through wrongful set-off by the employer, administration may provide enough time to claw back the set-offs and improve cash flow: *Smallman Construction* v *Redpath Dorman Long* (1988) 47 BLR 15.

5. Administration relieves the pressure on companies to settle claims for less than they are worth. It is probable that realisations in the insolvency of Mitchell Construction referred to in Chapter 7 would have been greater had the administration procedure been available during the 1970s.

There are two major hurdles which have to be overcome before administration can be feasible. First, the insolvency practitioner must be satisfied that there is a real prospect that one of the statutory objects of the procedure can be achieved. As so much of the contractor's value is locked up in long term contracts, none of the statutory objects may be possible where the company's contracts are terminated. It is desirable for the practitioner to know in advance whether the employer is prepared to co-operate and waive automatic termination or re-instate the employment of the company to allow the company to continue trading during administration.

The second major difficulty is in funding the company's working capital. In most cases, inadequate working capital will have contributed to the company's failure and it is often difficult to persuade creditors to increase their exposure to give the administration a chance of success. A secured lender is only likely to do this where the company's activities have been thoroughly reviewed and detailed cash flow projections prepared. The court had to consider both aspects in *Re Harris Simons* (1989) BCC 11. Lord Hoffman summarised the position as follows:

> "The company carries on business as builders. Over the past four years there has been a spectacular increase in turnover, from £830,000 in the year to April 1985 to £17 million in the year to April 1987 and £27 million in the year to April 1988. Almost all of its increased turnover has come from one client, a property developer called Berkely House Plc with which the directors had a close relationship. Recently the relationship has turned sour. There are disputes over a number of contracts and Berkely House has purported to dismiss the company and require its employees to leave their sites. It is also withholding sums running into several million pounds which the company says are due and in respect of which Berkely House says it has cross-claims. The effect on the company's cash flow has been that it is unable to pay its debts as they fall due and several writs and a statutory demand have been served. If no administration order is made, the company cannot carry on trading. There is no debenture holder who can be invited to appoint a receiver. The company will have to go into liquidation more or less immediately. The workforce will have to be dismissed and the contracts and work in progress will become a tangle of disputes and probably litigation. The report of the proposed administrator says that in those circumstances it would be extremely difficult to sell any part of the business. If an administration order is made, the company will have what is usually called a breathing space but unless some sort of funding can be found, will continue to have serious respiratory problems with its cash flow. It has however been able to negotiate at least an armistice with Berkely House by which the latter will, conditionally upon the administration order being made, provide sufficient funding to enable the company to complete four current contracts on condition that it quietly removes itself from the other sites in dispute. It is hoped that the four remaining contracts will produce a profit and that it may thereby be possible to stabilize and preserve a business which can either survive or be sold to a third party. In the meanwhile, it may be possible to arrive at a negotiated settlement of the underlying dispute with Berkely House" (at 12).

Hoffman J accepted that on this evidence there was a real prospect either of the survival of the company and the whole or part of its undertaking as a going concern or a more advantageous realisation of its assets than would be effected on a winding-up.

There were several other construction cases in the early years of the procedure. In *W F Fearman* (1988) 4 BCC 139 an insolvent contractor was involved on five or six sites in the London area. A practitioner supported the making of an administration order but had yet to complete his report. A quantity surveyor interviewed the managing director of the company and its employers and concluded that there was no prospect of continuing work on those sites. As a result, the proposed administrator changed his mind and was appointed provisional liquidator instead to safeguard the assets. In *Re Goscott (Groundworks) Ltd* (1988) 4 BCC 372 a contractor unable to comply with a statutory demand sought advice from an insolvency practitioner who advised it to cease trading. When a creditor petitioned to wind up the contractor, it applied for an administration order shortly before the Christmas shut-down. The directors hoped that it would be possible to complete contracts after the shut-down but this was insufficient to justify an administration order and again a provisional liquidator was appointed.

Where there is clear evidence that the company has current contracts which are profitable and that, by continued trading in the short term, offers for the assets and goodwill of the company could realise more than would be available in a liquidation, the court is prepared to make an administration order. In *Re Cavco Floors* [1990] BCC 589 Harman J abridged time between presentation and hearing of the petition. Only about £13,000 was owed to the contractor's bank who declined to appoint an administrative receiver. No one could be prejudiced by the abridgement of time:

> "the directors (having been warned of the dangers of trading while insolvent) have said that they are not prepared to carry on the business of the company even for some two or three days during which, the evidence of Mrs. Harvey makes it plain, it is vital that the company continues to perform its building contract; that the bank has withdrawn support and will not finance the business for that short time, and therefore that unless an administrator is appointed forthwith there is a serious risk that the company will suffer the substantial difficulties that arise in the building trade, which it is notorious are quick to be snatched [sic] by prime contractors when a sub-contractor fails to perform according to his contract" (at 590).

In that case the object of the administration was a better realisation than liquidation. In *Re SCL Building Services* (1989) 5 BCC 746 the court considered a building, mechanical and electrical engineering contractor. The company was insolvent and its bank had refused further credit. Its problems stemmed from financial assistance given to an associated company of which nearly £800,000 was outstanding and thought to be irrecoverable. The practitioner's report

> "proceeded on the footing that the administrator will sell the business carried on as a going concern. The company was said to be concentrating its activities on two substantial contracts, one at St Vedast House in the City carried out on a day work basis averaging £100,000 per month, yielding a gross profit of £40,000, and another in Dulwich Village, there being £1 million of work to carry out within four months of 14 April, and a gross profit of £150,000 being anticipated on that contract. The Dulwich Village contract has now been mutually determined without that profit being realised. Mr. Goldstein reports that the company is now trading profitably and is generating a net surplus of about £25,000 per month. He says he is cautiously optimistic about new work. He says that funding initially will be from the collection of book debts, but he says 'clearly the company can become self-financing in the near future'" (at 747).

Peter Gibson J granted an administration order on the better realisation than liquidation ground, the evidence being insufficient to show a real prospect of the survival of the company and its business in whole or part as a going concern. The company was bound to go into insolvent liquidation even after a sale on a going concern basis and it would have to continue trading over a long period to restore it to solvency. There was no cash flow forecast, no evidence on the likely duration of the remaining contract nor of the likelihood of further work being obtained. There was no evidence of support from the Crown and the alleged support of trade creditors was not supported by the evidence. "At least a hope" was not enough.

The procedure has been quite widely used with construction companies but there has been little empirical research. In the early days, it was possible to take advantage of a lacuna in JCT 80 whereby administration was not included as a termination event. Eclipse Copper, a fitting-out contractor, entered administration before Amendment 4 (July 1987) added administration to the termination clause. This enabled the administrators to complete some of the contracts and negotiate settlements with employers who had wrongly thrown the contractor off site.

In a research paper comparing the administrations of Smallman, Harris Simons, C J Pearce and Burlingway there were voluntary arrangements with distributions to creditors after administration in two cases and a better realisation than on liquidation was achieved in the others (Grogan 1992). For three of the companies, a major cause of insolvency was the wrongful set-off of sums due, while for the fourth it was the rising cost of an arbitration. Survival and company voluntary arrangement were the grounds for the administration order in three cases with better realisation accompanying them in two cases and the sole purpose in one. The whole board of directors was retained in all cases together with the majority of employees. Only in one case was bank finance available during the administration. In the others, the company traded on credit from sub-contractors and suppliers. In three cases retention was collected while in the fourth there was a need to insure against latent defects to obtain release of retention. In three cases litigation or arbitration was necessary. The study concluded that administration had been effective as an insolvency procedure and that problems with collection of retention, retention of title, set-off and defects liability caused less difficulty than might have been anticipated. It is impossible to say from such a small survey but the proportion of companies successfully undergoing administration may be no better and no worse in construction than other industries. It is, however, more suited to the larger company able to bear the cost of the procedure. Other construction administrations have included the Ward Group (1992), a serial administration since the Ward Group had previously purchased Smallman from the administrators, Brignell (1992) whose contracts were novated to Amey, Dean Jesmond, a cladding specialist, David Meek Plant (1992), Ellis (1996), Brazier (1997), Maxim (1998).

The most successful construction administration so far has probably been Smallman Construction. Smallman was a specialist steel erection sub-contractor working on the Broadgate development in the City of London. It had a high concentration of work for one contractor who wrongfully set off against money due to the company. The company experienced a liquidity crisis and was forced into administration. The administrator took proceedings against the contractor to recover the sums set off and was substantially successful. One aspect of the administration is reported at (1988) 4 BCC 784. In the meantime, the company was able to continue trading and to win new work. As a result of the administration, the creditors were paid in full and a surplus returned to the shareholders. The case is a heartening example of how administration can work even in a difficult industry.

Company Voluntary Arrangement (CVA)

CVAs have been used in the construction industry both with and without the support of the administration procedure. Examples of successful CVAs without administration are:

- HLM, an architectural practice, where the CVA apparently worked since there were comparatively few creditors, the directors were prepared to invest in the company through a management buy-out, the buy-out would generate sufficient funds to finance a dividend and the directors were prepared to reduce salaries and overheads;
- Charles Gregory, and various subsidiaries, civil engineering contractors, which were bought by the Miller Group in July 1992. The creditors agreed to accept a dividend of 35 pence in the pound through a CVA. It appears that the sale was conditional on the agreement of a CVA and that the creditors were influenced in their decision by the assurance of payment of the dividend from the proceeds of sale. Miller's chairman was quoted as saying that he thought CVAs would become a growing trend in the industry;
- Ebor, a Yorkshire construction group, entered a CVA under which secured and preferential creditors were to be paid in full and unsecured creditors would receive a dividend after agreeing to reschedule their debt. The CVA was prompted by the company's bank halving its overdraft limit and refusing a request for further facilities.

Construction companies which have used a CVA as an exit from administration include:

- Smallman Construction went into administration following wrongful set-offs by its employer. The administrators recovered the set-offs through litigation and the creditors agreed to a CVA. The administrators became the supervisors under the CVA and paid 100 pence in the pound to the creditors. They were also able to return to the shareholders an amount in excess of the shareholders' equity at the date of the administration order.
- SCL Building Services, where the company petitioned for an administration order based on the survival of the company, the approval of a CVA or a better realisation of assets than liquidation. The administration order was made only on the basis that it would enable a better realisation of assets. The CVA purpose was rejected because there was no evidence in

support from the main creditors, and one creditor with less than 10% of the overall debts of the company opposed it. However, the administrators later successfully applied to the court to add a CVA as an additional purpose and the creditors later agreed. A first dividend of 60 pence in the pound has been paid. The final outcome is not known.

- Ellis Construction, where there was an anticipated return for creditors of 20%. The grounds for the CVA over a liquidation were lower professional costs, greater flexibility to agree creditors' claims, and the ability to obtain higher rates of interest on realisations.

The Society of Practitioners of Insolvency has recommended changes to the CVA procedure by removing technical obstacles and introducing a new form of CVA with a moratorium. The technical obstacles relate to the need for shareholder approval even when all shareholders' funds have been lost, the position of unknown or unascertainable creditors and the voting rights of partly secured and contingent creditors. The new form of CVA would be activated by the company applying to the court for an order for suspension of payments. An insolvency practitioner would consent to act but would have no duty to supervise the company's business. The moratorium would last for 30 days during which time the insolvency practitioner would report to the court on whether a creditors' meeting should be held. The directors' proposals would be passed if approved by a majority of two-thirds in value of the creditors. Secured creditors' rights would be respected. The SPI have made it clear that even these proposals

> "would not benefit those companies whose business has come to the end of its useful life and cannot be made viable, nor those that are so dependent on customer confidence that the initiation of an insolvency process would cause the business irreparable damage" (SPI Bulletin 17).

There have been a large number of papers issued in reaction to the DTI's consultation document on possible changes to the CVA and administration procedures. The DTI is currently considering all the responses.

It has been suggested that

> "for a small company which is likely to be able to enter a CVA but which cannot afford the control of an insolvency practitioner, an adjournment of say three or six months [of an administration petition] in appropriate cases can and should in proper cases be granted to enable the CVA to be put in place" (Moss 1998).

Section 9(4) of the Act allows the court to adjourn the hearing of an administration petition, s 10(2) preserves the power of a floating charge-holder to appoint an administrative receiver, and s 17(2) would enable the court to give directions to the administrator to allow the existing management to stay in place subject to a minimum of supervision.

Conclusion

Boom and bust cycles in the industry make it essential for contractors to be able to manage change. It has been said that "the construction industry, more than almost any other, faces continuous and at times violent changes in work load, in work mix and in the method of managing the process. It is almost by definition changing its product all the time" (Hillebrandt and Cannon 1989, at xix). Management of change means adapting strategy to the prevailing industrial climate: growth, recession, recovery and so on (Lansley 1987 at 5, 141). Failure to meet the need for constant strategic revision is a prime cause of insolvency in this sector.

The industry has a strong identity and possesses financial characteristics which make it vulnerable to insolvency. However, there is no necessary reason why any of the available informal or formal procedures cannot be used successfully in the case of a contracting company. In cases where the directors leave it too late or where the company has no viable business, there may be little that can be done. But in the absence of these two fatal factors, there is a wide range of possibilities. Administration should not be equated with receivership. Receivership could be viewed more positively. The company voluntary arrangement procedure is still a rarity and deserves more consideration, especially for the smaller contractor whose other alternative is probably voluntary liquidation. Construction is a tough industry in which to work but it is full of survivors. If the people working in the industry were more aware of what can be done, there would be many more cases of contractors trading through insolvency.

Chapter 9

· Termination ·

Introduction

If a contractor fails to complete the works, it loses more than the balance of the contract sum. This is because of the extended termination clauses found in the standard forms. As well as the right to terminate, the employer is given wide powers over the contractor's property to facilitate the completion of the works. These powers can mean that a company with a substantial book value can become virtually worthless on the appointment of a receiver. The detention of substantial work in progress over long periods of time and the effect of termination clauses are special features of construction contracts.

A termination can have other important consequences. The contractor's failure to complete may cause the failure of the project, and this can lead to the insolvency of the employer and have a knock-on effect on anyone else involved. Termination creates conflict between creditors with proprietary rights or security interests and those with purely contractual rights against the insolvent company, who in turn may have to choose between rights given by the contract and other rights available under the general law (Carter 1989, 1990, 1991; Opeskin 1990).

Termination at common law

"Termination" is not a term of art: it has no fixed meaning in law. In this chapter, it is used in the broadest sense to include discharge, determination of employment, acceptance of repudiation and release from performance.

> "The three sets of circumstances giving rise to a discharge of contract are: (1) renunciation by a person of his liabilities under it, (2) impossibility created by his own act, (3) total or partial failure of performance. In the case of the first two, the renunciation may occur or the impossibility be created either before or at the time for performance. In the case of the third it can occur only at the time or during the course of performance.

Moreover, if the third is partial, the failure must occur in a matter which goes to the root of the contract. All these acts may be compendiously described as repudiation, though that expression is more particularly used of renunciation before the time for performance has arrived": *Heyman* v *Darwins* [1942] AC 356 at 397.

In the first situation, a renunciation can be a refusal to carry out an obligation which is due for performance or a statement that the obligation will not be performed when it becomes due. If there is no evidence of a clear refusal, the test is whether the person's actions would lead a reasonable person to conclude that it no longer intended to be bound by the contract. This also applies where a person does intend to carry out the contract but only in a way inconsistent with its obligations or by requiring the other person to do something it is not contractually obliged to do. In *Universal Cargo Carriers* v *Citati* [1957] 2 QB 401 at 437, Devlin J stated:

> "But unwillingness and inability are often difficult to disentangle, and it is rarely necessary to make the attempt. Inability often lies at the root of unwillingness to perform. Willingness in this context does not mean cheerfulness; it means simply an intent to perform. To say: 'I would like to but I cannot', negatives intent just as much as 'I will not'."

The second type of termination, inability to perform, occurs where one person through its own act or omission makes it impossible for itself to complete its side of the bargain. Examples are where an owner sells a ship it has previously agreed to charter or where goods which a vendor has agreed to sell are seized by a sheriff before they can be delivered to the purchaser. The third type of termination is perhaps the most common in the industry. Whether a person is so seriously in breach as to lead the other to conclude that it had no intention of carrying out its obligations is a question of degree. The position is complicated by the principle in *Woodar* v *Wimpey* [1980] 1 WLR 277 that a wrongful termination based on a bona fide but mistaken interpretation of the contract, without intending to abandon it, will not necessarily be a repudiation. The case arose out of the collapse of the Stern group in the recession of 1974. A seller of a car who asks for more than the agreed price on delivery in mistaken reliance on a term entitling it to charge its list at that time whatever the circumstances was not in repudiation and could keep the buyer's deposit on his failure to complete: *Vaswani* v *Italian Motors* [1996] 1 WLR 270. The same applies to a termination based on a mistaken view that the term in question was part of the contract: *Design Company* v *King* (1992) 8 BLM 1. If the renunciation or impossibility occurs before the time for performance has arrived, it is known as an "anticipatory breach". Unless the exception in *Woodar* v *Wimpey* applies, if one person wrongly treats the other's conduct as repudiatory, it may find itself in repudiation entitling the other to claim damages: *Bedfordshire County Council* v *Fitzpatrick Contractors* (1998) 62 Con LR 64.

Consequences of repudiation

If one person is in repudiation in any of the three aspects referred to in *Heyman* v *Darwins* [1942] AC 356, the other has the option either to accept the repudiation and claim damages or to affirm the contract and call on the person to perform.

If repudiation is accepted, the unperformed obligations of both parties are released and those of the person at fault are replaced by a liability to pay damages: *Photo Production* v *Securicor* [1980] AC 827. Acceptance must normally be communicated by some unequivocal act, but inactivity can in context be sufficient:

> "Postulate the case where an employer at the end of the day tells a contractor that he, the employer, is repudiating the contract and that the contractor need not return the next day. The contractor does not return the next day or at all. It seems to me that the contractor's failure to return may, in the absence of any other explanation, convey a decision to treat the contract as at an end": *Vitol* v *Norelf* [1996] AC 800 at 811.

If the contractor's failure to return was caused by its insolvency, for example, acceptance may not be inferred. Acceptance is irrevocable. If it later turns out that a repudiation accepted by the other person was not in fact a breach, the acceptance may still be valid if there were at that time another repudiatory breach, even if the person was not aware of it. The exception to this is where the person at fault is prejudiced by lack of notice, perhaps because it could have remedied the breach.

Affirming the contract is also irrevocable, with the possible exception of anticipatory breach (Treitel 1998). Affirmation can be express or implied from an unequivocal act. Simply protesting about the repudiation and calling on the other person to change its position and honour the contract is not necessarily an affirmation and there may be a half-way house for the innocent person to occupy while it decides what to do:

> "The law does not require an injured person to snatch at a repudiation and it does not automatically lose its right to treat a contract as

discharged merely by calling on the other to reconsider his position and recognise its obligations": *Yukong Line* v *Rendsberg* [1996] 2 Lloyd's Rep 604 at 608.

After affirmation, both parties retain previous causes of action and the contract remains alive for the benefit of them both.

Insolvency and repudiation

It is sometimes argued that insolvency is an anticipatory breach entitling the other person to terminate the contract. Acceptance of the breach would release both parties from further performance and entitle the innocent person to damages without having to wait until the time for performance has expired. "What anticipatory breach really means is that a party is in breach from the moment that his actual breach becomes inevitable" (Oditah 1992 at 495).

Insolvency could be an anticipatory breach if the construction contract was personal to the parties or of a long term nature: *Re Asphaltic Wood Pavement Co* (1885) 30 Ch D 216. Millett J commenting on this case in *Re Charge Card Services* [1986] 3 All ER 289 at 311 said that "the winding-up no doubt amounted to an anticipatory breach of contract." An anticipatory breach can be accepted by conduct even where the act constituting acceptance would otherwise be a breach of contract. Where the innocent person does not affirm, acceptance could be inferred from either taking action incompatible with continued performance or a simple failure to perform further: *Vitol* v *Norelf* [1994] 1 WLR 1390.

The main difficulty is that at common law, insolvency, whether formal or informal, is not necessarily a breach: *Re Agra Bank, ex parte Tondeur* (1867) LR 5 Eq 160. "The appointment [of administrative receivers] may be consistent with the firm intention to continue the contract rather than to abandon it, especially if it is profitable": *Laing and Morrison-Knudson* v *Aegon Insurance* (1997) 86 BLR 70 at 91. It is unlikely that a term will be implied allowing termination for insolvency: *Re Premier Products* [1965] NZLR 50. It would be possible for the parties to agree not to become insolvent but the standard forms do not take this approach. In *Twin City* v *Penwood Construction* (1980) 44 NSR (2d) 418, the court implied a term that the employer would pay progress payments within a reasonable time and that the contractor had an implied right to terminate the contract on the employer's failure to do so.

Unless it is an anticipatory breach or causes something to happen or fail to happen which is in conflict with the parties' intentions, insolvency has no legal effect on a contract. If the insolvency practitioner can find a way for the company to continue performing, the employer can do nothing about it. As insolvency is usually progressive over time, it is crucial for employers to understand the warning signs and weigh them up as potential breaches. The following are typical:

- failing to pay direct labour, sub-contractors and suppliers leading to disruption and delay
- supervisory staff leaving the company and not being replaced leading to defective work
- requests for advance or accelerated payments.

The employer needs to be careful, *e.g.* "going slow" by the contractor is not necessarily a repudiation: *Hill* v *London Borough of Camden* (1980) 18 BLR 31. If the contract excludes the common law, and provides for automatic termination and other remedies on the appointment of an administrative receiver to the contractor, the employer loses any right to treat the receivership as an anticipatory breach: *Perar* v *General Surety* (1994) 66 BLR 72.

Termination under the contract

To avoid any difficulty over the tests for common law termination, construction contracts almost always include an express term allowing either or both parties to terminate on various grounds. Termination events in general can be wider or narrower than or the same as those at common law. They can include ordinary and repudiatory breaches, events which are not breaches at all, something not happening (*e.g.* *Total Gas* v *Arco* [1998] 2 Lloyd's Rep 209), and termination at the option of either person.

Procedural requirements

Any person wishing to terminate under the contract must do so without undue delay but in practice this can be months or, it seems, even years: see *Laing and Morrison-Knudson* v *Aegon Insurance* (1997) 86 BLR 70. A person relying on a contractual termination clause needs to act strictly in accordance with its requirements as to the statement of grounds, period of notice, method of service etc or risk being in repudiation itself: *Hill* v *London Borough of Camden* (1980) 18 BLR 31. Where the contract lays down time periods for the giving of notices, it can be a repudiation if notice is given prematurely: *Afovos Shipping* v *Pagnan* [1983] 1 WLR 195. Particular care is required where the employer wishes to serve notice but has agreed to the assignment of the benefit of the contract to a third person: consider *Linden Gardens* v *Lenesta Sludge* [1994] 1 AC 85 at 105. If the contract allows termination only after a certificate, a person will be in repudiation if the certificate is invalid: *Nelson Carlton* v *Hatrick* [1965] NZLR 144. The same might apply where the contract required a notice to show cause why it should not be terminated, but it was not given, or was insufficiently connected to the notice of termination in terms of its content or timing: *Architectural Installation Services* v *James Gibbons Windows* (1990) 16 Con LR 68. If the default referred to in the notice to show cause has been remedied, the contractor may be able to obtain an injunction restraining the employer from serving the notice of termination: *Robert Salzer Constructions* v *Elmbee* (1991) 10 ACLR 64.

Wrongful termination by one person sometimes leads to the other's insolvency. If it can be proved that the insolvency was the natural and probable consequence of the breach of contract, then in principle the costs of the relevant insolvency procedure are recoverable as damages. A major problem is that there are likely to have been other causes of insolvency, such as under-capitalisation. Even if the costs of the procedure were irrecoverable, the court might penalise the wrongdoer, *e.g.* the exemplary damages awarded against the employer in *Egan* v *State Transport Authority* (1982) 31 SASR 481, considered in Chapter 4.

The standard forms take many different approaches. Termination may be automatic, automatic for some grounds but on notice for others, on notice only, on notice to the other contract person and a third person, *e.g.* a beneficiary under a warranty or direct agreement, on notice only after notice to show cause, or on notice plus a certificate from a third person. Termination clauses often confer rights wider than the common law to the person with greater bargaining strength. For example, the suspension of payment under JCT forms until the final account of the completion contractor has been agreed improves the employer's position at common law, unless it could have avoided having to pay sums accrued due to the insolvent contractor by an equitable set-off. Termination under a contractual provision does not prevent the person terminating from recovering an accrued unpaid stage payment as a debt even if the buyer obtains no benefit under the contract: *Stocznia* v *Latvian Shipping* [1998] 1 All ER 883. There was no failure of consideration as the contract was for the design, construction and delivery of a ship. Although it was terminated before the ship was delivered, the builder had carried out design and construction work in relation to it. A contractor who becomes insolvent and repudiates before completing the works still remains entitled to payment for work done before the termination. In *Coba Industries* v *Adams* (1987) 15 BCLR (2d) 68, the contract was informal but allowed the builder to invoice monthly in arrears. When the employer accepted the builder's repudiation, about $800,000 was outstanding. The employer could have had the works completed to the original design using an alternative contractor but instead opted to abandon the project. To avoid paying the contractor, it argued that, despite the agreement to make progress payments, the contract was entire and the contractor was due nothing. The argument was rejected and the matter referred back to the trial judge to deal with issues concerning set-off and quantification of loss.

Relation to the common law

The general rule is that clear words are necessary in order to exclude the common law. It follows that if a contract says nothing about the common law, its terms are in addition to and not in substitution for it: *Gilbert-Ash* v *Modern Engineering* [1973] 3 All ER 195. Occasionally the court has found an implied exclusion of the common law but this is very rare: *Lockland Builders* v *Rickwood* (1995) 77 BLR 38. It follows that words such as "without prejudice to the parties' rights and remedies at common law" are "legal verbiage": *Architectural Installation Services* v *James Gibbons Windows* (1990) 16 Con LR 68 at 73, Carter (1990) at 107. The danger of including them is that, if common law rights are preserved in one context, *e.g.* the power to terminate, the court might construe the whole contract as excluding the common law apart from the termination clause. This is the "argument from redundancy" criticised by Lord Hoffman in *Beaufort Developments* v *Gilbert-Ash* (1998) 88 BLR 1 at 10. In *Perar* v *General Surety* (1994) 66 BLR 72, the Court of Appeal observed that clause 27 of JCT 81 reserved common law rights when setting out termination events but did not repeat the reservation in a sub-clause conferring post-termination rights. The court concluded that the post-termination rights were exclusive of common law and amounted to a complete code. This problem has been rectified by clause 27.8 of

JCT 98 which preserves the common law in respect of the whole termination clause. It has been held that the preservation of common law rights makes it clear that the termination clause offers an alternative to acceptance of repudiation: *Tern Construction* v *RBS Garages* (1992) 34 Con LR 137 at 145. It also keeps alive the innocent person's right to elect to affirm the contract or accept the repudiation even after operating the termination clause: *Laing and Morrison-Knudson* v *Aegon Insurance* (1997) 86 BLR 70. This is a key issue in construction insolvency since so much depends on the successful completion of long term contracts.

Where the termination event is a repudiatory breach, and the contract does not exclude the common law, could the innocent person both terminate under the contract and accept a repudiation? The two remedies are not inconsistent although the damages recoverable may be different: *Financings* v *Baldock* [1963] 2 QB 104. The problem is that, on one view, in order to terminate under the contract, the innocent person has to rely on the termination clause, *i.e.* affirm the contract, thereby disabling itself from accepting the repudiation. Thus in *Johnstone* v *Milling* (1886) 16 QBD 460 a claim for damages for anticipatory breach failed as a tenant had previously treated a lease as being in existence by relying on its terms in terminating it.

In *Laing and Morrison-Knudson* v *Aegon Insurance* (1997) 86 BLR 70, a sub-contractor went into administrative receivership before completion. The management contractor terminated "the sub-contract work" pursuant to an express term and claimed damages from the sub-contractor's bondsman representing the cost of completion. The termination clause allowed the contractor to take possession of the sub-contractor's plant and materials but did not confer any right to compensation for loss caused by the termination. The contractor therefore argued that its reliance on the clause was acceptance of a repudiation which had preceded the insolvency, and claimed full repudiation damages.

It was held that the termination under an express clause was neither an acceptance of repudiation (because the clause provided for the termination of the works not the contract) nor an affirmation of the contract (because the contractual rights were expressly without prejudice to the parties' common law rights). It was a neutral event, a holding action to allow the innocent person to consider its position: "clearing the decks to enable [the contractor] to be able to do that which [the sub-contractor] was not going to do" (at 112). The court held the defendant bondsman liable because:

1. It was asked to assume that at the time of the termination, the bonded sub-contractor was in repudiatory breach.

2. The repudiation was accepted by the Statement of Claim in the action.

3. As a consequence the contractor was not limited to the restricted relief allowed by the termination clause, but could recover full damages for repudiation.

The bondsman argued that the contractor's loss (the cost to complete) was incurred as a result of the contractual termination, which had removed the sub-contractor's right to continue work, rather than the repudiation which was not accepted until long after the loss had been incurred. This reasoning was not accepted by the court since it became necessary for the contractor to incur the cost to complete as soon as the sub-contractor repudiated. The sub-contractor remained in repudiation after the contractual termination of the works. The fact that the repudiation was not accepted until after the loss was incurred was immaterial. For other points on the decision see (1998) 15 BLM 6, and generally van Deventer (1993, 311-319).

The notice of termination in *Laing and Morrison-Knudson* only referred to the termination clause not the common law, and the event relied on (the receivership) was not a repudiation. In *Kennedy* v *Collings Construction* (1991) 7 BCL 25 at 39, a notice of termination under an express clause also referred to the builder's repudiation and some of the termination events were also repudiatory. It was held to be an effective acceptance of repudiation. This seems to have been the case in *Bovis* v *Whatlings Construction* (1995) 75 BLR 1, where the House of Lords spoke of repudiation damages in the context of a termination under an express term. If the employer writes saying it is having the works completed by someone else in view of the contractor's failure to perform, the court may in context treat the employer's letter either as an acceptance of repudiation or a notice of termination: *Gibbs* v *Tomlinson* (1992) 35 Con LR 86 at 118.

If the termination event is not a repudiatory breach, it is crucial to examine the contract carefully. The innocent person will be limited to such relief as the clause allows (or which had already accrued due), which might be less than the damages recoverable on a repudiation: *Thomas Feather* v *Bradford* [1953] 52 LGR 30. If the termination clause was improperly operated, but there happened to be a repudiatory breach in existence when notice was given, the innocent person could rely on the notice as acceptance of the repudiation, even if unaware of it at the time: compare *Sheffield* v *Conrad* (1987) 22 Con LR 108.

If the parties go to the trouble of specifying certain events as entitling them to terminate the contract, does that mean that they must have intended them to have effect as conditions (as opposed to warranties or intermediate terms)? If so, it would mean that the occurrence of any of these events would be a breach of condition and give rise to an election to accept a repudiation or affirm the contract. In principle, simply nominating events as entitling one person to terminate ought not to elevate a term into a condition. The court would probably expect the parties to have articulated this intention by an express term: *Lombard North Central* v *Butterworth* [1987] QB 527.

The court has jurisdiction to make a declaration as to whether the party is entitled to terminate the contract, but in *Midland Land* v *Warren Energy* [1997] CILL 1222 the court declined to do so on the basis that it might encourage a flood of applications. The court was satisfied that the buyer under a gas supply agreement was solvent on the balance sheet basis under s 123(2) Insolvency Act 1986. The seller wanted to be certain in advance that a termination for insolvency under the contract would be valid.

The standard forms

Ever since termination clauses were introduced, a distinction has been made between terminating the contract and terminating the contractor's right to continue work on site.

Examples of the former include clauses which set out defined events and then either declare the contract void or give the employer power to avoid it, should any of the events occur: *e.g. Munro* v *Wivenhoe and Brightlingsea Railway Company* (1865) 12 LT 656. The contract is terminated under MF/1 and GC Works/1 (2nd edition). Examples of the latter fall into three groups. First, the JCT forms state that the contractor's employment under the contract is terminated: see the comparative table in Totty and Moss at H6.02. Secondly, the ICE forms entitle the employer to enter upon the site and expel the contractor from it. Thirdly, many older cases allow the employer to take the works "out of the contractor's hands" and have them completed by others: *e.g. Pauling* v *Mayor of Dover* (1855) 10 Ex 753. There is no substantial difference between these expressions: the intention is to give the employer power to terminate the contractor's right to continue the works without avoiding the contract. The use of the word "employment" suggests that the contractor loses both the right and the duty to continue work, but is not released from its other liabilities under the contract.

Important consequences flow from this since subsequent non-performance of work on site cannot be repudiatory because the contractor's right to continue has been terminated: *Perar* v *General Surety* (1994) 66 BLR 72.

> "I think that if a contract, whether it be for building or for anything else, provides for automatic termination in a certain eventuality, termination as a result of that term is in accordance with the contract and not in breach of it": *Samuel Properties* v *London Borough of Richmond* (unreported, 22 July 1983).

This has an impact on the question whether there has been a default for the purpose of liability under a bond or an insurance policy or a limitation defence: *Burns & Dutton* v *Yule* (1969) 8 DLR (3d) 683, *McPhail* v *Cunninghame District Council* (1985) SLT 149.

Automatic termination

Some forms make termination automatic on insolvency but optional in relation to other events, or automatic for some insolvency events but not for others. Automatic termination can perhaps help an employer who pays a certificate in ignorance of the occurrence of an insolvency event. As the termination suspends the employer's duty to pay, it may be able to recover the payment as having been paid under a mistake of fact. On the other hand, automatic termination removes any chance of accepting the contractor's conduct after the insolvency event as a repudiation, at least as far as it concerns the completion of the works: *Perar* v *General Surety* (1994) 66 BLR 72. It is arguable that automatic termination would not affect the employer's right to accept a repudiation which occurred before the insolvency event: *Laing and Morrison-Knudson* v *Aegon Insurance* (1997) 86 BLR 70 (which concerned a termination on notice).

It is possible that the court would not uphold a term providing for automatic termination if satisfied that it was activated by an event within one of the parties' control: *New Zealand Shipping* v *Société des Ateliers* [1919] AC 1 at 9, Carter (1990, at 97-8). If so, it would take effect as a term giving a right of termination to the innocent person. Conceivably, this could be the case in the event of a voluntary liquidation, administration (if sought by the company) or receivership where the appointment is made at the borrower's request. It has been suggested that it is "just conceivable" that an automatic termination clause could constitute a preference under s 239 Insolvency Act 1986 (Totty and Moss at H6.02). This possibility is considered in chapter 15.

Automatic termination on informal insolvency suffers from the problems inherent in the automatic crystallisation of a floating charge (Lightman and Moss 1994). How can a third party know when the event has occurred? What happens if the contractor manages to trade out of its difficulties? In view of these and other potential problems, provision for automatic termination on informal insolvency is best avoided.

Consensual termination

Where it is recognised by employer and contractor that the contractor will not be able to complete, the parties sometimes agree to terminate the contract: *e.g. Leyland Motors v Napier Harbour Board* [1930] NZLR 113 at 118. If a payment is made by a contractor to get out of a contract and the payment is influenced by a desire to improve the employer's position on the contractor's liquidation, it may have to be repaid by the employer as a preference (see Chapter 15). It was the consensual termination of contracts which led to the investigation of Norwest Holst Limited under s 165(b) Companies Act 1948 (DTI 1981).

Termination on notice

Termination where the employer is insolvent is not automatic but on notice under JCT 80 or FIDIC (4th edition). The contractor has no express power to terminate in the event of the insolvency of the employer under JCT 81, GC Works/1 or ICE (5th edition). Employer and contractor are given reciprocal rights to terminate on notice for the insolvency of the other under ACA 82 (3rd edition).

JCT contracts provide that the notice must not be given "unreasonably or vexatiously". It is probably not unreasonable to terminate under the contract even if this increases or fails to reduce loss: Opeskin (1990, at 314), *Thomas Construction v Grafton Furniture* [1988] 2 SA 546 at 560. How could this provision apply to an insolvency event? It would be reasonable for a contractor to terminate its employment if its employer were insolvent and unable to make any further payments under the contract, as in *Comco Constructions* v

Westminster Properties (1990) 2 WAR 335 at 344, where the contractor terminated its employment on the employer having execution levied against it. But if the employer through its insolvency practitioner were able to continue the contract and honour all its payment obligations, it would be unreasonable for the contractor to terminate, especially as it would not have had the right under the general law. If the employer were in administration, the court might consider it unreasonable or vexatious for the contractor to terminate in view of the purpose of the administration procedure and the fact that the contractor as a creditor of the employer, actual or contingent, has an interest in the outcome of the procedure.

In Australia an express power to remove the contractor from site by reason of insolvency is subject to an implied duty to exercise it reasonably: *Hughes* v *Trustees of the Roman Catholic Church* (1994) 10 BCL 335. It would usually be reasonable to terminate for insolvency, but not in all cases, *e.g.* where a winding-up petition has been issued against the contractor vexatiously. The implied term as to reasonableness imposes a duty on the employer to enquire about the surrounding circumstances before exercising its power.

> "Examples can be multiplied. A contractor may be in the process of having the proceedings against it disposed of by agreement ... [or] where the [employer] has engineered or encouraged the commencement of the proceedings against the contractor" (at 362).

In that case, the court found that the power had been exercised reasonably. The petition had been issued by unpaid nominated sub-contractors and statutory demands had been served. The contractor argued that its inability to pay had been caused by the employer but this was not supported by the evidence.

Waiver and withdrawal of termination

Where termination is not automatic, the right to terminate must be exercised within a reasonable time of the event relied on, otherwise the employer may be taken to have waived it: *Marsden* v *Sambell* (1880) 43 LT 120. What amounts to a reasonable time will depend on all the facts of the case. JCT contracts make automatic termination subject to re-instatement by agreement with the insolvency practitioner. The employer should be wary of re-instatement being inferred from all the circumstances where this is not intended. This may occur where an insolvency practitioner is allowed to retain possession of the site after his appointment and is likely where the insolvency practitioner is allowed to continue the contract to the knowledge of the employer. If a notice of termination is expressly subject to withdrawal on fulfilment of a condition, ceasing work after the condition has been satisfied will be a repudiation: *e.g. Ellis Tylin* v *Co-Operative Retail Services* [1999] BLR 205 at 216, 220. This could occur where a receiver persuades an employer to withdraw a termination notice if it can obtain a bond in support of the completion of the works.

Insolvency events

The standard forms range widely in the scope of insolvency events giving rise to termination. Some are restricted and limit the events to bankruptcy or liquidation. Others are more comprehensive and include events short of formal insolvency *e.g.* simply "becoming insolvent". Nineteenth century contracts commonly included "insolvency" as a termination event: *e.g. Davies* v *Mayor of Swansea* (1853) LJ Ex 297. The court has generally upheld such clauses: *Byblos Bank* v *Al-Khudairy* (1986) 2 BCC 549 at 560-4. This applies even now to FIDIC (4th edition) and the Scottish Supplement to the JCT forms: "becoming apparently insolvent" (see s 7 Bankruptcy (Scotland) Act 1985). This can be useful where an employer fears that a contractor may be insolvent and likely to default but cannot otherwise terminate the contract without risking liability for damages. An Australian case concerned a sub-contract which allowed the contractor to remove the works from the control of the sub-contractor on notice on the sub-contractor "becoming insolvent." The contractor served a notice but on a different ground not available at the time. Nevertheless, it was held that the contractor had validly terminated since the sub-contractor had been informally insolvent at the date of the notice. It was irrelevant that the contractor was unaware of the fact: *Minion* v *Graystone* (1990) 2 ACLB 7.

The widest term in current use is probably clause 63.1 of FIDIC (4th edition):

> "If the Contractor is deemed by law unable to pay his debts as they fall due, or enters into voluntary or involuntary bankruptcy, liquidation or dissolution (other than a voluntary liquidation for the purposes of amalgamation or reconstruction), or becomes insolvent, or makes an arrangement with, or assignment in favour of, his creditors, or agrees to carry out the Contract under a committee of inspection of his creditors, or if a receiver, administrator, trustee or liquidator is appointed over any

substantial part of his assets, or if, under any law or regulation relating to reorganisation, arrangement or readjustment of debts, proceedings are commenced against the contractor or resolutions passed in connection with dissolution or liquidation or if any steps are taken to enforce any security interest over a substantial part of the assets of the Contractor, or if any act is done or event occurs with respect to the Contractor or his assets which, under any applicable law has a substantially similar effect to any of the foregoing acts or events, or if the Contractor has contravened sub-clause 3.1 [assignment and sub-contracting], or has an execution levied on his goods ...".

Although intended for use on international projects, the FIDIC contract is construed in accordance with English law. Clause 63.1 ought to be sufficient to cover most insolvency regimes world wide, but some legal systems invalidate termination clauses operative on insolvency, and local advice will be essential in each case. Other possible events are the receipt of a statutory demand under s 123 Insolvency Act 1986, the dishonouring of a cheque or the execution of a bill of sale, but they may backfire on the employer. The more technical the event, the less relationship the event has to the solvency of the contractor or sub-contractor, and the further away it is from being repudiatory at common law, the stricter will be the court's construction of the clause.

The JCT forms have a comprehensive list of events, with the exception of the appointment of a receiver under a fixed charge. This is in contrast with ICE (6th edition) in which the only insolvency event relevant to a company is liquidation. Administration has been added as an insolvency event but (it seems) on the assumption that the contractor is an individual. The court may, however, construe the term as applying to any person acting in the capacity of contractor. When dealing with individuals, the clause has maintained the receiving order as an event, even though the concept was abolished with the repeal of the Bankruptcy Act 1914.

Some clauses require an architect's certificate of sufficient cause to terminate following an insolvency event. It has been held that the fact that

"the contract could be fully and adequately completed by the trustee may well (in the absence of some ulterior motive) be good reason why the architect would not in the circumstances execute such a certificate. For that reason ... the architect would first have to determine whether the contract could be completed by the trustee and hence the need for his certificate": *Casson* v *Laing Construction* (1974) 18 CBR 133 at 142, upheld on appeal on this point at (1975) 19 CBR 89.

Sub-contracts

One of the major risks to contractors arising out of employer insolvency is liability to sub-contractors. A common way of managing this risk is to insert a clause in the sub-contract allowing the contractor to terminate it on termination of the main contract. As a result, the contractor's inability to give access to the sub-contractor will not be a breach of the sub-contract. As a further way of reducing its loss, the termination clause may limit the compensation payable to the sub-contractor. Such transfer of risk involves a narrowing of the sub-contractor's rights at common law. The court always requires clear wording in order to achieve such a result. In practice, this can only be achieved by the harmonisation of main and sub-contract termination clauses.

To the layman, there is no real difference between the methods of termination adopted in construction contracts: terminating the contract, terminating the contractor's employment or excluding the contractor from site without avoiding the contract. The particular formula seems to have little effect on the consequential rights conferred by the contract, which tend to follow a similar pattern. If those rights mirrored or were wider than the common law, the court might be willing to treat these approaches as having the same effect. Since termination clauses in sub-contracts often cut down the sub-contractor's common law rights, however, subtle differences in approach between main and sub-contract termination clauses have been construed in favour of the sub-contractor. It is important to remember that the main function of a sub-contract termination clause in this context is to allow the contractor to deny the sub-contractor future access to site without being in repudiation of the sub-contract. As presently drafted, neither the engineering nor the building standard forms achieves this result.

Under clause 63(1) of ICE (5th and 6th editions), the employer is entitled in certain circumstances to enter the site and expel the contractor "without thereby avoiding the contract or releasing the contractor from any of his obligations or liabilities under the contract …". The FCEC form of sub-contract allows the contractor to terminate the sub-contractor's employment on notice "if the main contract is determined for any reason whatsoever". The compensation allowed to the sub-contractor after termination excludes loss of profit. The court has refused to regard the employer's entry on site as a "determination of the contract". As a result, it will be a repudiation of the sub-contract entitling the sub-contractor to full repudiation damages: *ER Dyer* v *Simon Build, Peter Lind Partnership* (1982)

23 BLR 23. In *Iezzi Constructions* v *Currumbin* (1994) BCL 408 a contractor terminated the main contract where the employer was insolvent. The contractor then repudiated a sub-contract by denying the sub-contractor access to the site. The repudiation was accepted. The contractor could not rely on a pay when paid clause as a defence to a claim for a *quantum meruit* following the termination. On its true construction, the clause related only to progress payments payable while the primary obligations under the contract were still alive and could not apply to a claim for a *quantum meruit*.

The JCT forms use the concept of "termination of employment". For example, clause 31.2.1 of NSC/4A provides that if the employment of the contractor is determined under the main contract then the employment of the sub-contractor shall thereupon also determine. The sub-contract also limits the sub-contractor's rights to compensation. If the main contract is repudiated by the employer, it will not be treated as a termination of the contractor's employment. If follows that the contractor will also repudiate the sub-contract entitling the sub-contractor to full repudiation damages: *Scobie & McIntosh* v *Clayton Bowmore* (1990) 49 BLR 119. Although the layman might assume that acceptance of repudiation would terminate the contractor's employment since the greater includes the lesser, the need for exceptionally clear words to exclude the common law enables the court to take a literal approach.

In a recent case, a sub-contract provided:

> "In the event that the main contract is terminated by the employer for any reason attributable to the contractor, then the contractor hereby undertakes to reimburse, on demand, all costs and expenses incurred by the sub-contractor as a result of such termination".

The failure to provide for termination meant that the sub-contract was repudiated by the contractor on the same day as the employer's repudiation of the main contract since the contractor could no longer give access to the sub-contractor: *Milburn Services* v *United Trading Group* (1995) 2 Con LR 130.

A peculiarity of DOM/1 and NSC/4 is that neither form allows the sub-contractor to terminate its employment on the insolvency of the contractor. The forms are inconsistent in this respect as the sub-contractor's employment is terminated on its own insolvency (on notice under DOM/1 and automatically under NSC/4). There seems to be no obvious justification for the absence of reciprocal rights of termination. A domestic sub-contractor is denied loss and expense where its employment is terminated on termination of the contractor's employment under the main contract. This apparently unreasonable provision is mirrored in NAM/SC. It is hard to understand this distinction between domestic and nominated sub-contracts. The termination would not affect the sub-contractor's accrued rights: *Westralian Farmers* v *Commonwealth Agricultural Service Engineers* [1935] 54 CLR 361.

In practice, sub-contractors may not exploit the fact that they are no longer obliged to continue working on site unless they want to get out of the contract or to re-negotiate their rates. From the point of view of an insolvency practitioner appointed over an employer, this can make it more difficult to rescue the project. Even if the employer is already the assignee of the benefit of existing sub-contracts, this will be of little use where the sub-contractors are no longer obliged to perform. A receiver appointed over the contractor will also be handicapped because any assignment of the benefit of a sub-contract as part of a novation package will be of limited value to a purchaser after the sub-contractor's employment has been terminated. In this situation, however, the automatic termination of sub-contracts may assist the employer in approaching the sub-contractors direct without risk of a claim by the receiver based on the tort of interference with contract: compare *Remm Construction* v *Allco* (1990) 53 SASR 471, discussed in Chapter 4.

Checklist of steps for sub-contracts

1. Use the same terminology in the main and sub-contracts.

2. Make sure the sub-contract accurately reflects the processes of the main contract.

3. Ensure the sub-contract anticipates a main contract repudiation as well as contractual termination.

4. Ensure the sub-contract termination procedure can be activated whoever terminates the main contract.

5. Be careful when using an engineering sub-contract form with a building main contract form and vice versa.

6. Ensure a sub-contract termination can be activated even if the main contract termination is disputed.

Post-termination rights

The consequential rights given by termination clauses are of very long standing and have generally been upheld by the court. They derive from building leases and infrastructure contracts in the first half of the 19th century, *e.g. Roach* v *Great Western Railway* (1841) 1 QB 51. The major benefit to the employer is a major change in its payment obligation: (1) the duty to pay is suspended and then postponed until after the final account of the completion contractor has been agreed, (2) the suspension then supports two further changes to the employer's duty, in that (3) it is made contingent on there being a net amount due to the contractor after setting off the cost to complete against the outstanding balance of the contract sum, and (4) to the extent that the employer makes direct payments, the duty to pay the contractor is converted into the rights to pay sub-contractors and suppliers and to set off equivalent amounts against the contractor (see Chapter 12).

The full range of consequential rights is as follows:

- to repossess the site
- to make alternative arrangements for completion of the work by engaging a completion contractor
- to suspend further payments to the contractor until after the works have been completed and a final accounting exercise has been done
- to use the contractor's plant, equipment and materials for the completion of the works
- to use designs whose copyright is vested in the contractor or others
- to call a demand bond
- to forfeit a security deposit, trust account or escrow account
- to set off the cost to complete and losses following termination against the balance of the contract sum and any other monies due or to become due to the contractor
- to pay sub-contractors, suppliers and leasing companies direct and set the payments off against money due to the contractor
- to compel the assignment of all contracts entered into by the contractor with others relating to the works
- to sell materials and plant after the works have been completed and set off their value against the loss caused to the employer by the termination

- to require the contractor to remove unwanted items, such as site accommodation, or to sell them if the contractor fails to do so
- to forfeit extracted material which would otherwise belong to the contractor
- to deem money already paid to the contractor as having been received in full and final satisfaction of all claims under the contract
- to deduct liquidated damages from sums due to the contractor until the works are finally completed.

Possession of the site

A contractor is entitled to exclusive possession of the site while it carries out the work. If its employment is terminated it can no longer carry out the work. The employer would say that it follows that the contractor must leave the site. If the contractor resists it may apply to the court for an injunction preventing the employer from removing it, or the employer may seek an injunction ordering the contractor to leave. Such orders are treated as specific performance of the contract. When hearing applications for specific performance, the court pays particular regard to the nature of the project and the reasons for termination.

Outside an insolvency situation, the court has often refused specific performance of construction contracts on the following grounds: damages would be an adequate remedy, the works to be done were not sufficiently defined, the court could not supervise them, if the employer wanted to abandon the project it should not be forced to continue, the balance of convenience or the merits were against the applicant, or the court could not form a view on them without a full trial. Even so, the court has a discretion to order specific performance of a building contract and will do so where it thinks it appropriate: *Wolverhampton Corporation* v *Emmons* [1901] 1 KB 515.

During the 19th century, orders for specific performance were consistently made in two situations:

1. In consideration of the sale of land on which to lay track, railway companies promised to build roads or bridges for the land owner connecting the severed parts of the estate.

2. In consideration of the construction of houses on its land, an owner promised to convey an interest in the land to the builder on completion.

In the first case, the works were part of the consideration for the grant of the land. In the second, the grant of land was consideration for the works (Jones and Goodhart 1996). The same would apply to a sale of land where the vendor agreed to lay drains and sewers on her own land for the benefit of the land being transferred: *Carpenter's Estates* v *Davies* [1940] Ch 160.

In the ordinary situation where the works are not connected with a grant of land by or to the builder, it is hard to lay down any general principles. The court has refused to grant an injunction ordering the contractor to leave site following termination of its employment: *London Borough of Hounslow* v *Twickenham Garden* [1971] Ch 233. Most later decisions have gone the other way, and the criteria for an injunction have since been lowered, making it easier for the employer to remove the contractor in this situation (Lightman & Moss 1994). Where the works are ongoing, however, the case will be decided on its merits. In *Channel Tunnel Group* v *Balfour Beatty* (unreported, 27 November 1991), the contractor threatened to suspend part of the works unless it was paid for a substantial variation. At first instance the court made it clear that, had the contractor not given an undertaking to give at least 14 days' notice of any cessation of work, it would have granted an injunction restraining the contractor from suspending (*i.e.* ordering him to continue) the work. The suspension would have had "vast financial consequences" for the employer for whom damages would not have been an adequate remedy. The work in question was well defined, and the injunction would be primarily effective to stop the suspension being instructed at management level. The Court of Appeal would also have granted an injunction had it not concluded that the English court lacked the jurisdiction to make it: (1992) 56 BLR 18 at 41. The House of Lords acknowledged that the injunction would have been equivalent to an order for specific performance, but the employer failed on jurisdictional grounds: (1993) 61 BLR 38. The law on specific performance was reviewed by the House of Lords in *Co-Operative Insurance* v *Argyll Stores* [1997] 2 WLR 898. A distinction was drawn between ordering a person to carry out a contract "to achieve a result" and "to carry on activities" such as running a business. A construction contract would fall within the former category and therefore remain capable of an order of specific performance if justified by the circumstances.

If the contractor is insolvent, two questions arise:

1. Could the employer obtain an order that the contractor complete the works?

2. Could the contractor force the employer to continue the contract and prevent the employer re-entering the site?

In *Macleod* v *Alexander Sutherland* (1977) SLT 44, a contractor bought land and covenanted with the vendor to carry out works on it. This is the reverse of the situation in *Carpenter's Estates* v *Davies*. The contractor went into receivership and the court refused to order the receiver to complete the works as it would involve expenditure for which the receiver might become personally liable. In *Anders* v *O/Y Lovisa Stevedoring* [1985] STC 301 at 306, it was stated that:

> "Commercial life would be subjected to new and unjust hazards if the court were to decree specific performance of contracts normally sounding only in damages, simply because of a party's insolvency".

There are few English cases in this context. In the Canadian case of *Grayson-Robinson* v *Iris Construction* (1960) 168 NE 2(d) 377, the court ordered a land owner to construct part of a shopping centre and grant a lease even though there was evidence that 27 lending institutions had refused to advance the construction cost against a mortgage of the property. Where the works are being carried out other than on the employer's land, the court has refused specific performance of a right of entry on to the contractor's premises in order to complete them: *Merchants' Trading* v *Banner* (1871) LR 12 Eq 18 (a shipbuilding case).

If the insolvency practitioner can satisfy the court that the contractor has the resources to complete the works, would the contractor be entitled to specific performance of the employer's obligations? As the employer's obligation is primarily to pay certified sums, the position ought to be simpler than an order to complete the works. Perhaps an order against the employer would be possible if it could be shown that the contractor could only obtain a grant of property from the employer or a third party where it had completed the work. This is analogous to relief from forfeiture.

Relief is available only where the rights under forfeiture are proprietary or possessory rather than contractual: *Sport International* v *Inter-Footwear* [1984] 2 All ER 321. Relief was granted in *Underground (Civil Engineering) Ltd* v *London Borough of Croydon* (1990) BLM 7, where the contractor was to be entitled to a 125-year lease within one month after practical completion. The contract allowed the employer to re-enter and take possession of the contractor's plant and materials if the contractor failed to complete within 12 months or such extended period as the contract allowed. The contractor failed to complete in time because it had ceased work on learning from the employer that the site was to be compulsorily purchased. Nevertheless, the employer re-entered when only three weeks' work was outstanding. The court held that the termination clause was not a penalty but did grant relief from forfeiture.

> "I am persuaded by counsel for the corporation that in an ordinary building contract the licence granted by the building owner to the builder is for the benefit of the owner as opposed to giving the builder any kind of 'beneficial' right or interest in the land. For that reason I do not consider that a builder in such a case would have a possessory or proprietary right such as would give the court jurisdiction to grant relief: the builder would have a 'mere' licence. In other words, the requirement in the authorities binding on this court that the jurisdiction to grant relief from forfeiture arises only in relation to contracts concerning the transfer of proprietary or possessory rights is not satisfied in an ordinary building contract. There are a number of features in this agreement which distinguish it from an ordinary building agreement. Although to an extent one can say that the agreement is in two separate parts, for the purpose of deciding whether the court has jurisdiction to grant relief, the whole document must be construed as one agreement. The company went into occupation of the land with a view to becoming a long leaseholder of it. It had an insurable interest in the building. It had the right to specific performance of the corporation's obligation to grant the lease. It had the right to use the agreement as security for financial arrangements. It was required to observe the provisions of the lease as if it had been granted. Thus, as it seems to me, under this agreement, when the company goes into occupation it does so for its own benefit as well as for the benefit of the corporation. None of these factors would apply in the case of an ordinary building contract. To hold that the concept applied in this case would not, in my judgment, breach the principle which determines where the boundary fence should be drawn. By reason of the factors just referred to I take the view that the company was granted sufficient interest in the land and building thereon to satisfy the 'possessory or proprietary interest' requirement and that the concept of relief from forfeiture applies in this case."

Where the employer is insolvent, issues arise whether: (1) the employer can force the contractor to complete the works, and (2) the contractor can force the employer to continue the contract by preventing it regaining possession of the site. The court is not likely to order a contractor to work for an insolvent employer, at least in the absence of a secure mechanism for payment. If the receiver of the employer decides not to complete the project, specific performance will not be ordered against him: *Munroe* v *Wivenhoe & Brightlingsea Railway* (1855) LT 655. This is under the principle that the court will not grant specific performance if it would mean forcing an employer to accept a building or a contractor it no longer wished to have. If the property market is such that the receiver decides to suspend the project, pending an improvement in the situation, the position is less clear. A contractor can improve its prospects of retaining possession of the site by electing not to terminate its employment or deciding to affirm the contract if the employer is in repudiation. In this situation, contractors sometimes say they are exercising a "builder's lien". In English law, however, there is no lien whether possessory or non-possessory. In America and Canada, contractors have rights to a lien in certain circumstances, but this affects the title to the land and does not confer any right to remain in possession (Odams 1996).

Assignment of sub-contracts

It is important for the employer to have direct access to the sub-contractors on the contractor's insolvency. Construction contracts often provide that after termination the contractor is obliged to assign to the employer the benefit of any contracts with sub-contractors or suppliers. This could be useful to the employer as until these contracts are terminated the sub-contractors or suppliers are bound to perform them. This device is only likely to work where the sub-contractor has been paid up to date and has no other claim against the contractor at the date of receipt of notice of assignment from the employer. The device will not work where the sub-contract automatically terminates on termination of the main contract or has a non-assignability clause. Before Amendment 11 (1992), JCT contracts provided that the employer could then assign the benefit although the sub-contractor was given the right to object to a further assignment: *e.g.* clause 27.4.2.1 of JCT 80. This reflected the purpose of the clause, namely to enable the employer to assign the benefit of the sub-contract to the replacement contractor. The Australian JCC-1994 forms supplement compulsory assignment by making the employer the contractor's attorney, allowing it to execute the assignment on the builder's behalf.

As the benefit of contracts with third parties falls within the wide definition of "property" in s 436 Insolvency Act 1986, the enforced assignment on bankruptcy or liquidation is invalid in contravening the *pari passu* rule. The position would be different if before bankruptcy or liquidation the contractor had declared a trust of the benefit of its sub-contracts to the employer (see Chapter 6). Still more problematic are terms which enforce a novation following a contractor's insolvency. As novation requires the consent of employer, contractor and sub-contractor, it is not possible in the main contract to enforce a novation without the sub-contractor's consent (see Chapter 10). Further, as the identity of the replacement contractor is not established until after the contractor's default and the terms of the proposed novation are usually not prescribed, the agreement may be void for uncertainty. The normal solution is to require the sub-contractors to enter into direct agreements with the employer at the inception of the project with draft forms of novation annexed.

Liquidated damages

After the works have been completed by an alternative contractor, can the employer claim liquidated damages to the date of completion from the insolvent contractor? The answer is usually "no" because it would be beyond the contractor's power to stop damages running and within the power of the employer to continue them by delaying completion. In *British Glanzstoff* v *General Accident* [1913] AC 143 the date for completion under the completion contract was one month before the date for completion under the original contract but the works were not completed until after the latter date. It was held that the termination clause allowing the employer to re-enter the site after the contractor's bankruptcy was incompatible with an entitlement to liquidated damages, which could only apply where the works had been finished by the original contractor (see also *Chanthall Investments* v *F G Minter* [1976] SC 73, Burke (1986) at 84-85). Where the works are completed by another contractor following an acceptance of a repudiation "time ceases to have relevance. Damages thereafter flow from the repudiation resulting from non-performance and the need to provide for substituted performance": *Bovis* v *Whatlings Contractors* (1995) 75 BLR 1 at 9. In other words, the employer can only recover liquidated damages up to the date of the repudiation. As was pointed out in *Tower Housing* v *Technical & General Guarantee* (1997) 87 BLR 82 at 94,

> "the revenue predicted by the contractual rate might have materialised for reasons unconnected with the determination or it might in fact be less

than the contractual rate used (the contractor's obligation under clause 26 to pay liquidated damages is of course replaced by the code in clause 27: Perar) even if the rate were representative of loss of return on capital employed it would have to be justified as being the actual loss caused to be recoverable under clause 27.6.6.1".

The terms of both original and completion contracts are crucial and can in context allow the employer to recover liquidated damages even if the contract is completed by another person. Where the works were completed by the contractor's guarantor and the agreement between the guarantor and the employer provided that the original contract was to remain in being as if the completion contract had not been made, the employer was entitled to deduct liquidated damages from retention: *Re Yeadon Waterworks* (1895) 72 LT 832. This is so even if the delay was caused by the original contractor and not the guarantor: damages could be deducted until the works were completed by the guarantor. In *Baylis v Mayor of the City of Wellington* (1886) 4 NZLR 84 an employer was allowed to deduct liquidated damages even where the works were completed by another contractor. The original contractor abandoned the works but instead of accepting the contractor's repudiation, the employer terminated under an express clause which entitled it to damages in respect of the period of delay before the abandonment and during the completion contract but not the time taken mobilising the completion contractor. In an Australian case where the majority of the work had been performed and the contractor left site in the mistaken belief that completion had been achieved, the employer had the works completed by another contractor and it was held entitled to liquidated damages against the original contractor to the date of completion: *Williamson v Murdoch* [1912] WAR 54.

Suspension of payments

One of the most valuable rights given to an employer after termination is the right to suspend payment to the contractor of sums which are already due and payable: *Thomas Construction v Grafton Furniture* [1986] 4 SA 510 at 519-520, affirmed [1988] 2 SA 546. This right prevents the receiver from arguing that the cost to complete and any consequential losses could not exceed a given proportion of the claim and obtaining summary judgment or an interim payment. This effectively frustrates the collection of book debts by a receiver. The suspension of payment only relates to sums payable by the employer. If the contractor were liable for liquidated damages before the termination, the employer could recover them even before the cost to complete had been ascertained: *Tower Housing* v *Technical & General Guarantee* (1997) 87 BLR 82 at 94.

There are two exceptions. First, payment is not suspended under the clause where automatic termination occurs after practical completion: *Emson Eastern* v *EME Developments* (1992) 55 BLR 114. Secondly, there is an implied term in JCT 80 that where a contractor goes into administrative receivership and the employer abandons the project rather than engaging a completion contractor the suspension of payments under clause 27 should come to an end: *Tern Construction* v *RBS Garages* (1992) 34 Con LR 137. The employer is liable thereafter to pay previously certified sums. This situation is now dealt with by clause 27.7 of JCT 98.

What happens where termination occurs between the issue of a cheque and its payment? If the employer stops the cheque, it is arguable that it would be unjust to allow the contractor the benefit of the normal rule that there is no defence to a claim brought on a cheque other than fraud or failure of consideration: *Willment Brothers* v *North West Thames RHA* (1984) 26 BLR 51 at 64. The contractor may defend by arguing that the suspension is void on the ground that the termination clause infringed the *pari passu* rule. This point is discussed later in this chapter.

Security deposits

The contractor may have to deposit a sum of money with the employer as security for performance of the contract: *Official Assignee* v *Mayor of City of Wellington* [1885] 3 NZLR 159, *Goodman* v *Napier Harbour Board* [1939] NZLR 97, *Amman Aviation* v *Commonwealth of Australia* [1988] 92 ALR 601 at 606, 626, 649. This may be in addition to other forms of security which have been provided, *e.g.* bonds and guarantees. Security deposits are an effective form of security to employers: *Public Bank* v *Perbadanan* [1980] 1 MLJ 214, compare *Kratzmann* v *University of Queensland* [1982] Qd R 682. They are a feature of the Australian standard forms. In the UK a cash deposit is more common in support of a counter-indemnity to an insurance company in respect of a surety bond than as security for performance of the contract. Occasionally the forfeiture of a deposit has been held to be a penalty: *Bysouth* v *Shire of Blackburn* [1928]

VLR 562 at 574, Beale (1988). It is important to specify how an advance payment is to be taken into account. In *John Dee* v *WMH (21) Limited* [1997] BCC 518, affirmed [1998] BCC 972, the contract provided for a down payment and two kinds of monthly payments, one in advance and the other in arrears. The contract was silent on how the down payment was to be taken into account. It was held that in context it was not a payment on account of the other types of charge, but a kind of security deposit repayable only on completion or termination of the contract.

Copyright

Outside insolvency, the issue is likely to be whether a work qualifies for copyright protection under the Copyright Designs and Patents Act 1988 or whether copyright has in fact been infringed. In insolvency, the questions turn on the ownership of the work and the extent to which third parties have acquired rights in it. Copyright subsists independent of registration in plans and drawings, models for buildings and buildings themselves (artistic copyright) and in reports, explanations on plans and drawings and computer software (literary copyright), but not in the construction process. An employer who pays for the work will become the owner of it but he does not acquire an interest in the copyright in the absence of specific agreement, *e.g.* outright assignment, a licence or by way of security. However, he will usually have an implied licence to use the plans etc for the purpose for which they were prepared and in accordance with them. Similarly, a contractor has an implied licence in respect of work created by a sub-contractor and so on (Wheeler 1991).

The RIBA form of agreement between client and architect (SFA/92) gives the employer the right to copy the architect's design where he has completed the design and all his fees have been paid, but it does not explain the consequences of non-payment. One writer considers that payment is a condition precedent to copyright under this form (Delemore 1994, at 95, 107). The same point arises under the CIOB Facilities Management Contract (1999) under which the facilities manager grants an irrevocable copyright licence to the client "subject to the client having paid all sums due" under the agreement. It is not clear whether the licence is irrevocable once granted even if the client stops paying or whether its irrevocability is conditional on the client continuing to pay. The position is clearer in SFA/99 which expressly allows the architect to suspend the licence for non-payment on giving seven days notice. "Use of the licence may be resumed on receipt of outstanding amounts" (clause 6.2.3). There is also an absolute non-assignability clause. This is very valuable in this context. The ACE Conditions (2nd edition, 1998) allow the engineer to revoke the licence for non-payment on seven days' notice (clause 7.1).

How is the implied licence affected by the insolvency of the licensee? In *Hunter* v *Fitzroy Robinson* (1977) 10 BLR 84, an architect was owed £46,000 for design work to an existing building which remained outstanding when the employer went into receivership. The receiver sold the building and its associated business to a purchaser who engaged other architects to complete the project. The architect failed in an application to prevent the new firm using part of his original design. It was strongly arguable that the original employer had an implied licence which had been assigned to the purchaser. Even if the assignment were subject to the architect's claim for payment, he could suffer no loss by allowing the building to be completed, and could pursue his claim for payment at the trial (at 93). The case highlights the negative nature of copyright. The architect could only try and prevent his design being used. He could not assert his debt as a claim against the new owner; he could only use it as a defence to a claim brought by the purchaser based on the assignment, but there was no need for the purchaser to bring such a claim. Even if the architect recovered damages for infringement at the trial, he could still not recover his original debt. By refusing the injunction, the court prevented the architect from using copyright as a commercial bargaining counter to recover a pre-receivership debt. Had the application been brought by the new owner (*e.g.* for delivery-up of the designs themselves), the position might have been different. Also, had there been a non-assignability clause in the architect's retainer, he could have required payment of the pre-receivership debt as a condition of an assignment to the purchaser. A similar situation arose in the receivership of Land & Property Trust, before the site had been sold, although the issue was settled between the parties (Wheeler 1994).

Ng v *Clyde Securities* [1976] 1 NSWLR 443 is an Australian case on similar facts. An architect submitted a proof of debt for unpaid fees in the liquidation of a developer but a dividend was unlikely. He therefore sued the mortgagee of the development, who had gone into possession, in an attempt to use his copyright as a lever to recover his pre-liquidation debt, but failed. Once granted, the licence was irrevocable and it had passed to the mortgagee pursuant to the developer's implied right to assign.

"The withdrawal of the licence would not merely affect the future activities of the licensee, but, by preventing the completion of a building, would render valueless what might be an enormous past investment in the building. Looking at the matter in terms of business efficacy, I find it unthinkable that an owner would agree to a licence revocable if a possibly temporary difficulty prevented him from paying his architect at the agreed time. Unless an architect expressly stipulated for such a devastating right of revocation to enforce actual payment, it is more reasonable to regard him as giving the licence in return for a debt recoverable, if unpaid, by ordinary litigious processes. He is essentially selling something, *viz*, his plans and a licence to build in accordance with them, in return for a promise of future payment, and the ordinary basis of a sale is that it gives the vendor a right in the event of non-payment to sue for recovery of the purchase price, not a right to deprive the purchaser of the enjoyment of the object sold, or to complain of the use by the purchaser of the article sold prior to payment for it" (at 446).

The effect of a repudiation of the architect's retainer on a copyright licence of this kind has not been formally considered by the English court, but dicta suggest that the view in *Ng* v *Clyde Securities* may well be followed: see *Stovin-Bradford* v *Volpoint* [1971] Ch 1007 at 1018. The licence will probably be regarded as a right vested in the licensee which neither a repudiation nor a termination under the contract could destroy.

In *High Mark* v *Patco Malaysia* (1984) 28 BLR 129 a turnkey contract was terminated at the completion of the design stage but before work had commenced on site. The court granted an injunction to the contractor restraining the employer from using drawings prepared by consultants engaged as sub-contractors and from entering into direct contracts with them. The position might have been different had the construction work already been under way. From a practical point of view, infringement of copyright in this area is perhaps not as serious as in others: the designer is unlikely to be able to prevent the building being constructed as damages would normally be an adequate remedy (*Hunter* v *Fitzroy Robinson* (1977) 10 BLR 84), and damages will probably be limited to a fair fee for the licence (*Charles Church* v *Cronin* [1990] FSR 1).

Final accounts

The insolvency of a contractor mid-way through a project can cause substantial delays and increase in cost. It may be several years before an insolvency practitioner will know whether there will be a net balance payable in favour of the contractor. In one case, a receiver had to wait three years before the contractor's final account was agreed. The account showed a balance due to the contractor of part of its retention but this was successfully claimed by a prior assignee: *Earle* v *Hemsworth RDC* (1929) 140 LT 69.

The standard forms differ in their approach to the ascertainment of the employer's loss. Broadly, they take two different approaches:

1. The employer's losses are added to the amount already paid to the contractor and then both are deducted from the amount which would have been payable to the contractor had it completed the contract in accordance with its terms (clause 27.4.4 of JCT 80).

2. The employer's losses are added to the amount already paid to the contractor and both are deducted from the value of the contractor's works as at the date of termination (clause 57(2) of GC/Works/1).

The second approach is vulnerable to attack as a penalty because it fails to bring into account the balance of the contract sum: *Corporation of the City of Adelaide* v *Jennings Industries* [1984] 156 CLR 274 at 294. The usual measure of damages for failure to complete is the difference between the cost to complete and the balance of the contract sum: *Mertens* v *Home Freeholds* [1921] 2 KB 526, *Ventura* v *Svirac* [1961] WAR 63.

The question arises whether any of these provisions contravene the *pari passu* rule. Where the contractor's property is used as payment for the cost to complete, the procedure is confiscatory because the employer would always have had to pay the completion cost whether the contractor's employment were terminated or not. This has been described as "too greedy an approach to take on a termination clause" (Carter 1990 at 117). This is the reason why standard forms require a notional final account to be drawn up of what would have been due to the contractor had it completed the works. The liquidator is not entitled to re-write the contract and, subject to the *pari passu* rule, is bound by its terms: *Re Scheibler, ex parte Holthausen* (1874) LR 9 Ch App 722 at 726. The position seems to be that no challenge can be made to the employer's set-off provided it is restricted to non-confiscatory items, *e.g.* expense flowing from the termination. Similarly, there is nothing objectionable in the suspension of payment, unless conceivably the absence of liability for interest during the period of suspension could taint it. These issues are reviewed in the South African case of *Thomas Construction* v *Grafton Furniture* [1988] 2 SA 546.

Where the general law is not excluded, the employer is entitled to abate the amount which would have been payable to the insolvent contractor by the value of any defective work: *Lintest Builders* v *Roberts* (1978) 10 BLR 120, affirmed (1980) 13 BLR 38. An employer who wrongfully repudiates a contract is entitled to abate the contractor's claim by the value of defective work carried out before the termination: *Slater* v *Duquemin* (1992) 29 Con LR 24. In JCT Practice Note 24 it is stated that the reference to verification of accounts within a reasonable time in clause 27.4.4 of JCT 80 means agreement with the insolvency practitioner or his representatives (at 33). In *Kennedy* v *Collings Construction* (1991) 7 BCL 25 at 43 the court allowed a set-off for rent, the cost to complete and a bank charge. In *Ferguson* v *Sohl* [1992] *The Times*, 24 December, a completion contractor finished the works for less than the original contract sum after the original contract had been repudiated. Despite this, the Court of Appeal allowed the employer's claim for an over-payment before the repudiation. In assessing damages for repudiation, the court takes into account that a business has spare capacity during a recession. In *Western Webb Offset Printers* v *Independent Media* [1995/6] CILL 1122, the Court of Appeal allowed the innocent party to recover its gross profit without making any reduction for labour costs and overheads.

Deemed settlement

Some contracts provide that payments previously made to the contractor shall be deemed to be the full value of its work executed to the date of termination and accepted by the contractor in full and final satisfaction of all claims: *Davies* v *Mayor, Aldermen and Burgesses of Swansea* (1853) 22 LJ Ex 297, *Goodman* v *Napier Harbour Board* [1939] NZLR 97. In *Roach* v *Great Western Railway Company* (1841) 1 QB 51 this was to be the position even if no payments had been made at all. A clause of this type has been held to be a penalty (*Bysouth* v *Shire of Blackburn* [1928] VLR 562), and is not found in the standard forms. However, a term that on termination for insolvency the contractor should accept all sums previously paid together with all sums then payable in full satisfaction of its claims was upheld in *Thiess Watkins White* v *Commonwealth of Australia* (1998) 14 BCL 61. Under the Australian NWPC3 (1981) form, on the contractor's insolvency the employer has the option of taking over the works or cancelling the contract. Under the former, there is an accounting under which the employer gives credit for all sums received on account of its loss, including proceeds of bond calls or sums owed to the contractor. But if the contract is cancelled, the employer becomes entitled to forfeit all cash deposits and bonds without having to account for the excess they may represent over its actual loss.

> "That may work to the advantage of the [employer], but it will work to its disadvantage if it thereafter discovers that the extra cost of completing the work exceeds the amount forfeited. There is no later accounting between them. In this way the [employer] and the contractor agree upon a means by which there can be an immediate end to their relationship. There will be a clean break in which the contractor knows where it stands and the [employer] takes the risk that it will be worse off than if it had taken over the work rather than cancel the contract. The result may be arbitrary but it is understandable that the bargain of the parties should include it" (at 76).

In the 19th century the employer expressly reserved the right to forfeit extracted material which would otherwise belong to the contractor: *Garrett v Banstead Downs and Epsom Downs Railway Company* (1865) 12 LT 654.

Validity of termination clauses

In practice, the validity of a termination clause which takes effect on bankruptcy or liquidation is taken for granted (*Re Sneezum, ex parte Davis* (1876) 3 Ch D 463 at 471, *Shipton v Micks, Lambert & Co* [1936] 2 All ER 1032), but there is little direct authority and the question probably remains open for argument (Totty and Crystal 1982). The issue is whether the clause has the effect of confiscating the contractor's property in breach of the *pari passu* rule. Section 436 Insolvency Act 1986 defines "property" as including

> "money, goods, things in action, land and every description of property wherever situate and also obligations and every description of interest, whether present, or future or vested or contingent, arising out of, incidental to, property".

The benefit of a contract falls squarely within "things in action". In the absence of a termination clause, a contractor would have had a claim for damages if the employer had re-entered the site on its liquidation.

Re Walker, ex parte Barter (1884) 25 Ch D 510 concerned a contract to build a ship which provided that all materials bought or ordered for the ship should become the property of the buyer subject to the builder's lien for unpaid purchase money. On default by the builder, or on his bankruptcy, the buyer could enter the builder's yard and employ others to complete the ship using the builder's materials for that purpose. The Court of Appeal held that the contract vested materials in the buyer as soon as they were bought or ordered for the ship but that on the facts there were grounds to justify an inquiry whether, after the builder's bankruptcy, the buyer had used other materials which had belonged to the builder but were now vested in the trustee. On that assumption, the Court of Appeal decided that seizure and user clauses would have been invalidated by insolvency law:

> "But, in our opinion, a power upon bankruptcy to control the user after bankruptcy of property vested in the bankrupt at the date of the bankruptcy is invalid. ... It was strenuously argued before us that the clause in question is clearly for the benefit, and not to the detriment, of the creditors, because, it is said, the completion of the ship will lessen the amount for which the [buyer] might otherwise prove against the bankrupt's estate. But this argument appears to us fallacious, because, in the absence of the clause in question, the trustee in the bankruptcy would have had the election to complete the ship or not as might seem best for the creditors, but the presence of this clause has transferred that election to the buyer, and put them in possession of a power to complete the ship when the trustee might prefer to abandon it" (at 519).

There is a long line of cases invalidating clauses allowing the employer to seize and use the contractor's goods after bankruptcy, but this is the only authority which invalidates the employer's right of re-entry in that event. The court did not construe the right of re-entry as a forfeiture of property but as a removal of the trustee's right to elect whether to complete the contract or not. The decision may be distinguished from liquidation since, unlike a trustee in bankruptcy, a liquidator is not personally vested with the company's property. The case concerned a trustee's claim to goods and it may be that the court's decision on the right of re-entry was *obiter*: even if the re-entry had been valid, the seizure of the goods would not have been.

If *Re Walker* is correct, and extends to liquidation, the termination clauses in the standard forms are void as against a contractor's trustee or liquidator. It is hard to see any difference between a right of re-entry and the termination of the contractor's employment. The respective positions of the parties would be as follows. The other person could (1) apply to the court to rescind the contract under s 186 Insolvency Act 1986, or (2) if the liquidator will not undertake to meet current and future obligations, accept the liquidator's conduct as repudiatory and claim damages, or (3) apply to the liquidator requiring him to decide whether he intends to disclaim under s 178(5) Insolvency Act 1986. The liquidator could (1) disclaim the contract as onerous property under s 178 Insolvency Act 1986, or (2) if the other person has committed a repudiatory breach, accept the repudiation and claim damages, or (3) claim specific performance of the contract.

Challenges to Re Walker

The invalidity of a termination clause may only become important to the employer where the liquidator decides to continue the contract against its wishes. This occurs so rarely that it has never become necessary to challenge *Re Walker*. The first point to consider is whether the termination clause is simply a limit placed by the employer on property granted to the contractor.

> "The general distinction seems to be that the owner of property may, on alienation, qualify the interest of his alienee by a condition to take effect on bankruptcy; but cannot, by contract or otherwise, qualify his own interest by a like condition, determining or controlling it in the event of his own bankruptcy, to the disappointment or delay of his creditors" *Whitmore* v *Mason* (1861) 2 J & H 204 at 210.

On this principle, a clause terminating a lease on the tenant's liquidation has been held valid: *Civil Service Co-Operative Society* v *Trustee of McGrigor* [1923] 2 Ch 347. An employer under a construction contract grants exclusive possession to the contractor. This has been analysed as a contractual licence to the site: *London Borough of Hounslow* v *Twickenham Garden* [1971] 1 Ch 233. It would follow that the right of re-entry in *Re Walker* was an implied revocation of that licence. The difficulty with this reasoning is that *Whitmore* v *Mason* seems to have contemplated the grant of an interest in property.

Another perhaps more convincing challenge to *Re Walker* is that

> "in 'ordinary contracts' it is difficult to identify who is the owner of what. So long as there are unperformed obligations by either person, they are both creditors or 'owners' of each other's obligations. There is therefore simply no occasion for invoking the rule that any owner of property could limit his grantee's interests. Rather, acceleration and rescission clauses are built-in limitations on each party's entitlement to the other's unperformed obligations" (Oditah 1992 at 499).

In other words the contractor's right to continue the works is conditional on the absence of the employer's right to terminate: *Laing and Morrison-Knudson* v *Aegon Insurance* (1997) 86 BLR 70 at 112.

This raises the question of the effect of *British Eagle* v *Air France* [1975] 1 WLR 758 (see Chapter 12). In his article in the *Law Quarterly Review*, Dr Fidelis Oditah comments that:

> "the decision remains very difficult to understand. ... If one were to pursue *British Eagle* to its logical end many contractual self-help remedies, particularly those encountered in building contracts, will not survive the insolvency of the builder" (Oditah, 1992 at 466).

It is useful to compare the effect of *British Eagle* on termination clauses and direct payment clauses (see Chapter 12). There is a line of authority holding that direct payment clauses are valid as an in-built limitation on the contractor's right to payment. But there is another, and more persuasive, line which holds them invalid, since in substance they acknowledge there is a sum due to the contractor but subject to set-off after liquidation in respect of amounts paid direct to sub-contractors. When applied to termination clauses, the first line of argument is the more convincing.

It has been held that the *pari passu* rule can also apply in context to the administration procedure. An administrator may therefore be able to rely upon *Re Walker* and resist the termination of the contractor's employment on its entry into administration. The administrator might also argue that the termination clause, and in particular the employer's consequential rights conferred by the clause, is in the nature of a security and can only be enforced with his permission or with leave of the court (Carter 1990). If termination clauses on administration are valid, it has been argued that they should be invalidated by statute, at least where the contractor is not otherwise in default (Homan 1989). The *pari passu* rule does not apply to receivership under a fixed or a floating charge. The employer's right to terminate is an equity subject to which the contractor's assets pass to a charge-holder on the crystallisation of a floating charge (see Chapter 13).

Checklist of steps before termination

Consider the contract:

- does it have a termination clause which covers the situation?
- does it preserve common law rights?

- what procedural requirements have to be followed?
- is there time to follow them?
- does the termination clause confer adequate compensation rights?
- is someone else's permission needed before the notice of termination can be served?
- what effect will the termination have on sub-contracts or associated contracts?

What is the common law position:

- how are common law rights affected by the contract?
- is the termination event relied on a repudiatory or other breach of contract?
- how much time has gone by since the breach occurred?
- could you already have affirmed the contract?
- what documents are available to support your position?
- what oral evidence could be given to support your contentions?
- could you have accepted repudiation already informally, *e.g.* at a meeting, in course of a letter on another topic, by issuing proceedings, by not continuing your side of the contract etc.

Keeping options open:

- what rights have already accrued (on both sides)?
- is it better to wait until further rights accrue due?
- are the breaches remediable or not?
- can a letter terminating under the contract be widely expressed so as to also act as acceptance of repudiation?
- what are the knock on effects of terminating under the contract or accepting repudiation as far as bonds, guarantees, insurance and warranties are concerned?

Conclusion

Termination for insolvency raises complex questions on the relation between express terms and (1) the common law of repudiation, and (2) the *pari passu* rule under insolvency law. The court seems to have adopted different criteria for the exclusion of the common law in this area from others, *e.g.* set-off. This is an undesirable development and causes uncertainty. A number of questions remain on the position where a termination event is also a repudiatory breach. The court has stated that insolvency can in context be an anticipatory breach, but it is hard to predict when this will be the case. Termination clauses operating on bankruptcy and liquidation, and possibly administration, are void according to 19th century case law. In practice, however, they are almost always treated as valid by insolvency practitioners and by the court. The question arises whether *Re Walker* would be decided the same way today, and as to its real effect. The employer's extensive post-termination rights, notably suspension of payment, effectively postpone the realisation of construction receivables and work in progress until the entire project has been completed by an alternative contractor. There may be a case for crediting the insolvency practitioner with interest from the date of termination on these amounts.

Chapter 10

Novation and
Completion Contracts

Introduction

The leading work on the law of contract devotes nearly 40 pages to assignment but only one to novation (Chitty 1994). In practice they are both important. The law developed in a series of cases involving the dissolution of partnerships and the transfer of business between insurance companies. The issue was whether liability for a debt had been transferred. In *Rouse* v *Bradford Banking* [1894] 2 Ch 32 at 53, novation was described as "a substitution of debtors". As with the law of assignment and security, it is sometimes difficult to apply the principles from these debt cases to the complex terms found in construction contracts.

Novation is currently used in a wide range of situations in the industry. Most commonly, it is the means of transferring to a contractor prior contracts entered into by the employer with consultants, nominated sub-contractors and, formerly, quantity surveyors: see *North* v *Bassett* [1892] 1 QB 333. Other examples are arrangements whereby the employer, the contractor or a sub-subcontractor agrees to novate its contract to a funder in certain situations and on an insolvency where novation is the preferred vehicle for transferring contracts to a purchaser. This chapter also reviews other means whereby an employer can procure a completion contract following the insolvency of the contractor.

Nature of novation

It may be useful at the outset to compare novation with other processes such as assignment, sub-contracting, dissolution and subrogation.

Assignment differs from novation in three important respects:

1. Assignment is a transfer of rights under a contract which continues to exist after the assignment: novation brings an existing contract to an end and creates a new one in its place (*Scarf* v *Jardine* (1882) 7 App Cas 345 at 351).

2. Assignment can only transfer the benefit of a contract: under a novation with all parties' consent the burden can also be transferred: such a transfer is not an assignment of the burden but a novation of the contract.

3. Consideration is not generally required for an assignment but is necessary on a novation as a new contract is being formed: consideration is normally implicit in a novation agreement.

A sub-contract is the delegation of work to another by a separate contract. The sub-contract does not release the contractor from liability for that work under the main contract. The main contract is not terminated or the benefit assigned. Nor does the sub-contractor assume any contractual liability direct to the employer as there is no privity. A sub-contract is not a substitute for part or whole of the main contract.

The dissolution of a construction company transfers its property to the Crown as *bona vacantia* but the Crown does not assume the company's obligations or accept any active duties regarding the property. If the company is later restored to the register under s 651 or 653 Companies Act 1985, its property is transferred back to it together with any causes of action but prior arbitrations are not preserved: *Morris* v *Harris* [1927] AC 252. Dissolution has the effect of substituting the Crown as owner of property but without releasing the company or its debtors from liability in the event that the company is restored. It therefore lacks the essential elements of a novation.

If A owes a liability to B which is discharged by C, in certain circumstances C is entitled by subrogation to enforce B's rights against A. It is immaterial whether A's liability is in contract or in tort: *Castellain* v *Preston* (1883) 11 QBD 380. In order to allow C to sue in its own name, B may legally assign its claim against A. Alternatively, C may issue proceedings in B's name in exercise of its rights of subrogation. A typical example is where an insurer issues proceedings in the name of an insured against a third party whose actions caused the loss. This process is different from novation in that it concerns the enforcement of a contract, *e.g.* an insurance policy or a guarantee, rather than a substitution of one by another.

Criteria for novation

"Novation is the substitution of a new contract for an old by the agreement of all parties to the old and the new": *Tito* v *Waddell* (No 2) [1977] Ch 106 at 287. There are two aspects to substitution. The first is where the parties to an existing contract agree to cancel it and substitute a new contract in its place. The second is where they agree that one of them will be released from its obligations and a new contract formed between the survivor and the newcomer: "the process by which a contract between A and B is transformed into a contract between A and C": *Linden Gardens* v *Lenesta Sludge* (1992) 57 BLR 57 at 76 (Court of Appeal). Most novations following insolvency are of this second type. Most of the cases concern implied rather than express novation. Even now, cases on express novation are rare.

In order to establish a novation, "what the Plaintiff has to prove is conduct inconsistent with a continuance of his liability, from which conduct an agreement to release him may be inferred": *Rouse* v *Bradford Banking* [1894] 2 Ch 32 at 54. In *Le Grys Building Services* v *Sealand Associates* (unreported, 29 March 1990, noted in (1994) 11 BLM 9) a sub-contractor successfully obtained judgment against the employer after the contractor went into liquidation on the ground that there had been a novation under which both main and sub-contracts had terminated and a new contract created between the employer and the sub-contractor. In *Chatsworth* v *Cussins* [1969] 1 All ER 143 the Court of Appeal considered a building contract where, after practical completion, the contractor assigned all its assets including the contract to a purchaser who undertook to discharge all its liabilities. The purchaser then changed its name to that of the contractor. On defects appearing in the works, the employer issued a writ against the purchaser in the mistaken belief that it was the original contractor. The purchaser admitted it had given an undertaking to the contractor to discharge all its liabilities but refused to accept liability as it had made no direct promise to the employer. The purchaser argued that it had not assumed any liability under the contract as the employer was unaware of the undertaking and had not consented to a novation. The court held the purchaser liable to the employer on the basis of an implied novation. From the brief report it seems that the decision was made on the basis of unusual facts and at an interlocutory stage when the matter was not fully argued. The original contractor was effectively unable to enforce the undertaking against the purchaser. Lord Denning MR said novation was "very easy to infer", but there was no evidence that the original contractor had been released. The decision seems likely to be confined to its facts.

The court reached the opposite conclusion on similar facts in *Westminster City Council* v *Reema Construction* (No 2) (1990) 24 Con LR 26 which concerned a defects claim by a local authority. The contractor became informally insolvent and hived down its assets to a purchaser and subsequently went into compulsory liquidation. The council claimed against the purchaser on the basis of implied novation, an implied contract or an implied term that the purchaser would fulfil the unperformed obligations of the insolvent contractor. The claim failed. There was no implied novation: although there was an express obligation in the hive down agreement that the purchaser would discharge the contractor's burden in the defects liability period in order to collect the remaining receivables which it could then keep outright, there was no direct agreement with the council who imagined it was dealing with the insolvent contractor throughout. It could not be inferred that the purchaser had given an undertaking to the council or that the council had accepted any undertaking. The court would not impute to the council notice that it was dealing with a different company simply because correspondence from the purchaser showed a different company number. It is interesting to note that before formal novation agreements became the norm, insolvency practitioners appointed over contractors used assignment coupled with an undertaking as the means of disposal of on-going contracts.

In *Far East Consortium* v *Airedale* (unreported, 27 December 1991, Hong Kong Court of Appeal), the court struck out third party proceedings brought by Airedale as sub-contractor against Henry Boot as substitute sub-sub-contractor. The claim related to defective work. Airedale's claim alleged that Henry Boot had, by a joint venture agreement, agreed to be jointly and severally liable with the existing sub-sub-contractor who had since dropped out of the picture. The novation was partly oral, partly in writing and evidenced by conduct. The evidence disclosed that, although an agreement was sent to the sub-contractor, it was never signed and an internal memorandum disclosed that one of Airedale's directors considered it was an internal matter for the original sub-sub-contractor and Henry Boot. The fact that Airedale operated one of the elements of the novation agreement by apparently making payments to Henry Boot was immaterial since it was within the sub-sub-contractor's power to dispose of the whole or part of the benefit of the contract. Airedale had to establish that Henry Boot had assumed the burden but could not do so on its own evidence.

In *Star-Trans* v *Norske-Tech* [1996] ADRLJ 62, a guarantee stated that the rights of the principal under the contract could be exercised by the guarantor and the obligations of the principal would be discharged if performed by the guarantor. It was held that, construing the contract and the guarantee together, the effect of the guarantee was *inter alia* to make the guarantor an additional party to the contract. It was not a novation of the contract since the principal was not discharged from liability.

The court is not likely to infer a novation where the circumstances are inconsistent with it, *e.g.* if it would mean the creditor losing the benefit of a security. For example, novation was refused where a life assurance company claiming to have been released had granted a charge over its assets securing payment of an annuity (*Re Endowments Society* (1870) 5 CL App 118) and a company had provided a cash deposit securing its performance of a contract that still remained executory (*Aktion Maritime* v *Kasmas* [1987] 1 Lloyd's Rep 283).

See also *Westminster City Council* v *Reema Construction Ltd* (No 1) (1990) 24 Con LR 16 (on the pleading of an implied novation), *Creasey* v *Breachwood Motors* [1992] *The Times*, 29 July (corporate veil lifted to enable former employee to sue purchaser of his employer). There have been a number of relevant overseas cases: *Alberta Mortgage & Housing Corp* v *Strathmore Investments* (1992) 6 Alta LR (3d) 159 (novation not established), *HEB Contractors* v *Verrissimo* [1990] 3 NZLR 754 (novation not established), *Doolaege* v *Solid Resources* (1990) 74 Alta LR (2d) 406 (novation established), *Allied-Signal* v *Dome Petroleum* (1991) 81 Alta LR (2d) 307 (novation established), *National Trust* v *Mead* [1990] 2 SCR 410.

Statutory novation

A novation can be effected by statute in many ways. The burden of a bond or insurance policy can be novated without the beneficiary's consent under Schedule 2C Insurance Companies Act 1982. A company reconstruction can take place under the Companies Act 1985. Novation could occur where a company incorporated by a private Act becomes insolvent and is re-incorporated: *e.g. Earl of Jersey* v *Great Western Railway* (1893) reported as a note to *Fortescue* v *Lostwithiel and Fowey Railway* [1894] 3 Ch 621. A statute may reorganise local government so that one local authority's contracts are taken over by another: *e.g. McPhail* v *Cunninghame* (1985) SLT 149.

Novation and construction contracts

"Novatio" under Roman law required evidence of an intention to novate and the substitution of one liability for another: *Wilson* v *Lloyd* (1873) LR 16 Eq 60, *Olsson* v *Dyson* [1970] 120 CLR 365. In its simplest form novation occurs when with the consent of A as creditor B is replaced as debtor by C: see Figure 10.1.

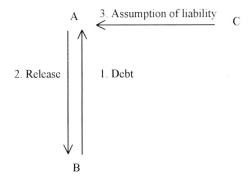

Fig 10.1

If C owes B a sum equal to or greater than B's debt to A, a novation could occur where A accepts C as debtor in the place of B: Halsbury 9(1)/1037. This is novation rather than assignment since a new contract is formed between A and C which extinguishes C's liability to B: see Figure 10.2.

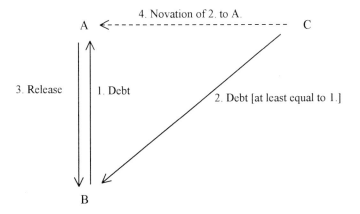

Fig 10.2

These situations assume that A owes no further obligations to B. In the 19th century cases, A may have supplied goods to B or be a client of B as a solicitors' firm or an insurance company. The release of B comes before A's acceptance of C in its place: *Re United Railways* [1960] 1 Ch 52 at 85. Under a construction contract, the parties owe each other mutual obligations, and a novation has to take account of the benefit and burden of both A and B.

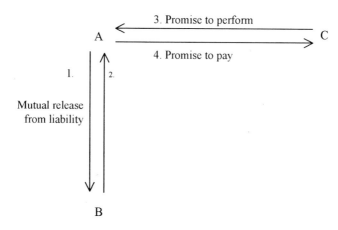

Fig 10.3

Figure 10.3 assumes a straightforward novation whereby one contractor is substituted for another. This time, as between A as employer and B as contractor, two releases are required to terminate the old contract. There are four stages:

1. The employer releases the contractor from liability.

2. The contractor releases the employer from liability.

3. C as purchaser promises the employer to complete the contract.

4. The purchaser accepts the employer's promise to pay for the work.

Stages 1 and 2 terminate the old contract; stages 3 and 4 create the new one. In consideration of its release, the contractor arranges for the purchaser to assume its responsibilities; and in consideration of its release, the employer accepts the purchaser in the contractor's place. The correct analysis is probably that the mutual releases between A and B come first followed by the mutual promises between A and C.

Novations of consultancy agreements or nominated sub-contracts work in a slightly different way. A as employer has a contract with B as designer and intends to enter into a design and build contract with C as contractor. B agrees to novate its contract to C on execution of the design and build contract and C agrees to accept a novation of the design contract in that event. The novation agreement is indicated in dotted lines in Figure 10.4.

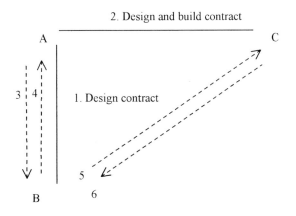

Fig 10.4

Here there are three main stages:

- execution of the design contract which B agrees to novate to C on execution of the design and build contract in the form of an agreement annexed to the design contract
- the execution of the design and build contract in which C agrees to accept a novation of the design contract from B in the same form
- a novation between A, B and C with the same four steps as in Figure 10.3.

In this context, novation is a way of merging one contract into another, although the novated design contract will take effect as a new sub-contract for which C will be vicariously liable to A. It has been pointed out that novation agreements drafted by employers sometimes omit stage 3 from Figure 10.4. In other words, although the employer is released, the designer is not (McNicholas 1993). On the face of it, this means the employer could sue the designer or the contractor for breaches in connection with the design although its cause of action against the designer would be limited to claims accrued before entering into the design and build contract. This is presumably the employer's intention. It could have been intended to apply to work carried out by the designer for which the contractor does not assume responsibility, *e.g.* planning matters. It could also be extra informal security against the risk of the contractor becoming insolvent before paying any award of damages for failures in the design.

It has been argued that the court could fill the gap as it were by inferring a release either as the common intention of the parties derived from all three agreements or on the ground that the arrangement falls within the situation in Figure 10.2 (McNicholas 1993). The first possibility would depend entirely on the construction of the three documents. The second is less likely since it is an example of inferred novation, whereas the example in Figure 10.4 is an express novation. In the absence of rectification, the court is likely to assume the parties intended the designer to remain potentially liable to the employer. Does the lack of a release avoid the novation for want of consideration from the employer? The court is concerned to find consideration for the new contract: *Rasbora v JCL Marine* [1977] 1 Lloyd's Rep 645 at 650. In this context, the consideration for the release of the old could be supplied by the design agreement since the agreement to novate in the form of the annexed draft was one of its express terms. Perhaps this is, however, a good reason to execute a novation agreement as a deed. If the novation is not executed as a deed, it is important for the draft novation agreement to be annexed both to the design agreement and the design and build contract.

Insolvency novations

The background was set out in Chapter 8. If possible, the insolvency practitioner wants to novate all of the company's contracts to the same purchaser. Prospective purchasers may be asked to put forward two bids: the first unconditional on the basis that he keeps the consideration whether or not the purchaser negotiates a novation with each client; the second conditional where the price allocates specific sums to individual contracts which only become payable on novations being achieved. Once informal agreement is reached, the terms are expressed in a sale agreement which is kept private between the insolvency practitioner and the purchaser, which sets out the consideration and the scope of the purchaser's obligation to procure the novations. A draft form of novation agreement is often included as a schedule to the sale agreement. The purchaser then approaches each individual client with the aim of negotiating a novation on the terms of the draft agreement. If clients impose more onerous terms in the novations than anticipated by the sale agreement, the purchaser may attempt to renegotiate the price with the insolvency practitioner.

Consequences of novation

Since novation is a contractual process, its effect can only be understood by examining the documents concerned. There are several areas of controversy. The first concerns the status of a novation where the parties omit an essential ingredient such as the release referred to earlier or introduce entirely new obligations which are not contained in the old contract. In this case, Halsbury would prefer to call such an agreement a "variation", reserving the term "novation" to cases where the existing terms remain unchanged. The position is analogous to a guarantee where the parties agree to cut down the defences available to the surety at common law. The court would still refer to the document as a guarantee: *Perry* v *National Provincial Bank* [1910] 1 Ch 464. It seems preferable to use "novation" even with agreements which are not in pure form.

A second area of difficulty concerns the newcomer's liability for breaches occurring before the novation. In a pure novation, the newcomer is liable as if it had been named as a party at the inception of the original contract. It is rather like a person who becomes liable for damages immediately on signing a contract which has retrospective effect. In order to exclude this result, very careful drafting is required. The position is the same where the surviving party was in breach before the novation. The surviving party would be liable for the loss actually suffered by the newcomer rather than such damages as its original contracting party would have suffered. In this respect novation differs from assignment. Likewise, rights of set-off ought not to be affected by a novation, but these questions should ideally be addressed in the novation agreement.

A novation can release a guarantor from liability: *Commercial Bank of Tasmania* [1893] AC 313, *Housing Guarantee Fund* v *Yusef* [1991] VR 17. Many guarantees anticipate this and expressly preserve the guarantor's liability in the event of a novation. Similarly a consensual termination of a contract will release a debtor's liability to an assignee if the assigned debt can only become due if the contract is performed in full: *Babson* v *Village of Ulysses*, 52 NW Rep (2d) 320 (1952).

Formal insolvency usually terminates the contractor's employment. Novation agreements sometimes expressly reinstate the employment before going on to effect a mutual release between employer and contractor. This is not strictly necessary and can reactivate an employer's duty to pay nominated sub-contractors direct, *e.g.* under clause 35 of JCT 80: Construction Award No 9 (1988) [1995] 2 Con L Yb 103. Among other things, it was the reinstatement that led the arbitrator in that case to construe the novation as a variation of the original contract. The facts are set out in Chapter 12.

Completion contracts

On the insolvency of the contractor, the employer has various options. These are set out in several industry publications: JCT Practice Note 24 (1992), SBCC Insolvency Practice Guide (1991), and the RICS Construction Insolvency Information Paper (1997), which has some useful flow charts. The possibilities for the employer are:

1. Invite the original tenderers to bid for the completion of the works.

2. Send the works out to open tender.

3. Ask contractors working on adjacent sites if they would be willing to undertake the completion contract at favourable rates.

4. Approach a contractor with whom it had worked before.

5. Complete the work itself if the employer has the resources.

6. Allow the insolvency practitioner to complete the contract using existing staff and sub-contractors under the same or varied contractual arrangements.

7. Allow the insolvency practitioner to assign the benefit of the contract to another contractor and appoint the assignee as the agent of the insolvent contractor for the purpose of completing the works.

8. Agree a novation with the insolvency practitioner who negotiates a price from the incoming contractor for procuring the novation.

9. Allow a guarantor to complete the work or arrange a novation.

Completion using a direct contractor

If options (1) to (5) are chosen it is important to note that the same care is needed when procuring a completion contract as any other. There are cases where completion contractors have defaulted: *Mertens v Home Freeholds* [1921] 2 KB 526, *Vigers v Swindell* [1939] 3 All ER 590, *Stanley Brown v Maryland Casualty Co* 442 SW 2d 187 (1969), and *F G Minter* (information supplied by the late Len Mann). The JCT recommends its own Form of Prime Cost Contract (1992) in cases where the employer prefers a negotiated contract with a replacement contractor (Practice Note 24, p.21). The precise procurement method can affect the recoverability of the completion cost by way of set-off against the insolvent contractor. This can occur where the insolvency practitioner argues that the employer has failed to mitigate its loss. This is considered later.

The employer's duty to provide warranties to tenants of a commercial development as and when units are let can be advantageous to a new contractor negotiating a novation as well as a contractor trying to mitigate its loss on an employer insolvency. The employer on a commercial development may have pre-let the building on terms that prospective tenants complete their leases within a certain period after practical completion and it may be a condition of the agreement for a lease with prospective tenants that a warranty in their favour be provided by the contractor. Tenants may refuse to accept an insurance policy in lieu of the warranty. Prospective tenants in a falling market may use the absence of a warranty as a ground for re-negotiating the terms of the lease or for withdrawing altogether. In this respect at least, the demand for collateral warranties can offer a benefit to contractors.

Completion by insolvency practitioners

This is likely only where a relatively small amount of work has yet to be done and there is a probability of a significant profit from the conversion of work in progress into debt. Completion of the contract can only be achieved by an insolvency practitioner who is able to inspire confidence in the employer and the contractor's staff, sub-contractors and suppliers. It has been seen that formal insolvency events are not in themselves breaches of contract. However, as almost all construction contracts contain termination clauses, it will in practice be impossible for an insolvency practitioner to complete the works unless the employer agrees to reinstate the contractor's employment or waives the termination by allowing the company to continue. If these hurdles can be overcome, the insolvency practitioner may attempt to re-negotiate the contract terms, by providing for weekly or fortnightly payments or by limiting or excluding the employer's right of set-off. Care is required in these negotiations as the employer may be entitled to treat such attempts at re-negotiation as a repudiation. Amendment 11 (1992) to JCT 80 introduced an interim arrangement procedure whereby an employer can agree terms on a temporary basis with a receiver while considering its options. This is now contained in clause 27.5.3 of JCT 98. No particular terms are specified except that "any right of set-off which the employer may have shall not be exercisable in respect of any payment due from the employer to the contractor under such interim arrangement". It should be noted that abatement for defective work performed under the interim arrangement has not been excluded (see Chapter 5). The JCT Practice Note 24 suggests that employers should consider:

> "retaining funds in excess of the contractual retention until the defects have been rectified but taking into account any performance bond that may be available and obtaining an undertaking from the insolvency practitioner that funds paid to him in respect of the contract will be applied to completing the works" (p 20).

Repudiation arguments are very common in this context, especially in a falling market. *Forth Shipbuilding* v *Tonnevold* (1923) 14 Ll L Rep 554 is a good example of how things can go wrong. A shipbuilder agreed to construct a ship for a Norwegian owner for £245,000 payable in six equal instalments. Completion was due by October 1920 otherwise liquidated damages would become payable at the rate of £100 per week. It appears that the whole works were sub-contracted to two sub-contractors, one responsible for the hull and the other for the engines. The chronology ran as follows. The contract was signed in December 1919. During the following year there was a slump in the shipping industry which damaged the shipbuilder's financial position. Strikes apparently caused delays to the works. On 17 February 1921 the owner issued a writ claiming rescission of the contract for fraudulent misrepresentation and the return of instalments already paid of £122,500. By mid-May the shipbuilder's directors realised the company was insolvent. By the end of May, the company's liabilities exceeded £1 million and the directors resolved to cease trading and convened a shareholders' meeting for 9 June to place the company into voluntary liquidation. On 1 June the owner's proceedings were settled on terms that the contractor was to keep instalments already paid and agreed to reduce the contract sum by £20,000 and to undertake to complete the works "with all possible expedition", while the employer was to pay two instalments previously withheld totalling £81,666 within 14 days. On 9 June the shipbuilder went into voluntary liquidation. On 15 June the owner discovered the shipbuilder's insolvency and refused to pay the £81,666. On 11 July the owner stated that he wanted no more to do with the ship. On 29 September the owner refused to agree a scheme of arrangement or to pay the £81,666. On 27 October the liquidator issued a writ for the £81,666 which was later amended to claim damages. On 13 December a scheme of arrangement was completed without the owner's co-operation. In January 1922 the liquidator ordered the sub-contractors to proceed to complete the ship without the owner's agreement. Practical completion of the ship was achieved in July 1922.

The evidence was that the owner had agreed a price of £245,000 at the peak of a shipping boom and that on its completion in July 1922 the ship was worth only £57,000. The report suggests that the contract was front-end loaded. By the start of the liquidation, the sub-contractors had been paid £90,200, were due £50,500, and their future work would cost £67,900. On these figures, and assuming that all the work had been sub-contracted, the shipbuilder would have made a profit of £37,400. As following the settlement reached in June 1921 only £102,500 remained payable by the owner, and the sub-contractors were due a total of £118,400, presumably the sub-contractors agreed to complete the ship for £67,900 (the value of their remaining work) and prove for the balance which would have left the liquidator with a profit of £34,600. This situation can be compared with *Re Thames Ironworks* (1912) WN 66 in which a court-appointed receiver was directed by the court not to complete a contract where the cost to complete exceeded the amount owed to a creditor.

In the proceedings, the liquidator claimed the balance of the contract price or damages and the owner counterclaimed for the return of the £122,500 he had already paid. By this time, he no longer wanted the ship. The trial judge held in favour of the owner but was reversed by the Court of Appeal who decided that both owner and builder were equally at fault, that the loss should lie where it fell and that both the claim and counterclaim should be dismissed. The end result was that the owner had spent £122,500 and received nothing in return and the liquidator had apparently paid £67,900 to the sub-contractors for the privilege of obtaining a ship valued at £57,500 which may have been unsaleable.

The liquidator's claim failed because he could not show that the builder had been ready, willing and able to complete. The shipbuilder's delays had been unreasonable breaches of contract and had been caused not through non-payment by the owner but by difficulties in putting the scheme of arrangement in place. The liquidator could have accepted the owner's conduct of 15 June and 11 July 1921 as repudiations but instead had chosen to affirm the contract. The counterclaim failed because the owner was also unable to show he had been ready, willing and able to complete the contract. He could not show total failure of consideration as the ship had been completed, nor could he demonstrate repudiatory conduct by the liquidator which he had accepted. All he could show was a substantial delay but that would only ground a claim for damages. Even that claim would not succeed because the owner could show no loss as a result of the delay because the value of the ship was dramatically lower than the contract price and had not effectively changed between June 1921 and July 1922.

Scrutton LJ held as an alternative that, in the context of the delays which had already occurred on the contract, the delay between 1 June and 11 July 1921 while the liquidator made up his mind what to do was non-repudiatory although it might have been sufficient to ground a claim for damages. This can be compared with *Creditel* v *Terrace Corporation* (1983) 50 CBR 87 where a trustee in bankruptcy failed in a claim because of unreasonable delay in deciding whether to perform. The court in *Tonnevold* held that delay between 1 June 1921 and 14 January 1922 was "sufficient to justify Tonnevold in treating the contract as frustrated and repudiated by that date. Seven months delay on a rapidly falling market may make the delivery of the ship quite a different delivery, so frustrate the original contract". Against such a background, it is difficult to overcome the negative attitude shown towards insolvency practitioners working in the industry.

Completion by guarantors

The timing and extent of a guarantor's liability to the employer depends on the terms of the guarantee. Many guarantees (*e.g.* under the ICE standard form) do not provide for completion by the guarantor; instead they commit the guarantor to compensate the employer for losses flowing from the contractor's default. In North America, and in some guarantees offered by US and Canadian insurance companies in the United Kingdom, the guarantor offers or has the right to procure completion (McDevitt 1985, at 15, 26, Scott and Reynolds 1994). This is to the guarantor's advantage because it gives it control over the selection of the completion contractor, the agreement of the cost to complete and the timing of the completion contract. It also enables the guarantor to spread the period over which it has to outlay the cost to complete.

Many employers are not prepared to cede control of the works to guarantors, apprehensive lest they minimise cost at the expense of quality. Completion by guarantors has its advocates in the United Kingdom and is part of the traditional scene in the United States. As the guarantor has no better rights against the employer than the contractor has, it may find itself in dispute with the contractor's bank or assignee or the employer in relation to receivables which become payable on completion, particularly retention: *Royal Bank of Canada* v *Wilson* (1963) 4 CBR 300, *Re Yeadon Waterworks* (1895) 72 LT 538, *Alexander* v *Administrator Transvaal* [1974] 2 SA 248, *Corrans* v *Transvaal Government* (1909) TS 605.

Novation by insolvency practitioners

Many of the decided cases concern situations where, following a novation, either the original debtor or the newcomer become insolvent. The majority of novations in the context of construction insolvencies are those negotiated by the insolvency practitioner. The practitioner will often wish to be a party to the agreement in order to receive indemnities from the purchaser and exclude personal liability: see Figure 10.5.

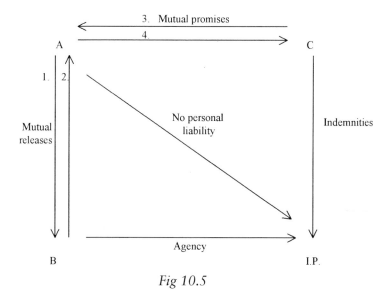

Fig 10.5

In the course of negotiations the parties need to work out the intended allocation of risk under the new contract. If the old contract is to be used as a basis for the new, any revisions should be clearly drafted and included as a schedule to the novation agreement. It will usually be necessary to revise the date for completion and to extend the newcomer's time for completion by reason of the delay resulting from the insolvency. The parties may also take the opportunity to make changes in the following respects:

- pricing provisions
- the scope of the works
- liability for liquidated and ascertained damages already incurred
- availability of plant and materials on and off site
- liability for retention of title claimants
- liability for existing patent and latent defects
- liability for past and continuing breaches
- liability for sub-contractors' claims
- willingness of sub-contractors and suppliers to novate their contracts
- enforceability of bonds and guarantees
- the effect of the Transfer of Undertakings (Protection of Employment) Regulations 1981
- availability of the professional team for novations (if design and build).

The JCT Practice Note 24 and the SBCC Insolvency Practice Guide for use in Scotland both have specimen forms of novation agreement. The contractor acts through its insolvency practitioner who will normally wish to be a party to the novation agreement, especially if the contractor has continued trading while the novation was being negotiated. This is to enable the insolvency practitioner to be released from any personal claims which the other parties may have and to take the benefit of any indemnities and warranties which have been negotiated.

Where a contractor has a number of on-going contracts at the date of a receivership, and some of them are bonded, one of the receiver's priorities will be to have the bonds discharged by novating the contracts thereby releasing any security the contractor may have given to the bondsman. This is especially important if the security ranks in priority to the charge under which the receiver was appointed, e.g. cash on deposit in an escrow account. The bondsman may be prepared to offer some of the cash deposit to the purchaser if it agrees to take on all uncompleted contracts and assist the bondsman in getting its existing bonds released by the employers. The receiver will try to prevent this by making it a term of the negotiations that the purchaser does not make any direct approaches either to the bondsman or the employer. The suggestion is sometimes made that an existing bond be novated by substituting the purchaser for the insolvent contractor as joint and several obligor. In practice, new bonds are normally issued.

The insolvency surveyor's review may reveal that in some cases the contractor has been working without a binding contract. There may be a letter of intent or a written payment undertaking from the employer or in simple cases an implied promise to pay arising from a request to carry out work. All of these give rise to a receivable, even if only a claim in quasi-contract for a *quantum meruit*. The risk of misrepresentation by the receiver or a member of his staff makes it important in this context to agree to sell only such title to the receivables as the company may have.

Sub-contractors

As the major part of a project is carried out by sub-contractors, it is important that a prospective purchaser from a receiver appointed over a contractor is aware of their position. Questions of particular relevance as far as sub-contractors are concerned are as follows. How much is still owed to the sub-contractor? Did the employer pay the insolvent contractor this amount before the receiver was appointed? If not, would the employer be prepared to pay this sum to the new contractor or make a direct payment to the sub-contractor? How much further work is required of the sub-contractor? Are there any special items of plant or materials on or off site which could be difficult to obtain from another source? Is there specialist labour on site which it would be difficult to replace? Does the sub-contractor own the copyright in plans or drawings in which the contractor has no licence? Are there any trust or retention of title claims?

Unless the new contractor is satisfied that it can deal with these issues, it could find itself unable to resource the works in accordance with the terms of the new contract. One factor which can help a purchaser dealing with the unpaid sub-contractors is to take an assignment from the receiver of the benefit of the sub-contracts. This assignment can be included in the novation agreement itself. By virtue of the assignment, a sub-contractor would owe the new contractor a duty to carry out work under the old sub-contract while only being able to look to the insolvent contractor for payment. In practice, of course, the sub-contractor would be likely to cease work in the absence of a promise of payment by the new contractor but, as assignee of the benefit of the sub-contract, the new contractor does have a certain hold which it may be able to use to its advantage. This would only assist the new contractor in cases where the old contractor had reached a binding contract with the sub-contractor which has not automatically terminated on the main contract termination. If work were being done under a letter of intent, the sub-contractor would normally owe no obligation to continue.

In deciding which sub-contractors should be approached with a view to a novation, the new contractor will probably disregard those whose works are neither specialist nor significant, whose materials have already been fixed or whose works are completed. The same would apply to trades in plentiful supply on the market at the time. Having identified those sub-contractors whose services are still required, the new contractor will then negotiate a cost to complete using such commercial pressure as is available to avoid paying the amount left unpaid by the insolvent contractor. Sub-contractors seek to recover their unpaid debt by enhancing their rates to the new contractor who may be prepared to accept some enhancement as the price for retaining a particular sub-contractor or supplier.

Returning to the example of the design agreement at Figure 10.3, it is possible to envisage a series of novations:

1. The design agreement is novated to the contractor on the execution of the design and build contract.

2. On the insolvency of the contractor, the benefit of its agreement with the designer is assigned to the employer.

3. The employer then novates the agreement with the designer's consent to the completion contractor (McNicholas 1993).

For a practical example see "Carry on contracting" (*Building*, 22 January 1993), which concerned Callendar Square, Falkirk. In that case the original contract was a management contract, the completion contract was design and build and the original design team's conditions of engagement were novated to the incoming contractor.

The design team would have preferred a completion contract based on construction management.

Mitigation of loss

Following a termination, if the employer fails to act reasonably in minimising its loss, its claim for damages will be calculated as if it had acted reasonably: *Sotiros Shipping* v *Sameiet Solholt* [1983] 1 Lloyd's Rep 605. It is always possible that the completion contractor will complete for less than the original contract sum: *Ferguson* v *Sohl* (1993) 62 BLR 95. An employer would not recover damages for any part of its loss flowing from the breach which could have been avoided by taking reasonable steps. But if reasonable steps are taken, the employer can recover any additional expense incurred in taking them. The standard required of the employer in these circumstances is not a high one since the contractor is the wrongdoer:

> "The law is satisfied if the party placed in a difficult situation by reason of the breach of a duty owed to him has acted reasonably in the adoption of remedial measures, and he will not be disentitled to recover the cost of such measures merely because the party in breach can suggest that other measures less burdensome to him might have been taken": *Banco de Portugal* v *Waterlow* [1932] AC 452 at 506.

See also *Popular Homes* v *Circuit Developments* [1979] 2 NZLR 642, *Goodman* v *Napier Harbour Board* [1939] NZLR 97 (where the contract gave the employer "uncontrolled discretion as to price and method to employ any person" to complete the works).

In *Kamlee Construction* v *Town of Oakville* (1960) 26 DLR (2d) 166, a contractor was engaged to construct a storm relief sewer but left site before the works were completed. It appears from the report that the contractor experienced financial difficulties without becoming formally insolvent. Within a week, the employer invited tenders to complete the work and received one offer of a fixed price and another at cost plus 15%. The second offer was accepted but, after completion, it was found that the works had cost substantially more than the fixed price offer. The original contractor argued that the employer had failed to mitigate its loss. The contractor's submission was rejected because: (1) completion was urgent as winter was approaching, (2) the cost plus contractor had available resources in the locality, (3) the employer's decision was taken on the engineer's advice that the likely final account on a cost plus basis would be close to the fixed price bid, and (4) the fact that the engineer's estimate proved to be completely out of line with the result did not mean that the employer had acted unreasonably.

The employer was not to be penalised because its adviser had inaccurately estimated the sum which would become due on completion of the works. *Kamlee* can be contrasted with *Payzu* v *Saunders* [1919] 2 KB 281, a non-construction case where a refusal to accept an offer of a substitute contract was held to be unreasonable.

In *Samuel Properties* v *London Borough of Richmond* (unreported, 22 July 1983), after a contractor went into receivership, the employer appointed a new contractor as caretaker on the basis of cost plus 10% but the completion contractor also went into receivership and had to be replaced by a third before the works were completed. The employer was in joint venture with a local authority and it was a term of their agreement that the employer would act with diligence and take appropriate steps to complete or procure the completion of the works. It was held that the employer had complied with this duty in selecting the defaulting second contractor. The employer had worked with the contractor before and had no reason to doubt an encouraging bank reference which properly reflected the bank's views at the time. "If [the employer] had called for a company search, I do not think that it would have altered the position. Many development and building companies are heavily dependent upon their banks and have to rely upon them to act reasonably." Cost plus is appropriate for emergency work, where speed is more important than economy or where the employer is unclear as to the precise eventual requirements (Capon 1990, 17). In *Kraft Construction* v *Guardian Insurance* (1984) 57 AR 118 the contractor was held to have acted reasonably in hiring an alternative sub-contractor on a cost plus basis in view of the "knock on effect" on the project of the failure of a significant sub-contractor and the inactivity of the guarantor. In *City of Moncton* v *Aprile Contracting* (1977) 17 NBR (2d) 678 it was held not unreasonable for a local authority to have sent out the works to competitive tender rather than engaging an alternative contractor on a cost plus basis. See also *Canadian General Insurance* v *Dube* (1982) 39 NBR (2d) 484 at 492.

A claim for reduction of damages on the ground of failure to mitigate is difficult to pursue unless the plaintiff has been obviously unreasonable. There need to be strong facts for an insolvency practitioner to have a fair prospect of success:

"Now, when a contractor gets into difficulties which culminate in bankruptcy, and the employer is in consequence put to the extreme inconvenience and annoyance of having himself to complete the work, I think the employer should be allowed a large discretion in the way in which he completes it, and that the contractor, in the absence of fraud or extreme negligence, cannot complain if the work be carried on in an uneconomical manner ... where a contractor by his own default does not perform his contract, but compels the [employer] to complete the work himself, if the contractor, or those claiming under him, wish to enforce claims arising out of the contract, they should be prepared with very plain evidence, both of the existence of such claims and of their precise extent and nature, and that every allowance should be made in considering the conduct of the [employer] in the position in which the default of the contractor has placed him": *Fulton* v *Dornwell* (1885) 4 SC 207 at 210.

In that case, the contractor's trustee had not brought sufficient evidence to show that the cost to complete incurred by the employer was unreasonable. If it had been unreasonable due to "an extravagant and largely unnecessary remedial scheme", the employer may be able to recover from its professional team the damages it could not claim against the insolvent contractor for failure to mitigate: *e.g. Equitable Life* v *Kenchington Ford* [1996] CILL 1163.

In *Bank of East Asia* v *Scottish Enterprise* (unreported, 19 June 1992) the employer, who was the successor of the Scottish Development Agency, engaged a contractor to design and build three factories for £500,000 (Figure 10.6). The difficulty was that the employer had no access to the money until the following financial year, *i.e.* by 15 May 1990. The contractor agreed to fund the work by deferring the employer's duty to pay monthly instalments until then. The contractor's normal bankers, who held a floating charge over its undertaking, refused to advance further working capital. But the contractor was able to obtain a facility of £450,000 from the plaintiff bank. As part of the arrangement, the employer agreed to pay the contractor interest on the deferred stage payments plus a facility fee and consented to the contractor assigning the benefit of the contract to the plaintiff as security for the new facility. Notice of the assignment was given to the employer.

Shortly after 15 May 1990, receivers were appointed over the contractor which automatically terminated its employment under the building contract. At that time, £415,000 was due to the plaintiff as assignee in respect of the value of work done together with interest and the facility fee. It was, however, discovered that there were significant defects in the work. It apparently cost the employer £500,000 to have

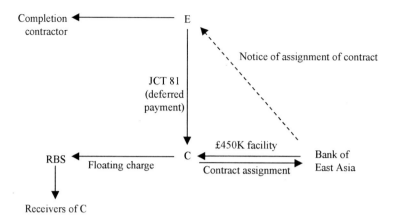

Fig 10.6

the defects rectified and the works completed by another contractor. The employer refused to pay the assignee on the ground that the cost of rectifying and completing the work exceeded the amount otherwise due to the contractor. The dispute was referred to the Official Referee and a Scott schedule was prepared.

The contract was governed by Scots law under which the employer was entitled to set off the cost of rectifying the contractor's defective work but not the cost of having the works completed. The court assessed the cost of rectifying defects at £170,000, making a balance due to the assignee from the employer of £245,000 together with interest and costs. The employer had to prove in the insolvency for the balance of its loss. The case is a stark reminder to employers of the dangers in allowing the benefit of the contract to be assigned.

Of particular interest is the rigorous approach taken by the court in disallowing aspects of the completion contractor's cost on the ground that the employer had failed to mitigate its loss. The failure to mitigate was in the context of the defective work but would seem to have applied equally to the incomplete work. Separate quantity surveyors were appointed by the receivers and the bank. Their combined evidence, which was accepted by the judge, was that:

1. It was unreasonable of the employer to have agreed a negotiated contract with its usual contractor instead of sending the works out to four contractors on competitive tender, and the employer's claim would be reduced by 7.5% as a consequence.

2. The rates in the original contract were increased by 7% in negotiations between the completion contractor and the employer. Since the tender price index had actually fallen during the relevant period, this increase was disallowed.

3. Numerous items such as additional security, loss of rent through delayed completion etc were disallowed as having been caused by the termination of the contractor's employment rather than by the defective work.

Had the benefit and burden not been split, the employer may well still have had its claim reduced through failing to act reasonably but it would have been able to recover the cost of the completion as well as the remedial work by way of set-off against monies otherwise payable to the receivers.

An insolvency practitioner may argue a failure to mitigate by not accepting his offer to complete the contract. The contract may have provided for the automatic termination of the contractor's employment on the appointment of the receiver or the employer may have exercised a right of termination shortly afterwards. Time will have gone by between the termination and the practitioner's proposal. In order to succeed on a mitigation argument, the receiver would probably have to undertake to meet any loss caused by the termination even if it continued to accrue after the receiver resumed working on site, and to take account in the proposal of any change in circumstances following the termination: *McIlwee* v *Foley Brothers* (1916) WWR 5.

One standard form gives the employer a choice in the event of the contractor's insolvency of terminating the contract or of giving the insolvency practitioner "the option of carrying out the contract subject to his providing a guarantee for the due and faithful performance of the contract up to an amount to be agreed": clause 13 of Model Form A/1976/1978 (Home Contracts with Erection). If the second option is followed and the termination clause is invalid (or invalidly invoked), the demand for the guarantee could amount to repudiatory conduct by the employer. It will normally be reasonable to require a bond or a guarantee as a condition of allowing the contractor to continue. The employer will be expected to give details of the additional cost to complete, especially where it is considerably more than the outstanding balance of the contract sum and includes extras or expenses incurred as a result of damage to the works or theft after the termination: *Tower Housing* v *Technical & General Guarantee* (1997) 87 BLR 82 at 94.

Conclusion

The law of novation remains comparatively undeveloped. There is little guidance on the construction and effect of express novations. The main difficulty is in the question of liability and the measure of loss for breaches occurring before the novation. The authorities mainly concern situations of debtor and creditor, in which the creditor has already performed its obligations. A novation of a construction contract has to deal with unperformed obligations on both sides. Novation remains a useful process before and after an insolvency, but is probably better understood by insolvency practitioners than industry professionals. It may not always be the most appropriate way of procuring a completion contract but the options need careful thought.

Case study*

Background

In an ideal world, the investigating team appointed to a contractor collates the relevant information on its contracts before insolvency occurs so that a strategy for each contract and an assessment of the collectability of debts can be made in advance. However, in practice the team often has limited access to the key staff (estimators, surveyors and contracts managers), and the details have to be taken from management accounts and debtor ledgers which can be very inaccurate or omit the essential information. Obtaining the right information and interpreting it correctly is critical if the course of an insolvency is to run smoothly and the recovery of assets maximised.

Base data

Management accounts are normally taken from a rolling series of figures, with profit and loss projections taken from tender estimates, adjusted for reserves and accruals. This does not give an appropriate view of a contract on which a decision can be made. For this purpose, a snapshot or "freeze-frame" approach needs to be taken. If the company cannot or will not provide the basic information then this should sound

---

* by and © Neil Burton, partner, GVA Grimley

double warning bells. Key information on a contract by contract basis is needed as set out below for both contracts in progress (CIP) and completed contracts (CC).

1. **Estimated final account.** This should be a realistic assessment of the total amount that will be received on the contract net of any discounts and with amounts assessed for claims for loss and expense or damages for late completion clearly identified and allowed for within the figure.

2. **Value of work done.** This should be assessed on the basis of the cumulative gross value certified or applied for, plus a reasonable assessment of work in progress (WIP) between the certificate and the snapshot date. It should be noted that WIP can be negative, and often is on design and build contracts, if the stage payments are front-end loaded. An allocation between fixed and floating charge assets can be undertaken if the WIP figure is known.

3. **Sums previously paid.** This should be the cumulative total paid as at the snapshot date. If a large sum will become due for payment in the near future, *i.e.* shortly after the snapshot date, this should be taken into account in considering when a decision should be taken on a particular contract.

4. **Completion dates.** For CIPs a realistic anticipated completion date is required so that this can be looked at in comparison to the amount of work still to be done. It is also valuable in assessing the value of claims for loss and expense or the amount of damages for late completion. For CCs the actual completion date is needed to give a view of when the defects liability period might expire.

5. **Retentions.** Although desirable it is not normally essential to identify retentions separately. The exception is for main contractors where nominated sub-contractors are involved as their retention may be held by the client in trust. In these cases the amounts should be separately identified and deducted from any balances shown due.

6. **Client name and contract.** Details of the client and the project enable a view to be taken as to the grouping of contracts and debts with a particular client and work type.

7. **Other information.** If it is readily accessible other information should also be obtained such as:

- form of contract
- date and number of last certificate
- estimate of costs to complete
- warranties and guarantees
- bonds.

However, care must be taken not to take too much time at the early stages obtaining information which is desirable rather than essential, otherwise the initial consideration of the key issues will be delayed.

Presentation of findings

The tabular presentation of key statistics enables a clear review of a portfolio of contracts to be undertaken. Typical figures for a small to medium sized main contractor are set out in Figures 10.7 and 10.8.

A. Contracts in progress

A	B	C	D	E	F
Client and contract	Estimated final account	Value of work done	Previously paid	Value to complete (B-C)	Completion date
1. Local authority school extension	2,000	100	0	1900	Aug 2000
2. Housing association (20 units refurbishment)	1,200	1,000	500	200	Sept 1999
3. Housing association (30 units new build)	1,500	750	600	750	March 2000
4. Manufacturer new warehouse	1,000	200	0	800	March 2000
		2,050	1,100		
		(1,100)			
Balance due		950			

Fig 10.7

B. Completed contracts as at 30 July 1999 (all figures in thousands)

A	B	C	D	E
Client and contract	Estimated final account	Previously paid	Balance (B-C)	Completion date
5. Local authority sports facility	2,000	1,800	200	April 1999
6. Housing association 10 new build	600	500	100	June 1999
7.Developer office block	1,900	1,400	500	Sept 1988
8.Manufacturer new workshop	1,300	1,100	200	Jan 1999
		Total balance	1,000	

Notes

1. Assumes no nominated sub-contractors involved.
2. Figures are exclusive of VAT.
3. Figures are rounded to thousands only for ease of presentation.

Fig 10.8

Insolvency practitioner's options for contracts

From the basic statistics presented for the contracts, various possible options can be explored. It is important to remain mindful of common clients for both CIPs and CCs where there will be a risk of set-off between one and another. In the example given it will be important to ensure there is no linkage between the contracts in these three groups: (1) contracts 2, 3 and 6, (2) contracts 1 and 5, and (3) contracts 4 and 8.

Contracts in progress

Contract 1. With a distant completion date, a large value to complete and a nominal amount outstanding, this contract will either be abandoned or novated as part of a package if there is sufficient profit in the value to complete.

Contract 2. If detailed investigations and negotiations ensured that the £500,000 outstanding were definitely due, then with a close completion date and only £200,000 of work to do this may be a prospect for completion by the insolvent company or a novation to a third party for a sensible consideration.

Contracts 3 and 4. With only nominal amounts outstanding and significant amounts of work to complete over an extended period, these contracts will either be abandoned or novated for nominal amounts as part of a package.

Completed contracts

Contracts 5, 6 and 8 look fairly straightforward in terms of reasonable balances of final account and retentions outstanding for a relatively short period of time. Debt collection for these, on the assumption there are no major defects, should be a relatively simple case of agreeing final accounts and reasonable client contra charges.

Contract 7 is more difficult in that a significant amount is shown as due and has been for some time since completion. A detailed investigation may reveal claims and counterclaims, defective work or a difficult client. Key company staff may need to be retained to assist with the collection of this debt.

Arrangements for debt collection can include incentivised deals with existing staff, sale of contract debts for a lump sum or a percentage of recovery, and the appointment of third party agents on hourly rates or percentage based fees. Care needs to be taken in structuring any arrangements for debt collection to allow for the long time scale that the process takes when a company is no longer trading.

Realisable assets

Basic book values for contract debts are not recovered on a pound for pound basis in insolvency situations. Clients have a duty to mitigate loss and substantiate the amounts they are seeking to deduct from monies due to an insolvent company. However, there are many items which legitimately reduce the asset value. These include but are not limited to:

- excess completion costs
- additional professional fees

- absence of warranties
- inability to pursue claims
- inability to defend counterclaims
- enhanced costs of rectifying defects
- set-off between contracts
- negotiable settlements.

A statistical analysis of main and sub-contractor's debts and collectability using data from insolvencies handled by my firm shows that over a 10-year period recoverability in the range of 5% to 69% was achieved, with an average rate of 19%. In the case study, Figure 10.9 sets out a good result representing a return of 23% to 38% (figures in thousands):

	Balance due	Recoverable
CIP	950	250 – 350 (assuming novation)
CC	1,000	200 – 400
TOTALS	1,950	450 – 750

Fig 10.9

Chapter 11

· **Trust Claims** ·

Introduction

Most trust claims made in the industry concern the JCT retention trust. Common issues are whether the trust has been properly constituted and the scope of the trustee's right of recourse. The case law has explored the relationship between construction trusts and fixed and floating charges. This chapter also considers sub-contract terms which have attracted trust arguments, *e.g.* "name borrowing" provisions and terms requiring the contractor, at the sub-contractor's request, to obtain for its benefit any applicable rights or benefits of the main contract. General principles of trust law, and an outline of the trust of the contract sum, are set out in Chapter 6. Imaginal aspects are considered in Chapter 18.

The retention trust

The nominated sub-contractor trust

The earliest case on the retention trust concerned an application by nominated sub-contractors in the liquidation of a main contractor: *Re Tout and Finch* [1954] 1 All ER 127. The contractor was involved in the construction of flats for a local authority under an RIBA contract with quantities. Ten per cent retention was withheld. The sub-contract was in the Green Form and provided as follows:

> "If and to the extent that the amount retained by the employer in accordance with the main contract includes any retention money the contractor's interest in such money is fiduciary as trustee for the sub-contractor [and if the contractor attempts or purports to mortgage or otherwise charge such interest or his interest in the whole of the amount retained aforesaid (otherwise than by floating charge if the contractor is a limited company), the contractor shall thereupon immediately set aside and become a trustee for the sub-contractor of a sum equivalent to the retention money and shall pay the same to the sub-contractor on demand; provided that upon payment of the same to the sub-contractor

the amount due to the sub-contractor upon final payment under this sub-contract shall be reduced accordingly by the sum so paid]".

A fiduciary is not necessarily a trustee in the full sense of the word: such a person can have obligations towards another's property even though it may not be vested in him. The nature and extent of a fiduciary's duties are variable and depend on the circumstances of each case. However, in this contract, the words "fiduciary as trustee" are sufficiently clear to show that a trust is intended with the sub-contractor as beneficiary.

There was no evidence in this case that the contractor had attempted to charge its retention; it had simply gone into liquidation before receiving it from the employer. Although that contingency had not occurred, the court held that the nominated sub-contractors were entitled to a declaration that the contractor's rights to retention were held in trust for them and that the liquidator was bound to pass over the proportion due to them on receipt from the employer. The judge observed that "on the face of it there are clear words used which are apt to create a trust which will operate by way of an equitable assignment of assets described as the contractor's interest in the retention money" (at 134).

The words in square brackets in the clause quoted above show that the trust was originally intended to prevent the contractor's creditors obtaining priority over the nominated sub-contractors in respect of retention. The exception in favour of floating charge-holders might have diluted the protection had the court not construed the first part of the clause as an effective assignment (see *MacJordan Construction* v *Brookmount Erostin* (1992) 56 BLR 1 considered later). The sanction of accelerated payment never seems to have been used in practice and was dropped in later contracts, *e.g.* clauses 4.29 of WC/2, 4.22.1 of NSC/C, which also introduced the requirement to set aside a fund on request. In *Re Tout and Finch* the contractor was already in liquidation and incapable of complying with an injunction to set aside a fund as its assets had become subject to the statutory trust in favour of creditors: *Ayerst* v *C & K (Construction) Ltd* [1976] AC 167. As the retention had not been paid to the contractor before its liquidation, the court could enforce the assignment by ordering retention to be paid direct to the sub-contractors or by ordering the liquidator to "pass it on" as soon as it was received by him.

In *Harry Bibby* v *Neill Construction* [1973] EGD 52 the main contract was in CCC/WKS/1 form (the precursor of GC/Works/1), and the sub-contract was in the Green Form. The contractor went into liquidation before receiving the retention from the employer, the Ministry of Public Building and Works. The Ministry released the retention to the liquidator apparently before the proceedings were issued by the sub-contractor. The Court of Appeal held, following *Re Tout and Finch*, that "the payment made by the Ministry to the liquidator in March 1970, was impressed in the liquidator's hands with a trust in favour of Harry Bibby". The report is unfortunately very brief but it seems the trust of the contractor's rights declared by the Green Form extended to the Ministry's cheque for the retention and the proceeds of the cheque held by the liquidator (see Chapter 6).

What is the position where a sub-contractor's retention is received by the contractor but not paid to the nominated sub-contractor before the contractor's liquidation? At first sight, unless the employer had received notice of the equitable assignment, it could not be compelled to pay the sub-contractor the same sum, *i.e.* to pay twice. Could the fact of nomination be actual or constructive notice? The question was considered in *Re Arthur Sanders* (1981) 17 BLR 125 in which Nourse J held:

> "Putting it at its lowest it seems to me to be clear that the employer requires and authorises the contractor to enter into a sub-contract in that form and that the employer has notice of its contents. The sub-contract therefore takes effect as an assignment to the sub-contractor, made with the authority and with the knowledge of the employer, of a due proportion of the contractor's beneficial interest in the retention moneys under clause 30(4)(a) of the main contract. In my judgment there can be no doubt that that is the effect of clause 11(h) of the FASS sub-contract" (at 138).

Although the employer is fixed with knowledge of the terms of the Green Form or NSC/4, it may not know whether a sub-contract incorporating them was in fact concluded: the contractor might have substituted its own terms and conditions or amended the standard form by omitting the trust clause. For this reason, a nominated sub-contractor concerned to protect its retention is best advised to give notice to the employer of the assignment effected by the sub-contract.

The ASI form of sub-contract includes the following clause:

> "6.41: All amounts retained will be held in trust by the employer in a separate banking account as money due to the contractor pending satisfactory completion of the work, and will include such money due to the sub-contractor".

The reference to "money due to the contractor" seems to suggest that only the contractor is the beneficiary, and there is no sub-trust or assignment as in *Re Tout & Finch*. The form seems to be a simplified version of NSC/4.

Rights of recourse

The sub-contract trust clause is subject to two equities:

1. Any right of recourse which the employer has over the whole retention, and

2. Any right of recourse which the contractor has against the retentions of the nominated sub-contractors.

If notice of assignment is given and the employer pays the sub-contractor's retention to it direct, the contractor will have been deprived of its right of recourse. Clause 23 of NSC/4 gives the contractor a right of set-off in respect of loss and/or expense actually incurred provided it complies with certain conditions. The architect is involved only where the cross-claim arises out of the sub-contractor's delay in completion. Even in that case, the architect may fail to notify the employer of the contractor's cross-claim. If the loss and expense is incurred as a result of a different breach neither the architect nor the employer would know of it unless notice were given by the contractor. In this situation, the employer should seek the contractor's confirmation that it claims no right of set-off against the sub-contractor before releasing the money. In the event of a dispute between contractor and sub-contractor, the employer should interplead. Interpleader proceedings enable the court to decide which of two or more claimants is entitled to property in the hands of a disinterested third party: *e.g. Drew* v *Josolyne* (1887) 18 QBD 590.

The employer's right of recourse contained in JCT 98 reads:

> "Notwithstanding the fiduciary interest of the Employer in the Retention as stated in clause 30.5.1 the Employer is entitled to exercise any right under this Contract of witholding and/or deduction from monies due or to become due to the Contractor against any amount so due under an Interim Certificate ..." (clause 30.1.1.2).

This right protects the employer in two ways: it may excuse it from having to set up a trust fund at all or, if an account is opened, it will enable the employer to make withdrawals from it without being in breach of trust.

The expression "right under this Contract of witholding and/or deduction" suggests that the employer's cross-claim must derive from a right given by the contract, rather than under common law. Sums expressly deductible include liquidated damages, the cost of employing others to carry out an instruction if the contractor refuses to do so (*e.g.* clause 4.1.2 of JCT 80, applied in *GPT Realisations* v *Panatown* (1992) 61 BLR 88), and a premium for personal injury insurance taken out by the employer if the contractor fails to do so, *e.g.* clause 21.1.3 of JCT 80. Claims for damages in tort are excluded. Damages for breach of contract also probably fall outside the scope of deductible claims, although there are dicta to the contrary: *Rayack Construction* v *Lampeter Meat* (1979) 12 BLR 30, 38. It is thought that the right of recourse given by the contract is exhaustive of the employer's rights of set-off against funded retention. There is an argument that "right under this Contract" means "under an express or an implied term" and, as the common law is implied unless excluded, it must apply even to funded retention. Although the words used might ordinarily be a restatement of the general law, this is unlikely here because, as trustee, the employer would normally have no rights against the retention, and the court will assume the parties had this in mind when using the expression "under the contract". *GPT Realisations* v *Panatown* (at 98) appears therefore to have been wrongly decided on this point.

The right of recourse is an inherent weakness of the chose in action representing retention: it constitutes the employer as an active self-interested trustee rather than a beneficiary of the trust with the contractor: *Wates* v *Franthom* (1991) 53 BLR 23, and Hayton CLY 1994. This is in contrast to other contexts where a commercial trustee has been found to be a co-beneficiary in respect of a right of deduction: *Re Lewis's of Leicester* [1995] 1 BCLC 428.

If the employer holds retention on trust for the contractor who in turn holds a proportion of its interest in the retention on trust for nominated sub-contractors, can the employer exercise its rights of deduction against the whole retention or only against the contractor's own proportion? The question arose in *Re Arthur Sanders* (1981) 17 BLR 125. In that case, a contractor had two contracts with the same employer. On the contractor's liquidation, one contract was virtually finished and retention of £11,086 was due and payable, of which £1,374 represented retention withheld against six nominated sub-contractors. On the other contract, the contractor owed £98,155 to the employer. The contracts were both in JCT 63 form which allowed the employer recourse against retention "for payment of any amount which he is entitled under the provisions of this contract to deduct from any sum due or to become due to the contractor". The liquidator conceded that the employer was entitled in principle to liquidation set-off of its claim against the retention (see Chapter 13). The issue was whether the employer could make the set-off against the nominated sub-contractors' proportion. At first sight this depended on the question of mutuality: if the contractor held the nominated sub-contractors' portion as trustee, it would be held in a different capacity to the remainder of the retention and be unavailable for liquidation set-off. Nourse J denied set-off to the employer, analysing the position as follows:

> "In the present case the effect of the equitable assignment was to create a trust in favour of the sub-contractor of the company's equitable interest in the retentions. In other words, the position as between employer, contractor and sub-contractor under the present RIBA conditions and the FASS sub-contract is that the employer holds a due proportion of the retentions on trust for the contractor as trustee for the sub-contractor. ... It is not the retentions which are expressed to be subject to the right of the employer to have recourse thereto, but the contractor's 'beneficial interest' therein. In my judgment once a sub-contract has been entered into the contractor no longer has a beneficial interest in the sub-contractor's due proportion of the retentions. At that stage his only interest in that proportion is as a trustee for the sub-contractor ... Once that stage is reached I do not see how the proportion in question can really be said to be 'due' to the contractor at all. It may strictly still be payable to him under the terms of the main contract, but he must immediately pay it over under the sub-contract. ... To hold otherwise would necessarily involve the consequences that the sub-contractors were deprived of the security which this elaborate scheme of things was clearly intended to give them at the very moment when they most needed it, that is to say on the insolvency of the contractor" (at 138-140).

The court seems to have reached the right result but for the wrong reasons. Liquidation set-off allowed the recourse against the main contractor's proportion of retention since there was mutuality between contractor and employer. But as between the employer and the nominated sub-contractors, liquidation set-off was not available because the trust scheme only allowed the employer to set off against the nominated sub-contractors' proportion of the retention in respect of claims against the contractor on the same project. In this case the employer's cross-claim arose under a different contract. Lack of mutuality between the employer and the sub-contractors was not the issue in the case.

The purpose of the retention trust is to protect the contractor against employer insolvency or the sub-contractors against contractor (and indirectly employer) insolvency. It is not intended to rewrite the contract. Nourse J has not taken the employer's right of recourse into account in his analysis. This view is supported by a decision of the High Court of Hong Kong where an employer was allowed to set off against the whole retention in respect of losses arising from a nominated sub-contractor's default. No question of insolvency arose. The court distinguished *Re Arthur Sanders* in the following passage:

> "The phrase 'any sum due or to become due to the main contractor' is almost a term of art in this contract. It simply covers all certified payments payable to the main contractor. I do not see how its meaning can be affected by any equitable assignment. To say that the assignor, main contractor, 'must immediately pay it over' seems to me with respect wrong. It ignores the provisions of Clause 13 subject to which the assignment was made. As its initial recipient, the main contractor has an interest in the whole fund. The interest in 'his' part is admittedly beneficial. But although he may hold other portions as trustee for particular nominated sub-contractors, in no case is he simply a bare trustee. Clause 13 gives him the right to retain or set off for his own benefit. I therefore conclude that for the purposes of Clause 30(4), the main contractor has a 'beneficial interest' in the whole retention fund. Accordingly in my judgment, the employer's right of recourse under Clause 30(4) extends to the whole retention fund, and no valid distinction can be drawn between the main contractor and the nominated sub-contractors' portions of it. Such recourse may be based on a right to deduct arising under any term of the contract, *e.g.* Clauses 2(1), 19(1)(c), 22 or 27(c). In each case the effect is the same. Up to the total amount of the permitted deduction the employer's obligation to set aside ceases; as does *pro tanto* the relationship of trustee and beneficiary. The trust continues to apply only to the balance if any" (*Hsin Chong Construction* v *Yaton Realty* (1986) 40 BLR 119 at 129).

In *Harrington* v *Co Partnership* (1998) 88 BLR 44, considered later in this chapter, the Court of Appeal applied the reasoning of Nourse J to the trust in the JCT 87 form. In so doing, the court again ignored the employer's contractual rights of recourse. The problems with JCT trust clauses arise because of a failure to work out the relationship between retention and set-off under the main and sub-contracts. In a decision on the retention trust provisions in the Australian SC JCC A (1985) sub-contract, it was held that the contractor's right of set-off against sub-contractors' retention was "one of the terms of the trust qualifying the builder's obligations as trustee and limiting the sub-contractor's beneficial entitlement" (*KBH Construction* v *Lidco* (1991) 7 BCL 183, 191).

Main contract retention trusts

JCT 63 introduced a trust of retention in favour of the main contractor. Clause 30(4) of this form reads:

> "The Employer's interest in any amount so retained shall be fiduciary as trustee for the Contractor (but without obligation to invest), and the Contractor's beneficial interest therein shall be subject only to the right of the Employer to have recourse thereto from time to time for payment of any amount which he is entitled under the provisions of this Contract to deduct from any sums due or to become due to the Contractor".

The fundamental difficulty is the apparent lack of trust property. In the Green Form quoted earlier, the "amount so retained" was identifiable as the main contract retention and the trust property consisted in the contractor's rights to that retention. In the JCT 63 clause, the "amount so retained" refers to the debt owed by the employer but the employer cannot have a right against itself. Nevertheless, the clause has been construed as imposing "an obligation on an employer to appropriate and set aside as a separate trust fund a sum equal to that part of the sum certified in any interim certificate as due in respect of work completed which the employer is entitled to retain during the defects liability period": *Rayack Construction* v *Lampeter Meat* (1979) 12 BLR 30, 37. The retention trust clause of JCT 98, the current edition of the Standard Form of Building Contract, runs as follows:

> "30.5 The Retention shall be subject to the following rules:
>
> .1 the Employer's interest in the Retention is fiduciary as trustee for the Contractor and for any Nominated Sub-Contractor (but without obligation to invest);
>
> .2.1 at the date of each Interim Certificate the Architect shall prepare, or instruct the Quantity Surveyor to prepare, a statement specifying the Contractor's retention and the Nominated sub-Contract retention for each Nominated Sub-Contractor deducted in arriving at the amount stated as due in such Interim Certificate;
>
> .2.2 such statement shall be issued by the Architect to the Employer, to the Contractor and to each Nominated Sub-Contractor whose work is referred to in the statement.

.3   The Employer shall, to the extent that the Employer exercises his right under clause 30.4, if the Contractor or any Nominated Sub-Contractor so requests, at the date of payment under each Interim Certificate place the Retention in a separate banking account (so designated as to identify the amount as the Retention held by the Employer on trust as provided in clause 30.5.1) and certify to the Architect with a copy to the Contractor that such amount has been so placed. The Employer shall be entitled to the full beneficial interest in any interest accruing in the separate banking account and shall be under no duty to account for any such interest to the Contractor or any sub-contractor."

As payment of retention is deferred under the building contract, release of the equivalent amount to the employer under the funding agreement is usually witheld on the same terms, although the funding agreement may impose as a further condition a certificate from its surveyor that all defects have been made good. This is well understood in the industry and may be the reason for the request envisaged by clause 30.5.3. The rationale is that the employer should not be expected to fund a payment it has not received itself. If the parties deleted this sub-clause, the court would still give effect to the trust wording in the main contract and order an equivalent amount to be set aside. The sub-clause is "merely machinery for giving effect to the trust": *Herbert Construction* v *Atlantic Estates* (1993) 70 BLR 46, 65. As a fiduciary the employer cannot use retention as part of its own working capital: *Wates Construction* v *Franthom* (1991) 53 BLR 23.

Where the form is unamended, but no request is made to set money aside, it has been argued that the trust wording will extend to any right the employer has to "retention" under the funding agreement (Hayton CLY 1994). If it can be shown that the employer knows that a receivable under the funding agreement will represent the retention it agreed to hold on trust for the contractor, it is reasonable to conclude that the employer holds that chose in action on trust for the contractor, subject to its rights of deduction: see *Pullan* v *Koe* [1913] 1 Ch 9. Once payment is made by the funder to the employer, it will become subject to the trust, in substitution for the original chose, and the contractor will have tracing rights in respect of it.

In *Re Jartay Developments* (1982) 22 BLR 134, the employer went into liquidation before having set aside retention. The court rejected the contractor's claim that the main contract trust clause was an assignment of the employer's rights under a development agreement. Unlike the position with nominated sub-contractors, there was no express assignment in the building contract of the employer's rights under the development agreement and it was not made a condition of the development agreement that the building contract include a trust clause. Nor could any assignment be implied:

> "The provisions for retentions under clause 30 of the RIBA conditions have no reference to the retentions under the development contract. They take effect de novo as between [the contractor] and [the developer]. Moreover, as Mr. Hegarty for the liquidator pointed out, the provisions in the two contracts which deal with certificates and payments, retentions, practical completion and release of retentions are entirely different. The retentions were different in amount, being £30,000 under the development contract and about £46,000 under the building contract. In my judgment this is not a case where it can be said that [the developer] and [the contractor] must have intended that there should be assignment to [the contractor], either in whole or in part, of [the developer's] contractual right as against the [the fund] to the retentions of £15,000. It is clear to me that if I were to hold that that must have been their common intention I would be making for the parties a contract which they could have made, but did not make, for themselves" (at 142).

A development agreement will often mirror the building contract. For example, in *Banque Paribas* v *Venaglass* [1994] CILL 918, a freeholder terminated a development agreement on the developer's insolvency. The bank was assignee from the developer of the benefit of the agreement. The termination clause obliged the freeholder to pay the value of the work carried out as quantified by an independent quantity surveyor. It was held that the *quantum meruit* approach was correct: the freeholder's liability was not limited to such amount of the development value of the site as had been released by the termination date.

Inconsistencies between funding and building contracts to the extent of those in *Re Jartay Developments* are comparatively rare. The funding agreement is much more likely to mirror the payment terms of the building contract, as in *Finnegan* v *Ford Sellar Morris* (No 2) (1991) 27 Con LR 41, 51. Funders are likely to make approval of the building contract a condition of the loan, as in the *MacJordan* case considered later. The only significant difference is the interposition of the funder's surveyor's approval as a condition of release of retention, over and above the certificate of making good defects. Professor David Hayton views the surveyor's approval as a restriction on the chose owed by the employer: it cannot negative a trust of that chose. As soon as the surveyors gave their approval, the chose would mature into a debt. If the employer had no rights of deduction, it would hold the debt as bare trustee for the contractor and there is an implied equitable assignment as in *Re Tout and Finch*. If the contractor then gave notice of the assignment, the funder could only get a good discharge by paying the contractor. The same presumably applies where the surveyor's approval or the architect's certificate are wrongly withheld.

JCT forms impose no duty on the employer to invest funded retention. This means that the employer keeps any interest earned on it, even if retention is released in full at the end of the defects liability period. This is unjust as not only does the contractor have to suffer withholding of its retention but it also has to finance it. A fairer approach would be to say that interest should follow the retention so that if the retention is released in full the contractor should be entitled to the interest. If on the other hand, the employer has a cross-claim which cannot be met in full by the retention, it should be entitled to the benefit of any interest required to meet the balance of the cross-claim. Under the Australian AS 2124-1992 form the account is in the joint names of employer and contractor and withdrawals have to be sanctioned by both of them. Interest on the retention belongs to the contractor. It is interesting to note that this was the position in the predecessors of the JCT forms. For example, clause 25(d) of the RIBA contract (1931 edition) obliged the employer, on the architect's certificate, to open a trust account in joint names once the retention reached £1,000. The fund thereby created was to be held "together with all interest upon trust for the Employer as security for the due completion of the Works". The retention and accrued interest was then paid to the contractor on completion in two stages. This was expressly subject to the employer's right to any liquidated damages for delay. The clause also dealt with the situation where the employer became insolvent or repudiated the contract: in either case, the retention and accrued interest had to be paid to the contractor. This clause, and indeed the contract as a whole, is refreshingly clear and shows how a standard form, while essential in an industry like construction, becomes progressively more unwieldy as time goes by. The only disadvantage was that the retention trust was an optional clause in the RIBA form, whereas it is integrated within the JCT forms.

Management contract trusts

When the JCT introduced a form of management contract, it was decided to extend the protection of the retention trust to the management contractor and to all works contractors. It is possible for the trust to be limited to one particular group of works contractors to the exclusion of the others if the drafting is clear enough, but if there is no express trust clause, the court will not imply a trust simply because the subject matter is retention: *Herbert Construction* v *Atlantic Estates* (1993) 70 BLR 46.

As with JCT 80, retention is only funded under JCT 87 on request. In the unreported case of *H L Smith Construction* v *Albany Estates* (noted in Dean 1996), the contractor contended it had performed its function by passing on the request even though the employer had not opened the trust account. Despite the lack of privity, the works contractor obtained a mandatory injunction against the employer to set up the account. There were common directors between the employer and the management contractor and the court was satisfied that the employer had actual or constructive notice of the request.

The scheme is closely analogous to JCT 80. On the basis of the interlocking provisions of the management and works contracts and the extensive case law on the retention trust it might have been expected that once an account had been set up, the employer would hold it (subject to its own rights of deduction) on trust for the management contractor to hold (subject to its rights of deduction against the works contractors) as sub-trustee for the works contractors as tenants in common in proportions ascertainable from certificates issued under the management contract. According to the Court of Appeal in *Harrington* v *Co Partnership* (1998) 88 BLR 44, this is not the case.

Harrington was a works contractor under WC/2 with John Lelliott as management contractor. Harrington's work was completed early on in the project and it was agreed that the defects liability period under their works contract had expired. The project had been practically completed, but defective work by other works contractors meant that there had been no project-wide certificate of completion of making good defects. The latter certificate was a condition to the release of the second half of retention to the works contractors, including Harrington. The employer had set aside a retention fund which stood at nearly £300,000 when Lelliott went into administrative receivership. Under JCT 87, Lelliott's employment was automatically terminated. The architect certified under the management contract termination clause that the employer's loss following termination was just over £650,000. The employer exhausted the retention account in partial satisfaction of its claim. Harrington claimed direct from the employer in respect of about £20,000 as its proportion of the money which had been in the account. The court at first instance decided that the employer's right of recourse was limited to retention withheld against the management contractor's fee and could not be exercised against retention held for works contractors since such retention could never have been money due or to become due to the management contractor. The decision was upheld on appeal. In giving the judgment of the court, Morritt LJ stated:

> "Down to the date of practical completion there were two parallel provisions for retentions, namely the retentions under the Management Contract pursuant to and in respect of the items specified in clause 4.6.2 and the retentions under the Works Contract pursuant to and in respect of the items specified in clause 4.23. The latter retentions never had been money due to the Management Contractor for they were specifically excluded from the interim certificates to be issued under clause 4.6 of the Management Contract. From the time the respective retentions were made they were held in one fund by the Employer in trust in the amounts of the respective retentions for the Management Contractor and the Works Contractor pursuant to clause 4.8.1 of the Management Contract. After practical completion the Management Contract retentions did become due by the Employer to the Management Contractor for the authority to retain them ceased at that stage and at the later stage of the certificate of completion of making good defects. Thus the right of set-off of the Employer under clause 7.4.4 was exercisable against those retentions. But in my view it is clear that such right was never exercisable against the Works Contract retentions. Those retentions had not been and never became 'money due to the Management Contractor' (see Chapter 3). They were held by the Employer in trust for the Works Contractor. By the time for the preparation of the interim certificate prescribed by clause 4.11 of the Management Contract the Works Contract retentions should have been released because the authority to retain them had lapsed pursuant to clause 4.23. In that event clause 4.3.2 could not be applied for the Employer would no longer hold the retention. But if for some reason the certificate of completion of making good defects had not been granted at the time when the certificate required by clause 4.11 was prepared it would make no difference. At all times since the Works Contract retentions had been made they had been held by the Employer in trust for the Works Contractor. The interim certificate required by clause 4.11 could not operate so as to make the Works Contract retentions due to the Management Contractor rather than the Works Contractor" (at 54).

Under the management contract, the employer agrees to pay the management contractor the prime cost of the project and a management fee. The prime cost is defined as including all sums due to works contractors, which must include their retention. All sums payable to the management contractor are channelled through interim certificates issued by the architect. The employer has no right to pay works contractors direct, other than after termination, and even then there needs to be a contractual set-off against money due or to become due to the contractor. It follows that retention like all other payments to works contractors begins life as a sum due to the management contractor.

The employer's right of recourse is linked with the trust retention clause in the management contract which specifically states that retention in that context includes works contractors' retention, thereby ousting the contract definition of retention as that withheld against the management fee. The existence of the trust seems to have blinded the Court of Appeal to the ordinary contractual restrictions on release of retention. As no certificate of making good defects for the project had been issued prior to termination no works contracts retention was due for release. This is a condition precedent and there was no allegation that the certificate had been wrongly withheld. The court appears to have regarded the trust as freeing retention from its conditionality, but there is no justification for this. The only machinery for release of works contract retention after making good defects of the project is by interim certificate under clause 4.11. That certificate can only be for money due to the management contractor in the first instance. It is true that, if employer and contractor confirmed that they had no rights of deduction, the works contractor could call for payment direct, the contractor stepping out of the picture as bare trustee. But that did not happen here since the employer had a right of deduction under the main contract termination clause.

The effect of Lelliott's receivership was to automatically terminate the employment of the management contractor and all works contractors. In each case, the termination is without prejudice to the accrued rights or remedies of either party, which would include their rights as beneficiaries under the retention trust subject to other relevant terms of the management and works contract forms. Such terms would include the automatic suspension of payment to the management contractor and the employer's right to recover termination losses by way of set-off. The termination clause in the management contract replaces the normal payment provisions, including those relating to retention, since the employer's set-off is to be made against "the total amount which would have been payable on due completion in accordance with this Contract" *i.e.* the prime cost. As with JCT 80, the purpose of the trust is not to re-write the contract terms relating to retention but to change the status of payer-payee from that of debtor-creditor to trustee-beneficiary. It is possible that the court may have confused the expiry of the defects liability period under the works contract with the defects period for the project as a whole. Had the employer been attempting to use its right of recourse to satisfy a cross-claim arising against Lelliott under a separate contract, it would have been right to order release of retention to the works contractors: *Re Arthur Sanders*. The court may have been misled by the approach of Nourse J in that case, who held that the proportion of retention attributable to nominated sub-contractors could not be due to the main contractor. The court also rejected the employer's submission that the contractor's right to deduct a cash discount of 2.5% from all payments implied that retention must have been due to the contractor, perhaps through a misapprehension that retention becomes automatically due for release on the certificate of making good defects for the project without the need for a further interim certificate.

This case can be contrasted with an earlier decision of the Court of Appeal, *Rafidain Bank* v *Saipem* (unreported, 2 March 1994), which is considered in detail later. The court ordered payment out of the trust of the second half of retention to a contractor even though the contractor could not provide one of the documents required by the trust agreement. In that case, the document was regarded as a formality, not as an equity qualifying the contractor's proprietary interest in the fund. The employer as engineer had issued a final acceptance certificate, had no cross-claim and apparently accepted that the document in question was merely evidence of something the employer already knew to be the case. In *Harrington*, the court, naturally concerned to arrive at the just result, overrode the employer's equity. Admittedly, the contrary result would have been hard on works contractors, especially those who finish their packages early in the project. It is hard on innocent works contractors to be deprived of retention because of defaults by the management contractor or by other works contractors. That is, however, how the JCT retention scheme works: *Hsin Chong Construction* v *Yaton Realty* (1986) 40 BLR 119. The position is analogous to a claim by a sub-contractor pursuant to a lien law. A claim can only succeed to the extent of any surplus owing to the contractor after the employer has set off the cost to complete (see Chapter 17). There is a potential conflict between the notions of "retention" and "trust". Retention protects the employer against the contractor's insolvency, in particular by making the issue of a making good defects certificate a condition precedent for its release. A trust protects the works contractors against the insolvency of the contractor and the employer, but cannot alter the nature of the trust property as defined by the contract: compare *Balfour Beatty* v *Britania Life* [1997] SLT 10 discussed in Chapter 17.

Mandatory injunctions

In practice, employers do not set aside retention into a separate account requested to do so. Research suggests that employers regard such requests as insulting (Hopper 1996). If the employer refuses to open a trust account, the court has power to grant a mandatory injunction ordering it to do so. The application may be made *ex parte* in urgent situations but otherwise on notice or on an application for summary judgment. The court requires evidence that the parties entered into a contract containing a trust clause, or conceivably that such a term was incorporated by a course of dealing (*Harry Bibby* v *Neill Construction* [1973] EGD 52), that retention has been withheld and that the employer has refused a request to fund it. The affidavit should also give all relevant details surrounding the application, *e.g.* a description of the works, the stage they had reached, the amount of the contract sum received on account and any cross claims which had been raised by the employer, and disclose any special circumstances. In that regard:

> "It is ridiculous to suggest that the main contractor can only insist on the trust being set up if it can adduce evidence of some shakiness in the employer's financial position. If the main contractor had to wait till such evidence was forthcoming it would often by then be too late to take steps which would result in the fund being secured. Rather than requiring the main contractor to show that the horse is showing signs of bolting, the courts allow it to take steps to have the stable door shut while there is still no suggestion of anything being amiss. In asking for a trust fund to be set up, the main contractor is merely acting prudently": *Concorde Construction* v *Colgan* (1984) 29 BLR 125, 135.

Even so, there are limits it seems, and injunctions were refused partly for lateness in *GPT Realisations* v *Panatown* (1992) 61 BLR 88. It was an extreme case in that of the three contracts between the parties two had already reached practical completion and the other had been terminated. The court has granted injunctions after practical completion before and this ought not to be a problem especially in view of the kind of relief being sought. Termination ought not to be regarded as a bar since only the contractor's employment is terminated, and the termination clause does not suspend the employer's duty to fund retention, only its duty to pay sums due. The court seems to have been influenced more by the fact that the contractor was in receivership and refused to give an undertaking in damages and was also dragging its feet in arbitrations against the employer. Against this however it can be argued that the insolvency of the beneficiary (and its consequential difficulty with an undertaking in damages) could not prejudice the employer as its property will be preserved in the account pending the resolution of the dispute. The case seems to come down to the court's perception that the application was at heart a tactical one. As the injunction was refused in the end because the employer had rights of recourse exceeding the retention, it is not persuasive authority on these issues.

The court has granted injunctions on the eve of the employer's formal insolvency: *Finnegan* v *Ford Sellar Morris* (No 2) (1991) 27 Con LR 41. If it turns out that the employer is genuinely unable to comply with the injunction, the court can always discharge the order leaving the contractor with other remedies such as winding-up or personal claims against the directors. In *MacJordan Construction* v *Brookmount Erostin* (1992) 56 BLR 1, considered later in this chapter, the court was concerned with an application against an employer who was already in receivership. In passing, Scott LJ expressed the view that to grant an injunction where the employer was informally insolvent would be a preference of the contractor. This issue is discussed in Chapter 15.

The court will not grant an injunction if satisfied that the employer is entitled to exercise a right of recourse in excess of the retention for two reasons:

1. It would be pointless to set aside a fund for it to be immediately exhausted.

2. If the employer exercised its right of deduction there would be no retention capable of being funded.

Where the employer claims liquidated damages, the court has refused an injunction where the architect had certified non-completion under JCT 63 (*Henry Boot* v *The Croydon Hotel* (1985) 36 BLR 41), but not where the employer had given notice of non-completion under JCT 81 (*Finnegan* v *Ford Sellar Morris* (No 1) (1991) 53 BLR 38). Where the employer only has an unsubstantiated claim for defects, an injunction will be granted: *Concorde Construction* v *Colgan* (1984) 29 BLR 125. In one case, where ordering an employer, who was a private individual, to open a trust account, the court directed that the employer could not exercise any right of recourse against the fund without an order of the court: *Tolent Construction* v *Kustow* (unreported, 28 June 1994). It seems to follow from the decision in *Harrington* v *Co Partnership* (1998) 88 BLR 44 that the employer under JCT 87 would have to fund works contractors' retention in full notwithstanding any right of recourse it may have against the management contractor. As a request by one works contractor is deemed to be a request by them all, would the court discriminate between performing and defaulting works contractors when ordering the fund to be set aside, if satisfied that the employer's right of recourse against the contractor was not attributable to its default? This would be impracticable on an injunction application, and highlights one of the problems with the decision in *Harrington*.

In order to avoid setting up a fund, the directors of the employer may assure the contractor that it has funds available to pay retention as and when it became due. If the assurance is given dishonestly or recklessly, it may ground an action in deceit against the directors personally if it later emerges that the assurance was untrue. Other alternatives are to ask the employer to procure a bond from the funder, an assignment or attornment from the funder or a parent company guarantee from the employer, although only a demand bond would give the same protection as a properly funded trust.

Trust or charge?

The Lovell case

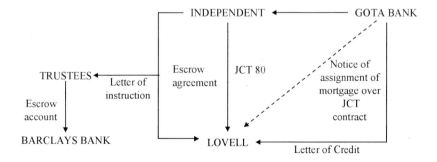

Fig 11.1

So far, the only authority on the trust of the contract sum is *Lovell Construction* v *Independent Estates* [1994] 1 BCLC 31. The facts of this case are instructive: see Figure 11.1. Independent was incorporated in 1989 at the height of a property boom. During the year, it acquired numerous properties for redevelopment by borrowing from Gota Bank and other Scandinavian lenders. At the end of 1989, Independent purchased a property in London NW1 for £14 million with funding from Gota Bank against a mortgage on the property and all present and future contracts relating to it. In the middle of 1991, Lovell agreed to redevelop the property for a contract sum of £16 million on condition that interim payments were channelled through an escrow account. The contract was in the JCT 80 form, amended to allow Lovell to terminate its employment if payments were not made in advance into the escrow account and to require the architect to send copies of his certificates to the parties' solicitors.

The escrow agreement stated that its purpose was to facilitate payment under the building contract through an account to be opened at Barclays in the names of the parties' solicitors. The account was to continue until the final certificate or earlier termination for insolvency, in which case the architect was to value the works in accordance with the termination clause in the contract and, if appropriate, certify further payment to Lovell. On receipt of the architect's certificate, the trustees were to pay Lovell by telegraphic transfer and the trust would terminate, any surplus in the account being repaid to Independent. The escrow agreement stated that any money paid into the account was "deemed to be impressed with a trust in favour of Lovell" although interest was to be for Independent's sole benefit. Payments into the account were to be made in accordance with an agreed schedule. Any certificate by the architect after an insolvency termination could only have been issued under the escrow agreement as the termination clause in JCT 80 is silent on the point.

The parties then instructed their solicitors to open an account in the solicitors' names and to transfer sums to Lovell immediately on receipt of interim certificates provided there were sufficient funds in the account to enable them to do so. The only exception was where the architect had certified Lovell to be in delay, when the solicitors were to abate payment by the amount of any liquidated damages levied by Independent. By early 1992, the property market had collapsed and the project was no longer viable. Lovell requested additional security and Independent procured from Gota Bank a standby letter of credit for £1 million payable on demand on receipt of Lovell's certificate that an interim certificate had not been honoured "by reason of there being no sum standing to the credit of the escrow account" and that Independent had failed to honour the certificate in whole or in part. The letter of credit was to expire at the end of June 1992. In early March, the bank served Lovell with notice of the assignment of the benefit of the building contract and the escrow agreement which had been effected by the mortgage executed by Independent several years previously. At the end of March, the bank appointed receivers in respect of the site and the agreements. Lovell mistakenly believed that fixed charge receivership entitled them to terminate their employment and they served notice purporting to do so. The same day Independent convened a meeting of creditors under s 98 Insolvency Act 1986. Liquidators were appointed at a creditors' meeting held towards the end of April. At this point, the architect issued a certificate in favour of Lovell under the escrow agreement for final payment out of the account. However, the certificate was ineffective since the architect's power to issue it only arose on a valid termination of the building contract. It had become clear to Lovell that sums due to them would exceed the amount in the account and they would have to make a call on the standby letter of credit. The difficulty was that the architect had issued an invalid certificate and was concerned at its position, and the fact that it might not be paid in view of the employer's insolvency. By this time, there were only two weeks left before the letter of credit was to expire.

At this point, the liquidator claimed the balance standing in the account by challenging the status of the escrow agreement. He argued that the agreement amounted to a floating charge of the credit balance standing in the account from time to time as security for Independent's duty to pay under the building contract. As the charge had not been registered under s 395 Companies Act 1985, it could not be binding on him. Gota Bank had a valid security over the escrow agreement, and so it seems that the liquidator's efforts could only have benefited the bank. The bank was also exposed under the letter of credit. Lovell decided to take the initiative and served a fresh notice of termination under the contract, relying this time on the fact that Independent had gone into creditors' voluntary liquidation. Lovell immediately issued proceedings before the Official Referee which were primarily intended to procure the architect's certificate under the escrow agreement, non-payment of which was a condition precedent to a valid call under the letter of credit. Lovell then applied for leave to amend its proceedings to claim a declaration that the escrow account was not a registrable charge under the Companies Act 1985. In the end, this was the only issue which had to be decided by the court. The application was against the company in liquidation, the bank and the receivers. The liquidator was joined so as to ensure compliance with any direction to the architect to issue a certificate under the escrow agreement and to enable the court to hear his submissions on the security issue. The receivers were joined as claimants to the money in the escrow account and as parties interested in the architect's power to certify under the agreement. Neither they nor the bank played an active role.

The liquidator argued that Independent's right to any surplus in the account after payment had been made in full to Lovell was an equity of redemption. He argued that Independent's right to have liquidated damages deducted from payments out of the account was inconsistent with a trust. On its true construction, the whole arrangement was a security because Independent never lost its right to pay Lovell under the building contract. If it chose to do so, it would be entitled to redeem the money standing in the account to the extent of the interim certificate it had paid. If the arrangement did amount to a trust, it was a trust by way of security similar to that in *Compaq Computer* v *Abercorn* [1993] BCLC 602. Lovell argued in reply that, taken together, JCT 80 and the escrow agreement were simply the means of payment and, even if the trust were a security, it was not registrable under s 396. After hearing detailed argument, the court held in favour of Lovell:

> "It was the intention of the parties that the joint account should be a conduit by which monies due from Independent to Lovell pursuant to certificates issued by [the architect] should be channelled to Lovell. This was not in substitution of any rights Lovell had under the JCT contract. These were additional rights and in one sense can be described as a form of security, but it appears reasonable to infer that it was the intention of the parties that Lovell would look to the joint account rather than to their rights under [the building contract] for the honouring of certificates ... I have reached the conclusion that the machinery established by the escrow agreement was for effecting payment and was not for establishing security. Since on the happening of certain events moneys in the account might be paid out either to Lovell or Independent, both had a beneficial interest in the monies. I find that the escrow agreement established a trust and not by way of charge under which the legal interest was in the trustees and the beneficial interests were in Lovell and Independent" (at 36-37).

There was no need for the court to consider whether, had the trust been a charge, it would have been registrable. The upshot was that the architect certified again under the escrow agreement, the balance in the account was paid out to Lovell who were also able to claim under the letter of credit before it expired. The decision is in line with previous authorities such as *Carreras Rothmans v Freeman Matthews Treasure* [1985] 1 All ER 155.

This case has a number of interesting features. First, the correct analysis of the escrow agreement was that it constituted a trust to pay Lovell in accordance with certificates issued under the building contract. Secondly, the claim that the trust of the account was a charge over a book debt was misconceived. To fall within s 396 Companies Act 1985, the charge had to be in respect of debts owed to the chargor, *i.e.* Independent. In this case, the account was a debt owed by the bank to the trustees, who were primarily accountable to Lovell. It is true that Independent was entitled to any surplus in the account after the contract sum had been paid, but even this is unlikely to be accepted as a book debt: *Re Brightlife* [1987] Ch 200 and subsequent cases. It is only ascertainable after the "secured" obligation has been fully discharged, when the solicitors have become bare trustees in favour of Independent, dropping out of the picture as between Independent and Barclays. If it were intended as security, it seems that a trust can only take effect as an equitable mortgage not a charge (Anderson 1992). Thirdly, Lovell's position would have been easier if fixed charge receivership had been an insolvency termination event under JCT 80. Gota Bank had a floating charge over the undertaking of Independent, but only chose to appoint receivers under their fixed charges. Fourthly, although the escrow agreement was tied in to the payment clause of JCT 80, it was not fully integrated with the termination clause, in that quantification of the amount due to the contractor on termination for the employer's insolvency was not dealt with. The architect was not made a party to the escrow agreement and was concerned about his jurisdiction to issue the certificate.

The retention trust

The question whether the retention trust operates as a charge has not so far been raised in the case law. The fact that a charge over retention might cause practical difficulties in the industry is not necessarily a reason against it: compare *Re Welsh Irish Ferries Ltd* [1985] WLR 610. An argument might run as follows:

1. By paying money into a separate account, the employer has appropriated property for the discharge of a debt and charged the account as security for payment of retention.

2. The equity of redemption would be the right to withdraw the money in the account by satisfying the retention from another source.

3. The arrangement has other characteristics of a charge: the contractor is given a right in the fund; the contractor's interest has been conferred by the employer rather than reserved by it; the arrangement restricts the employer's rights of disposition of the money in the account; interest on the fund is payable to the employer.

This view is supported by a retention of title case which held that a clause constituting the buyer as trustee of hire charges arising from use of the goods until the seller had been paid was a registrable charge: *Tatung* v *Galex* (1989) 5 BCC 325.

Against this it can be argued by analogy with the *Lovell* case that the parties intended to create a trust as the means of payment of the retention. The trust device can be seen as the most appropriate vehicle to fulfil this purpose as it identifies the retention, recognises the claims of contractor and employer and protects the money in the event of the employer's liquidation. As the retention accrues, the employer's contractual duties in respect of it are discharged by payment into the account. The contractor's right to payment from the account arises by operation of the trust provisions: see *Swiss Bank* v *Lloyd's Bank* [1980] 2 All ER 419, 426. If this is correct, the contractor's remedy if the employer fails to release retention when it becomes payable is not to sue the employer in debt but to seek a declaration that it has performed the contract and an order that the fund be paid out to it. In a retention of title case, the House of Lords tested whether a seller had a security interest by asking whether it retained the ultimate right to the goods: *Armour* v *Thyssen* [1990] 3 All ER 481. In this context the contractor has the ultimate right to the fund, subject to the employer's rights of deduction. The employer only has a right to the fund on the contractor's default. This is the reverse of the position which would have applied had the trust operated as a charge. The fact that the employer cannot mix its own money with the retention fund also points towards a trust: *Re ILG Travel* [1995] 2 BCLC 128, 156.

A trust is more consistent with the intention of the parties as expressed in the JCT forms. If the retention trust is a charge, is it registrable? It is not registrable as a book debt: see the earlier discussion on the Lovell trust. A retention trust clause is similar to a floating charge in that both exist mainly in potential. Just as the charge is an incomplete assignment until a receiver is appointed, so the trust clause is a purely contractual right until money is set aside. However, there the resemblance ends because the charge-holder has complete control over the receiver's appointment, whereas the contractor is dependent on the employer's co-operation, or the court's assistance, to constitute a trust. In the interim the borrower is entitled to dispose of assets falling within the floating charge provided it does so in the ordinary course of business, whereas if the employer makes no attempt to segregate retention and simply uses it as working capital, it does so in ordinary breach of contract. It appears therefore that a security over retention would not be registrable.

The MacJordan case

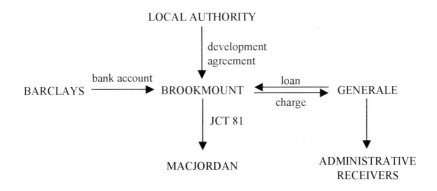

Fig 11.2

The difference between these two devices is highlighted in *MacJordan Construction* v *Brookmount Erostin* (1992) 56 BLR 1 which concerned a contest between a contractor and administrative receivers of an employer over money standing in the employer's general bank account: see Figure 11.2. Brookmount agreed with the local authority to develop land. Brookmount approached Generale Bank for funding, who agreed in principle subject to three conditions: that the terms of the intended building contract be satisfactory to the bank; that a certified copy of the building contract be given to the bank after execution; and that Brookmount give as security a floating charge over its undertaking. All three conditions were satisfied. The contract with MacJordan was in the JCT 81 form, which includes the standard retention trust clause. Before completion of the contract, Generale appointed administrative receivers to Brookmount under its floating charge and MacJordan gave formal notice terminating its employment. The statement of affairs disclosed a shortfall under the bank's security of £2 million, and a claim by MacJordan for £1 million which included retention of £110,000. The retention had not been set aside into a trust by the time the receivers were appointed. Brookmount had over £150,000 cash at bank with Barclays. It was this account which formed the subject of the dispute. Until it saw the statement of affairs, MacJordan was unaware of the cash at bank.

On the face of it, the bank account fell squarely within Generale's floating charge over Brookmount's undertaking. The onus was on MacJordan to satisfy the court why it should grant an injunction setting aside £110,000 of the £150,000 in the account into a separate trust fund. In order to do this, MacJordan had to show either that a trust had been formed in some way before the receivership or that its right to have the money segregated was an equity subject to which the bank took the borrower's property by equitable assignment on the appointment of the receivers.

MacJordan put its case in three ways. First it argued that the trust clause gave it an interest in a notional fund which took priority over the floating charge. The contractor raised the maxim that "equity looks on as done that which ought to be done". The problem for MacJordan was that the maxim was only effective against Brookmount, not against a third party like the bank who had given consideration for its security. It was true that Nourse J. had treated retention as notionally set aside in *Re Arthur Sanders* (1981) 17 BLR 125, but that could not assist MacJordan since in *Re Arthur Sanders* it was the contractor who was insolvent not the employer-trustee (compare *G & T Earle v Hemsworth RDC* (1928) 140 LT 69). The second argument was that MacJordan had an equitable interest in the bank account at Barclays. The precise basis for the claim was not elaborated and it had to be rejected because, apart from the rough parity between the amounts, there was no link between the retention and the bank account. Even if Brookmount had declared itself trustee of £110,000 of the £150,000, the trust would have failed for lack of identifiable subject matter. It might have been possible, however, for MacJordan to have argued that it had an equitable charge over the account under the principles explained in *Re Diplock* [1948] Ch 465 (see Hayton LQR 1994). It was the third argument that caused the court to pause. This was that the trust clause was an equity binding on Generale since it had notice of it before accepting the floating charge.

Generale had specifically made it a condition of providing finance to Brookmount that it approved the form of the building contract and it must be taken to have known of the existence and legal effect of the retention trust clause. There was binding authority in the form of *De Mattos* v *Gibson* (1858) 4 De G & J 276 in support of the view that a person obtaining an equitable right aware of a prior equity must take subject to that equity.

The court accepted that, when the floating charge was granted, Generale's rights against Brookmount's property were subject to MacJordan's rights under the building contract, including the right to have retention funded. Funding the retention would have been an act in the ordinary course of Brookmount's business. The bank was or ought to have been fully aware of this possibility. Unfortunately for MacJordan, on the appointment of the receivers, the floating charge crystallised and became a fixed charge on Brookmount's property, including the bank account at Barclays. In law, crystallisation took effect as an equitable assignment to Generale of all the property covered by the floating charge. It followed that, after the receivers' appointment, Brookmount had no cash available to it from which to fund the retention and the court would not make an order in vain. There were two further points: on crystallisation, the property caught by the floating charge became subject to the rights of preferential creditors, such as Customs & Excise, who took priority over Generale. It was possible that the money in the account would be required to pay preferential creditors. Last, and controversially, the court observed that to grant an injunction against an informally insolvent employer would be to prefer the contractor. This aspect has been heavily criticised (Moss 1992, Lightman and Moss 1994), on the ground that, provided liquidation has not intervened, the court is always ready to assist one creditor over another in perfecting its rights, following *Roberts Petroleum* v *Kenny* [1983] 2 AC 192. This point is considered further in Chapter 13. The *MacJordan* case demonstrates that the value of retention trust clauses is lost unless enforced early on in the contract.

There is no reported case on the position where the employer goes into administration before having set aside a retention fund. It is possible that a contractor's prospects of obtaining an injunction depends on which of the four statutory grounds forms the basis of the order. If it were to achieve a better realisation of assets than on a liquidation, then an injunction ought to be refused because the administration would be a quasi-liquidation and ought to attract the *pari passu* rule. In *Re Polly Peck (No 2)* [1998] 3 All ER 812, the Court of Appeal applied the *pari passu* rule to liquidation and administration. The court refused to impose a remedial constructive trust over the assets of a company in administration. "You cannot grant a proprietary right to A, who has not had one beforehand, without taking some proprietary right away from B" (at 831). Although the contractor's right to have a trust funded can be specifically enforced, it is contractual not proprietary in nature. Where the administration is ordered on other grounds, the position remains open.

Sub-contract benefits

In addition to the retention trust, there are two other ways in which a nominated sub-contractor might be able to claim priority in the insolvency of the contractor: "name-borrowing" and the procurement of the benefit of the main contract. "Name-borrowing" is the right to bring an arbitration in the contractor's name against the employer where the sub-contractor is dissatisfied with an architect's instruction, an extension of time or the amount of a certified sum. In all three cases:

> "Subject to the Sub-Contractor giving the Contractor such indemnity and security as the Contractor may reasonably require the Contractor shall allow the Sub-Contractor to use the Contractor's name and if necessary will join with the Sub-Contractor in arbitration proceedings at the instigation of the Sub-Contractor to decide the matter as aforesaid" (clauses 2.7, 3.11 and 4.20 of NSC/C).

An example of the second avenue open to a nominated sub-contractor is clause 1.13 of NSC/C which provides:

> "The Contractor will so far as he lawfully can at the request of the Sub-Contractor obtain for him any rights or benefits of the provisions of the Main Contract so far as the same are applicable to the Sub-Contract Works and not inconsistent with the express terms of the Sub-Contract but not further or otherwise".

"Benefit" in this context extends to bringing an arbitration, but if the employer becomes insolvent before meeting the award, the contractor remains liable to pay the sub-contractor. It cannot argue that the "benefit" was the right to payment rather than payment itself: *Birse Construction v Co-Operative Wholesale Society* (1997) 58 BLR 58 at 77. A clause 1.13 claim applies to the whole of the main contract and an arbitration brought under it would be between the main contractor and the employer and under the control of the contractor. A "name borrowing" arbitration is limited to three heads of claim and takes effect as an arbitration by the sub-contractor in the name of the contractor but under the control of the sub-contractor: *Gordon Durham* v *Haden Young* (1990) 52 BLR 61. In the *Gordon Durham* case, a "name borrowing" arbitration was completed and the arbitrator granted the sub-contractor an extension of time and loss and expense. The employer was ordered to pay the sub-contractor direct "as effective claimants herein" within 14 days in full and final satisfaction of their claim. The award was issued by consent between the employer and the sub-contractor. No insolvency was involved.

If the contractor were insolvent, and the sub-contractor succeeded against the employer, or the contractor obtained a benefit for the sub-contractor under clause 1.13, could the contractor's insolvency practitioner claim the benefit from the sub-contractor? The answer turns on the construction of NSC/C. Take first the name borrowing procedure. A claim is usually brought in the name of another by (1) an insurer exercising a right of subrogation in the name of the insured, (2) an equitable assignee suing in the name of the assignor, or (3) a beneficiary of a trust claiming in the name of the trustee. In each case the nominal claimant would receive any damages subject to the other's proprietary interest: an equitable lien or charge in the case of subrogation (*Napier and Ettrick* v *Hunter* [1993] 1 All ER 385): a trust in the other two cases. Such an interest would protect the sub-contractor against the contractor's insolvency. The right to use the other's name is a consequence of an existing proprietary right. But if the right to sue in another's name is conferred by contract, and is not the consequence of a proprietary interest, the beneficiary only has a personal claim for the damages. The name borrowing provision could be seen as consistent with privity of contract, its purpose being to enable an arbitrator "to decide the matter" referred to him.

Outside the name-borrowing context, the courts have consistently rejected the notion that the contractor receives money from the employer representing sub-contractors' work as trustee for the sub-contractors. The question arose in *George E Taylor* v *G Percy Trentham* (1980) 16 BLR 15 where a contractor claimed a sum which had been withheld by the employer under a certificate. The sum represented a claim which the employer had against a sub-contractor under a direct warranty under which the sub-contractor was liable to the employer for delay. The employer had no right of set-off under the main contract in respect of this sum but it argued that the contractor had no beneficial interest in the money since it would have been bound to pass it on to the sub-contractor. This argument was rejected by the Official Referee, although he went on to speculate that the employer might have been able to set off the cross-claim against the sub-contractor had the sub-contractor made a claim for direct payment under the warranty.

An argument that a name borrowing clause took effect as a trust of the claim might be met by two defences:

- if the parties had intended a trust, they would have used clear language as in the retention trust clause
- there is a strong presumption against importing trust obligations into commercial contracts unless the context is clear.

On any view, the approach taken in NSC/C is not clear. A contractor receives a nominated sub-contractor's proportion of certified sums in its own right, unless they concern retention. The same applies to any loss and expense certified by the architect. It would seem strange that a nominated sub-contractor could alter this situation by invoking the "name borrowing" procedure. Such a result would adversely affect the contractor's rights of set-off in respect of cross-claims against the sub-contractor. The clause provides the sub-contractor with one of the rights of a trust beneficiary, but without constituting a trust. The court in *Lorne Stewart* v *William Sindall* (1986) 35 BLR 109 rejected an argument that the arrangement was an assignment (at 128). The language falls short of either assignment or trust and it seems more probable that the court would hold the "name borrowing" provision to be an elaborate contractual device which is not intended to disrupt the normal payment chain. It is not an express equivalent of the implied term that led to the equitable lien in *Napier's* case, *i.e.* that the insured would pay to the insurer any damages received from a third person attributable to the insurance proceeds it had received (at 409). The sub-contractor faces similar difficulties with a clause 1.13 claim (see *Schott-Kem* v *G Percy Trentham* (unreported, 15 May 1985, Court of Appeal) discussed in Chapter 12).

Alternatively the sub-contractor might argue that the contractor entered into the main contract for its benefit. In such a case, the contractor would hold the benefit on trust for the sub-contractor: *Lloyd's* v *Harper* (1880) 16 Ch D 290. The example in that case was of a broker entering into an insurance policy for the benefit of others. The judge stated: "I consider it to be an established rule of law that where a contract is made with A for the benefit of B, A can sue on the contract for the benefit of B, and recover all that B could have recovered if the contract had been made with B himself" (at 321). The principle was later applied by Lord Denning MR to enable a man to recover damages for loss of his holiday on behalf of himself and his family even though the booking was in his sole name: *Jackson* v *Horizon Holidays* [1975] 1 WLR 1468 at 1473. Construing the sub-contract as a whole it is not in this category. The question is whether it could fall within the principle in *Lloyd's* v *Harper* to the limited extent of clause 1.13. It is hard to resist the conclusion that all clause 1.13 does is to prevent the contractor sitting on its rights under the main contract: to the extent that they overlap and are consistent with a nominated sub-contract, it is reasonable that they should be exercised against the employer. But to the extent that the claim is successful against the employer, the contractor accounts to the sub-contractor in its own right for the proceeds and not as trustee or assignor. Clause 1.11 expressly excludes privity of contract as between the employer and the sub-contractor.

The same principles apply to clause 10(2) of the FCEC form of sub-contract which provides:

> "... the Contractor shall take all reasonable steps to secure from the Employer such contractual benefits, if any, as may be claimable in accordance with the Main Contract on account of any adverse physical conditions ... On receiving any such contractual benefits from the Employer ... the Contractor shall in turn pass on to the Sub-Contractor such proportion if any thereof as may in all the circumstances be fair and reasonable."

It has been stated that the duty to "pass on" a proportion of the benefit "imposes a legal obligation on the main contractors": *Mooney* v *Henry Boot* (1996) 80 BLR 66 at 78. A legal obligation can co-exist with an equitable obligation in the same transaction: *Barclays Bank* v *Quistclose* [1970] AC 567 at 581. The way that the words apparently reify the proportion could lead to an argument that it must be held on trust for the sub-contractor. But the language is commercial and is more likely to reflect the industry's linear idea of payment discussed in Chapter 3. In other words, although the contractor's claim may be calculated by reference to the sub-contractor's claim, it is not advanced as trustee for the sub-contractor.

On the contractor's insolvency, could the nominated sub-contractor still use the contractor's name or obtain specific performance of clauses 1.13 or 10(2)? The obvious analogy is with the right of a charge-holder to use the borrower's name in proceedings to realise property caught within a charge. This right survives the borrower's entry into liquidation but is only available to the charge-holder by reason of the security. Similarly a liquidator of an insured was ordered to co-operate with the insurer to obtain payment of money to which the insurer was entitled by subrogation: *Re Miller Gibb & Co* [1957] 2 All ER 266. But where the sub-contractor only has a contractual right against the company, the liquidator has a discretion whether to co-operate and cannot be compelled to do so. An insolvency practitioner may decide to seek an injunction preventing the sub-contractor from using the company's name or possibly do nothing and claim the benefit as soon as an award is issued. The only solution seems to be for the sub-contractor to ask the liquidator for an assignment of the cause of action against the employer.

Breach of trust

There are no reported cases in English law of breach of trust in connection with construction contracts. This is partly because trusts are rarely set up whether for retention or the whole contract sum and breach of trust is exceptional, and partly because insolvency practitioners lack the funds and solvent contractors the desire to pursue defaulters. There are breaches, however, and they fall into two kinds: unauthorised withdrawals from trust bank accounts and the misappropriation of cheques representing trust property. In either case tracing will be available in principle, subject to the usual rules as to identifiability of trust property. If tracing is not an effective remedy, *e.g.* where the money was paid in to an account which was already overdrawn by an amount in excess of the payment in, the beneficiaries of the trust may have personal claims against the companies concerned and their directors for knowing receipt or knowing assistance.

For example, in one case which was not pursued by the contractor, an employer asked a funder to pay an amount representing retention to its parent company who paid it into its overdrawn bank account and then went into liquidation. The employer had acknowledged it had no right of deduction in respect of the amount and on ordinary trust principles could only have received the cheque as bare trustee for the contractor: *e.g. International Factors v Rodriguez* [1979] QB 351. The authorisation to the funder to pay the parent company was a breach of trust, and the employer and those directors and employees concerned would be personally liable as constructive trustees for knowing assistance. If the parent was aware of the breach of trust, or turned a blind eye to the obvious, or failed to make the enquiries an honest person would make, it would also be personally liable to the contractor for knowing receipt and the relevant directors and employees would be liable for knowing assistance. Where the employer held its right to retention from the funder as bare trustee (and consequently as equitable assignor) and the contractor gave notice of that fact to the funder, the funder could only get a good discharge for the payment by paying the contractor. It follows that it is important for a contractor to give notice to anyone liable to pay money to the employer which could represent retention to prevent it being paid to the employer and then dissipated.

In addition, a bank and its relevant officers could be made liable for knowing assistance for demanding that retention received from a funder should be applied in reduction of an overdraft. In the absence of English authority, it is instructive to note a line of Canadian cases where banks have been held liable for breach of a statutory construction trust (see Glaholt 1999). In *Fonthill* v *Bank of Montreal* [1959] OR 451 a bank manager knew that deposits came from homeowners for whom the contractor was carrying out building work. The bank was presumed to know about the statutory trust and the fact that such deposits could only be used to pay sub-contractors. The bank had dishonoured cheques and knew that the contractor was in serious financial difficulties. It also knew that the contractor had not paid suppliers whose debts were due for payment. The manager had pressed for payment to reduce the contractor's overdraft and was aware that the contractor's wife had personally guaranteed the overdraft. It was held that in the circumstances, the bank had accepted deposits in reduction of the overdraft at the expense of trade creditors and for the benefit of the bank and the customer's wife. The deposits had not been received in the ordinary course of business and there were ample circumstances which should have put the bank on enquiry.

In England there is no statutory trust and a bank will not be on notice of a trust simply because its client is a builder. A contractor might use non-standard contracts or, even if the standard form is used, the parties may have deleted the retention trust clause. However, if after entering into the contract, the contractor immediately requested the employer to set aside retention as it became due and gave notice to the bank, the bank would be placed in a difficult position. If it were not funding the employer on the development concerned, it would have no knowledge whether particular receipts represented retention or not. It would impose a considerable burden on the bank if it had to enquire of the employer whether a cheque represented retention and it is not suggested that the bank would be under any such duty. However, if immediately before a cheque from a funder representing retention became due, the contractor put the bank on notice of that fact, it is submitted that the bank would have to make enquiry as to the nature of the payment to avoid potential liability for knowing assistance, particularly if it would otherwise have been paid into an overdrawn account.

Termination of trusts

A trust terminates either pursuant to an express power of revocation or when its purpose has been fulfilled. Construction trusts are usually irrevocable and fulfilment depends on the parties' performance of their contractual obligations. Fulfilment of the trust depends therefore on completion of the contract, and difficulties will arise where either or both parties become insolvent before completion. The termination clause in JCT contracts does not expressly deal with retention in that situation.

Numerous cases of employer insolvency arose in the early 1990s after retention had been set aside. In some cases, receivers opted to "mothball" the project, awaiting an improvement in the market and appropriate changes of use. Contractors were apparently left without a remedy. Although their retention was protected, it was depreciating over time because the employer in receivership was entitled to the interest.

The court might conclude that it was an implied term of the trust that where the contractor lost possession of the site on the employer's insolvency, practical completion should be deemed to have occurred at that moment, allowing part of the retention to be paid out to the contractor, with the balance becoming payable once the period for rectifying defects had expired. Otherwise:

> "it may well be that a Chancery judge will intervene to prevent the trustee-employer from unconscionably exploiting the strict contractual terms in its own favour well beyond what the parties contemplated when allowing the trustee-employer to have the benefit of the retention trust. This may enable the judge to impose a term that could not have been implied as a matter of contract at common law" (Hayton CLY 1994).

A possible solution is for the trustees to apply to the court under RSC Order 85 for guidance or for extra powers under s 57 Trustee Act 1925 or the court's inherent jurisdiction: see *Rafidain Bank* v *Saipem* (unreported, 2 March 1994) and Figure 11.3.

In that case, an Italian consortium as contractor agreed to build a pipeline for an Iraqi state-owned organisation (SCOP) as employer for

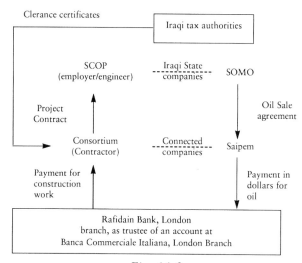

Fig. 11.3

about $500 million. The employer was named as engineer under the project contract. The contractor was to be paid from a trust account at Banca Commerciale Italiana in London on presentation of invoices to the trustee (Rafidain Bank) which had been approved by the employer in its capacity as engineer and certified by the Central Bank of Iraq. The project had been completed and the only remaining sum due to the contractor was the second half of its retention. It was a condition of final payment to the contractor that it obtained clearance certificates from the Iraqi authorities in relation to income tax, social security and customs as proof that the contractor had discharged its obligations to make these payments pursuant to the project contract. The contractor applied for the clearance certificates but before they were issued the Gulf war intervened and the pipeline was destroyed by allied bombing. Iraq passed legislation preventing payment to foreign contractors and international sanctions were imposed against Iraq. The trust account was funded by another Iraqi state-owned organisation (SOMO) from the proceeds of sale of oil to an Italian company (Saipem) linked with the consortium. In the absence of the clearance certificates, the employer would not approve the contractor's final invoice and the Central Bank of Iraq would not certify payment. On the contractor's application under RSC 85 as a beneficiary of the trust, the court directed Rafidain as trustee to pay the contractor its retention from the account, despite the absence of the requisite documents. The decision was upheld on appeal on different grounds. In the leading judgment, Hobhouse LJ had to consider the inter-action between the project contract, the finance agreement and the trust agreement. The trust agreement created both contractual and proprietary rights. He considered the contractor's claim in two stages:

1. Was the contractor entitled to payment from the account pursuant to the contractual obligations in the trust agreement?

2. If not, was it entitled to payment pursuant to its equitable proprietary rights in the fund?

The answers were "No" and "Yes" respectively.

In contract, the contractor argued that the mechanism for payment had broken down and that where a contractual condition had become impossible to fulfil, the court had jurisdiction to step in and provide a remedy. The argument failed since, although extremely unlikely, it remained a possibility that the Iraqi authorities would issue the clearance certificates. Even if there were impossibility, the court would not intervene because it had not been caused by the employer. It was common ground that the employer was not in breach of the project contract. The trustee was in the same position as the issuer of a demand guarantee or a letter of credit. Provision of documents in the correct form was a condition of liability intended to protect the paying parties. The court rejected an implied term excusing the contractor from providing the documents. The trust agreement was part of the overall contractual matrix: provision of documents was not simply procedural but conditioned the contractor's right to payment.

The arguments which were rejected when put in contract terms were accepted when advanced by the contractor as a beneficiary under the trust. The contractor was exclusively beneficially entitled to the account. "It was an equitable title which came into existence as an interest in possession at the time that the proceeds of the sale of the crude were paid by Saipem AG into the account" (at 46). The finding that the contractor had a vested interest in property cast a different light on the matter. The property vested under the terms of the trust agreement. The trust was to pay the contractor, in other words "to discharge, *pro tanto*, the obligations of [the employer] under the project contract" (at 48). As between the contractor and the employer, the retention was due for payment: the evidence was that the contractor had paid the local taxes. The court concluded that the duty to provide documents to the trustee was "part of the machinery of the administration of the trust, and not a qualification on the contractor's equitable proprietary right in the account" (at 49). The requirement for invoices approved by the employer as engineer and certified by the Central Bank of Iraq was a contractual term governing the exercise of the trustee's powers, not the existence of the trust or the interest of the contractor in the fund (at 51). To order payment to the contractor could not prejudice anyone. Even if it could, the contractor had given indemnities under the trust agreement which would cover the position. The court has jurisdiction to enable the purpose of a trust to be fulfilled in this kind of case by virtue of *Re New* [1901] 2 Ch 534:

> "Where some event or development unforeseen, perhaps unforeseeable, and anyhow unprovided against by the settlor or testator, threatened to make shipwreck of his intentions: and it was imperative that something should be saved from the impending wreck. These are often referred to as the 'salvage' cases …".

What was an absolute bar to recovery in contract was only an administrative detail in trust. The case is an excellent example of the status of property in English law. With only a contractual right to payment, the creditor has an uphill struggle and will be defeated by clearly expressed contractual conditions to its release. Where the creditor also has a vested right in the fund from which payment will be made, the court will take a broader view and intervene to rescue the creditor (or rather its property) if that is the just result in all the circumstances. The case is exceptional, arising out of extreme facts, but shows how overlaying a trust on a contractual matrix can enlarge the court's jurisdiction to deal with what was essentially a contractual problem.

Conclusion

As used in the construction industry, a trust is the means of payment offering informal security to the creditor. When overlaid on a contractual obligation, a trust also allows the court to do justice as it sees it in the light of all the facts. The analysis of *Re Arthur Sanders, Harrington* v *Co-Partnership* and *Rafidain Bank* v *Saipem* in this chapter shows how difficult it can be for the court to do justice and to follow precedent at the same time. The trust can also be seen as alleviating against the excessive individualism of freedom of contract. It is an authentic English remedy. The trust has a place in construction contracts as the means of payment since it reflects in law the image of payment which is commonly held by the industry.

Chapter 12

· Direct Payment ·

Introduction

Any disruption to cash flow has a potential knock on effect for the project. It is in the employer's interests that the contractor pays sub-contractors on time. Payment may be delayed for a number of reasons:

1. A contractor may deliberately delay payment so as to earn more interest.

2. A contractor under pressure from its bank may be forced to apply certified sums in reduction of its overdraft.

3. A contractor in a state of formal insolvency loses both the ability and the right to pay.

4. The terms of payment may be altered by the circumstances.

In the first two situations, the project may be delayed through sub-contractors suspending work in retaliation or through their own lack of working capital. In the others, the project may be put at risk by sub-contractors repossessing materials and plant or leaving site altogether.

In an attempt to manage these risks, employers include direct payment clauses in main contracts. They are a special feature of the standard forms. At first sight, they operate by allowing the employer to by-pass or leap-frog the contractor, but in reality they allow the employer to make payments to sub-contractors with one hand and take an equivalent amount from the contractor with the other. In legal terms, the effect of these clauses is not to divert payment but to convert the employer's duty to pay into a right, or rather two rights: to pay sub-contractors direct and then set off an equivalent amount against sums due to the contractor. As will be seen, the first of these rights is worthless without the second.

Where the contractor is solvent

The fact that construction work is carried out using chains of contracts gives rise to the idea that payment is linear. Sub-contractors often complain that certified sums are not being "passed on" to them. The FCEC form of sub-contract even uses this expression (see Chapter 11). The image is of payment as a thing to be divided by the contractor between itself and all the sub-contractors, and then sub-divided among the sub-sub-contractors and so on down the line. In law, a right to payment is a chose in action enforceable by bringing proceedings against the debtor. There is nothing to be "passed on". When the contractor's right to be paid is converted into a credit balance in its bank account, the contractor is solely beneficially entitled to it. Even though they are linked in a number of ways with the main contract, sub-contracts set up an autonomous right to payment against the contractor which is unrelated (other than in amount) to the contractor's rights against the employer. For example, in *Schott-Kem* v *G Percy Trentham* (unreported 15 May 1985, Court of Appeal) a nominated sub-contractor claimed about £50,000 from the contractor and also sought a declaration that, under the main contract, the contractor was owed at least £125,000 by the employer. The contractor defended on the basis that the sub-contractor had been paid everything that was due to him. There was no unpaid certified sum outstanding. The Court of Appeal rejected the sub-contractor's application. His difficulties:

> "were essentially inherent in the nature of the original contractual arrangements into which the sub-contractor – presumably with its eyes open – originally entered. These contractual arrangements seem to me clearly, carefully and deliberately designed so that the building owner will not be exposed to any kind of direct contractual obligation to the sub-contractor" (Slade LJ).

Where a trust is used, a sub-contractor has both contractual and equitable proprietary rights as explained in Chapter 6. By contrast, direct payment clauses are purely contractual and do not normally confer an actionable right in the sub-contractor. They operate down the chain by giving the employer power to calm any disruptions to payment. Trust rights usually operate up the chain by conferring equitable rights in property as an informal security for payment. In addition, as each contract in the chain is regarded as separate from the others, an employer can only obtain a good discharge by paying the person with whom it is in contract. If it pays a person further down the line it remains liable to pay the same sum to its own contracting party.

Where the contractor is solvent, a direct payment provision will be effective provided that the debt owed to the contractor is greater than or equal to the amount of the direct payment. But some kinds of formal insolvency change the beneficial ownership of the contractor's property, including the right to be paid the value of work carried out by sub-contractors. There are difficulties here whether or not the contract contains a direct payment clause. Take first the situation where there is no express right to pay direct. In *Re Holt, ex parte Gray* (1888) 15 LJQB 5, a contractor was instructed to spend a provisional sum of £137 and the items were supplied and fixed before the contractor went bankrupt. At that time, the £137 had not been certified for payment and the supplier asked the employer to pay direct. On the supplier giving indemnities to the architects and the employer against any claim by the contractor's trustee, the architects issued a certificate and the employer paid the supplier. It was held that the employer was liable to pay the same sum to the trustee. Lord Coleridge CJ said: "It seems clear to me that, without any real dispute, this is an attempt on the part of the architects to interfere with the division of the bankrupt's estate and with the bankruptcy laws" (at 7). Cave J considered that the architects' action in certifying payment to the supplier was "a pure piece of impertinence".

Several points call for comment. No authority was cited for the decision on this aspect of the case, which suggests that it was the first time that the court had had to consider whether a direct payment could infringe the *pari passu* rule. The goods appear to have been fixed to the building by the time the contractor went bankrupt: if so, the employer did not have to make any payment to the supplier as the supplier had lost title to the chattels when they became converted into land on incorporation. This is an important aspect of construction contracts and is considered in Chapter 4. The case is sometimes cited as authority for the proposition that an employer can make a direct payment to a sub-contractor or supplier if the contract so provides. It would be more accurate to say that the case decided that an employer cannot pay a supplier direct where the contractor is bankrupt as it would amount to a distribution of the bankrupt's assets in a manner contrary to insolvency law. There is nothing in the judgment to support the view that the direct payment would have been valid if the contract had sanctioned it in the event of the contractor's bankruptcy; the substance of the decision is, if anything, to the contrary. Nevertheless, in the absence of insolvency, a properly drawn direct payment clause avoids the risk of the employer paying twice for the same work. In *Vigers Sons & Co v Swindell* [1939] 3 All ER 590, the sub-contractor failed in its argument that an employer was liable to pay under an order placed by the architect because it was held that the employer had not authorised the architect to place the order nor had she ratified the order after learning of it. The contractor went into liquidation several months after the contract was formed and was replaced by one of the contractor's former directors who agreed to continue on the same terms. The new contractor was not involved in placing the order with the sub-contractor. Although normally the sub-contractor would have had a cause of action against the architect for breach of warranty of authority, the architect was also insolvent. It appears from the report that the completion contractor also became insolvent, or at least received money from the employer which included a sum destined for the sub-contractor and misapplied it.

Construction of direct payment clauses

Normally, the only way in which an employer will be able to pay a sub-contractor and be released from paying the contractor the same sum is by an express term in the main contract. A direct payment clause gives a dual right to pay direct and to set off the amount paid against money due or to become due to the contractor. This is an example of contractual set-off in the strict sense as the contract is conferring a right of set-off where none exists under the general law. The position is therefore different from *Gilbert-Ash v Modern Engineering* [1974] AC 689 where a failure to follow contractual set-off machinery was not fatal as the set-off was saved by the general law, which had not been excluded. Here the general law is not excluded but it does not permit this type of set-off.

Because this device interferes with cash flow and is an exception to privity of contract, it is strictly construed by the court: *Milestone v Yates Brewery* [1938] 2 All ER 439. That case concerned the RIBA Standard Form (1909 edition) which included the following term:

> "The provisional sums mentioned in the specification for materials to be supplied, or for work to be performed by special ... tradesmen or for other work or fittings to the building shall be paid ... to and in favour of such persons as the architect shall direct, and the sums so expended shall be payable by the contractor without discount or deduction or ... by the employer to the said ... tradesmen."

The contractor went into liquidation after having completed the majority of the work and having received payment of certified sums part of which represented work done by nominated sub-contractors, but before having paid the sub-contractors. The liquidator claimed the balance of the contract sum but the employer argued that it was entitled to pay the sub-contractors direct and that no further sum could become due to the contractor. The architect had issued a certificate to the contractor but then proceeded to issue certificates for the same work in favour of the nominated sub-contractors. It was held that the certificates in favour of the sub-contractors were invalid and the employer was liable to the liquidator on the ground that the direct payment clause was to be strictly construed as giving the employer the right to elect between them. By paying the contractor, the employer had elected not to exercise the right to pay the sub-contractors direct. Milestone was followed in *Cone Textiles* v *Mather & Platt* [1981] 3 SA 565. The right to certify in favour of either contractor or sub-contractor was removed in later editions of the standard forms. In *Hobbs* v *Turner* (1900) 17 TLR 83, (1901) TLR 235 the Court of Appeal had some difficulty in ascertaining the identity of payer and payee and held that the contractor had acted as the employer's agent in entering into the sub-contract.

The court in *Milestone* referred to an earlier case of *British Investment Trust* v *Foundation* (unreported, 15 December 1930) which evidently concerned a similar type of clause, although it appears that the RIBA form was not used. Maugham J considered how best to approach the matter in the following passage:

> "Further, I think that a number of circumstances must be borne in mind in considering the operation of such a clause. It is plain that there may be disputes between the contractor and the tradesman in which the building owner may have no concern. It is plain that the terms of credit between the contractor and the tradesman may be of a special kind. In this case, as in most cases, the contractor is, in the first instance, paid on the certificate only a percentage of the total amount due. In the first case, he is paid 80%, then perhaps another 10% after a period of maintenance, while the tradesman may, and very often would, be entitled to the whole of the amount due to him from the contractor. Further, I think that it is not unreasonable to remember that the contractor may be at a particular moment in very urgent need of money to be paid on his certificates, partly by reason of the fact that he is being paid only in part for the work which he has done, and partly in consequence of unforeseen circumstances. All these grounds lead me to think that a clause entitling the building owner to pay a sub-contractor, with whom he has no

contractual relation, for work done and materials supplied ought, I think, to be strictly construed" (quoted in *Milestone* at 442).

This passage is the genesis of the way in which direct payment clauses have developed since the 1930s. Maugham J has recognised that the contractor may dispute the sub-contractor's entitlement to be paid, perhaps because of defective work entitling the contractor to abate the sub-contractor's payment. This factor is now recognised in the standard forms and the contractor is given an opportunity to justify why he has not paid the sub-contractor, *e.g.* clauses 59.5 of FIDIC (4th edition) and 59C of ICE (5th edition). The case also acknowledges the importance of cash flow, the absence of privity and the fact that the terms as to credit in the main contract and sub-contract may not be back to back. In *Milestone*, and possibly also *British Investment Trust*, the contractor had gone into liquidation. The court did not have to consider whether a payment would infringe the *pari passu* rule as the liquidator succeeded in his claim.

Public policy considerations

Direct payment clauses arose out of provisional sums and prime cost sums inserted in bills of quantities, which reflected the role played by specialist sub-contractors in 19th century contracts, especially in mechanical and electrical works. The rationale was that, having chosen the sub-contractor, the employer should have a right to pay it direct. The importance of specialist sub-contractors is even greater now than it was then and an obvious policy reason behind direct payment clauses is the need to ensure that these sub-contractors perform their works on time. In construing clauses of this kind, the courts have over the years taken account of what are strictly considerations of public policy rather than principles of law. For example, in *Re Wilkinson, ex parte Fowler* [1905] 1 KB 713, the court upheld a direct payment clause on the bankruptcy of the contractor on the grounds that the clause:

- benefited the employer as much as the sub-contractor
- promoted the satisfactory performance of public works contracts
- enabled the employer to make contracts more advantageously when sub-contractors and suppliers knew there was a reasonable probability of payment
- placed the employer in a better position when inviting tenders on future projects.

It can be inferred from the judgment that the major policy consideration was that the clause fostered competition between sub-contractors and benefited the employer by ensuring a good spread of competitive tenders. In English case law the predominant public policy consideration is that it is desirable that the employer should be protected. In other jurisdictions, public policy lays the emphasis on protecting the rights of those who actually carry out the work by granting a charge or lien on the land and on monies payable to the contractor as security for payment (see Chapter 17). Until it was repealed in 1988, a similar position applied in New Zealand under legislation which applied to sums due to suppliers, sub-contractors or the contractor's employees. It did not apply to government contracts but, as a concession, they included a right to pay direct at the Government's discretion. In *H M Attorney General* v *McMillan & Lockwood* [1991] 1 NZLR 53 the New Zealand Court of Appeal upheld the judge at first instance who had declared direct payment provisions to be void as infringing the *pari passu* rule but disapproved the judge's conclusion that so long as the legislation remained in force the clauses could not be considered contrary to public policy. The court considered that the direct payment clauses were:

> "... sensible commercial provisions which were given particular significance during the wages protection legislation era by the desire to provide sub-contractors under Crown contracts with a measure of the protection they had under that legislation in respect of private contracts. But in circumstances where the Crown was not bound by the wages protection legislation, so where Parliament in expressing the public interest did not give statutory protection to such sub-contractors, it would not be right to elevate those commercial concerns into public policy considerations."

It was not a matter of balancing different public policy considerations as in that case the court was dealing with the *pari passu* rule which is a legal principle. In the context of public policy in commercial contracts where both parties are solvent, however, the court approved the approach taken in *Re Wilkinson*. As the right to pay direct arises only through some default of the contractor, there was no reason on policy grounds why the contractor should be protected.

What is the position where the contractor goes into receivership? Does the administrative receiver's statutory duty to pay preferential creditors in priority to floating charge-holders under s 40 Insolvency Act 1986 override an employer's rights under a direct payment clause?

In practice the problem may not arise since the "sum due or to become due" to the contractor is likely to be a certified sum falling within a fixed charge on book debts. If the receivable is, however, subject to a floating charge, the charge-holder receives it subject to equities, in this context the employer's contractual right of set-off, so it will never be an asset "coming to the hands of the receiver" under the section (compare Totty and Moss H6.03). This argument avoids having to resolve the issue whether the contractor's right to payment in this situation is conditional or is absolute subject to set-off.

It has been suggested that direct payment clauses are contrary to the spirit of the provisions of the Insolvency Act 1986 as far as the administration procedure is concerned (Totty and Moss H6.03). While it is true that the exercise of set-off rights damages the financial position of a company in administration, if it had been Parliament's intention to suspend set-off rights during an administration, it is reasonable to assume that the Act would have made it clear. Even so, set-off has a security function and as the Act focuses on the functional aspects of a security rather than its strict legal classification (Bridge 1991), it remains to be seen what attitude the judges of the Companies Court will take to contractual rights of set-off in this context. Regardless of public policy considerations, as a matter of commercial practice, the usefulness of direct payment clauses is self-evident (UN 1988, 32).

Discretionary direct payment

There are two main types of discretionary direct payment clause in common use. The first applies during the contract where the contractor fails to honour payment obligations to sub-contractors and suppliers. This clause is frequently restricted to nominated sub-contractors. The second type of clause applies after termination of the contract or the contractor's employment where the right to make a direct payment is one of a bundle of rights expressly given to the employer.

During the contract

The clauses commonly in use today can be grouped into four categories. The first gives the architect power to refuse certification of payment in respect of the sub-contractor's work until the contractor has paid the sub-contractor. For example, an American Institute of Architects form provides:

"The Architect may also decline to certify payment or, because of subsequently discovered evidence or subsequent observations, the Architect may nullify the whole or any part of any Project Certificate for Payment previously issued to such extent as may be necessary, in the Architect's opinion, to protect the Owner from loss because of ... failure of the Contractor to make payments properly to Subcontractors, or for labor, materials or equipment [provided that when payment has been made to the Subcontractors] payment shall be made for amounts withheld ..." (clause 9.6.1 of AIA Document A201/CM-1980).

The second approach permits the employer to pay sub-contractors from the debt owed to the contractor as if the contractor had assigned its rights to payment to the sub-contractors. An example is the form of government contract used in New Zealand set out later in this chapter. The third category, and probably the most common in practice, is where the employer pays the sub-contractor from its own resources but then sets off the payment against money due to the contractor. A typical example is clause 27(c) of JCT 63 which provides:

"Before issuing any certificate under clause 30 of these Conditions the Architect may request the Contractor to furnish to him reasonable proof that all amounts included in the calculation of the amount stated as due in previous certificates in respect of the total value of work, materials or goods executed or supplied by any nominated sub-contractor have been duly discharged, and if the Contractor fails to comply with any such request the Architect shall issue a certificate to that effect and thereupon the Employer may himself pay such amounts to any nominated sub-contractor concerned (to which amounts the Employer may add an amount for any value added tax which would have been properly due to the nominated sub-contractor) and deduct the same from any sums due or to become due to the Contractor."

Other variants entitle the employer to make the deduction from "any sums due or which become due" (ICE and FIDIC) or "from the next certificate due to the contractor" (*Re Wilkinson*). The fourth approach is that taken by JCT 80 (now replicated in JCT 98). Clause 35 states that once the architect has issued his certificate:

"... the amount of any future payment otherwise due to the Contractor ... shall be reduced by any amounts due to Nominated Subcontractors which the Contractor has failed to discharge ... and the Employer shall himself pay the same to the Nominated Subcontractors concerned ...".

What does "reduction" mean in this context? It seems to point towards the conditional nature of the contractor's right to payment rather than to confer a distinct right of set-off. The reduction is automatic after the architect's certificate of non-payment.

After termination of the contract

Clause 25(3)(b) of JCT 63 provides:

> "In any case, the Employer may pay any supplier or sub-contractor for any materials or goods delivered or works executed for the purpose of this Contract (whether before or after the date of determination) insofar as the price thereof has not already been paid by the Contractor. The Employer's rights under this paragraph are in addition to his rights to pay nominated sub-contractors as provided in clause 27(c) of these Conditions and payments made under this paragraph may be deducted from any sums due or to become due to the Contractor."

Under JCT 80, a similar right is given to the employer but it cannot be exercised where the contractor has become bankrupt or gone into liquidation. As an alternative to set-off, the direct payment is also "recoverable from the contractor by the employer as a debt", presumably to establish a right to submit a proof. The right to pay direct on termination was removed in its entirety from JCT 80 by Amendment 11 (1992), only to be partially restored by Amendment 13 (1994). Direct payment is now permitted on an insolvency termination except on bankruptcy or liquidation or the filing of a petition alleging insolvency which is subsisting. This remains the position under JCT 98.

Neither ICE nor FIDIC expressly provides for direct payment on termination. Clause 57(1)(d) of GC Works/1 Edition 3 provides simply that "the Authority may pay to any sub-contractor or supplier any amount due to him which the Project Manager certifies as included in any previous advance to the Contractor. The amount so paid shall be forthwith recoverable by the Authority from the Contractor". The SIA form takes a different approach (Wallace 1986). Under clause 32(8)(c) of this form the employer is deemed to make the direct payment as agent for the contractor and has the option to deduct an equivalent amount from sums to become due to the contractor, otherwise the payment "shall be deemed to be a part of the cost of completing the Works".

Effect of bankruptcy and liquidation

Because of their effect on the contractor's cash flow, clauses operative during the contract have numerous pre-conditions which must all be satisfied before a payment and subsequent set-off can be made. In the absence of case law, the court is likely to adopt the same approach to direct payment clauses as it shows to set-off clauses. Any failure to comply with the conditions ought in principle to invalidate the set-off. The consequences of receivership and administration have been considered earlier. The effect of bankruptcy or liquidation on direct payment clauses is a difficult and controversial question. This is an important subject in practice and an area where uncertainty is undesirable. At the moment, employers are inhibited by concern about the validity of direct payment clauses with the result that they are rarely used, to the ultimate detriment of sub-contractors and suppliers.

There are two distinct lines of authority both for and against the validity of direct payment clauses on bankruptcy or liquidation. It is proposed to start with the arguments for their validity by examining the English cases on this point. The earliest case is *Re Holt, ex parte Gray* (1888) 15 LJ QB 5 discussed in the first section of this chapter. That case invalidated a direct payment made after the contractor's bankruptcy; however, the contract did not contain a direct payment clause. The first case where the validity of such a clause was questioned was *Re Wilkinson, ex parte Fowler* [1905] 2 KB 713 where a contractor agreed to carry out engineering work for an employer at a price to be paid by monthly instalments on the certificate of an engineer. The contract also required the contractor at his own cost to provide all materials, machinery and plant which might be necessary for the completion of the works. Clause 54 of the contract provided:

> "At each and every certificate in which the engineer shall deem proper to include a sum or sums for machinery, the contractor shall, upon measurement being made, produce to the authorised officer a receipt showing that he has paid the machinery makers the net sum to be included, notwithstanding that he has not at the time of paying of such machinery makers received the said sums from the council. If the engineer shall have reasonable cause to believe that the contractor is unduly delaying proper payment of the firms supplying the machinery, he shall have power if he thinks fit to order direct payment to them and shall deduct from the next certificate issued to the contractor the money so paid, provided that no payment in the manner referred to shall be held to relieve the contractor from any of his liabilities under this contract."

The court considered that the payments could be made direct notwithstanding the bankruptcy on the public policy grounds mentioned earlier and because:

"... [the clause] amounts to an authority given by the contractor - that is to say, by the bankrupt in this case - to the engineer representing the council to dispose of money, which would otherwise come to the bankrupt, in a certain way under certain circumstances. It is an authority which, in my opinion, it was not competent for the bankrupt to withdraw, and it was never contemplated that he should withdraw it; and indeed it is not contended on behalf of the trustee that the authority was one that could be lawfully withdrawn. It is an authority, therefore, which the bankruptcy of the contractor did not annul" (at 720).

The idea seems to be that the employer has "a power coupled with an interest" (Oditah 1992, at 477). It is significant that no argument was made based on the *pari passu* rule or bankruptcy set-off, *Re Holt ex parte Gray* was not cited in argument and the trustee conceded that the authority given by the direct payment clause was irrevocable. Given that the effect of the concession was to accept that the contract could disturb the realisation and distribution of the bankrupt's property in the absence of a security interest, it is questionable whether this case was correctly decided.

It was followed, however, in *Re Tout & Finch Limited* [1954] 1 All ER 127 in which the court considered clause 21(c) of the RIBA form which stated as follows:

"Before any such certificate is issued to the contractor he shall, if requested by the architect, furnish to him reasonable proof that all nominated sub-contractors' accounts included in previous certificates have been duly discharged, in default whereof the employer may pay such accounts upon a certificate of the architect and deduct the amount so paid from any sums otherwise payable to the contractor ...".

The court considered an application by a nominated sub-contractor in the winding-up of a contractor for a declaration that the employer was entitled to make a direct payment to the sub-contractor of the balance remaining unpaid of amounts included in previous certificates representing its work. The judge dealt briefly with this issue holding that the case was on all fours with *Re Wilkinson*. The only argument put forward by the liquidator was that the certificate referred to in clause 21(c) could only be interim not final. In passing, the judge commented that:

"... the council has a right - and the matter is entirely one for the council - to pay such account on a certificate being duly given by the architect and, as mere necessary machinery, deduct the amount so paid from any amounts otherwise payable to the company".

These words suggest that the judge was not referred in argument to liquidation set-off or conditionality. This decision has been relied upon by the UK Government as validating the direct payment provision on termination in GC Works/1 (HMSO 1974). *Re Tout and Finch* is of limited value because it concerned an entitlement to a direct payment of retention which the judge held in any event to be the subject of an equitable assignment. The employer was bound to pay direct because the subject matter of the assignment did not constitute property of the company in liquidation.

The English cases have been followed in Australia. In *Re C G Monkhouse Properties* [1968] SR (NSW) 429 the New South Wales Court of Appeal considered a direct payment clause in virtually identical terms to JCT 63. The court rejected a claim that payments to nominated sub-contractors constituted preferences and stated as follows:

> "This is not a case where the building owner paid the sub-contractor out of monies which were then due or would certainly become due to the building company. If it were, then there might be much to be said for the submission made on behalf of the appellant; but it is fundamental to this case that the monies, the subject of the claim, were not due to the builder and could not, on the terms of the contract, become due so long as clause 21(c) of the contract operated. The right of the builder to receive the certificate from the architect and his right to be paid on that certificate is governed under this contract by clause 25, and clause 25 specifically makes it clear that the builder is not entitled to any certificate or to any payment except subject to clause 21(c) of the contract. That being so, the payment made by the building owner cannot be described as a payment made out of monies for the builder. It is a payment made out of the building owner's own monies which, if the contract were strictly carried out, would never become due to the builder." (at 431-432)

This case was followed by the Supreme Court of Western Australia in *Gericevich Contracting* v *Sabemo* [1984] 9 ACLR 452 which sanctioned direct payments to the sub-contractor's employees following the contractor's liquidation on the ground that the employer's debt to the contractor was limited to the balance, if any, remaining after the direct payments had been made. The court held that the contractor's property capable of disposal could only be ascertained after compliance with the contract terms affecting the debt, *i.e.* the debt was conditional. See also *Victorian Railway Commissioners* v *Williams* (1969) 44 ALJR 32. The Irish High Court adopted a similar approach in *Glow Heating* v *Eastern Health Board* (1992) 8 Const LJ 56 which is discussed later.

The other stream of authorities which invalidate direct payment clauses operating on a contractor's bankruptcy or liquidation comprises cases decided in South Africa, New Zealand, Singapore, Northern Ireland and Hong Kong. These will now be considered in turn. In 1947 and 1953, the South African courts considered two cases where injunctions were obtained by judicial managers appointed over a contractor restraining an employer from making direct payments to nominated sub-contractors. In both cases, the parties had used a standard form of building contract which was in substantially the same terms as JCT 63. In *Norman Kennedy* v *Norman Kennedy Ltd* [1947] 1 SA 790 the court upheld the injunction. Although there was no privity of contract and the court followed *Re Wilkinson* in holding that the contractor's authority to the employer could not normally be revoked, it exercised its discretion under the South African Companies Act against the nominated sub-contractors on the grounds that they had no legal right to payment, the employers had not appeared at the hearing to object to the granting of the injunction, and the court paid great regard to the submissions of judicial managers as court appointees who spoke in the interests of the general body of creditors. This case was overruled by the South African Court of Appeal in *Wire Industries* v *Certes* [1953] 2 SA 531 on the ground that although there was no privity of contract, the sub-contractor had a material interest that the employer should not be restrained from paying direct which the court would protect.

It was not until 1968 that the South African Court of Appeal ruled on the question whether an employer could pay direct and set off the amount of the payment against sums otherwise due to the contractor after the contractor had gone into liquidation. In *Administrator, Natal* v *Magill Grant & Nell* [1969] 1 SA 660 a liquidator applied for directions when an employer claimed to set off sums paid after the commencement of the liquidation to two nominated sub-contractors. The court refused set-off on the following grounds:

1. The absence of privity of contract meant that the sub-contractors could not compel the employer to pay them direct.

2. The authority given to the employer was not automatically terminated upon insolvency or liquidation of the contractor.

3. The main contractor was not merely a conduit for payment of money due to nominated sub-contractors.

4. The contractor's right to payment was not contingent on itself paying the sub-contractors.

5. The set-off would disturb both the realisation of assets and distribution to creditors contrary to the *pari passu* rule.

The court left open the question whether, had the set-offs been made before liquidation, they would also have been invalidated but it was conceded by counsel for both parties that the set-offs would have been valid. In a powerful dissenting judgment, Wessels JA stated:

> "The amount of the administrator's indebtedness in the circumstances postulated would, therefore, not only depend upon the valuation of 'all the work done up to' the date of the valuation in terms of the contract, but also (1) upon the performance by the contractor of the further contractual obligation above referred to, and (2) the payment by the administrator to a nominated sub-contractor of the amount due to him, such payment being made pursuant to an election made by the administrator in terms of the provisions of clause 21(b). ... pending the exercise by the administrator of his contractual right to elect to make a payment to a nominated sub-contractor, the defaulting contractor would, in my opinion, have no legally enforceable claim based solely on the valuation of the work done by him. On the proper construction of clause 21, sub-para (b) in effect provides for an alternative 'manner' in which the administrator may perform the contractual obligation imposed upon him by clause 2 of the contract between the parties. In the circumstances postulated in clause 21 of the conditions of contract the administrator makes a payment in terms of the contract when he exercises his right of election and makes a payment to the nominated sub-contractor ... the true effect of the payment made pursuant to an election to make such payment is to reduce pro tanto the amount due to and claimable by the contractor in terms of the contract" (at 674).

In other words, Wessels JA considered that the contractor had only a conditional right to payment and, as the condition was never fulfilled, the direct payments were not made from the property of the contractor but from the employer's own assets.

In *H M Attorney General* v *McMillan & Lockwood*, the New Zealand Court of Appeal had to construe the following clauses in a government contract:

> "19.10 The [Architect] shall not be bound to certify that any payment is due to the Contractor until the Contractor has satisfied him that payment has been duly made of all sums due and payable by the Contractor in respect of: (a) Wages to persons employed on the Works; (b) Progress

payments or other sums due to sub-contractors; (c) Sums due to any person for services supplied or for Materials, Plant, or prepared work (or cartage thereof) incorporated in the Works or used in connection therewith or brought upon the Site or placed on or near thereto for the purposes of being used in or upon the Works; (d) Premiums in respect of policies of insurance of any nature required in terms of the contract. 19.11 The Minister may at his discretion and notwithstanding the exercise by him of all or any of the other powers conferred on him by the contract pay to any employee of the Contractor or to any sub-contractor, supplier, or other person to whom any moneys as specified in the last preceding clause are due [by the Contractor] the whole or any part of such moneys as if such persons were a lawful assignee of the Contractor in respect of such moneys. Any such payment may be made out of moneys then due or accruing due to the Contractor and the Minister shall have no further liability to the Contractor in respect of any amounts so paid."

The court declared these clauses void as infringing the *pari passu* rule. The reasons were:

1. As work is done the entitlement of the contractor and the associated obligations of the Crown accrued, and those obligations existed before the time for payment arrived.

2. The assignment deemed by clause 19.11 assumed that the contractor had property in those monies.

3. As at liquidation, the company had an existing chose in action, measured by the value of the work done under each contract and as yet unpaid, even though the time for payment had not arrived.

4. As a result of the *pari passu* rule and the decision in *British Eagle* v *Air France* [1975] 2 All ER 390, it was not open to the employer to make payments out of monies due to the contractor and the clauses were therefore void,.

5. The English and Australian cases were distinguishable on the ground that the direct payments were not made out of monies which were due or to become due to the builder nor were they payments on behalf of the builder.

6. It was not a matter of balancing public policy considerations as the *pari passu* rule applied absolutely on liquidation.

The suggested distinction between these decisions and the English and Australian cases is perhaps more apparent than real: there is no difference between a payment made "out of monies due" to the contractor and a set-off "against monies due" to the contractor as the latter is merely a deemed payment or discharge by set-off and is equally inconsistent with the *pari passu* rule.

In *Joo Yee Construction v Diethelm* [1990] MLJ 66 the High Court of Singapore heard an application for directions issued by a liquidator appointed over a contractor. The employer wished to make direct payments to four nominated sub-contractors and the liquidator sought a direction whether they could validly be made. After reviewing the authorities, Thean J concluded that the proposed payments would contravene the *pari passu* rule. He declined to follow the English cases on the ground that the *pari passu* rule had not been raised in argument and that, had Bigham J been alerted to the principle, he would not have considered the contractor's authority in *Re Wilkinson* to be irrevocable. It has been noted that retention trust cases were not cited in argument on the scope of the decision in *British Eagle* (Powell-Smith 1991); however, they do not seem relevant to this issue. Under a trust or an assignment (in the case of a sub-contractor) the contractor loses its beneficial interest in the debt. In the normal situation where a sub-contractor is seeking a direct payment, the contractor still has the beneficial interest in the debt owed by the employer representing the certified sum.

These decisions were followed by the Court of Appeal of Northern Ireland in *Mullan v Ross* (1996) 86 BLR 1. The case concerned an application by an ordinary sub-contractor for a direction in the liquidation of a contractor that the employer could make a direct payment pursuant to clause 27.4 of JCT 81. The court refused to authorise the direct payment, holding that the receivable formed part of the contractor's property and was payable to the liquidators. The English and Irish cases were distinguished, the court preferring the other line of cases culminating in *Joo Yee Construction*. Although the contractor went into administrative receivership over three months before it entered voluntary liquidation, the receivers were not joined as a party to the application. Presumably the benefit of the main contract was either not charged or had already been released from the security.

The High Court of Hong Kong followed the decision in *Mullan v Ross* in the recent case of *Golden Sand v Easy Success Enterprises* (unreported, 31 March 1999). Over a year before it went into compulsory liquidation, the contractor agreed with the employer and a number of nominated sub-contractors that the employer should pay the sub-contractors direct. The agreement was evidenced by contemporary correspondence. The court seems to have held that the arrangement was an equitable assignment to the sub-contractors of relevant proportions of future certificates and therefore payments falling due after the liquidation could not be the contractor's property. Interestingly, the evidence was that the parties did not intend the agreement to affect any of their existing rights and obligations. It is possible that the arrangement amounted to no more than an agreement by the contractor that the employer should act as its agent in the payment of the sub-contractors, in which case it would, on the court's own analysis of the authorities, have been invalidated by the *pari passu* rule.

Summary of the current position

There are therefore two lines of authority: England, Australia and the Irish Republic, on the one hand, and South Africa, New Zealand, Singapore, Northern Ireland and Hong Kong on the other. The English cases were both decisions at first instance and in neither case was the possible conflict with the *pari passu* rule argued. *Re Wilkinson* rests on a concession that the authority given to the employer to pay direct was irrevocable even on the contractor's bankruptcy. The decisions are unsatisfactory and should not be followed. Only the Australian decisions (and the dissenting judgment of Wessels JA in the *Magill* case) grapple with the real issue: is the contractor's property a debt subject to reduction by set-off following direct payment or only such amount as is left after the direct payment and set-off have been made? It seems immaterial whether the direct payment is made out of the debt owed to the contractor (as in *McMillan & Lockwood*) or made out of the employer's own funds and then set off against a debt due to the contractor. The effect is the same. In other words, the issue is whether the debt owed by the employer is absolute subject only to contractual set-off or conditional so that it cannot arise if the contract conditions governing its accrual are never fulfilled.

A similar question was considered by the House of Lords in *British Eagle v Air France* [1975] 2 All ER 390. The issue was whether the claim against Air France was the property of British Eagle or IATA. The court had to rule whether the liquidator was bound by a clearing house arrangement whereby British Eagle and Air France agreed that debts arising between them should only be dealt with through the medium of the clearing house. With some hesitation, the House of Lords decided that the clearing house arrangement was void as against the liquidator of British Eagle. The debt was owned by British Eagle not IATA. The question of the ownership of the debt was the main issue in the case

(Goode 1988). Philip Wood has argued forcefully that *British Eagle* is just one in a long line of cases holding that a creditor cannot help himself to a debtor's property after insolvency unless he has a charge or unless the debt owed by the employer is a "flawed asset". In other words, it will only become payable if there are no unpaid sub-contractors at the commencement of the liquidation or there are unpaid sub-contractors but the employer decides not to exercise its right to pay direct (Wood 1989, 214-232). No doubt there are circumstances where a flawed asset arrangement would be valid in the event of liquidation. But a close reading of the cases on direct payments does not support a construction that all the employer owes is a conditional debt. Reading *British Eagle* with these clauses in mind, one is driven to the conclusion that their intended effect is to allow the employer to help itself to the contractor's property and pay one of the contractor's own creditors.

Most contracts have discretionary clauses permitting a direct payment both during and on termination of the contract. The question arises whether the former could be operated where the latter is invalidated. There could be difficulties because first, it is not necessary for a clause or contractual arrangement to be operative only on insolvency to infringe the *pari passu* rule and secondly, as the contract has provided what is to happen in the event of termination it is thought that the employer's direct payment rights may be restricted to those contained in the termination clause in that event.

In view of the absence of modern English case law, and the conflict between the two lines of authority, the position could be summarised thus:

1. A direct payment clause, whether operated during the contract or after termination, which has the effect of paying one particular group of creditors from the property of the contractor will, if operated after bankruptcy or liquidation, offend against the pari *passu rule* because the money ought to be distributed rateably among all the contractor's creditors. This is the case whether the clauses provide for payment by the employer from its own resources and subsequent set-off against money due to the contractor or payment from money due to the contractor.

2. Whatever the merits of the public policy considerations in *Re Wilkinson*, they must yield to the *pari passu* rule. For considerations of public policy to prevail over the rule, they would have to be enshrined in statute: see *e.g. Farrier-Waimak v Bank of New Zealand* [1965] NZLR 426.

3. Even if expressed to be irrevocable, an authority given by a contractor to an employer to pay direct and set off will be defeated by the *pari passu* rule. In *British Eagle*, notice to the clearing house of any credit or debit for clearance was said to "constitute an irrevocable authority to Clearing House to clear the same and for that purpose to collect or pay (as the case may be) the amount thereof in accordance with the Regulations and current clearing procedure and to make all necessary sets off in that behalf and to pay any ultimate balance due as a result of the clearance effected." Despite this irrevocable authority, the House of Lords on a majority of 3:2 decided that the clause was not binding on the liquidator (see Prentice 1983, Oditah 1992).

4. To regard the contractor's right to payment as conditional or contingent on the operation of the direct payment clause as was held in *Monkhouse* would be wrong as that would be applying the very term in the contract which offended the *pari passu* rule.

In view of current uncertainty the prudent draftsman would still include the right to pay direct in the event of liquidation or bankruptcy but before exercising such right an employer should obtain legal advice on its position. The employer should seek an indemnity from the sub-contractor, secured if necessary, for the return of the payment if the employer is forced to pay the same amount to the liquidator. If the contractor's obligations had been guaranteed, it is advisable either to obtain the guarantor's approval beforehand or legal advice that the direct payment will not affect the guarantor's liability. In *Doe* v *Canadian Surety* (1937) 1 SCR 1, a guarantor was discharged from liability partly because the employer had made direct payments to sub-contractors with the contractor's consent. To avoid any problems over ownership of materials or equipment whose value is included in the direct payment, a form of agreement should also be prepared in which the sub-contractor gives a warranty as to title and agrees that title will pass to the employer on payment unless the goods have already been incorporated.

Mandatory direct payment

So far this chapter has considered contracts which give an employer power to make a direct payment to a contractor at its discretion. However, there are occasions when direct payments are mandatory. This can arise in a number of ways: under the main contract, under a direct contract between the employer and the sub-contractor, under a court procedure for attachment of debts, under statute and following assignment.

Main contract

In *Glow Heating* v *Eastern Health Board* (1992) 8 Const LJ 56, the main contract contained a mandatory direct payment clause which operated where a contractor could not prove it had discharged sums due to nominated sub-contractors from previous certificates. The sub-contract was based on the Green Form, but in addition it provided that all sums received by the main contractor in respect of the sub-contract work were to be held in trust. On the contractor's entry into liquidation, the liquidator decided to complete the works. Before the liquidation, a payment of £6,617 was certified and made to the main contractor who dissipated it. The sub-contractor had no tracing remedy but successfully claimed a direct payment from the employer under the main contract in the same amount. In effect, the employer compensated the sub-contractor for the main contractor's breach of trust. The liquidator challenged the consequential set-off against the contractor's retention in respect of the amount of the direct payment but the court held that the effect of the direct payment clause was to impose "a contingent liability on an asset of the main contractor, the monies in the retention fund, namely, a liability to suffer a reduction in the event of a specified default on the contractor's part. The liquidator, in my opinion, took the retention fund subject to this liability" (at 61). The absence of privity was no defence to the employer, the court referring to *Re Tout & Finch*. However, in that case, the employer had not yet made the payment and was abiding the court's decision as to whether to pay the liquidator or the nominated sub-contractors. In this case, payment had already been made in accordance with the main contract.

Direct contract

There has long been a practice for specialist sub-contractors to enter into direct design warranties with the employer. In return for the warranty, the employer may undertake to pay the sub-contractor to the extent that the contractor fails to do so. The warranty for use with JCT 63 was known as the "grey form". The employer's undertaking was amended in NSC/2 and NSC/2A introduced to accompany JCT 80.

This was necessary because the intervention of British Eagle led the JCT to remove the duty of the employer to make a direct payment where the contractor was in bankruptcy or liquidation. NSC/2 provides:

> "7.1 The Architect/The Contract Administrator and the Employer shall operate the provision in regard to the payment of the Sub-Contractor in clause 35.13 of the Main Contract Conditions. 7.2 If, after paying any amount to the Sub-Contractor under clause 35.13.5.3 of the Main Contract Conditions, the Employer produces reasonable proof that there was in existence at the time of such payment a petition or resolution to which clause 35.13.5.4.4 of the Main Contract Conditions refers, the Sub-Contractor shall repay on demand such amount."

Although this appears to be a comparatively simple procedure, problems arise in practice. First, is the clause intended to apply on the presentation of a winding-up petition, rather than the making of an order? Reading the clause literally, the employer could make a direct payment, ascertain later that a petition had been issued before the payment was made, even though it was later withdrawn, and then demand the return of the payment, thereby stultifying the operation of NSC/2 at a time when it was most needed. Perhaps the problem would be remedied when dealing with the following certificate. Secondly, JCT 80 provides that the employer is only obliged to make the direct payment to the extent that there is money available from future payments due to the contractor. What happens where the architect has over-certified so that no future payments become due? This would work unjustly against the sub-contractor where it has carried out work since the last certificate. Thirdly, in view of the limited fund available, if more than two sub-contractors are unpaid, they will presumably share pro-rata. On a substantial project, there may be numerous nominated sub-contractors who are owed significant amounts. The employer's undertaking would be of limited value to them.

The employer's undertaking only arises where the architect has certified that the contractor has failed to provide reasonable proof of prior payment. What happens where the architect fails to issue the certificate? Can the employer rely on the absence of the certificate as a defence to a claim by the sub-contractor? An example of this type of situation is reported in Construction Award No 9 (1988) [1995] 2 Con L Yb 103. After the contractor went into receivership, the architect refused to certify under clause 35 of JCT 80 that the contractor had failed to pay the amount attributed to a nominated sub-contractor in the previous interim certificate. The contractor then went into compulsory liquidation but between the petition and the winding-up order, the main contract was novated and a further interim certificate issued. The contractor was only released from liabilities arising after the date of the novation and the employer agreed not to deduct from any sums due to the incoming or the insolvent contractor any amounts unpaid to nominated sub-contractors. The sub-contractor brought an arbitration against the employer under NSC/2 claiming the amount of the direct payment and won. The employer relied on clause 35 under which the duty to pay direct ceases if at the date when it "would otherwise be made" there is a petition to wind up the contractor. This argument was rejected on the ground that, had the architect issued his certificate promptly after receiving the sub-contractor's request, payment would have been due under NSC/2 several weeks before the petition was issued. The employer was in breach of NSC/2 in failing to procure that the architect operated clause 35 and should not be allowed to profit from its own wrong. The employer also argued that the receivership had activated the employer's post-termination rights which replaced clause 35 and released the employer from its obligations under NSC/2. The arbitrator disagreed and held that the novation took effect as a reinstatement and variation of the original contract. This is an unusual finding based on the specific terms of the novation (which are not set out in full in the award) and made it unnecessary for the arbitrator to consider the effect of the termination clause.

NSC/2 fails to deal with the situation where the contractor is in receivership and liquidation at the same time. For example, if administrative receivers are appointed before the winding-up commences, the set-off following direct payment to the sub-contractor will not be made from property of the company under the liquidator's control, but from the receivable assigned to the charge-holder on the receiver's appointment. If the contractor were to go into liquidation before the direct payment, it would be wrong to deprive the sub-contractor of the benefit of it. Clause 7.2 was inserted to deal with *British Eagle* and the *pari passu* rule, but this does not apply where the whole undertaking of a company passes to the debenture holder on the crystallisation of a floating charge. Against this, a liquidator may argue that the assignment to the debenture holder is for the purpose of security and the contractor has a contingent interest in any property which is not required to discharge the secured indebtedness. It would be a preference over other creditors for a sub-contractor to be paid from (or for an employer to set off against) property which it later emerged was not needed to discharge the security. The answer may be that it is a question of timing: the charge-holder is entitled to the benefit of all the property falling within the charge until the security is paid off. If that means that the employer has access to a receivable for the purpose of set-off which it would not have had in the event of the contractor's liquidation, that is merely the consequence of the differing natures of receivership and liquidation: *Hargreaves* v *Action 2000* [1993] BCLC 1111.

Other forms of direct agreement have been produced, *e.g.* the Model Form of Employer/Specialist Contractor Collateral Warranty Agreement published in February 1991 by the Confederation of Construction Specialists. This is intended for use with any standard form and provides that:

> "The Employer undertakes to take all reasonable steps to ensure that the Specialist Contractor receives interim payments from the Main Contractor within the time period stipulated in the Sub-Contract Agreement. In the event that any payment from the Main Contractor to the Specialist Contractor is still overdue at the time of the next valuation the Employer on notification by the Specialist Contractor will forthwith pay such amount directly to the Specialist Contractor."

It is worth noting that there is no right of set-off of the amount of the payment.

Attachment of debts

If a sub-contractor issues proceedings and obtains judgment against a contractor, it can enforce the judgment by attaching any debt owed to the contractor. This is achieved by issuing garnishee proceedings. This is a two stage process: in the first stage, the sub-contractor obtains a garnishee order nisi. This is done without reference to the contractor and the order fixes a date when the contractor and the contractor's debtor must appear to show cause why the order should not be made absolute. At the hearing, the court will either make the order absolute or discharge the previous order. The crucial factor with garnishee proceedings is that the attachment must have been completed before the start of the winding-up, otherwise it cannot be relied on by the sub-contractor who will remain an unsecured creditor: s 183 Insolvency Act 1986.

In *Wilson* v *Metropolitan Property* [1975] 2 All ER 814 the Court of Appeal refused to allow a sub-contractor the benefit of attachment. This case was one of several arising out of the collapse of the Stern Group in the recession of the early 1970s. The contractor was a subsidiary in the group whose parent company had gone into voluntary liquidation. The creditors of other group companies had agreed on a six-month moratorium of their debts to enable a scheme of arrangement to proceed. The sub-contractor refused to participate in the scheme and obtained a garnishee order nisi. The contractor went into voluntary liquidation and later the garnishee order was made absolute. The Court of Appeal held that the order should not have been made absolute as it conferred a preference on the sub-contractor (see Chapter 15). The court also approved *Hudsons Concrete* v *Evans* (1961) 105 Sol J 281 where the facts were similar, although there was no resolution or winding-up petition, only an originating summons seeking the sanction of the court to a scheme of arrangement.

Garnishee proceedings are only available where there is a debt which is "due or accruing due" even though it may not be immediately payable. Under the traditional lump sum building contract with interim payments payable under a certificate, no debt can arise for the purposes of attachment until a certificate has been issued: *Dunlop & Ranken* v *Hendall Steel* [1957] 3 All ER 344. Uncertified work in progress does not constitute a debt in this context. It has also been decided where a sub-contractor sought a garnishee order against retention under the main contract after the main contract had been terminated, that retention was not a debt due or accruing due: *Grant Plant Hire* v *Trickey* (1961) 105 Sol J 255. In that case, the contract provided that after termination the employer was not bound by any other provision to make any payment to the contractor. Retention would only become a debt if, after the cost to complete had been ascertained and set off against the balance of the contract sum, there were found to be a net balance payable to the contractor. Viewed in the context of attachment applications, both decisions make sense but so far as they purport to hold that no debt exists before a certificate is issued they are too wide and are inconsistent with decisions of the Court of Appeal in other contexts: *Earle* v *Hemsworth RDC* (1928) 140 LT 69, *Drew* v *Josolyne* (1887) 18 QBD 590. This is especially so in the case of construction book debts (see Chapter 3).

Statute

English law gives certain limited rights to third parties in the event of a contractor's insolvency. A person who suffers loss may be able to claim direct against the contractor's insurers under the Third Parties (Rights against Insurers) Act 1930. An unpaid employee of an insolvent contractor may have a claim against the National Insurance Fund under the Employment Rights Act 1996. But in general, statute does not come to the aid of an unpaid sub-contractor or a direct supplier. Other jurisdictions treat sub-contractors and employees differently (see Chapter 17).

Assignment

In Chapter 6 it was seen how one of the functions of assignment is the resistance of creditor pressure. Where the creditor is a sub-contractor, it may bargain for an outright assignment of sums due or to become due from the employer under the main contract. If the assignment is effective, the employer will only obtain a good discharge by paying the sub-contractor. Assignment can therefore operate as a direct payment authorised by the contractor. If the assignment is validly made before the contractor goes into liquidation, it is binding against a receiver who would have to remit the payment to the sub-contractor if the employer paid the receiver by mistake: *Ashby Warner* v *Simmonds* [1936] 2 All ER 697, *Kon Struct* v *Storage Developments* (1990) 6 BCL 171, *Golden Sand* v *Easy Success Enterprises* (unreported, 25 March 1999, High Court of Hong Kong).

As the effect of the assignment is to remove the assigned property from the ownership of the contractor, a subsequent payment to the sub-contractor cannot infringe the *pari passu* rule. In the event of assignment before a liquidation, however, it is more common for the liquidator to challenge the assignment itself as a preference and claim the payment from the sub-contractor on that ground. This type of claim is considered further in Chapter 15. It is not uncommon for arrangements to be made for the direct payment of sub-contractors which fall short of an assignment: see *Re Right Time Construction* (1990) 52 BLR 117, where payments were invalidated as post-petition disposals. Similarly, an arrangement whereby the contractor is paid direct by a funder may simply be for administrative convenience and have no effect on an employer's liability to fund retention, even if the payments are made on invoices issued to the funder by the contractor: *Finnegan* v *Ford Sellar Morris* (No 2) (1991) 27 Con LR 41.

Conclusion

Direct payment is a useful device in a main contract. It acknowledges the popular image of money being "passed down" the chain while recognising that this is not the correct legal analysis. Yet in practice it is comparatively rare that such rights are exercised. This is understandable where the contractor is bankrupt or in liquidation as it seems likely that English law will follow that of Northern Ireland in holding direct payment in this situation to be an infringement of the *pari passu* rule. Employers remain apprehensive in other contexts. Administrative receivers sometimes pressurise employers not to make a direct payment by raising the argument based on s 40 Insolvency Act 1986, referred to earlier. Administrators tend to be more even-handed, at least perhaps until a test case can be brought.

This chapter has shown two distinct approaches taken by the courts internationally to direct payment clauses. This is an area where it is hard to be dogmatic since comparatively subtle changes in the wording of the clause may affect the outcome. It has been argued that the *pari passu* rule should yield to a public policy favouring contractual mechanisms which promote the integrity of a project (McGaw 1992). Sir Michael Latham considered that employers' reluctance to make direct payments could be overcome by introducing a secondary trust in favour of the first line of sub-contractors into all construction contracts by statute (Latham 1994). He also recommended that construction contracts be made exempt from the rule in *British Eagle* through an amendment to the Insolvency Act 1986. This was by analogy with the exception made in favour of market contracts in the Companies Act 1989 (McCormack 1997). The government accepted that a trust would overcome the problem caused by *British Eagle*, and therefore opposed any amendment to the Insolvency Act 1986, but was not prepared to introduce legislation on trust funds without further consultation (DOE 1995). The Contracts (Rights of Third Parties) Bill is unlikely to improve the position of sub-contractors since it will not apply where, on a proper construction of the relevant contract, it appears that the parties did not intend the direct payment clause to be enforceable by the sub-contractor. The European Commission (1997) recommended that sub-contractors should have the right to direct payment in "cases of unjustified non-payment by the principal contractor". In the absence of such radical solutions, this will remain an especially intricate area of construction law.

Chapter 13

· **Set-off in Insolvency** ·

Introduction

The question of set-off is one of the most important in insolvency law. Whether formal insolvency makes any difference to the position depends in part on the procedure. The bankruptcy or liquidation of one party to a contract sweeps away all contractual or common law rights of set-off and substitutes a statutory procedure. By contrast, the position in administration is neutral: ordinary principles apply (Chapter 5). As receivership takes effect as the assignment to the debenture holder of the property comprised in the charge, questions of set-off turn more often than not on whether the cross-claim is an equity subject to which the assignment was made. Apart from bankruptcy and liquidation, therefore, set-off in insolvency can only be understood by first ascertaining the position under the general law and then enquiring whether the insolvency procedure has changed the position.

Receivership set-off

It was explained in Chapter 8 that the effect of the appointment of an administrative receiver is to crystallise the floating charge under which the appointment is made. At that moment, the charge becomes fixed on the assets included in the charge. The assets are assigned in equity to the charge-holder and the administrative receiver is entitled to claim them on the charge-holder's behalf. It follows that set-off where one party is in receivership is as much a question of the law of assignment as set-off. The charge-holder, or the receiver on its behalf, must give notice to the debtor to prevent further build-up of set-off rights. Letters sent by receivers on their appointment sometimes say that a debtor cannot rely on any right of set-off which arises after the date of the appointment. Strictly, this is inaccurate as the relevant moment from the debtor's point of view is receipt of the notice.

The debtor can set off a cross-claim for legal set-off which arises between the appointment and receipt of the notice even though the mutuality has been destroyed because, owing to the statutory origins of legal set-off, mutuality is by reference to the legal title to the two claims. "The question then becomes whether it is unconscionable for the debtor to rely on this right of set-off otherwise available at law when the equitable title to one of the debts is in someone else" (Derham 1996, 568).

As explained in Chapter 6, giving notice is beneficial to the assignee for two reasons. First, after receiving notice, the debtor can only obtain a good discharge by paying the assignee. Where the assignee is the holder of a floating charge, this is unimportant as the assignor will be under the control of the receiver who acts as its agent and is entitled to use its name for the purpose of collecting in the charged assets. Secondly, the debtor cannot raise as a defence to the receiver's claim any equities which arise after the date of receipt of notice of appointment: *Stephens* v *Venables* (1862) 30 Beav 625. It is as if a line had been ruled under the claim after notice was given. This is of crucial importance to an understanding of a debtor's right of set-off against a claim by a receiver.

"Subject to equities"

An equity is any defence or remedy which a debtor has against an assignor at the date of receipt of notice of assignment: *Roxburghe* v *Cox* (1878) 17 Ch D 520. Equities in construction cases can be divided into three types:

- a right to avoid a contract
- arbitration and non-assignability clauses
- set-off and abatement (see generally Oditah 1991).

Rights to avoid a contract on the ground of mistake, misrepresentation, fraud, duress or undue influence are all equities binding an assignee. An employer successfully defended a claim brought by an assignee of its contractor in *Wakefield & Barnsley Banking Co v Normanton Local Board* (1881) LT 697. A dispute arose between the contractor and employer over a contract to build a reservoir where the employer alleged that certain work was defective and incomplete. The dispute was settled on the basis that the employer was to take immediate possession of the site and pay an agreed sum on a particular date. The contractor assigned this sum as security to its bank and gave notice to the employer. When the employer failed to pay, it was sued by the bank as assignee. After the settlement, the employer had discovered that the contractor had colluded with the engineer in the issue of fraudulent certificates. It appears from the report that the contractor had removed stone from the reservoir and substituted concrete. It was held that the employer had a good defence to the claim because the settlement agreement had been obtained by fraud (Tettenborn 1987).

Other equities consist of the right to rely on a non-assignability clause as a defence or to refer a claim to arbitration: *Rumput v Islamic Republic of Iran* [1984] 2 Lloyd's Rep 259. Non-assignability clauses are commonly found in construction contracts (Chapter 6). If the receiver is making a claim in right of the debenture holder as equitable assignee, at first sight the debtor could defend by pointing out the non-assignment clause. This objection could be overcome on the ground that the receiver has power to bring proceedings in the name of the company to realise charged assets. The debtor could counterclaim for damages for breach of the covenant not to assign but it is thought that, by analogy with breach of an arbitration agreement, such damages would be nominal as the debtor would normally suffer no loss: *Doleman v Ossett Corporation* [1912] 3 KB 257.

The third group of equities consists of rights of set-off and abatement which have arisen or are in existence at the date of receipt of notice of assignment. The question when a claim comes is in existence is not entirely straightforward (Grantham 1989). The easiest conceptually are cross-claims for legal set-off and abatement. The law is clear that both must be in existence before receipt of the notice. In the case of abatement, the right to make a claim for defective work accrues when the work is carried out: *Lintest Builders v Roberts* (1980) 13 BLR 38. A claim for legal set-off must be liquidated or ascertainable with certainty (*Watson v Mid Wales Railway* (1867) LR 2 CP 593) and payable at the time the defence is filed: *Stein v Blake* [1995] 2 All ER 961 at 964. Such a claim was rejected in *Hargreaves v Action 2000* (1992) 36 Con LR 74. A debtor defended a receiver's claim for recovery of a book debt by asserting cross-claims based on sums due under several other contracts. The debtor had instructed a surveyor to re-value those contracts and relied on his valuation of the work done, as well as omitted and defective work. Such claims could only be ascertained by litigation or arbitration. By the time the claim was made, the company was also in compulsory liquidation. The debtor argued it was entitled to the benefit of liquidation set-off. This was rejected on the ground that mutuality was destroyed on the appointment of the receivers, by analogy with *Re Asphaltic Wood Pavement Company* (1885) 30 Ch D 216.

The position is different with equitable set-off where, provided the cross-claim "impeaches" the claim, it will be allowed against a receiver even though it arises after the date of the notice. This is best illustrated by considering the facts of cases where equitable set-off has been allowed against an assignee. The plaintiff contractor in *Young* v *Kitchen* (1878) 3 Ex D 127 was an assignee. The court had little difficulty in holding that the employer was entitled to equitable set-off because the cross-claim had arisen before the assignment was made. In the leading case of the *Government of Newfoundland* v *Newfoundland Railway Company* (1888) 13 App Cas 199 the Privy Council considered a claim by assignees of monies due to a contractor under an agreement to construct 340 miles of railway within five years and thereafter to maintain and operate it in return for a subsidy of $180,000 per annum in half yearly payments for a period of 35 years "such annual subsidy to attach in proportionate parts and form part of the assets of the said company, as and when each five-mile section is completed and operated, or fraction thereof." In addition to the subsidy, the employer agreed to grant 5,000 acres of land per mile of track completed "upon completion of each section of five miles of railway, or fraction thereof." After five years work, the contractor had only completed 85 miles of track. The government had granted land and paid the subsidy as each five mile portion had been completed. The contractor failed to complete the work but the assignee claimed the balance of the subsidy and land grants. It was held that the employer was entitled to an equitable set-off against the assignee's claim of the cost to complete the railway:

> "... the obligation to construct the whole is so intimately connected with the obligation to pay for a portion, as to give rise to a forcible argument that one is a condition precedent to the other; so intimately that their Lordships have serious difficulty in disengaging them, and can only do so by modifying the language of part of the contract" (at 211).

The right to each payment and portion of land was dependent or conditional on the completion of five-mile portions of track. Not only did the cross-claim flow out of the dealings giving rise to the claim, but it was inseparably connected with them and '"impeached" the plaintiff's demand. This case was followed recently in *John Dee* v *W M H (21) Ltd* [1997] BCC 518 at 530.

There are many cases where disputes arise following a sale and lease-back or charge-back of commercial property. In two Canadian cases, the consideration for the land was partly in cash, part by assumption of an existing first mortgage and the balance left on a second mortgage to the vendor. In *Coba Industries* v *Millie's Holdings* [1975] 6 WLR 14 the whole agreement was subject to the vendor taking a lease under which the rent was double the amount payable under the two mortgages. The vendor assigned the second mortgage some weeks later. Before taking the assignment, the assignee was aware of the vendor's arrangement with the purchaser. The purchaser gave the vendor 12 post-dated cheques for the mortgage money which were handed over to the assignee. When the vendor defaulted in payment of rent under the lease, the purchaser stopped the mortgage cheques. It was held that there was a fundamental connection between the vendor's obligation under the lease and the purchaser's obligation under the mortgage such that the price for the building had been determined by the cash flow to be generated by the lease. "In cases where equitable set-off is justified, the assignee takes an impaired title." Set-off was not limited to the arrears of rent owed at the date of receipt of notice of assignment but included damages flowing from a repudiation of the lease which occurred some months later. Because of the very close link between the lease and the mortgage obligations, even rent and other sums accruing due after notice of assignment was received could be set off. This can be contrasted with other authorities where rent becoming due after assignment was held not capable of set-off against an assignee.

In *Re Ovington Investments* (1975) 5 OR 320 the vendor also agreed to complete the construction of the building in a good and workmanlike manner and warranted its fitness for purpose for one year. The issue was whether the purchaser was entitled to a caution against the mortgagee's title. It was held that the caution should be vacated but the underlying assumption in the judgment is that the purchaser had an equitable set-off. In *Mercantile Bank of Canada* v *Leon's Furniture* (1989) 42 Business Law Rep 1 a receiver was appointed over a manufacturer under a fixed charge on book debts which were owed by a retailer. The contract allowed the retailer a volume rebate, an advertising allowance, warranty and service entitlements and the manufacturer always unquestioningly accepted back any damaged goods. The receiver claimed the book debts but refused to allow the rebate or perform any of the manufacturer's obligations. The manufacturer accrued liabilities under warranties in its accounts at the time that products were sold. It was held that the receiver was not entitled to collect the receivables without allowing for the discount and the value of the other obligations even though the discount itself was not payable until after the year end. The claim and cross-claim were so closely bound together as to make it unconscionable to allow one and exclude set-off of the other.

In all these cases there was a close nexus between claim and cross-claim, much more than the simple fact that they both arose out of the same transaction. These cases are examples of equitable set-off where the criterion of impeachment is present. In some cases where the English courts have allowed a cross-claim on the basis of an equitable set-off, there is no obvious nexus with the claim apart from the fact that both arose out of the same contract or transaction: *Bankes* v *Jarvis* [1903] 1 KB 549, *Morgan* v *Martin Johnson* [1949] 1 KB 107, *Hanak* v *Green* [1958] 2 QB 9.

A contractual set-off is likely to be effective even if it arose after the notice provided that it arose from a pre-notice obligation. Where the debt is contractually conditional on the performance of another obligation, the receiver will be unable to recover it without performing the obligation.

Fixed charges on book debts

It is commonplace for a lender to seek a fixed charge on book or other debts of its borrower. Such a charge attaches to all receivables falling within this description currently due or which come into existence after its creation. This is different from an assignment because a charge does not transfer property in the receivable but merely burdens it with satisfaction of the borrower's liabilities. Assignment is only the means of enforcement of the charge. Accordingly, it is not thought that a fixed charge prevents a debtor building up set-off rights, whether aware of the charge or not (Goode 1984). This view has been challenged on the ground that the charge does give the charge-holder a proprietary interest in the debt so that a debtor should not be entitled to a set-off after receiving notice of the charge (Oditah 1991, Derham 1996). Perhaps set-off should only be denied to a trade debtor where in all the circumstances it would be unconscionable to allow it an advantage (Grantham 1989). This is a complex area where the law is in an unresolved state.

Receivership trading

It is often necessary for a receiver to continue trading to preserve the company's goodwill while a buyer is found or to convert work in progress into book debts. A receiver appointed over a contractor may decide to build out where there is a comparatively small amount of work still to be done. It is of concern to the receiver that receivables arising from trading during the receivership are not reduced by set-off of cross-claims arising before or during the receivership (*e.g.* this is the reason for clause 27.5.3 of JCT 98). Equally, those trading with a company which goes into receivership are concerned to preserve their rights of set-off against debts which become payable to the company in receivership through trading with the receiver. Unless the position is altered by agreement after the receivership, a receiver who continues to provide services under a pre-receivership contract is entitled to the benefit of any clause excluding set-off in that contract. This is so even in respect of sums accruing due to the company after the contract has been terminated: *John Dee* v *W M H (21) Ltd* [1997] BCC 518.

Where a receiver allowed the company to continue trading by delivering goods pursuant to a pre-receivership obligation, it was held that the debtor was entitled to legal set-off of a cross-claim which it had before the receiver's appointment: *Rother Iron* v *Canterbury Precision Engineers* [1974] QB 1. Where a receiver realised a charged asset by selling it to a pre-existing creditor of the company, however, it was held that the pre-existing debt could not be set off against the price of the asset: *Felt and Textiles* v *Hubrich* [1968] NZLR 716. In the former case, the receiver had incurred the post-receivership debt by delivering goods without previously agreeing that the purchaser would not make a set-off against the price. In the second case, the purchaser freely contracted in the knowledge that the receiver was selling an asset in the enforcement of the charge for the benefit of the debenture holder.

In a further case, a tenant lent money to its landlord to finance the construction and operation of a building and mortgaged the debt to its bank: *West Street Properties* v *Jamison* [1974] 2 NSWLR 435. The bank appointed a receiver who went into occupation of the premises. The landlord claimed rent from the receiver who was allowed legal set-off of the loan which had been charged to the bank. This case can be contrasted with *Robbie* v *Witney Warehouse* [1963] 1 WLR 1324 where a receiver succeeded in a claim against a pre-receivership debtor of the company who had bought another's claim against the company after receiving notice of appointment. These cases are not wholly logical in their reasoning. Although the concept of mutuality has generally been relied on, the courts appear to be applying a doctrine of unfairness and to look carefully at the facts in each case without applying dogmatic rules.

If a receiver continues to trade, receivables through trading are probably subject to set-off rights acquired in the course of the post-receivership trading: compare *Rendell* v *Doors & Doors* [1975] 2 NZLR 191. This is notwithstanding the fact that as soon as the receivables are created, they automatically fall within the (then) fixed charge over book debts and there is therefore no mutuality between the debtor and the creditor-assignee. From a debtor's point of view, it is always desirable to reach an express agreement with a receiver before continuing a contract post-receivership, otherwise a set-off problem may well arise.

Bankruptcy set-off

The law of bankruptcy set-off has been clarified by the House of Lords in *Stein* v *Blake* [1996] AC 243. Assume that A and B have mutual claims against each other. On A becoming bankrupt, his claim against B passes to his trustee by operation of law. The effect of s 323 Insolvency Act 1986 is to extinguish the claim and the cross-claim and to substitute a claim to the balance owing after setting them off against each other. The trustee has to strike an account of the mutual claims as at the date of the bankruptcy. Where a claim against the bankrupt is not yet due, or is contingent or unascertained, the trustee must make an estimate of it for this purpose. Even before the account is taken, the trustee has power to assign the right to the ultimate net balance. If B claims to be the net creditor, it is advisable for any such assignee to join the trustee in the proceedings.

Bankruptcy set-off will not apply where a creditor goes bankrupt after assigning a debt. In that case, the debtor's right to a legal or equitable set-off against the assignee depends on the continued existence of its cross-claim against the assignor. If the assignee delays issuing proceedings until after the assignor has been discharged from bankruptcy, it may recover its claim in full against the debtor, as the cross-claim will have been released under s 281 Insolvency Act 1986 (see Derham 1996 at 580).

If a joint bankruptcy petition is presented by all members of an insolvent partnership, bankruptcy set-off will apply to the partnership liabilities: Insolvent Partnerships Order 1994. Similarly, liquidation set-off will apply where a partnership is being wound up as an unregistered company.

Voluntary arrangments

Unlike any other formal insolvency procedure, a voluntary arrangement is a contract between the debtor and its creditors. Like any other contract, a voluntary arrangement can expressly modify common law rights of set-off. Thus if the debtor tried to improve its position after an arrangement has been sanctioned by taking an assignment from another creditor bound by the arrangement, it would probably find itself unable to resist payment to the supervisor since its cross-claim would of necessity be subject to the terms of the arrangement. Where the assigning creditor is not bound by the arrangement the position is more complicated.

Liquidation set-off

Where one of the contracting parties goes into liquidation, the general law or the parties' own contractual set-off arrangements are replaced by a mandatory set-off applied by r 4.90 Insolvency Rules 1986 which provides:

> "(1) This Rule applies where, before the company goes into liquidation there have been mutual credits, mutual debts or other mutual dealings between the company and any creditor of the company proving or claiming to prove for a debt in the liquidation. (2) An account shall be taken of what is due from each party to the other in respect of the mutual dealings, and the sums due from one party shall be set off against the sums from the other. (3) Sums due from the company to another party shall not be included in the account taken under paragraph (2) if that other party had notice at the time they became due that a meeting of creditors had been summoned under Section 98 or (as the case may be) a petition for the winding-up of the company was pending. (4) Only the balance (if any) of the account is provable in the liquidation. Alternatively (as the case may be) the amount shall be paid to the liquidator as part of the assets."

"Debt" is defined very widely and includes a liability which is "present or future, whether it is certain or contingent or whether its amount is fixed or liquidated, or is capable of being ascertained by fixed rules or is a matter of opinion": s 382(3) Insolvency Act 1986. Liquidation set-off is therefore much wider than the general law. The requirement for mutual credits, debts and dealings is normally satisfied in a construction contract: *Willment v North West Thames RHA* (1984) 26 BLR 51 at 62. It is unnecessary for a creditor to deliver a formal proof of debt to be eligible for liquidation set-off: it is enough if the creditor has the right to prove. Since only the balance is provable after an account has been taken by the liquidator of the mutual dealings, it is not possible for the liquidator to assign the debt owing to the company without taking into account a debt owed by the company: *Farley* v *Housing and Commercial Developments* (1984) 26 BLR 66. This position is the same as bankruptcy set-off: *Re Bank of Credit and Commerce International (No 8)* [1997] 3 WLR 909. Both apply automatically and are self-executing: *Stein* v *Blake* [1996] AC 243. The set-off is compulsory and the parties cannot contract out of it: *Halesowen Presswork* v *National Westminster Bank* [1972] AC 785.

As it is rare for a liquidator to continue trading in the construction industry, the usual components of liquidation set-off where the contractor goes into liquidation are certified sums and the amount of uncertified work in progress and loss and expense owed to the contractor and the employer's claims arising out of the completion contract. It is not unusual for the cost to complete to exceed the balance of the contract sum resulting in a net debt owed to the employer. The account is taken at the date when the contractor goes into liquidation. If the liquidator declines to continue and the employer has to arrange for a completion contractor to finish the works, it could take some time before the liquidator can take the account. Until the works have been completed and the balance is ascertained, the employer is a contingent creditor in the liquidation. The amount of the debt will be valued by the liquidator under r 4.86 Insolvency Rules 1986 or, in the event of a dispute which could impact on the recovery of other creditors, by means of an arbitration (*Farley* v *Housing and Commercial Developments* (1984) 26 BLR 66 at 79), or an appeal by the employer against rejection of proof.

The Rules allow a creditor to prove in the liquidation for a contingent liability owed by the company. If the contingency occurs after the start of the liquidation the full debt can be proved: *Ellis* v *Dixon-Johnson* [1924] 1 Ch 342 at 357. What is the position where a contingent liability is owed to the company? In *MPS Constructions* v *Rural Bank of New South Wales* (1980) 4 ACLR 835, a contractor went into liquidation and the liquidator decided to complete the contract in order to release retention from a trust account. The account was held by both parties on trust for the employer subject to completion by the contractor. After the works were completed, the employer refused to release the retention relying on set-off of a prior separate debt owed by the contractor. The court upheld the employer's set-off. At the date of the liquidation, the contractor's right to the retention was contingent and there was no provision allowing the liquidator to value it as if it were a "sum due" or to allow it in full on the occurrence of the contingency. The result seems unjust, and in conflict with *Re Asphaltic Wood Pavement* (1885) 30 Ch D 216 considered later, but is in line with other cases. It is to be hoped that the court will reconsider the law in this area and allow a set-off in cases where the contingency does occur (Derham 1996 at 237-244).

Where a contractor is in financial difficulty, the fact usually becomes known on site some time before the contractor becomes formally insolvent. Employers feel it prudent in such circumstances to delay payment and occasionally stop cheques before payment after learning of the contractor's liquidation. It has been held that, because of the liquidation set-off provision, the liquidator cannot obtain judgment by suing on the cheque because, by virtue of r 4.90, the employer's contingent claim has to be brought into account. The liquidator only has a net claim for such balance as is later found to be due to the contractor: *Willment* v *North West Thames RHA* (1984) 26 BLR 51, *Re Jason Construction* (1972) 17 CBR 158.

The contractor may also owe sums to sub-contractors which have been certified together with the value of uncertified work done since the last valuation date. A sub-contractor would also be entitled to losses flowing from the contractor's breach of contract which could include the cost of removing plant and equipment and materials from site (assuming the sub-contractor is not engaged by the completion contractor), and loss and expense caused by the termination. If one of the standard forms has been used, only a nominated sub-contractor is entitled to loss and expense following the termination; whether nominated or not, the sub-contractor would be entitled to any loss and expense which had been incurred before the termination. The certified sum may not have been immediately payable but the contractor's liquidation accelerates the debt to make it payable immediately. The same applies to the uncertified work in progress. Other claims will be unliquidated and require valuation by the liquidator. The contractor may also owe debts to its direct suppliers and damages for breach of contract. Payment of the debts will be accelerated and the damages will have to be assessed. In the case both of sub-contractors and suppliers, the liquidator may reduce their proofs of debt on the ground that they had acted unreasonably in refusing offers of engagement from the completion contractor. As the completion contractor commences work, defects may be found in the works which will constitute additional contingent liabilities requiring valuation and proof at a later date. The employer may also sustain additional losses as a result of the termination, *e.g.* loss of rent.

Liquidators should be aware of two peculiarities in the industry: the entire contract and the letter of intent. If the contractor is entitled to payment only on completion of the works (with no express or implied provision for progress payments), there will be no sum due to the liquidator to set off against the employer's claim for breach of the contract. Generally, only small contractors operate on entire contracts. The potential injustice of this rule is mitigated to an extent by the doctrine of substantial performance but this will only apply where the works have been practically completed.

Where the value of work in progress justifies the cost of obtaining advice, the liquidator may be prudent to investigate whether a contractor or sub-contractor has been working under a letter of intent. If so, it is probably the case that the employer or contractor as the case may be would not be entitled to prove for damages as a result of the failure to complete. And, more importantly, the liquidator could be entitled to claim payment in the form of a reasonable sum under a *quantum meruit* against which the employer would have no right of set-off, although it would have a right of abatement: *Farnsworth* v *Garrard* (1807) 1 Camp 38. Each letter must be carefully examined because, although called a letter of intent, it may in fact be a contract.

The requirement for mutuality means that there must be identity of parties and the mutual debts must be owed between them in the same capacity. Liquidation set-off will not apply where a claim is owed to a company as trustee but by a company in its personal capacity. In the United Kingdom, this problem is most likely to arise in relation to a retention trust. Set-off against money held under a retention trust is discussed in Chapter 11.

Executory contracts

Assume a contractor goes into liquidation and has two contracts with the same employer. The first is front-end loaded and 75% complete. The cost to complete would exceed the eventual receipts. The second contract is not front-end loaded and the cost to complete is less than the anticipated receipts. Subject to the effectiveness of any termination clause, the liquidator has power to continue the second contract and abandon the first: *Asphaltic Limestone* v *City of Glasgow* [1907] SC 463. This process is known as "cherry-picking". By failing to complete the first contract, the liquidator is not barred from recovering the full value of the second contract on completion. The employer is not entitled to withhold payment as security for its claims under the other contract or for prospective claims under the adopted contract.

The employer could in such circumstances apply to the court for an order rescinding the contract and the court may in its discretion consider in all the circumstances that it is just to do so under s 186 Insolvency Act 1986. Each case depends on its facts but where the liquidator is able to demonstrate an ability to complete the court will not grant rescission as of course. Rescission is perhaps more likely where there is a significant amount of work still to be done.

Where a liquidator continues a contract but is unable to satisfy the maintenance obligations, the employer is entitled to prove for its costs in doing so. Where the employer is entitled to prove, it is entitled to liquidation set-off. This situation arises with long term contracts. In the leading case of *Re Asphaltic Wood Pavement* (1885) 30 Ch D 216 the contractor agreed to pave a street and keep it in repair for two years and, if during that time the employer gave notice, to maintain the street for a further 15 years for an agreed fee. Before the work was completed, the contractor went into liquidation. The liquidator completed the works but was unable to ensure that the company would perform its maintenance obligations. The liquidator's claim to payment was therefore defeated by the employer's set-off of its damages claim as a contingent liability of the contractor.

Set-off in administration

The making of an administration order is not likely to affect the parties' rights of set-off (Goode 1997, 307). Set-off (at least if it is equitable or contractual) is not a "proceeding" within s 11 Insolvency Act 1986: see *Re Olympia & York* [1993] BCLC 453. Derham (1996, 152) makes an exception of legal set-off on the ground that it applies only to money claims which are enforceable by action, and actions against a company in administration cannot be brought without the consent of the administrator or leave of the court under s 11 of the Act.

Conclusion

Insolvency practitioners experience difficulties with set-off in construction insolvencies in a number of areas. This is partly because of the wide definition of equitable set-off in building cases given in

Hanak v *Green* [1958] 2 QB 9, and the uncertainty of when a cross-claim maturing after receipt of notice of a receiver's appointment will qualify for equitable set-off. The other major difficulty is in the area of contingent liabilities owed by and to the insolvent company.

Chapter 14

· **Bonds and Guarantees** ·

Introduction

Bonds and guarantees have been required in connection with construction contracts for centuries (Salzman 1952). They provide an informal security for performance by the contractor and occasionally by the employer. There is an enormous range of documents: many are drafted specifically for individual projects; there are some standard forms but they tend to be amended by the parties; and many bondsmen do not have their own forms.

Although these documents are short, they often cause confusion. There are a number of reasons for this. Mainstream construction law concerns contract and tort whereas the law relating to guarantees is derived from equity. The case law has arisen from other commercial spheres such as banking or international sale of goods which have their own terminology. This has led to a plethora of terms used in different contexts to describe the same thing. The industry has persisted in the use of the conditional bond, a form of obligation which has become obsolete for most other purposes. Bonds and guarantees are often dealt with last, and are not properly integrated in the procurement process. Compromises during negotiations can leave them in a highly ambiguous state.

Sir Michael Latham recommended they should use modern language, have a clear end date, allow the beneficiary to obtain payment without the need for litigation and be enforceable on default rather than demand (Latham 1994). This chapter examines the legal concepts underlying such documents to see whether his idea is feasible.

The three variables

These documents can be considered by reference to three variables: the form in which they are expressed, the commercial function they are intended to perform and the legal obligation they contain (Figure 14.1).

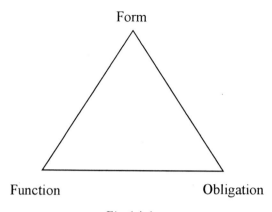

Fig 14.1

It is important in this context to make a distinction between primary and secondary obligations. A primary obligation is one in which the person undertaking the obligation (the obligor) is liable to the person benefiting from it (the obligee) without reference to the liability of any other person. An example is an indemnity by which an obligor promises to make a payment on a certain date or event. An obligation is secondary where its enforceability is contingent on a breach of an obligation owed to the obligee by a third person. This is a suretyship obligation or guarantee. The court has also referred to hybrid obligations: *General Surety v Francis Parker* (1977) 16 BLR 16. These arise where primary and secondary obligations feature in the same document or where it mixes terminology associated with them both. The court then has the difficult task of making sense of apparently contradictory language.

Where the obligation is ambiguous, the court has sometimes been influenced when construing it by the form in which it is expressed: a letter, a formal contract document or a bond. These documents can contain any form of obligation. In practice, a letter is the form preferred by banks and usually contains a primary obligation, whereas contracts and bonds are used for secondary obligations, but this is not necessarily so. The banking letter is an anomaly: it could be classed as a single bond but for the fact that it is not usually executed as a deed and it could be regarded as a contract but for the apparent absence of consideration. It is either a contract between the bank and the obligee, the consideration being implied as the obligee's promise to enter into the construction contract (compare *Jaks (UK) Limited v Cera Investment Bank* [1998] 2 Lloyd's Rep 89) or an autonomous payment undertaking not requiring consideration (Goode 1995 at 77, 986-987).

In construing a document, the court will take account of its commercial function. Bonds and guarantees perform both general and specific functions (Chapter 2). The most common general function is protection against insolvency: a primary obligation is a source of cash flow to finance the completion of the project while a secondary obligation is a source of compensation once the project has been completed and the obligee's loss ascertained. The other general function is protection against default: in this context a primary obligation allows the obligee to call for payment on account of its loss without delay ("pay now, argue later"), whereas a beneficiary of a secondary obligation has to wait until liability has been proven and quantum of loss established. Specific functions range between obligations of performance in general and payment in particular. Performance obligations include the completion and maintenance of the works, the achievement of required efficiency and output levels, the duty to enter into a contract following a successful tender and statutory duties under the Highways Act 1980 and in relation to public utilities. Payment obligations concern advances, retention, stage payments, payment to sub-contractors and suppliers, liquidated damages and customs duty.

There is little uniformity in the titles given to bonds and guarantees. Broadly, those containing primary obligations are called "on demand" bonds or demand guarantees, while secondary obligations tend to be called default bonds or suretyship guarantees. The range of expressions used is set out in Figure 14.2.

PRIMARY OBLIGATION	SECONDARY OBLIGATION
on demand bond	surety bond
demand guarantee	conditional bond
bank guarantee	default bond
standby letter of credit	parent company guarantee
documentary demand bond	guarantee
single bond	insurance bond
payment undertaking	suretyship guarantee
performance bond	performance bond

Fig 14.2

"Performance bond" is perhaps the most confusing, as it is used freely to describe both types of obligation: bankers use it to describe a primary obligation, contractors use it for secondary obligations. Issuers are described as obligors, bondsmen or guarantors. Those receiving bonds and guarantees are called obligees or beneficiaries. The person on whose behalf the document is issued is known as the principal debtor or the account party.

Primary obligations

A construction contract contains primary obligations: for example, the contractor's duty to carry out the work and the employer's duty to pay for it. On international sale of goods contracts, the means of payment is often by letter of credit issued by the buyer's bank. The credit is paid on the seller presenting documents to the bank. Since it does not depend for its enforceability on the liability of a third person, the credit is a primary obligation. The bank takes an indemnity from the buyer for the amount of the credit and may require a cash deposit or some other form of security.

In the 1970s, employers on international construction projects began to require security for performance in the form of a primary obligation from the contractor's bank (Pierce 1993). This obligation was expressed in the form of a letter in which the bank promised to pay up to a fixed amount on receipt of the employer's first written demand without making any enquiry as to the position under the contract. These letters were originally called performance bonds. Although primary in obligation, they are secondary in function since unlike letters of credit they are not intended as the means of payment but as a source of compensation should the contractor fail to perform. Nevertheless, in the earliest reported case on these documents, Lord Denning MR equated primary obligations of this kind with letters of credit: *Edward Owen* v *Barclays Bank* [1978] 1 QB 159. The court has treated demand guarantees as if they were the means of payment ever since.

> "The first principle which the cases establish is that a performance bond, like a letter of credit, will generally be found to be conditional upon the presentation of one or more documents, rather than upon the actual existence of facts which those documents assert. If the letter of credit or bond requires a document asserting that goods have been shipped or that a contract has been broken, and if such a document is presented, the bank must pay. It is nothing to the point that the document is untruthful,

and that the goods have not been shipped or the contract not broken":
I E Contractors v *Lloyd's Bank* (1990) 51 BLR 1 at 7.

There are signs that the court is now relaxing this approach: see
Themehelp v *West* [1995] 4 All ER 215, *Kvaerner* v *Midland Bank*
(1998) CLC 446, *Wahda Bank* v *Arab Bank* (unreported, 16 June
1999) discussed later.

The bank may be liable to pay on receipt of a simple demand but it
is becoming common for more to be required, for example an
assertion that the contractor is in breach or a statement of the nature
of the breach. Although these additional requirements are sometimes
referred to as conditions (so that CUP 1994 refers to a "conditional
demand bond"), they impose little extra burden on the employer,
especially where the document provides that statements by the
employer are conclusive evidence of their own validity and that the
amount claimed is legally payable: *Bache* v *Banque Vernes* [1973] 2
Lloyd's Rep 437. Provided the issuer's liability depends on the
presentation of a document, it will remain primary in character. So a
requirement for a demand to be accompanied by a certificate of a
third person, *e.g.* an engineer, will not alter the fundamental nature of
the obligation, even if the third person has to state that the contractor
is in breach, citing relevant clause numbers and details of the factual
background. The issuer's obligation is primary even where the
demand has to be accompanied by a copy of a court judgment or
arbitration award. This kind of document is primary in obligation but
secondary in function.

A bond could be enforceable on receipt of a demand accompanied by
a copy of a notice of the receiver's appointment or a winding-up order.
It may, however, be difficult to obtain such a bond, especially if the
contractor is already financially unstable, as in that event the contractor
may lack the necessary cash cover or net asset value, and the market
may decline the risk. Figure 14.3 shows how the type of document
required will gradually move the function of the obligation from
indemnity towards suretyship, while remaining primary in character.

Standard forms

A few of the standard forms of guarantee are primary obligations, *e.g.*
those annexed to JCT 98 in respect of advance payment and off-site
materials, World Bank standard bidding documents and contracts
published by the Institution of Chemical Engineers. The I Chem E Red

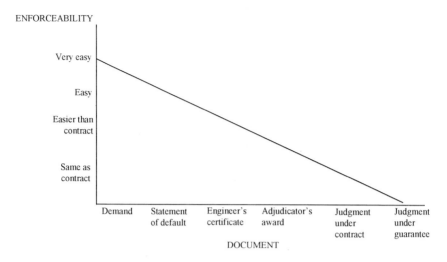

Fig 14.3

Book (2nd edition) gives the parties the option of requiring different documents to be served with the demand, ranging from a statement of breach to an arbitration award. In its demand the employer has to state that it has given the contractor 14 days' written notice of intention to claim under the bond. The International Chamber of Commerce has developed a sophisticated set of rules to accompany model forms of on demand guarantee (ICC 458 and 503E). The rules can be incorporated by reference into the bond. The main innovation is Article 20 by which the beneficiary, when making a demand, has to state that the contractor is in breach and describe the nature of the breach. An ICC bond can be enforced even where a breach has not occurred, but Article 20 is intended to encourage the honest and fair use of such documents. Unfortunately, banks are not very enthusiastic about issuing guarantees in the ICC forms: they are apprehensive about becoming involved in disputes between the contract parties.

Secondary obligations

Under an open contract of guarantee, all that is required is that there be some form of words which the court can construe as a "contract to answer for the debt, default or miscarriage of another" (Halsbury 20/101). In modern English, the guarantor's obligation is to see to it that one person (the principal) does something for another person (the beneficiary) or to perform the principal's obligation if he does not: *Moschi* v *Lep Air* [1973] AC 331. If the guarantor fails to do this, he is liable in damages to the beneficiary. The guarantor's primary duty is not to pay damages in the event of the principal's default but to ensure the performance of the principal's obligations, unless the guarantee expressly limits the guarantor's obligation to the payment of damages.

General principles of suretyship

A guarantor's liability is secondary to that of the principal, contingent rather than actual, unless and until the principal defaults (the accessory principle); and a guarantor is liable to the same extent as the principal is liable to the creditor (the principle of co-extensiveness). Both aspects can be altered by the terms of the guarantee itself (Moss and Marks 1999). A guarantee must be made in writing and signed by the guarantor or by someone with his authority: Statute of Frauds 1677. As a contract, it must be supported by consideration or be by deed. In some jurisdictions, suretyship law is enacted in legislation, *e.g.* Malaysia and India. A guarantee involves two contracts (the guarantee and the contract being guaranteed), and three people (the guarantor and beneficiary under the guarantee, and the beneficiary and principal of the underlying contract: see Figure 14.4.

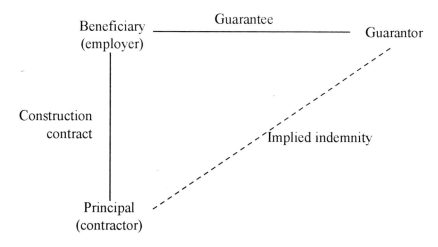

Fig 14.4

Where the contract is under hand, but the guarantee is by deed, the guarantor will be liable for 12 years in respect of a breach, even though the beneficiary would have lost its right to sue the contractor: *Carter* v *White* (1883) 25 Ch D 666. Where the contract is by deed, but the guarantee is under hand, the position is not so clear. The court might say that, by adopting different modes of execution, the parties intended that the guarantor should be released before the principal.

Any breach of contract by the principal will be a breach of guarantee by the surety. Exactly what is a breach of a construction contract in this context is not entirely straightforward: compare *Guinness* v *CMD Property Developments* (1995) 76 BLR 40 with *Oval (717) Ltd* v *Aegon Insurance* (1997) 85 BLR 97. The surety becomes immediately liable without any need for the beneficiary to serve a demand. The beneficiary will not usually take action against the guarantor unless the principal fails to remedy the breach. Guarantees are also construed strictly but all the circumstances are relevant. The court will not re-write a guarantee simply because the parties have not addressed their minds to certain contingencies (Chitty 42-1032). Nor is any favour given to the guarantor if it proposed the form of wording or negotiated it with the beneficiary: *Mercers Company* v *New Hampshire* [1992] 2 Lloyd's Rep 365.

The surety is entitled to be relieved from liability (exonerated) under the guarantee to the same extent as the principal has defences to liability under the contract. A surety will be relieved from liability in certain cases by reason of the creditor's conduct. If the creditor alters the obligation which the surety has guaranteed, without the surety's consent, he risks releasing the surety altogether: *Holme* v *Brunskill* (1878) 3 QBD 495. The case concerned a lease of a sheep farm in Wales. There was a guarantee for the redelivery of the flock of sheep in good condition at the end of the lease. Unknown to the guarantor, the tenant surrendered one of the fields in return for a reduction in rent. Even though the variation made no substantial difference to the lease, the guarantor was wholly discharged from liability. The court said:

> "... if it is not self-evident that the alteration is unsubstantial, or one which cannot be prejudicial to the surety, the court ... will hold that in such a case the surety himself must be sole judge whether or not he will consent to remain liable notwithstanding the alteration, and that if he has not so consented he will be discharged" (at 505).

In recent times, this rule has been softened so that there is an absolute discharge only where the beneficiary's breach is repudiatory. In the case of an ordinary breach, the guarantor's liability will be reduced to the extent that the beneficiary's claim becomes irrecoverable as a result: *National Westminster Bank* v *Riley* [1986] BCLC 268, *Mercers Company* v *New Hampshire* [1992] 2 Lloyd's Rep 365.

Further areas of concern are cases where guarantors have been released through the beneficiary giving additional time to the contractor to pay or to perform (*General Steam Navigation* v *Rolt* (1859) 6 CB (NS) 550), or where the employer releases retention early, giving up an asset against which set-off could have been made, and increasing the likelihood of a claim against the guarantor: *Calvert* v *London Dock Co* (1838) 2 Keen's Rep 638. In practice, these protections to sureties conferred by equity in the 19th century are excluded by the express terms of the guarantee. As with any attempt to exclude the general law, however, the words used must be clear and unambiguous: *Trafalgar House* v *General Surety* [1996] AC 199. An act which benefits the contractor will not necessarily benefit the surety. Other examples of the surety being discharged are the making of direct payments to sub-contractors where this is not allowed by the contract (*Doe* v *Canadian Surety* [1937] SCR 1), and the novation of the contract where the contractor is released absolutely from liability (*Commercial Bank of Tasmania* [1893] AC 313, *Housing Guarantee Fund* v *Yusef* [1991] VR 17). It is also possible for a surety to be discharged if the creditor enters into a voluntary arrangement with the debtor: see *Johnson* v *Davies* [1998] BPIR 607.

If the surety carries out the principal's obligation, he is entitled to all the rights the creditor had against the principal. In other words, the surety is subrogated to the creditor's rights. If the creditor held security to support his rights, then the surety is also subrogated to the creditor's security. As against the principal, the surety has a right of indemnity to the extent he has discharged the principal's obligation. If there is more than one surety for the same obligation, the surety who discharges the obligation is entitled to look to the other for a contribution. The proportion varies depending on the terms of the guarantees. This is worth bearing in mind where an employer has the benefit of a parent company guarantee and a surety bond: if the employer chooses to enforce only against the bondsman, who meets the claim in full, the bondsman can call on the parent company for contribution, *e.g. Stimpson* v *Smith* [1999] 2 WLR 1292.

Where the guarantor undertakes a performance obligation and also indemnifies the employer against all losses flowing from breaches by the contractor, to what extent can the indemnity expose the guarantor to a wider liability than the guarantee obligation set out earlier in the clause? This depends in each case on the words used. The court has sometimes construed an indemnity in this context as simply mirroring in financial terms the guarantor's obligation to procure performance by the contractor or through itself: *Western Credit* v *Alberry* [1964] 2 All ER 938.

Parent company guarantees

A parent company guarantee (PCG) is a contract between a parent company and a beneficiary by which the parent guarantees the performance of one of its subsidiaries under a separate contract between the subsidiary and the beneficiary. The term is commercial rather than legal since the guarantee may be given by an intermediate parent or the ultimate holding company rather than the immediate parent and the words used can make the parent's liability wider than that of the subsidiary. It is often the case that a guarantee issued by an insurance company is less onerous than a PCG. This is partly because surety companies have developed a practice of requiring notices of breaches of the guarantee within a set period after the breach and of imposing strict deadlines for the issue of proceedings. It is commercially difficult for a parent company to justify giving a guarantee of its subsidiary's performance which is of a lower standard of obligation than the construction contract. Many forms used in the industry impose a higher obligation, *e.g.* by making the parent liable even where part of the construction contract becomes unenforceable.

Although at first sight it may seem advantageous to ask for a guarantee from the parent or the ultimate holding company in the group, this will not necessarily be effective if the only assets of the guarantor are shares in its subsidiaries. Where a subsidiary becomes insolvent, the guarantor as shareholder is subordinated to the interests of the creditors, receiving such sum as may be left after all the creditors have been paid in full. The answer is to obtain a guarantee from a company within the group which owns significant assets, but it can be very difficult to ascertain where control and ownership of assets really lies. The expression "parent company guarantee" tends to assume the simple model of a holding company owning 100% of the shares in its subsidiaries, but with a major project it is likely that the contractor will be a member of a large group of companies. If a multinational is involved, there may be literally hundreds of companies within the group. Such a group has a molecular structure rather than the familiar rake or pyramid.

A PCG reduces the effect of abusive or unfair treatment of a subsidiary by other companies in the group. Andrew Muscat has identified four ways in which a subsidiary can be mistreated (Muscat 1996). The first is "subservience" where the subsidiary acts to its detriment in the interests of the holding company, another group company or the group as a whole. A subsidiary's interests may be sacrificed in favour of a policy of maximising the profit of the group; there may be a policy of transfer pricing which obscures the real cost of transactions between group companies (*e.g.* providing services to another group company at less than market value or leasing equipment from the other group company for more than its rental value); a business opportunity won by the subsidiary might be diverted to another group company; its assets may be mixed with those of other group companies without adequate records being kept to enable them to be separated later; its assets may be transferred and re-transferred at convenient times; it may be subject to bogus service charges or forced loans at uncommercial rates; it may have to give guarantees and security in support of liabilities of other group companies (upstream or cross-stream guarantees). The detriment can be a reduction in the profitability or the net asset value of the subsidiary.

The second kind of mistreatment is under-capitalisation where the subsidiary is set up with an inadequate or a "creditor-proof" financial structure. Instead of taking a shareholder's risk by injecting equity, the holding company might finance the subsidiary through debt in the form of secured loans from itself, or the subsidiary may own no property but take everything on lease from the holding company terminable on the subsidiary's insolvency. Thirdly, there is isolation in an integrated economic enterprise where a business is sub-divided into a number of separate legal units. For example, vertical or horizontal integration can be abused by separating functions or assets to an uncommercial degree and isolating them in specific subsidiaries. Last, there is misrepresentation, a group persona situation where the group gives the false impression that creditors are dealing with the holding company or that the holding company is prepared to back the subsidiary. By contrast, some construction groups expressly constitute their subsidiaries as trading agents for the holding company, although this may not be clearly communicated to outsiders. It is possible for a parent company to recover as damages for breach of contract losses sustained by one of its subsidiaries who is not a party to the contract.

The damage would be measured by the loss of value of its shareholding in the subsidiary: *Fischer* v *Multi Construction* (1995) BCC 310.

A PCG recognises the existence of a group of companies as an enterprise in its own right even though the law still focuses on individual entities within the group, *e.g. Adams* v *Cape Industries* [1990] BCLC 479. A PCG expresses the commercial reality for which the law has yet to evolve a framework. Suing a parent can force a quick settlement, especially if the timing is right, *e.g.* issuing proceedings just before the parent intends to sign an agreement with underwriters for a rights issue. A creditor may have little or no knowledge about the parent's affairs, and the proceedings may be a "shot in the dark", but they can be devastatingly successful. Apart from proceedings, simply alerting the parent to the subsidiary's predicament can stimulate a change of attitude by the subsidiary's directors. A dissatisfied trading partner might consider a claim in tort against the parent or a Mareva injunction freezing the parent's assets. There are also statutory claims which a liquidator appointed over an insolvent subsidiary can bring against the parent (Chapter 15), but these are speculative and more problematic than a direct remedy against the parent in contract, hence the popularity of PCGs. Forms used in the Far East give the beneficiary but not the guarantor a discretion to refer a dispute to arbitration, and the guarantor agrees to have its dispute referred to an arbitrator appointed or to be appointed under the contract.

Conditional bonds

A bond is a deed containing a promise to pay money immediately or on a future date. There are two kinds of bond: single and double. A single bond is an undertaking to pay a sum of money without any conditions. Single bonds have largely become obsolete. A double bond consists of two parts: first, an obligation to pay a sum of money and secondly, a condition which contains the real agreement between the parties (Halsbury 12/1385). Bonds are construed strictly, under rules relating to deeds (Halsbury 12/1418). In *Fairclough* v *Cigna Insurance* (unreported, 11 September 1991), the conditions of the bond were full performance by the sub-contractor or payment of damages by the surety "on written notice by the Main Contractor to the Surety of default by the Sub-Contractor (such notice to provide full comprehensive and irrefutable evidence in substantiation of the default)". The court held that these words changed the ordinary standard of proof of balance of probability to that of "irrefutable evidence", which the court suggested (without specifically holding) meant the criminal burden of proof "beyond all reasonable doubt".

The condition could be the performance of another obligation which the bond is intended to secure, so that on performance of the condition, the bond will be void. Double bonds of this kind are called conditional bonds and referred to as "conditioned for" the performance of particular obligations: *Tins Industrial* v *Kono Insurance* (1987) 42 BLR 110. If the bondsman is the same person as the contractor, the bond will take effect as an indemnity. If, as is now almost always the case, the bondsman is a third person such as a surety company (or the contractor and surety company are made jointly and severally liable as bondsman), and the condition of the bond is the proper performance of the building contract, it will contain a secondary obligation and take effect as a guarantee: *Trade Indemnity* v *Workington Harbour and Dock Board* [1937] AC 1. Such a guarantee is often called a surety bond (Scott and Reynolds 1994). The relation between a bond and a guarantee is explained in Figure 14.5.

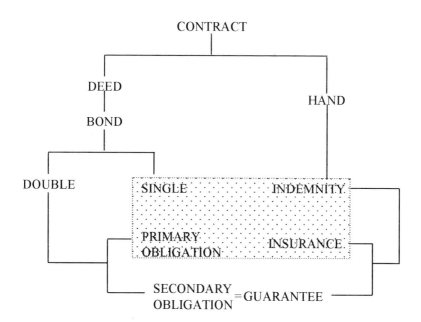

Fig 14.5

Disputes have arisen where the parties have used the conditional bond form for a primary obligation. In a recent case involving an advance payment bond, of five judges who considered the document, one construed it as a guarantee of the underlying building contract, two as an on demand bond, while the remainder (who constituted the majority in the Court of Appeal) construed it as a guarantee by the bondsman of a contractor's obligation as co-obligor under the bond to earn the amount of an advance payment received in connection with the contract: *Mercers Company* v *New Hampshire* [1992] Lloyd's Rep 365. The employer paid the contract sum in advance in order to avoid liability for VAT which was shortly to be extended to refurbishment contracts. The bondsman, jointly and severally with the contractor (Rush & Tompkins), promised to repay the advance of £4.5 million, on condition that if the advance were "liquidated in accordance with the terms of [the contract] and faithfully employed for the purpose of [the contract]" then the bond would be void. The contractor carried out work worth £1 million before going into receivership and the employer demanded immediate payment of the balance of £3.5 million. The bondsman defended on two grounds: first that the document was a secondary obligation and the employer had to prove loss; secondly, that it should be discharged from liability since the contract had been varied by consent when possession of the site was deferred for longer than the contract allowed. It was held that delay in giving the contractor access to the site was not a variation but a simple breach of the contract, which did not affect the employer's rights under the bond. Bonds of this kind are still being used in the industry. In another case, the inappropriate use of the recitals in a conditional bond led to a finding that the insurance company named in the bond was not liable to the beneficiary: *Guyana and Trinidad Mutual Fire Insurance* v *Plummer* (1992) 8 Const LJ 171. The complexity of these documents tends to lead to unfortunate accidents of this kind.

To the layman, the layout of a surety bond gives the impression of enforceability without proof of loss. Thus, in a recent case a contractor working under JCT 81 became insolvent and the employer made a claim under a conditional bond. The claim failed because the employer failed to appreciate that insolvency, although a termination event under the contract, is not in itself a breach of it (Chapter 9). A breach would only result if, the contract having been completed and the losses arising from the termination ascertained, the contractor were to fail to pay any net balance due. The accounting exercise had not taken place by the time the claim was made: *Perar* v *General Surety* (1994) 66 BLR 72, effectively overruling *Northwood* v *Aegon Insurance* (1994) 10 Const LJ 157. The position is different, however, where there are pre-existing breaches of contract before the intervention of insolvency: *Nene Housing Society* v *National Westminster Bank* (1980) 16 BLR 22.

It has been argued that surety companies are keen on conditional bonds as their language and structure increase the prospect of avoiding liability (Wallace 1986). There have been some cases in which the bondsman has avoided liability on technical grounds, *e.g.* failure by the employer to notify the bondsman of all breaches within one month of their coming to its attention: *Oval (717) Ltd* v *Aegon Insurance* (1997) 85 BLR 97. But it seems more likely that the conditional bond has survived because of the conservatism of the construction industry and because, on a deeper level, "conditional bond" accurately represents the psychological relation between employers and contractors.

Standard forms

The industry received a shock in 1994 when the Court of Appeal construed a bond in the ICE (5th edition) form as a primary obligation: *Trafalgar House* v *General Surety* (1994) 66 BLR 42, until the decision was overruled by the House of Lords: [1996] AC 199. Following this case, the Association of British Insurers (ABI) decided to produce a new guarantee in the form of a contract document rather than a conditional bond. Old habits die hard, however, and the document was entitled a "Guarantee Bond". It was issued in September 1995 in conjunction with a Guidance Note from the National Joint Consultative Committee for Building (NJCC).

One of the problems with the ABI bond is that it does not resolve the difficulty caused by the *Perar* decision (see Chapter 9). Employers have therefore made amendments to the form. In *Tower Housing* v *Technical & General Guarantee* (1997) 87 BLR 82, such amendments did not work and the employer failed in a claim for summary judgment against the bondsman following the receivership of the contractor. The bond provided that the surety would

> "... in the event of a proven breach of the contract by the contractor and/or in the event of the determination of the contractor's employment under the contract for reasons of insolvency whether such determination is automatic or otherwise ... satisfy and discharge the net damages sustained by the employer as established and ascertained pursuant to and in accordance with the provisions of the contract, after taking into

account all sums due or to become due to the contractor thereunder and all retention monies held, provided that nothing therein contained shall oblige the employer to await completion of the works prior to making any proper demand hereunder."

For reasons which are not explained in the judgment, the employer issued proceedings against the bondsman before the completion contract had reached practical completion and the additional cost to complete had been quantified. It may be that the employer, as a housing association, lacked access to funds to bring the works to completion without a contribution from the bondsman. The proviso did not enable the employer to recover from a bondsman before the works had been completed since no "proper demand" could be made under clause 27 of JCT 81 until that had happened. The proviso could only refer to a sum due to the employer under some other provision of the contract. If an employer needs help with cash flow to fund the completion contract, it either needs to stipulate for an on demand bond or a hybrid bond, perhaps along the lines of the draft ICE bond, entitling it to a payment on account. Compare *Paddington Churches* v *Tower & General Guarantee* [1999] BLR 244 in which it was held that the reference to determination in the bond did not accelerate the bondsman's liability, which remained conditional on the employer's statement under clause 27.

The ABI bond imposes a secondary obligation to pay damages in the event of a breach by the contractor. Its purpose is to serve as a financial long-stop, primarily in the event of a financial failure (NJCC 1995). It is in the form of a deed, but is expressed as a contract rather than a bond. It is interesting to note the ways in which it favours the issuer by cutting down the obligations found in an open contract of guarantee. First, the obligation guaranteed is not to perform the contract in the place of the contractor but to pay damages in lieu, and there is a maximum cap on liability. Secondly, although not absolutely clear from the words used, it appears that the beneficiary must first obtain an award against the contractor before pursuing the guarantor (or possibly obtain a certificate under the contract, assuming it is not challenged). This could be a significant disadvantage to employers. Thirdly, the expiry provisions attempt to ensure that the guarantor is released on expiry (anticipated as practical completion or earlier sectional completion) unless there has been both a breach and notification of a claim before that event. Under the general law, depending on the precise words of the expiry provision, the guarantor would remain liable for the limitation period: *National House-Building Council* v *Fraser* [1983] 1 All ER 1090; compare *National Westminster Bank* v *Hardman* [1988] FLR 302, approved in *Royal Bank of Scotland* v *Slinn* (unreported, 10 March 1989).

In contrast, the document attached to the ICE (6th edition) has retained the form of a conditional bond. This bond is interesting in containing an arbitration agreement whose ambit is any dispute or difference between employer and contractor concerning the date or otherwise as to the withholding of the defects correction certificate. FIDIC (4th edition) has several standard forms of guarantee. It is curious, given that this form is intended for use internationally, that the draftsman has chosen the conditional bond form. Both the FIDIC performance guarantee and the performance bond contain secondary obligations. In the first, it is a condition of the guarantor's liability that the employer obtains an award against the contractor, an exception to the normal law of guarantees. The performance bond follows American precedents in apparently making the guarantor's liability conditional on the employer having performed its obligations under the contract; and entitling the guarantor to complete or obtain bids from completion contractors. Under this bond, the employer loses a certain amount of control. The International Chamber of Commerce has issued forms of secondary obligation (ICC 524). They are being used increasingly in a wide range of jurisdictions, notably Japan. The New Engineering Contract (now called The Engineering and Construction Contract) published by the ICE has an optional clause G1.1 in relation to performance bonds. The use of the present tense in this clause creates unnecessary difficulty: see [1994] CILL 960. Other forms with secondary obligations are those used in connection with the MF/1 and G/90 main contracts, and issued by FASS, CCS and CECA for use with sub-contracts.

Hybrid obligations

The commonest kind of hybrid obligation is where the document mixes terminology associated with primary and secondary obligations. For example, in *Esal Commodities* v *Oriental Credit* [1985] 2 Lloyd's Rep 546, the document stated: "We undertake to pay [$487,300] on your written demand in the event that the supplier fails to execute the contract in perfect performance …". The issuer argued that it was a secondary obligation. In construing it as a primary obligation, the court was influenced by the function of the document.

"If the performance bond was so conditional, then unless there was clear evidence that the seller admitted that he was in breach of the contract of sale, payment could never safely made by the bank except on the judgment of a competent court of jurisdiction and this result would be wholly inconsistent with the entire object of the transaction, namely to enable the beneficiary to obtain prompt and certain payment" (at 549).

In *United Trading* v *Allied Arab Bank* [1985] 2 Lloyd's Rep 554, the court stated that "to delay payment under such documents strikes not only at the proper working of international commerce but also at the reputation and standing of the international banking community" (at 561). Wording such as that used in *Esal Commodities* is used in illustrative forms issued to customers by some of the clearing banks.

The other kind of hybrid obligation occurs where the same document contains primary and secondary obligations in different clauses. *Harmon* v *Cigna Insurance* (unreported, 16 April 1992) concerned a conditional bond for £22 million which contained the following additional clause: "Notwithstanding the foregoing, Obligee may demand 5% of the value of the bond subject to written notice of 10 days to the Principal specifying the reasons for the calling of the bond, with an additional 14 days (after the expiration of the initial 10 day notice period) for the right of the Principal to begin remedy". Although at first sight a primary obligation, the clause was construed as secondary in the light of its reference to "remedy". The court reached the same conclusion in *TBV Power* v *Elm Energy* (unreported, 21 November 1995) which concerned a conditional bond for £3.8 million. After setting out the conditions of the bond, there were two provisos. The first stated that, if the employer served a written demand stating that a sum of money was due pursuant to a certificate issued under certain clauses of the contract, the bondsman's obligation would be to discharge the amount stated in the certificate either on the expiry of the time limit for serving an adjudication notice or, where a notice was served, on the issue of the adjudicator's decision. The obligation under the bond would not become null and void until after all payments due under this proviso had been made. The second proviso contained an arbitration agreement similar to that found in the ICE bond.

The employer made a demand under the first proviso for the whole of the bond value. The court concluded that, construing the bond as a whole, the first proviso did not remove the bondsman's right under the conditions to make the bond null and void by paying damages. By including an arbitration agreement in the bond, the parties had recognised the possibility that such damages could be less than the bond value.

> "With the possibility that Seaboard's liability to pay damages in a sum less than the amount of the bond, a requirement that Seaboard should make full payment now and then seek repayment of some or all of the moneys at a later date does not suggest a construction that the parties intended … The absence of any provisions in the bond for repayment militates against [it] being other than a contract of guarantee" (Judge Fox-Andrews).

The bond in this case can be contrasted with the retention bond issued by the Civil Engineering Contractors Association (CECA) for use with GC and PC/Works/1 with Quantities (1998) Sub-Contract. This form begins as a conditional bond under which the sub-contractor and the surety are jointly and severally bound to the contractor in a specific sum (a secondary obligation). However, clause 3 sets out a primary obligation to pay the contractor up to the whole of the bond value on receipt of its written demand. If the demand is for the whole bond value, the contractor can deduct retention from future progress payments. The bond states that it will be discharged on the fulfilment of the conditions of the secondary obligation or on the satisfaction of a demand made under the primary obligation. Although likely to cause confusion to sub-contractors, there is no reason why a document cannot contain both kinds of obligation, and there may be good commercial reasons why the contractor would choose to enforce the secondary obligation first. The primary obligation could be abused since it is for the whole retention, rather than gradually accruing as the contract proceeds. In theory, a contractor could call the bond in full at an early stage of the sub-contract, and then start withholding retention in the normal way. The contractor would be forced to issue proceedings for an interim payment to recover some of the bond proceeds but this may be impractical, and the sub-contractor may have to wait until agreement of its final account before getting any refund.

A default bond sometimes also contains a primary obligation activated on the principal's insolvency so as to entitle the beneficiary to demand up to a fixed amount as an interim payment on account of the surety's liability. The employer may be required to apply the money for the purpose of the contract by paying it into a trust account and reporting to the surety periodically as to how the money has been spent. Alternatively, the default bond may include an expert procedure available to the beneficiary at its discretion enabling it to obtain provisional payments on account. The procedure may thus take effect as a primary obligation: *Odebrecht* v *North Sea Production Co* (unreported, 10 May 1999).

A similar process is at work in a parent company guarantee which, after setting out a secondary obligation in easy to understand language, constitutes the parent a "primary obligor" and goes on to say that the parent shall be liable to the beneficiary as if it had been the principal debtor. It is a question of construction in each case whether this wording imposes a collateral indemnity obligation on the parent independent on its duty as guarantor. Such a term is found in the form of parent company guarantee included with the CECA sub-contract referred to above.

Retention bonds

Retention is a special feature of the industry (Chapter 3). In return for its early release or payment gross without deduction, contractors often provide a retention bond. The Institution of Chemical Engineers considers the purpose of this to be

> "to allow the contractor to realise his profit at the earliest moment so long as he continues to fulfil his contractual obligations, and secondly that the purchaser is entitled to reverse the position at any moment at his discretion if he has cause to object to the contractor's performance. It must be emphasised that the rights and obligations of the parties are not affected by either the giving or calling of the bond" (I.Chem.E 1980 at 47).

This statement may be the commercial position but does not accurately reflect what happens in law.

1. Unless the contract clearly states otherwise, the proceeds of a bond call belong absolutely to the employer, subject to an implied duty to give credit for them when agreeing the contractor's final account. They will not necessarily revert to the status of retention for the purpose of release at practical completion and the making good of defects, in the absence of specific rights of recourse in the employer.

2. Retention gradually increases as the relevant percentage, say 5%, is withheld from the gross value of monthly certificates and it will take some time before the employer owes a significant debt against which it can set off a cross-claim. If retention is not withheld, and

the retention bond is for 5% of the contract sum from the start, the employer is better off receiving a bond.

3. Retention bonds are normally expressed as primary obligations, enforceable on presentation of a statement by the employer that the contractor is in default under the contract even though the contractor may have performed satisfactorily. Had retention not been bonded, the contractor might have been able to obtain an interim payment or even summary judgment in respect of retention. While the employer might be ordered to make an interim payment in an amount equivalent to the proceeds of the bond call, it is less likely since the court prefers not to interfere with primary obligations, even where the relief is directed to the proceeds.

4. If the contract limits the employer's right of recourse against retention, for example, to express rights of deduction rather than rights of set-off under the general law, and retention is bonded, the employer may argue that its right to make a demand under the bond is unfettered. Although the bond is a substituted obligation it does not necessarily follow that restrictions in the contract will also apply to the bond: *Costain International* v *Davy McKee* (unreported, 25 November 1990).

5. The contractor can be prejudiced if the terms of the bond do not accurately reflect the contract. This is especially so with reduction and expiry provisions. For example, a bank may refuse to reduce the bonded sum where there is no requirement under the contract to issue the certificate required under the bond, or where the bond purports to refer to a certificate issued under the contract but mis-describes it. If the bond has a dispute procedure, the contractor may find itself having to pay for the continued existence of the bond, and the cost of the dispute procedure, and remain on risk longer than it should have been.

6. On a major project, retention may be bonded in tranches, as it reaches pre-agreed levels. As a result, there may be more than one retention bond. This opens up the possibility of delays in reduction and expiry, and also problems in enforcement, especially where the terms of the bond, or the identities of the bondsmen, are different. It may be arguable that they reduce (or are to be called) pro rata or consecutively.

7. If retention is withheld, the employer owes the contractor a conditional debt which is defeasible by its own rights of recourse.

If retention is bonded, the employer has a contingent asset in the form of the right to call the bonds. If a bond is called, the contractor becomes a contingent creditor of the employer in respect of a claim for repayment under the contract. If the employer is insolvent at the time the call is made, the directors could become personally liable by creating the contingent debt in respect of retention. A claim might be framed in fraudulent trading, wrongful trading or misfeasance (Chapter 15).

It has been held in Australia that evidence that a demand was made to pressurise a contractor to settle a dispute will not vitiate a primary obligation or amount to fraud allowing the contractor to obtain an injunction: *Wood Hall* v *Pipeline Authority* (1978) 141 CLR 443. Where the contract provided for a bond instead of retention and the contractor procured a bank guarantee but went into receivership before completing the works, it was held that the employer was entitled to set off against bond monies amounts representing direct payments made to sub-contractors and that the employer was obliged to pay any surplus to the contractor rather than the bank: *Australian Conference* v *Mainline* (1978) 141 CLR 335. Occasionally, on demand bonds require any part of the demand which is not needed to compensate the beneficiary to be repaid to the issuing bank. These decisions have been distinguished in a line of authority in which the Australian courts have granted injunctions restraining the employer from calling a retention bond. The basis for the decisions is that the construction contract contains a restriction on the employer's right to call the bond (Chapter 17).

Tender Bonds

The tender process on a construction project may take months and involve the employer (and tenderers) in considerable cost. Tender bonds, or bid bonds, compensate the employer for losses sustained if the contractor fails to follow through the tender process to the end. The form of bond varies widely but usually allows the client to call it: (1) if the contractor withdraws its tender before the bond expires without the employer's consent, (2) if the contractor is the successful tenderer but fails to enter into a formal contract, (3) if the successful tenderer enters into a contract but fails to provide a performance or payment bond in accordance with it (Jones 1990). The usual reason for withdrawal of tenders is that a contractor realises it has made a serious pricing error. In an extreme case, the error could lead to insolvency if the contractor is compelled to enter into a contract at its tender rates.

The provision of a performance bond is sometimes a condition precedent to the formation of a building contract, so that non-provision after the contract has been entered into can entitle the employer to rescind: *Swartz* v *Wolmaransstad* [1960] 2 SA 1. If the contractor experiences financial difficulties between the submission and acceptance of its tender, it may find itself with inadequate cash cover or asset value to support the amount of the performance bond. In that event, the contractor may be able to persuade the employer to accept an increased retention or reach some other arrangement whereby no call is made on the bid bond. Can a call be made against a tender bond if the employer fails to enter into the contract, *e.g.* by reason of insolvency? As a call will not be prevented in the absence of clear and established fraud, a contractor ought to insert as a condition of the bond that the employer must have remained willing and able to enter into a contract. Article 6 of the Uniform Rules goes some way to tackling this problem by providing that the bond expires "in the event of the beneficiary expressly deciding that he does not intend to place a contract" (ICC 458).

The amount stated in the bond may be a specific sum or a percentage of the tender price (between 1% and 5%) subject to a maximum sum. Bid bonds are usually primary obligations. It has been suggested that the sum covered by a bid bond could be viewed as the "agreed price for the privilege of being permitted to tender" (Capper 1990). Where a bid bond provides that a performance bond must be procured if the tenderer is successful, it is important to ensure that the latter comes into effect only when the former has expired. Otherwise, a contractor may find its bonding capacity exhausted because of unreturned bid bonds on projects it has no hope of winning. It has been known for a tender bond to be called to compensate an employer for losses allegedly incurred on another contract. If a bank issues a bid bond, it will not necessarily issue the replacement performance bond, at least without a commitment fee, if the nature of the risk alters in the meantime. Like on demand performance bonds, tender bonds have historically been a creature of international rather than UK contracting. However, with changes in procurement methods, and perhaps as a consequence of the 1990s recession, they are becoming more common. One of the earliest was required in connection with the Midland Metro project (*Construction News*, 28 May 1992).

Advance payment

Advance payments are sought to cover mobilisation of plant and equipment, particularly items of high capital value which have to be designed and manufactured specifically for the project. They can also cover the cost of transportation and housing of labour where immigrant workers are required and, where necessary, the cost of stockpiling materials in advance of need. Unless the employer has a right of control or approval of the use made of an advance payment it may find it difficult to ensure that it is in fact used for the project and not diverted to some other use or simply paid into the contractor's overdrawn bank account. The bond protects the employer against abuse of this kind.

Commercial factors

Expiry

In the construction industry, it is common for a guarantee to make express reference to expiry on one of the following: a fixed date, the issue of a certificate under the contract, an event anticipated by the contract, or if the contract is terminated before completion a fixed period after termination.

   If the guarantee is a secondary obligation and expires on one of the events given above, the beneficiary can sue the guarantor after expiry in respect of a prior breach: *National House-Building Council* v *Fraser* [1983] 1 All ER 1090. To make expiry a true cut-off point, the guarantee would have to say that after expiry the guarantor ceased to be liable to the beneficiary absolutely, even in respect of accrued causes of action, unless the beneficiary had already issued proceedings. In *De Vere Hotels* v *Aegon Insurance* [1998] CILL 1346, the surety provided a conditional bond for £1.6 million in support of a contract in JCT 81 form. The surety would be released from its obligation under the bond on the issue of the statement of practical completion of the works. Any proceedings to enforce the bond had to be brought within six months after the date of practical completion named in the statement "and thereafter shall be absolutely barred". The contractor went into receivership before practical completion could be achieved and the employer had the works completed by another contractor. Proceedings were issued more than six months after practical completion of the completion contract. On a preliminary issue, the court held that the employer was not barred since the proviso could only refer to practical completion under the original contract. After the contractor's employment was terminated on its receivership, practical completion could never occur. The employer was under no obligation to enter into a completion contract or to do so on the same terms and with the same practical completion mechanism as the original contract. The completion contract may, and in this case did, not include the whole of the works under the original contract.

When issuing a primary obligation, a bank usually insists on a fixed expiry date, partly for ease of administration and partly so that it can control its capital adequacy ratio, but the contract may require the bond to continue until practical completion or later. The solution is to insert a fixed date in the bond but require the contractor to procure the renewal of the bond or its replacement within a certain period before its expiry for as many times as is necessary until completion has been achieved. Were the contractor to refuse, the employer could treat the contractor's refusal as a breach of contract and call the bond. If so, and the contract is nearing completion or it is obvious that the employer is the net debtor, the contractor may immediately issue proceedings for repayment under the contract on the ground that, although technically in breach in failing to renew the bond, the employer's damages would be nominal. The employer occasionally stipulates for liquidated damages in respect of this breach but it is hard to see how they can be a genuine pre-estimate of loss. Where an employer instructs the bondsman to extend the period covered by a bond or pay, the court is unlikely to regard such conduct as fraud: *Harbottle* v *National Westminster Bank* [1978] QB 147. An 'extend or pay' ultimatum is given in connection with all kinds of bonds, but particularly bid bonds where a prospective employer wants to keep all the tenderers in the frame and play them off against each other. Cover is available from the Export Credits Guarantee Department against the risk of unfair or abusive calls of this kind.

Government contracts

H M Treasury has stated that bonds are not always necessary on government contracts and are no substitute for considered judgements about the risks of a particular contract and the capabilities and financial resources of the available contractors (CUP 1994). In response to pressure from the industry to ban the use of on demand bonds with government contracts, the Department of the Environment set up an inter-departmental working group to carry out research and recommend best practice. In its report, the working group recommended that on demand bonds should only be used in connection with government contracts for specific purposes, *e.g.* advance payments or retention. Departments should not normally use bonds but instead rely on effective pre-qualification and vetting procedures. The report has model forms of performance bond, retention bond, advance payment bond and parent company guarantee (DOE 1996). Neither publication is mandatory and government departments retain a discretion over the use of bonds and guarantees.

Sub-contracts

There is little standardisation of sub-contract bonds and guarantees. They are derived from a number of sources: adaptations from main contract precedents, the contractor's own form, the sub-contractor's preferred form, and occasionally one of the ICC forms. On a major project, sub-contract bonds can have a high value and require careful consideration. The issues which arise are analogous to those concerning the relation between the main contract and the sub-contract. These include:

- whether sub-contract bonds are properly back to back with bonds which the contractor has provided to the employer
- whether reduction and expiry provisions are properly tied in to significant events under the main contract or whether they depend on certificates, events or dates relating only to the sub-contract
- whether they are freely assignable.

It may be necessary for the contractor to assign the benefit of sub-contract bonds to the employer or allow them to be charged to project funders.

Special issues arise in connection with management contracting. In a recent case, on the insolvency of a works contractor, the management contractor had the works completed at considerable extra cost and made a claim under a surety bond. The bondsman defended arguing that, as the management contractor could only be liable to the employer to the extent that it recovered damages from the works contractor, the management contractor had suffered no loss and therefore had no claim under the bond. The court rejected this argument. If the management contractor had not yet recovered the additional cost of completion from the employer, the bondsman would be liable. If recovery had been made, the management contractor could recover from the bondsman provided the employer asserted a claim against the management contractor: *Laing Management and Morrison-Knudson* v *Aegon Insurance* (1997) 86 BLR 70.

A sub-contractor may be required to share part of the burden of the indemnity required by the contractor's bank. A sub-contractor's bond may expressly be enforceable if a bond provided by the contractor is called. The CBI has suggested various options to sub-contractors:

1. The sub-contractor could seek joint venture status with the contractor, and become a party to the main contract.

2. The sub-contractor's bond ought to be enforceable only on the sub-contractor's default.

3. In lieu of a bond, a sub-contractor could offer an insurance policy indemnifying the contractor against the sub-contractor's insolvency.

4. If insurance is available from ECGD, the sub-contractor could be made joint insured.

Alternatively the contractor could agree to pass on an appropriate proportion of the proceeds of a successful claim. This will only apply in the event of an unfair call.

Personal guarantees

Where directors gave a personal guarantee to the NHBC as a condition of the company being admitted as a probationer to the National Register of House-Builders, they were found liable when the company defaulted under its obligations under the NHBC agreement: *National House-Building Council* v *Fraser* [1983] 1 All ER 1090. Guarantees are required from sub-contractors as a condition of obtaining exemption under the tax deduction scheme discussed in Chapter 16.

Joint ventures

The principal might be a corporate or a contractual joint venture. If corporate, the employer may require a PCG from each of the shareholders. If contractual, PCGs may be required from the parent of each of the companies comprising the principal. In each case, the employer needs to be clear whether each guarantor is liable for any default or has a limited responsibility, *e.g.* for a specific part of the works. Even if not mentioned in the guarantee, these matters may need to be dealt with in the consortium agreement by indemnities between the members. If the joint venture is contractual, and the members are jointly and severally liable to the employer, the employer may be prepared to accept some limitation on its recourse, *e.g.* if there are three members in the consortium, the employer may accept that the liability of their respective parents shall each be limited to one third of the consortium's total liability.

If the member of the consortium is the ultimate holding company of a group, the employer may dispense with the requirement for a group guarantee. Alternatively it may require an upstream guarantee from the company in the group which owns most assets or in an extreme case require cross guarantees from all of the group companies. If there are co-guarantors, it is useful for the employer to reserve the right to reach a settlement with one without affecting its rights to recover the balance against the others. If the PCG provides for co-guarantors, but not all of them execute the document, the guarantee may be unenforceable if, on its true construction, it was a condition precedent to its coming into effect that all the guarantors should sign it: *James Graham* v *Southgate Sands* [1986] QB 80.

Assignment

If the guarantee is assigned, but the underlying contract is not, the assignee will not be able to pursue a claim. This is because a creditor cannot convert one obligation into two: the original contract duties owed to himself and the guarantor's duties owed to the assignee. There is no English authority but the principles are set out in the Australian case of *Hutchens* v *Deaville Investments* (1986) 68 ALR 367. An assignment of a contract will not necessarily assign a guarantee issued in relation to it. It is important to deal specifically with the assignment of the guarantee. It is an open question whether the assignment of an on demand bond vests the right in the assignee to make a demand under the bond, to call on the assignor to make the demand or merely passes the right to the proceeds of a successful call (see Chapter 6). In civil law jurisdictions an assignment of a primary obligation only passes the right to the proceeds, as is the case with assignments of letters of credit under the Uniform Customs and Practice (Bertrams 1993).

Link with the contract

As an autonomous obligation, a primary obligation ought to refer to the contract only so as to distinguish it from other obligations. Care is necessary where the document uses terms which are defined in the contract. The contract sometimes contains a term restricting the employer's right to call the primary obligation. For example, it may lay down a notice procedure whereby the contractor is given the opportunity to remedy an alleged default before a call can be made. This approach was taken by London Underground on the contracts for the Jubilee Line extension. Where the employer fails to follow such a procedure before making a call, it is conceivable that the court would grant an injunction restraining the employer from making a demand, although the facts would probably have to be exceptional.

In *Kvaerner* v *Midland Bank* (1998) CLC 446, a contractor agreed to supply materials and design services for the construction of a chemical plant in Indonesia. The contract provided that if the contractor defaulted and the employer gave 14 days' written notice of its intention to call a standby letter of credit specifying the details of the default, then the beneficiary could draw down under the credit. The ICC Uniform Customs and Practice for Documentary Credits (1993 revision) was incorporated into the credit. The beneficiary made a claim under the credit stating that the notice had been served, whereas in fact it had not been. The contractor obtained an injunction against the bank restraining payment and against the beneficiary from receiving payment, which was upheld *inter partes*. The injunction was varied so as not to preclude the service of a further compliant demand. Cresswell J stated:

> "In the wholly exceptional case where a demand under a performance bond or standby credit purports to certify that a written notice has been given as required by the underlying agreement; when it plainly has not been given, the court will, in the exercise of its discretion, grant an injunction to restrain the beneficiary from maintaining the demand accompanied by what is in fact a false certificate. To grant an injunction

in such a case, is not inconsistent with the general principles set out above. It is, in my view, clearly arguable in the present case that the only realistic inference is that the demand was made fraudulently and it is, in my view, further arguable that it is, in the circumstances, dishonest to maintain the demand. I emphasise that this is a wholly exceptional case for the reasons that I have identified."

"Calling the bond"

In *Workington Harbour* v *Trade Indemnity (No 2)* [1938] 2 All ER 101 it was held that, where the contractor was in breach, the beneficiary of a conditional bond could obtain judgment for the entire bond value as long as some loss could be proved, the judgment standing as security for the recovery of damages for future breaches. This was an exception to the normal rule whereby fresh proceedings have to be brought if a cause of action arises after the first action. In *Bold* v *BGK Metals* (unreported, 21 May 1997) the court has clarified that it will only grant a declaration as to a current breach and give judgment for loss which can be proved. Future breaches will have to be pursued in separate proceedings.

Procedural requirements

Under an open contract of guarantee, the guarantor is liable immediately a breach occurs of the underlying contract. However, the guarantee may provide that the guarantor's obligations only arise on service of a notice from the beneficiary. The guarantee may oblige the beneficiary to notify the guarantor within a certain period of any breach of the underlying contract which comes to the notice of the beneficiary. This apparently onerous provision was upheld as a condition precedent in *Clydebank* v *Fidelity & Deposit Company of Maryland* [1916] SC 69. This applies to all "non-performance or non-observance" and is not restricted to the particular event giving rise to the claim. For example, where a contractor working under JCT81 goes into receivership and the employer has the works completed by an alternative contractor, and the receiver refuses to pay the net sum found due after the agreement of the completion contractor's final account, the bondsman can still resist payment of this sum on the ground that it had not been notified of the original contractor's failure to complete by the date for completion within one month: *Oval (717) Limited* v *Aegon*

Insurance (1997) 85 BLR 97. There were a number of reasons why a guarantor might require such notice, and where it was expressly made a condition precedent liability in the bond, the court would uphold the condition. The notice requirement was not unfair under the Unfair Contract Terms Act 1977. Even if the Act could apply, the term was reasonable. The notice provision in the *Oval* case can be compared with a requirement in an insurance policy that an occurrence giving rise to a claim should be notified "as soon as possible". The court held that this was not a condition precedent to the insurer's liability: *Alfred McAlpine v BAI* [1998] 2 Lloyd's Rep 694. This was a claim against insurers under the Third Parties (Rights Against Insurers) Act 1930 by a main contractor in respect of a liability of a sub-contractor which had gone into liquidation.

The counter-indemnity

Under a contract of indemnity, there is an undertaking to pay if a person suffers a loss or incurs a liability: *Yeoman Credit* v *Latter* [1961] 1 WLR 828. There is no need to show who caused the loss or why or how it was caused, only that it was caused and was of the kind for which the indemnity was given: *Gulf Bank* v *Mitsubishi* [1994] 2 Lloyd's Rep 145. Broadly speaking, an indemnity exposes the issuer to wider liabilities than a guarantee, does not give rise to common law defences, has a different effect on assignment and on limitation, and is likely to be easier to enforce than a guarantee.

Where a bank issues an on demand bond, it may require its customer to provide a cash deposit which can be drawn down in case the bond is called unless the contractor's net worth is such that an indemnity is sufficient and the bond is given against a special credit facility. Alternatively the indemnity may give the bank the right to call for a cash deposit if the principal is in breach of one of its terms. On an international contract, local law may require the bond to be issued by a bank based in the country of performance of the works (the issuing bank). This is put in place by a chain of indemnities: after the contractor has deposited cash cover or given an indemnity, its bank gives a primary obligation to the issuing bank which then provides the bond (Figure 14.6). If the bond is called, so is the indemnity and the cash cover is forfeited. Where a secondary obligation is given, it is more likely to be given by an insurance company who would not require cash cover but issue the bond against a premium.

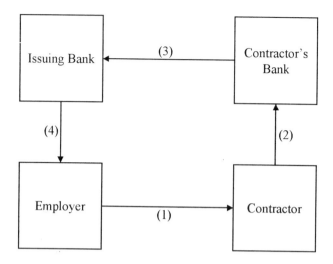

(1) Construction Contract
(2) Counter-Indemnity
(3) Indemnity/Performance Bond
(4) Performance Bond

Fig 14.6

In a case decided by the Hong Kong Court of Appeal, *Bollore* v *Banque Nationale de Paris* [1983] HKLR 78, the contractor provided a bank bond analogous to the ICE bond in respect of an advance payment. The bank obtained indemnities in respect of the bond from the contractor and its director against all liabilities arising out of the bond whether before or after the expiry date.

The words of the indemnity were so wide as effectively to convert the bond into a primary obligation. This was because the indemnities rendered the bank immune from suit from the customer if it paid out wrongly under the bond. The moral for contractors is that it is just as important to scrutinise the wording of the indemnity given to the bank as the wording of the bond given to the client. On a large project, the local bank may issue a bond backed by an indemnity agreement which has been syndicated to a group of participating banks (Kronfol 1983).

In *Wahda Bank* v *Arab Bank* (unreported, 16 June 1999) the contractor's bank refused to honour a counter-indemnity given to an issuing bank in support of four performance bonds provided to a

Libyan Government agency. The counter-indemnity was governed by Libyan law. The agency had issued proceedings against the issuing bank in Libya which had been dismissed. Nevertheless, a further claim had been intimated. The contractor's bank was entitled to refuse to pay since the evidence was overwhelming that the contractor had fully performed the contract long since, the demand had no basis and could not be made honestly.

Indemnities sometimes oblige the contractor to pay on demand any sum which the bank has paid which was "properly due" or "in accordance with" the primary obligation. This provides a safeguard to the contractor. However, indemnities required by some of the clearing banks do not have this protection, and expressly provide that the bank will be entitled to enforce the indemnity on demand even if it is not clear whether a valid demand has been made against them. Similarly, the members may have executed a counter-indemnity to a bank providing bonds to the employer and agreed that their liability under the indemnity should be several: one might be liable for 70% of a demand, and the other for 30%. If either failed to pay its relevant proportion, the bank could not call on the other to make up the difference.

Liability under a counter-indemnity issued in support of a bid bond will be shared in fixed proportions by the joint venturers, under the consortium agreement or a separate letter of indemnity. The indemnity might confer a right on the participator to object to the form of tender bond offered before it is executed and make its consent a condition to the extension or replacement of the tender bond by other bonds.

Arbitration

The power of an arbitrator to make an order preventing a call under a demand guarantee is uncertain. It can only derive from the rules under which he is operating. There is very little authority. In *Bocotra Construction* v *Attorney General of Singapore* [1996] ADRLJ 312 an arbitrator granted an injunction restraining a call *ex parte*, only to withdraw the order and make an interim declaration to the same effect at the hearing *inter partes*. The order was declared void by the Singapore Court of Appeal on a number of grounds, but in particular that it did not fall within the scope of the arbitrator's general powers to make orders for the "preservation of property".

In the American case of *Sperry* v *Government of Israel* (689 F 2d 301, 1982) the contractor had to procure a letter of credit which could be drawn down by the employer on its own certification that it was "entitled to the amount covered by such a draft by reason of a clear and substantial breach" of the contract. The contractor referred disputes to arbitration which the employer defended and counter-claimed. In the course of the arbitration, the contractor obtained an order restraining the employer from calling under the letter of credit. The award was overturned by the court and a call successfully made but the arbitrators then issued a further award ordering that the proceeds of the credit be held in an escrow account in the joint names of employer and contractor. There have been a number of cases where interim relief has been granted under articles 8(5) and 11 of the ICC Rules, but they are of limited value since the reports are unclear and frequently fail to give the bond wording or to state whether the contract referred to the bond in any way.

Resolving disputes

Proper law

If there is no express choice of law in the guarantee, the court will consider the circumstances in which the guarantee was given to see whether there is an implicit choice of law, or, if there is no implied choice, adopt the legal system of the country with which the guarantee is most closely connected. If there is no express choice of law, the position in the majority of cases is likely to be as follows. A secondary obligation will follow the law of the obligation or contract guaranteed: *Broken Hill* v *Xenakis* [1992] Lloyd's Rep 304. A primary obligation such as an on demand bond is autonomous and will not necessarily follow the contract pursuant to which it was provided. The most common test will be its place of performance, *i.e.* the place where payment is to be received: *Attock Cement* v *Romanian Bank* [1989] 1 WLR 1147. If the bond is silent, the proper law will therefore depend on the exercise of the beneficiary's discretion as to the place of payment. A counter-guarantee will usually follow the law of the on demand bond: *Turkiye* v *Bank of China* [1993] 1 Lloyd's Rep 132, *Wahda Bank* v *Arab Bank* [1996] 1 Lloyd's Rep 470.

These common law rules are now subject to the Contracts (Applicable Law) Act 1990 which incorporates the Rome Convention

1980. The Convention also applies the close connection test, but there is a presumption that the guarantee will be most closely connected with the country where the issuer has its principal place of business. The presumption can be disregarded in some cases and care is needed (Petkovic 1995).

Unfair calling

The separation of an on demand bond from the underlying contract inevitably opens up the possibility of its being used unfairly. The most effective remedy for the contractor in this context is an injunction restraining the issuing bank from honouring a demand. Normally, an applicant for an injunction has to show three things: that there is a serious issue to be tried (*i.e.* that there is a cause of action), that damages would not be an adequate remedy and that, on a balance of convenience, it would cause less harm to grant the injunction than to preserve the status quo: *American Cyanamid* v *Ethicon* [1975] 1 All ER 504. These principles do not apply to on demand bonds since the courts have chosen to equate them with letters of credit which, as autonomous obligations, must be honoured unless it can be shown that the demand was fraudulent: *Edward Owen* v *Barclays Bank* [1978] 1 QB 159. The burden of proof is a high one: it is not sufficient to show that there is a strongly arguable case of fraud; the applicant for an injunction must be able to show that the only realistic inference from the facts is that the demand was fraudulent and that the bank was aware of the fraud: *GKN Contractors* v *Lloyds* (1985) 30 BLR 48, *United City Merchants* v *Royal Bank of Canada* [1983] 1 AC 168, *United Trading* v *Allied Arab Bank* [1985] 2 Lloyd's Rep 554. See *Kvaerner* v *Midland Bank* (1998) CLC 446, considered earlier, for a rare example of the fraud exception being established.

The position may be different where the application is to restrain the beneficiary from making a demand. In a recent case, the Court of Appeal upheld an injunction restraining a demand being made under a demand guarantee: *Themehelp* v *West* [1995] 4 All ER 215. The facts were unusual in that the fraud alleged concerned a misrepresentation which induced the underlying contract. The fraud did not relate to the demand guarantee or to a demand which was anticipated under the guarantee. The position is much less clear where the contractor is relying on grounds other than fraud as a basis for the injunction against the beneficiary. Despite the distinction referred to earlier between applications to restrain banks and beneficiaries, and the absence of public policy considerations in the latter case, English law has shown its conservative face on the few occasions when the courts have commented on this issue. Andrews and Millett (1996) contains a thorough review of the authorities world wide on this subject.

In addition, the court has consistently refused to imply a term in the underlying contract that a demand will only be made under the bond where there is evidence of default or when there is reasonable and just cause. Lord Denning once observed however that

> "The only term which is to be imported is that the buyer, when giving notice of default must honestly believe that there has been a default on the part of the seller. Honest belief is enough. If there is not honest belief, it may be evidence of fraud. If there is sufficient evidence of fraud, the court might intervene and grant an injunction": *State Trading Corporation of India* v *Man* [1981] Com LR 235.

The case seems to say that no inference other than fraud should be capable of being drawn from the beneficiary's conduct. The only other relevant early authority is *Elian* v *Matsas* [1966] 2 Lloyd's Rep 495 in which the Court of Appeal granted an injunction restraining a call. Danckwerts LJ said:

> "It seems to me that if the shipowners were entitled immediately after obtaining the undertaking to claim a fresh lien and use it for the purpose of the undertaking, it would amount at least to a breach of faith in regard to the arrangement between the parties. Whatever may be the final result of the case, it seems to me that this is an instance where the court should interfere and prevent what might be an irretrievable injustice being done to the plaintiffs in the circumstances" (at 498).

This finding was not made on the basis of an implied term but Lord Denning also referred to the understanding underlying the provision of the demand guarantee (that it was to release goods from a lien on the understanding that no further lien would be imposed). The case could perhaps be explained on the basis that it was an implied term of the arrangement (part of which was the provision of the demand guarantee) that the guarantee was in consideration of a waiver of all rights to lien, past present or future, regarding the goods. One can see obvious distinctions between this case and others as the demand guarantee was put in place only half way through the transaction for a specific purpose which it seems the beneficiary then tried to subvert.

The court has also refused to imply any term into the bond itself: *Erimis* v *Banque Indosuez* (unreported, 26 February 1997). The court has upheld an implied term of the contract that the beneficiary will account to the contractor for any excess of the bond proceeds over its actual loss, but this does not affect the principle of "pay now, argue later" or give the contractor any right to an injunction restraining payment in the meantime: *Cargill* v *Bangladesh Sugar* [1996] 4 All ER 563, affirmed [1998] 2 All ER 406. It remains a possibility, however, that the *Cyanamid* principles can still be relevant where an injunction is sought on the ground that the bond has expired (*Gibraltar Homes* v *Agroman* (unreported, Gibraltar CA 15/96, Sir Brian Neill), or where there is an arguable case that the engineer is threatening to interfere with the underlying contract (*Press Construction* v *Penspen*, unreported, 16 April 1996) or it can be shown that the beneficiary would not be able to repay the bond proceeds after the dispute between the parties has been resolved: *Bristol Meci* v *Ericsson* (unreported, 25 October 1996). In bond cases, damages are often not an adequate remedy to the contractor. This is because bond calls are comparatively rare and the contractor's reputation could be damaged if a bond call became widely known: *Hawker Siddeley Power* v *Peterborough Power* (unreported, 9 May 1994). Invitations to tender often require contractors to state whether any bonds have been called against them.

Dispute resolution clauses

The presence of a dispute resolution clause in a bond can affect its construction: see *TBV Power* v *Elm Energy* (unreported, 21 November 1995) discussed earlier in connection with hybrid obligations. Disputes arising under bonds and guarantees are decided by the court since there is not usually an arbitration clause in the bond, or if there is, it is limited in scope, as with the ICE bond (see Moss and Marks 1999 for precedents with ICC arbitration clauses). It is often open to an employer to sue a guarantor in court while at the same time arbitrating against the contractor to recover the same loss. There is a risk of inconsistent findings and wastage of costs. In *Alfred McAlpine* v *Unex* (1994) 38 Con LR 63, the court refused to intervene to stay the court action pending the outcome of the arbitration, although this is an exception to the court's usual approach: *University of Reading* v *Miller Construction* (1994) 75 BLR 91.

Disputes under bonds and guarantees tend to focus on the beneficiary's entitlement to call, which in turn is likely to depend on the issue of documents under the bond or the contract. For example, in order to make a valid call, an employer may have to serve with its written demand a certificate of the engineer that the contractor is in breach. From the contractor's perspective, it may be possible to argue that the certificate was fraudulent or that the engineer's independence has been compromised. As the certificate was issued for the purposes of the bond, there is a certain logic in hearing this dispute by an arbitrator appointed under the bond. Other things may also depend on the issue of a certificate by the employer's agent, *e.g.* the increase or reduction in the bonded amount or the date of expiry of the bond. In such cases, a dispute may arise as to whether the contractor is entitled to the certificate, which a bond arbitrator could decide.

In October 1995, the ICE issued a draft form of bond for consultation which contains provision for adjudication where the bondsman disputes a claim. The purpose of the bond is explained in the guidance notes as providing security against default in general and protection against cash flow problems in particular. The bond attempts to combine the functions of the financial long-stop and cash flow protection. The adjudicator's jurisdiction is limited to deciding whether an event of default has occurred and/or the amount of the employer's loss. Both informal and formal insolvency are included in the events of default. The document is not expressed as a bond in the traditional way. The adjudicator's decision is final for the purpose of the bond only, leaving it open to the parties to have their dispute heard in another forum after the bond has been paid. Since the reference to an adjudicator takes place after a call has been intimated, there could be more than one adjudication under the bond. The bond enables an employer in theory at least to obtain payment of a sum representing a future loss provided that the sum is claimed in good faith. Clearly this could be open to abuse, even with the power to refer to adjudication.

The bond contains a provision that set-off is not allowed against a bond claim unless it has been certified by the engineer. In contrast to the NJCC form, it appears that claims are possible under this form of bond in respect of breaches occurring before expiry, even where the claim is made after expiry. The ICE has not yet issued a new form based on the draft. The form of sub-contract bond published by the Confederation of Construction Specialists (1992) also contains an adjudication provision. The bond is conditional on the sub-contractor's failure to remedy a default after service of two notices from the contractor. The adjudicator's jurisdiction is to decide on the basis of documents only whether the sub-contractor has rectified the default and, if not, the amount payable by the guarantor. The adjudicator's decision is binding on the parties until the dispute is referred to arbitration or to the court.

The International Bar Association has issued illustrative forms of demand guarantee which approach the problem of unfair calling from a different perspective (IBA 1992). The forms require the beneficiary to state that the principal is in default and set out the nature of the breach, but go further by deferring the bank's obligation to honour the call until either the principal confirms that it does not object or the beneficiary applies to the International Chamber of Commerce for a pre-arbitral reference on the validity of the call. The bank must then defer payment until the ICC gives its decision or until the beneficiary gives a counter-guarantee, if sooner. The bank is not concerned with the reference, but only with documents. Bonds also sometimes contain an expert procedure: *Odebrecht* v *North Sea Production Co* [1992] 2 All ER (Comm) 405. Under the Danish standard form AB 92, if the contractor wishes to challenge a call, it can ask the Building & Construction Arbitration Board in Copenhagen to appoint an expert to rule on its validity and, if necessary, the amount which should be paid.

Relation to other securities

How do bonds and guarantees compare with other informal kinds of security? Consider the following statements:

1. I promise to pay you up to £1 million on 1 June (single bond).

2. I promise to pay you up to £1 million if you ask me in writing (on demand bond).

3. I promise to pay you up to £1 million on receipt of your written demand accompanied by an arbitration award or a judgment in your favour for the amount of your demand (documentary demand bond).

4. I promise to pay you the cost of reinstating the works if they are damaged by fire (insurance).

5. I promise you that I will perform my contract with Peter (collateral warranty).

6. I promise to pay you up to £1 million on condition that if I perform my contract with you my promise is void (conditional bond with primary obligation).

7. I promise to pay you up to £1 million on condition that if Peter performs his contract with you my promise is void (conditional bond with secondary obligation).

8. I promise that my son Peter will perform his contract with you (parent company guarantee).

The obligation is primary in statements 1 to 6, and secondary in 7 and 8.

Conclusion

At the beginning of this chapter, it was questioned whether the criteria for bonds and guarantees recommended in the Latham Report were feasible in practice. It seems that the law has yet to evolve an instrument which could meet all of them. There is no difficulty in using modern language. As far as a clear end date is concerned, the industry's wish for expiry on an event or a certificate can be accommodated in a number of ways. But there is an irreconcilable conflict between the aims of allowing a beneficiary to obtain payment without litigation and having a bond which is enforceable on default rather than demand. This is because the law regards these two aims as needing different kinds of obligation, primary and secondary. Attempts at hybrid obligations have not been successful. Those reviewed in this chapter have either been ambiguous, thus increasing the likelihood of litigation, or an uneasy compromise by which the same document contains primary and secondary obligations in the alternative, while the primary obligation is almost certainly going to be chosen by the beneficiary, or allowing the beneficiary to call part of the bonded sum on demand on account of its loss, which has to be proved in the normal way at a later date.

The better course is to spend longer at the prequalification and tender stages, carefully appraising the relevant risks, and only requiring a bond or guarantee where absolutely necessary. The government's policy on its own contracts of reducing the need for such documents is welcome, but unfortunately the overall trend is in the opposite direction. It is not entirely clear why this has happened. International practice, the insolvency of large contractors in the early 1990s, the increasing use of joint ventures, and the sheer size of modern infrastructure projects are all relevant factors. Perhaps the major driving force, though, has been the PFI initiative which has required contractors to shoulder additional risk and provide greater security (Haley 1999). Haley speculates that increased competition between funders might reduce these factors. Perhaps the closest approach to Latham's idea is that taken in the oil and gas industry, where bonds of primary or secondary obligation have included expert procedures.

Chapter 15

· Insolvency Claims ·

Introduction

On an insolvency, various causes of action become available to administrators, liquidators and others. The public policy underlying these claims varies in the light of their differing historical origins. Many concern the avoidance of transactions entered into by the company before its insolvency which conferred an unfair advantage on one creditor over the others. Some claims are remedial in character and enable the company to recover property which has been misappropriated and compensation from directors and others charged with a duty to the company to deal honestly with creditors and to take their interests properly into account when the company becomes informally insolvent. Some claims are continuations of those available to the company and to third parties even before the company becomes insolvent (Goode 1997).

The underlying policy affects the entitlement to the proceeds of the claim. Broadly, claims based on the avoidance of transactions are for the benefit of the company as a whole, including secured creditors: *Re Yagerphone* [1935] Ch 392. Claims of a remedial nature are for the benefit of the general body of unsecured creditors: *Re Oasis Merchandising* [1997] 1 All ER 1009. Figure 15.1 sets out the range of claims available, and who stands to benefit from them.

Most claims are brought by liquidators against directors. As is explained in Chapter 16, a person may be a director for the purpose of an insolvency claim if appointed as a director by the company (*de jure*), by holding himself out as such to third parties (*de facto*) or by controlling the actions of the company from behind the scenes (shadow director). Many of the claims can, however, be brought by a person other than the liquidator against persons other than the directors. This chapter briefly summarises insolvency claims and gives examples of situations occurring in the industry giving rise to them.

BENEFICIARY	PROCEEDING	IA SECTION
Unsecured creditors	Fraudulent trading	212
	Wrongful trading	214
	Preference	239
	Transaction at an	238
	undervalue	423
	Transactions in fraud of	244
	creditors	
	Extortionate credit	
	bargain	
The company (including	Misfeasance	213
secured creditors)	Post-petition disposals	127
	Invalidated floating	245
	charges	
	Unregistered registrable	395(Companies
	charges	Act 1985)
	Contravention of *pari*	107
	passu rule	

Fig 15.1

Fraudulent trading

Fraudulent trading gives rise to civil and criminal liability. In this exceptional case, the courts apply the criminal burden of proof beyond reasonable doubt to civil claims. It arises where "any business of the company has been carried on with intent to defraud creditors of the company or creditors of any other person or for any fraudulent purpose": s 213 Insolvency Act 1986. Where this can be shown, the court has jurisdiction to declare that any persons who were knowingly parties to the carrying of the business are liable to contribute to the company's assets. Liability is not restricted to directors but to any participators in the fraud. Fraudulent trading is a criminal offence whether or not the company is in liquidation: s 458 Companies Act 1985. Fraudulent trading can result from a single act or transaction (*Re Gerald Cooper* [1978] Ch 262), *e.g.* in creating a contingent liability in the form of an implied duty to account for the excess of bond proceeds over actual loss by causing an insolvent employer to call an on demand bond (see Chapter 14).

In *Mowlem* v *Eagle Star* (1992) 33 Con LR 131, an employer went into receivership a few weeks before an arbitrator issued an award ordering it to pay over £12 million to a contractor. The contractor sued the architect and one of the shareholders of the employer in tort alleging that they had interfered with the contract and procured the employer to break it. It was alleged that the architect was aware of the employer's insolvency and, to avoid committing it to further payments, certified that the contractor owed significant liquidated damages and was in default such as to allow the employer to terminate the contract. The allegations were not proven but, if they had been, they might have been sufficient to ground a claim by a liquidator of the employer in fraudulent trading. A further industry example is where a labour only sub-contractor engages workmen on a self employed basis but absconds before paying them. Such actions could constitute fraudulent trading if it could be shown that the directors of the sub-contractor acted intentionally or recklessly in instructing the workmen knowing they were not going to pay them.

Wrongful trading

"Wrongful trading" was introduced by s 214 Insolvency Act 1986. It uses the civil burden of proof of the balance of probabilities and is easier to establish than fraudulent trading. The section provides that the court can order a director or a shadow director to make such contribution to the company's assets as it thinks proper where it can be shown that a company has gone into insolvent liquidation and at some time beforehand the director "knew or ought to have concluded that there was no reasonable prospect that the company would avoid going into insolvent liquidation." It is not necessary to prove dishonesty.

A director will not be liable if he can show he has taken "every step with a view to minimising the potential loss to the company's creditors ... as he ought to have taken": s 214(3). A director is judged not simply by his own skill and experience but also by the knowledge, skill and experience of a reasonably diligent person performing his function in the company: s 214(4). The court first looks to see whether the director acted properly to the best of his own ability (subjective test) and then whether he acted as a person with his role in the company ought to have done (objective test). The greater the director's responsibility within the company, the stronger is the risk of personal liability.

In the earliest reported case, *Re Produce Marketing* (1989) 5 BCC 569, the company went into liquidation in October 1987. The court held that the directors knew or should have known that liquidation was inevitable by July 1986 and ordered them to pay compensation based on the credit incurred since then. The court made the following observations:

1. Account had to be taken of the nature of the business concerned: a higher standard would be expected from a director of a large company with sophisticated accounting procedures than a director of a small company in a modest way of business.

2. The court would look at facts which were ascertainable by the directors as well as those actually known to them.

3. The section was compensatory rather than penal although the court left open whether it could make a punitive award.

4. The absence of fraud should be taken into account but would not of itself justify a reduction in the award.

5. Relevant factors were that the directors had ignored the auditor's warnings, lied to creditors and taken trade credit to reduce an overdraft which one of them had guaranteed.

Re Produce Marketing concerned a fruit importer. It was quickly followed by a construction case. In *Re DKG Contractors* [1990] BCC 903 the court considered a groundworks sub-contractor whose directors and shareholders were a Mr and Mrs Gibbons. Mr Gibbons began business as a sole trader. They formed the company in 1986 and it was contended that Mr Gibbons continued to run his own business in parallel with the company, supplying it with labour, materials and plant for which he rendered invoices.

The company became informally insolvent in February 1988. Liquidation became an inevitability two months later. Between May and November 1988, 16 creditors obtained judgment and there were 10 visits from the bailiff. The company went into liquidation in December 1988 owing creditors over £160,000. During the previous 10 months, it had paid Mr Gibbons over £400,000. No proper accounts were kept. The court rejected Mr Gibbons' claim that the company was dormant between 1986 and 1988. During 1987, it had obtained its own headed notepaper on which tenders were submitted and correspondence entered into with main contractors, who paid the company gross of tax in reliance on a 714 certificate in Mr Gibbons' name until the company obtained its own certificate in January 1988 (see Chapter 16). Both directors were liable for wrongful trading and ordered to contribute to the company's assets a sum representing credit incurred after the end of April 1988. They were also liable for misfeasance and preference (see later). This is perhaps an extreme case in view of the fact that the directors took no independent advice. They acted unreasonably but not dishonestly. Other situations which might give rise to wrongful trading in the industry arise from the nature of the trading vehicle or the funding structure, *e.g.* joint ventures and charitable trusts (Davis 1988).

Wrongful trading uses the balance sheet test as the criterion of insolvency: s 214(6). This was considered in Chapter 7. It can be difficult to apply where an unliquidated claim has been made against the company. Should the whole claim be brought into account as a contingent liability when the directors are monitoring the company's position in order to avoid wrongful trading? It is difficult to give a clear answer but English law disapproves of directors taking a sanguine view of the outcome of such claims (Cork 1982, at 214 and 1295).

Where a company is insolvent, it is sometimes argued that the directors risk liability under s 214 by continuing to allow it to defend proceedings rather than leaving the decision to a liquidator, the measure of compensation being the plaintiff's legal costs and interest accruing on the claim. In *Taylor* v *Pace Developments* [1991] BCC 406 the Court of Appeal refused to order a director of an insolvent developer to pay the plaintiff's costs. It would only be in rare cases, perhaps where the company's defence was not made in good faith, that the director would be made liable. This was not a wrongful trading claim but the situation is analogous: provided the director receives professional advice that the company has a substantial defence, he should not be made personally liable for the costs if the defence fails. Professor Goode has devised a 12 point plan for directors wishing to minimise the risk of liability (Goode 1997, at 472).

Some Australian states have similar legislation. In *Pioneer Concrete* v *Ellston* [1985] 10 ACLR 289 the court held a director personally liable to a concrete supplier. When applying for credit, the director had falsely represented that the company's assets were substantial whereas in fact they were marginal. The supplier petitioned to wind up the company four months after placing it on its stop list. It was argued on behalf of the director that the court should look at the circumstances prevailing in the industry and in particular the fact that suppliers of materials were slow to enforce trading terms. This submission was rejected by the court on the ground that the issue had to be decided by reference to the parties' legal relationship. Giving excessive credit and poor debt collection did not dilute the supplier's legal rights.

Preference

By s 239 Insolvency Act 1986 a preference occurs if the company does or suffers anything to be done which has the effect of putting a creditor into a better position than it would have been in in the event of the company's liquidation. The company must have been "influenced in deciding to give it by a desire" to produce the preference. Where the creditor is "connected with" the company (as defined in s 249), the burden is on the creditor to disprove the desire. As with transactions at an undervalue, it must be shown that the company was insolvent at the time of the preference or became so as a result. The time limits are stricter for this claim since it can only be brought in respect of a preference made within six months before the start of liquidation (or two years where the creditor is a connected person).

The mental element in preference is a question of some subtlety. It was considered in *Re M C Bacon* [1990] BCC 78. Millett J observed:

> "A man can choose the lesser of two evils without desiring either. ... A man is not to be taken as desiring all the necessary consequences of his actions. Some consequences may be of advantage to him and be desired by him; others may not affect him and be matters of indifference to him; while still others may be positively disadvantageous to him and not be desired by him, but be regarded by him as the unavoidable price of obtaining the desired advantages" (at 87).

The classic defence to a preference claim is that it was given in response to pressure applied by the creditor rather than any desire to improve that creditor's position. This often occurs where the creditor is paid after issuing, or threatening to issue, a winding–up petition which is withdrawn after payment.

Probably the most common preference in construction as in insolvency generally, is a payment into the company's overdrawn bank account which has been guaranteed by the director. The liquidator issues proceedings against the bank as the preferred creditor which then issues third party proceedings against the director under the guarantee.

In *Re DKG Contractors* [1990] BCC 903, over £400,000 was paid to the director in the ten months before the company went into voluntary liquidation in respect of goods apparently supplied and services rendered by him to the company. As he was a connected person, the burden of proving a preference was reversed. The court was prepared to accept that some payments "may well have been influenced by commercial considerations such as the advantages of completing rather than abandoning the contracts" (at 910). However, the desire to prefer was present. The company had been insolvent when the payments were made. The director was ordered to repay the £400,000 concurrently with an order in the same amount as a misfeasance.

Preference arguments sometimes arise in connection with direct payments (Chapter 12). The idea behind a direct payment is that, for various reasons, an employer may wish to pay another person in the contractual chain rather than the contractor. The concept originated in the use of nominated subcontractors in the 19th century. There are two elements: the contract permits a payment by an employer to a person who is in contract with the contractor and the amount of the payment is then set off by the employer against sums otherwise due to the contractor. The court would need to be satisfied that there was an act resulting in a preference and that the act was influenced by the desire to prefer. The act of preference could be the contractual term allowing direct payment, the payment itself or the set-off following the payment. If the contract does not provide for direct payment, a collateral agreement by which the contractor consented to it being made could also be a preference.

The issue was considered in *Re C G Monkhouse* (1968) 69 SR(NSW) 429 which concerned a direct payment made within six months before the contractor went into voluntary liquidation. The terms of the contract were similar to JCT 63. The liquidator argued that the sub-contractor had been preferred on the ground that the payment had been made on behalf of the contractor. In rejecting the liquidator's claim, Jacobs JA held that "the payment made by the building owner cannot be described as a payment made out of monies for the builder. It is a payment made out of the building owner's own monies which, if the contract was strictly carried out, would never become due to the builder" (at 432). The rationale for the decision was that the contractor only ever became entitled to such sum as remained after the direct payment had been made. This aspect is considered in Chapter 12. In a later Australian decision, *Gericevich v Sabemo* [1984] 9 ACLR 452, the court rejected a preference claim on similar grounds. A preference was established in the Canadian case of *British Columbia Hydro v Hallcraft Construction* (1986) 6 BCLR (2d) 74.

In *Analogy v Bell Basic Industries* (1996) 12 BCL 291, a direct payment by a contractor (Leighton) to a sub-sub-contractor (Boral) was held a voidable preference at the suit of the liquidator of the sub-contractor (Analogy). Boral withdrew from site on the ground of non-payment by Analogy of $450,000. Analogy claimed to be owed $650,000 by Leighton for work done before March 1989, and $130,000 for work done during March. Leighton wanted Boral to return to site and finish its work. An agreement was reached between the three of them whereby Leighton agreed that $100,000 was due to

Analogy for the work done in March and agreed to make a further payment of $200,000 on account of Analogy's disputed claims on condition that Boral immediately returned to site. Analogy agreed to allow Boral to contract directly with Leighton for the balance of the work. Analogy executed an authority directing Leighton to pay these sums to Boral and Leighton undertook to Boral to make the payments in accordance with that direction. Leighton paid $100,000 to Boral who returned to site and completed the work. Boral claimed payment of the $200,000 but Leighton replied saying that payment depended on Analogy proving an entitlement under the sub-contract for at least that sum. A receiver and manager was then appointed to Analogy, followed shortly afterwards by a liquidator. The court analysed the position as follows.

> "In the arrangement Boral had a promise from Leighton that Leighton would pay to Boral $300,000 of Analogy's indebtedness to Boral in return for Boral's promise to remobilise and complete the work. For its part, Analogy had an express or implied promise from Boral that Boral would receive the payments from Leighton in reduction of Analogy's indebtedness to Boral. The consideration for that promise was Analogy's agreement to forego its entitlement to be paid $100,000 by Leighton, and to permit Leighton to make the payment direct to Boral".

It followed that the payment of $100,000 was made from "Analogy's money" and therefore a preference. The same could not apply to the $200,000 as it was an advance for the specific purpose of payment to Boral and fell within the principle in *Barclays Bank* v *Quistclose* [1970] AC 567. In addition, Leighton was indebted to Boral for that amount. The case also has the characteristics of an attornment (see Chapter 6).

A preference can only be given to a creditor or a guarantor of the insolvent contractor: s 239(4) Insolvency Act 1986. Could the set-off be a preference on the ground that the employer is a contingent creditor pending completion of the works? Although a creditor in the context of preference claims includes a contingent creditor the set-off is unlikely to be a preference because it is an automatic consequence of entering into the contract. It cannot be said to have been influenced by a desire to prefer the employer in that situation. Could the contract be a preference? In practice, this is extremely unlikely, at least where entered into in the ordinary course of business, as the employer normally specifies the form of contract when inviting tenders.

Totty and Moss suggest it is just conceivable that "automatic termination provisions or similar clauses" could be a preference (at

H6.02). It is very difficult to see how this could be so. The issue is whether a preference places the employer in a better position at the expense of other creditors but the right to terminate is an integral part of the value received by the employer in return for its promise to pay the contractor. The argument rests on the assumption that by the clause the contractor is allowing the employer to terminate its employment on a liquidation, depriving the liquidator of the opportunity of completing the works: an example of the contractor "suffering something to be done" within s 239. Aspects of this argument were considered in Chapter 9. Perhaps there could be a preference where the employer is connected and the contract was entered into shortly before the contractor went into liquidation. The employer might then get the benefit of fixed materials and work in progress without having to pay for them, by raising a termination set-off. Even a payment by the contractor in return for the employer's promise not to terminate for insolvency is unlikely to be a preference provided the amount of the payment does not exceed the value to the contractor of retaining its employment (compare Goode 1997 at 397).

Preference is sometimes raised as an argument where a company declares itself trustee of property shortly before becoming insolvent. In two cases decided before the Insolvency Act 1986 changed the criterion for preference, such claims were rejected: *Re Kayford* [1975] 1 WLR 279 and *Re Chelsea Cloisters* (1981) 41 P & CR 98. Some aspects of these decisions may no longer be correct (Anderson 1992). To what extent could a construction trust be vulnerable to such a claim? It is necessary to decide what action amounts to the preference: entering into the contract containing the trust provisions, voluntarily setting up a fund on request, complying with the court order to do so, or making payments from the trust account in accordance with the contract. The only real prospect of preference in this area consists in the action of setting aside the fund. As the test is subjective, and a mixed motive could be sufficient, the possibility that setting aside retention could be a preference cannot be completely ruled out. If an employer has half a dozen contracts with different contractors using the same JCT form, has the funds to set aside retention in respect of them, is asked to do so by all of the contractors, but does so only for one of them, it could be inferred that the employer was influenced by desire to place that contractor in a better position than the others on a liquidation. Such authority as there is in the general commercial context suggests that preference arguments in respect of a trust are not likely to succeed: *Re*

Lewis's of Leicester [1995] 1 BCLC 428. The dicta in *MacJordan Construction* v *Brookmount Erostin* (1992) 56 BLR 1 at 18 to the contrary are doubtful. This argument is similar to *John Holland Construction* v *Majorca Projects* (1996) 12 BCL 135 in which a judge awarded summary judgment to a contractor but stayed the drawing up of the order because of concern about the employer's solvency and the risk of giving a preference to the contractor. The decision was reversed on appeal since otherwise the contractor would be hindered "in its legitimate desire to obtain and retain payment of a debt due from a debtor whose financial position was admittedly doubtful" (at 137).

Avoidance of transactions

The court has power to set aside a transaction entered into at an undervalue: s 238. This applies where the company receives no consideration or the value given is significantly more than that received. The company must have been insolvent at the time or have become so as a result, but this is presumed where the transaction is with a connected person, *e.g.* a director or a company controlled by him. An administrator or liquidator can bring the claim. There is a defence that the transaction was entered into in good faith for the purpose of carrying on the company's business and there were reasonable grounds for believing that it would benefit the company. It must have taken place within two years before the start of the insolvency procedure. The court has power to make such order as it thinks fit to restore the status quo.

If a house-builder transfers a land bank or specific properties for less than full value, the transfer could be set aside on this ground. The difficulty is obtaining clear valuation evidence. In practice, claims tend to proceed only where the divergence in value is so great that it can only be explained as an undervalue. A guarantee given by a subsidiary to a creditor of its parent can also be a transaction at an undervalue. In the industry this occurs where a profitable plant hire subsidiary is asked to guarantee the liabilities of a loss-making contractor. The directors' actions could also be a misfeasance. "Upstream" guarantees of this kind are more open to attack than guarantees "downstream" where the parent is supporting its subsidiaries (Lingard 1988). An undervalue may also occur where a lease is granted by the company shortly before formal insolvency at below market rent or with an option to review on better terms than generally available: *Kinsela* v *Russell* (1986) 4 NSWLR 722.

In addition the court can set aside a "transaction in fraud of creditors" under s 423 Insolvency Act 1996. This is very similar to a transaction at an undervalue but with two significant differences:

1. It must be shown that the purpose of the transaction was to put assets beyond the reach of the claimant and was intended to prejudice the interests of the claimant in relation to its claim, although dishonesty need not be proved.
2. Unusually, the relief is not restricted to the liquidator but is available to any victim of the transaction.

A victim is any person who is or is capable of being prejudiced by it. Where the company is in liquidation, the victim needs leave from the court to bring proceedings: *Arbuthnot Leasing* v *Havalet Leasing* [1990] BCC 627. The remedy should be considered by those involved in litigation with a company where there is evidence of risk of dissipation of assets. Proof of insolvency is not required.

Misfeasance

Misfeasance is the liquidation equivalent of a claim by the company for breach of fiduciary duty (Oditah 1992). It applies where a director or other person concerned in the promotion, formation or management of the company "has misapplied, or retained or become accountable for, money or other property of the company, or has been guilty of any misfeasance or breach of fiduciary or other duty in relation to the company": s 212 Insolvency Act 1986. The court has power to order that person to repay, restore or account for the money or property misapplied with interest or to contribute such sum to the company's assets by way of compensation as it thinks just. The misfeasance remedy does not create any new cause of action which would not have existed before the insolvency: *Re B Johnson & Co (Builders) Ltd* [1955] 1 Ch 634 at 647. Its purpose is to provide a comparatively quick and efficient remedy in the liquidation. It applies to directors or anyone involved, even informally, in the running of the business. Unusually, any creditor or shareholder can bring a claim but the duty must have been one owed to the company.

Many misfeasance claims concern the misappropriation of the company's money. *West Mercia Safetywear* v *Dodd* [1988] BCC 250 concerned a person who was a director of a parent and a subsidiary which both had accounts at the same bank. The director guaranteed the parent's overdraft and was advised that in view of the financial difficulties of both companies, their bank accounts should not be operated. Nevertheless, he transferred £4,000 from the subsidiary's account to reduce its debt of £30,000 owed to the parent, thereby reducing his guarantee liability by the same amount. The payment was a misfeasance and the director was liable to repay the £4,000 to the liquidator with interest.

One of the directors of DKG Contractors considered earlier in connection with wrongful trading and preference was also held liable in misfeasance. The company had received over £400,000 in the 10 months before it went into liquidation. Instead of paying the money into the company's bank account, the director misappropriated it by

- paying cheques made in favour of the company into his personal account
- transferring money from the company's account to his own
- drawing cheques on the company's account in his favour
- drawing cheques to cash and keeping the money.

In breach of his fiduciary duty the director was also acting as a labour only sub-contractor to his own company which meant that "the general creditors were competing on unfair terms with one creditor" (at 908). He was ordered to repay the £400,000 to the liquidator.

Construction cases often concern the diversion of contracts from the company to the directors or a company controlled by them. In *Schott Kem v Bentley* [1990] 3 All ER 850 the Court of Appeal reviewed the criteria for an interim payment on account of such claims. Schott Kem was a plumbing contractor with a special expertise in glass drainline pipework. The directors submitted artificially high tenders to prospective clients following them up with lower unsolicited tenders on their own behalf. As time went by, they stopped bidding on behalf of the company and switched all enquiries direct to their own company. They removed materials from site and appropriated payments in respect of labour supplied by the company. The Court of Appeal awarded substantial interim payments against the directors on account of claims for damages for breach of contract, the return of money paid under a mistake of fact, money had and received and damages for conspiracy to defraud and the misuse of confidential information. A further common misfeasance in construction cases is the use of company resources for personal purposes, *e.g.* building, extending or repairing the directors' homes: *Halls v O'Dell* [1992] 2 WLR 308.

Other claims

Any disposition by the company after a winding up petition has been issued against it is void unless validated by the court: s 127. An application for validation can be made before or after the disposition has been made. This provision has an important effect on the company's bank account, which is liable to be frozen by the bank following the issue or advertisement of a petition, as well as on other transactions: *Re Gray's Inn Construction* [1980] 1 All ER 814. In the industry, direct payments made to nominated sub-contractors after presentation of a petition to wind up the contractor were invalidated in *Re Right Time Construction* (1990) 52 BLR 117.

The section applies to all dispositions, even those made in the ordinary course of business (Goode 1997 at 424). In the industry, the section could invalidate a retention trust whether set up voluntarily or pursuant to an injunction: *Re Flint* [1993] Ch 319. Perhaps the court had this problem in mind in *Finnegan* v *Ford Sellar Morris* (1991) 53 BLR 38 where an injunction was granted but apparently not to be enforced for a period of time in case the employer entered formal insolvency within that time (Blackler 1998 at 768). The same applies to a contractual set-off and payments due by the company under a garnishee order previously made against it. A validation order can be sought from the court, ideally before the issue of the petition: *Re S & D Wright* [1992] BCC 503.

Where a floating charge is granted within 12 months before the start of a liquidation (two years if in favour of a connected person) and the company was insolvent at the time or became so as a result (unless they are connected) and the company did not receive value in return, it is liable to be invalidated on an application by the liquidator: s 245 The remedy is also available to an administrator. Giving a floating charge for no consideration when the company is insolvent could also constitute a misfeasance or be relevant to the question of disqualification.

Conclusion

The influence of insolvency claims is far reaching. Not many are actually brought in practice, reflecting difficulties over funding and evidence (Milman and Parry 1997), but their existence affects the way contracts are drafted and administered, and the attitude of the court in enforcing them. They have a strong influence over rescue procedures, and the actions directors and lenders take with companies which are informally insolvent.

Chapter 16

· **People** ·

Introduction

In law, a company is a person who is liable to others to the extent of the net proceeds of its property, but unlike an individual, a company lies dormant until animated by others. Only then can it become known, through its place of business, products, property and brands: apart from these manifestations a company exists only in the acts of people which the court is prepared to attribute to it: *Meridian Global Funds* v *Securities Commission* [1995] 3 All ER 918. In the context of insolvency, those most relevant are company directors, employees and insolvency professionals. This chapter takes a brief look at each of these groups.

Directors

Many epithets are used for directors: *de jure*, *de facto*, managing, executive, non-executive, alternate, nominee, shadow, and others indicating a function in the company, *e.g.* contracts, development, finance. A *de jure* director is a person properly appointed as a director by the company. A director *de facto* acts as if he had been appointed and can be disqualified or be made liable for wrongful trading in the same way as a *de jure* director: *Re Hydrodam (Corby) Ltd* [1994] BCLC 180. In that case the court considered that to be a de facto director the person has to be held out as such by the company, but this may not be necessary: *Re Richborough Furniture* [1996] 1 BCLC 507 at 522. English law has not made a distinction between executive and non-executive directors. A non-executive also owes active duties to the company: *Re Continental Assurance* [1996] BCC 888.

Directors nominated to the board of a subsidiary or a joint venture company can find themselves in a potential conflict of interest. The test is whether a course of action desired by the appointor can reasonably be said to be for the benefit of the company: *Charterbridge* v *Lloyd's Bank* [1969] 3 WLR 122. The appointor owes no duty to the company's creditors to take care that nominee directors act diligently and competently: *Kuwait Asia Bank* v *National Mutual Life Nominees* [1991] AC 187.

A director owes duties to the company rather than its shareholders, creditors or employees. His duty is to act bona fide in the best interests of the company. It demands honesty and the amount of care, skill and diligence which an ordinary man might be expected to take in his own affairs, but no greater degree of skill than can reasonably be expected from a person of his knowledge and experience: *Re City Equitable* [1925] 2 Ch 407. The duty is based on principles of agency law. As a fiduciary, a director must not put himself in a position where his duty to the company conflicts with his personal interests, so he must disclose any personal interest he may have in contracts entered into by the company and cannot obtain a loan from the company subject to a few exceptions: ss 330, 334 Companies Act 1985. He is an officer and agent of the company and not personally liable for his actions unless he fails to disclose his agency. Where the director is in breach of his duty, the cause of action lies with the company. Examples include claims for breach of fiduciary duty, the rescission of any contracts entered into, an account of secret profits, restoration of misappropriated property or an injunction restraining the director from disclosing confidential information. Under English law, the duties expected of a director are lower than in other jurisdictions, but this is changing (Wheeler and Wilson 1998).

Duties to creditors

To what extent is the position altered when a company becomes insolvent? The court has said that, where a company is informally insolvent, the directors owe a duty to the company to take the creditors' interests into account, but English law has not yet evolved a duty on the directors which is owed to the creditors themselves. In *West Mercia Safetywear* v *Dodd* [1988] BCC 250, the Court of Appeal approved an Australian case in which it was stated that:

> "Where a company is insolvent the interests of the creditors intrude. They have become prospectively entitled, through the mechanism of liquidation, to displace the power of the shareholders and directors to deal with the company's assets. It is in a practical sense their assets and not the shareholders' assets that, through the medium of the company, are under the management of the directors pending either liquidation,

return to solvency, or the imposition of some alternative administration" (*Kinsela* v *Russell Kinsela* (1986) 4 NSWLR 722 at 730).

The argument that, where the company is insolvent, the directors are under a duty to realise assets in the best interests of the creditors was expressly rejected in *Re Welfab Engineers* [1990] BCC 600. The directors had sold the company's assets for £110,000 and the purchaser had taken on the entire work force including the directors themselves. The liquidator's claim that the directors had acted in breach of duty in giving priority to the preservation of the business and their own jobs and should have obtained a higher price was not accepted.

Shadow directors

Several insolvency claims can be made against a person other than a properly appointed director. For example, a fraudulent trading claim can be brought against any participator in the fraud and a misfeasance claim made against any person involved in the management of the company (Chapter 15). The Insolvency Act 1986 extends liability for all claims which can be made against a director to a shadow director who is defined by s 251 as "a person in accordance with whose directions or instructions the directors of the company are accustomed to act (but so that a person is not deemed a shadow director by reason only that the director acts on advice given by him in a professional capacity)." *In Re Hydrodam (Corby) Ltd* [1994] 2 BCLC 180 it was held that the statutory definition assumes the existence of a board of directors, and "a pattern of behaviour" in which the board failed to exercise its own independent judgment.

The concept of shadow directorship applies to construction companies in several ways. Where the contractor receives so much of its work from one particular employer that it effectively receives instructions from it, the employer and its directors could find themselves in the position of a shadow director. This example could apply to any other party in the contractual chain. Overdependence on one client was identified in Chapter 7 as a cause of insolvency and is not uncommon where a contractor wishes to grow its business. Also, a parent may be a shadow director of other companies in the group. However, apart from that situation, a parent company is regarded as an entirely separate entity from its subsidiaries and is not liable for their debts: *Adams* v *Cape Industries* [1990] Ch 433. Hence the widespread use of parent company guarantees (Chapter 14).

A director may owe a duty of care to a co-director. Thus where A and B entered into a joint venture for the carrying on of a business through the medium of a special purpose vehicle company C, with A as continuing guarantor of C's liabilities, it was at least arguable that B owed A a duty to conduct himself as a director of C in such a way as not, except in good faith, to increase A's liabilities under his guarantee: *Elliott* v *Wheeldon* [1992] BCC 489.

Liability in tort

Although English law has not developed a general duty to creditors so as to allow them to sue directors direct, certain causes of action are available to the creditors in tort or under statute.

A director can become liable in the tort of deceit where he makes a representation which he knows to be false, or is reckless as to its truth, intending another person to act on it, and the person does so act on it and incurs loss. In *Thomas Saunders* v *Harvey* (1989) 30 Con LR 103 a director of a sub-contractor was held liable in deceit and negligent misstatement for confirming to a contractor that its proprietary flooring met with a certain specification. It became evident after installation that the flooring did not conform and that the representation had been false. The director was liable even though the representation had been made on behalf of the company in his capacity as managing director. Similarly in *Wong* v *Ratesharp* [1994/5] CILL 1001, a director was held liable for damages in deceit for representing that his company had the expertise and skilled people for the work whereas it had only just been formed and had no working capital, and for falsely telling the employer that work to a particular stage, which triggered a further payment in advance, had been done when it had not. Compare *Convent Hospital* v *Eberlin* (1989) 14 Con LR 1 where a claim in deceit against a director of a contractor failed because, although there had been a fraudulent misrepresentation, it was not an inducing cause of the contract. There had been a similar representation by the contractor's quantity surveyor which had been relied on, but it could not be proved that the director had authorised it and he could not be held vicariously liable for torts which he had not authorised. The false representation was that the contractor had procured a performance bond. The contractor later went into receivership. The architect was found liable to the employer for failing to ensure that the bond had been provided but failed in its claim to pass on liability to the director.

If the director gave negligent rather than fraudulent advice, he would only be liable to a customer of the company who acted on the advice and suffered loss if objectively he assumed personal responsibility for the advice and the customer reasonably relied on his assumption of responsibility: *Williams* v *Natural Life Health Foods* [1998] 2 All ER 577. In that case, the House of Lords refused to award as damages the loss suffered by the plaintiffs following the liquidation of a company they had formed to take up a franchise from the defendant company.

A director can be made liable in the tort of trespass to goods for misapplying the property of another. This could happen where an unpaid supplier removes goods which had been fixed to the building where it had no contract with the landowner entitling it to enter for that purpose. Although the act is that of the supplier, the directors can be held liable in certain circumstances. This would normally require proof that the director expressly directed or procured the tortious acts: *Mancetter Developments* v *Garmanson* (1986) 2 BCC 98924.

Where a director signs an order or a cheque without using the correct name of the company, he can be made personally liable under s 349 Companies Act 1985 to the addressee for the amount concerned unless it is paid by the company: *e.g. Rafsanjan* v *Reiss* (1990) 7 CLD 7.30.

Statutory relief

Where a director or other officer of the company is found liable in proceedings in respect of negligence, default, breach of duty or breach of trust, but under s 727 Companies Act 1985

> "has acted honestly and reasonably, and that having regard to all the circumstances of the case (including those connected with his appointment) he ought fairly to be excused ... [the] court may relieve him, either wholly or partly, from his liability on such terms as it thinks fit."

This relief was sought but refused in the wrongful trading cases discussed in Chapter 15. Relief was granted in *Re D'Jan of London* [1993] BCC 646 in which the court found that "conduct may be reasonable for the purposes of s 727 despite amounting to lack of reasonable care at common law" (at 649).

A company can take out insurance against its directors sustaining liability of the kind mentioned above (Doyle 1992). It may also indemnify the director against liability incurred in defending proceedings brought against him (provided he is successful in his defence) or with an application for the relief referred to in the previous section: s 320(3) Companies Act 1985. Directors and officers' liability policies commonly exclude cover where the director is found to have been dishonest or has been fined and careful attention needs to be paid to policy wording.

Disqualification

The Company Directors Disqualification Act 1986 gives the court power to disqualify any person from acting as a director or being concerned in the promotion, formation or management of a company. The power arises where a director is convicted of an offence or persistently fails to file accounts or annual returns or where the director has been fraudulent in the course of the company's winding up. Where it is satisfied that the conduct of a director of an insolvent company makes him "unfit" to be concerned in the management of the company, the court must make a disqualification order of between two and fifteen years. The application has to be made within two years after the start of the formal insolvency. The criteria of unfitness include:

- breach of duty
- misapplication of money or other property of the company
- the extent of the director's responsibility for a transaction at an undervalue
- the company's failure to maintain proper records
- failure to comply with obligations to provide information to insolvency practitioners.

What is the purpose of disqualifying a director?

> "The primary purpose of the section is not to punish the individual but to protect the public against the future conduct of companies by persons whose past records as directors of insolvent companies have shown them to be a danger to creditors and others. Therefore the power is not fundamentally penal:" *Re Lo-Line Electric Motors* [1988] Ch 477.

Incompetence or negligence can be sufficient for disqualification. The court also considered that non-payment of Crown debts is not necessarily evidence of unfitness.

> "But what is relevant in the Crown's position is not that the debt was a debt which arose from a compulsory deduction from employees' wages

or a compulsory payment of VAT, but that the Crown was not pressing for payment, and the director was taking unfair advantage of that forbearance on the part of the Crown, and, instead of providing adequate working capital, was trading at the Crown's expense while the companies were in jeopardy. It would be equally unfair to trade in that way and in such circumstances at the expense of creditors other than the Crown. The Crown is the more exposed not from the nature of the debts but from the administrative problem it has in pressing for prompt payment as companies get into difficulties": *Re Sevenoaks Stationers* [1990] BCC 765 at 779.

The Court of Appeal has issued guidelines on the period of disqualification. Two to five years is appropriate where the case is not very serious. Six to 10 years would apply for serious cases and disqualification for over 10 years should be reserved for particularly serious cases, *e.g.* where the director had previously been disqualified: *Re Sevenoaks Stationers* [1990] BCC 765. There could be an analogy between non-payment of Crown debts and an employer's non-payment or failure to make provision for retention: see *Re Stanford Services* (1987) 3 BCC 326 at 334. Contravention of a disqualification order makes a director personally liable for all the debts of the company incurred after the contravention: s 15 Company Directors Disqualification Act 1986. He will also commit an offence punishable by a fine or imprisonment.

There have been a number of cases involving directors of construction companies. In *Re Carecraft Construction* [1993] 4 All ER 499, a builder carrying on business as a sole trader formed five different companies all of which went into liquidation a couple of years later. No accounts or annual returns were filed. Nor were returns made for National Insurance or PAYE. Crown debts were allowed to accrue, in some cases from the date of incorporation. No proper books of account were kept, and a sanguine view was taken of cash flow difficulties which arose six months before the main trading company, Carecraft Construction, went into liquidation. The case proceeded on agreed facts and a disqualification order was made for the minimum period of two years. The Official Receiver had evidence which might have warranted a longer period, but chose not to bring it in the light of the director's concession that they were unfit for the purposes of the Act.

A disqualification of two years was also ordered in *Re Grayan Building Services* [1995] BCC 554. The company worked as sub-contractor on three sites for the same contractor whose terms included a pay when paid clause. The company did not operate a pay when paid system with its sub-contractors. On two of the contracts, the main contractor agreed to certify payment on a fortnightly basis in return for a financing charge. On one contract where the company had a substantial loss and expense claim, the contractor was not paid by its client and therefore relied on its pay when paid clause. On the company's entry into liquidation, the contractor entered into direct contracts with the company's sub-contractors. Shortly before the liquidation, the directors made substantial payments into the company's overdrawn bank account, which they had personally guaranteed. Preference proceedings were brought by the liquidator which were settled. Another payment to an associated company was declared a preference. The directors had caused the company to trade for six months after the point when they knew or ought to have known that it was bound to go into liquidation. The company wrote to its own sub-contractors six months before liquidation informing them it was in financial difficulty. Similar difficulties in the following months were confirmed in the report distributed at the creditors' meeting. The contractor was only making payments on condition that the company paid its sub-contractors. The directors failed to keep accounting records which would enable them to allocate overheads and costs to particular contracts. Arden J made no disqualification order, but she was reversed on appeal. One of the relevant facts was the extent to which the directors had incurred credit after "the point of no return". The company had substantial claims against the contractor, and believed they would be met, but that was not an adequate reason to continue taking credit from sub-contractors and supplies.

A director of four companies involved with damp-proofing, glazing, heating and plumbing was disqualified for 10 years in *Re T & D Services* [1990] BCC 592. The main grounds were the fact that the companies had been partly funded by non-payment of Crown debts, there had been preferences and the sale of a building at an undervalue to the director. The director also withdrew substantial sums from the company's account, ostensibly to pay wages and to buy materials, but this was not verified by the company's records. Likewise, a director of a building company who ignored an investigating accountant's report and wilfully misinterpreted a bank's willingness to extend an overdraft facility as evidence of the company's solvency was disqualified for three years in *Re GSAR Realisations* [1993] BCLC 409.

Employees

As with directors, there is no all-embracing definition of an employee. Whether a person is employed or self-employed has a number of consequences. Outside insolvency, only an employee can claim an immunity from proceedings in an industrial dispute, give rise to an obligation on the employer to contribute a levy to the Construction Industry Training Board, impose a duty to deduct tax at source under the PAYE system (outside the construction industry), bring a claim under the Employment Rights Act 1996 for unfair dismissal, redundancy etc. On a construction insolvency, the distinction between an employee and a self-employed person is relevant in three areas: the right to prove in a liquidation as a preferential creditor, the right to a claim under the Transfer of Undertakings (Protection of Employment) Regulations 1981, and certain aspects of the tax deduction scheme operated in the industry.

Preferential debts

A preferential creditor takes priority over other unsecured creditors and floating charge-holders: s 386 Insolvency Act 1986. Where the assets are insufficient to meet them in full, preferential debts abate rateably: s 175 Insolvency Act 1986. Schedule 6 of the Act lists categories of debts which are accorded preferential status. Category 1 includes sums due to the Inland Revenue in respect of deductions which should have been made from sums payable to sub-contractors working in the construction industry. Category 5 includes remuneration owed to an employee in respect of the whole or any part of the period of four months before the commencement of a formal insolvency procedure subject to a maximum of £800 together with accrued holiday pay, and money advanced to pay either of the above claims which would otherwise have been preferential debts.

Category 1 debts will be considered later. For the purposes of Category 5, the Act does not define an employee, but it does define remuneration as a sum "paid as wages or salary (whether payable for time or for piece work or earned wholly or partly by way of commission) in respect of services rendered to the debtor". On its face, the Act therefore excludes self-employed workmen and labour only sub-contractors.

Money advanced to pay wages and used for that purpose will be a preferential debt to the extent that the employees' preferential claims have been reduced: *Re Primrose Builders* [1950] Ch 561. Thus, in *Re C W & A L Hughes* [1966] 1 WLR 1369, a contractor obtained an overdraft to operate a wages account. When the contractor went into voluntary liquidation, it was found that part of the overdraft represented payments to labour only sub-contractors made within four months before the winding-up resolution. It was held that the liquidator was correct in refusing to treat the payments as being made "on account of wages or salary" within s 319(4) Companies Act 1948.

The TUPE Regulations

Under the Transfer of Undertakings (Protection of Employment) Regulations 1981, where a business is sold the purchaser takes over all of the vendor's rights and duties under any contract of employment except in relation to an occupational pension scheme (see Lightman and Moss 1994). As a result, an employee of the vendor becomes the employee of the purchaser. An example of how the Regulations can apply to the industry arose in *Rolfe* v *Amey Construction* (unreported, 13 November 1992). Following the appointment of administrative receivers to Farr plc, 33 out of its 39 contracts were novated to Amey. Some of Farr's employees were not taken on by the purchaser and applied to an industrial tribunal for compensation for unfair dismissal. It was held that there had been a relevant transfer under the Regulations entitling the employees to claim compensation from Amey. The determining features were that:

1. There had been an express assignment of goodwill.
2. The reason why six contracts were not novated was because employers refused to accept a novation, not because Amey did not want to novate.
3. Disruption was kept to a minimum by Amey's agreeing to pay sub-contractors direct.
4. Before entering into the sale agreement with the receivers, Amey had offered employment to key site and head office staff.
5. Amey took over part of Farr's premises under a separate agreement.

The tax deduction scheme

The self-employed are taxed under Schedule D of the Income and Corporation Taxes Act 1988 which entitles them to defer payment of tax. Employees are taxed under Schedule E by which tax is deducted under the PAYE system. The self-employed have a cash flow advantage over the employed, and Schedule D is also open to abuse if the tax-payer absconds without paying the tax. Self-employment has historically been high in the construction industry. In order to deal with widespread evasion of income tax, the Finance Act 1971 introduced a system whereby contractors have to deduct tax before making payments to sub-contractors unless the sub-contractors obtain a certificate from the Inland Revenue entitling them to be paid gross. These are known as "714 certificates". The system is now contained in the 1988 Act as amended by Sched 27 Finance Act 1995 and in the Income Tax (Sub-Contractors in the Construction Industry) Regulations 1975 as amended.

It applies to all payments to sub-contractors relating to construction operations. Under s 560 of the 1988 Act, a contractor is any person carrying on a business which includes construction operations. The definition of sub-contractor is wide enough to include the self-employed and labour only sub-contractors. It is possible that a direct payment by an employer to a sub-contractor would fall within the scheme. At least, a failure to consider whether tax should be deducted could lead to a double payment.

As from 1 November 1999, tax exemption certificates 714 are being replaced by "gross payment certificates" CIS 5 and CIS 6. These will only be issued to sub-contractors whose turnover exceeds certain levels. This means that many sub-contractors who currently hold tax exemption certificates will not qualify under the new scheme. This will adversely affect a sub-contractor's cash flow since the labour element of its payments will be reduced by 23% (Sadler 1999). Even if the sub-contractor does not qualify under the scheme, and thus has to be paid net of tax, it now has to obtain a registration card from the Revenue in order to be entitled to be paid at all. A contractor is liable to a penalty if payment is made to a sub-contractor without a registration card. This requirement is intended to address the problem of "the lump" by giving the Inland Revenue access to information as to who is working in the industry and what they are earning.

There are two insolvency implications of the scheme. First, tax not deducted within 12 months before the start of the insolvency procedure is a preferential debt under Category 1. Secondly, if an insolvency practitioner continues trading and pays sub-contractors gross, there is a risk that, if the sub-contractors later default, the company could become liable to pay the deduction to the Inland Revenue, unless it can be shown that the payment was made in good faith and the practitioner exercised reasonable care in making it. If the court finds that insufficient care has been exercised, it is possible that the deduction could be a pre-preferential claim in the insolvency procedure.

Criteria for an 'employee'

There is a substantial body of case law on the relevant criteria on when a person working in the construction industry is an employee (Ryley and Goodwyn, forthcoming). Some of these cases were reviewed in the first edition of this book. As part of its revision to the tax deduction scheme, the Inland Revenue has issued several leaflets giving its view on this question: IR 148/CA 60, IR 157, CA 80 and CIS 1. The criteria include:

- the amount of control the person has over how he does his job
- whether the person supplies his own equipment
- how long the person has been working for the contractor
- whether the person runs his own business from separate premises
- the degree of risk of non-payment undertaken by the person
- whether the person tenders on a competitive basis.

These factors were taken into account by the Court of Appeal in *Lane* v *Shire Roofing* (1995) IRLR 493. Mr Lane was self-employed for tax purposes but held to be an employee for the purpose of claiming damages for a serious accident at work. However, just as the meaning of "debt" depends on the context, whether a person is held to be an employee seems to depend on why you are asking the question.

Insolvency professionals

Before the Insolvency Act 1986, the insolvency profession was largely unregulated. For example, no qualifications were required to take an appointment as a liquidator. Unfortunately, this meant that some insolvency administrations were not properly conducted. It also harmed the reputation of the insolvency profession as a whole. Accordingly, s 389 of the Act now requires a person to be authorised by a recognised professional body before acting as an insolvency practitioner. Authorising bodies are the Chartered Association of Certified Accountants, the Institute of Chartered Accountants in England and

Wales, the Institute of Chartered Accountants of Scotland, the Institute of Chartered Accountants in Ireland, the Insolvency Practitioners Association, the Law Society and the Law Society of Scotland. New entrants into the profession have to take the Joint Insolvency Examination which concerns personal and corporate insolvency law and practice. "Acting as an insolvency practitioner" is defined by s 388 as taking appointments as a liquidator, provisional liquidator, administrator, administrative receiver, supervisor, trustee in bankruptcy, interim receiver. The only procedure which remains unregulated is taking an appointment as a receiver under a fixed charge.

The regulation of the profession has dramatically increased its confidence and reputation. The Society of Practitioners of Insolvency runs training sessions for its members, produces regular technical bulletins, and has a number of committees with responsibility for specific areas. Most insolvency practitioners are chartered accountants, but there are some lawyers. The Insolvency Lawyers Association is open to all lawyers who have demonstrated an interest in insolvency administration, whether barristers or solicitors, and is not limited to licensed insolvency practitioners.

It publishes a journal, the *Insolvency Lawyer*, holds conferences and seminars and has recently published some valuable research papers. In the construction context, the insolvency surveyor plays an important role. The insolvency practitioner relies heavily on the surveyor for his appraisal of the value of current contracts and the likelihood of being able to collect debts due on completed contracts. The surveyor may well be involved in negotiating novations and the settlement of claims. The surveyor's appraisal is particularly important where the equity in the contract is greater than the cost required to complete, *e.g.* in confirming that the work has not been over valued. Where there are insufficient funds in the insolvency to engage a lawyer, the surveyor may also be asked for advice on legal aspects.

Chapter 17

· International Aspects ·

Introduction

Insolvency is a feature of construction industries across the world. This includes the Far East where for example the bankruptcy of Muramoto Construction owing Y590 billion in 1993 was one of the biggest insolvencies recorded in Japan at that time. In Western Europe the largest Finnish contractor Haka went into liquidation in 1994 (caused in part by loss of market in Russia and the Middle East) and there have been a number of contractors in financial difficulty in Spain and Italy. Eastern Europe has seen a shake up with the privatisation of formerly state-owned contractors. A large number of construction insolvencies also occurred in Canada in the early 1980s and the early to mid 1990s (Reynolds 1996).

As the construction process is similar wherever it occurs, and standard forms used in other countries broadly follow the same pattern as those used in the United Kingdom, it is useful to compare the approach taken by other jurisdictions. This is especially so in areas where English law denies remedies to contractors and sub-contractors through privity of contract, the rule that anything attached to the land becomes part of it, or the policy not to interfere with the calling of on demand bonds. This chapter takes a dual approach, partly conceptual partly geographical. Some ideas, such as the construction lien, are widespread and it is more convenient to look at them conceptually. Others are specific to individual jurisdictions and these are treated locally.

Construction liens

Sub-contractors are the major victims of the knock-on effect following contractor insolvency. They bear a significant amount of the total risk generated on a project and are the most vulnerable section of the industry.

Some jurisdictions have passed legislation giving sub-contractors (and contractors) statutory lien remedies against the landowner, *e.g.* United States, Canada, Australia and New Zealand. It tends to need frequent amendment to take account of changing social and legal conditions. Difficulties have been experienced in every jurisdiction in putting it into practice, and some have since abandoned their legislation, but it remains an important source of protection to sub-contractors. It has various names: construction lien, builders' lien, or mechanics' lien.

Theoretical basis of the lien

There appear to be two theories at work: (1) that law has a distributional goal, and (2) that law has an economic function. The former is apparent from the report of the committee which led to the enactment of the Ontario Construction Lien Act 1983.

> "It seems to the Committee to be unfair that where an owner runs into financial difficulty he loses his property, the persons who worked on the property go unpaid and the mortgagee of that property gets not only the property but also the benefit of the unpaid suppliers' labour and materials" (at 192).

Thus, one purpose of lien legislation is to promote fair treatment between the parties to a project. The lien acts as "a statutory correction of a common law aberration." (McGuinness 1983 at 11).

The second basis of the lien is the application of construction economics to legal principles. In his book on the Ontario legislation, Kevin McGuinness comments:

> "Stated in its most basic terms, the purpose of this statute is to accord preferential treatment to one group of creditors (namely, construction industry suppliers) over all other creditors. There is no apparent moral or social benefit to be derived from giving construction industry creditors such a preference. The justification, if there is one, must be an economic one, namely that by giving special protection to the construction industry, mechanics' lien law enhances the efficient operation of the provincial economy. Economic efficiency is, of course, an inherent social benefit. In an efficient economy, there is optimal utilisation of society's scarce resources, with the result that the utility derived by society as a whole from those resources is maximised. Since mechanics' lien law is a field of law primarily concerned with the debtor and creditor relationship, we should concentrate our attention upon the credit aspect

of construction. The adoption of the economic analysis line of reasoning requires us to begin with two assumptions. First, it is assumed that the law should seek to achieve efficient allocation of the risks arising from the construction of an improvement, between the many parties involved in or affected by the construction of that improvement. Second, it is assumed that the law should be structured so as to enhance the efficiency of credit granting within the construction industry. It is implicit in these assumptions that, in order to accomplish these two objectives, the law must balance the interests of construction industry creditors against the interests of non-construction industry creditors" (at 9-10).

His thesis is that, without the lien, the parties involved in the construction process would become involved in countless individual contracts all attempting to achieve the same end. These high transaction costs would outweigh the disadvantages of a lien law (at 110-116). Common law and statute provide a remedy in other situations by giving liens to unpaid vendors, repairers, warehousemen, shipbuilders etc. McGuinness argues that a lien is necessary for construction because there is no other alternative: privity of contract prevents direct action by sub-contractors; pricing the risk is unrealistic because it would make the sub-contractor less competitive; and the transaction costs of arranging a mutual insurance scheme on a project-by-project basis would be exorbitant. Viewed in this way, the construction lien, by giving the contractor a security interest in the employer's property, confers both the power to coerce payment and the right of salvage in the event of the employer's insolvency. The same applies to sub-contractors and those working under them in the event of the contractor's insolvency.

The Ontario legislation

The Ontario legislation assumes that the lien over the employer's interest in the land is insufficient on its own to achieve the desired distributional goal and perform the required economic function. The lien is reinforced by three other devices. First, the trust concept is applied to all monies receivable by the contractor or received by the employer in relation to the project. Secondly, a holdback is required by which the employer retains 10% of monies payable to the contractor until a specific period after completion in order to secure the lien. This is necessary in case the equity in the land is insufficient to discharge the lien claims. Retention in Canada performs a completely different function from its English equivalent. It is intended from the outset to act as protection for sub-contractors and suppliers in the event of the contractor's insolvency. Thirdly, there is the right to apply to the court for the appointment of a trustee to act as receiver and manager over the property under s 70 Ontario Construction Lien Act 1983. All four remedies working together were thought by the Ontario legislature to constitute a valuable security for those working on the improvement.

It is interesting to note that none of the submissions made to the Committee advocated the abolition of the existing lien law. Lien legislation was introduced in Ontario in 1873 and had become an established part of the construction industry. The Committee's reluctance to alter existing arrangements was one reason why the new legislation reinforced rather than undermined the lien. In the United Kingdom, the preservation of the status quo would be a reason against the introduction of a new law. However, any consideration of means by which statute could mitigate the rigours of the *quicquid plantatur* rule should take account of the McGuinness analysis and the structure of the Ontario legislation as well as lien laws in other jurisdictions.

Nature of the lien

The lien is a non-possessory right against the owner of the land. With few exceptions, lien laws do not give a right to possession; they confer a right to a charge on the land as security for payment. The charge requires registration and enforcement by proceedings, normally within strict time limits.

In the United States, sub-contractors and suppliers who have supplied goods or services to a construction project are entitled to register a mechanics' lien against the property. This operates as an equitable charge and can be enforced by foreclosure proceedings, resulting in the sale of the property and payment of the lien-holder. Each state has its own procedure. In California, for example, a sub-contractor has to file a preliminary notice with the employer, contractor and funder within 20 days after furnishing its materials and register its claim within 20 days of completion of the works (Cushman and Blick 1988). To preserve the lien, the sub-contractor must then take proceedings to foreclose it within 90 days after registration against the contractor and the landowner. The effect of this is to convert the sub-contractor into a secured creditor to the extent of any equity in the property.

The first lien law was introduced in Maryland in 1791 and was intended to encourage the development of the construction industry by giving protection to those who actually carried out the work (Sweet 1994). The rationale is that the sub-contractor has helped to create an improvement which enhances the value of the land. In order to avoid registration of liens, American contracts provide that before becoming entitled to a progress payment, the contractor must either show it has paid sums due to sub-contractors or produce lien waivers signed by them (Cushman and Blick 1988). Lien holders may also be bought off by the provision of a bond covering the value of their claims.

Disadvantages of liens

One disadvantage of the lien procedure is that it tends to generate litigation. This is partly because of the drafting of the statutes themselves and partly from changes in social conditions and commercial innovations. Although there are many problems of implementation, none is so serious as to undermine the concept.

The question whether to introduce a lien law was considered by Western Australia in 1974, but the Law Reform Commission decided against it:

> "Liens legislation has, in the Commission's view, the fundamental objection that the registration of a lien against land may be detrimental to an owner who is in no way at fault. A registered lien operates as an encumbrance and may inhibit the owner's right to transfer, mortgage or otherwise deal with his land. A person relying on a mortgage to construct a dwellinghouse could find that because the land was encumbered by a lien, the mortgagee refused to advance further money since the recovery of those further advances would be postponed to the lien. This would be likely to cause hardship, particularly if the registration of one lien resulted in the registration of other liens, as commonly occurs in South Australia" (at para 35).

These criticisms view the position entirely from the landowner's standpoint. It is curious that the report makes no reference to the *quicquid plantatur* rule (which also applies in Australia), and that the lien received very little support from those making submissions to the Commission.

There were other objections: building societies thought that a lien might be a prior mortgage which would mean that they could not make an advance on the property.

> "Problems could also arise for an owner of land due to the actions of third parties over whom he has no control. For example, a lien could be registered over an owner's land, to the extent of the interest created by a lease, because of work done for the lessee. Again, a person who buys a newly completed house ... could find his land becomes encumbered by a lien for work performed by the previous owner" (at para 36).

These objections could be overcome by restricting the right to register a lien against the interest of the employer, *i.e.* the lease, rather than the freehold. The obligation to register the lien, and the ability to search the register of liens prior to purchase, ought to satisfy the second objection.

The biggest practical objection is that the employer may have fully mortgaged the property as security for a development loan. As the lien only attaches to the equity and does not impose a personal obligation on the employer for the excess, it would be of little use in that situation. For this reason, many jurisdictions supplement the lien by giving subcontractors a security interest in money payable from lender to employer or from employer to contractor.

Stop notices

This is a procedure available in some American states whereby a subcontractor or supplier can serve notice on the construction lender that it has not been paid. The notice prevents the lender from parting with funds allocated to the project pending the hearing of the subcontractor's claim. Some states permit stop notices to be served on the employer preventing it from making any further payments to the contractor pending hearing of the claim. The rationale for the procedure is as follows:

> "Although the work of the laborer and goods of the materialman do not directly enhance the value of the loan fund, that fund is commonly secured by a trust deed upon the real property where the improvement is constructed. By enhancing the value of that realty, the laborer and materialman also increase the security of the fund": *Connolly* v *Superior Court of Merced County*, Supp 132, Cal Rptr 477 (1976).

The stop notice procedure was introduced because construction lenders obtained priority over liens by registering their security interests before work started on site. The Supreme Court of California stated:

> "This protective policy continues to serve the needs of the construction industry. As was pointed out in *Cook* v *Carlson* ... 'labor and material

contractors [in the construction industry] are in a particularly vulnerable position. Their credit risks are not as diffused as those of other creditors. They extend a bigger block of credit, they have more riding on one transaction, and they have more people vitally dependent upon eventual payment. They have much more to lose in the event of default. There must be some procedure for the interim protection of contractors in this situation.' Without such interim protection, the improvement may be completed, the loan funds disbursed, and the land sold before the claimant can obtain an adjudication on the merits of his claim" (at 493).

It was felt in that case that the landowner suffers a minor deprivation by reason of the lien or stop notice because he still retains possession and use of the land. The stop notice could be justified on the ground that it only concerns funds already allocated exclusively to the project. The requirement that preliminary notice be filed of any lien gives the landowner an opportunity to obtain an injunction preventing its registration in appropriate cases. The sub-contractor would suffer prejudice as an unsecured creditor after having enhanced the value of the property for no reward.

A stop notice served on a lender (as opposed to an employer) must be bonded, otherwise it will have no effect. The obligation on the owner or lender to withhold funds terminates unless the sub-contractor takes enforcement proceedings within a certain period. The restriction on an employer's ability to sell or charge its own property is justified in the eyes of state legislatures because:

1. The employer will always gain through having the value of its property enhanced by the sub-contractor's work.
2. The labourer is not only worthy of his hire but entitled to security for his wages.
3. The protection is temporary in that the sub-contractor must act quickly to preserve its charge by taking proceedings.
4. The lien may be waived or removed by the provision of a bond.

Against this, it is argued that "even a slight delay in releasing frozen construction funds can destroy the project and result in the debtor's loss of his property" which is particularly undesirable where domestic property is concerned. In addition, it is said that:

"In almost all disputes of this nature, the creditor alleges improvement of the property and the debtor alleges that the creditor has failed to perform in a satisfactory manner the work contracted for ... Yet the majority assume the conclusion that there has been an enhancement, thereby depriving the debtor through a prompt, post-taking hearing, constitutionally required, of the opportunity of showing that no improvement has occurred or that if it does it is of substantially less in value. Thus the hearing required to establish the nature, if any, of the benefit, enhancement, or improvement is circumvented because the creditor has 'improved' the property ... Thus a conclusive presumption of improvement is created thereby obviating a hearing:" *Connolly* v *Merced County* at 502.

The stop notice is like the English Mareva injunction in that it freezes funds otherwise available for use but goes beyond the Mareva jurisdiction in giving the applicant security over specific funds pending a full hearing: compare *Cretanor Maritime* v *Irish Marine* [1978] 1 WLR 966.

Statutory charges

Some jurisdictions have passed legislation imposing a statutory charge on money payable to the contractor. An example is the Queensland Subcontractors Charges Act 1974 which entitles every sub-contractor to a charge on the money payable to the contractor to secure payment of all money payable or to become payable for work done under the sub-contract. The total amount recoverable is limited to the amount payable by the employer to the contractor. Although the statute says that sub-contractors are entitled to a charge, no charge actually exists until a notice of claim is served on the employer giving particulars of the amount and nature of the debt and the notice has been copied to the contractor and filed at the court. Notice can be given before the debt due to the sub-contractor becomes payable but there are time limits within which it must be given after completion of the work. There are different time limits depending whether the sum payable is a progress payment or retention. The effect of service of the notice is that the employer must retain the amount in the notice from the contractor or risk personal liability. The contractor must reply admitting or disputing the charge and in default will be deemed to have admitted it. The employer can pay the amount into court if in doubt as to what to do. Otherwise the charge can be enforced by action which must be brought within strict time limits after service of the notice otherwise the charge is deemed to be extinguished. Proceedings taken by one charge-holder are deemed to be taken on behalf of all: it becomes a class action. Anyone prejudicially affected can apply for relief and a sub-contractor can be liable in some circumstances for damages if the notice of claim is vexatious. Proceedings are taken in the magistrates' court.

The claim can be defeated if no money is payable to the contractor when the notice is given or if the contractor has the right of set-off or abatement or any other reason under the sub-contract for withholding payment. Where neither employer nor contractor has a good reason for non-payment, however, the sub-contractor can still claim a charge even after the contractor has gone into liquidation: *Ex parte Pavex Constructions* [1979] Qd R 318. There are important restrictions to the remedy. Direct suppliers to the contractor are not within the Act. The charge only applies to money payable to the contractor under the contract. Claims for damages, *quantum meruit* or a security deposit fall outside the Act: *Road Surfaces* v *Brown* [1987] 2 Qd R 792. The Act does not apply to a commercial development of a block of flats since it falls within "domestic building work": *Watpack* v *K-Crete Industries* (1996) 12 BCL 103. Despite its problems, the legislation is apparently effective but sub-contractors surveyed expressed the preference for a system of direct payment by the employer (Lance 1987).

The sub-contractor has to elect whether to rely on the security of the statutory charge or to prove in the contractor's liquidation. In *Seventeenth Canute* v *Bradley Air-Conditioning* [1987] 1 Qd R 111 both contractor and sub-contractor were in liquidation (perhaps an example of the knock-on effect). The sub-contractor's liquidator considered that it was unlikely that any money would be recoverable under the charge and submitted a proof as part of a scheme of arrangement organised by the contractor's liquidator. Under the scheme, the contractor's debts had been assigned to a third party and the sub-contractor recovered a dividend. The sub-contractor's liquidator later received five times the amount of the dividend direct from the employer pursuant to the charge and was held liable to pay it to the assignee under the scheme of arrangement as money had and received. The liquidator had elected to prove rather than to claim under the statutory charge.

Other jurisdictions have combined lien and charge remedies, *e.g.* the Workmen's Liens Act 1893 which applies to South Australia and the Northern Territory. The status of the charge was considered in relation to the New Zealand Contractors' and Workmen's Lien Act 1892 as follows:

> "A statutory relation, quite independent of contract, is thus created between the employer and the workmen. If this principle is established, it

must be plain that the general principle of the law of bankruptcy, which is to provide for the equal distribution of the bankrupt's assets among all his creditors, cannot apply; for this principle can have no legitimate application save with regard to what might, by the bankrupt himself, or by the ordinary process of law, be made available for his ordinary creditors ... The true meaning of all the sections taken together appears to be that the lien or charge is created by this Act, and not by the notice, but that until the notice is given the charge is a floating charge and is liable to be defeated to the extent and in the manner provided by the statute": *Re Williams, ex parte Official Assignee* (1899) 17 NZLR 712 at 720.

The New Zealand statute was replaced in 1939 and has since been repealed.

The statutory charge was criticised by the Law Reform Commission of Western Australia (1974 at paras 41-57). It is said that the possibility of registration of a charge could cause delay to the work or to the issue of certificates because the employer would want to be certain that there were no charges before making payment to the contractor. If the employer plays for safety by making a payment into court, costs are increased and the ultimate sum available to the sub-contractor is reduced. The procedure takes many months to reach a conclusion. The charge remedy may restrict the contractor's ability to finance the works as the statutory charge has priority over a floating charge. This is two-edged: it might be regarded as beneficial in that it deters some contractors from trading thereby reducing the industry's fragmentation; on the other hand, it might exacerbate the financial position of those already trading and may not deter contractors determined to trade with inadequate capital. It may be of doubtful worth on the contractor's insolvency in view of the extended termination clause usually contained in construction contracts or the entire contract rule. This is unfortunate because it is on the contractor's insolvency that the charge is really needed and it is often only in that event that the sub-contractor is brave enough to serve notice of claim on the employer.

The remedy may also be circular and self-defeating in that after one notice of claim is served, others may follow. As a result, the employer will not pay the contractor who then loses all incentive to complete the works which may result in the extinguishment of any amount due to the contractor by set-off of the employer's cost to complete. It is possible that it also discriminates against later sub-contract packages *e.g.* finishing trades. This is because the finishing sub-contractor may be disrupted or delayed by earlier events on the contract which entitled earlier sub-contractors to a charge; and it is more likely that the employer will make a claim towards the end of a contract. The Queensland legislation has been criticised (Macklem 1983, Baird 1978), but it may be that this is more because of inadequacies in drafting than matters of principle. While there is substance in some of these objections, it is suggested that the basic and fundamental objection is a question of policy: should an employer be entitled to the benefit of the sub-contractor's work without incurring any obligation to the sub-contractor or any disbenefit which is of advantage to the sub-contractor?

Statutory trusts

In addition to a construction lien, many jurisdictions provide for a statutory trust (see *e.g.* Glaholt 1999). The trust applies to all sums received by a contractor or a sub-contractor on account of the contract price. These sums make up a trust fund in the hands of a contractor or sub-contractor for the benefit of those named in the statute. The contractor or sub-contractor is trustee of the sums received until all the beneficiaries have been paid and cannot appropriate or convert the sums to its own use or to any use not authorised by the trust. Statutory trusts are intended to supplement the lien remedy in recognition of the fact that the lien is useless where there is no equity in the property:

> "The [British Columbia Mechanics' Lien Act] is designed to give security to persons doing work or furnishing materials in making an improvement on land. Speaking generally, the earlier sections give to such persons a lien on the land, but that is limited to the amount of money owing by the owner to the contractor under the contract ... for obvious reasons this is but a partial security; too often the contract price has been paid in full and the security of the land is gone. It is to meet that situation that s.19 has been added. The contractor and sub-contractor are made trustees of the contract moneys and the trust continues while employees, materialmen or others remain unpaid": *Minneapolis-Honeywell* v *Empire Brass* [1955] SCR 694 at 696.

The remedies are independent and are not intended to result in double payment to the sub-contractor. Where a sub-contractor claimed a lien against the land, it had to allow trust monies received against the value of the lien, otherwise it would be paid twice. The sub-contractor is obliged to appropriate trust monies to the contract under which they arose rather than to the oldest invoice: the presumption in *Clayton's*

Case does not apply in this situation. The trust remedy cannot rescue sub-contractors who have failed to register a lien. In one case, a contractor went bankrupt and the lien holders appointed the trustee in bankruptcy as their trustee to sell the land. There was a surplus after payment in full of all the lien-holders, and suppliers who had failed to register a lien argued that the surplus was held in trust for them. It was held that the surplus was not money received by the trustee "on account of the contract price" and that the suppliers could not fall back on the trust as it was a separate remedy: *Re Burch Construction* (1967) 10 CBR 307.

An employer who fails to retain money after receiving notice of a trust claim can be made to pay twice: *Bre-Aar* v *D'Angela Construction* (1975) 21 CBR 260. Where trust money is misapplied, it may give rise to a claim for breach of trust. It should be observed that a claim for breach of trust presupposes the creation of a trust. This only happens where trust property has been identified. Under a statutory trust, if a sub-contractor is barred from asserting a claim because the limitation period has expired, no trust can arise of which it could hold a third party in breach. A bank which applies a cheque in reduction of an overdraft in the ordinary course of business without notice of the fact that the customer is in financial difficulty and without applying pressure for payment is unlikely to become liable for breach of trust: *Standard Electric* v *Royal Bank of Canada* (1960) 1 CBR 64. Legislation varies as to whether the beneficiary can only look to its immediate superior in the contractual chain or whether it can claim against a party at the head of the chain.

The trust concept was rejected in the report of the Law Reform Commission of Western Australia on the ground that:

> "In order to render it effective, money the subject of the trust would be required to be paid into a central fund or be guaranteed by a bond. ... a scheme providing payment of trust money into a central fund would be an administrative nightmare. To guarantee payment of the trust money by a bond, in addition to its cost, would be little different from payment bonding" (at para 77).

Some American states restrict the trust provision to public works and to receipt of money by contractors; others extend it to all private construction work and impose similar duties on sub-contractors to pass money down the chain. A feature of the legislation is that it imposes a criminal sanction in the event of default (Lewis 1989). Where legislation does not expressly confer a civil cause of action, it has been construed as a penal provision benefiting civil claimants through its deterrent effect; in some cases the courts have "filled the gap" by construing the statutes as conferring a civil right of action. The legislation is intended to prevent contractors using money received from one project to meet commitments on another or of an entirely different kind, *e.g.* liability for federal taxes or interest on loans. By "ring fencing" projects in this way, the legislation adversely impacts on the contractor's cash flow and is a striking illustration of the policy in the United States of protecting those who actually carry out work on a construction project.

Holdback

Canadian statutes further support the construction lien by requiring the employer to hold back a specific percentage of the contract price as a fund to which sub-contractors can resort if the security of the lien proves insufficient. Holdback is similar to retention under other forms of contract in that it represents a proportion of the contract price withheld by the employer. It differs from them in that the function of the holdback is to give extra protection to sub-contractors and is not intended to give any protection to the employer. Sub-contractors are given a charge on the holdback as it is retained, *e.g.* s 21 Ontario Construction Lien Act 1983.

Statutory assignment

In New South Wales, the Contractors' Debts Act 1897 provides an additional post-judgment remedy to sub-contractors. On judgment being entered, the judge issues a certificate that a certain amount is due and payable. The certificate is served on the contractor who must disclose the employer's identity. The judgment is then enforced by serving it on the employer together with the judge's certificate with a notice obliging the employer to pay the sub-contractor "out of any moneys now due or from time to time becoming due" to the contractor. "The statute, therefore, operates to make a statutory assignment of such moneys, namely, 'moneys due or to become due' to the contractor to the amount specified. If there are no such moneys due or to accrue due no obligation of any kind is imposed upon [the employer]": *Concrete Constructions* v *Barnes* [1938] 61 CLR 209 at 217.

Like a legal assignment, the sub-contractor is entitled to sue the employer in its own name and the assignment is subject to equities (Chapter 6). The statute enables sub-contractors to gain priority over a secured creditor. In one case, a sub-contractor obtained a statutory assignment of monies to accrue due in the future. It was held that the assignment was valid against a receiver appointed after the assignment but before the money became due: *Costain Australia* v *Superior Pipe* [1975] 1 ACLR 209.

It is doubtful whether the Contracts (Rights of Third Parties) Bill when enacted will be of use to contractors or sub-contractors in this context. The Bill currently allows a person who is not a party to a contract to enforce any term which purports to confer a benefit on him. Several provisions in construction contracts could fall within these words but the Act does not apply if on a proper construction of the contract it appears that the parties did not intend the term to be enforceable by the third party. The law reports are already littered with failed applications of this kind.

There are two further Australian statutes of interest. The Building Contracts (Deposits) Act 1962 requires any builder accepting a pre-payment for work to a house to pay it into a special purpose account in a bank in the joint names of the owner and the builder. Secondly, there is the Trust Accounts Acts 1923-1959, s 3E of which requires a builder receiving money on terms requiring him to apply it in or towards defraying the price of any contract to pay it into a trust account at a bank. The account need not be in joint names but the statute is penal and non-compliance can result in a fine or imprisonment: *R* v *Webb* [1960] Qd R 443, *Centre* v *Downie* [1970] Qd R 414.

Restraining bond calls

There is a line of authority in Australia concerning such applications arising out of standard contract terms, *e.g.* "If the principal becomes entitled to exercise all or any of his rights under the contract in respect of the security the principal may convert into money the security that does not consist of money". In *Pearson Bridge* v *State Rail Authority of New South Wales* (1982) 1 Aust Const LR 81, the bond was an unconditional payment undertaking. The court construed the bond and the contract together and concluded:

> "A perusal of the contract as a whole leaves a firm impression that the parties intended that, where the contractor was in default and in

consequence the defendant suffered damage, then where necessary it should have recourse to the retention monies and only to the security if the former should prove insufficient."

In *ADI* v *State Electricity Commission of Victoria* (1997) 13 BCL 337, which concerns similar contract wording, the court granted an injunction restraining the employer from calling an on demand bond lodged in lieu of a security deposit. The balance of convenience lay in favour of the contractor, in that its finances and commercial standing would be harmed, even though the court did not restrain a demand under retention guarantees for much larger sums. An injunction restraining a demand was also made in *Read Construction* v *Kheng Seng* (1999) 15 BCL 158 on the ground that the beneficiary of the on demand bond had promised in the contract only to make a call "whenever the [employer] shall be entitled to the payment of moneys by the Builder under or in consequence of this Agreement or whenever the [employer] shall be entitled to reimbursement of any moneys paid to others under this Agreement." The employer made a demand under a maintenance bond after practical completion even though the architect had confirmed that the contractor had made good all defects. Note that the Australian forms also require the employer to exhaust any right of set-off against debts due to the contractor before making a demand on a bond *e.g.* clause 5.06 of JCC-D (1994).

Injunctions have also been granted in the Far East. In Malaysia, for example, the court restrained the making of a demand in *Royal Design Studio* v *Chang* [1991] 2 MLJ 229. See also *Kirames* v *Federal Land* [1991] 2 MLJ 198, *Esso* v *Kago Petroleum* [1995] 1 MLJ 149 and the Singaporean cases of *Kvaerner Singapore* v *UDL Shipbuilding* [1993] 3 SLR 350 and *Rajaram* v *Ganesh* [1995] 1 SLR 159. These decisions are analysed in Andrews & Millett (1995 at 464). On the whole, Singapore has taken a bolder line and widened the basis for an injunction in this context from fraud to unconscionability: *Bocotra Construction* v *Attorney General* (No 2) [1995] 2 SLR 733. In *Raymond Construction* v *Low Yang Tong* (unreported, Suit No 1715 of 1995), the court stated that:

> "The concept of "unconscionability" to me involves unfairness, as distinct from dishonesty or fraud, or conduct so reprehensible or lacking in good faith that a court of conscience would either restrain the party or refuse to assist the party."

An injunction restraining a demand or payment on the ground of unconscionability was granted in *Min Thai* v *Sunlabel* [1999]

2 SLR 368, later affirmed by the Singapore Court of Appeal. The underlying contract concerned the sale of white rice growing in China. The rice could not be delivered in view of the exceptional flooding in China in 1998 and the court held there was a serious issue to be tried whether the supplier had been relieved from performance by a *force majeure* clause in the contract.

It is also worth noting *Chip Hua Poly-Construction* v *Housing and Development Board* [1998] 2 SLR 35 in which the Singapore Court of Appeal granted an injunction restraining a call under a bond which entitled an employer to make a demand "in satisfaction of moneys due from the Contractor to the Board under the provisions of any other contract made between the Contractor and the Board". On its true construction, the bond did not allow the employer to make a demand in respect of a claim under a contract entered into by the contractor jointly with another person. This was despite the presence of a "conclusive evidence" clause in the bond and the express right in the employer to apply the bond proceeds as it thought fit, even in satisfaction of a liability of the contractor under a different contract.

Payment bonds

On American federal projects, it is compulsory for the contractor to procure payment bonds in favour of sub-contractors and suppliers. The United States is by no means alone in this requirement. This is the practical effect of the German Contractors' Security Law of 1993 (Minogue 1994), under which security for payment has to be provided by employers on request, and by contractors on request by sub-contractors. The Western Australia Law Reform Commission concluded that bonding was the best alternative to liens, charges and trusts (at para 74). It was the means of security most favoured by submissions to the Commission. One disadvantage was that the cost would be passed on to the owner thereby increasing the cost of building. Another possible disadvantage was that some contractors might be driven out of the industry because they could not finance the cost of obtaining the bond.

Payment bonding has its advocates in the United Kingdom and is a feasible alternative to the construction lien and its ancillary remedies. Kevin McGuinness suggests that it could make the construction industry dependent on the bonding industry (1983 at 257). If the latter were risk adverse, it could stultify new construction or financing techniques. Bonding would also be difficult to achieve if it were decided to protect sub-sub-contractors and others further down the chain because, if the bondsman were to underwrite the creditworthiness of sub-contractors, it would insist on obtaining similar back to back bonds which would increase the overall cost.

Third party benefit

Under English law, the privity doctrine prevents a person who is not a party to a contract from relying on its terms even if the contract obliges one of the parties to pay a sum of money to a stranger. Other jurisdictions permit a stranger to sue under the contract in certain restricted circumstances. Broadly, this position will arise where A contracts with B on terms that it is a condition of the contract or consideration for it that B confers some advantage on C. If C consents to avail himself of the advantage, the contract cannot be revoked. This has been explained as follows in an American case:

> "In undertaking to determine whether an advantage for a third party has been provided by a contract between others, the following factors are important: (1) the existence of a legal relationship between the promisee and the third person involving an obligation owed by the promisee to the beneficiary which performance of the promise will discharge; (2) the existence of a factual relationship between the promisee and the third person, where, (a) there is a possibility of future liability either personal or real on the part of the promisee to the beneficiary against which performance of the promise will protect the former; (b) securing an advantage for the third person may beneficially affect the promisee in a material way; (c) there are ties of kinship or other circumstances indicating that a benefit by way of gratuity was intended": *Merco* v *McMichael,* 372 F Supp 967 (1974).

This concept is derived from Roman law and has been adopted by many American states.

There are two scenarios disclosed by the cases:

- where a contractor is a third party beneficiary of a contract between the employer and the architect
- where a sub-contractor is a third party beneficiary of a contract between the employer and the contractor.

Whether the principle applies will depend on the construction of the contract concerned. There is a crucial difference between a benefit which is intended to be conferred on the third party concerned and a benefit which is merely incidentally conferred on it. Only in the former case will the principle apply. The provision must have been inserted in the contract directly or primarily for the benefit of a particular person. Terms normally found in construction chain contracts are generally insufficient to invoke the principle. The intended beneficiary must be in a legal relationship with the promisee in some other way.

Restitution

If there is no right to a lien, or if the right has been lost through non-registration, could a sub-contractor make a claim against the landowner in restitution on the basis that the landowner has been unjustly enriched? In England, such a claim would fail:

> "for if a stranger builds on my land knowing it to be mine, there is no principle of equity which would prevent my claiming the land with the benefit of all the expenditure made on it. There would be nothing in my conduct, active or passive, making it inequitable in me to assert my legal right": *Ramsden* v *Dyson* (1866) LR 1 HL 129 at 140.

This is one of the harshest rules of English common law. Other jurisdictions have accepted claims in restitution.

In *Atlas Cabinets* v *National Trust* (1990) 68 DLR (4th) 161, when a contractor ran into financial difficulties, sub-contractors threatened to reduce their workforce. A manager employed by the lender (which had a first charge on the property) assured the sub-contractors that the lender would continue to make advances and that it was retaining a holdback. On the strength of these representations, the sub-contractors completed the project. The lender knew the contractor was in financial difficulties and it was concerned that the project might be abandoned to its detriment if the sub-contractors walked off site. It was not obliged to retain a holdback under the relevant legislation and did not do so. When the sub-contractors claimed payment from the lender, it argued that it was entitled to retain undrawn money for its own security. The sub-contractors succeeded on the ground that the lender had been unjustly enriched. Three things had to be proved:

- that the lender had been enriched
- there had been a corresponding deprivation of the sub-contractors
- there was no juristic reason for the enrichment: *Pettkus* v *Becker* (1980) 117 DLR (3rd) 257.

The British Columbia Court of Appeal concluded that:

> "The completion of the job enhanced [the lender's] mortgage security. That security was later realised when [the lender] foreclosed on the mortgage and took title. But it was the completion itself which constituted the benefit and the enrichment. That enrichment had its inter-connected counterpart in the corresponding deprivation of the sub-contractors who continued to work and incur costs for materials and labour for which they were not compensated. The only juristic reason that could be advanced for the enrichment lay in the clause of the commitment letter and the clauses in the mortgage document which made it clear that [the lender] had a discretion to refuse to make further advances. In my opinion, by the assurance given to [the sub-contractors] which was relied on and acted on by [them], [the lender] waived its rights to rely on those contractual terms and is estopped from doing so. As a result there was no juristic reason for the enrichment. In my opinion the element of injustice or want of commercial good conscience which should guide the application of the three-part test in *Pettkus* v *Becker* in a commercial context is established in this case" (at 172).

In a dissenting judgment on this point, Southin JA reviewed some of the sub-contractors' claims and held that several of them had improved their position as a result of continuing work. The judge also held that no action would lie on the facts of the case for money had and received, an equitable lien on the land, a quasi-contractual implied promise to pay, a promise to answer for the debt of another, assignment by the debtor of a fund coming to him, in deceit or negligent mis-statement, for breach of an express statutory or resulting trust, for breach of a promise to create a trust or on other grounds.

Alternatives to retention

The settled practice of not funding retention in the United Kingdom was disturbed by the Court of Appeal in *Wates* v *Franthom* (1991) 53 BLR 23. This may reduce the number of marginal projects where developers are unable to finance the periodic deposit of retention as the works proceed. Weeding out undesirable players in the market has been put forward as a policy reason in favour of statutory intervention. Apart from this issue, there is a need to clarify the relationship between main and sub-contracts. In what circumstances can the employer set off a cross-claim against retention held in respect of sub-contractors' work? In view of the sophisticated nature of these contracts, and the importance of set-off, it is surprising that this issue is not addressed in the standard forms. The whole question needs to be re-examined and overseas experience considered before the JCT decides whether to retain, replace or abandon the retention trust concept (see Chapter 11).

In Chapter 3, reference was made to an Australian standard form which suggests the use of a cash deposit or a bond instead of retention. Bonded retention does appear to be a feasible alternative. The Ontario Committee considered owner payment bonds as a form of guarantee in respect of the holdback. They were rejected because the proposal met with little enthusiasm from the local bonding market which was apparently quite small. The Canadian construction industry did not consider it advisable to make the provision of a bond a condition precedent to contract formation. The bonding industry was conservative and, where the project was even slightly speculative, might refuse to underwrite it. It was also feared that bonds could introduce into lien actions the defences of discharge by variation or material non-disclosure which are common in disputes relating to guarantees and insurance policies. Bonding could also impose additional cost and administrative burden on employers (McGuinness 1983 at 171-181). These considerations would probably not be so significant in the United Kingdom.

The Ontario Committee considered credit insurance but no detailed proposal was formulated partly because of the absence of a model in other jurisdictions. The Committee also considered letters of credit as a means of securing the holdback. It appears that the English equivalent would be documentary demand bonds which can be called on production of specified documents. These are issued by banks which require cash cover for the amount of the bond and would be an expensive means of funding which many developers would be unable to obtain. A further possibility was the establishment of a public repository to which employers would be required to deposit holdback as it accrued. This alarming suggestion would have involved the engagement of full time administrative staff to supervise the payment in and out of the holdback. Not surprisingly, the proposal received limited support.

Interestingly, the Committee rejected the idea of a joint trust account as unrealistic. Banks were not keen because they felt that trust accounts would be difficult to operate in practice. There would be no way of ensuring that payments had been properly made into the account especially where the employer and the contractor were associated companies. There was a fear that courts would be overloaded with applications to establish the trust. The administrative and direct cost to employers was thought to outweigh the advantages to contractors. Some employers were involved in a substantial number of contracts and would have to employ local staff to administer the holdback accounts. The solution adopted by the Ontario legislation was the holdback secured by the lien and the trust remedy. Under this scheme, the employer is not obliged to fund the retention which operates as a deferred debt which the employer is not required to pay until the final stages of the contract. The lien remedy is reinforced by s 80 of the Act which gives the lien holder an interest in the land in priority to a lender secured by a mortgage on the property.

Many American states have legislation dealing with retention. In a few cases, 10% retention is mandatory on public works contracts. The State of Texas even requires a 10% retention on private contracts where a mechanic's lien can be claimed. Apart from these cases, however, the legislation is intended to protect the contractor:

- by laying down a maximum percentage which can be deducted
- by requiring retention to be released once half of the works have been completed provided that the contractor has made satisfactory progress
- by requiring retention to be paid by the employer into an escrow account either absolutely or on the contractor's request.

Stockenberg and Woodbury (1996) consider that "unnecessary retainage actually slows down the progress of the job rather than insuring progress" (at 46). They recommend "line item release", *i.e.* release of retention to sub-contractors as they complete their work to avoid sums due to earlier trades being used to finance the project. They recommend that retention should be reduced at practical completion to 150% of the estimated value of snagging items in dispute if this is lower than the percentage provided by the contract. They also point out:

> "No other industry has a concept like retention. Who besides contractors will tolerate withholding of payments for an excessively long period of time for work that has been satisfactorily performed? Do patients withhold 10% of their doctor's bill for a year to see if the operation really worked?" (at 48).

Nevertheless, they consider it impractical to advocate its abolition, and instead have drafted a model bill including the items discussed above (at 51).

The US Federal Government has a policy of not deducting retention unless and until circumstances make it necessary.

> "Retainage should not be used as a substitute for good contract management, and the contracting officers should not withhold funds without cause. Determinations to retain and the specific amount to be withheld shall be made by the contracting officers on a case-by-case basis" (Federal Acquisition Regulation 32.103).

Other protective devices

Preferential status

The purpose of the lien is to make a person who has contributed to the improvement a secured creditor. As an alternative, the person could be given preferential status like Customs & Exercise and the Inland Revenue up to a maximum amount or proportion of his debt. Quebec law operates a system of this kind by giving a construction privilege to a certain class of creditor. The privilege is limited to the additional value given to the land by the work or materials supplied by the particular creditor concerned. The preferential claim is against only part of the insolvent estate (Marklen & Bristow 1990). The prospect of giving construction industry creditors in the United Kingdom preferential treatment must be remote since the trend is towards the reduction of preferential debts rather than an increase.

Caveat system

Some standard forms in New South Wales contain a clause by which the employer charges the land with payment to the contractor of all monies due under the contract or in connection with the works. Such a clause has been construed as an equitable charge on the land: *Griffiths v Hodge* (1979) 2 BPR 9474. The contractor can protect its charge by registering a caveat against the title which takes effect as a statutory injunction. The contractor has to take steps to have the amount due under the contract confirmed by an arbitrator or a judge: *Venios v Macon* (1986) 3 BCL 171. The right to register a caveat survived the termination of the contract where a progress payment had accrued due and was unpaid since the debt was contractually supported by the charge which had also survived the termination: *McCosker v Lovett* (1996) 12 BCL 146.

Licensing

Some jurisdictions operate a system whereby only licensed contractors can carry on business. A report to the Queensland government on security of payment (1997) stated that an effective licensing system for contractors was "a fundamental element of any regulatory framework to improve security of payment and enhance industry performance" (at 17). The report recommended changes to the Building Services Authority Act 1991 to enhance the existing licensing system including increasing its financial requirements. These included satisfying a 1:1 liquidity ratio and levels of net tangible assets set for nine categories of contractor by reference to turnover.

Disclosure regulation

It is possible to operate a system whereby the contractor is required to prove that all sub-contractors and suppliers have been paid from sums received under prior certificates before the current certificate will be paid by the employer. Where the prior certificate has included off-site materials, this is common practice in the United Kingdom. Such "pay to be paid" clauses are used in the United States where in certain circumstances an affidavit is required from the contractor that it has discharged debts due to those lower down the chain from previous progress receipts. This ensures that funds are not diverted away from the project.

Direct payment

It was seen in Chapter 12 that direct payment by employers to sub-contractors is mandatory in certain situations. Before the modern standard form had developed, it appears to have been commonplace for the architect to have had the option of certifying payment either to the contractor or direct to the sub-contractor.

Set-off

Algons Engineering v *Abigroup Contractors* (1998) 14 BCL 215 is the latest in a line of authorities in which the Australian court has construed a sub-contract as impliedly excluding the common law of set-off. The factors influencing the court are unlikely to have the same effect in England. For example, the Australian court considers that the existence of the common law of set-off is inconsistent with an express term allowing the sub-contractor to suspend or terminate for non-payment: *Triden Contractors v Belvista* (1987) 3 BCL 203; or a term that, if there were a dispute that went to arbitration, both parties would continue the contract in the meantime, *i.e.* the employer would continue to pay without set-off until the final account has been agreed: *Sabemo v De Groot* (1991) 8 BCL 132; or that the contract did not expressly allow a deduction from progress payments of the type of cross-claim advanced by the employer: *L U Simon Builders v Fowles* [1992] 2 VR 189 (an argument made by Lord Reid who was in the minority in *Gilbert-Ash v Modern Engineering* [1974] AC 689); or that the contract provides for payment of certified sums within a set time frame. It is hard for an English reader of these cases to resist the conclusion that the Australian courts have reverted to the "Dawnay's principle" (Chapter 5). The Irish courts have taken a similar approach, although there the authorities are divided on the issue.

If a cross-claim qualifies for equitable set-off in that it impeaches the claim, there does seem a good argument that it should be allowed unless set-off has been expressly excluded. The Australian approach would not be justified simply to deal with legal set-off as it is not particularly common, at least in the UK construction industry. However, the frequent references in the cases to claims for liquidated damages under sub-contracts suggest the situation is different in Australia.

New Zealand has taken an ambivalent approach, notionally following the approach in *Gilbert-Ash*, while actually imposing such a high threshold for any equitable set-off claimed against a certified sum that the result is close to the Dawnay's principle. For example, in *Savory Holdings v Royal Oak Mall* [1992] 1 NZLR 12, a contractor sought summary judgment on a certified sum and the employer cross-claimed in respect of credits which had not been given, unapproved costs, disputed time extensions and defects. Smellie J expressly followed the House of Lords' decision in *Gilbert-Ash v Modern Engineering* [1974] AC 689 while holding that the certificate was "clearly an admission of a special and formal kind. It emanates from quantity surveyors and architects ... whose judgment in these matters the parties expressly agreed to accept" (at 23). He also quoted from one of the cases which were impliedly overruled in *Gilbert-Ash*. He accepted that some elements of the employer's cross-claim raised triable issues but nevertheless granted summary judgment of the whole claim, staying execution for a month on terms that the contractor co-operated in the prompt resolution of the outstanding disputes. The court considered the following factors to be relevant:

1. As the certificate was only an approximation of what was owing, to grant summary judgment on it would not be a final decision on the financial position between the parties.

2. This was especially so as the employer had taken steps to refer its cross-claims to arbitration, which could not be affected by entering summary judgment at this stage.

3. The employer's quantity surveyor had given evidence that it had agreed a final account balance in favour of the contractor which was greatly in excess of the amount of the unpaid certificate.

4. The certificate had been outstanding for over a year.

5. The cross-claims related to work covered by a previous certificate which had been paid in full and was not the subject of the application for summary judgment.

6. The employer had dismissed the quantity surveyor and this was likely to cause further unnecessary delay.

The approach taken in this case was later approved by the New Zealand Court of Appeal in *Hempseed* v *Durham Developments* [1998] 3 NZLR 265. The Court of Appeal considered it was arguable that the standard form issued by the New Zealand Institute of Architects impliedly excluded the common law of set-off, although it made no specific finding on the point. This suggests that the New Zealand courts may in the future follow the direction taken by the Australian courts. On the facts in *Hempseed*, set-off was denied since the contractor's application for summary judgment was based on a final certificate which enshrined an arbitrator's award. The employer had given the impression that the arbitration had included all claims which it had against the contractor. Further, the architect did not support the employer's contentions, and it remained open to the employer to pursue its cross-claims by separate proceedings if it so desired. This is a straightforward case of the court disallowing a shadowy cross-claim. In *Gough* v *Timbalok* [1997] 1 NZLR 303, the court took the more orthodox approach and allowed an employer's cross-claim for equitable set-off for defects and delay.

In Singapore, it seems that the court has adopted the English law position both as to the principle in *Gilbert-Ash* and the criteria for equitable set-off: *Aurum Building Services* v *Greatearth Construction* [1994] 3 SLR 330 and *Kum Leng* v *Hytech Builders* [1996] 1 SLR 751. A rare industry cross-claim for legal set-off was considered in *OCWS Logistics* v *Soon Men Construction* [1999] 2 SLR 376. The claim was for the difference between amounts previously paid and the value of materials supplied by the contractor to a sub-contractor, and was admitted. The cross-claim was brought by a sub-contractor in respect of work done under a later contract. It was disallowed because it appeared that the sub-contractor had simply placed a figure on what was, in reality, an unliquidated cross-claim. In any event, the contractor also had a claim it wished to set off under the later contract. It appeared that the contractor's claim under the later contract qualified for equitable set-off and therefore overtopped the sub-contractor's cross-claim on the later contract, thereby extinguishing the cross-claim advanced by way of legal set-off.

Joint cheque agreements

In the United States, parties sometimes agree that cheques should be issued by the contractor in favour jointly of sub-contractors and their suppliers. This ensures that payment is not diverted by the sub-contractors. The procedure is apparently subject to abuse where commercial pressure is applied by one of the joint payees to obtain a release from the other without the appropriate transfer of funds. Even if no funds are transferred, the court may hold that both payees have been paid thereby denying a defrauded payee of the right to seek payment from the contractor.

Nevertheless, the arrangement can benefit the sub-contractor if the contractor becomes insolvent. In *D&H Distributing* v *United States*, 102 F 3d 542 (Fed Cir 1996), a sub-contractor was concerned about the contractor's credit and persuaded the employer to agree to issue joint cheques. The employer paid the contractor direct, presumably by mistake. On the contractor's insolvency, the employer was held liable to pay the same sum to the sub-contractor as a third party beneficiary.

Joint control

A further variant operated in the United States is the joint control system whereby an agent acts as recipient of construction funds to ensure that they are properly disbursed. The joint control agreement is made between the agent, the employer and the contractor. The employer assigns the construction funds to the agent who disburses them to the order of the contractor on receipt of lien waivers signed by sub-contractors and suppliers. The agent opens a separate bank account for each project. Joint control ensures that marginal projects are screened out because the agent will refuse to act unless the project is viable. It acts as a preventative service. This method, as with the other methods discussed above, will doubtless be opposed by the contractor since it deprives it of the use of receipts from the employer on the money market before it has to pay the sub-contractors.

Appointing a trustee

Section 70 of the Ontario Construction Lien Act 1983 gives a sub-contractor power to apply to the court for the appointment of a trustee to act as receiver and manager of the premises or revenue produced by them. The appointment of a trustee is the logical means of enforcement of the charge given by the construction lien.

Right to information

Section 39 of the Ontario Construction Lien Act 1983 enables a supplier to ascertain whether there is equity in the property. The objective is to enable the supplier to make a reasoned decision whether or not to pursue a lien claim. Access to information of this kind leads to the avoidance of unnecessary or vexatious applications for registration of a lien.

Prompt payment legislation

In the United States, the Prompt Payment Act 1982 enforces payment to contractors by government employers within 30 days of invoice and by contractors to sub-contractors within seven days of receipt. Similar legislation has been passed in many states.

Liquidation agreements

This is an American term for settlement agreements by which the contractor agrees to "pass through" a sub-contractor's claim direct to the employer (Calvert and Ingwalson 1998). This has some similarities to the name borrowing and direct benefit clauses discussed in Chapter 11.

Impaired bonding claims

Some American courts have allowed contractors to recover as damages for breach of contract, losses resulting from impaired bonding capacity (Snider 1999). Typical breaches have included non-payment or wrongful termination. The claimant has to show that its bonding capacity was reduced or lost as a result of the breach, causing further damage. One example is a claim for loss of opportunity from the inability to tender for work through lack of capacity to obtain a necessary bid bond. However, a number of such claims have been rejected for want of foreseeability.

Bonds and arbitration

The extensive use of bonds in the United States has resulted in a body of case law on the question of current arbitration under the contract and litigation under the bond. The traditional solution has been to stay the bond action pending the outcome of the arbitration, and then to use the action to enforce the arbitration award (McGill 1994, at 22). American practice differs from English law, however, in at least two respects:

1. The surety may be bound by the arbitration award even though it was not made a party to the arbitration: *Modern Brokerage* v *Massachusetts Bonding & Ins Co*, 54 F Supp 939 (SD NY, 1944).

2. The American courts are more ready to find that the arbitration agreement in the contract has been incorporated by reference into the bond to enable the court to compel the surety to arbitrate: *Exchange Mutual* v *Haskell*, 742 F 2d 274 (6th Cir, 1974). Thus, the surety may be compelled to participate in the arbitration as a condition of court proceedings being stayed against it: *Henderson Investment Corp* v *International Fidelity Ins* Co, 575 So 2d 770 (Fla App 5 Dist, 1991).

Chapter 11 reorganisations

The procedure for Chapter 11 in the United States is sometimes compared to the administration procedure in the United Kingdom. It is, however, very different in that the directors remain in office. It does not seem to have offered much assistance to insolvent contractors. Lewis, Franks and Rowland (1995) report that "we have been unable to find one documented case of a contractor successfully rehabilitated under Chapter 11 of the Bankruptcy Code" (at 41). One of many difficulties is that, if contracts have already been terminated for failure to perform before the petition for bankruptcy has been filed, they are not classed as executory and therefore fall outside the protection given by the Code. If the process has not yet become irreversible, *e.g.* where the employer has only taken steps to invoke the termination clause by serving notice to show cause, filing for bankruptcy can at least buy time. In such a case, the contract is treated as executory, and the contractor has until confirmation of its reorganisation plan to decide whether or not to "assume the contract": *Moody* v *Amoco Oil*, 734 F 2d 1200 (7th Cir), cert denied 469 US 982 (1984). Apart from the cost of the proceedings, Chapter 11 is hard to apply to contractors because the power to assume a contract once the bankruptcy process has commenced depends on the contractor being able to provide adequate assurances that current breaches can be corrected and that it will be able to perform in future.

Griffin (1997) recommends that contractors only apply for bankruptcy after having agreed a plan through negotiating with employers and sureties. Ideally, under each contract, the plan would provide that:

- the employer will extend time and waive any damages for delay
- the surety will agree to any bonds in favour of the employer remaining in force
- the surety will honour obligations under its payment bonds to sub-contractors and suppliers
- the contract price is increased so as to make it profitable to the contractor to complete the work, the increase being less than the employer's potential loss in engaging a completion contractor.

Griffin considers that the lack of reported cases of Chapter 11 involving contractors is either because terms are negotiated in this way or negotiations fail and the case has to be converted to a Chapter 7 liquidation (at 57).

It is possible that the automatic stay on creditors' taking possession of the debtor's property under Chapter 11 could prevent the employer from exercising any post-termination rights which might otherwise be available, *e.g.* in respect of the contractor's plant and materials. There are apparently no reported cases on this point (Griffin 1997, at 28). The aim of the procedure is to allow the contractor sufficient time to carry out a contract review of the kind referred to in Chapter 10 so as to enable a plan to be drawn up of profitable contracts to pursue and unprofitable ones to reject. As with administration, the aim is to release resources tied up in unprofitable contracts so they can be put to better use. Filing a petition before contracts have been terminated may also improve the contractor's prospects of arguing that sums earned but unpaid before the bankruptcy are its property under the Code (Griffin 1997, at 32).

Other methods

Other methods used include release bonds, escrow accounts, lien recovery funds, title insurance and the equitable lien.

Far East

A number of cases from the Far East have been referred to earlier in this book. Reference should also be made to Robinson, Lavers and Tan (1996). There have been a number of recent cases in Hong Kong and Singapore which raise issues not dealt with elsewhere.

In Hong Kong, an unpaid employee can seek payment in certain circumstances under the Employment Ordinance from a debtor of their employer. The direct payment to the employee then becomes a debt due by their employer to the third person. In *Re Finbo Engineering* [1998] 2 HKLRD 695, a sub-contractor (AMEC) paid the employees of a sub-sub-contractor (Finbo) direct and then presented a winding-up petition against Finbo based on a statutory demand in respect of the debt. The petition was dismissed on the ground that Finbo had an arguable cross-claim for legal or equitable set-off in excess of the petition debt and that, in all the circumstances, it would not be just for the court to exercise its discretion and make a winding-up order.

The claim for legal set-off was in respect of unpaid interim payment applications and the value of authorised variations. AMEC argued that legal set-off had been abolished in Hong Kong by the Application of English Law Ordinance (No 2 of 1966), but it was held inappropriate to decide the issue on the hearing of the petition. AMEC also argued that equitable set-off could not apply where the claim was a statutory debt arising under the Employment Ordinance, relying on *Pysogea* v *Rightfairs Development* [1991] 1 HKC 341. The court held that there was *prima facie* evidence that AMEC had caused or contributed to Finbo's failure to pay its employee by "constricting its cash flow" (at 703). Also, as Finbo was a small company with limited cash flow, AMEC had agreed to buy materials on its behalf subject to a handling charge of 2.5%. Finbo alleged it had suffered loss from delays resulting from late delivery of the materials by AMEC.

It is also worth noting *Re UDL Holdings* [1999] 2 HKLRD 817 in which the court adjourned a winding-up petition against a large construction and shipping group to allow a proposed scheme of arrangement supported by a substantial majority in value of the creditors to proceed. One of the issues concerned was a substantial claim by Nishimatsu against UDL pursuant to a parent company guarantee of a contract with one of UDL's subsidiaries on the Chek Lap Kok airport development. As so often happens, the claim had been disputed by the subsidiary and as a result Nishimatsu were denied the right to appear at an earlier hearing of the petition against UDL on the ground that its claim against the parent was a disputed debt.

Bouygues v *Shanghai Links* [1998] 2 HKLRD 479 concerned an escrow account which was intended as the means of payment of the contract sum. The contract concerned a substantial development with a contract sum of US$ 33.25 million. The employer was a special purpose vehicle company formed under the law of the PRC and had no assets apart from the development. Its parent was incorporated in the British West Indies and its sole asset was the right to use the land to which the development related for 70 years. It was a condition of the contract that the contractor's duty to start work depended on its receiving satisfactory arrangements for payment. The contractor was satisfied by a letter in the following terms from the employer's parent:

> "We advise that under an agreement entered into by the [defendant], all of the funds required to pay the US$ 33.25 million contract price will be deposited in a segregated US dollar account of the [defendant] at Standard Chartered Bank in Hong Kong. Payment of the contract price under the contract will be made from this account and funds can be paid out of this account by the signature of Barry Hansen and one other director of the [defendant]."

The contractor accepted the escrow account in lieu of a payment guarantee. Before the contract was completed, there were mutual allegations of termination. The contractor claimed $3 million in respect of an unpaid certified sum and a further \$11 million for losses following the termination. Both the contractor's claims and the employer's cross-claims were being pursued in arbitration.

The contractor brought proceedings claiming a declaration that the parent held the account, a US dollar account opened in the parent's name, on trust to pay whatever was found due to the contractor in the arbitration and an injunction preventing any withdrawals from the account pending the arbitrator's award. If the trust claim failed, the contractor argued that the parent had agreed that the account would only be used to pay sums due from the employer under the construction contract and that the injunction should be granted to prevent a breach of the parent's agreement. The court rejected both the contractor's claims that the arrangement amounted to a trust and the parent's defence that the letter was not contractually binding, that it was a mere "letter of comfort" that money would be set aside which could be used to pay the contractor. The court held the letter to be an actionable promise by the parent that the matters referred to would be carried out. The account was a security in the sense that it could not have been the parties' intention that the parent could have removed funds from it before the contract price had been paid in full. However, the court found that "the contract price" was a term of art and meant "the totality of the sums payable to the plaintiffs for the performance of their obligations under the construction contract" (at 496), and could not extend to sums due to the contractor after the contract had been terminated. In that event, the account was intended to finance a completion contract, otherwise "in the absence of other sources of funding the construction of the development would grind to a halt" (at 497). Investors had also written to the contractor in similar terms to the parent's letter but with an additional clause:

> "We agree that payment of the contract price will be made to you according to the terms and conditions of the construction contract ..."

The court construed these words as referring only to the timing of payments rather than to any sums which might become due in connection with the contract. This seems a harsh result, but the evidence was that the contractor had only raised the question of security for payment at a late stage so as not to put the employer off. Had it pressed for clearer wording, or a properly constituted trust, there was a risk it would not have obtained the contract.

Two further cases from Singapore concern the retention trust and contingent payment. *Nam Fang Electrical* v *City Developments* [1997]

1 SLR 585 concerned a successful claim by a nominated sub-contractor against the employer for the second half of retention. The architect had issued a final certificate of payment of about $200,000 to the contractor of which about $170,000 was retention due to the plaintiff and the balance payable to other nominated sub-contractors and suppliers. Both the main contract and the plaintiff's sub-contract had been properly completed. The employer refused to pay under the certificate since it had received a notice from the Inland Revenue ordering it to account direct for $230,000 in respect of tax unpaid by the contractor "from any monies held ... or due to" the contractor. The employer chose to pay the Revenue from the final certificate sum. It was held that the employer had to pay twice to the extent of the $170,000 claimed by the nominated sub-contractor as that sum did not constitute monies due to the contractor. The sub-contract had a trust provision similar to the Green Form. Since the project had been satisfactorily completed, the contractor had no right of recourse against the sub-contractor and therefore was entitled to payment from the employer as bare trustee. The statutory deduction was not a right of recourse for this purpose.

In *Interpro Engineering* v *Sin Heng Construction* [1998] 1 SLR 694, the High Court of Singapore took a robust line in upholding a pay when paid clause in a sub-sub-contract. The clause was as follows:

> "[The Plaintiff's] entitlement to payment of the net sum each time shall arise progressively as and when a progress payment ... is received from [the contractor]".

The court considered the clause to be "reasonably straightforward and unambiguous" (at 698). Because the contractor had not been paid the amount in question, the claim by the sub-sub-contractor had to fail. The court observed:

> "While the courts will readily wrap a caring arm around the weak and the meek, they cannot do so in every instance. Everyone negotiates his own contract. He is at liberty to give and take as much as he can mutually agree with the other side. The sub-contractor *per se* is not a special species which requires special principles of law to give him a generous dose of legal protection" (at 698).

This case is perhaps the high water mark of decisions upholding pay when paid clauses.

Finally, *Engineering Construction* v *Attorney-General* [1994] 1 SLR 687 is the latest in a long line of authorities denying the employer the right to claim liquidated damages after the contract has been terminated. In this case, the government's actions in wrongfully terminating a contract were treated as a repudiation which was accepted by the contractor. The superintending officer issued a certificate of delay and the government claimed liquidated damages. It was held that the officer had no authority to issue the certificate and the government's right to liquidated damages could not therefore arise after the acceptance of repudiation.

Scotland*

> "On March 25 1707, the Scottish Parliament last met ... and adjourned as a prelude to its incorporation in the Westminster Parliament under the Act of Union. This decision was deeply divisive in its own time and was one in which the people of Scotland had no say ... In contrast, today, July 1 1999, sees a new democratic Scottish Parliament take on legislative and executive power in Scotland." (Sir David Steel, Presiding Officer, at the opening of the Scottish Parliament).

And so the Scottish Parliament was re-opened this year, following a lengthy adjournment, accompanied by a mixture of nationalist fervour and weary cynicism throughout the Scottish business community. This cynicism may be well placed: the Parliament was expected to make legislation on all appropriate matters of immediate consequence for the Scottish economy, including the construction industry. However, it is not so: although personal bankruptcy is a matter upon which legislation is proposed by the new Scottish Parliament, corporate law and insolvency is a reserved matter for Westminster.

Notwithstanding this, an urgent need for intervention by the Scottish Parliament in relation to corporate insolvency is not immediately apparent: the enthusiasm for the Parliament is accompanied at this time by evidence of a lively Scottish economy, and the construction industry in Scotland has very much shared that experience. The tight margins on traditional contracting which beset the industry at the end of the last decade and led to its downturn in the early 1990s still remain. However, the survivors have now turned towards:

1. Higher risk projects, involving the contractor taking more of a developer-type role, sometimes requiring the investment of equity,

---

* by Vincent Connor and Sharon Fitzgerald, Masons, Glasgow

and often taking a PFI or PPP procurement route, particularly in the health, water and education sectors; or

2. Lower risk, high volume, repetitive projects in the form of partnering-type arrangements, particularly in the leisure sector; or

3. A combination of the two.

The statistics available for the period 1998-99 indicate a level of activity in liquidations, receiverships and administrations considerably lower than that experienced in the early 1990s. Receiverships are considerably fewer, partly because of improvements in the Scottish economy and partly because of a perceived desire on the part of Scottish banks to use their own teams, many of whom are recruits from accountancy firms practising in insolvency, to work with companies in financial jeopardy with a view to realising key financial objectives, thus decreasing the need for a formal procedure.

Notwithstanding the above, construction insolvency or the threat of it remains a part of the industry in Scotland and many of the themes examined elsewhere in this book are just as relevant in Scotland as they are in the rest of the United Kingdom. We propose in this section to examine those areas of construction insolvency law and practice in Scotland which differ from that of England and Wales, dealing in particular with the following issues:

- the legislative framework relating to insolvency in Scotland
- the Scottish provisions of the Insolvency Act 1986
- diligence
- set-off (or compensation) and the balancing of accounts in bankruptcy
- determination of employment due to insolvency
- some Scottish construction insolvency cases.

The legislative framework

In Scotland, personal insolvency is governed by the provisions of the Bankruptcy (Scotland) Acts 1985 and 1993. It is not proposed to deal with personal insolvency in this section (see the bibliography). The legislative framework which governs the regulation of corporate insolvency in Scotland consists of the following:

- Insolvency (Scotland) Act 1986
- Insolvency (Scotland) Rules 1986 as amended. The Rules contain detailed provisions on the procedural aspects of

company voluntary arrangements, administration procedure, receivers and winding-up
- Receivers (Scotland) Regulations 1986. These Regulations set out the forms to be used for the purposes of the provisions of the 1986 Act.

Chapter II of the 1986 Act extends to Scotland only. Section 51 deals with the powers to appoint a receiver in Scotland. Section 52 deals with the circumstances justifying an appointment. A receiver may be appointed by the holder of the floating charge pursuant to a power contained in the charge or after 21 days have expired following a demand for payment, after interest due and payable has remained unpaid for two months, on winding-up of the company or on the appointment of a receiver under another floating charge.

There is no Official Receiver in Scotland. When a winding-up order is made by the court, an interim liquidator is appointed. Section 138(3) requires an interim liquidator to summon separate meetings of the company's creditors and contributories for the purpose of choosing a liquidator of the company to act in his place. If no liquidator is appointed at the meetings, then the court will appoint the interim liquidator as liquidator of the company.

In Scotland, a transaction at an undervalue is referred to in s 242 as a "gratuitous alienation". The periods of challenge are longer in Scotland than they are in England and Wales. A claim can be brought in respect of alienations within two years before the commencement of a winding-up or an administration, or five years if it had the effect of favouring an "associate", within the meaning of the Bankruptcy (Scotland) Acts. A preference is referred to in s 243 as an "unfair preference" and can be invalidated if committed within six months before the commencement of the winding-up or the making of an administration order.

Diligence

No discussion of construction insolvency in Scotland would be complete without consideration of the unique Scots law of diligence. Diligence is a form of security for a pursuer in a court action intended to prevent the defender disposing of his assets: effectively, it gives the pursuer security for his claim. In the slump in the construction industry in Scotland in the early 1990s, diligence was a prominent feature of litigation. Much of that diligence was cut down, as many defenders went into receivership or liquidation, on the basis of the rules highlighted below. Since then, diligence has continued in use but its applicability in the construction industry has been reduced by the effect of the *Costain* decision. If the Scottish Law Commission has its way, it will be restricted to even fewer circumstances.

There are two principal types of diligence:

- diligence in execution, *e.g.* arrestment of bank accounts, an individual's earnings, belongings etc, which proceeds on a decree (or judgment)
- diligence on the dependence of a court action which proceeds on the court's warrant granted when the action is raised.

The main forms of diligence are arrestment affecting money or moveable property and inhibition affecting heritable property, *e.g.* land and buildings. In the Scottish construction industry, with the exception of developers or housebuilders, arrestment is the more important.

Arrestment is a procedure whereby a pursuer freezes sums of money or moveable property owed to the defender (the arrestee) in the hands of third parties within the jurisdiction of the Scottish courts. This prevents the arrestee from paying over the sums attached: *Lucas' Trustees* v *Campbell and Scott* (1984) 21 R 1096. The arrestment takes place the moment the schedule of arrestment is served on the arrestee. Only the duty to account owed at that time is caught. There is no duty on the arrestee to account for interest: *Glen Music* v *City of Glasgow District Council* (1983) SLT 26. More than the sum sued for may be caught by the arrestment, in which case it may be restricted by agreement or by order of the court. An arrestment may be recalled by the court if it is "nimious and oppressive" or is incompetent: compare *Levy* v *Gardner* (1964) SLT (Notes) 68, *West Cumberland Farmers* v *Ellon Hinengo* (1988) SLT 294. A claim for wrongful use of arrestment is competent (*Laidlaw* v *Smith* (1836) 16 F 267), but unusual, and proceeds on the exacting test of malice, lack of probable cause or irregularity. Four specific areas are worth mentioning: insolvency practitioners, bonds and guarantees, certified sums and monthly certification.

A liquidator has a preference over anyone whose diligence is not complete. Arrestment is not regarded as a complete diligence in itself. It requires the procedure of "furthcoming" raised by separate court proceedings for this purpose, by compelling the arrestee to make over to the pursuer/creditor the monies or goods arrested. Section 37(4) Bankruptcy (Scotland) Act 1985, as amended by s 185(1) of the 1986

Act, provides that no arrestment of the estate of the company executed within a period of 60 days before the commencement of the winding-up and whether or not subsisting at that date, or on or after the commencement of the winding-up, shall be effectual to create a preference for the arresting creditor, and the estate so arrested, or the proceeds of the sale, must be handed over to the liquidator: *Hertz* v *Itzig* (1865) 3 M 813, *Commercial Aluminium Windows Limited* v *Cumbernauld Development Corporation* (1987) SLT 91. Where a receiver wishes to sell assets subject to a floating charge which are affected by an effectively executed diligence, he must ask the consent of the creditor or, if this is withheld, apply to the court for authority to sell: s 61 Insolvency Act 1986, *Lord Advocate* v *Royal Bank of Scotland* (1977) SC 155. After an application has been made for an administration order, no diligence may be commenced or continued without the leave of the court: *Taymech* v *Rush & Tompkins* (1990) SLT 681.

With a view to maintaining the security obtained by way of arrestment, a bond or guarantee from a bank or indeed a parent company guarantee may be provided. If in sufficient terms and of sufficient value, monies arrested should be released voluntarily ("loosed") by the pursuer/arresting creditor. If not, a motion may be made to the court for release. Very often, bonds or guarantees issued by banks will incorporate provisions which enable the terms to be enforced against the bank (or in some instances the insurance company) even where the defender/debtor has become insolvent. This is certainly advantageous from the point of view of the claimant: arguably it gives him a degree of security greater than that which the law would allow him as a matter of right.

The pursuer in a dispute under a construction contract which provides for the certification of sums owed by a third party before they become owing, and for the review of such certification by a third party such as an arbiter/arbitrator, cannot lodge arrestments on the dependence of those sums if not yet so certified: *Costain* v *Scottish Rugby Union* (1994) SLT 573. The same principle applies where a right to payment is contingent upon satisfaction of a condition precedent such as a pay when paid clause or other "condition of payment" provision: *Taymech* v *Trafalgar House Construction* (1995) SLT 202. It is important to distinguish between the question whether a creditor has a right to bring proceedings and whether the receivable sued for is arrestable: see *Taylor Woodrow* v *Sears Investment Trust* (1991) SLT 421.

Care should be exercised when ascertaining the amount of money caught by an arrestment served against a party who is paid by way of interim certificates. If an arrestment is lodged on, say, the 10th day of the month, does it catch only monies due up to that date? The answer strictly speaking is "yes", but due to the impracticality of ascertaining the extent of the obligation to account as at that date - does it depend only on what has been valued and certified at that date or could it extend to unvalued work in progress? - the view should be taken that the entirety of the next certificate has been caught by virtue of that arrestment. Alternatively, on a lump sum contract, one arrestment in the course of the contract may be enough to freeze the entire entitlement to payment under the contract. These questions are relevant when ascertaining the extent of a company's estate available for the benefit of creditors in an insolvency situation.

The Scottish Law Commission's Report on Diligence on the Dependence and Admiralty Arrestments (1998, No 164) has recommended that in future, warrant to arrest on the dependence of an action will be granted only following appearance before a sheriff or judge and the presentation of information to justify the necessity of arrestment as a means of security. This is likely to mean fewer opportunities to arrest since in many cases the procedure is used simply to force parties to negotiate by starving them of cash or by embarrassing them into settlement. Those which are granted on reasonable grounds, *e.g.* the defender's precarious financial position, may initially be successful in catching monies, but be cut down by a subsequent receivership or liquidation (depending upon the time limits detailed above).

Compensation and balancing of accounts in insolvency

The Scottish legal term for "set-off" is "compensation", although "set-off" is also in common use. The principles of set-off are as follows:

- the debts to be set-off must be of the same nature
- the debts to be set-off must be due at the same time
- the debts must both be liquid claims and capable of immediate ascertainment
- there must be *concursus debiti et crediti, i.e.* the parties must be debtor and creditor not only at the same time but in the same capacity.

Where one of the parties is bankrupt or in liquidation, the principle of balancing accounts in insolvency may be applied which effectively overturns the first three of these points, so that:

- the claims may be of a different nature
- a debt presently due can be set off against a future claim
- an illiquid claim may be set off against a liquid claim.

The reader should beware, however, of express contractual terms which exclude this principle.

Insolvency termination

Most standard forms of Scottish building or civil engineering contract include provisions for either the automatic (without notice) or discretionary (usually on notice) determination of a contractor's employment upon the occurrence of an insolvency event. The Insolvency Practice Guide published by the Scottish Building Contract Committee (1991) is a useful commentary in this area and is in similar terms to JCT Practice Note 24.

Scots case law

A number of Scottish cases are considered elsewhere in this book. In addition, it is worth noting cases on the following areas: the use of plant and equipment following determination, retention trusts, and the ownership of materials.

In *Melville Dundas* v *Team Management* (unreported, 1 December 1994, Edinburgh Sheriff Court), Team were the principal contractors, on behalf of the University of Edinburgh, for the construction of student residences. One of the sub-contractors went into receivership. Melville bought all temporary buildings, plant, equipment and tools from the sub-contractor's receiver. Melville wrote to Team to ask for access to the site to remove them. There was a delay, but eventually Melville were allowed to remove the items from site. Melville then sued Team for their unauthorised use during this period of delay. Team argued that on the determination of the sub-contract they had a right to use the items on site and that the sub-contractor had breached the sub-contract by selling them to Melville. It was held that the sub-contract had effectively conferred a right on Team, on determination of the sub-contract, to use all temporary buildings and plant brought on site by the sub-contractor, and imposed a duty on the sub-contractor not to interfere with such use. By selling the items, the sub-contractor had breached the sub-contract provision. Any claim, however, lay against the sub-contractor in receivership unless it could be established that Melville had committed the delict (tort) of inducing the sub-contractor or its receivers to breach the sub-contract by selling the items in question.

In *Balfour Beatty* v *Britannia Life* [1997] SLT (OH) 10, a management contractor entered into a contract for the redevelopment of residential properties and engaged Balfour Beatty and Stewart McGlashen as works contractors. The management contractor then went into receivership. Prior to that, the works contractors had completed their work and had been paid all sums due apart from retention. The management contract was in the form of the SBCC Scottish Management Contract (March 1988) with Scottish Supplement to JCT 87. Clause 4.29 of the works contracts stated that: "The Management Contractor's interest in the Works Contractor's Retention … is fiduciary as trustee for the Works Contractor (but without obligation to invest)." The management contractor's employment was determined on the appointment of the receivers. The works contractors brought an action against the novated employers and the receivers, seeking declarator that the retention monies had been held in trust for them and payment of those sums, failing which they should be set aside in separate bank accounts for their exclusive benefit. Britannia Life argued there had been no setting aside of sums so as to create a trust fund in respect of which a trust could exist. The receivers argued that clause 4.8 of the management contract was inapplicable as its phraseology was directed to retentions under the management contract and not the works contract, and that, in any event, there was nothing on the face of the interim certificates to show that money was held in trust for the benefit of the contractor for no provision of intimation was made. It was held, dismissing the action, that:

- "retentions" under clause 4.8 clearly comprised retention in respect of the works contract as well as the management contract;
- it could not be said that as at the date on which retention monies were quantified and identified, there existed in the hands of the employer a fund capable of being the subject of a valid and effective trust according to Scots law, the provisions in effect purporting only to create fiduciary obligations in

respect of the employer's obligation, not in respect of any asset derived from it or related to it and being ineffective to achieve any further purpose;

- reading the contract provisions as a whole, the intention was that determination of the contract superseded in full the payment provisions which would otherwise apply in terms of clause 4 of the management contract conditions, so that the defenders were not obliged, in terms of clause 4.8.3, to place the retention monies relative to the respective contracts in separate bank accounts;
- similarly, the receivers were not obliged to make a request of Britannia Life that the sums of retention should be set aside for the pursuers' benefit, as the determination of the contract effectively evacuated clause 4.8.3 in its entirety and there was no substantial underlying basis for setting aside retention;
- upon determination of the contract, any trust which did subsist in favour of the works contractors terminated and was of no continuing substance, for such determination brought clause 7 of the management contract conditions into play which made the protection of the employer's interests paramount;
- the employer was entitled to apply all sums held by him by way of deduction or set-off against his claims against the management contractor, so that the pursuers had no right to have the share of retention held for them protected against the employer's claims related to areas of the contract for which the works contractors had no responsibility.

On the question of ownership of materials, *Archivent v Strathclyde Regional Council* (1984) 27 BLR 99 is considered in Chapter 4. *Modern Structural (Scotland) Plastics v Tayloroof* (unreported, 3 December 1990, Edinburgh Sheriff Court) concerned almost identical facts. A supplier of goods under retention of title to a sub-contractor obtained an interim interdict (injunction) against a contractor restraining it from intromitting (converting) its goods or removing them from site, and an order that they be delivered up, following the sub-contractor's entry into liquidation. The orders were overturned on appeal, on the contractor giving evidence that it had paid the sub-contractor for the goods in question before the commencement of the winding-up, and had an arguable defence under s 25 Sale of Goods Act 1979. The contractor stated that the inability to use the supplier's goods would cause eight weeks' delay to the project and, under the main contract, liquidated damages of £10,000 per week of delay would be payable, and it might also be liable for disruption to other trades. Two- thirds of the goods claimed by the supplier had already been fixed before the sub-contractor went into liquidation. The balance of convenience lay with the contractor and the interdict was recalled (discharged).

Conclusion

As with notions of a new democracy in Scotland, there might be said to be more than a little naivety in predicting anything other than a deceleration of growth in the Scottish economy and the construction industry itself within the next five years. If that be the case, the principles of Scottish construction insolvency law as set out above will continue to be of significance and their practical application will almost certainly increase. A more realistic anticipation for the Scottish market is that the combination of the benefits of the forms of procurement described in the introduction, a restriction on warrants to arrest being granted as freely as at present and an increased use of ADR including adjudication will encourage enhanced management of disputes and therefore result in less resort to insolvency save where unavoidable due to wider considerations. Pending the further transfer of powers from Westminster (if that is ever to happen), that will require to suffice!

Ireland*

Irish law is based on the common law, which, together with the court structure and the legal profession, came to Ireland with the Anglo-Normans and has developed in parallel with the English legal system ever since. Following independence in 1922, Irish legislation continued to borrow quite heavily from United Kingdom statutes. The increasing importance of EU law contributed to this trend, but in areas not governed by EU law, the two systems are now becoming increasingly divergent. Irish case law has also relied heavily on English precedents, especially when interpreting similar statutory provisions, *e.g.* company and insolvency law. United Kingdom practitioners working in these areas will find much in Ireland with which they are already familiar.

---

* by Niav O'Higgins, Masons, Dublin

This section provides an overview of the situation in Ireland and highlights a few of the differences which do exist.

The construction industry in Ireland

The Irish construction industry operates within a smaller market than in the United Kingdom but is subject to the same forces and pressures. Cash flow is as vital to the construction industry in Ireland as it is anywhere else. The Irish standard forms of contract contain comparable mechanisms in relation to payment and termination for insolvency to those found in the United Kingdom. The most commonly encountered standard forms are issued by the Royal Institute of Architects of Ireland (RIAI), the corresponding Government Departments and Local Authorities (GDLA) contracts for use in the public sector, as well as those issued by the Institute of the Engineers of Ireland (IEI). Broadly speaking, the RIAI and GDLA contracts can be compared with the JCT forms and the IEI contracts with the ICE conditions.

Irish insolvency law

The principal sources of company and insolvency law are the Companies Acts 1963 to 1990. The principles of the Bankruptcy Act 1988, which refers mainly to individual insolvency, are incorporated by reference into the corporate insolvency regime. Many of the procedural rules governing the winding-up of companies are to be found in the Rules of the Superior Courts. Insolvency procedures and other arrangements operating in Ireland are very similar to those in the United Kingdom, *e.g.* voluntary and involuntary liquidation, schemes of arrangement and receivership. Notices of creditors' meetings, winding-up orders and other insolvency matters are published in the Official Gazette (Iris Oifigiúil). Advertisements in relation to petitions are generally published in any of the national papers, the most prominent being *The Irish Times, Irish Independent* and *The Examiner*. Lists of judgments and details of the appointment of receivers and liquidators tend to be published in *Stubbs' Gazette* and the *Irish Trade Protection Association Gazette.*

The main difference is examinership, which most closely equates to administration in the United Kingdom, which was introduced by the Companies (Amendment) Act 1990. Examinership has as its objective the rescue of the whole or part of a company. This is achieved by placing the company under the protection of the court and imposing a moratorium while an investigation is carried out into the company's prospects by an independent person known as an "examiner" who decides whether a survival package for all or part of the company is viable. A petition for the appointment of an examiner can be presented in circumstances where there is no existing order or resolution for winding-up on the ground that the company is, or is likely to be, unable to pay its debts as they fall due. The petition may be presented by the directors, a creditor or a member with at least a 10% shareholding. The onus is on the petitioner to show that the company is unable to pay its debts, but the burden is less onerous than on a petition for an administration order. For example, it is not necessary to adduce any evidence that the examinership would be likely to assist the survival of the company. The petitioner must simply show good reason for the order, although what constitutes "good reason" will vary from case to case. Once the petition has been presented, the company is given three months' protection from creditors, a receiver cannot be appointed, the company cannot be wound up and no security can be enforced against it. The examiner acts as an officer of the court and is charged with putting together a rescue proposal. If at the end of his investigation he concludes that all or part of the company can be rescued, he will prepare a draft scheme of arrangement for approval by the creditors and sanction by the court.

The examiner has limited powers although these can be extended on application to the court. A significant difference between examinership and administration is that the examiner does not take over the management of the company and his powers are more limited. He may, however, apply to the court for them to be extended to include all those exercisable by the directors and may be able to intervene to some extent in the management of the company by proposing a certain course of action. Similarly, the court has discretion to give the examiner all the powers of a liquidator. He has quite extensive powers to enable him to gather the necessary information and he can question the officers and employees of the company under oath and require the production of documents. The power of certification is perhaps the most controversial power in the examiner's armoury. This enables him to certify certain expenses incurred during the three-month period which take priority (along with his remuneration and legal costs) over all other debts owed by the company, including sums due to secured creditors. Thus, unsecured creditors can obtain priority for goods and services supplied to the company during the protection period and gain priority over secured creditors. Such a power enables the company to continue trading as it reassures essential suppliers that they will be paid, but it has come under severe criticism from secured creditors. Because of the far-reaching nature of this power, it is likely to be exercised cautiously.

The appointment of an examiner does not affect pre-existing contracts. However, he will become personally liable for any contracts which are novated to him or entered into in his own name or in the name of the company after his appointment. An examiner must therefore take care to ensure that any contracts entered into after his appointment expressly exclude any personal liability. There is an option for the company to affirm or repudiate existing contracts where there remains an obligation to be performed other than the payment of money. If a contract is repudiated, the court may determine the amount of damages suffered by the other party as a consequence who will then stand as an unsecured judgment debtor. The court also has wide powers to make any further orders it considers appropriate, including a declaration of the rights of any other person affected by the repudiation. The powers to affirm or repudiate will only arise when a scheme of arrangement is to be entered into and the determination in this context of the amount of damages due as a consequence of that repudiation will have a direct impact on the voting rights of that party at any subsequent meetings of creditors, including voting on any scheme of arrangement proposed by the examiner. The examiner also has powers similar to those given to an administrator by s 15 Insolvency Act 1986. This raises problems similar to those which have been encountered in the United Kingdom where the property in question is subject to third party rights, such as a fixed charge.

If it is not possible to rescue the company, the examiner's costs and expenses will take priority over other claims in the subsequent liquidation, including the costs of the liquidator. To hold otherwise would undermine the aims of the Act of 1990, namely to ensure the success of examinerships by having suitably qualified people appointed to that role: *In the Matter of Springline Limited* (in liquidation), 17 August 1998, *The Irish Times*, Supreme Court. However, the examiner must be able to justify all costs and expenses incurred as having been necessary to enable him to carry out his duties.

Irish construction insolvency

Much of this book will be directly relevant in Ireland. There are some areas where Irish law and practice does not follow the United Kingdonapproach. Briefly they are as follows:

- pay when paid clauses, which have recently been outlawed outside insolvency in the United Kingdom, are still prevalent in Ireland but voices are being raised against them
- it remains usual for sub-contractors to be nominated, although this practice is also changing
- the question of direct payment by employers in the event of a main contractor's insolvency is a very live issue
- the same applies to trusts over retention
- the trust device is also used in respect of the whole contract sum in the CIF sub-contract: see *Murphy Brothers* v *Morris* (unreported, 6 October 1975)
- the Irish courts are more ready to imply the exclusion of the common law of set-off by reference to all of the contract terms.

It is worth looking in a little more detail at the last two differences. Clause 11(d) of the Construction Industry Federation (CIF) form of sub-contract intended for use with nominated sub-contractors, but often used with domestic sub-contractors, provides:

> "Payments made to the Contractor in respect of work done and materials used by the Sub-Contractor shall until received by the Sub-Contractor be deemed to be money or moneys worth held in trust but without obligation to invest by the Contractor for the Sub-Contractor to be applied in or towards payment of the Sub-Contractor's account, subject always to the right of adjustment by the Architect/Engineer in the event of his certifying that adjustment is necessary."

This provision, together with the provisions creating a retention trust in the sub-contractor's favour and allowing direct payment by the employer, survived a claim that they were contrary to the *pari passu* rule in *Glow Heating* v *Eastern Health Board* (1992) 8 Const LJ 56 (see Chapter 12).

In Ireland, the same principles relating to legal and equitable set-off as set out in this book will apply. Likewise, the parties to a contract may seek to limit the right of set-off and such limitations can be found in the standard forms, such as the RIAI forms of main and sub-contract. The Irish courts have held that where the parties have expressly provided for the circumstances in which certain sums may be set off, this can, depending upon the construction of the particular contract, exclude any wider rights of set-off which might exist at common law. The test of whether or not set-off is applicable is "not whether the common law right of set-off has, by the terms of the building contract, been unequivocally excluded, but rather as to whether all the relevant terms of the building contract are in any event inconsistent with the exercise in that event of such a right of set-off": *John Sisk & Son* v *Lawter Products* (unreported, 15 November 1976), followed in *Rohan Construction* v *Antigen* [1989] IRLM 783.

The provisions considered to be relevant were the contractor's right to payment of certified sums subject only to certain deductions such as liquidated and ascertained damages, the contractor's right to claim interest on unpaid certified sums, the contractor's right to suspend works for non-payment of certified sums and both parties' rights to refer disputes to arbitration. This approach appears to be confirmed by the GDLA form of contract which expressly provides for the operation of legal set-off in relation to sums due under different contracts. However, it should be noted that the decisions in the High Court are inconsistent on this point: *Hegarty* v *Royal Liver Friendly Society* (unreported, 11 October 1985). The Supreme Court has yet to rule on this issue.

Liquidation set-off also exists in Ireland: para 17, First Schedule, Bankruptcy Act 1988 as incorporated into the statutory framework for corporate insolvency by virtue of s 284 Companies Act 1963. But whereas Rule 4.90 of the United Kingdom Insolvency Rules 1986 is mandatory and requires that an account of mutual dealings "shall" be taken, the equivalent Irish provision provides that "where there are mutual credits or debts as between a bankrupt and any person claiming as a creditor, one debt or demand may be set off against the other and only the balance found owing shall be recoverable on one side or the other", suggesting a discretion in the application of liquidation set-off. Specifically, it seems that it is possible to contract out of the right to set off mutual dealings. In the event of legal advice being required in Ireland, a solicitor should be consulted.

The Kentz examinership

In early 1994, a number of companies in the Kentz Group went into receivership. The construction group was a significant employer in Ireland. As there was a possibility of it being sold as a whole, an examiner was appointed, thereby terminating the prior receiverships. A series of extraordinary hearings ensued, in which the debentures under which the receivers had been appointed were construed as creating floating rather than fixed charges over book debts: *Re Holidair* (7 March 1994, Supreme Court). It was also held that the examiner could exercise the borrowing powers of the company without obtaining the consent of the debenture holders, and that the proceeds of book debts which had been collected by the receivers should be paid to him. It was open to the examiner therefore to use the company's receivables as security for future borrowing and the payment of his costs and expenses in priority to the claims of other secured or unsecured creditors. Although the floating charge granted by the company had crystallised on the appointment of the receivers, the court held that it had de-crystallised on the examiner's appointment. The failure of the Kentz Group had important repercussions in the United Kingdom, where it was carrying out a number of contracts. The group's bondsman incurred significant liability and Kentz' insolvency was the cause of the litigation which resulted in *Laing and Morrison Knudson* v *Aegon Insurance* (1997) 86 BLR 70, discussed in Chapter 9.

France

There are two French laws dealing with construction: 16 July 1971 (amended 23 December 1972) which concerns retention on private projects; and 31 December 1975 which concerns direct payment to sub-contractors (Thomas 1997). The retention law applies to main and sub-contracts, imposes a maximum limit of 5% of the contract sum and is restricted to cross-claims for defects. As it accrues, retention has to be protected by payment to an agreed third party and is released a year after the equivalent of practical completion, unless the employer or contractor objects. The law of 1975 applies to private and public contracts. On a private contract, a sub-contractor is given a right of action against an employer in the event of non-payment by the contractor. Provided the employer has no cross-claim against the contractor, the sub-contractor can gain priority over the contractor's general creditors to the extent of its debt by serving the notice of non-payment on the employer. This right is similar to the stop notice procedure in the United States. On a public contract, sub-contractors are given the right to be paid direct during the contract. The law aims to alleviate the effect of the insolvency of contractors in the industry.

Conclusion

Construction is an industry of place. More perhaps than any other, its practices reflect the history, traditions and culture of its country. Attitudes towards financial protection are very different between common law and civil law jurisdictions, between North America and the rest of the world, and between states in countries with a federal constitution. Such differences need to be respected.

Against this array of ideas and protective devices, it is even more striking that English law has maintained a strict view of privity of contract and the *quicquid plantatur* rule, without seeing the need to interfere with the parties' freedom of contract. Even the Housing Grants, Construction and Regeneration Act 1996 only regulates ordinary contractual terms and does not introduce any new proprietary rights. The Contracts (Rights of Third Parties) Bill is unlikely to affect relations between employers, contractors and sub-contractors.

Chapter 18

Images of Construction Insolvency

Introduction

Lying beneath the law is a stream of images which give life to its language and concepts. The stream flows by largely unnoticed, occasionally bubbling up in a metaphor in a judgment or statute. One of the metaphors of the Insolvency Act for example is of drying out, of liquid turning solid. Where is the image that informs this metaphor? As I write, I have a mental picture of a dried up river, and a person of indeterminate sex gazing at the stones and debris on the river bed. Suddenly the person is lying face down on the stones and water is seeping from him-her. As suddenly, the figure is standing ankle deep in water, and then falls through the river bed down to the bottom of the sea. What is it saying, this strange and powerful image? This last chapter gives a voice to the images of construction insolvency.

The legal imagination

The way the law uses images makes them seem ordinary, it takes away their power. We may have heard a thousand times that set-off is a shield and not a sword but it doesn't occur to us that we are in the midst of a battle. A few moments of reflection and we realise how much legal work is a ritualised battle: claims and counterclaims, defences, breaches. Or consider "insolvency" – why does the law employ this image of drying-up? Isn't it strange that insolvency is followed by "liquidation" and then "dissolution"? At this point (if not before) the legal mind protests: "what does it matter? I know what the words mean in law", but this is very revealing of the mind trained by the legal method. The inference is that all that matters is the definition. The fact that a word may have roots deep in our culture and be expressing something profound is neither here nor there. But again the legal mind objects: "I don't deny that, but it's not relevant to my work as a lawyer." The legal mind has become cut off from its cultural roots. Meanings wider than the legal definition are for poets not lawyers, who take refuge in the matter in hand. The legal mind is well aware of this. Its intelligence makes it a formidable debater. But it pays a high price for such exclusion by definition. Benjamin Sells (1994, 1999) shows the consequences in the feelings of isolation, depression and loss of emotional life experienced by many lawyers.

The legal method has a way of pinning down its material "like a patient etherised upon a table". Remorselessly, the law shines its searchlight into every obscurity on its way to the resolution of the issue. But the law's explanatory approach somehow fails when confronted with images because they do not want to be explained but to be noticed and understood. They are the voice of the imagination and are not susceptible to analysis. At least, they will not reveal their secrets that way. There is something in this combination of construction, law and insolvency that is elusive, and yet has a Siren call, so why not put aside "problem solving" and the legal method and let the images informing this subject speak for themselves?

The image of the limited company

This book mainly concerns corporate insolvency. The notion of a company being liable to creditors only to the extent of the proceeds of sale of its property first appeared in the Limited Liability Act 1855 (Fletcher 1996). This was a significant legal and psychological moment in that it marked a shift from person to property. Instead of dealing with a natural person and relying on his reputation and that of his family or tribe, the trader could now deal through and with an artificial person relying on its own material resources. Companies had existed for several centuries but from now on they would deal with each other as personified property. Through the medium of share ownership, it became possible to own a legal person without being responsible for its acts, an advantage over slavery which was finally abolished only in the 1830s. Trade could be conducted between "artificial persons" whose primary connection was the flow of goods, services and money. The Act of 1855 and its successors allowed commercial men to do through their companies things they could never have done as individuals, although it was not until the 20th century and the rise of the corporate group that its full potential would be realised.

Although the legal method can be constricting, the law has an imagination which is profound, fertile and archaic. To the law a limited company is as much a person as you or me. The judges speak of directors as the "conscience" or the "mind and will" of the company. Statutes refer to a company's "seat" and "head"' office. Writers and lawyers employ the metaphor of the family: "parent" and "sister" companies. To the construction industry cash flow is the "life blood" of the company. A company "enjoys" a right to something, and "suffers" a burden. The law also speaks of the "veil of incorporation" and "pierces" or "lifts" it in cases of fraud. In *El Ajou* v *Dollar Land Holdings* [1993] 3 All ER 717 at 743 Millett J commented:

> "In my judgment, where the knowledge of a director is attributed to a company, but is not actually imparted to it, the company should not be treated as continuing to possess that knowledge after the director in question has died or left its service. In such circumstances, the company can properly be said to have 'lost its memory'."

This imagery is used quite casually as a convenient way of speaking. After all, "it's only an image". The real attitude of the law is demonstrated by the speech of Lord Hoffmann in *Meridian Global Funds* v *Securities Commission* [1995] 3 All ER 918 at 922:

> "A company exists because there is a rule (usually in a statute) which says that a *persona ficta* shall be deemed to exist and to have the powers, rights and duties of a natural person. But there would be little sense in deeming such a person to exist unless there were also rules to tell one what acts were to count as acts of the company. It is therefore a necessary part of corporate personality that there should be rules by which acts are attributed to the company. These may be called 'the rules of attribution'. ... There is in fact no such thing as the company as such, no 'ding an sich', only the applicable rules. To say that a company cannot do something means only that there is no one whose doing of that act would, under the applicable rules of attribution, count as an act of the company."

Lord Hoffmann then referred to previous judicial statements which likened the company to a human being, and continued:

> "But this anthropomorphism, by the very power of the image, distracts attention from the purpose for which Viscount Haldane said he was using the notion of directing mind and will, namely to apply the attribution rule derived from s 502 to the particular defendant in the case. ... Once it is appreciated that the question is one of construction rather than metaphysics, the answer in this case seems to their Lordships to be as straightforward as it did to Heron J."

In this speech, Lord Hoffmann acknowledged the power of the image. He was interpreting a statute that required a person to take a certain step as soon as he "knew or ought to know" something, and was careful to limit his terms of reference accordingly. He restricts what he says to the question of statutory interpretation. Anthropomorphism as such is a gift of the imagination. It is open to us to ask: what if a company really were human? How would it be with others inside and outside the family? It is worth articulating the law in such terms, to appreciate "the power of the image."

Until recently, every company required at least two parents, but could have had an unlimited number. Now, a company can be born of just one parent. Every parent has a share or portion of the company and can decide its fate. Depending on the kind of company it is, a parent can sell its shares to a stranger or may have to offer them to another member of the family first. If the stranger has the money and the parents wish to sell, the company can be cast out of the family and sold into slavery. A company can reproduce itself without limit, become the parent of a sibling or even of its own parent. A company can have property of its own, and must reveal it every year, especially its money. If part of a large family, the company may find that its property is taken away from time to time and not returned. It may be stolen by the parents, or given away to a sibling on their instructions or on the orders of the head of the family. The patriarch may order the company to marry (joint venture) or merge with another. On a merger, the new company may turn round and swallow the patriarch (reverse take-over) only later to disgorge it and its offspring. A company may be deprived of food by a parent (divided declaration) and murdered by it (members' voluntary liquidation). Or a parent may order the company to commit suicide (creditors' voluntary liquidation) or stand by and do nothing while strangers kill an offspring (compulsory liquidation). A parent may then claim part of the child's dismembered body to eat (submit a proof of debt) and vice versa. A parent can offer its shares in the company as a hostage for the payment of money (give security). If the parent fails to pay, the creditor acquires the power of life and death over the company. The patriarch can order his sons and daughters to do likewise (cross-collateralisation) with their offspring, and to offer themselves as hostages (sureties) for each other's debts. The family may be permanently engaged in like activities with other families. The State is constantly trying to stop them dominating the market but encourages them to fight each other as much as possible. Once allowed to speak, the images latent in company law disclose a world very like that of the Greek myths. The law's imagination is mythic and takes unpredictable twists and turns, drawing us deeper into itself the closer our involvement with it. Let us now turn to some specific images of insolvency.

The nature of forfeiture

Insolvency has always been dominated by images of forfeiture. Historically the idea applied to the person of the debtor. In pre-classical Greece, a person could be sold or enslaved for non-payment of a debt. In many cultures, loans were made on condition that the borrower pledged his services as security. If the lender's terms were not met, the value of the debtor's services would not be credited to the repayment of the loan, reducing the debtor and his children to hereditary debt bondage (*New Encyclopaedia Britannica*: "Servitude"). In England, personal insolvency was punished by imprisonment from the Statute of Acton Burnell 1283 until the Debtors Act 1869 (Lester 1995). In the Middle Ages, if a debtor absconded or fraudulently concealed his property from his creditors he could be executed. Insolvency was a crime as well as a sin and bears a stigma even today. Six hundred years of statutory forfeiture must have had some effect on the collective psyche.

We saw examples of forfeiture in the image of the company, *e.g.* how hostages are taken as security (the floating charge) or as a surety (the guarantee). In construction insolvency, the prime example is the termination clause, which is still known in some contexts by its former name of "forfeiture clause". The termination of sub-contracts on the contractor's insolvency is experienced as a forfeiture by the sub-contractors. In addition to contracts, forfeiture affects plant and materials, bonds, debts and cash deposits. The possibility of forfeiture hangs over the contractor like the "Sword of Damocles". The phrase has become part of the language, but what does it mean? and who exactly was Damocles?

The story comes down to us from Cicero's "Discussions at Tusculum". Cicero was the leading lawyer of his time until circumstances forced him to retire to his villa at Tusculum outside Rome. There he took refuge in philosophy and the "Discussions" represent imaginary conversations on the subject of happiness as the outcome of moral goodness. To prove his point that "the wise are always happy", Cicero recounted episodes from the life of Dionysus, the tyrant of Sicily. One of them concerns Damocles, who is described as "a flatterer". On being saluted by Damocles as "the happiest of men", Dionysus invited him to see for himself whether it was true by affording him all the pleasures of the court.

> "Damocles thought himself a truly fortunate person. But in the midst of all this splendour, directly above the neck of the happy man, Dionysus arranged that a gleaming sword should be suspended from the ceiling to which it was attached by a horsehair. [He lost his appetite] ... Presently the garlands, of their own accord, just slipped down from his brow. In the end he begged the tyrant to let him go, declaring that his desire to be happy had quite evaporated. Dionysus was indicating clearly enough that happiness is out of the question if you are perpetually menaced by some terror" (V, 21, 61, trans Grant).

As so often happens, the story reveals more than first appears. The sword belongs not to Damocles but Dionysus. Its purpose was not to terrorise Damocles but to show how the Saturnine possession of wealth, pleasure and power does not contribute to happiness. Dionysus attributes to Damocles his own state of perpetual fear. Cicero affords us other glimpses of Dionysus' lifestyle:

> "Round his own bedroom he arranged for a wide trench to be dug; it could only be crossed by a wooden gangway, which he himself drew inside the door every time he wanted to shut himself in. As for his official appearances, he did not dare to appear on the public platform, but used to climb up a high tower whenever he wanted to address his subjects" (V, 20, 59, trans Grant).

Dionysus was an historical figure who ruled Sicily from 405 to 367 BCE.

> "Personal power at home and abroad was Dionysus' aim, and this provides a key to understanding his 38-year rule. His methods were often singular. He collected the normal revenues of a Greek state but he also resorted to every possible device to raise emergency funds when he needed them, just as he freely commandeered labour for arms manufacture and fortification. ... All this has a certain intrinsic interest, but it is important too in that it indicates how completely personal the rule of Dionysus was, and was meant to appear. In this respect he created something new in the Western world, anticipating the practice of Hellenistic monarchs in the centuries after Alexander the Great" (Finley et al, 1986, p 21).

The stories about him may not have a basis in fact but it hardly matters since they survive by virtue of their mythic power - and as testimony of Cicero's abiding contribution to Western culture. In the light of them, it is worth considering again the panoply of protective measures listed in Chapter 2. What is happening when the employer, whether or not prompted by the funder, demands so much security? Could he be experiencing the "happiness" of Dionysus?

In *Order in the Court*, Benjamin Sells tells how he once gave a talk to the partners of a large law firm. Things were going well for them financially, but the pressure of work was causing lack of satisfaction.

> "I asked them why they didn't just work less. They were in charge of the firm; if they wanted to drop the yearly hours expected by the firm, then all they had to do was say so. One man immediately said that was impossible because of the overhead in the firm. Although I didn't see it at the time, I now see that this defensive move bespeaks a very unsettled soul. If you live life to satisfy something hanging over your head, then you will live a subservient and nervous life, a life especially hard on the spirit of the lawyer" (p 187).

The image of the sword of Damocles now seems to dominate much of commercial life.

Trust and transferability

Dionysus suffered from a pathological lack of trust. According to the dictionary, trust can have three meanings: to place reliance in someone, to sell goods on credit, and to consign property to another without misgivings. All three are features of the construction industry. First, every interaction requires a certain level of reliance in the honest operation of the contract terms. Pre-qualification means that the employer leaves less to trust than the contractor does. The *quicquid plantatur* rule discussed in Chapter 4 means the contractor cannot retain title to his materials and has to trust the landowner not to take advantage. Secondly, the whole industry is based on credit flowing up the contract pyramid to the employer. Ultimately, the industry is based on the trustworthiness of the employer to pay the contract sum.

The third meaning is directed to a trust in the legal sense, in which a "settlor" trusts a "trustee" to deal honestly with its property. In the industry the legal trust is used in two contexts: to protect retention and as the means of payment of the contract sum. Is it not ironic that one form of trust is used to support another? The legal device points up the lack of trust in the other senses. For example, retention has been described as a kind of forced loan (McGuinness 1983). Taking credit by force is not trust but rape. The reliance element in the legal trust does exist between settlor and trustee, but in the JCT retention trust the employer fulfils both roles. As between trustee and beneficiary, the relationship is the same as the contract. Retention is still conditional on completion and defeasible by the employer's rights of deduction. Since in practice defeasibility is more likely than the employer's insolvency, the retention trust is but a limited form of protection to the contractor. Trust which is either forced or confined cannot really be described as trust at all. Perhaps Latham was right after all: in this industry, trust is only experienced as its opposite and manifests as security.

Transferability disregards the person and, like defeasibility, undoes the bond between the contracting parties. In their more extreme forms, construction contracts allow assignment by the employer but not the contractor. A stranger is allowed to take the benefit of the contractor's credit, leaving the burden with the employer. There has been a transfer of power without responsibility: Damocles can remain at the banquet, but the hair from which the sword hangs over him has been passed to someone else.

A dialogue on construction

"Construction" is derived from the Latin *struere*, "to pile up", which also gives us "destruction" and "instruction". The prefix "con" means "together". Thinking imaginatively, construction has several meanings: combining separate elements to make a new thing, communal action for the common good, as in "constructive suggestion". The elements need not be physical as in building bricks one on top of the other. We speak also of constructing an argument, in the sense of ordering thoughts in a way others can understand and as a means of persuasion. The court often has to construe an agreement, *i.e.* analyse the words to ascertain its meaning. As a metaphor, construction holds within it the outward physical activity of the building site and the inner mental activity of the lawyer's office.

But here the legal mind revolts: "I see that, but I don't see the point of these semantics. In reality, the construction industry and the legal profession are completely different. All you are doing is finding linguistic similarities."

All right, of course they are different. Let's consider the differences, and come back to the argument later. Perhaps you'd like to take over at this point?

"With pleasure – I'll confess to you I was getting impatient with your 'poetic' approach. You say that construction and law share the same metaphor. I point to the concrete realities. Construction assaults the senses, all five of them, including taste – I'm thinking of the dust in the air that dries the mouth. Then, construction is manual, it's still a craft. Contractors are emotional. Remember all that childish contract correspondence beginning "we *totally* refute … "? The thinking is done by the designers. It's element is earth, fixing things to land. There are three or four differences to begin with, and important ones I would have thought."

Thank you. It's useful to have the differences pointed out. You imply that thinking is not a function of the body, but I prefer to say that a builder thinks with his hands, like a weaver or a potter. As a lawyer you do this too, as you write your arguments down on paper or, these days, type them on to a computer screen. You also weave ideas in your mind. It occurs to me that we don't have the ways of understanding these connections that the ancients did. Did you know that the Goddess Athena was patroness of war, intellectual activity and weaving? She also invented the jury. When we lost contact with the Gods, the aspects of life which only They could hold together fell apart, leaving us floundering.

"That's an interesting thought. While you were speaking, I had another idea. Construction is about handling things, real things made from earth. Hence, the maxim *quicquid plantatur solo, solo cedit*. Incidentally, I have never understood why contractors complain about this: anything they fix to the land must become part of it as it originally came from it. Anyhow, construction could be said to be an activity concerning matter, in the sense of the body, the earth, and the way it changes one thing into another. Law, on the other hand, is an activity of the spirit, in the sense of the mind, the air, the abstract, the way it organises ideas in a structured way towards a particular end. It needs words as construction needs hands. They are distinct but each needs the other to be able to function."

I think you've hit on something there. Construction and law appear as opposites to us in the same way as matter and spirit are opposites. We know they are inseparable but live as if they were not. Maybe this is why lawyers like to fasten on specific areas like construction: it's something concrete for the law to apply to, and vice versa. The construction process is so material it seeks out law's abstraction to hold it together. Hence all those standard forms.

"In another way, though, both of them are materialist: construction physically, and law figuratively. The law reifies everything, including intangibles. For example, you remember how lawyers describe a contract as a bundle of rights and obligations?"

I think I see what you mean. As usually practised, they both seem rather literal even though one is concrete and the other abstract. You see a connection between them in their literalness. To me though, there is something missing that I can't quite grasp. That seems a convenient moment. Shall we end our conversation there?

"Fine. I am left wondering how insolvency relates to them both and whether a synthesis of the three of them could constitute some other metaphor."

The love of money

Money is neither good nor evil: it is neutral, and therein lies its beauty. Unless you are holding it in the form of coins, paper or plastic, money exists only in the imagination or, as the law would say, as a chose in action. Money is an unattainable dream, a fantasy of security, power, achievement, freedom, sex, love, anything or anyone. If money is neutral these images must originate from us. We can attribute anything to money but usually it is something we don't know, or don't wish to know, about ourselves:

> "Money is a tremendous projection carrier. Because is so faceless, so neutral, we tend to project on it more easily. But because it is so important, we have great difficulty knowing where projections start and where money itself begins" (Guggenbuhl-Craig 1982).

How we are with money reveals our psyche. The construction industry has a real thing about money. When a contractor tenders for new work, he is interested not so much in the profit he will earn, but in the cash flow. He likes to see money coming in as early and as frequently as possible, and he likes spending it. This inevitably brings its opposite, insolvency, which is more prevalent in construction than almost any other industry.

Likewise, the law sees everything of value as money. I don't just mean lawyers and their fees. In English law, if a person breaks his contract, he is not likely to be held to it because any breach can be compensated in money: damages are regarded as a surrogate for performance, without involving any moral opprobrium. If anything can be converted into money, money is latent in all things. Money is able to receive our projections to such an extent as to equate to the psyche itself.

It therefore appears that construction, law and money stand in symbolic relations to each other. Construction is matter as law is spirit as money is soul. It is tempting to see them dancing together like the three Graces. The psychologist James Hillman (1982) says:

> "I see money as an archetypal dominant that can be taken spiritually or materially, but which in itself is neither. … Just as animals were spirits or Gods in material forms, so too is money, a kind of third thing between only spirit and only the world, flesh and devil. Hence, to be with money is to be in this third place of soul, psychic reality. … That money is the place where God and Caesar divide shows that money is a "third thing" like the soul itself, and that in money are both the inherent tendency to split into spirit and matter and the possibility to hold them together."

If soul leaves the dance, harmony is broken and spirit and matter are split apart. Psyche too is lost and dark times lie ahead. It is time for us to go into insolvency.

Images of insolvency

It might reasonably be asked why the standard forms go to such lengths to protect the employer on the contractor's insolvency. The court, as it is wont to do, resorts to economics for an answer: because of the inevitable increase in costs in having the works completed by someone else, and the delay, and the inconvenience and so on. But I question whether the severity of the response can be attributed to such a cause. Bear in mind that the law does not deprive a bankrupt of the tools of his trade, whereas the standard forms take everything away. In some of the standard forms, termination is even made automatic on insolvency and on notice for other causes. At the moment of the contractor's greatest vulnerability, the employer uses his most powerful weapon. The standard forms are sometimes seen as a kind of "extra-parliamentary statute", but a law which confiscates property in this way is tyrannical and against the nature of law. So what is it about insolvency that brings out the tyrant? Let us consider the context.

When a contractor gets into financial difficulty, it starts to delay payment to others, the main contract programme slips behind, problems occur with the quality of its work. The contractor begins to break its contracts. The employer then begins to withhold payment, makes sure items are not removed from site, under-certifies the value of work being done, and starts preparing to call the contractor's bond. The latent "money-nature" of all things becomes visible. This is a very common situation and yet it has a numinous, archetypal quality. What is really happening here? Let us take our cue from the language. There are many different metaphors present: movement slowing down and stopping, liquid beginning to harden into a solid, wetness becoming dry, bonds being loosened, a structure beginning to deteriorate, stability becoming unbalanced. These metaphors and the images that lie behind them are mythical. They takes us back to our origins and inform us of the psychic patterns at work in this subject.

Bonds

In *The Origins of European Thought* (1951), R B Onians demonstrates how the metaphor of binding and loosing is derived from the primordial image of the Fates, the three sisters responsible for the length of a man's life, who allotted the span, and spun, wove and cut the thread on which life depends. Thus was man bound to his fate, a fact which even the Gods could not alter. Homer refers to a network of bonds fastened over warring armies. The metaphor occurs in the law (as laws themselves, or binding decisions of the court), in construction (cords and fastenings were used to hold a structure together, and keep doors and chests closed), in diseases (the bond of fate paralyses its victim, mentally or physically, as he is bound by a God), and in competition (the wreath awarded to the victor of the games). The garlands slipping down Damocles' brow of their own accord may be an echo of this.

So much for binding, but what of loosing? This meant death for the individual or defeat for the army, and most likely both. Commercially, loosing the bond consisted in payment of a debt, an equation which still exists in the form of the conditional bond. Loosing in terms of payment also survives in the legal expression *debitum in praesenti, solvendum in futuro*, a present debt payable [*i.e.* to be loosened] in the future (see Chapter 3). Loosing also meant atoning for an offence by undoing the harm done or by suffering like harm yourself. Loosing is Homer's word for the breaking up of an assembly of men: in our terms, liquidating a company. In the same mould is the termination of the contract as a portion of life.

This talk of loosing means that the God Dionysus (after whom Dionysus the tyrant named himself) cannot be far away. When he was captured by pirates they could not tie him to the mast as the ropes would not hold their knots. Perhaps he is the God of the breakdown following insolvency. Many of his myths tell of dismemberment, including his own: the Titans tore him apart when he was a baby and boiled the parts up, but he was reconstituted by Rhea. Dionysus also has connections to construction as God of destruction (or demolition) and, with Hermes, of transformations (plans and drawings into reality, materials into land). Dionysus is linked with the earth Goddesses Gaia and Demeter with whom construction must also be intimately bound.

Novation

The metaphor of binding and loosing is most obvious in a novation (Chapter 10). The insolvent contractor is released as a new contractor agrees to be bound. The two events happen simultaneously. The process is reminiscent of the Centaur Chiron's exchange with Prometheus, as recorded by Apollodorus. Chiron was accidentally wounded in the knee by one of Heracles' arrows:

> "Distressed at this, Heracles ran up to him, pulled out the arrow, and applied a potion which Chiron gave to him, but when the wound turned out to be incurable, Chiron withdrew to his cave. He wanted to die, but was incapable of doing so because he was immortal. Only when Prometheus offered himself to Zeus to become immortal in his place was Chiron able to die" (II.5.4 trans. Hard).

For Chiron, the bond from which he seeks release is life as an immortal or, at least, such a life if passed in eternal pain. The insolvent contractor seeking a release from his contract will probably be dissolved all the same, but in this metaphor a contract is a portion of life. For Prometheus, it was not an act of altruism. Later, Apollodorus tells us that Zeus had long relented over his punishment of Prometheus for giving fire to man by chaining him to a rock and sending a vulture each day to tear out his liver. The problem was that:

> "Prometheus's sufferings were destined to last until some immortal should voluntarily go to Tartarus in his stead; so Heracles reminded Zeus of Chiron, who was longing to resign the gift of immortality ever since he had suffered his incurable wound" (Graves, II.p 149).

Zeus agreed and Heracles shot the vulture and set Prometheus free. So by surrendering his immortality, Chiron did Prometheus a favour and enabled him to be released from eternal torment.

The myths say so much. Chiron and Prometheus were both released from suffering by each becoming bound. But how is the insolvent company bound and the newcomer released by the novation? The myths are right: the insolvent contractor is bound by the promises it makes in return for money from the newcomer; and the latter is released from the lack of work (*penia*) that was binding him to seek out the novation.

Chiron and Prometheus come from different mythic worlds. The first is of the imagination (healer, teacher) who longs for the underworld, death, the reality of the image. The other is of the practical (benefactor of man, giver of fire) who aspires to the upperworld of the Gods, the place of nectar and ambrosia. Mysteriously, their exchange provides each with what they need: they are a resource (*poros*) for each other. Could this myth be an image of Construction Insolvency?

A company is a person, but it is not human. In a sense it is immortal. As immortals in need, the companies participating in a novation have far more in common than they might suppose. Only by liquidation and other forms of release like novation can the insolvent company leave the register and be dissolved, and thus ensure that any lingering fragment of life passes from it.

Termination and repudiation

The forms of release are apt to describe the processes of liquidation and novation, but not termination, especially under an express clause of the contract, which is more like the fall of Damocles' sword than a release. There could be an archetypal difference between express termination and common law acceptance of repudiation. The sword falling is an attack, an intensification of the bond, that removes the contractor from the action but keeps him bound as surety for the consequences of his removal, "clearing the decks" as the court has put it, to allow the victim as terminator to find a rescuer for the project. Termination is like receivership (another tensing of the bond). The employer goes into possession like a mortgagee but without the benefit of formal security.

An acceptance of repudiation is very different. The contractor is the aggressor: the employer as victim is entitled to defend himself by releasing the bond represented by the primary obligations of the contract and substituting another for the payment of damages, i.e. a preparation for loosing. It is the contract draftsman of the 19th century who invented the termination clause and insisted on the bond remaining until dissolution.

Dryness and wetness

Dryness had many associations in the ancient world. It is primarily associated with disease, old age and death. I think of the story of Tithonus in the Homeric Hymn to Aphrodite. He was a youth beloved by Eos (the Dawn) who persuaded Zeus to grant him immortality. But she forgot to ask Zeus to give him eternal youth. "Tithonus became daily older, greyer, and more shrunken, his voice grew shrill, and, when Eos tired of nursing him, she locked him in her bedroom, where he turned into a cicada" (Graves, I p 150). Graves records that the golden cicada was an emblem of Apollo as the sun God. The Greeks saw the life-force as a liquid which gradually diminished in amount over time. This liquid was identified with the sap of plants and trees. "The Greeks also knew that most mature plants inevitably pass through a season of dryness, saplessness, of rest or death, but also that most seeds need to become dry, as it were dead, before they will germinate" (Onians 1951, p 269). Once steeped in water, new life would come.

Apart from the loosing aspect, there is another link between water and binding. According to Greek cosmology, the river Okeanos was believed to be a bond around the earth, in the form of a serpent, a form also taken according to early writers by the psyche. Also, "when a man is in trouble or pines or is wasting physically as well as in spirit he may be said to 'melt', 'dissolve' his [breath/soul], or to 'waste it away' …" (Onians 1951, p 48). There was a direct link between dryness and poverty. Dryness was also associated with consciousness and intelligence while sleep was conceived as a liquid or moist vapour. Awakening from sleep to normal consciousness was a process of drying out.

Pathology

Reading the Greek myths is like poring over "The Home Doctor". Every other page, it seems that we have caught some rare disease. The metaphor of illness is often used in connection with insolvency: "financial distress", "company doctor", "intensive care", "corporate recovery". This echoes the attitude towards insolvency in ancient Greece.

> "Poverty in the ancient world had all the dignity of a sickness. … According to the ancient theory, the two concepts [of] *nosos* (illness) and penia (poverty) cannot be separated, any more than *hygieia* (health) and ploutos (wealth). So sickness is equivalent to poverty, and health to riches" (Meier 1967).

Sickness had dignity since it was the consequence of divine action, which could be cured only by a God or another divine action. There was a God in the sickness and in the remedy. The sick person slept in the sanctuary of the temple, and waited for a dream from the God, from which he might be cured. The modern company can be traumatised, but can it also dream?

In his classic work "Commercial Law" (1995), Professor Roy Goode compares the differing approaches of judges and textbook writers. The judge acts intuitively, he:

> "feels his way to the right conclusion and, within the limits permitted by prior authority, shapes his statement of principle to reach that conclusion. ... The textbook writer, on the other hand, is not called upon to adjudicate on a concrete dispute. His concern is to extract, criticise and reduce to order statements of principle enunciated in cases already decided and to speculate on the likely or desirable outcome on such other issues as may occur to him ... In short, the textbook writer tends to be preoccupied with the pathology of law" (p 22).

This striking phrase, "the pathology of law" is a complex metaphor. It shows an analogy between the facts which come to the court for resolution and diseases which are brought to a doctor for cure. In this context "facts" are not data, but pieces of soul. In the context of a law book, it refers to the pathology of the writer that leads him to write, and to choose this or that particular subject as his medium, and also of the reader, who chooses to hold this book rather than another. Professor Goode could also have had in mind the pathology of the law itself as manifested in its methods and its tendency to ossify and dry out, and its effect on the legal profession and the lives of lawyers. The metaphors are evident here: disputes over breaches of contract leading to litigation (from the Latin *litigare* "to quarrel") are forms of tightening, just as the law hardens when following precedent leads to injustice, and the writer is fixed to his book. Jung once wrote that "the Gods have become diseases". As a psychologist, he had in mind the psyche (or soul), and the fact that modern man regards as disease what the ancients considered as of divine origin. It is possible for us to see in the law reports the archetypal background of the unconscious, and to re-connect with the images which are embedded in the law. Like poetry they can enable us to re-enter mythical space and time.

Poverty

In the *Symposium* of Plato, Poverty is personified, and plays a crucial role in the beautiful myth of the parentage of Eros:

"On the day that Aphrodite was born the gods were feasting, among them Contrivance [*poros*] the son of Invention; and after dinner, seeing that a party was in progress, Poverty [*penia*] came to beg and stood at the door. Now Contrivance was drunk with nectar – wine, I may say, had not yet been discovered – and went out into the garden of Zeus, and was overcome by sleep. So Poverty, thinking to alleviate her wretched condition by bearing a child to Contrivance, lay with him and conceived Love [*eros*]. Since Love was begotten on Aphrodite's birthday, and since he has also an innate passion for the beautiful, and so for the beauty of Aphrodite herself, he became her follower and servant" (trans Hamilton).

Other words used of Penia are want, lack, need, deprivation. I have not found a classical representation of her, but one thinks of the statues and paintings of Psyche after her abandonment by Eros. As a mythical person Penia should not be thought of literally. She could be very well dressed, exquisitely so, and yet be recognisable by the sadness in her eyes or her round shoulders or the downward cast of her lips and features. Can she be seen in the tired features and greyness of the over-working lawyer, narrowed and hardened by all that defining? Penia is an image of the soul who has lost her connection with spirit and body.

Is she not also present in the legal method, shorn of images in the interests of clarity? Images do occur in the law reports and in open court but they are often strangulated, twisted to drive an argument home or crushed into a form of shorthand: "Let's call that the Penia point". Is the law in a state of penury when it does this? Or when it clings to precedent instead of doing justice? Or perhaps Penia casts her shadow over the modern approach to drafting contracts whose over-complexity and excessive length obscure the fact that two or more persons (corporate or otherwise) have come together for their common good.

Poros is variously translated as Contrivance or Resourcefulness. He is inventive like his father, crafty, has plenty of material or knows where to get it, he will always find a way. Aren't contractors like that? Substituting different materials of the same standard to keep the cost down, filling in the gaps of the architect's design by their workmanship, distributing profit to the earliest work, as well as the more shadowy aspects of extras and payment of sub-contractors. In the union of Contrivance and Poverty, do we have another image of Construction Insolvency?

Dissolution

On the completion of a liquidation, or on being struck off the register for some other reason, a company is "dissolved". Property owned by the company at that time passes to the Crown who can sell, disclaim or ignore it. In certain cases, an application can be made to the court for an order declaring the dissolution to be void by persons "interested" or "aggrieved": ss 651, 653 Companies Act 1985. If an order is made, the company revives and is restored to the register. "Dissolution" reverberates with meaning. It was used by the alchemists of the 17th century as a stage of the alchemical process or *opus* (the work). Now it is the corporate equivalent of death, but the fact that a company can be brought back to life by order of the court makes one ponder on the nature of dissolution.

To the Greeks, it would have referred to Hades, the underworld where the souls of the dead were consigned, a place of utter darkness ruled by the God whose name was also Hades, who was invisible but whose conversation was so compelling that no-one wanted to leave. This aspect is also suggested by Hades' other name of Ploutos, wealth, in the sense of the riches of the imagination (Hillman, 1979). This playing with "dissolution" and the Companies Acts also brings to mind one of the greatest myths of the ancient world, the Rape of Persephone. Persephone was abducted by Hades, and as a result, her mother Demeter caused the earth to grow barren with her grief. After a long sojourn, she persuaded Zeus to prevail on his brother Hades, and her daughter was restored to her. But Persephone had eaten a pomegranate seed before leaving Hades which meant she had to spend every winter there. In our corporate terms Demeter is the "person aggrieved", her daughter is the company, Zeus is the court, and Hermes is Demeter's advocate. Hades acts (invisibly) in person.

It cannot be denied that insolvency has an emotional setting. The process is saturated with loss: directly in terms of money, employment, firms, homes; indirectly in terms of personal relationships and self worth; and in terms of contractual rights, *e.g.* to occupy the site and continue working. Further, we might add the loss experienced when projections onto money or a company are forcibly removed by insolvency. In his work on construction law, now in its 11th edition, Alfred Hudson (1891) commented:

> "The cases in this work tell such a tale of loss as could not be equalled by any class of persons entitled to the protection of the laws of this country" (p 7).

He was writing about the situation which then prevailed of a certifier's opinion being binding on the contractor and not open to review by an arbitrator. Peter Fenn charted the decades of mistrust between employers' and contractors' organisations on this issue earlier (Chapter 1). Which brings us back to Dionysus the tyrant ruling over a country where conditionality is king.

The myth of construction insolvency

This brief excursion to the ancient world shows how the apparently disparate elements of this book are governed by a community of related images. When seen against their mythic background, concepts of forfeiture, trust, assignment, bonds and guarantees, security, novation, termination and repudiation, dissolution and conditionality take on a different colour. We can now tentatively suggest why the life of a company so often consists of formation, solvency, insolvency, liquidation and dissolution.

The formation of the company is marked by its entry on the register and the issue of a certificate of incorporation. Both events record the naming of the company. Name and soul are intimately connected in many cultures. Naming the company and the subscription of capital are perhaps the equivalent of the moment when Athena first breathed psyche into man. Solvency, which the law sees as the flow of the company's blood, corresponds to the liquid life-principle of the Greeks. While the company is solvent it can be said to be whole: there is no split between body, soul and spirit. We can see insolvency as a process of drying out, a tightening of the bonds of fate, as manifested in the termination and litigation which often accompanies it. Insolvency is a loss of soul, a state of depersonalisation, a crisis caused by the loss of the "projection carrier". Liquidation is the loosing, the dismemberment of the company as represented by its property, its conversion into money and the payment to creditors of their portions. Dissolution is perhaps the complete release of the company's psyche from its fetters. What are we to make of all this? It is hard to resist the idea that in the image of the company the business world is re-enacting ancient myths of the origin and life of man.

"The Gods have become insolvency procedures"

The law sees a company as a person but a liquidator sees it as an aggregate of properties. A company is like money in being neutral and able to take virtually all our projections. As such, a company can be an image of the psyche. As well as the dismemberment of a body or the division of aggregated property, liquidation is an image of the disintegration of the psyche, such as occurs in sleep, death (or madness). James Hillman describes dreaming as the process whereby the waking ego is replaced by a dream ego, "which is another name for the imaginal ego" (1972, p 186). The three main insolvency procedures are different myths, involving different Gods, but all concern the displacement of the directors, representing the waking ego of the company.

In a liquidation, the directors are permanently ousted by the liquidator as the ego of the company. He looses the bonds and dissolves the boundaries of inside and outside by inviting all persons with a money claim to submit a proof of debt – employees, the former directors, other group companies, as well as external creditors. The company is freed of its burdens, and, in the person of the liquidator, stands outside itself. An administrator also ousts the directors but they will probably be kept on as his consultants. He wants everything to carry on as normal either to save the company or preserve the value of its property for a liquidator. He sees the company more as a person than as property. He preserves the boundaries as agent of the company, officer of the court and representative of the creditors. An administrative receiver is different. He invades the company on behalf of a foreign power and ousts the directors while pretending that nothing has happened. He strips the company of its valuables and hands anything he doesn't want to a liquidator. He also preserves the boundaries but only long enough for him to convert the company's property to cash. Then he is off.

What myths are they enacting, these insolvency practitioners? I suggest three divine figures are involved. The God of liquidation is Dionysus for reasons already explored. What of administration? The language of "turnaround" and "corporate rescue" gives the clue, as does the title of a recent American book *Restructuring: how to extract value from a distressed enterprise*. I would nominate Heracles as the patron of administration, the hero charged with seemingly impossible tasks (under the protection incidentally of Athena). Receivership is more complex and harder to characterise: its God could well be Hermes, the thief, the patron of commerce, who stands at the boundary, and delights in changing shape. It is no accident that these three divinities all visited Hades at one time or another. In many respects Hades and Dionysus are the same.

The fear of insolvency

It is often said that the ability of a contract to anticipate and deal with insolvency is the sign of good drafting, but insolvency not only affects the structure of contracts; it has been a major force determining the course of development of commercial law across the world.

> "Bankruptcy is an emotional subject, because it involves the ancient politics and resentments of creditors and debtors ... Bankruptcy is a destroyer and a spoliator. By reason of the fact that on insolvency there is not enough money to go round, the law has to decide who it will protect – the debtor or the creditors – and, because of the depth of feeling involved in bankruptcy, this taking of sides was likely to be a useful indicator of legal culture" (Wood 1998).

Philip Wood's financial maps (1997) show how the nature of a country's financial and commercial law depends on whether the jurisdiction took the side of the debtor or the creditor against the terror of insolvency.

Perhaps the outcome of this dilemma depended on the degree to which the relevant culture was in contact with the Dionysian archetype at the relevant time. One might expect Mediterranean countries to have favoured the debtor for this reason, and, by and large, they do. English law on the other hand has long been dominated by the Apollonian archetype, and it shows: our commercial law strongly favours the creditor, *e.g.* in the specifically English inventions of the floating charge and the trust. Wood's maps show also how the English spread their strongly pro-creditor attitudes throughout the Empire, and how their former possessions have retained them.

Opting for the creditor can be seen as a crucial psychological step. Fear of insolvency seems to have affected commercial men in the same way as terror of the tiger affects Indian villagers. But rather than convert it to awe and even worship of the tiger as divine, the fear of insolvency went the way of Dionysus the tyrant into a maximum security prison. So it is that the "banker's mind", which now has such a strong influence on the modern construction project, has come to be so obsessed with the extermination of risk. It is as if the English saw the "God in the disease" of insolvency and instinctively withdrew.

Construction insolvency is also telling us something about commonalty and community. The metaphor of co-operation is at work in the essentially communal process of building, now known as "teamwork". The same thought is expressed in the word "company" which is derived from *cum panis* referring to the sharing of bread by "companions". Similarly, liquidation, the paradigmatic insolvency procedure, is by nature collective. When a winding-up petition is presented, it is deemed to have been issued on behalf of all the creditors of the company. In theory at least, the *pari passu* rule is designed to achieve rateable distributions to creditors. The meeting of creditors called to appoint the liquidator is likely to be the first time they will have met together. At the imaginal level, Hillman speaks of the "collective nature of the soul's depths" (1972, p 24) and shows how the Dionysian mode of consciousness is participative (1972, p 296).

There are other aspects of construction insolvency which point to aspects of the Dionysian: the way it concerns the incomplete and the imperfect, the inferiority felt by the construction industry compared with others, the lowly status of insolvency practitioners until the legislative reforms of 1986 and the creation of the modern profession, and the surprising fact that the enthusiasm shown by academics towards insolvency law also post-dates 1986.

The numinosity of law

We have lost the connection with the numinosity of law. In the *Symposium*, Diotima tells Socrates that:

> "there are some whose creative desire is of the soul, and who long to beget spiritually, not physically, the progeny which it is the nature of the soul to create and bring to birth. If you ask what that progeny is, it is wisdom and virtue in general; of this all poets and such craftsmen as have found out some new way may be said to be begetters; but far the greatest and fairest branch of wisdom is that which is concerned with the due ordering of states and families, whose name is moderation and justice" (trans. Hamilton, p 90).

In an earlier passage, Diotima said that "all the processes in all the crafts are kinds of poetry, and all those who are engaged in them poets" (p 85). For the Greeks "craft" embraced building as well as weaving.

Thus, we may conclude with grateful thanks to Diotima and to all those through whom she speaks. Law and construction are branches of wisdom "which it is the nature of the soul to create and bring to birth". Soul has appeared to them in the guise of insolvency, and through us she wishes to re-connect with them and re-unite them with their origins and their own essential natures. If the person in the image at the beginning of this chapter could speak, I think he-she might say "look into the water". In other words, although the river appears to be dry, it is an image, like money or the company or construction insolvency, of the psyche.

For too long the law has been operating on its own terms and without contact with its roots. One of the ways in which contact can be re-established is by entering the myths underlying the law, and one of the best ways of doing this is through the archetypal psychology of Jung and Hillman which is devoted to the psyche or soul. For as Marsilio Ficino, one of the great men of the Renaissance, whose death 500 years ago we commemorate this year, once wrote:

> "For how can we understand anything else fully unless we understand the soul itself, through which everything must be understood? Does not a man abuse the soul by not devoting himself to its study, when it is by means of the soul and for its sake that he wants to understand everything else?" (Letters, I-107)

· Glossary ·

This glossary consists of simplified definitions to assist the general reader and should not be taken as a complete explanation of the concepts involved for which reference should be made to the text.

Abatement: Defence that value of work done or goods supplied should be reduced because of defects.

Adjudication: Interim dispute procedure in construction contracts.

Administration: Formal court-based insolvency procedure with the aim of rescuing a company.

Administrative Receiver: Insolvency Practitioner appointed by the holder of a floating charge.

Administrator: Insolvency Practitioner appointed by the court to take control over a company in administration.

Assignee: Person to whom an asset is assigned.

Assignment: Procedure for transferring assets.

Assignor: Person who assigns.

Attachment: Enforcing a judgment by ordering a person who owes a debt to a judgment debtor to pay it direct to the judgment creditor.

Back to back contracts: Where the terms of one contract are referred to or mirrored in another to promote easier enforcement of rights.

Balance sheet test: Test of insolvency where the value of a company's assets is compared with the amount of its liabilities, including contingent and prospective liabilities.

Bankruptcy: Formal insolvency procedure for individuals rather than companies or partnerships.

Bankruptcy set-off: Mandatory set-off of all mutual dealings where one party is bankrupt.

Benefit of contract: Rights which one party to a contract has against the other.

Bills of quantity: Schedules containing each item of work and materials required in the construction process individually priced by the contractor.

Bill of sale: Document transferring ownership of a chattel.

Bond: Undertaking under seal to pay money.

Bondsman: Person who gives a bond.

Book debt: Debt arising in the course of a business which would normally be entered in the books of the type of business concerned.

Building out: Completing an unfinished structure after a contractor defaults.

Burden of contract: Obligations which one party under a contract owes to the other.

Cash flow test: See going concern test.

714 certificate: Certificate entitling a sub-contractor to be paid gross.

Certified sum: Money certified for payment to a contractor or a sub-contractor by an architect or an engineer normally on a monthly basis.

Charge: Form of security whereby an asset of a debtor is identified and appropriated towards payment should the debtor fail to pay.

Charge-holder: Person to whom a charge is given.

Chattel: Any property except land and choses in action.

Chose in action: Property right enforceable by proceedings, e.g. a debt, a claim for damages, an insurance policy, copyright.

Collateral warranty: Separate contract often between an employer and sub-contractor to overcome the absence of privity of contract.

Completion contract: Contract entered into with a new contractor after the original contractor's failure to complete.

Compulsory liquidation: Formal court-based insolvency procedure started by winding-up petition.

Construction (of a contract): Ascertaining the intention of the parties by interpreting the words used.

Construction management: Means of procuring construction work by employing a contractor to manage the work where the employer rather than the contractor enters into contract with sub-contractors.

Contingent liability: Liability under an existing obligation subject to a contingency which may or may not happen.

Contract sum: The sum for which a contractor agrees to carry out construction work.

Contractor: Person or company that carries out or procures construction work for an employer.

Contractor's employment: The contractor's right and duty to carry out the works.

Conversion: Tort of interfering with another's goods.

Cost-plus contract: Contract where the contractor is paid his costs plus an agreed percentage for overheads and profit.

Court of Session: High Court (Scotland)

Crown debts: Debts owed to the government, e.g. VAT, National Insurance contributions, PAYE.

Crystallisation: Conversion of a floating charge into a fixed charge.

Debt: Right to payment of money enforceable by action.

Deceit: Tort of fraudulent misrepresentation.

Declarator: A declaration by the court of a person's right, made in an action for declarator. The declarator does not itself actually enforce the rights (Scotland).

Decree: The judgment of a court or arbiter (arbitrator) in civil procedings (Scotland).

Defects liability period: Period between practical completion and final completion on a building contract.

Defender: Defendant (Scotland).

Delict: Tort (Scotland).

Diligence: The methods of obtaining security and/or enforcing unpaid debts due under decrees of the Scottish courts.

Direct payment: Payment made by an employer to a sub-contractor or a supplier by-passing the contractor.

Disqualification: Procedure resulting in a court order forbidding a director from acting in the management of a company for a specific period.

Disruption: Interference to the regular progress of construction work, measured by the degree of alteration caused to the contractor's programme.

Dividend: Proportion of creditor's debt receivable from an insolvency procedure where the assets are insufficient to pay the debt in full.

Employer: Client who wishes to procure construction work.

Entire contract: Contract where nothing becomes payable to the contractor until it is substantially completed.

Equitable assignment: Transfer of personal property where formalities have not been complied with.

Equitable set-off: Set-off of a cross-claim so closely connected with the claim it would be unjust not to allow the set-off.

Equity of redemption: The right of a debtor to recover property offered as security on performing the secured obligation.

Estimator: Person employed by contractor to prepare and cost tenders.

Execution: Enforcement of a judgment by the seizure and sale of the assets of the judgment debtor.

Factoring: Sale of debts for less than their face value in return for immediate payment.

Fixed charge: Charge over a specific asset preventing its owner from dealing with it in the ordinary course of business.

Floating charge: Charge over an asset permitting its owner to deal with it in the ordinary course of business.

Fluctuations clause: Contractual term entitling a contractor to recover increases in the cost of labour and materials since the date of his tender.

Formal insolvency: Legal procedures under which an Insolvency Practitioner assumes control of a company or partnership or an individual's property for the benefit of creditors, e.g. receivership, liquidation, administration, bankruptcy.

Fraudulent trading: Carrying on business with intent to defraud creditors.

Furthcoming: An action raised for the recovery of money or property arrested in the hands of a third party (Scotland).

Garnishee: Person ordered to pay another's judgment creditor rather than his own creditor.

General law: Common law.

Going concern test: The ability to pay debts as they fall due.

Guarantee: Contract whereby a person agrees to answer for the debt or default of another.

Guarantor: Person who gives a guarantee.

Holdback: Fixed percentage retained from progress payments payable to a contractor for the benefit of persons unpaid by the contractor who are entitled to a lien on the property being developed (Canada).

Improvement: Building or other construction work added to land capable of generating a lien (United States, Canada).

Indemnity: Document giving right to compensation on the occurrence of an event.

Informal insolvency: Failure to pass either the going concern test or the balance sheet test.

Inhibition: An order by the Court of Session called "letters of inhibition", forbidding a debtor to burden or part with heritage to the prejudice of a creditor (Scotland).

Injunction: Court order compelling a person to act or preventing a person from acting in a particular way.

Insolvency: Inability to pay debts.

Insolvency Practitioner: Person licensed to act as Administrative Receiver, Liquidator: Administrator or Trustee in Bankruptcy.

Intellectual property rights: Rights protecting inventions, designs, drawings, e.g. copyright.

Interim certificate: Certificate issued by an architect or an engineer showing the amount payable by the employer in respect of the work done by the contractor during the previous month.

Interpleader: Court procedure whereby a person in possession of property not his own which is claimed by two or more persons can apply to the court to decide who owns it.

Knock-on effect: Phenomenon where a company or an individual becomes insolvent as a consequence of the insolvency of another.

Legal assignment: Transfer of personal property which complies with the formalities of the Law of Property Act 1925.

Legal set-off: Set-off of independent mutual debts which are both liquidated or ascertainable by the time the defence is due.

Letter of intent: Written instruction to a contractor to commence work against an undertaking to pay a reasonable sum for it if a contract is never concluded with the employer.

Licence to the site: Right to temporary possession of a construction site for the purpose of carrying out the works.

Lien: (1) Security interest entitling holder to retain property until payment. (2) "Mechanics' lien": a contractor's charge on the employer's property as security for payment (United States, Canada).

Liquidated and ascertained damages: A genuine pre-estimate of loss agreed by the parties in advance.

Liquidation: Formal insolvency procedure leading to the dissolution of the company.

Liquidation set-off: Mandatory set-off of all mutual dealings where one party is in liquidation.

Liquidator: Insolvency Practitioner appointed to conduct a liquidation.

Loss and expense: Compensation payable to the contractor under the terms of a construction contract for delay or disruption to the work.

Main contract: Construction contract between the employer and the contractor.

Maintenance period: Period between substantial completion and final completion on an engineering contract.

Management contract: Means of procurement whereby the contractor does no site work but manages the works entering into sub-contracts for that purpose.

Mechanics' lien: A form of charge on the employer's property to secure payment to a person who has provided work or materials for the project (United States, Canada).

Misfeasance: A claim against a director for breach of duty owed to the company brought by a liquidator.

Mitigation of loss: Minimising loss caused by breach of contract by acting reasonably.

Moratorium: Suspension of creditors' rights for an agreed period.

Mortgage: Form of security where property is transferred to a creditor on terms that it be transferred back to the debtor after the debt is paid or the secured obligation is performed.

Mutuality: The position where two persons have claims against each other in the same capacity.

NHBC: National House-Builders' Council.

Negative pledge: Contractual term where a person agrees not to grant security over his assets.

Negligence: Tort of breach of a duty of care.

Negotiated contract: Contract where an employer agrees a construction contract with a contractor without inviting tenders.

Nemo dat quod non habet: Legal maxim meaning: "you cannot give what you do not have".

Nominated sub-contractor: Sub-contractor appointed on an architect's instruction expending a prime cost sum.

Non-assignment clause: A contractual term restricting the transfer of the benefit of the contract.

Notice of assignment: Notice given by an assignee to a debtor following an assignment removing the debtor's right to obtain a good discharge by paying the assignor.

Novation: Three-way agreement where one party to a contract is released by the other in consideration of a third person agreeing to be bound as if it had been named as a party originally.

Official Referee: Former name of a judge in the Queen's Bench Division of the High Court designated to hear construction disputes (now designated as judges of the Technology and Construction Court).

***Pari passu* rule:** Rule that all unsecured creditors are paid the same proportion of their debts out of sums remaining after payment of secured and preferential creditors and the costs and expenses of the liquidation.

Pay when paid clause: Clause in a sub-contract that the sub-contractor will become entitled to payment only after the contractor has been paid (also known as a "contingent payment" clause).

Payee: Person to whom money is paid.

Penalty: Contractual term imposing financial consequences out of proportion to the breach which activates it.

Permanent works: Construction works forming the subject matter of an engineering contract where FIDIC or ICE is used (see Table of Standard Forms).

Pledge: Form of security where possession of property is given to a creditor as security for payment of a debt, entitling the creditor to sell the chattel if the debtor defaults.

Post-petition disposal: Disposal of property by a company after the issue of a winding-up petition against it which is void unless validated by the court.

Practical completion: Completion of building work to a stage where the employer can go into occupation.

Preference: Payment made to a creditor (or surety of a creditor) within a defined period before the start of liquidation or bankruptcy which is influenced by the desire to improve the creditor's position in that event.

Preferential debt: Class of debt given priority by the Insolvency Act 1986 over amounts due to the holder of a floating charge or to unsecured creditors.

Prime cost sum: Amount included in a construction contract to be expended on work to be carried out by a nominated sub-contractor.

Privity of contract: Rule of law that only a party to a contract can sue or be sued under it.

Procurement: Contractual method chosen for the construction process (e.g. management contract).

Progress payment: Periodic payment made by an employer to the contractor on account of the contract sum.

Proof of debt: Creditor's claim to have a debt admitted by a liquidator.

Proprietary right: A right or interest in property.

Provisional liquidator: Liquidator appointed by the court in urgent situations before a winding-up petition is heard.

Provisional sum: Sum inserted in a construction contract to cover work whose scope is uncertain at the time of tender.

Pursuer: Plaintiff (Scotland).

Quantity surveyor: Person qualified to prepare bills of quantity and measure and value construction work.

Quantum meruit: Reasonable sum for work done and materials supplied at the request of another.

Quicquid plantatur solo, solo cedit: Legal maxim meaning 'anything fixed to the land becomes part of it'.

Receivable: Sum payable or to become payable.

Receiver: Person appointed by a secured creditor to enforce security.

Receivership: Procedure for the enforcement of a security by the appointment of a receiver over the asset charged.

Remeasurement contract: Contract where the contract sum is not ascertained until after completion when the work done is valued by an engineer.

Repudiation: Conduct by one party to a contract showing an intention no longer to be bound by its terms entitling the other to claim damages or to compel the other's performance.

Reputed ownership: Bankruptcy concept (now repealed) whereby goods apparently in the ownership of a bankrupt could be claimed by a trustee in bankruptcy in priority to the real owner.

Retainage: American word for retention.

Retention: Fixed percentage of the contract sum withheld from each progress payment until the end of a construction contract.

Retention of title: Term in a sale of goods contract where the seller withholds ownership until the goods have been paid for.

Retention trust: Term contained in some building contracts that the employer holds the retention on trust for the contractor.

Right of re-entry: Right to enter on another's property for the purpose of re-possessing goods or land.

Ring-fencing: Protecting a company or an asset from the effects of insolvency.

Secured creditor: Creditor with a security interest in the debtor's property.

Security for costs: Court procedure where a plaintiff who is insolvent can be ordered to pay money into court in respect of the defendant's costs as a condition of continuing its claim.

Security interest: An interest in another's property enforceable in the event of default but which comes to an end if the obligation secured is performed.

Set-off: Procedure whereby a debtor pays a debt by using its own claim against its creditor.

Shadow director: A person in accordance with whose instructions and directions the directors are accustomed to act.

Sheriff: Judge (Scotland).

Sheriff court: County court (Scotland).

Specific performance: Court action to compel the carrying out of a contract.

Standard forms: Agreed forms of contract published by industry bodies comprising the parties involved in construction work.

Statutory demand: Demand for payment of a debt which is due and payable and exceeds £750 non-compliance with which deems the debtor to be insolvent.

Statutory scheme: Order of priority of payment to creditors in a liquidation laid down by the Insolvency Act 1986.

Sub-contractor: Individual, partnership or company to whom a contractor contracts out part of the work.

Substantial completion: *See* Practical completion.

Summary judgment: Court procedure for obtaining final judgment at an early stage in the action.

Surety: See Guarantor.

Temporary works: Works of a temporary nature necessary to construct the permanent works on an engineering contract.

Trustee: A person who holds property on behalf of another.

Trustee in bankruptcy: Insolvency Practitioner appointed by the court to conduct the bankruptcy of an individual.

Under-certification: Where an architect or engineer includes as the gross value of the contractor's work a sum less than the true value of the work properly done.

Vesting clause: Contractual term giving the employer a security interest or proprietary right in the contractor's plant or materials.

Voluntary liquidation: Form of liquidation initiated by the directors in which the creditors choose the liquidator.

Winding-up petition: Document presented to the court seeking a compulsory liquidation.

Work and materials contract: Contract for the supply and fixing of goods.

Wrongful trading: Civil claim brought by a liquidator against directors for compensation in respect of credit incurred by the company after the date when they knew or must have known there was no reasonable prospect of avoiding insolvent liquidation.

· Bibliography ·

Chapter 1: The Construction Industry

Acland, A: (1990) *A Sudden Outbreak of Common Sense*, Hutchinson Business Books, London

Baden Hellard, R: (1988) *Managing Construction Conflict*, Longman, London

Ball, M: (1990) *Rebuilding Construction*, Routledge, London

Banwell: (1964) *The Placing and Management of Contracts for Building and Civil Engineering Work*, HMSO

Bowdery, M: (1997)"New age contracts" in Uff, J (ed) *Construction Contract Reform: A Plea for Sanity*, Construction Law Press, King's College, London

Davis, Langdon and Everest: (1996), *Contracts in Use: A Survey of Building Contracts in Use During 1995*, The Royal Institution of Chartered Surveyors

CIEC (Construction Industry Employers Council): (1994) Final Report by the CIEC to Sir Michael Latham

DoE (Department of the Environment): (1990) *Housing and Construction Statistics 1979-1989: Great Britain*, HMSO

DETR (Department of the Environment, Transport and the Regions): Construction Market Intelligence Division, http:// www. construction. detr.gov.uk

Fenn, P and O'Shea, M and Davies, E: (1998) *Dispute Resolution and Conflict Management: An International Review*, E & F N Spon, London

Ferry and Brandon: (1983) *Cost Planning of Buildings*, Granada, London

Fleming M C: (1980) *Construction and the Related Professions,* Pergamon Press

Harvey, J: (1992) *Urban Land Economics*, Macmillan

Higgins and Jessop: (1965) *Communications in the Construction Industry*, The Tavistock Institute, London

Hillebrandt, P: (1984) *Analysis of the British Construction Industry*, Macmillan

Hillebrandt, P: (1985) *Economic Theory and the Construction Industry*, 2nd ed, Macmillan

Hillebrandt, P and Cannon, J (eds): (1989) *The Management of Construction Firms: Aspects of Theory*, Macmillan

Hillebrandt, P and Cannon, J: (1990) *The Modern Construction Firm*, Macmillan

Hillebrandt, P and Cannon, J and Lansley, P: (1995) *The Construction Company in and out of Recession*, Macmillan

Ison, W: (1978) *The Georgian Buildings of Bristol*, Kingsmead Press, Bath

Ison, W: (1980) *The Georgian Buildings of Bath*, Kingsmead Press, Bath

Latham, M: (1994), *Constructing the Team*, HMSO, London.

Mackie, K J: (1991), *A Handbook of Dispute Resolution*, CEDR, London.

Raftery, J: (1991) *Principles of Building Economics*, BSP, London

Smith and Wiede Nebbeling: (1986) *The Shadow Economy in Britain and Germany*, Anglo-German Foundation, London

Tillotson, J: (1985), *Contract Law in Perspective*, Butterworths, London

World Bank: (1984), *The Construction Industries: Issues and Strategies*, World Bank, Washington DC.

Chapter 2: Financial Protection

Goode, R M: (1988) *Legal Problems of Credit and Security*, 2nd ed, Sweet & Maxwell

Halsbury's Laws of England, 4th ed, Butterworths, London

Hughes, W, Hillebrandt, P and Murdoch, J: (1998) *Financial Protection in the UK Building Industry*, E & F N Spon, London

Jones, D F: (1992)"How the construction contract can protect those in the construction industry from the effects of insolvency" (1992) 8 BCL 246

Kharbanda, O P and Stallworthy, E A: (1983) *How to Learn from Project Disasters: True-Life Stories with a Moral for Management*, Gower

Kharbanda, O P and Stallworthy, E A: (1986) *Management Disasters and How to Prevent Them*, Gower

Latham, M: (1993)"Trust and money", unpublished paper

Latham, M: (1994), *Constructing the Team*, HMSO, London.

Lightman, G and Moss, G: (1994) *The Law of Receivers of Companies*, 2nd ed, Sweet & Maxwell

May, A: (1995) *Keating on Building Contracts*, 6th ed, Sweet & Maxwell

Neate, F W: (ed): (1990) *Using Set-off as Security*, Graham & Trotman and International Bar Association

Odams, AM: (1996)"Lien, charge and payment security" in *Security for Payment*, Davis R and Odams A M, (eds) Construction Law Press, King's College, London

Oditah, F: (1992)"Assets and the treatment of claims in insolvency" (1992) 108 LQR 459

Wallace, I N D: (1995) *Hudson's Building and Engineering Contracts*, 11th ed, Sweet & Maxwell

Wallace, I N D: (1986) *Construction Contracts: Principles and Policies in Tort and Contract*, Sweet & Maxwell

Chapter 3: Payment

Banwell: (1964) *The Placing and Management of Contracts for Building and Civil Engineering Work*, HMSO

Cork, K: (1982) *Insolvency Law and Practice: Report of the Review Committee*, HMSO

County NatWest Securities: (1991) *Cash flow update* 1990/1991

Davis, R: (1996)"Insolvency and the bill", *Building*, 22 March 1996

DoE (Department of the Environment): (1995) *Fair Construction Contracts*

Goldsmith, I and Heintzman, TG: (1988) *Goldsmith on Canadian Building Contracts*, 4th ed, Carswell

Goode, R M: (1983) *Payment Obligations in Commercial and Financial Transactions*, Sweet & Maxwell

Goode, R M: (1988) *Legal Problems of Credit and Security*, 2nd ed, Sweet & Maxwell

Halsbury's Laws of England, 4th ed, Butterworths, London

Hayton, D: (1994 CLY)"The significance of equity in construction contracts" [1994] 2 Con L Yb 19

Hillebrandt, P and Cannon, J (eds): (1989) *The Management of Construction Firms: Aspects of Theory*, Macmillan

Hosie, J:"How will pay when paid clauses be affected by the Construction Act?" (1997) 8(7) *Construction Law* 236

Hughes, W, Hillebrandt, P and Murdoch, J: (1998) *Financial Protection in the UK Building Industry*, E & F N Spon, London

Keating, D: (1983)"Sub-contracts under English law" in *Selected Problems of Construction Law: International Approach*, University Press, Fribourg and Sweet & Maxwell

Lloyd's Bowmaker: (1990) *Performance Comparisons*

Lyndon, R: (1996)"Can a contractor's failure to perform a contractual obligation constitute an acceptance of an anticipatory breach by the employer?", Society of Construction Law paper

McCosker, B: (1995) "Back to back payment clauses: 'if and when'" [1995] CILL 1029

McGuinness, K P: (1983) *Construction Lien Remedies In Ontario*, Carswell Legal Publications

Murphy, H J: (1989)"Pay when paid clauses in construction sub-contracts: conditions precedent or terms of payment?" (1989) 4 ICLR 207

Oditah, F: (1991) *Legal Aspects of Receivables Financing*, Sweet & Maxwell

Pilcher, R: (1985) *Project Cost Control in Construction*, Collins

Price, J: (1994) *Sub-Contracting under the JCT Standard Forms of Building Contract*, MacMillan

Salinger, F R: (1991) *Factoring Law and Practice*, Sweet & Maxwell

Stebbings, S:"Performance bonds" (1997/8) 8(10) *Construction Law* 336

Sweet, J: (1994) *Legal Aspects of Architecture, Engineering and the Construction Process*, 5th ed, West Publishing Company

Upson, A: (1987) *Financial Management for Contractors*, BSP Professional Books

Wood, P R: (1989) *English and International Set-Off*, Sweet & Maxwell

Wright, J D: (1997)"Credit insurance for the construction industry" (1997) 8(1) *Construction Law* 25

Chapter 4: Plant and Materials

Ballard, D: (1994)"Payment for materials or goods not yet incorporated into the works" (1994) 10 Const LJ 203

Barber, P: (1998)"Title to goods, materials and plant under construction contracts" in Palmer N, McKendrick, E (eds) *Interests in Goods*, 2nd ed, LLP, London

Buckland, WW: (1963) *A Textbook of Roman Law from Augustus to Justinian*, Cambridge University Press

Cooper, D: (1991)"Retaining title to fixtures" (1991) 4 Auckland Univ LR 477

Crowther: (1971) Report on the Committee on Consumer Credit, Cmnd 4596

RIBA: (1978) *Retention of Title (Ownership) by Suppliers of Building Materials and Goods*, RIBA

Feld: (1992)"Retention of title: Seller v Receiver", (1992) LSG 1 July

Goode, R M: (1989) *Proprietary Rights in Insolvency and Sales Transactions*, Sweet & Maxwell

Goode, R M: (1995) *Commercial Law*, 2nd ed, Penguin, London

Goode, R M: (1997) *Principles of Corporate Insolvency Law*, 2nd ed, Sweet & Maxwell

Goode, R M: (1992)"Bills of sale" in *Halsbury's Laws of England*, 4th ed, Butterworths, London

Goodhart, W and Jones, G: (1980)"The infiltration of equitable developments into English commercial law" (1980) 43 MLR 489

Guest, A G and Lever, J: (1963)"Hire-purchase, equipment leases and fixtures" (1963) 27 Conv 30

Holdsworth, W: (1956) *A History of English Law*, 7th ed, Methuen, London

Hudson, A: (1891) *The Law of Building and Engineering Contracts*, 1st ed, Sweet & Maxwell, London

ICC (International Chamber of Commerce): (1993) *Retention of Title*, 2nd ed, Publication No 501

Latham, M: (1994) *Constructing the Team*, HMSO, London.

McCormack, G: (1995) *Reservation of Title*, 2nd ed, Sweet & Maxwell, London

Newman, P: (1998)"Plant vesting under civil engineering contracts" (1998) 9(6) *Construction Law* 195

Palmer, N: (1996)"ICE (5th) conditions: title to plant and contractor's insolvency" (1996) 13 BLM 1

Palmer, N: (1997)"Employer's rights over plant: Cosslett in the Court of Appeal" (1997) 14 BLM 1

Parris, J: (1986) *Effective Retention of Title Clauses*, Collins

Pike, A: (1982) *Engineering Tenders, Sales and Contracts*, E & F N Spon and Sweet & Maxwell

Tettenborn, A M:"Reservation of title: insolvency and priority problems" (1981) JBL 173

Wallace, I N D: (1995) *Hudson's Building and Engineering Contracts*, 11th ed, Sweet & Maxwell

Weathered, J: (1992)"Administrative receivers and leased assets" (1992) 8 IL & P 3

Williams G A: (1987)"Reservation of title in the construction industry: who wants it: some economic perspectives on risk allocation" (1987) 40 *Current Legal Problems* 233

Wylie, O P: (1978)"Reservation of ownership: a means of protection for unsecured creditors of bankrupt builders" (1978) 42 Conv 37

Chapter 5: Set-Off, Abatement and Deduction

Aeberli, P: (1992)"Abatements, set-offs and counterclaims in arbitration proceedings" [1992] ADRLJ 130

Barrett, K J: (1998)"Withholding payment under the Housing Grants, Construction and Regeneration Act 1996" (1998) 14 Const LJ 180

Bowles, S and Reingold, J: (1999)"Channel Tunnel Rail-Link: all aboard for the restructuring" (1999) 10 *Practical Law for Companies* 21

Derham, S R: (1996) *Set-Off*, 2nd ed, Clarendon Press, Oxford

Farrer, J H: (1970)"Contracting out of set-off" (1970) 120 NLJ 771

Furmston, M, Norisada, T and Poole, J: (1998) *Contract Formation and Letters of Intent*, John Wiley & Sons

Gardner, S: (1996)"Knowing assistance and knowing receipt: taking stock" (1996) 112 LQR 56

Goode R M: (1990)"Formation of contracts and pre-contractual liability" in ICC Publication No 440/9

Goode, R M: (1988) *Legal Problems of Credit and Security*, 2nd ed, Sweet & Maxwell

Jones, D: (1990) "Bonds in relation to the formation of contracts and their possible confiscation" in ICC Publication No 440/9

Jones, N F: (1999) *Set-Off in the Construction Industry*, 2nd ed, Blackwell Science

Judge, J A M and Grottenthaler, M E: (1991)"Legal and equitable set-offs" (1991) 70 Can Bar Rev 91

LLoyd H: (1992)"Hong Kong rejects weak set-off link", *Building*, 1 May 1992

McKendrick, E: "Unascertained goods: ownership and obligation distinguished" (1994) 110 LQR 509

Meagher, R P, Gummow, W M C, and Lehane, J R F: (1992) *Equity: Doctrines and Remedies*, 3rd ed, Butterworths, Sydney

Neate, F W (ed): (1990) *Using Set-Off as Security* (Graham & Trotman and International Bar Association)

Shea, A: (1986)"Statutory set-off" [1986] 3 JIBL 152

Spry, I C F: (1969)"Equitable set-offs" (1969) ALJ 265

Uff, J (ed): (1997) *Construction Contract Reform: A Plea for Sanity*, Construction Law Press

Wood, P R: (1989) *English and International Set-Off*, Sweet & Maxwell

Chapter 6: Trust and Transferability

Allcock, R: (1983)"Restrictions on the assignment of contractual rights" (1983) CLJ 328

Cartwright, J: (1990)"The assignment of collateral warranties" (1990) 6 Const LJ 14

Cartwright, J: (1993) "Remedies in respect of defective buildings after *Linden Gardens*" (1993) 9 Const LJ 281

Chitty on Contracts: (1994) 27th ed, Sweet and Maxwell, London

Davis, R: (1996)"Payment issues and legislation" in *Security for Payment*, Davis, R and Odams A M, (eds) Construction Law Press, King's College, London

Goode, R M: (1979)"Inalienable rights?" (1979) 42 MLR 553

Goode, R M: (1976)"The right to trace and its impact in commercial transactions: Part I" (1976) 92 LQR 360, (Part II) (1976) 92 LQR 528

Hayton, D J: (1994)"The significance of equity in construction contracts" [1994] 2 Con L Yb 19

Hayton, D J: (1995) *Underhill and Hayton: Law Relating to Trusts and Trustees*, 15th ed, Butterworths, London

Jones, G and Goodhart, W: (1996) *Specific Performance*, 2nd ed, Butterworths

Latham, M: (1994), *Constructing the Team*, HMSO, London

McCormack, G: (1997) *Proprietary Claims and Insolvency*, Sweet & Maxwell, London

Megens, P and Ang, B: (1994)"Assignment, novation and sub-contracting: who cares what you call it?" [1994] BCL 319.

Millett, P J: (1991)"Tracing the proceeds of fraud" (1991) 107 LQR 71

Prentice, G: (1983)"Remedies of building sub-contractors against employers" (1983) 46 MLR 409

Stebbings, S: (1997/98) "Performance bonds" (1997/8) 8(10) Construction Law 336

Tettenborn A M: (1987)"Fraud, cross-claims and the assignment of choses in action" (1987) Conv 358

Chapter 7: Informal Insolvency

Adamson, S: (1991) "Restructuring", unpublished paper

Banwell: (1964) *The Placing and Management of Contracts for Building and Civil Engineering Work*, HMSO

BCIS (Building Cost Information Service): (1994) BCIS News No 74, September 1994

Ernst & Young: UK GAAP *(Generally Accepted Accounting Practice in the United Kingdom)*, 6th ed, 1999

Goode, R M: (1988) *Legal Problems of Credit and Security*, 2nd ed, Sweet & Maxwell

Goode, R M: (1997) *Principles of Corporate Insolvency Law*, 2nd ed, Sweet & Maxwell,

Grant Thornton: (1999) *Industry Watch on Construction*

Hillebrandt, P M: (1977)"Going bust: what are the facts?" (1977) 232 *Building* 52-53

Hillebrandt, P M: (1984) *Analysis of the British Construction Industry*, MacMillan

Kent, P: (1997)"Corporate workouts – a UK perspective" (1997) 6 Int Insolv Rev 165

Lee Beng Tat: (1993)"Claiming a pound of flesh as a contingent or prospective creditor under the Companies Act" [1993] *Singapore Journal of Legal Studies* 144

Morrell, D: (1987) *Indictment: Power and Politics in the Construction Industry*, Faber and Faber

Oditah, F: (1995)"Winding-up recalcitrant debtors" [1995] LMCLQ 107

RICS: *Statements of Asset Valuation Practice and Guidance Notes*, 3rd ed, (RICS, 1990)

Slatter, F: (1984) *Corporate Recovery: A Guide to Turnaround Management*, Penguin Books, London

SPI (Society of Practitioners of Insolvency): (1999) Company Insolvency in the United Kingdom

Summerson, J: (1978) *Georgian London*, 3rd ed, Barrie & Jenkins, London

Totty, P and Moss, G: (1986) Insolvency, Longman

White, J: (1998)"Rescue v Insolvency: the lawyer's perspective", unpublished paper

Chapter 8: Formal Insolvency

Anderson, L R and Anderson, J C:"The construction industry looks at the new Bankruptcy Code" (1981) 1(3) *The Construction Lawyer* 1

Bennett:"Anticipating what happens when the project turns sour: bankruptcy or receivership" (1988) 26 CLR 141

Bennett:"The insolvency of a general contractor on a construction project" (1990) 35 CLR 256

Blanchard, P: (1989)"The contracts of a company in receivership" (1989) NZ Univ LR 237

Brown, D: (1996) *Corporate Rescue: Insolvency Law in Practice*, John Wiley & Sons

Cork, K: (1982) *Insolvency Law and Practice: Report of the Review Committee*, HMSO

Griffin, D S and Macauley, W F: (1983)"General contractor in Wonderland: selected problems in reorganisation under the Bankruptcy Code" (1983) 4(3) *The Construction Lawyer* 1; 4(4) 3

Grogan, F: (1992)"A review of the administration order procedure in the context of the construction industry incorporating case studies", unpublished thesis, King's College, London

Hillebrandt, P and Cannon, J (eds): (1989) *The Management of Construction Firms: Aspects of Theory*, Macmillan

Homan, M: (1989) *A Survey of Administration under the Insolvency Act 1986: The Result of Administration Orders Made in 1987*, Institute of Chartered Accountants in England and Wales

Hunter, M: (1988) *Muir Hunter on Personal Insolvency*, Stevens & Sons

Hunter, M and Graham, D: (1979) *Williams and Muir Hunter on Bankruptcy*, 19th ed, Stevens & Sons

Institute of Chartered Accountants in England and Wales: (199*) *Company Investigations*

Lightman, G and Moss, G: (1994) *The Law of Receivers of Companies*, 2nd ed, Sweet & Maxwell

Moss, G: (1998)"Administration orders really do work", unpublished paper

Oditah, F: (1991) *Legal Aspects of Receivables Financing*, Sweet & Maxwell

Phillips, M: (1996)"The administration procedure and creditors' voluntary arrangements: the case for radical reform", *Insolvency Lawyer*, June 1996, p 14

Simmons, M: (1996)"The statutory declaration of solvency: voluntary winding-up of companies: members or creditors? (1996) 9 *Insolvency Intelligence* 33

SPI (Society of Practitioners of Insolvency): (1993) Bulletin 17

SPI: (1999) Company Insolvency in the United Kingdom

Totty, P and Crystal, M: (1982) *Corporate Insolvency*, McGraw-Hill

Upson, A: (1987) *Financial Management for Contractors*, BSP Professional Books

White, J: (1998) "Rescue v Insolvency: The Lawyer's Perspective", unpublished paper

Chapter 9: Termination

Beale H:"Penalties in termination provisions" (1988) 104 LQR 355

Bridge S, Candi, E and Wyburn, M: "Copyright and architecture" (1987) BCL 94

Burke T M: (1986) "The liability of the contractor for late completion" in LLoyd, H (ed) *The Liability of Contractors*, Longman,

Carter J W: "The effect of discharge of a contract on the assessment of damages for breach or repudiation" (1989) JCL 113 and 249

Carter J W: "Termination clauses" (1990) 3 JCL 90

Carter, J W: (1991) *Breach of Contract*, 2nd ed, Sweet & Maxwell, London

Cohen, A: (1999) "Counterparty risk – termination of contracts on insolvency [1999] 1 *Insolv* L 26

Countryman: "Executory contracts in bankruptcy" (1973) 57 Minn LR 439; (1974) 58 Minn LR 479

Delemore, C L: (1994) *Copyright Explained*, RIBA Publications, London

Jones, G and Goodhart, W: (1996) *Specific Performance*, 2nd ed, Butterworths

Homan, M: (1989) *A Survey of Administration under the Insolvency Act 1986: The Result of Administration Orders Made in 1987*, Institute of Chartered Accountants in England and Wales

Keating, D: (1986) "Employer's remedy for delay: termination" in LLoyd, H (ed) *The Liability of Contractors*, Longman,

Knox, J A: "What constitutes a default sufficient to justify termination of the contract: the surety's perspective" (1981) 2(1) *The Construction Lawyer*, 1

LLoyd, H: (1990) "Termination clauses, worth more than a moment's thought", *Building*, 25 May 1990

Meyers, R L and Albers, M F: (1984) "The contractor in bankruptcy: protecting the interests of the owner" (1984) 5(2) *The Construction Lawyer*, 1

Nimmer, R T: (1983) "Executory contracts in bankruptcy: protecting the fundamental terms of the bargain" (1983) 54 Univ of Colorado Law Rev 507

Oditah, F: (1992) "Assets and the treatment of claims in insolvency" (1992) 108 LQR 459

Opeskin, R: (1990) "Damages for breach of contract terminated under express terms" (1990) 106 LQR 293

Rubin, R A: (1984) "Bankruptcy from the vantage point of the contractor" (1984) 5(2) *The Construction Lawyer*, 9

Rubino-Sammartano, M: (1983) "International construction agreements: employer's breach and consequent right of the contractor to withhold delivery of the site" (1983) IBL 143

Sheak, J C and Korzun, T J: "Liquidated damages and the surety: are they defensible?" (1989) 9(2) *The Construction Lawyer*, 19

Sims, J and Powell-Smith, V: (1985) *Determination and Suspension of Construction Contracts*, Collins

Totty, P and Moss, G: (1986) *Insolvency*, Longman

Van Deventer, R: (1993) *The Law of Construction Contracts*, John Wiley & Sons

Wheeler, P: (1991) "Copyright in construction drawings and works of architecture" (1991) 7 Const LJ 75

Wheeler, P: (1994) "Copyright – the Cinderella of construction agreements - Part 2" (1994) 5(1) *Construction Law* 27

Wheeler, P and Boyson, K: (1999) "Copyright – an accident waiting to happen?" (1999) 10(5) *Construction Law* 24

Chapter 10: Novation and Completion Contracts

Chitty on Contracts: (1994) 27th ed, Sweet and Maxwell, London

Halsbury's Laws of England, 4th ed, Butterworths, London

McDevitt, K: (1985) *Contract Bonds and Guarantees*, CIOB

McNicholas, P: (1993) "Novation of consultants to design build contractors" (1993) 9 Const LJ 263

RICS: (1997) Construction Insolvency Information Paper

Megens, P and Ang, B: (1994) "Assignment, novation and sub-contracting – who cares what you call it?" [1994] BCL 319

Newman, P: (1992) *Insolvency Explained*, RIBA Publications, London

Scott, K and Reynolds, B: (1994) *Scott and Reynolds on Surety Bonds*, Carswell Legal Publications, Toronto

Capon, G: (1990) *Construction Industry*, Institute of Chartered Accountants in England and Wales

Chapter 11: Trust Claims

Anderson, H: (1992) "The treatment of trust assets in English insolvency law" in McKendrick, E (ed) *Commercial Aspects of Trusts and Fiduciary Obligations*, Clarendon Press, Oxford

Critchlow, J and Mulla, Z: (1996) "Nominated sub-contractors: the trouble with name-borrowing" (1996) 7(3) *Construction Law* 96

Dean, C: (1996) "The JCT retention trust: an effective means of protecting a contractor's right to his own money?" in *Security for Payment*, Davis, R and Odams A M, (eds) Construction Law Press, King's College, London

Glaholt, D: (1999) *Construction Trusts*, Carswell Legal Publications, Toronto

Hayton, D J: (1994) "Uncertainty of subject-matter of trusts" (1994) 110 LQR 335

Hayton, D J: (1994) "The significance of equity in construction contracts" [1994] 2 Con L Yb 19

Hopper, R: (1996) "Construction sector retention survey" in *Security for Payment*, Davis, R and Odams, A M, (eds) Construction Law Press, King's College, London

Lightman, G and Moss, G: (1994) *The Law of Receivers of Companies*, 2nd ed, Sweet & Maxwell

Moss, G: (1992) "Retention trusts" (1992) 5 *Insolvency Intelligence* 25

Chapter 12: Direct Payment

Bridge, M G:"Company administrators and secured creditors" (1991) 107 LQR 394

Cushman, R F and Blick, G L: (1988) *Construction Industry Forms*, Wiley Law Publications

DoE (Department of the Environment): (1995)"Fair construction contracts": Consultation Paper issued by the Department of the Environment

European Commission: (1997)"The competitiveness of the construction sector"

Giocanti, X: (1986)"Security for performance: conditional and on-demand bonds: the position of French law" in LLoyd, H (ed) (1986) *The Liability of Contractors*, Longman

Goode, R M: (1988) *Legal Problems of Credit and Security*, 2nd ed, Sweet & Maxwell

HMSO (1974): Commentary on GC/Works/1

Latham, M: (1994) *Constructing the Team*, HMSO, London

McCormack, G: (1997) *Proprietary Claims and Insolvency*, Sweet & Maxwell, London

McGaw, M: (1994)"Insolvency, project integrity and the JCT Standard Forms" (1994) 10 Const LJ 266

Oditah, F: (1992)"Assets and the treatment of claims in insolvency" (1992) 108 LQR 459

Powell-Smith, V: (1991)"Payment of sub-contractors when main contractor is insolvent" [1991] 2 ICLR 241

Prentice, G: (1983)"Remedies of building sub-contractors against employers" (1983) 46 MLR 409

Totty, P and Moss, G: (1986) *Insolvency*, Longman

UN: (1988) UNCITRAL *Legal Guide on Drawing up International Contracts for the Construction of Industrial Works*, United Nations

Wallace, I N D: (1986) *Construction Contracts: Principles and Policies in Tort and Contract*, Sweet & Maxwell

Wood, P R: (1989) *English and International Set-Off*, Sweet & Maxwell

Chapter 13: Set-Off in Insolvency

Derham, R: (1996) *Set-Off*, 2nd ed, Clarendon Press, Oxford

Goode, R M: (1984)"The effect of a fixed charge on debts" [1984] JBL 172

Goode, R M: (1997) *Principles of Corporate Insolvency Law*, 2nd ed, Sweet & Maxwell, London

Grantham, R B: (1989)"The impact of a security interest on set-off" [1989] JBL 377

Oditah, F: (1991) *Legal Aspects of Receivables Financing*, Sweet & Maxwell, London

Tettenborn A M: (1987)"Fraud, cross-claims and the assignment of choses in action" (1987) Conv 358

Wood, P R: (1989) *English and International Set-Off*, Sweet & Maxwell, London

Chapter 14: Bonds and Guarantees

Andrews, G and Millett, R: (1995) *Law of Guarantees*, 2nd ed, FT Law & Tax

Bertrams, R: (1996) *Bank Guarantees in International Trade*, 2nd ed, Kluwer/ICC Publishing SA

Cahill, F: (1988)"Security for performance clauses" (1988) BCL 18

Capper, P: (1990)"Bonds and guarantees: their various types and problems" in *International and ICC Arbitration, Centre of Construction Law & Management*, King's College, London

CUP (Central Unit on Procurement): (1994) No 48 Bonds and Guarantees, HM Treasury

Chitty on Contracts: (1994) 27th ed, Sweet and Maxwell, London

DoE (Department of the Environment): (1996) *The Use of Performance Bonds in Government Construction Contracts, Inter-Departmental Work Group for the Construction Sponsorship Directorate of the Department of the Environment*

Goode, R M: (1986)"Unconditional bonds: the common law" in LLoyd, H (ed), *The Liability of Contractors*, Longman, London

Goode, R M: (1992) Guide to the ICC Uniform Rules for Demand Guarantees, No 510, ICC Publishing SA, Paris

Goode, R M: (1995) *Commercial Law*, 2nd ed, Penguin, London

Haley, G: (1999)"PFI contractors: some emerging principles" (1999) 15 Const LJ 220

Halsbury's Laws of England, 4th ed, Butterworths, London

Herzfeld, E:"Security for payments under major overseas projects" [1986] JBL 446

Horn, N: (ed): (1989) *The Law of International Trade Finance*, Kluwer

IBA (International Bar Association): (1992) *International Business Lawyer*, May 1992

ICC (International Chamber of Commerce): (1986) "Model Forms for Issuing Contract Guarantees" No 406

ICC: (1992) ICC Uniform Rules for Demand Guarantees, No 458, ICC Publishing SA, Paris

ICC: (1993) ICC Uniform Customs and Practice for Documentary Credits, No 500, ICC Publishing SA, Paris

ICC: (1993) ICC Uniform Rules for Contract Bonds, No 524, ICC Publishing SA, Paris

ICC: (1994) ICC Model Forms for Issuing Demand Guarantees, No 503E, ICC Publishing SA, Paris

Jack, R: (1993) *Documentary Credits*, 2nd ed, Butterworths

Jones, D: (1990) Section in *Formation of Contracts and Pre-Contractual Liability*, ICC Publication No 440/9

Kronfol, Z A: (1983-84)"Legal theory and practice of guarantee bonds in the Arabian Gulf" (1983-84) 1 ICLR 218

Latham, M: (1994), *Constructing the Team*, HMSO, London.

McDevitt, K: (1985) *Contract Bonds and Guarantees* (CIOB)

Moss G, and Marks, D: (1999) *Rowlatt on Principal and Surety*, 5th ed, Sweet & Maxwell, London

Muscat, A: (1996) *The Liability of the Holding Company for the Debts of its Insolvent Subsidiaries*, Dartmouth, Aldershot

NJCC (National Joint Consultative Committee for Building) (1995): Guidance Note 2: Performance Bonds

Petkovic, D: (1995)"The proper law of letters of credit" [1995] 4 JIBL 141.

Pierce, A: (1993) *Demand Guarantees in International Trade*, Sweet & Maxwell, London

Rowe, M: (1987) *Guarantees, Standby Letters of Credit and Other Securities*, Euromoney Publications

Rubino-Sammartano, M:"Performance bonds: primary or secondary obligations?" (1985) IBL 125

Rubino-Sammartano, M:"Performance bonds: injunctions" (1981) LSG, 4 February

Salzman, A: (1952) *Building in England Down to 1540*, Oxford University Press

Scott, K and Reynolds, P: (1994) *Scott & Reynolds on Surety Bonds*, Carswell Legal Publications, Toronto

Wallace I N D: (1986) *Construction Contracts: Principles and Policies in Tort and Contract*, Sweet & Maxwell

Wood, P R: (1995) *Comparative Law of Security and Guarantees*, Sweet & Maxwell, London

Wunnicke, D B and Turner, B S: (1996) *Standby and Commercial Letters of Credit*, John Wiley & Sons Inc

Chapter 15: Insolvency Claims

Anderson, H: (1992)"The treatment of trust assets in English insolvency law" in McKendrick, E (ed) *Commercial Aspects of Trusts and Fiduciary Obligations*, Clarendon Press, Oxford

Blackler, A: (1998)"Retention monies in UK building contracts" in Palmer N, McKendrick, E (eds) *Interests in Goods*, 2nd ed, LLP, London

Cork, K: (1982) *Insolvency Law and Practice: Report of the Review Committee*, HMSO

Davis, R: (1988)"Wrongful trading and the construction industry" (1988) 4 Const LJ 185

Goode, R M: (1997) *Principles of Corporate Insolvency Law*, 2nd ed, Sweet & Maxwell, London

Lingard, J: (1988) *Bank Security Documents*, 2nd ed, Butterworths, London

Milman, D and Parry, R: (1997) *A Study of the Operation of Transactional Avoidance Mechanisms in Corporate Insolvency Practice*, Insolvency Lawyers Association Research Report, GTI Specialist Publishers

Oditah, F: (1992) "Misfeasance proceedings against company directors" [1992] LMCLQ 207

Totty, P and Moss, G: (1986) *Insolvency*, Longman, London

Chapter 16: People

Clark, G de N: (1967) "Industrial law and the labour-only sub-contract" (1967) 30 MLR 6

Drake, C D: (1968) "Wage slave or entrepreneur?" (1968) 31 MLR 408

Inland Revenue Consultative Document: (1991) "Taxation of sub-contractors in the construction industry"

Hillebrandt, P M: (1971) *Small Firms in the Construction Industry*, HMSO

Mordsley, B I: (1975) "Some problems of the lump" (1975) 38 MLR 504

Phelps Brown, E H: (1968) Report of the Committee of Inquiry into Certain Matters Concerning Labour in Building and Civil Engineering, Cmnd 3714, HMSO

Pollard, D: (1994) Tolley's *Employment and Pension Rights in Corporate Insolvency*, Tolley, Croydon

Rear, J: (1972) "Self employment in the building industry" (1972) 2 HKLJ 150

Ryley, M and Goodwyn, E: (forthcoming) *Employment Law for the Construction Industry*, Thomas Telford, London

Sadler, L: (1999) "The CIS – what will the changes mean?" (1999) 10(5) *Construction Law* 16

Sealy, L S: (1993) *Disqualification and Personal Liability of Directors*, 4th ed, CCH Editions, Bicester

Tuite, T: (1983) *The Construction Industry Tax Deduction Scheme*, Tolley

Wallace, I N D: (1988) "The lump and the landlord as exits from Anns: the *D & F* case" (1988) 4 Const LJ 100

Wheeler, S and Wilson, G: (1998) *Directors' Liabilities in the Context of Corporate Groups*, GTI Specialist Publishers

Chapter 17: International Aspects

Australia

Cahill, F: (1988) "Security for performance clauses" (1988) BCL 18

Calvert, C A and Ingwalson, C F: (1998) "Pass through claims and liquidation agreements" (1998) 18(4) *The Construction Lawyer* 29

Dorter, J B and Sharkey, J J A: (1990) *Building and Construction Contracts in Australia: Law and Practice*, 2nd ed, Law Book Company, Sydney

Griffin, D S: (1997) "Post-termination bankruptcy considerations for the defaulted contractor" (1997) 17(1) *The Construction Lawyer* 24

Hendrick, D R, Spangler, J I and Wedge, R B: (1996) "Battling for the bucks: the great contingency payment clause debate" (1996) 16(3) *The Construction Lawyer* 12

Hill, W M and Evans, D M: (1998) "Pay when paid provisions: still a conundrum" (1998) 18(2) *The Construction Lawyer* 16

Hughes, L W and Dunning, B A: (1996): "Holding on to what you have been paid: defending a preference action against a contractor, sub-contractor or supplier" (1996) 16(1) *The Construction Lawyer* 15

Hunt, R: (1987)"Remedies of the builder: the use of caveats to secure payments under building contracts" (1987) 3 BCL 239

Kinsella, F: (1987)"The standard sub-contracts" (1987) 3 BCL 315

Kirksey, G B and Brown, S L: (1991/1992) "The pay-when-paid/pay-if-paid dichotomy and the Florida trilogy: bright line or murky fog?" (1991) 11(4) *The Construction Lawyer* 8; (1992) 12(1) *The Construction Lawyer* 1

Lance, S J: (1987)"Sub-contractors' charges legislation" (1987) 3 BCL 6

Lance, S J: (1988)"Re sub-contractors' rights: the Sub-Contractors' Charges Act 1974" (1988) 4 BCL 240

Law Reform Commission of Western Australia Project, No 54: Report on Contractors' Liens

Lewis, J T, Franks, J M and Rowland, J H: (1995) "Prepetition planning for contract sureties" (1995) 15(3) *The Construction Lawyer* 41

McGill, J G: (1994) "Bonds and arbitration" (1994) 14(2) *The Construction Lawyer* 18

Queensland Government: (1996) Discussion Paper:"Security of Payment in the Building and Construction Industry"

Queensland Government: (1997)"Securing our industry's future": Report of the Implementation Steering Committee on Security of Payment in the Queensland Building and Construction Industry

Sessler, R J: (1992) "Bottom of the totem pole: legal risks and payment problems of sub-contractors (1992) 12(4) *The Construction Lawyer* 23

Snider, W G: (1999) "Impaired bonding claims" (1999) 19(4) *The Construction Lawyer* 36

Stockenberg, R A and Woodbury, J S: (1996) "Retainage revisited: a time to revise and reform" (1996) 16(1) *The Construction Lawyer* 41

Zillmann, B: (1997) "A further erosion into the autonomy of bank guarantees?" (1997) 13 BCL 354

Canada

Baird, D E: (1978) "Statutory trusts liens priority over claims of secured creditors" (1978) 25 CBR 261

Bordan, G: (1989)"The law of construction privileges: corrective justice or distributive justice?" (1989) 2 Can J of Law and Juris 57

Ettinger, L P: (1989)"Trusts in the construction industry" (1989) 27 Alberta LR 390

Goldsmith, I and Heintzman, T G: (1988) *Goldsmith on Canadian Building Contracts*, 4th ed, Carswell Legal Publications, Toronto

Macklem, D N and Bristow, D I: (1990) *Construction Builders' and Mechanics' Liens in Canada*, 6th ed, Carswell Legal Publications, Toronto

McGuinness, K P: (1983) *Construction Lien Remedies in Ontario*, Carswell Legal Publications

Reynolds, B: (1996)"A Canadian approach to the minimisation of construction insolvencies" in *Security for Payment*, Davis R and Odams A M (eds), Construction Law Press, Kings College, London

Report of Ontario Law Reform Commission: The Mechanics' Lien Act 1966

England and Wales

Andrews, N H:"Does a third party beneficiary have a right in English law?" (1988) 8 *Legal Studies* 14

Davis, R: (1996)"Payment issues and legislation" in *Security for Payment*, Davis, R and Odams A M, (eds) Construction Law Press, King's College, London

Dean, C: (1996)"The JCT retention trust: an effective means of protecting a contractor's right to his own money?" in *Security for Payment*, Davis, R and Odams A M, Construction Law Press, King's College London

Fitzpatrick, F: (1991)"Retention funds in building contracts" (1991) NLJ 1007

Goode, R M:"The death of insolvency law" in *The Company Lawyer*, Vol 1, No 3, p 23

Goode, R M: (1983) *Payment Obligations in Commercial and Financial Transactions*, Sweet & Maxwell

Odams, A M: (1996)"Lien, charge and payment security" in *Security for Payment*, Davis R and Odams A M, (eds) Construction Law Press, King's College, London

Parris, J: (1985) *Default by Sub-Contractors and Suppliers*, Collins

Prentice, G H: (1983)"Remedies of building sub-contractors against employers" (1983) 46 MLR 409

Thomas, C: (1997)"Fair construction contracts: a reponse to the Consultation Paper" in Uff, J (ed) *Construction Contract Reform: A Plea for Sanity*, Construction Law Press, King's College, London

Ireland

Forde, M: (1990) *Bankruptcy Law in Ireland*, Mercier Press

Forde, M: (1992) *Company Law,* Round Hall, Sweet & Maxwell

Houghton, A R and Atkinson, N G (eds): (1993) *Guide to Insolvency in Europe*, CCH International

Keane, D: (1997) *The RIAI Contracts: A Working Guide*, 3rd ed, Royal Institute of Architects of Ireland

Keane, R: (1991) *Company Law in the Republic of Ireland*, 2nd ed, Butterworths

Lynch, I, Marshall, J and O'Ferrall, R: (1996) *Corporate Insolvency and Rescue: Law and Practice*, Butterworths

O'Donnell, J L: (1994) *Examinerships: The Companies (Amendment) Act 1990*, Oak Tree Press, Dublin

Sanfey, M and Holohan, W: (1992) *Bankruptcy Law and Practice in Ireland*, Round Hall, Sweet & Maxwell

Far East

Jewkes, R: (1988)"Sub-contracting under threat: a personal view" (1988) 5 ICLR 118

Robinson, N M, Lavers, A P and Tan, G K H: (1996) *Construction Law in Singapore and Malaysia*, 2nd ed, Butterworths

The Netherlands

Goudsmit: (1983-84)"Chain liability in the Netherlands" (1983-84) 1 ICRL 289

New Zealand

Smellie, R P: (1979) *Building Construction and Practice in New Zealand*, Butterworths

Scotland

Flint, D: (1990) *Liquidation in Scotland*, 2nd ed, Jordans

Houghton, A R and Atkinson, N G (eds): (1993) *Guide to Insolvency in Europe*, CCH International

Howlin, M: (1996) "English and Scots insolvency law: a comparative overview" (1996) *Insolvency Lawyer*, Special Issue, 21

Maher, G and Cusine, D J: (1990) *The Law & Practice of Diligence*, Butterworths

McKenzie Skene, D: (1998) "The past is a foreign country, they do things differently there" (1998) 14 IL & P 312

St Clair, J B and Drummond-Young, J E: (1992) *The Law of Corporate Insolvency in Scotland*, 2nd ed, Butterworths

Scottish Law Commission: (1982) Report on Bankruptcy and Related Aspects of Insolvency and Liquidation (No 68)

Scottish Law Commission: (1998) Report on Diligence on the Dependence and Admiralty Arrestments (No 164)

The Laws of Scotland: Stair Memorial Encyclopaedia: (1991) Vol 4, Butterworths

SBCC (Scottish Building Contract Committee): (1991) *Insolvency Practice Guide*

Wilson, W A and Forte, A D (eds): (1995) *Gloag & Henderson on The Law of Scotland*, 10th ed, W Green

South Africa

Loots, P C: (1985) *Engineering and Construction Law*, Juta & Co

Van Deventer, R: (1993) *The Law of Construction Contracts*, John Wiley & Sons

United States

Barrett, S R: (1988)"Joint check agreements" (1988) 8(7) *The Construction Lawyer* 6

Berman, J and Waitzer, E: (1980-81)"Which way to lien?" [1980-81] 5 Can Bus LJ 470

Berman, J and Waitzer, E: (1982-83)"Liening over backwards" [1982-83] 7 Can Bus LJ 129

Bocock, J H: (1978)"Oklahoma's trust fund provisions" (1978) 31 Oklahoma LR 199

Burch, J V: (1988)"Third party beneficiaries to the construction contract documents" (1988) 8(2) *The Construction Lawyer*, 1

Coleman, S L and Peltier, L J: (1980)"Mechanics' liens: review of Kentucky's statutory scheme" (1980) 68 Ky LJ 681

Comment [no author given]: (1958)"Mechanics' liens and surety bonds in the building trades" (1958) 68 Yale LJ 138

Cox, M and McCue, M: (1983)"The Nebraska Construction Lien Act: which way to lien?" (1983) 62 Neb LR 86

De Rungs, J A: (1983)"Statutory payment rights in public construction projects: South Dakota bond and lien rights" (1983) 29 S Dak LR 111

Dudley, F R, Buzzett, W A and Kearney, D K: (1991)"Construction lien law reform: the equilibrium of change" (1991) 18 Flo SULR 251

Frohlinger, T G: (1983)"Manitoba Builders Lien Act" (1983) Man LR 357

Gallagher, E G: (1990)"Unpaid sub-contractor's or supplier's right to payment out of contract funds" (1990) 10(1) *The Construction Lawyer*, 9

Gwyn, A H: (1990)"Contractor and sub-contractor payments" (1990) 8(1) *The Construction Lawyer*, 1

Keyes, M F: (1985)"The bankruptcy of public works contractors: what recourse for laborers, sub-contractors, and materialmen?" (1985) Idaho LR 561

Lewis, M F: (1989)"Criminal misapplication of construction funds: myth and reality" (1989) Florida BJ 11

Marsh, L: (1965)"The joint control industry and state regulation" (1965) 16 Hastings LJ 229

McGill, J: (1983)"Construction liens" (1983) 4(1) *The Construction Lawyer*, 3

McGuire, T J: (1989)"Construction contract proceeds as trust funds" (1989) Flo Bar J 31

McPherson, M: (1977)"Procedural due process and the California construction industry: the stop notice" (1977) 13 Cal WLR 489

Missling, T J: (1991)"Effect of a subsequent bankruptcy on construction project payments" (1991) 11(1) *The Construction Lawyer*, 10

Mulvaney, J M: (1981)"Contractor's rights against mortgage lenders" (1981) 2(1) *The Construction Lawyer*, 25

Perlman, M S: (1985-86)"Third-party beneficiary rights" (1985-86) 3 ICLR 483

Reitz, C R: (1981)"Construction lenders' liability to contractors, sub-contractors and materialmen" (1981) 130 U Pa L Rev 416

Robinson, J M and Griffith, E S: (1986)"Surety bonds: the law relating thereto and the use thereof in North America" in T*he Liability of Contractors*, LLoyd, H (ed), Longman

Siegfried, Mand and Sklar: (1990)"Overview of the Uniform Construction Lien Act" (1990) 10(3) *The Construction Lawyer*, 13

Sweet, J: (1994) *Legal Aspects of Architecture, Engineering and the Construction Process*, 5th ed, West Publishing Company

Treacey, G B: (1980)"The release bond statutes: achieving balance in the mechanics' lien laws" (1980) 28 UCLA Law Rev 95

Yarbrough, R A: (1980-81)"Rights and remedies under Mississippi's New Public Construction Bond Statute" (1980-81) 51 Miss LJ 351

Chapter 18: Images of Construction Insolvency

Apollodorus, trans Hard, R: (1977) *The Library of Greek Mythology*, Oxford University Press

Calasso, R: (1994) *The Marriage of Cadmus and Harmony*, Vintage Books, London

Cicero, trans Grant, M: (1971)"Discussions at Tusculum" in *On the Good Life*, Penguin, London

CIB (Construction Industry Board): (1996) *Constructing a Better Image*, Thomas Telford, London

Ficino, M, trans School of Economic Science: (1975) *The Letters of Marsilio Ficino*, Shepheard Walwyn, London

Finley, M I, Mack Smith, D and Duggan, C: (1986) *A History of Sicily*, Chatto & Windus, London

Fletcher, I F: (1996) *The Law of Insolvency*, 2nd ed, Sweet & Maxwell

Goode, R M: (1995) *Commercial Law*, 2nd ed, Penguin, London

Graves, R: (1960) *The Greek Myths*, 2 volumes, Penguin, London

Guggunbuhl-Craig, A: (1982)"Projections: Soul and Money" in Spring 1982, Spring Publications, Connecticut

Hillman, J: (1972) *The Myth of Analysis*, Northwestern University Press, Evanston

Hillman, J: (1975) *Re-Visioning Psychology*, HarperCollins, New York

Hillman, J: (1979) *The Dream and the Underworld*, Harper & Row, New York

Hillman, J: (1982) "A Contribution to Soul and Money" in Spring 1982, Spring Publications, Connecticut

Lester, V M: (1995) *Victorian Insolvency*, Clarendon Press, Oxford

Meier, C A: (1967) *Ancient Incubation and Modern Psychotherapy*, Northwestern University Press, Evanston

Onians, R B: (1951) *The Origins of European Thought*, Cambridge University Press

Plato, trans Hamilton, W: (1951) *The Symposium*, Penguin Books, London

Sells, B: (1994) *The Soul of the Law*, Element Books, Shaftsbury, Dorset

Sells, B: (1999) *Order in the Court*, Element Books, Shaftsbury, Dorset

Wood, P: (1997) *Maps of World Financial Law*, 3rd ed, Allen & Overy

Wood, P: (1998)"Maps of world financial law – background note" (1998) 14 IL & P 173

· Index ·

Abatement,
contractual terms, and, 27
payment, and, 128, 151
set-off, and, 132-134, 143-146, 150,
    373
termination, and, 290
Acceptance of repudiation. *See also*
    Termination of contract
common law, at, 240-244
conclusion, 275-277
contract, under, 244-249
final accounts, 269-272
introduction, 240
post-termination rights, 258-269
standard clauses, 249-254
sub-contracts, and, 255-257
validity of clauses, 272-275
Accounting process,
set-off, and, 134-135
Accrual of right to payment,
contractual terms, and, 27, 49-52,
    358-359
Adjudication,
dispute resolution, and, 21
payment, and, 73-74
Administration,
application to construction industry,
    231-236
commencement, 212-214
creditors' rights, 221-222
directors' role, 222-223
effect,
    current contracts, on, 218-219
    employment contracts, on, 223
    existing litigation, on, 220-221
    ownership of assets, on, 214-215
    secured creditors, on, 216-217
    set-off rights, on, 219-220, 383
    unsecured creditors, on, 217-218
imaginal aspects, 522
officeholder, status of, 215-216
purpose, 210-212
Administrative receivership,
application to construction industry,
    226-230
commencement, 212-214

Administrative receivership, *cont.*
creditors' rights, 221-222
directors' role, 222-223
effect,
    current contracts, on, 218-219
    employment contracts, on, 223
    existing litigation, on, 220-221
    ownership of assets, on, 214-215
    secured creditors, on, 216-217
    set-off rights, on, 219-220
    unsecured creditors, on, 217-218
imaginal aspects, 522
officeholder, status of, 215-216
purpose, 210-212
set-off, and, 371-378
Advance payment bond,
generally, 38
purpose, 398, 408
Alternative dispute resolution (ADR),
adjudication, 21
dispute resolution adviser, 20
dispute review boards, 19-20
generally, 17-18
mediation, 19
mini-trial, 20-21
partnering, 21
Arbitration,
assignment, and, 372
bonds, and, 417-418, 480
Assignment,
assignability
    generally, 166-171
    non-, 171-177
    qualified, 173-175
attornment, 176-177
benefit and burden, 164-166
bonds, and, 412-413
charge, by way of, 175-176
claim, of, 79
direct payment, as, 369
flawed, 177
formalities, 180-182
generally, 163-164
"no-loss" arguments, 177-180
    flawed assignments, 177
    qualified assignability, 173-175

Assignment, "no loss" arguments, *cont.*
  standard clauses, 171-173
  priorities
    money already earned, 183-184
    money yet to be earned, 184-185
  qualified assignability, 173-175
  trust, by way of, 175
Assignment of sub-contracts,
  termination of contract, and, 263-264
Attornment,
  transferability, and, 176-177
Avoidance of transactions,
  creditors, in fraud of, 435-436
  floating charge made within prior
    12 months, 438
  undervalue, at an, 435

Bailment,
  plant and equipment, 85, 94-95
Balance sheet test,
  insolvency, and, 187-188
  wrongful trading, and, 430
Bankability,
  pre-contract measures, and, 24
Bankruptcy,
  formal insolvency, and, 224-225
  set-off, and, 378
Bid bond. *See also* **Tender bonds**
  security for performance, and, 38,
    406-407
Bond calls,
  dispute resolution, and, 419-421
  generally, 414
  restraint, and, 466-467
Bonds,
  advance payment bonds
    generally, 38
    purpose, 398, 408
  arbitration, and, 389, 401, 417-418, 480
  assignment, and, 412-413
  calling the bond
    dispute resolution, and, 419-421
    generally, 74, 414
  contractual link, 413-414
  conditional bonds, 396-399
  counter-indemnity, and, 415-417
  default, *see* secondary obligations
  demand, *see* primary obligations
  dispute resolution
    clause construction, 421-423
    proper law, 418-419
    unfair calling, "the fraud
      exception", 413, 419-421, 467
  expiry, 408-409

Bonds, *cont.*
  functions
    cash flow, 35
    financial long-stop, 35
    group cover, 36
  general purposes, 36-38
  generally, 385-388
  government contracts, and, 409-410
  hybrid obligations, 401-404
  imaginary aspects, 514
  joint ventures, and, 411, 412, 417
  mitigation of loss, and, 301
  obligations
    hybrid, 401-404
    primary, 388-390
    secondary, 390-401
  parent company guarantees, and,
    394-396
  payment, 39, 468
  personal guarantees, and, 411
  primary obligations
    generally, 388-389
    standard forms, 389-390
  procedural requirements, 414-415
  restructurings, and, 205-206
  retention bonds
    generally, 38
    purpose, 404-406
  secondary obligations
    conditional bonds, 396-399
    generally, 390-391
    parent company guarantees,
      394-396, 404
    principles of suretyship, 391-394
    standard forms, 399-401
  security for performance, and, 35-39
  specific purposes, 38-39
  sub-contracts, and, 401, 403, 410-411
  surety bonds, 397
  tender bonds
    generally, 38
    purpose, 406-407
Book debts,
  fixed charges, and, 184, 376, 378, 501
  payment, and, 71-73, 330
Breach of contract,
  anticipatory, 242-244
Breach of trust. *See also* **Acceptance of
    repudiation**
  trust claims, and, 157-159, 338-340, 364

Cash flow test,
  insolvency, and, 186-187

Caveats,
 financial protection, and, 474
Certification process,
 contractual terms, and, 28
 under-certification, and, 196, 428-429
Charge, assignment by way of,
 transferability, and, 175-176
Charges,
 plant and equipment, and, 87-93
 security for performance, and, 31-32
  registration, 32-33
Cheques,
 claims where stopped, 146, 266, 375, 381
Choses in action. *See* **Payment,**
  Receivables, Set-Off
Claims on insolvency,
 avoidance of transactions
  creditors, in fraud of, 435-436
  floating charge made within prior
   12 months, 438
  undervalue, at an, 435
 dispositions after petition issued, 438
 fraudulent trading, 427-428
 misfeasance, 436-437
 preferences
  construction trusts, 434-435
  direct payments, 432-433
  generally, 430-431
  payments, 431-433
  set-off, 433
  termination clauses, 433-434
 transactions at an undervalue, 435
 transactions in fraud of creditors,
  435-436
 wrongful trading, 428-430
Commercial insolvency test,
 insolvency, and, 186-187
Companies,
 dissolution, 279, 519-521
 images, 504, 522
Company voluntary arrangements (CVAs),
 application to construction industry,
  236-239
 generally, 224
Completion contracts,
 direct contractor, by, 289
 generally, 288
 guarantors, by, 292-293
 insolvency practitioners, by, 289-292
Composition,
 informal insolvency, and, 201-202
Conditional bonds, 396-399
Conditionality, 275

Conditions precedent,
 contractual terms, and, 28
Construction liens,
 basis, 454-456
 disadvantages, 457-458
 nature, 456-457
Construction trusts,
 contract sum, trusts of the 160-161,
  326, 340, 499
 generally, 159-160, 308
 main contract, 364
 Quistclose trusts, 162, 337, 434
 retention trusts, 161-162, 308-325
 stakeholder accounts, 162
 trust accounts, 162, 326, 341
Construction industry,
 characteristics, 3-6
 contract, forms of
  ICE, 17
  JCT, 16-17
  RIBA, 15-16
 criticisms, 7-8
 definition, 2-3
 dispute resolution, 17-21
 entire contracts, 382
 features, 11-15
 structure, 8-10
Constructive trusts,
 assignment, and, 179
 preferences, and, 434-435
Contract, trusts of the,
 transferability, and, 160-161
Contractual liens,
 security for performance, and, 32
Contractual set-off,
 Dawnays' case, rule in, 137-138
 generally, 137
 modification of general law, 138-141
Contractual terms,
 exclusion of common law, 26-27
 expansion of common law, 27-30
 generally, 26
 restriction of common law, 26-27
Copyright,
 termination of contract, and, 267-269,
  295
Counterclaims,
 payment, and, 152-154
 set-off, and, 128
 winding-up petitions, and, 207
Counter-indemnity,
 bonds, and, 415-417
Creditors. *See* **Debts**

Cross-claims,
  defective work, 150
  delay, 147-149
  disruption, 149-150
  generally, 146-147
  over-valuation, 151-152
Current contracts,
  formal insolvency, and, 218-219
Customs and freight,
  security for performance, and, 39
CVAs,
  application to construction industry,
    236-238
  generally, 224

Debts. *See also* **Book debts, Payment,**
  Receivables, Set-Off
  accruing due, 51
  attachment of, 367-368
  conditional, 356, 361
  contingent, 187-190, 206, 209, 364,
    380, 383, 384, 391, 428
  defeasible, 53-55
  due and payable, 50, 309, 314, 320
  insolvency, and,
    composition, 201-202
    moratorium, 201
    rescheduling, 201
  preferential, 474
  prospective, 187-190, 206, 209
Deduction,
  contractual terms, and, 27-28
Default bonds. *See* **Bonds,** secondary
  obligations
Defective work,
  cross-claims, and, 150
Demand bonds. *See* **Bonds,** primary
  obligations
Delay,
  cross-claims, and, 147-149
Diligence,
  security, and, 488-491
Direct payments,
  bonds, and, 406
  clause construction
    generally, 347-349
    public policy, 349-351
  discretionary,
    during contract, 351-353
    post-bankruptcy, 353-361
    post-termination of contract, 353
    summary of case law, 361-363
  guarantees, and, 393

Direct payments, *cont.*
  international aspects, and, 475, 501
  mandatory
    assignment, under, 369
    attachment of debts, 367-368
    direct contract, under, 364-367
    main contract, under, 364
    statute, under, 368-369
  novation, and, 366
  preferences, and, 432-433
  solvent contractors, and, 345-347
  validity on formal insolvency, 350-351
Directors,
  disqualification, 445-447
  duties to creditors, 441-442
  liability,
    shadow directors, 442-443
    statutory relief, 444-445
    tortious, 431, 443-445
Discharge of contract. *See* **Termination of**
  contract
Dispositions,
  claims on insolvency, and, 438
  under sale of goods contract, 115-116
Disqualification of directors,
  generally, 445-447
Disruption,
  cross-claims, and, 149-150

Employees,
  direct payment to, 356, 482
  meaning, 451
  preferential creditors, as, 448-449
  tax, 449-451
  transfer of employment, 227, 449
Employment contracts,
  formal insolvency, and, 223
Equitable set-off, 131-132, 371-376
Equitable tracing claims,
  transferability, and, 157-158
Escrow agreements,
  security for performance, and, 35, 294,
    325-329, 483
Examinership, 496-498, 500
Existing litigation,
  formal insolvency, and, 220-221

Final accounts,
  termination of contract, and
    deemed settlement, 271-272
    generally, 269-271
Financial protection,
  bonds, 35-39

Financial protection, *cont.*
  charges, 31-33
  contractual terms, 26-30
  criteria checklist, 46
  escrow agreements, 35
  formal security, 31-32
  guarantees, 35-39
  informal security, 33-40
  insurance,
    payment, 41
    performance, 34-35
  liens, 32
  mortgages, 32
  non-assignment, 34
  pledges, 32
  pre-contract measures, 23-26
  retention trusts, 41-42
  security for payment, 40-42
  security for performance, 30-40
  set-off, 33
  use of, 43-46
  vesting clauses, 34
  warranties, 39-40
Fixed charges,
  book debts, on, 376
  plant and equipment, and, 87-90
  security for performance, and
    generally, 31
    registration, 32-33
Fixed materials,
  meaning of fixture, 111-113
  supplier's interest, 113-114
Flawed assignment,
  transferability, and, 177
Floating charges,
  plant and equipment, and, 90-93
  security for performance, and,
    generally, 31-32
    registration, 32-33
Forfeiture,
  insolvency, and, 507-509
Formal insolvency. *See also*
  Administration, Liquidation,
  Receivership
  application to construction industry,
    administration, 231-236
    CVAs, 236-239
    generally, 226
    liquidation, 230-231
    receivership, 226-230
  bankruptcy, 224-225
  commencement, 212-214
  conclusion, 238-239

Formal insolvency, *cont.*
  creditors
    rights, 221-222
    secured, 216-217
    unsecured, 217-218
  current contracts, 218-219
  CVAs, 224
  directors' role, 222-223
  employment contracts, 223
  existing litigation, 220-221
  introduction, 210
  IVAs, 225-226
  ownership of assets, 214-215
  procedure
    administration, 210-223
    bankruptcy, 224-225
    CVAs, 224
    introduction, 210
    IVAs, 225-226
    liquidation, 210-223
    receivership, 210-223
  secured creditors, 216-217
  unsecured creditors, 217-218
  voluntary arrangements
    company, 224
    individual, 225-226
France,
  construction law, 501
Fraud of creditors, transactions in,
  claims on insolvency, and, 435-436
Fraudulent trading,
  claims on insolvency, and, 427-428
Funding cash flow,
  "front-end loading", 303, 382
  working capital
    debt, 58-59
    equity, 59-61

Garnishee. *See* **Debts, attachment of.**
Going concern test,
  insolvency, and, 186-187
Goods and materials,
  fixed materials, 110-114
  insolvency practitioners, role of, 123-127
  remedies,
    damages in conversion, 123
    delivery up, 119-121
    injunction to restrain dealing with
      goods, 121-122
    removal of goods from site, 122-123
  retention of title clauses
    fixed materials, 110-115
    remedies, 119-123

Goods and materials, retention of title
　　clauses, *cont.*
　　　　unfixed materials, 114-119
　　unfixed materials
　　　　sale of goods contracts, 115-117
　　　　work and materials contracts, 117-119
Government contracts,
　　bonds, and, 409-410
Guarantees. *See also* **Bonds, Conditional**
　　　　Bonds, Parent Company Guarantees
　　completion by guarantors, 292-293
　　defences of guarantors, 392-393
　　functions, 35-36
　　general purposes, 36-38
　　secondary obligations, as, 390-391
　　security for performance, and, 35-39
　　specific purposes, 38-39

Holdback,
　　financial protection, and, 465
Housing Grants, Construction and
　　　　Regeneration Act 1996,
　　payment, and,
　　　　calculation mechanism, 62-63
　　　　instalment payments, 62
　　set-off, and, 143-146

Indemnities,
　　contractual terms, and
　　　　generally, 27
　　　　insurance, 28
Individual voluntary arrangements (IVAs),
　　formal insolvency, and, 225-226
Informal insolvency. *See also* **Insolvency**
　　composition, 201-202
　　merger, 201
　　moratorium, 201
　　operational changes, 200
　　rationalisation, 202
　　reorganisation, 200-201
　　rescheduling, 201
　　restructuring
　　　　lending criteria, 204-205
　　　　limitations, 205-206
　　　　refinancing, 203-204
　　　　standstill, 203
　　　　workout, 204
　　secondment, 201
　　take-over, 201
　　voluntary arrangements, 202
Informal security,
　　bonds, 35-39
　　escrow agreements, 35

Informal security, *cont.*
　　generally, 33
　　guarantees, 35-39
　　insurance, 34-35
　　non-assignment, 34
　　set-off, 33
　　vesting clauses, 34
　　warranties, 39-40
Insolvency. *See also* **Administrative**
　　　　receivership, Claims on insolvency,
　　　　Formal insolvency, Informal
　　　　Insolvency, Liquidation, Preferences,
　　　　Set-off, Voluntary arrangements
　　absence of entry barriers, 192
　　causes
　　　　contractual claims, 195-196
　　　　diversification, 197
　　　　economic cycles, 193
　　　　financial control, 193-195
　　　　structural, 191-193
　　conglomerates, 192
　　contractual claims, 195-196
　　CVAs, 224
　　dispositions after petition issued, 438
　　family firms, 192
　　financial control
　　　　"knock-on" effect, 194-195
　　　　lack of, 193-194
　　fraudulent trading, 427-428
　　indicators, 198-199
　　introduction, 186
　　IVAs, 225-226
　　management buy-outs, 192-193
　　meaning
　　　　balance sheet test, 187-188
　　　　cash flow test, 186-187
　　　　commercial insolvency test, 186-187
　　　　generally, 186
　　　　going concern test, 186-187
　　misfeasance, 436-437
　　pari passu rule, 190-191
　　valuation of liabilities, 188-190
Insolvency professionals,
　　regulation, 451-452
　　status, 524
Insolvency termination clause,
　　contractual terms, and, 29-30
Insurance,
　　security for payment, and, 41
　　security for performance, and, 34-35
Interest,
　　payment, and
　　　　defences, 77-78

Interest, payment, and, *cont.*
generally, 75-77
Interim payments,
contractual terms, and, 28
International issues,
bond calls, restraint of, 466-467
caveats, 474
construction liens,
basis, 454-456
disadvantages, 457-458
nature, 456-457
direct payment, 475
disclosure of payment, 475
holdback, 465
information rights, 479
joint cheque agreements, 478
joint funds control, 478
licensing contractors, 475
Mareva injunctions, 460
payment bonds, 468-469
preferential claims, 474
prompt payment regulation, 479
restitution, 470-471
set-off, 475-478
statutory assignment, 465-466
statutory charges, 460-463
statutory trusts, 463-465
stop notices, 458-460
third party benefits, 469-470
trustees, 479
Ireland, Republic of,
generally, 495
insolvency,
construction industry, 496, 499
Kentz examinership, 500

Joint cheque agreements,
financial protection, and, 478
Joint funds control,
financial protection, and, 478
Joint ventures,
bonds, and, 194,197, 204, 281, 411,
412, 417

Latham Report (1994),
bonds, and, 385
contracts, and, 17
direct payment, and, 370
dispute resolution, and, 21
Legal set-off, 135-136, 482
Letters of comfort, 483
Letters of credit, 326, 387-389
Letters of intent, 230, 382

Licensing contractors,
financial protection, and, 475
Liens. *See also* **Construction liens**
plant and equipment, and, 94
security for performance, and, 32
Liquidated damages,
retention trust, and, 324
security for performance, and, 39
termination of contract, and, 264-265
Liquidation. *See also* **Winding-up petitions.**
application to construction industry,
230-231
commencement, 212-214
creditors' rights, 221-222
disclaimer, 274
directors' role, 222-223
effect,
current contracts, on, 218-219
employment contracts, on, 223
existing litigation, on, 220-221
ownership of assets, on, 214-215
secured creditors, on, 216-217
set-off rights, on, 219-220
unsecured creditors, on, 217-218
imaginal aspects, 521
officeholder, status of, 215-216
purpose, 210-212
set-off, and, 379-383

Main contract trusts,
trust claims, and, 315-318
Maintenance bond,
security for performance, and, 39
Management contract trusts,
trust claims, and, 318-323
Mareva injunctions,
financial protection, and, 460
Materials. *See also* **Fixed materials.**
insolvency practitioners, role of, 123-127
remedies,
damages in conversion, 123
delivery up, 119-121
injunction to restrain dealing with
goods, 121-122
removal of goods from site, 122-123
retention of title clauses,
fixed materials, 110-115
remedies, 119-123
unfixed materials, 114-119
Scotland, and, 494
unfixed materials,
sale of goods contracts, 115-117
work and materials contracts, 117-119

Mediation,
  dispute resolution, and, 19
Merger,
  informal insolvency, and, 201
Mini-trial,
  dispute resolution, and, 20-21
Misfeasance,
  claims on insolvency, and, 436-437
Mitigation of loss,
  novation, and, 297-301
Moratorium,
  informal insolvency, and, 201
Mortgages,
  security for performance, and, 32

"Name-borrowing", 309, 334
Nemo dat non quod habet,
  goods and materials, and, 109
New Engineering and Construction
    Contract, 17
'No-loss" arguments,
  construction management, 179
  development agreement, 178-179
  duty of care deed, 179-180
  generally, 177-178
  inter-group assignment, 178
  management contracting, 180
  property assignment, 178
Nominated sub-contractor trusts,
  trust claims, and, 308-311
Non-assignability,
  assignment by way of charge, 175-176
  assignment by way of trust, 175
  attornment, 176-177
  flawed assignments, 177
  qualified assignability, 173-175
  standard clauses, 171-173
Non-assignment clause,
  security for performance, and, 34
Non-payment, remedies for,
  adjudication, 73-74
  interest
    defences, 77-78
    generally, 75-77
  security for costs, 78-79
  suspension of contract, 74-75
Novation,
  case study, 302-307
  completion contracts, and,
    direct contractor, by, 289
    generally, 288
    guarantors, by, 292-293
    insolvency practitioners, by, 289-292

Novation, *cont.*
  construction contracts, and,
    consequences, 287-288
    generally, 283-286
    insolvency novation, 286-287
  criteria, 280-282
  direct payment, and, 366
  imaginal aspects, 515-516
  insolvency practitioners, by, 293-295
  mitigation of loss, 297-301
  nature of, 278-279
  statutory, 282
  sub-contractors, and, 295-296

Operational changes,
  informal insolvency, and, 200
Over-valuation,
  cross-claims, and, 151-152, 373
Ownership of assets,
  formal insolvency, and, 214-215

Parent company guarantees,
  bonds, and, 394-396, 404
Pari passu rule
  insolvency, and, 84, 99-100, 161,
    190-191, 264, 270, 275-276, 334,
    349, 355, 363, 365-366, 369, 370
Partnering, 21
Payment. *See also* **Set-off**
  adjudication, and, 73-74
  advance, 87, 168-169, 387, 398, 408
  book debts, 71-73
  conclusion, 79-80
  counterclaims, and, 152-154
  cross-claims, and
    defective work, 150
    delay, 147-149
    disruption, 149-150
    generally, 146-147
    over-valuation, 151-152
  direct, *see also* **Direct payment**
    clause construction, 347-351
    conclusion, 369-370
    discretionary, 351-363
    introduction, 344
    mandatory, 363-369
    solvent contractors, 345-347
  funding cash flow,
    generally, 58
    working capital, 58-61
  Housing Grants, Construction and
      Regeneration Act 1996, under,
    calculation mechanism, 62-63

Payment, Housing Grants ... Act 1996, *cont.*
    generally, 61-62
    instalment payments, 62
  imaginal aspects, 513-514
  interest,
    defences, 77-78
    generally, 75-77
  non-payment, remedies for,
    adjudication, 73-74
    interest, 75-78
    security for costs, 78-79
    suspension of contract, 74-75
  pay-when-paid,
    background, 64-66
    condition precedent, 66-68
    generally, 63-64, 209
    international, 499
    statutory limitation, 68-71
  preferences, and,
    direct payments, 432-433
    generally, 431-433
  qualities,
    relational, 48
    structural, 48-49
    temporal, 48
  receivables,
    generally, 49-53
    quantum meruit, 57-58, 295
    retention, 53-57
  retention, right of,
    alternatives to, 56-57
    function, 54-55
    generally, 53-54
    significance, 55-56
  security for,
    generally, 40-41
    insurance, 41
    retention trusts, 41-42
  security for costs, 78-79
  suspension of contract, 74-75
  working capital
    debt, 58-59
    equity, 59-61
    generally, 58
Payment bond,
  international issues, and, 468-469
  security for performance, and, 39
Pay-when-paid,
  background, 64-66
  condition precedent, 66-68
  generally, 63-64, 109, 209
  statutory limitation, 68-71

Penalty arguments,
  deemed settlement, 271
  final accounts, 270
  plant, 98-99, 102
  security deposit, 266
Performance,
  security for,
    formal, 31-33
    generally, 30-31
    informal, 33-40
Performance bond,
  security for performance, and, 38
Personal claims,
  transferability, and, 158-159
Personal guarantees,
  bonds, and, 411
Plant and equipment,
  challenges to vesting clauses,
    bills of sale, 102-105
    conversion, 100-102
    disputed termination, 96-98
    generally, 96
    pari passu rule, 99-100
    penalty arguments, 98-99
  charges, and,
    fixed, 87-90
    floating charges, 90-93
  introduction, 81
  liens, and, 94
  not owned by contractor, where,
    generally, 105-106
    hired, 107-108
    sub-contractors' property, 106-107
    subsidiary company's property, 108
  pledges, and, 94-95
  rights against,
    contract, 83-84
    property, 84-86
    security, 86-87
  risk, and, 81-83
  Scotland, and, 492-493
  vesting clauses, and,
    challenges to, 96-105
    conclusion, 95-96
    fixed charges, 87-90
    floating charges, 90-93
    liens, 94
    pledges, 94-95
Pledges,
  plant and equipment, and, 94-95
  security for performance, and, 32
Pre-contract measures,
  bankability, 24

Pre-contract measures, *cont.*
  pre-qualification, 25-26
  procurement method, 24-25
  tender process, 26
Preferences,
  construction trusts, and, 434-435
  direct payments, and, 432-433
  generally, 430-431
  payments, and, 431-433
  set-off, and, 433
  termination clauses, and, 433-434
Preferential claims,
  employees, and, 448-449
  international issues, and, 474
Pre-qualification,
  pre-contract measures, and, 25-26
Priorities,
  assignment, and,
    money already earned, 183-184
    money yet to be earned, 184-185
Private Finance Initiative, 424, 487
Procurement methods,
  construction management, 179
  design and build, 179, 285, 296
  management contracting, 135, 180,
    197, 296
  pre-contract measures, and, 24-25
  prime cost, 289
Prompt payment regulation,
  financial protection, and, 479

Qualified assignability,
  transferability, and, 173-175
Quantum meruit,
  payment, and, 57-58, 140-141, 295
Quicquid plantatur solo, solo cedit,
  goods and materials, and, 109-111,
125-126, 502
Quistclose trusts,
  transferability, and, 162, 337

Rationalisation,
  informal insolvency, and, 202
Receivables,
  direct payment, and, 359
  factoring, 163
  generally, 49-53
  quantum meruit, 57-58
  retention, right of,
    alternatives to, 56-57
    function, 54-55
    generally, 53-54
    significance, 55-56

Receivership. *See* **Administrative**
  receivership
Recourse, rights of,
  trust claims, and, 311-315
Refinancing,
  informal insolvency, and, 203-204
Release from performance. *See*
  Acceptance of repudiation,
  Termination of contract.
Reorganisation,
  informal insolvency, and, 200-201
Repudiation of contract,
  consequences, 242-243
  effect of insolvency, 243-244
  generally, 240-242
Rescheduling,
  informal insolvency, and, 201
Restitution,
  financial protection, and, 470-471
Restructuring,
  informal insolvency, and,
    generally, 202-203
    lending criteria, 204-205
    limitations, 205-206
    refinancing, 203-204
    standstill, 203
    workout, 204
Retention bonds,
  generally, 38
  purpose, 404-406
Retention of payment, right of,
  alternatives to
    generally, 56-57
    international, 471-474, 501
  function, 54-55
  generally, 53-54
  recoverability, 183
  significance, 55-56
Retention of title clauses,
  fixed materials,
    generally, 110-111
    fixtures, 111-113
    supplier's interest, 113-114
  generally, 109-110
  incorporation in the contract, 118
  insolvency practitioners, role of, 123-127
  remedies,
    damages in conversion, 123
    delivery up, 119-121
    generally, 119
    injunction to restrain dealing with
      goods, 121-122, 494
    removal of goods from site, 122-123

Retention of title clauses, *cont.*
  unfixed materials,
    generally, 114-115
    sale of goods contracts, 115-117
    work and materials contracts, 117-119
Retention trusts,
  invalidity,
    post-petition disposition, 439
    preference, 435
  Scotland, and, 493
  security for payment, and, 41-42
  transferability, and, 161-162
  trust claims, and,
    case law, 325-334
    main contract trusts, 315-318
    management contract trusts,
      318-323
    nominated sub-contractor trust,
      308-311
    recourse, rights of, 311-315
    trust accounts, 323-325
Risk,
  plant and equipment, and, 81-83
Royal Institution of British Architects
    (RIBA),
  contracts, 15-16

Scotland,
  arrestment, 489, 495
  diligence, 488-491
  legislative framework, 487
  materials, 494
  plant and equipment, 492-493
  retention trusts, 493
  set-off, 491-492
  termination of contracts, 492
Secondment,
  informal insolvency, and, 201
Secured creditors,
  formal insolvency, and, 216-217, 427
Security for costs,
  payment, and, 78-79
Security deposits,
  termination of contract, and, 266-267
Security for payment,
  generally, 40-41
  insurance, 41
  retention trusts, 41-42
Security for performance,
  bonds, 35-39
  charges, 31-33
  escrow agreements, 35
  formal, 31-32

Security for performance, *cont.*
  guarantees, 35-39
  informal, 33-40
  insurance, 34-35
  liens, 32
  mortgages, 32
  non-assignment, 34
  pledges, 32
  set-off, 33
  vesting clauses, 34
  warranties, 39-40
Set-off,
  abatement, and, 132-134, 373
  accounting process, and, 134-135
  common law, at, 131-136
  contractual,
    Dawnays' case, rule in, 137-138
    modification of general law, 138-141
  contractual terms, and, 27
  deduction, and, 137, 140, 320-321
  equitable, 131-132, 371-376
  formal insolvency, and, 219-220
  insolvency, and,
    administration, 383
    bankruptcy, 143, 355, 378
    liquidation, 143, 313, 356, 379-383,
      500
    receivership, 371-378
    voluntary arrangements, 378-379
  international issues, and, 475-478, 500
  legal, 135-136, 373
  limitations
    common law, at, 146
    generally, 142
    HGCRA 1996, under, 143-146
    Insolvency Act 1986, under, 143
    UCTA 1977, under, 142
  payment, and,
    common law, 131-136
    contractual, 137-141
    limitations, 142-146
    quantifiability of claim, 130
  preferences, and, 433
  Scotland, and, 491-492
  security for performance, and, 33
  statutory, 135-136
Shadow directors,
  liability on insolvency, and, 442-443
Site possession,
  termination of contract, and, 259-263,
    274
Solvency warranties,
  contractual terms, and, 29

Specific performance,
  assignment, and, 166
  building contracts, of, 259-263
  duty to assign, of, 263
  plant risk, and, 93
Stakeholder accounts,
  transferability, and, 162
Standstill,
  informal insolvency, and, 203
Statutory assignment,
  financial protection, and, 465-466
Statutory charges,
  financial protection, and, 460-463
Statutory set-off. *See* **Legal set-off.**
Statutory trusts,
  financial protection, and, 463-465
Stop notices,
  financial protection, and, 458-460, 501
Sub-contractors. *See also* **Pay when paid.**
  contractual terms, and, 28-29
  novation, and, 295-296
Sub-contracts,
  bonds, and, 410-411
  plant and equipment, 106-107
  termination of contract, and, 255-257,
    263, 381
  trust claims, and, 334-338
Subject to contract,
  pre-contract measures, and, 26
Subrogation, 279, 336-338, 393
Surety bonds. *See* **Bonds,** secondary
  obligations, **Conditional bonds.**
Suppliers,
  contractual terms, and, 28-29
Suspension of contract,
  payment, and, 74-75
Suspension of payments,
  termination of contract, and, 265-266

Take-over,
  informal insolvency, and, 201
Tender bonds,
  generally, 38
  purpose, 406-407
Tender process,
  pre-contract measures, and, 26
Termination of contract,
  common law, at,
    consequences, 242-243
    effect of insolvency, 243-244
    meaning, 240-242
  checklist of steps, 275-276

Termination of contract, *cont.*
  contract, under
    common law, and, 246-249
    procedure, 244-246
  contractual terms, and, 29
  final accounts
    deemed settlement, 271-272
    generally, 269-271
  imaginal aspects, 516
  meaning,
    failure of performance, 241-242
    inability to perform, 241
    renunciation, 241
  post-termination rights,
    assignment of sub-contracts, 263-264
    copyright, 267-269
    liquidated damages, 264-265
    security deposits, 266-267
    site possession, 259-263
    suspension of payments, 265-266
  preferences, and, 433-434
  repudiation,
    consequences, 242-243
    effect of insolvency, 243-244
  Scotland, and, 492
  standard clauses,
    automatic termination, 250-251
    consensual termination, 251
    insolvency events, 253-254
    notice, termination on, 251-252
    "unreasonably or vexatiously", 251
    waiver of termination, 252-253
    withdrawal of termination, 252-253
  sub-contracts, and, 255-257
    retention trust, and, 321
  validity of clauses, 272-275
Termination of trusts,
  trust claims, and, 340-343
Third party benefit,
  international, 469
Title to product,
  contractual terms, and, 27
Tracing,
  transferability, and, 157-158
Transactions at an undervalue,
  claims on insolvency, and, 435
Transactions in fraud of creditors,
  claims on insolvency, and, 435-436
Transferability. *See also* **Assignment, Trusts**
  insolvency, and, 509-510
Trust accounts,
  transferability, and, 162
  trust claims, and, 323-325, 479

Trust, assignment by way of,
  transferability, and, 175
Trust claims. *See also* **Retention trusts**
  breach of trust, 338-340
  equitable tracing, and, 157-158
  personal claims, and, 158-159
  sub-contract benefits, 334-338
  termination of trusts, 340-343
Trusts. *See also* **Assignment, Construction
    trusts, Trust claims**
  bare, 317-318
  general principles,
    creation of trust, 156-157, 331-334
    equitable tracing claims, 157-158
    personal claims, 158-159
  salvage jurisdiction, 342
Trusts of the contract,
  transferability, and, 160-161

Undervalue, transactions at an, 435
Unfair Contract Terms Act 1977,
  set-off, and, 142
Unfixed materials,
  sale of goods contracts, 115-117
  work and materials contracts, 117-119
Unsecured creditors,
  formal insolvency, and, 217-218

Valuation,
  payment, and, 128-129
Vesting clauses,
  challenges to,
    bills of sale, 102-105
    conversion, 100-102
    disputed termination, 96-98
    pari passu rule, 99-100

Vesting clauses, challenges to, *cont.*
    penalty arguments, 98-99
  plant and equipment, and,
    fixed charges, 87-90
    floating charges, 90-93
    liens, 94
    pledges, 94-95
  security for performance, and, 34
Voluntary arrangements,
  formal insolvency, and,
    company, 224
    individual, 225-226
  informal insolvency, and, 202
  set-off, and, 378-379

Warranties,
  completion contracts, and, 185, 289,
    294, 304
  contractual terms, and, 27
  security for performance, and, 39-40,
    364-367
Winding-up petitions,
  contractors, against, 208-209
  direct payments, and, 231, 365
  employers, against, 207-208
  generally, 204, 211, 213, 230, 431,
    439, 524
Working capital,
  debt, 58-59
  equity, 59-61
  generally, 58
Workout,
  informal insolvency, and, 204
Wrongful trading,
  balance sheet test, and, 430
  generally, 428-430